CLIENT-CENTERED AND EXPERIENTIAL
PSYCHOTHERAPY IN THE NINETIES

STUDIA PSYCHOLOGICA

Leuvense Psychologische Reeks gesticht in 1953 door A. Michotte en J. Nuttin.
Redactieraad : J.M. Nuttin Jr., Voorzitter
G. d'Ydewalle, Redactiesecretaris
R. Bouwen
P. De Boeck
L. Delbeke
R. Van Balen

De Leuvense Psychologische Reeks "Studia Psychologica" is de voortzetting
van de "Études de Psychologie" opgericht in 1912 door A. Michotte.

CLIENT-CENTERED AND EXPERIENTIAL PSYCHOTHERAPY IN THE NINETIES

EDITORS

G. LIETAER
J. ROMBAUTS
R. VAN BALEN

Leuven University Press
1990

Coventry University

© 1990 Universitaire Pers Leuven / Leuven University Press / Presses Universitaires de Louvain, Krakenstraat 3 - B 3000 Leuven/Louvain, Belgium.

ISBN 90 6186 364 3

D/1990/1869/11

CONTENTS

8

Psychopathology and theory of personality change

Proposals for future research

Dialogue with other orientations

Part II. SPECIFIC PROBLEMS AND SETTINGS

10

PREFACE

This book has a long history. Twenty-five years ago, in 1964, Professor J. Rombauts founded the "Centrum voor client-centered therapie en counseling" at the Catholic University of Leuven. Attached to it was a two year half-time postgraduate training program which is still existing and flourishing. To celebrate this twenty-fifth anniversary, the staff of the Center organized the first "International Conference on client-centered and experiential psychotherapy" in September 1988. This book is an outgrowth of the Conference, although we believe it is much better than the usual "Conference book." It has been carefully prepared long before the Conference, by asking the cooperation of many well-known scholars in our field. A selection was made from the manuscripts presented and several accepted manuscripts have since been thoroughly revised. To this we added six contributions from Leuven, which had not been presented at the Conference. (At the time, we had more down-to-earth responsibilities for the practical organizational aspects of the Conference.)

The *scope* of the book can be described as follows. It covers exclusively the field of psychotherapy, and not the broader applications of the person-centered approach. It is a book which spans three generations, as it contains contributions from colleagues from the Chicago-period as well as from young colleagues, trained in the last ten years. The various orientations are heard: Classic Rogerians; client-centered therapists who favor some form of integration or even eclecticism; experiential psychotherapists for whom Gendlin's focusing approach is a precious way of working; client-centered therapists who look at the therapy process in terms of information-processing; existentially oriented therapists... Remarkable is that - for the first time in the history of client-centered/experiential psychotherapy - the European voice rings through forcefully: More than half the contributions were written by authors from the F.R. Germany, The Netherlands, Belgium, Great Britain, and Switzerland. And finally, it is a 'voluminous' book of 47 chapters, and a book in which theory, research and clinical practice are given a roughly equal share. All this makes the book into a good overview of what is burgeoning in our field in the Anglo-Saxon world and Western Europe.

The diversity just mentioned renders the book to a certain extent controversial: It does not represent one single vision; instead, the editors chose to give the floor to several points of view. These differences and the "tensions" which may occasionally result from them are mainly centered around problems of orthodoxy versus integration and around the conception of the therapist's role with polarities such as: Companion versus process expert; facilitating versus directing; observing versus participating; relation versus technique.

As far as the *content* is concerned, I shall briefly highlight the most important themes. Several chapters contain reflections on the evolution - past, present and future - of client-centered/experiential psychotherapy. Ample attention is given here to the intensive research into the process, which had a central place in the initial phase of client-centered therapy, with several creative studies and proposals for renewal. In numerous contributions we find efforts to build and further develop a theory of psychopathology, the client's process, the basic attitudes and task-oriented interventions of the therapist. The chapters dealing with clinical practice typically aim at the description of therapy with specific client populations and particularly severely disturbed clients. And finally a few fields are introduced which are new or barely explored within the client-centered/experiential approach: Working with dreams, health psychology, couple and family therapy.

All this makes it obvious that our therapeutic orientation is fully "in process," and that this book offers a good cross-section of this process on the edge of the nineties. We are convinced that the book will contribute to a deeper and more up-to-date knowledge of client-centered/experiential psychotherapy in therapists of our own and other therapeutic orientations. We also hope that it will contribute to the main goal of the Leuven Conference, i.e. restoring the balance between practice and science in client-centered/experiential psychotherapy.

*****

With much affection we dedicate this book to Carl Rogers, founder of client-centered psychotherapy. Carl Rogers always kept in close touch with the Department of Psychology in Leuven and has had a major influence on the shaping of its training program in clinical psychology: Already shortly after the second world war via his contacts with Professor J.R. Nuttin who, through his writings made Rogers' views regarding therapy well-known and who paved the way for a training program in "non-directive counseling"; via the publication, in 1959, in collaboration with a Leuven graduate, Dr. G.M. Kinget, of a work in Dutch: *Psychotherapie en menselijke verhoudingen. Theorie en praktijk van de non-directieve therapie;* via J. Rombauts' stay in Madison (1962-1963) and G. Lietaer's stay in La Jolla (1969-1970); via his visit to the Counseling Centrum in May of 1966, about which he wrote in one of his travel reports: "... The greatest professional fun was in talking with the young staff of the Counseling Centrum. It seemed like my first days in Chicago all over again"; and via meetings with many of our students in workshops all over the world in the last 15 years.

When, a couple of years before the Conference, we let him know about our plans, asking him to participate, he wrote to us: "Yes, if I am still around and in good health, I would like very much to attend and to participate." Unfortunately, he died in February of 1987, and we were unable to confer on him, during the Congress, the honorary doctorate of our University. May this book be a posthumous expression of respect for the man who meant so much to us and many others; and may it also be an enriching contribution to the fiftieth anniversary of client-centered therapy: Indeed, Carl Rogers situated its birth in 1940, more specifically on December 11th, when he gave a lecture at Minnesota University, entitled: *Newer concepts in psychotherapy.*

On behalf of the editors,
Germain Lietaer
Leuven, June 1989

ACKNOWLEDGEMENTS

The Editors wish to thank all those who have contributed, directly or indirectly, to the coming about of this book: The staff members of the Counseling Centrum for their editorial assistance and part of the typing: Paul Dierick, Els Heidbüchel, Mia Leijssen, Greet Vanaerschot, Els Vloeberghen; the authors for handing in their manuscripts on time and for their smooth cooperation during the editorial phase; especially the European authors for providing a translated version of their manuscripts; the Advisory Board of the Series *Studia Psychologica* under the presidency of Professor J.M. Nuttin, for their nearly blind faith in us when accepting this book for publication; Mrs. Maria Flamen for translating most of the Leuven contributions, Mrs. Anne Tracy for checking the language in most European manuscripts, Mr. Patrick Engelhardt for doing much of the correction work, and Mrs. Jessica Jager-van Ginneken for the general language revision of all chapters; Mrs. Betty Dang-Vanden Bavière for her valuable advice 'behind the scenes' and for checking the printer's proof of all chapters; Mrs. Hilde Lens of Leuven University Press for her smooth and competent handling of the print- and publication stages of the book; and above all Mrs. Dilly Wieërs who retyped all manuscripts, did her utmost to create a certain uniformity of layout, patiently made all corrections as the versions of the chapters became more final, and kept the book 'under control' with a strong sense of responsibility until the finishing line was reached.

PART I
THEORETICAL AND CLINICAL ISSUES

THE CLIENT-CENTERED APPROACH AFTER THE WISCONSIN PROJECT: A PERSONAL VIEW ON ITS EVOLUTION

Germain LIETAER
Katholieke Universiteit Leuven, Belgium

Which changes and shifts have taken place within the client-centered approach and its experiential offspring during the last twenty five years? In which direction have the theory and practice of client-centered therapy evolved? What has happened in the area of research? What should be expected in the nineties of this orientation in psychotherapy which has existed now for almost half a century?

I will try to answer these and other questions from a personal - and maybe European - vantage point without attempting to present an exhaustive picture of the client-centered scene. The present "trend analysis" will thus be limited in three ways. Firstly, I will focus mainly on psychotherapy and counseling, and only occasionally on the wider field of the person-centered approach. Secondly, I will take written material as my main source of information. Although this is undoubtedly the most valid avenue to what has been achieved on the scholarly and scientific level, it is not the only avenue to client-centered "life": Much that is valuable has been done without being written down. Thirdly, to a great extent my survey will be limited to the languages I am familiar with (English, German, Dutch and French). For a survey of the growing number of Japanese and Latin-American publications I can refer to: Murayama, Nojima, and Abe, 1988; Tassinari and Doxsey, 1987.

REFLECTIONS OF A GENERAL NATURE

Paucity of publications

While compiling a bibliography of client-centered therapy in the 1970's and the 1980's (Lietaer, 1988) I was struck by the fact that the client-centered contribution to the psychotherapy literature was rather limited in volume and shrinking with the passing of the years. American journals of clinical psychology and psychotherapy only sporadically included an article with a client-centered orientation. Psychological Abstracts mentioned roughly 10 to 15 references per year under the headings "client-centered therapy" and "experiential therapy," a negligible quantity when compared to the number of references on psychoanalytic therapy and on behavior therapy. Especially striking was the almost total absence of the client-centered approach from the literature on specific therapeutic modalities such as couple therapy, family therapy, and child therapy.

Big differences exist however among the language groups. I was amazed at the large number of German publications, in which the work of Reinhard and Anne-Marie Tausch (1981) at the University of Hamburg, and of Johannes Helm (1980) at the von Humboldt University of Berlin have a central place. The opposite could be said of the French publications: The French do not seem to be very receptive to the Rogerian message on psychotherapy. The productivity in The Netherlands and in Flanders may be described as "moderate but growing" (e.g. Lietaer, van Praag, & Swildens, 1984; Van Balen, Leijssen & Lietaer, 1986). The greatest number of contributions still comes from the English-speaking world (e.g. recently: Levant & Shlien, 1984; Combs & Avila, 1985; Patterson, 1985; Wright, Everett, & Roisman, 1986; Mearns & Thorne, 1988), but especially in the United States client-centered therapy seems to be losing the position it once had (Strupp, 1978, p. 16).

What are the causes of this decline in scholarly activity? The termination of the Wisconsin project (Rogers et al., 1967) seems to have been a crucial moment in the history of client-centered therapy. It was the end of what Barrett-Lennard (1979) calls "the school phase." Since 1965 no Mecca exists anymore where a team of therapists is endeavoring in a coordinated effort to expand client-centered theory, research and practice. The members of the Wisconsin team have disbanded (not entirely on friendly terms), and since then no large client-centered research projects have been undertaken. Furthermore, many client-centered therapists have evolved towards an eclectic way of working with clients (e.g. Howe, 1982). And finally, especially during the seventies, and partly under the influence of anti-academic tendencies within the Human Potential Movement, client-centered therapists seem to have concentrated on action and practice, and no longer took the time to put on paper what they learned from their experiences. I want to add however that since about 1983, there seems to be a revival of scientific reflection and writing.

Diversity and divergence

The 1970's produced a great diversity in thinking and working. The earlier unity around the central figure of Rogers gave way to different factions, i.e.: A group around Rogers in the Center for Studies of the Person, La Jolla; Gendlin and his collaborators; a group around Truax and Carkhuff; and the contributors to the book *Innovations in client-centered therapy,* with Wexler and Rice (1974) as the most important authors. These four subgroups seemed to go their own way and lost touch with each other's work. This of course brought about a remarkable diversity of views. On a theoretical level for example, Rogers (1977) continued to elaborate further his basic philosophy; Gendlin (1973) attempted to ground his work in the European existential philosophy; Wexler and Rice (1974) chose the cognitive learning psychology as a theoretical framework, while Truax and Carkhuff (and many after them) worked on an eclectic model of the helping relationship. There were also striking differences on the methodological and didactic level. Rogers (1980b) for example, chose to work in an unstructured way, even in workshops with large groups; Carkhuff (1972) and Gordon (1970) - among others - opted for a clearly structured approach when training people in relationship skills.

It might be mentioned in parenthesis that the diversity within the client-centered approach is even reflected in the profusion of names given to it. The French often use the term "non-directive therapy"; the Germans seem to use more readily "Gesprächspsychotherapie"; the Dutch usually speak of "Rogerian therapy." The term most frequently used is however undoubtedly "client-centered therapy," but more and more the La Jolla group is replacing it with the term "Person-centered approach," thus emphasizing the applicability of client-centered principles to the broader field of education, human relations and social organizations. Finally, Gendlin calls his approach "experiential psychotherapy" and defines it as a "method of methods" (1974b).

In my opinion, this diversity and divergence should be applauded. It is part of the richness of our approach, and is in fact the logical consequence of the client-centered basic philosophy, i.e. not to submit slavishly to authority but to seek one's own way in a personal and experiential manner. Rogers always tried to oppose doctrinarianism and dogmatism. Yet, I think it would be beneficial if there were more contact and coordination within the client-centered approach. Not the diversity itself is regrettable but the fact that few people know about other people's work, and the result is a lack of "cross fertilization." I am happy however with the appearance of the international journal *Person-centered Review.* I hope that the journal will increase the depth of client-centered thinking, stimulate the confrontation with other approaches, and become a medium of contact between client-centered therapists of all continents.

Few key figures

Client-centered therapy has existed now for over forty five years. When comparing it to other approaches, it strikes me how much it has been dominated by a few central figures. Carl Rogers was the dominant figure until the end of the fifties. Then for some time Gendlin and Rogers formed a duet (which may have looked more like a duel at times; see Kirschenbaum, 1979, pp. 281-287). In the 1970's and the 1980's as well, the most creative work was done by only a few people: Rogers, Gendlin and Rice. This does not mean that they were the only ones doing useful work, but it was for example Rogers who put the new findings on paper although he has always given credit to the stimulating influence of his colleagues. A lot of the work done by other authors promotes client-centered ideas rather than providing new directions. The handbooks of Reinhard and Anne-Marie Tausch (1977 and 1981), are good examples of this. While they are very good introductions to the Rogerian approach and have had an enormous impact on German psychotherapists, they do not contain many ideas which are really new.

ROGERS

Despite his advanced age Rogers has remained extremely productive until he died in February 1987. In addition to many articles he published six books after 1969: *Freedom to learn* (1969), *Carl Rogers on encounter groups* (1970), *On becoming partners* (1972), *Carl Rogers on personal power* (1977), *A way of being* (1980a), *Freedom to learn for the 1980's* (1983). To a large extent these books may be considered as the application of his fundamental vision on therapy to other areas of human relations. They are in part "variations on a theme," and are perhaps because of this not likely to survive as long as his pioneer work. Yet, Rogers has done more than simply applying the client-centered principles to new fields. He has gradually expanded his basic philosophy, mainly by explicating the political dimension of client-centered theory in the context of therapy and education, and extending it to life and work relations in general. He summarized his political ideology, a blueprint of a "silent revolution," as follows (1978):

> "I find that for myself, I am most satisfied politically: When every person is helped to become aware of his or her own power and strength; when each person participates fully and responsibly in every decision which affects him or her; when group members learn that the sharing of power is more satisfying than endeavoring to use power to control others; when the group finds ways of making decisions which accomodate the needs and desires of each person; when every member of the group is aware of the consequences of a decision, on its members and on the external world; when each person enforces the group decision through self-control of his or her own behavior; when each person feels increasingly empowered, strengthened; when each person, and the group as a whole, is flexible, open to change, and regards previous decisions as being always open for reconsideration."

Rogers was no longer active in conducting empirical-scientific research. His advanced age and his ambivalence about the research methodology in positivistic sciences (Lietaer, 1971) has undoubtedly played an important role in this. Personally, I have always had the impression that he was not well supported by the people at the Center for Studies of the Person (CSP) in his research activities. When I was there in 1969-1970 it struck me that only a few of his colleagues were really familiar with his work in a fundamental way, that many of them were not deeply interested in client-centered theory, and certainly not in client-centered research. Sometimes I think that Rogers must have experienced this as a lack. On the other hand, being a "Resident Fellow" of CSP was deeply satisfying to him: He had good personal contacts at the Center; he could work with therapists and group facilitators who were very different from him in style and orientation; and he could experiment with new ideas perhaps more easily than in a University setting. During the last two decades he had a rich and stimulating life (e.g. see Kirschenbaum, 1979).

GENDLIN

Eugene Gendlin has also been very active during the past two decades. Maybe the most characteristic aspect of his evolution is that he has detached himself from the client-centered approach by presenting his own approach - "experiential psychotherapy" - as an independent and broader method: A "method of methods" which is applicable to client-centered therapy as well as to other approaches (Gendlin, 1974b, 1986a). This departure from the client-centered orientation is most noticeable in Corsini's book "Current Psychotherapies" (1973). It contains a chapter on client-centered therapy, and a separate one on experiential psychotherapy, with no reference at all to Rogers' writings. It seems thus that Gendlin tries to strengthen his own identity. I find that he is partly correct in doing so; after all he has made an original contribution. On the other hand I believe that Rogers and Gendlin have a lot in common in their basic view of the therapeutic process, that they have influenced each other a great deal and that it would be a distortion of reality to consider their approaches as two separate orientations.

Another characteristic of Gendlin's recent work is his somewhat onesided attention to the self-exploration process of the individual, almost at the expense of the interpersonal context. When reading certain passages from his book *Focusing* (1981), it would seem that he still considers the quality of the relationship with another person as important in order to optimize the receptive process of inner listening to the "bodily felt sense". Yet in contrast to Rogers, his attention is mainly directed to the intrapsychic process of focusing and to the (self-) instructions which can facilitate it.

Furthermore, it is striking to see Gendlin move between being very concrete and being very abstract in his writings. He unites in his person the rare combination of a "philosopher-technician." His attempts at building a theoretical basis of experiential psychotherapy read like philosophical tracts which I often find difficult to swallow. On the other hand, his rules for constructive focusing and his instructions for listening are sometimes overly concrete.

THE INFORMATION PROCESSING APPROACH: RICE AND OTHERS

I had never heard of these authors prior to the publication of their book *Innovations in client-centered therapy in 1974* (Wexler & Rice). They form, together with some others, a separate wing within the client-centered orientation, in the sense that their theoretical framework borrows much from cognitive psychology. From this vantage point, they try to describe and further analyze the therapeutic process as a process of integrating information whereby the therapist - mostly by virtue of his empathic responses - functions as a "surrogate-information-processor"; as somebody who tries to evoke aspects of experiencing which the client has not yet fully integrated on the cognitive level.

These authors are not prolific but their writings are of high quality. For example, Rice's chapter about "the evocative function of the therapist" is, in my opinion, among the best writings of the last fifteen years. The book *Innovations in client-centered therapy* has been the most innovative but perhaps also the most contested contribution of the 1970's. Above all, Wexler's bulky chapter - which forms the theoretical substratum of the whole book - caused much polemic discussion. His opposition to Rogers seems more directed against the letter than against the spirit of Rogers' writings. Certain passages in the book seem too cognitive to me: I miss the psychodynamic dimension. Psychopathology and psychotherapy are described, respectively, as merely a question of deficient processing style and how to improve it. In my opinion, the importance of inter- and intra-personal conflicts as factors causing and maintaining such defective forms of information processing, is underestimated in this cognitive theory. I find it quite positive however that the authors have succeeded in bringing together the client-centered theory and academic psychology. They returned the empathic response to the limelight after the years of unrestrained glorification of transparency; and they clearly described how empathy can be instrumental in bringing about change. They proposed a typology of clients' styles of information processing, and differential ways for the therapist to respond to what the client communicates. And, they have underlined the vocal and paralinguistic aspects of the self-exploration process. Finally it should be acknowledged that these authors have been very active and creative in conducting microscopic process research: E.g. see in this volume the chapters of Iberg, Rice and

Greenberg, Sachse, Toukmanian, Zimring. In June 1988 Laura Rice was given the Distinguished Research Career Award by the Society for Psychotherapy Research.

TOWARDS PREVENTION AND SOCIAL ISSUES

When Rogers went to the Western Behavioral Sciences Institute in 1963, he left to a large extent the field of individual psychotherapy and started working with small and large groups. Many other client-centered therapists began to concentrate on prevention and social problems. They became - in the wake of the human potential movement - quiet revolutionaries, concerned with humanizing society. This shift was certainly influenced and supported by the fact that American society was plagued with rather disturbing problems at the end of the 1960's. However, it also was in line with client-centered theory not to make any sharp difference between therapy in the strict sense and personality development. Rogers always defined health in positive terms : Not as the absence of pathology but as continuing growth in realizing one's potentialities, a growth in "being in process." Moreover, Rogers has always emphasized that the professional-therapeutic relationship is only one type of growth enhancing relationship; that the basic attitudes of empathy, acceptance and authenticity are not the privilege of professional therapists but are in fact human qualities which can be displayed and developed by other people as well. Hence the easy switch from individual work to human relations in general. For a critical reflection on the dangers and shortcomings of these society-oriented initiatives, see Farson (1978) and Coulson (1984).

The encounter group

The small person-to-person group - "basic encounter group" or "experiential learning group" (Barrett-Lennard, 1974) - has been the most frequently used modality by client-centered facilitators. Rogers (1970) was so convinced of the power and impact of such groups that he called them "the greatest social discovery" of the twentieth century.

Only a small percentage of the publications on client-centered group work are about therapy proper (e.g. Mente & Spittler, 1980; Eckert &

Biermann-Ratjen, 1985), the majority referring to groups where personal growth is the main objective. Research shows that the difference between group therapy and growth groups should not be too strongly emphasized because the processes involved and problems handled in outpatient therapy groups and encounter groups are about the same. Nevertheless I feel that we have to face a certain deficiency within our orientation: We lack precise descriptions of the specific processes and problems encountered in longterm group therapy programs on a weekly basis. In this context, Yalom's handbook (1975) would be a good supplement to what the client-centered literature has to offer.

Very often, the encounter group has been used for objectives beyond the promotion of personal growth and self-actualization. As an experiential learning tool it often plays an important part in teaching and training in counseling, group therapy and human relations in general. Moreover, client-centered facilitators have tried to bring together in encounter groups select subgroups of people, particularly people living in conflict with each other or entertaining prejudices about each other, in the hope to improve communication between them. They worked for example with whites and blacks, with Catholics and Protestants from Northern Ireland, with parties in conflict about the drug problem, and with different interest groups within the health sector. During the last years of his life Rogers became very involved in his Peace Project (Rogers & Ryback 1984; *J. Humanistic Psychology,* 1987, whole issue no. 3, 275-384), and also within this context he used encounter groups to help people of conflicting political factions learn about one another "as people" (i.e. beyond their social and political roles).

Furthermore many client-centered workers have seen the encounter group as an ideal tool to assist life and work communities, as well as larger organizations, in developing themselves or solving their internal problems. These workers were, as agents of change, most often active in the non-profit sector, especially in the field of education. The best known project of this kind is the Immaculate Heart Project, an ambitious experiment "for self-directed change in an educational system." There is no consensus as to the results of this project. Rogers (1974) was rather positive about it, but Coulson (1972) was ambivalent: He believed that it was quite positive on the level of personal growth but that the mass introduction of encounter groups was too directive an intervention. In his opinion the project staff wanted to change too much too quickly. This brought about a polarization within the system which led to the termination of the project.

Person-centered communities and non-professional help

Client-centered facilitators also became interested in person-centered and therapeutic community building. At the Center for Studies of the Person the emphasis was on working with large groups (60 to 200 persons) of brief duration (1 to 3 weeks) (Rogers, 1980b; Bozarth, 1981; Wood 1984). The goal of such person-centered workshops was to learn to build self-regulating communities in which the individual would not get suffocated: "In these groups we have come to focus our efforts on providing a climate in which the participant can make his or her own choices, can participate equally with others in planning or carrying out activities, can become more aware of personal strengths, can become increasingly autonomous and creative as the architect of his or her own life" (Rogers, 1980b). In the same line - under the impulse of Devonshire - many intercultural workshops have been organized in Western and Eastern European Countries (Devonshire & Kremer, 1980).

Along with these, we find the "Changes Communities," set up under the direction of Gendlin, who had a more therapeutic objective in mind. It is in fact a form of local community work, with "peer counseling" being carried out in a structured manner. Mc Guire (1982) describes the Changes model in the following way:

> "Through a weekly community meeting, interested persons from a neighbourhood community are introduced to listening and focusing skills. They are provided the opportunity to arrange exchanges of listening turns with others in the Changes group. There is no distinction made between professionals and non-professionals, helpers and helpees, "well" persons and "sick" persons. As a person forms friendships through the exchange of listening turns, these friends begin to function as a supportive community for him or her throughout the week or in special times of crisis."

One of Gendlin's main concerns while developing the Changes model was "to give psychotherapy back to people". An important element in this was the introduction of the non-professional in community mental health programs. Many client-centered therapists have taken initiatives on this level. Bebout and Gordon (1972) carried out a large process and outcome study on groups which were led by non-professionals.

Goodman (1972) worked out a program of "companionship therapy":
He selected therapeutically talented young people on the basis of how
they functioned in small groups, gave them a short training, and
allowed them - during a period of 6 months and on the basis of 2 to 3
contacts per week - to develop a relationship with a problem child in
the local community. These and other examples (under the next point)
illustrate how client-centered workers have tried to introduce
intrinsically helpful people into the field of prevention-oriented
counseling work. For a survey I can refer to Larsons' book *Teaching
psychological skills: Models for giving psychotherapy away* (1984), in
which you find chapters by Gendlin, Goodman, Gordon, Guerney and
McGuire-Boukydis.

Didactic-experiential training programs

Rogers' basic hypothesis about the necessary and sufficient conditions
for constructive personality change, found an enormous response in the
world of psychotherapy, counseling and education. The basic attitudes
of authenticity, acceptance, and empathy became and are recognized by
many (also outside the client-centered orientation) as being core
conditions in every form of personal relationship and helping contact.
The question however remains as to how people can best be trained in
these relational skills. Some of Rogers' colleagues opted for a
structured-didactic way. The therapeutic attitudes - described by
Rogers as being more a way of being than a way of doing - were
translated concretely, molded into scaled steps and taught in short-term
training programs in communication skills. This wing in the client-
centered orientation is in fact strongly related to behavior and
communication therapy, which tends to teach "life skills" in a
cognitive-didactic way.

These programs were not only set up for professional and non-
professional health workers, but also for parents, teachers, paramedics,
partners... in short, for everybody who is involved in personal or
growth-promoting relationships. Some of these programs were applied
on a very large scale. Gordon is the first who comes to mind in this
context: His book *Parent effectiveness training* (1970) became a best-
seller; he has provided training for over half a million parents, teachers
and other helpers in the U.S. alone. Then there is the contribution of
Guerney (1977): Originally he trained parents of children suffering

from emotional difficulties but later on he worked out a program for partners in general. Also the didactic-experiential programs of Carkhuff and colleagues (1972) have been very influential, especially in the American training programs for counselors. Within the same - eclectic and integrative - approach we can also mention Egans book *The skilled helper* (1975), Martins book *Counseling and therapy skills* (1983), and Ivey's book *Developmental therapy* (1987). Many show scepticism about these "instant courses" on Rogerian basic attitudes. Above all the existentially-oriented client-centered therapists are afraid that Rogers' true message may become distorted. They point out the danger of teaching therapists hollow behavior, wooden techniques which are not anchored in a personal philosophy or way of being.

RESEARCH

Historical sketch

The client-centered tradition has always been on the frontline of research. Looking back at the last thirty years it strikes me how much Rogers' article on the "necessary and sufficient conditions of therapeutic change" (1957) has stimulated the research in psychotherapy: During fifteen years this hypothesis has been a dominant force in the field of psychotherapy research. Around 1973 however research on Rogers' basic hypothesis came to a standstill. Hence the seventies and eighties are mainly characterized by a multitude of reviews on previous research rather than by reports about new research projects.

One can pose the following question together with the authors of these reviews: What insights have twenty years of research on Rogers' conception of psychotherapy given us? What remains of his "process equation" (1961)? The early years of this sort of research were very hopeful. Rogers and his colleagues found in a number of studies a clear connection between the level of his triad of basic attitudes and the degree of therapeutic success. Rogers' hypothesis was further strengthened by the finding that very low levels of the basic attitudes correlated with deterioration. A review of the research of this productive period can be found in a chapter by Truax and Mitchell in Bergin and Garfield's handbook of 1971. These findings were confirmed in Europe in a vast amount of studies carried out by R. Tausch (e.g. 1975) and co-workers.

Attracted by these promising results, many researchers from different therapeutic orientations also became interested in Rogers' hypothesis. For example, the NIMH financed a large project - the Arkansas study under the direction of Mitchell, Truax, Bozarth and Krauft (1973) - in which 75 experienced therapists participated with 120 clients. In this project as well as in many subsequent studies, the former strong relations were no longer found; moreover there was no longer any association found between deterioration and low levels of basic attitudes. Thus the results became more and more disillusioning, and this gave rise to fundamental methodological and clinical-theoretical reflection. In retrospect, the earlier research results were perhaps not as positive as they seemed to be. When a more critical analysis was applied to the survey of Truax and Mitchell (1971), it seemed that Truax had the tendency of covering up negative findings. Additionally, in several publications on the same research, contradictory results were reported (Parloff, Waskow and Wolfe, 1978, pp. 242-252).

Reflections on the meager harvest

Many authors wrote critical reviews, with reflections on theoretical and methodological issues. The interested reader should consult the following articles: Bozarth, 1983; Gurman, 1977; Lambert, 1986; Lambert, Dejulio and Stein, 1978; Mitchell, Bozarth and Krauft, 1977; Parloff, Waskow and Wolfe, 1978; Watson, 1984. Patterson (1984) wrote a "review of reviews," in which he argues that many reviewers had a negative bias and hence have underestimated the evidence for the effectiveness of the Rogerian therapist variables. Whatever the final conclusion might be, the research data stimulated a "consciousness raising process" concerning the nature itself of Rogers' hypothesis. Almost all reviewers point out that Rogers' vision is formulated in too general a way, that it is not sufficiently differentiated as to the sort of client and the phase of therapy. According to them the Rogerian researchers have paid too little attention to the complexity of the therapeutic process, particularly to the interaction with other than relational variables. A few thoughts may illustrate this.

Some authors maintain that it is perhaps in the initial phase - where building up a good contact is central - that the basic attitudes are both "necessary and sufficient."Of course an optimal working alliance remains important during the whole course of therapy, but other capacities of the therapist come into play at later stages in the process: For example his ability to bring the client's problem into the here-and-now and to deal with it in a constructive way, his ability to make the client's decisions concrete and to support them... Deep empathy or bold self-expression can be too threatening for the client in the first phase of therapy... Gurman suspects that it is not so much the average empathy level of the therapist which is important, but his empathy level at those critical moments during therapy when the client reveals crucial material... Certain clients need above all warmth and acceptance, while empathy may be deepened only gradually; with other clients one must rather temper the warmth in order to preserve a work atmosphere... Confrontation and feedback can be very helpful for certain clients at certain moments, whereas for others it can be both disturbing and distracting... In short, these authors maintain - and I agree with them - that Rogers' hypothesis has been formulated in too general, too linear and too incomplete a way, and that there is little or no purpose in continuing further research on the relation between such isolated and very general variables and the outcome.

Besides stimulating a reformulation and refinement of Rogers' basic hypothesis, this chain of studies has contributed importantly to the broader field of psychotherapy and psychotherapy research. The fairly strong connection which was found between the client-perception of the relationship at the start of therapy and the outcome, points to how important it is to build up a good working alliance as a conditio sine qua non for effective psychotherapy. The research on eclectic and psycho-dynamically-oriented psychotherapy (Waterhouse and Strupp, 1984) also points more and more to the same direction. Client-centered research has also shown that there is a clear connection between the quality of the experiencing process and the outcome of therapy (Orlinsky and Howard, 1978, p. 305). This means that Rogers' and Gendlin's vision as to the characteristics of a fruitful self-exploration process seems to be a very valuable one. Finally these studies have led up to a sharpening of methodological questions and to the construction of a series of process scales which may be of permanent value; I especially think here of the Experiencing Scales of Klein, Mathieu and Kiesler (1986), and of the Relationship Inventory of Barrett-Lennard (1986).

Perhaps client-centered research has been too reductionistic

(Bozarth, 1983). There has been a certain "split" in the client-centered approach between the phenomenological-existential character of its practice and the strict-positivistic research methodology. The studies of the sixties burst with numbers and tables; the complex therapeutic process of flesh and blood threatens to be burried under it. I think that the research work already done must be supplemented by detailed process research, in which naturalistic observation and longitudinal case studies would seem to be methodologically more appropriate.

THE PRACTICE OF CLIENT-CENTERED THERAPY

The core of the client-centered approach remains constructive personality change and how to facilitate it as a therapist. But how is client-centered therapy actually practiced today? I would like to draw attention to some shifts in emphasis which seem to have occurred over the past two decades and are, in my opinion, clearly visible in the chapters of this book.

Most characteristic perhaps - at least in European countries - is the fact that client-centered therapists have shaken off their phobia of directing. The time of the "don'ts" (Gendlin, 1970b) has perhaps passed by forever. Most client-centered therapists no longer feel uneasy when defining their work as an active influencing process in which they try to stimulate the unfolding of the client's experiencing process through task-oriented interventions. As "process experts" they have found a way to intervene actively without falling into manipulation or authoritarian control. The central principle here is that the experience of the client has to remain the continuous touchstone for what is introduced by the therapist: The therapist must always be receptive and responsive to what his interventions have brought about in the client. Of course in order to achieve this, a good relationship is needed, but there should be no conflict between "relation" and "technique" (e.g. Rice, 1983; Tscheulin, 1983).

In line with what I just said, more attention has been given to aspects of the therapeutic work which go a little further than "maintenance reflections" or merely the creation of interpersonal safety. Rice for example describes the evocative function of the therapist as follows (1974, p. 298): "He simply tries to sense as accurately as possible 'this is what it was like to be the client at that moment'. It is this flavor of the total experience that he tries to give back to the client as concretely and vividly as possible. Hopefully, the client can then use this reflection to deepen and enrich his own awareness of the total experience and thus to broaden his construction of it." In doing this she sees the use of metaphors and vivid language as powerful tools. As for Gendlin (1981), his focusing instructions aim at drawing the client's attention to what is not yet clear, albeit directly and bodily felt. Even though both these authors follow a different road they have the same goal: To let something new take shape, to stir deeper layers of experiencing during the client's inner self-exploration process. Furthermore, the use of the therapist's here-and-now experience, of confrontation and feedback (Gendlin, 1967; Rogers, 1970; Carkhuff and Berenson, 1977; Kiesler, 1982) are increasingly described as active ways of deepening the process, as ways of helping the client move beyond his rigid perceptual or behavioral patterns.

In addition, there is a tendency to describe in more detail the specific interventions of the therapist with each type of client, in each type of setting, for each type of ongoing process, etc... Rogers has always restricted himself to the description of what he found essential, the "heart of the matter. "He left it to every therapist to give it its concrete form and thus certainly respected everybody's personal style. The other side of this "fundamentalism" was however a lack of differential description. For example, how does one begin a therapy with a poorly motivated client? How can we work with a psychosomatic client who does not experience any connection between his bodily symptoms and personal problems? How do we tackle the problems arising around the termination of therapy?... These kinds of specific problems are hardly ever touched upon in the client-centered literature. Of course cookbook recipes cannot be given, but concrete suggestions from therapists with many years of experience with a certain type of client could be extremely useful, as was for example Gendlin's excellent article on client-centered therapy with schizophrenics (1967). Today however, especially in Europe, there is a noticeable change towards more specification and differentiation. Innovative work of that type has been done in the following areas: Therapy with the severely disturbed (e.g. *Zeitschrift für Personenzentrierte Psychologie und Psychotherapie,* 1986, 5, whole issue no. 4, 361-480; Swildens, 1988; Prouty & Pietrzak, 1988; see also Part 2 of this book); dream therapy (e.g. Gendlin, 1986a; Vossen, see this book; Wijngaarden, 1985); health psychology and person-centered medicine (e.g. A. Tausch, 1981; A. Tausch & R. Tausch, 1985; Barnard, 1984; Jaspers, 1985; Speierer, 1985; Pfeiffer, 1986).

Finally, many client-centered therapists have evolved in the direction of a more eclectic attitude. Rogers' fear of orthodoxy seems increasingly unfounded. With minimal guilt and inner conflict, many client-centered therapists look for what can be borrowed from other orientations and integrated. And this seems to be a considerable amount (e.g. Martin, 1972; Howe, 1982; Peters, 1984; Tausch, see this volume)! There are hardly any techniques left which are not used by some client-centered therapists as part of their experiential work: E.g. psychodrama, hypnosis, behavior therapy procedures, Gestalt techniques, relaxation methods, the scream technique... As far as knowledge of psychopathology and process diagnosis are concerned, many allow themselves to be influenced by insights from psychodynamic, "systems" and behavior therapy... We are thus evolving towards a broadly conceived experiential psychotherapy whereby these techniques and insights can all be used as "fishing lines" (Gendlin, 1974a and 1974b). An illustration of this trend is to be found in Gendlin's book on experiential dreamwork (1986a): Many insights and procedures from other orientations are used here to help the client focus on the meaning of his dream. Without a doubt, this evolution bears witness to the ecumenical spirit working within our orientation, but it gives rise to questions about our identity, the communality in our approach and its differentiation from other orientations.

PROPOSALS FOR THE FUTURE

What does our orientation need and which developments should we stimulate in the nineties? At the Leuven Conference I formulated what I see as our most urgent needs and made some specific proposals for each. Here they follow, in seven points (For viewpoints of other colleagues: See Cain et al., 1989).

We need better organization and better communication channels

Since Rogers did not want a school, we remained to a great extent a "free association" on the international level. One of the serious problems in organizing the Leuven conference was to find the names and addresses of people who are deeply acquainted with, and interested in, client-centered/experiential psychotherapy. Therefore I propose that we:

- Create a *confederation* of already-existing associations and institutes. Each association or institute would be asked to send useful information about its activities to the other associations, which in turn could send the information to their members through their newsletters;
- Support a few (not many) high quality journals; and
- Organize - every three years - an International Conference on Client-centered and Experiential Psychotherapy, supported and coordinated by the already existing associations, institutes, research units, and training centers.

We need to accept and enjoy the fact that we are professional experts and foster (restore?) that image in society and in psychotherapy circles

To me there is no contradiction between creating a good helping alliance along Rogerian lines and being a process expert. To this end, I propose that we:

- Organize long-term training programs with high standards, programs which can be taken seriously by other orientations. This is a "vital" proposal: To make progress in practice, theory building and research, we need well-trained and highly competent client-centered/experiential therapists in the first place!
- Found psychotherapy associations or local networks in countries which do not yet have such an organization. When I look at the associations I am acquainted with (in Belgium, The Netherlands and Germany), I think they have been extremely important in providing mutual support, a place for exchange and stimulation of ideas, and a voice in society for psychotherapy issues.

We need a younger generation of scholars

In our orientation most of the work has been done by Rogers and his first generation of students. After the Wisconsin project we have been stagnating compared to other orientations. Not much has been written by younger colleagues.

If we wish to attract young scholars we will have to make meaningful contributions to the field, and make an effort not to lose our already weak position at the universities. Therefore I propose that we initiate a better dialogue with academic psychology and the other behavioral sciences. More specifically, I propose that every trainee should write a paper as a part of his training program . This will stimulate the intellectual development of our trainees and help us to identify those young talents who should be encouraged to publish their work.

We need to expand our therapy theory

Since 1965 not much work has been done on the level of theory building. Yet many aspects of our theoretical patrimony (e.g. our "image of man," our theory of personality change) are in need of further elaboration, refinement or correction.

As a first step, I think it would be very useful - after half a century of client-centered therapy - to collaborate on the publication of a *handbook* (in several volumes), in which contributions of our most creative authors would be integrated to form a balanced and harmonious new Gestalt. One should especially pay sufficient attention to the interpersonal (e.g. Anchin & Kiesler, 1982; van Kessel, 1975; Pfeiffer, 1987; Shlien, 1987; Van Balen, 1984) and the existential dimension (e.g. Yalom, 1980; Friedman, 1986; Swildens, 1988) of our approach. Such a handbook would meet the needs of many: It would be a useful didactic tool in education and training; for the interested outsider - and also for many therapists within our own circle - it would be an opportunity to get an up-to-date and integrated picture of client-centered/experiential psychotherapy. Finally it would offer us a renewed platform from which to continue working on the expansion of our therapy system.

We need to develop our view on working with couples and families

We do not have much literature on couple and family therapy; in this area the work of Van der Veen and Raskin (1970), Levant (1982), Auckenthaler (1983), Pavel (1984) and Greenberg & Johnson (1986) is an exception. This is indeed amazing, when we think that within the sector of prevention, training and education, the client-centered approach has always aimed at facilitating life and work relations (e.g.

Guerney, 1984; Levant, 1983). Do we have to leave to other orientations the therapeutic work with "stranded systems?" I rather believe that we have a voice of our own. Many client-centered psychotherapists practice couple therapy (though the number of family therapists within our circle is somewhat more limited). It would thus be interesting to make explicit what our basic premises are in psychotherapeutic work with existing systems, how we concretely work and what we experience as being specific in our approach. The chapters in this book on couple and family therapy may provide a stimulus in that direction.

We need more and meaningful research

Client-centered research no longer sets the tone in the world of psychotherapy research. One of the reasons for this decline is the fact that - in comparison with psychoanalytic and behavior therapy - client-centered therapy does not have a strong position in the universities: The power in clinical psychology and psychiatry departments is usually not in client-centered hands. In addition, there has been discontent with the prevailing positivistic research methodology. Yet, times are changing: There is a growing openness for hermeneutic and qualitative research methods. Within our orientation the creative work of Elliott, Greenberg and Rice (e.g. see Rice & Greenberg, 1984) may be a source of inspiration. If we wish to carry out meaningful research which will appeal to and influence the practitioner, we will have to return to an intensive and discovery-oriented analysis of the therapy process. In doing so we could get more insight in *when and under what specific conditions* certain interventions are effective or not; we could focus our analysis on micro-processes (Gendlin, 1986b), critical incidents and significant moments of change (instead of studying blindly selected 4-minute-segments); and we could learn much about how a specific client problem is approached throughout the different phases of therapy. This sort of research would at the same time supply interesting didactic material and meet the need for specificity and process diagnosis. It seems to me that it would be useful not only to study successful cases but failure cases as well. Let us hope that the client-centered/experiential orientation will renew its research tradition and that we will make new and important contributions to the field of psychotherapy in the coming years.

We need to define our family boundaries

- Do we need to exist as a separate orientation? YES, we are just too good to be absorbed (in a superficial way) by other orientations. Our richness should not be lost. Along with the psychoanalytic, "systems" and behavioral approaches, I think there remains a need for a more phenomenological-experiential-existential approach.
- What are our family boundaries? I am in favor of an *extended family* in which there is room for diversity, but one which has, as the corner stones of its identity, the triad of therapist attitudes and the focus on the experiential process.
- And what about psychotherapy integration? Client-centered therapy played an important role in the ecumenical movement between orientations. In fact Rogers' and Gendlin's views on personality change are metatheories: They do not emphasize specific procedures or contents, but rather general and formal process characteristics which they believe are true for *all* good therapy.

Along the lines of the above discussion I propose to follow two tracks: Expand our own system, yet, at the same time, make bridges to other orientations and look for possibilities of (partial) integration.

REFERENCES

Anchin, J.C., & Kiesler, D.J. (1982). *Handbook of interpersonal psychotherapy.* New York: Pergamon Press.

Auckenthaler, A. (1983). *Klientenzentrierte Psychotherapie mit Paaren.* Stuttgart: Kohlhammer.

Barnard, D. (1984). The personal meaning of illness: Client-centered dimensions of medicine and health care. In R.F. Levant & J.M. Shlien (Eds.), *o.c.* (pp. 337-351).

Barrett-Lennard, G.T. (1974). Experiential learning groups. *Psychotherapy: Therapy, Research and Practice, 11,* 71-75.

Barrett-Lennard, G.T. (1979). The client-centered system unfolding. In F.J. Turner (Ed.), *Social work treatment: Interlocking theoretical approaches* (pp. 177-241). New York: Free Press.

Barrett-Lennard, G.T. (1986). The Relationship Inventory now: Issues and advances in theory, method, and use. In L.S. Greenberg & W.M. Pinsof (Eds.), *o.c.* (pp. 439-475).

Bebout, J., & Gordon, B. (1972). The value of encounter. In L. Solomon &

B. Berzon (Eds.), *New perspectives on encounter groups* (pp. 83-118). San Francisco: Jossey Bass.

Bozarth, J.D. (1981). The person-centered approach in the large community group. In G. Gazda (Ed.), *Innovations to group psychotherapy* (2nd ed.). Springfield, IL: Thomas.

Bozarth, J.D. (1983). Current research on client-centered therapy in the USA. In W.R. Minsel & W. Herff (Eds.), *Research on psychotherapeutic approaches* (Vol. 2, pp. 105-119). Frankfurt a/M., Bern: Peter Lang.

Cain, D.J., Lietaer, G., Sachse, R., & Thorne, B. (1989). Proposals for the future of client-centered and experiential psychotherapy. *Person-centered Review, 4(1),* 11-26.

Carkhuff, R.R. (1972). Toward a technology for human and community resource developments. *The Counseling Psychologist, 3,* 12-30 (comments: 31-87).

Carkhuff, R.R., & Berenson, B.G. (1977). In search of an honest experience. Confrontation in counseling and life. In R.R. Carkhuff & B.G. Berenson, *Beyond counseling and therapy* (pp. 198-213). New York: Holt, Rinehart and Winston.

Combs, A.W., & Avila, D.L. (1985). *Helping relationships: Basic concepts for the helping professions.* Boston: Allyn & Bacon.

Coulson, W.R. (1972). The effect of encounter groups on systems. In W. R. Coulson, *Groups, gimmicks and instant gurus* (pp. 97-166). New York: Harper & Row.

Coulson, W.R. (1984). *Backlash against the person-centered approach. Toward understanding its causes in schools.* Unpublished manuscript.

Corsini, R. (Ed.). (1973). *Current psychotherapies.* Itasca: Peacock.

Devonshire, C.M., & Kremer, J.W. (1980). *Toward a person-centered resolution of intercultural conflicts.* Dortmund: Pädagogische Arbeitsstelle.

Eckert, J., & Biermann-Ratjen, E.-M. (1985). *Stationäre Gruppenpsychotherapie: Prozesse, Effekte, Vergleiche.* Berlin: Springer.

Egan, G. (1975). *The skilled helper: A model for systematic helping and interpersonal relating.* Belmont, CA: Wadsworth.

Farson, R. (1978). The technology of humanism. *Journal of Humanistic Psychology, 2,* 5-35.

Friedman, M. (1985). *The healing dialogue in psychotherapy.* New York: Aronson.

Gendlin, E.T. (1967). Therapeutic procedures in dealing with schizophrenics. In C.R. Rogers et al. (Eds.), *o.c.* (pp. 369-400).

Gendlin, E.T. (1970a). A theory of personality change. In J.T. Hart & T.M. Tomlinson (Eds.), *o.c.* (pp. 129-174).

Gendlin, E.T. (1970b). A short summary and some long predictions. In J.T. Hart & T.M. Tomlinson (Eds.), o.c. (pp. 544-562).

Gendlin, E.T. (1973). Experiential psychotherapy. In A. Corsini (Ed.), *Current psychotherapies* (pp. 317-352). Itasca: Peacock.

Gendlin, E.T. (1974a). The role of knowledge in practice. In G.F. Farwell, N.R. Gamsky, & F. Mathieu-Coughlan (Eds.), The counselor's handbook (pp. 269-294). New York: Intext.

Gendlin, E.T. (1974b). Client-centered and experiential psychotherapy. In D.A.

Wexler, & L.N. Rice (Eds.), o.c. (pp. 211-246).

Gendlin, E.T. (1981). *Focusing* (rev. ed.). New York: Bantam Books.

Gendlin, E.T. (1986a). *Let your body interpret your dream.* Wilmette, IL: Chiron.

Gendlin, E.T. (1986b). What comes after traditional psychotherapy research? *American Psychologist, 41,* 131-136.

Goodman, G. (1972). *Companionship therapy: Studies in structured intimacy.* San Francisco: Jossey-Bass.

Gordon, T. (1970). *Parent effectiveness training: The no-lose program for raising responsible children.* New York: Wyden.

Greenberg, L.S., & Johnson, S.M. (1986). Emotionally focused couples therapy. In W.S. Jacobson & A.S. Gurman, *Clinical handbook of marital therapy* (pp. 253-276). New York: Guilford.

Greenberg, L.S., & Pinsof, W.M. (Eds.). (1986). *The psychotherapeutic process: A research handbook.* London: Guilford Press.

Guerney, B.G., Jr. (1984). Contributions of client-centered therapy to filial, marital, and family relationship enhancement therapies. In R.F. Levant & J.M. Shlien (Eds.), o.c. (pp. 261-277).

Guerney, B.G., Jr. et al. (1977). *Relationship enhancement skill-training programs for therapy, problem prevention and enrichment.* San Francisco: Jossey-Bass.

Gurman, A.S. (1977). The patient's perception of the therapeutic relationship. In A.S. Gurman & A.M. Razin (Eds.), *Effective psychotherapy: A handbook of research* (pp. 503-453). New York: Pergamon Press.

Hart, J.T., & Tomlinson, T.M. (Eds.). (1970). *New directions in client-centered therapy.* Boston: Houghton Mifflin.

Helm, J. (1980). *Gesprächspsychotherapie.* Darmstadt: Stierhaupt.

Howe, J. (Ed.). (1982). Integratives Handeln in der Gesprächstherapie. Weinheim/Basel: Beltz.

Ivey, A.E. (1987). *Developmental therapy.* London: Jossey-Bass.

Jaspers, L. (1985). *Zieken en zorgen. Psychosociale begeleiding van patiënten en hun familie.* Leuven: Acco.

van Kessel, W. (1975). Van reflektie tot interventie: Een interpretatie van het proces van de client-centered therapie in interaktionele termen. *Tijdschrift voor Psychiatrie,* 17, 342-354.

Kiesler, D.J. (1982). Confronting the client-therapist relationship in psychotherapy. In J.C. Anchin, & D.J. Kiesler (Eds.), o.c. (pp. 274-295).

Klein, M.H., Mathieu-Coughlan, Ph., & Kiesler, D.J. (1986). The experiencing scales. In L.S. Greenberg & W. Pinsof (Eds.), o.c. (pp. 21-71).

Lambert, M.J. (1986). Future directions for research in client-centered psychotherapy. *Person-centered Review, 1,* 185-200.

Lambert, M.J., Dejulio, S.J., & Stein, D.M. (1978). Therapist interpersonal skills: Process, outcome, methodological considerations, and recommendations for future research. *Psychological Bulletin, 85,* 467-489.

Larson, D. (Ed.). (1984). *Teaching psychological skills: Models for giving psychotherapy away.* Monterey, CA: Brooks-Cole.

Levant, R.F. (1982). Client-centered family therapy. *American Journal of Family Therapy, 10,* 72-75.

Levant, R.F. (1983). Client-centered skills-training programs for the family: A review of the literature. *The Counseling Psychologist, 11(3),* 29-48.

Levant, R.F., & Shlien, J.M. (Eds.). (1984). Client-centered therapy and the person-centered approach: *New directions in Theory, Research and Practice.* New York: Praeger.

Lietaer, G. (1971). De opvattingen van Carl Rogers over wetenschappelijk onderzoek. *Nederlands Tijdschrift voor Psychologie, 26,* 233-250.

Lietaer, G. (1988). *The Client-centered/Experiential/Person-centered Approach 1950-1987: Bibliographical Survey.* Brochure (120 pp.). Centrum voor client-centered psychotherapie en counseling, K.U.Leuven (Address: Blijde Inkomststraat 13, 3000 Leuven, Belgium).

Lietaer, G., van Praag, Ph.H., & Swildens, J.C.A.G. (Eds.). (1984). *Client-centered psychotherapie in beweging.* Leuven: Acco.

Martin, D.G. (1972). *Learning-based client-centered therapy.* Monterey, CA: Brooks/Cole.

Martin, D.G. (1983). *Counseling and therapy skills.* Belmont, CA: Brooks/Cole.

McGuire, K.N. (1982). *Building supportive community: Mutual self-help through peer counseling.* (Available from: 3440 Onyx St. Eugene, OR 97405).

Mearns, D., & Thorne, B. (1988). *Person-centered counseling in action.* New York/London: Sage.

Mente, A., & Spittler, H.D. (1980). *Erlebnisorientierte Gruppenpsychotherapie* (2 Vols.). Paderborn: Junfermann-Verlag.

Mitchell, K.M., Truax, C.B., Bozarth, J.D., & Krauft, C.C. (1973). *Antecedents to psychotherapeutic outcome.* NIMH Grant Report (12306), Arkansas Rehabilitation Research and Training Center, Arkansas Rehabilitation Services, Hot Springs, Arkansas.

Mitchell, K.M., Bozarth, J.D., & Krauft, C.C. (1977). A reappraisal of the therapeutic effectiveness of accurate empathy, non-possessive warmth, and genuineness. In A.S. Gurman & A.M. Razin (Eds.), *Effective psychotherapy: A handbook of research (pp. 482-502).* New York: Pergamon Press.

Murayama, S., Nojima, K., & Abe, T. (1988). Person-centered groups in Japan: A selective review of the literature. *Person-centered Review, 3,* 479-492.

Parloff, M.B., Waskow, I.E., & Wolfe, B.E. (1978). Research on therapist variables in relation to process and outcome. In S.L. Garfield & A.E. Bergin, *Handbook of psychotherapy and behavior change. An empirical analysis* (pp. 242-252). New York: Wiley.

Patterson, C.H. (1984). Empathy, warmth and genuineness in psychotherapy: A review of reviews. *Psychotherapy: Theory, Research and Practice, 21,* 431-438.

Patterson, C.H. (1985). *The therapeutic relationship: Foundations for an eclectic psychotherapy.* Monterey, CA: Brooks/Cole.

Pavel, F.G. (1984). Integrative klientenzentrierte Therapie individueller und sozialer Systeme. *Zeitschrift für personenzentrierte Psychologie und Psychotherapie, 3,* 277-300.

Peters, H. (1984). *Client-centered therapie en gedragstherapie: Een aanzet tot integratie.* Lisse: Swets & Zeitlinger.

Pfeiffer, W.M. (1986). *Psychologie des kranken Menschen.* Stuttgart: Kohlhammer.

Pfeiffer, W.M. (1987). Uebertragung und Realbeziehung in der Sicht klientenzentrierter Psychotherapie. *Zeitschrift für personenzentrierte Psychologie und Psychotherapie, 6,* 347-352.

Prouty, G., & Pietrzak, S. (1988). The pre-therapy method applied to persons experiencing hallucinatory images. *Person-centered Review, 3,* 426-441.

Rice, L.N. (1974). The evocative function of the therapist. In D.A. Wexler & L.N. Rice (Eds.), *o.c.* (pp. 289-311).

Rice, L.N. (1983). The relationship in client-centered therapy. In M.J. Lambert (Ed.), *Psychotherapy and patient relationship.* Homewood: Dow Jones-Irwin.

Rice, L.N., & Greenberg, L.S. (1984). Patterns of change. *Intensive analysis of psychotherapy process.* New York: Guilford.

Rogers, C.R. (1957). The necessary and sufficient conditions of therapeutic change. *Journal of Consulting Psychology, 21,* 97-103.

Rogers, C.R. (1959). A theory of therapy, personality and interpersonal relationships as developed in the client-centered framework. In S. Koch (Ed.), *Psychology: A study of science* (Vol. 3, pp. 184-256). New York: Mc Graw Hill.

Rogers, C.R. (1961). The process equation of psychotherapy. *American Journal of Psychotherapy, 15,* 27-45.

Rogers, C.R. (1969). *Freedom to learn.* Columbus: Charles E. Merrill.

Rogers, C.R. (1970). *Carl Rogers on encounter groups.* New York: Harper & Row.

Rogers, C.R. (1972). *On becoming partners: Marriage and its alternatives.* New York: Delacorte.

Rogers, C.R. (1974). The project at Immaculate Heart: An experiment in self-directed change. *Education, 95,* 172-196.

Rogers, C.R. (1977). *Carl Rogers on personal power. Inner strength and its revolutionary impact.* New York: Delacorte.

Rogers, C.R. (1978). *My political view. A statement to the El Escorial Workshop.* Unpublished manuscript.

Rogers, C.R. (1980a). *A way of being.* Boston: Houghton Mifflin.

Rogers, C.R. (1980b). Building person-centered communities: The implications for the future. In C.R. Rogers, *o.c.* (pp. 181-206).

Rogers, C.R. (1983). *Freedom to learn for the 80's* (Rev. ed.). Columbus, Ohio: Charles Merrill.

Rogers, C.R. et al. (Eds.). (1967). *The therapeutic relationship and its impact. A study of psychotherapy with schizophrenics.* Madison: Univ. Wisc. Press.

Rogers, C.R., & Ryback, D. (1984). One alternative to nuclear planetary suicide. In R.F. Levant & J. M. Shlien (Eds.), *o.c.* (pp. 400-422).

Shlien, J.M. (1987). A countertheory of transference. *Person-centered Review, 2,* 15-49 (comments: 153-202/455-475).

Speierer, G.W. (1985). *Das patientenorientierte Gespräch. Baustein einer personenzentrierten Medizin.* München: Causa-Verlag.

Strupp, H.H. (1978). Psychotherapy research and practice: An overview. In S.L.

44

Garfield & A.E. Bergin, *Handbook of psychotherapy and behavior change. An empirical analysis* (pp. 3-22). New York: Wiley.

Swildens, J.C.A.G. (1988). *Procesgerichte gesprekstherapie. Inleiding tot een gedifferentieerde toepassing van de cliëntgerichte beginselen bij de behandeling van psychische stoornissen.* Leuven, Amersfoort: Acco/de Horstink.

Tassinari, M., & Doxsey, J. (1987). *The Latin American encounters: Recent trends in written material on the person-centered approach.* Unpublished manuscript (71 pp.). (Address: Rua Fonte de Saudade, 87, Lagoa, Rio de Janeiro, R.J. CEP: 22471, Brasil).

Tausch, A.-M. (1981). *Gespräche gegen die Angst. Krankheit: ein Weg zum Leben.* Reinbek: Rhowolt.

Tausch, A.-M., & Tausch, R. (1985). *Sanftes Sterben. Was der Tod für das Leben bedeutet.* Reinbek bei Hamburg: Rhowolt.

Tausch, R. (1975). Ergebnisse und Prozesse der Klientenzentrierten Gesprächspsychotherapie bei 550 Klienten und 115 Psychotherapeuten. Eine Zusammenfassung des Hamburger Forschungsprojekts. *Zeitschrift praktische Psychologie, 13,* 293-307.

Tausch, R., & Tausch, A.-M. (1977). *Erziehungspsychologie. Begegnung von Person zu Person.* Göttingen: Hogrefe.

Tausch, R., & Tausch, A.-M. (1981). *Gesprächspsychotherapie.* Göttingen: Hogrefe.

Truax, C.B., & Mitchell, K.M. (1971). Research on certain therapist interpersonal skills in relation to process and outcome. In A.E. Bergin & S.L. Garfield (Eds.), *Handbook of psychotherapy and behavior change. An empirical analysis* (pp. 299-344). New York: Wiley.

Tscheulin, D. (Ed.). (1983). *Beziehung und Technik in der klientenzentrierten Therapie.* Weinheim/Basel: Beltz.

Van Balen, R. (1984). Overdracht in client-centered therapie. Een eerste literatuurverkenning. In G. Lietaer, Ph.H. van Praag, & J.C.A.G. Swildens (Eds.), *o.c.* (pp. 207-226).

Van Balen, R., Leijssen, M., & Lietaer, G. (1986). *Droom en werkelijkheid in client-centered psychotherapie.* Leuven/Amersfoort: Acco.

Van der Veen, F., & Raskin, N.J. (1970). Client-centered family therapy: Some clinical and research perspectives. In J.T. Hart & T.M. Tomlinson (Eds.), *o.c.* (pp. 387-406).

Waterhouse, G.J., & Strupp, H.H. (1984). The patient-therapist relationship: Research from the psychodynamic perspective. *Clinical Psychology Review, 4,* 77-92.

Watson, N. (1984). The empirical status of Rogers' hypothesis of the necessary and sufficient conditions for effective psychotherapy. In R.F. Levant & J.M. Shlien (Eds.), *o.c.* (pp. 17-40).

Wexler, D.A., & Rice, L.N. (Eds.). (1974). *Innovations in client-centered therapy.* New York: Wiley.

Wijngaarden, H.R. (1985). *Luisteren naar dromen.* Meppel: Boom.

Wood, J.K. (1984). Communities for learning: A person-centered approach. In R.F. Levant & J.M. Shlien (Eds.), *o.c.* (pp. 297-316).

Wright, L., Everett, F., & Roisman, L. (1986). *Experiential psychotherapy with children.* Baltimore: John Hopkins University Press.
Yalom, I.D. (1975). *The theory and practice of group psychotherapy.* New York: Basic Books.
Yalom, I.D. (1980). *Existential Psychotherapy.* New York: Basic Books.

ROGERS' LATER MOVE TOWARD MYSTICISM: IMPLICATIONS FOR CLIENT-CENTERED THERAPY

Harry A. VAN BELLE
Redeemer College, Ancaster
Ontario, Canada

In this chapter I would like to explore the basic intent of Carl Rogers' writings on therapy. I will attempt to describe what Rogers "was up to" with all that he said, wrote and did. This is no easy task since his views on therapy kept changing continually until the day of his death, so it is hard to say what he was up to from beginning to end.

Nevertheless, I find that two themes are evident in his writings. The first is a profound respect for individual persons. The other is an almost religious reverence for growth. I believe the latter was more important to him than the former and I hope to show that his respect for persons was really a function of his reverence for growth.

To accomplish this task I will first attempt to situate Rogers in a cultural-historical context. In this discussion these two themes of his life will become more intelligible. Thereafter I will give a brief description of his successive positions on therapy and show that these are increasingly more incisive expressions of his basic intent. Then I will describe his latest move toward, what I call, "mystical universalism", as this comes to expression in his latest book, A way of being. Finally, I will explore the implications of this latest development for person-centered therapy.

To understand Rogers we must first place him in the cultural-historical context in which he lived, since this context defines the limits of his thought. I think, it is generally not recognized enough that Rogers was an American who was born and raised in a cultural climate in which the dilemma of the freedom of the individual over against conformity to society was dominant. As a nation the U.S.A. was founded on a belief in the freedom of the individual. Americans have always believed that if you leave an individual to himself he can always be counted upon to develop his inherent potential optimally (Potter, 1967; Lipsett, 1967).

This idea worked well during the time that America was still a nation of pioneers. But when its society became more complex, as it did toward the latter part of the nineteenth century, the question about the relation between individual freedom and conformity to society became more urgent. People became aware of the fact that this free and unfettered pursuit of individual happiness could at times run counter to the will of the majority, which as the sum total of all individual desires and opinions could also claim voluntary adherence from its members (Potter, 1967; Tocqueville, 1845; Bryce, 1893; Riesman, 1951).

The philosopher John Dewey inherited this cultural dilemma and grappled with it for most of his life. Next to William James, Dewey was perhaps America's most influential philosopher. He certainly had a profound effect on Rogers (Rogers, 1980). He attempted to resolve this dilemma by giving both the individual and society their relative due, dynamically. Dewey held that individuals are not born free, as was previously supposed, but rather that they can only become free by freeing society. Individuals become free by continually changing, or reconstructing society toward human ends (Bernstein, 1960; Dewey, 1958, 1963).

In his writings Rogers essentially reversed this formulation by arguing that society cannot be free unless it continually frees its individual members to actualize their potential. He advocated an approach to therapy that moves the individual away from societal control, thereby demonstrating his respect for individuals. This theme in his thinking was not unique to Rogers. He merely articulated an already existing shared cultural value (Van Belle, 1980).

Neither did he respect individuals as ends in themselves but rather because he saw in them the embodiment of the forces of growth evident in all living things. He respected individuals for their ability to actualize their potential. For him people were growth principles (Evans, 1975).

In his understanding of what growth means Rogers was heavily dependent on Dewey. Following Darwin, Dewey saw change rather than stasis as the primary characteristic of all that exists. This dynamic notion of reality allowed him to conceive of the order of the different "kingdoms" (or classes of things) in reality (i.e. rocks, plants and animals) as one of different levels of interactive complexity. For Dewey reality originally consisted of an infinite number of interactions. Things emerged when series of these interactions grouped themselves into organized wholes. When these wholes in turn began to interact with other wholes they made it possible for even more complex wholes to emerge.

For Dewey this ongoing process is characteristic of all that exists in nature. No organized interactive whole, or thing is ever complete in itself. Its meaning lies perpetually in the consequences it engenders in subsequent, more complex interactive wholes. Things are always in the process of becoming integrated into more complex things. Reality is thus perpetually (re)ordered or (re)constructed in a process that runs from lower to higher differentiation and integration. This dynamic order of ongoing naturally occurring differentiation and integration is what Dewey called growth (Bernstein, 1960; Dewey, 1958, 1965).

Dewey's and Rogers' conception of growth are virtually indistinguishable. However, on one significant point Rogers parted company with Dewey. This concerns the formative influence of human beings on the process of growth. Dewey held that on the human level of differentiation and integration the innovative activity of free individual human subjects can shape the process of growth and redirect it to its own human ends. Thus at that level of interaction the naturally occurring growth process becomes a historically formative process, governed by changes that have their purpose in a source outside the growth process itself. Simply put, Dewey held that people can form growth (Dewey, 1963).

While Rogers certainly recognized the existence of individual subjects, he denied that they exist external to the process of growth and thus he also denied that individuals can form growth to their own human ends. On the contrary, the growth process itself has formative power, and it naturally shapes the individual rather than the reverse (Van Belle, 1980). For Rogers everything that exists, including human beings, is taken up into this total evolutionary process of becoming. This growth process has its own ends in view and its own organizational principle within itself. It is a syntropic force, it has morphological properties. It forms and reforms itself dynamically (Rogers 1980). Individuals, as microcosms of this total process, each uniquely have the capacity to form themselves or to actualize their potentials but they have this capacity only insofar as they are open to themselves, thus only insofar as they function as the "organisms" or growth principles that they are (Van Belle, 1985). Here we have the one and only condition that Rogers posits for growth to occur. People have an incessant tendency to cultivate, to shape, to control, to change things as they are. As far as Rogers is concerned, when they do this, they only end up distorting reality. Only when we let things or people be what or who they are, do they naturally change themselves (Rogers, 1980). People should not form growth, they should let themselves be formed by growth.

It is this basic intent which caused Rogers, together with other Third Force psychologists to take a stand against the internal determinism of psychoanalysis and the external determinism of behaviorism. These "nothing but" psychologies reduce the human person to something less than he could be. Rogers argued that people are always more than the reduced picture we make of them. People are by their nature self-renewing, self-transcending and self-transforming growth principles. A healthy, fully functioning person is a person in the process of becoming.

Over against these traditional "nothing but" psychologies Rogers developed a "more than" psychology. "More than" is its basic paradigm. It is a thoroughgoing dynamic transcendentalism in which a person's reach must always exceed his grasp. It celebrates human potentiality and possibility. Its motto is *semper excelsior*. It is a height psychology as opposed to a depth psychology, a growth psychology as opposed to stimulus-response psychology. With its constant emphasis on novelty its picture of man is that of *homo novus* (Richards & Richards, 1973). Man is nothing if he does not grow.

DEVELOPMENT OF ROGERS' VIEWS ON THERAPY

We can illustrate this emphasis on growth by briefly describing the development of Rogers' views on therapy. This development is characterized by a movement from "structure bound" to "process oriented" thinking.

Initially Rogers adhered to a nondirective view of therapy. Its aim was to free individual persons. Its approach was to reflect the client's feelings and its outcome was catharsis, which according to Rogers inevitably leads to a reorganized, more comfortable self concept or personality *structure* (Rogers, 1942).

The aim of his subsequent client-centered view is essentially to free the growth process in the client. The therapist now frees or facilitates this process in the client by means of a total, unconditional trust in the client's capacity for growth. The client is now expected to do something. He is expected to take the attitude which the therapist has toward him and to apply it toward his inner experiential growth process. Thus, he is not only expected to become nondirective, empathic or open toward his own dynamic experience. In addition it is expected he will come to trust his experience to such an extent that he begins to identify with it. He will become experience-centered and will live his experience. In short, in client-centered therapy the client becomes the therapeutic process that was released in him. In successful therapy clients move from having a personality structure toward becoming a personality process (Rogers, 1951, 1961).

THE CONDITIONS

From a focus on the growth process that occurs in the client Rogers briefly returns to the therapeutic conditions that facilitate this process. He lists these conditions as empathic openness, unconditional positive regard and congruence, or the condition that the therapist transparently and genuinely be himself in the relationship. The latter is seen as the central condition of client-centered or person-centered therapy.

For Rogers one can only be genuinely oneself insofar as one changes continually. Congruence is therefore defined in terms of the growth process. In essence to be congruent in relation to the client means that the therapist already is the growth process that he seeks to facilitate in the client. Rogers in effect concludes that congruence facilitates congruence, which is identical to saying that growth facilitates growth (Rogers, 1957).

FROM INTRAPERSONAL TO INTERPERSONAL

At this point Rogers realizes that if the congruence of the therapist can facilitate the growth of the client, the client's congruence, insofar as it exists, can also facilitate the therapist's growth. I.e., he realizes that congruence is mutually growth facilitating in a relationship. From this point on his style of therapy moves more and more in the direction of encounter groups in which the therapist is less dominant as a facilitator and where the members mutually facilitate each other's growth (Rogers, 1970, 1973).

FROM THERAPY TO COMMUNICATION

As a result of his experience in encounter groups Rogers now also begins to focus his attention on what happens between people rather than what happens inside people. Thus for a while the topic of communication takes centre stage in his writings and he argues that when two or more people relate congruently to one another, they are not only open to their own experience but also open to the experience of the other in the relationship. As a result they are mutually influenced and changed by one another's experience, i.e. they communicate.

In fact Rogers holds that when communication is good the boundaries between communicators disappear. In effect they mutually and freely flow into and through one another. We might put it this way: If congruence means being able to think what you feel, and transparency means being able to say what you think you feel, then good communication exists when one person is able to say what the other in the relationship thinks he feels. With this formulation Rogers' view of the growth process has become fully interpersonal. Earlier he had stressed the fact that good interpersonal communication facilitates intrapersonal congruence or growth. Now he argues that intrapersonal congruence also promotes good communication (Rogers, 1959, 1961, 1969, 1970)

Thus, in every way Rogers sought to promote the occurrence of growth. It now is no longer a property of persons only. It also has become a characteristic of good relationships and of groups.

TOWARD MYSTICAL UNIVERSALISM

During the last decade of his life Rogers' thought turned more and more toward "mystical universalism." He increasingly became preoccupied with a mystical, spiritual world full of psychic phenomena. Why would Rogers, who by his own admission has never had a mystical, paranormal experience, drug induced or otherwise, move in this direction as he does in *A way of being* (p. 253)? This all the more because the vocabulary he now uses differs so much from the words he previously used. He talks about "being" rather than "becoming," "humankind" (p. 133) rather than "persons," "the wisdom of the group" (p. 182, 334) rather than that of the organism, of "participation in a larger whole" (p. 128) rather than being one's unique separate self.

That Rogers changed his position at all is due to his dynamic growth oriented conception of human life. He simply lived what he believed, also in his theorizing. Because of it his thinking was destined to change continually until the end of his days. But his move in the direction of mystical universalism was largely an outgrowth of his experience in encounter groups.

In these groups Rogers found that he was at his facilitative best when he was "in a slightly altered state of consciousness." At such times his "inner spirit seemed to reach and to touch the inner spirits of others." His "relationship with others in the group transcended itself and became part of something larger."

Rogers quotes a participant in one of his encounter groups who called it "a profound spiritual experience" in which people "felt, and spoke for one another ..., without the usual barricades of 'me-ness' or 'you-ness'" (p. 129).

Elsewhere he ascribes this experience to the "wisdom of group." It creates "a collective harmonious psyche almost spiritual in nature" (p. 182). Furthermore he states that there exists "almost telepathic communication" in the group. There is a "sense of something greater" than the group (p. 196), and an "awareness of together being part of a broader universal consciousness" (p. 197). Clearly the group for Rogers has many characteristics of mystical universalism. It is transpersonal in nature.

These and other experiences make Rogers question first of all whether our everyday reality is the only reality there is. It leads him to posit the existence of a deeper reality, an "inner world" (p. 101) about which we know nothing because it is "not open to the five senses" (p. 256). It only appears to us when we "shut out outer stimuli" (p. 313), as occurs in sensory deprivation. It can only be known when we are "passively receptive" to it (p. 256). The central characteristic of this world is "transcendent harmony and unity." It includes "mankind" (p. 133). It has no past, no present and no future. In it the barriers of time and space are gone (p. 256). To live in this world is to experience yourself "participating in a larger universal formative tendency" (p. 128), that itself is "up to something" (p. 313). It shows a "trend toward ever greater complexity" (p. 128). This is now no longer the impulse of life only but of the universe as a whole. All that exists, changes continually and participates in a kind of "cosmic dance" (p. 345).

IMPLICATIONS

Probably the greatest difficulty in assessing the import of Rogers' latest move for person-centered therapy lies in determining what changes in therapeutic approach it entails. Earlier developments in his thinking on therapy were always accompanied by parallel changes in the therapeutic conditions. But in his latest writings Rogers does not tell us what new things a therapist must do to facilitate this mystical, transpersonal experience in clients.

In his very readable book *No boundary*, Ken Wilber (1981) does give us some hints about what methods would elicit such an experience when he refers to meditation and "channeling." But with these methods we have also left the "third force" of humanistic psychology and entered the realm of "fourth force" transpersonal psychology. One may wonder therefore whether Rogers by his latest move has not turned his own person-centered therapy into a "has been" approach, in much the same way as he once relegated psycho-analysis and behaviorism to that status.

In a sense Rogers' move to mysticism was prefigured in his earlier writings. In them a preference for attitude rather than technique, for being and becoming rather than doing is already evident. This preference comes to its fullest expression in his latest publications. By moving from a way of doing to a way of being Rogers may have exceeded the bounds of therapeutic thought and may have given us a philosophy of life, a world view or even a religion instead. By making change or growth central to life he may have given us more than a way to change lives intrapersonally and interpersonally. By making growth an end rather than a means he may in fact be telling us how to live.

If so, then his latest view is more properly judged as a novel alternative to already existing world views and religions, but not as a better way to do therapy. One may even question the novelty of this new way of life since a cursory reading of history will show it has many historical precedents.

Personally I find Rogers' latest view rather esoteric and otherworldly. I wonder whether in essence it differs all that much from the worldavoiding fundamentalistic view of his parents which he abandoned as a youth. If we can access the world he envisions only by eliminating the report of our senses I wonder whether I would want to live in it. Such an experience may be out of this world, but I, for one, still prize the delight of slurping an ice cream cone, or the delight of my wife's body against mine in bed. I prize the reality of such experiences, as well as the awareness that the one is not the other.

My appreciation for the earlier Rogers stems from the fact that he steadfastly refused to intellectualize and always respected the colourful particularity of his experience. I am afraid his later emphasis on the experience of unity eradicates all that and I wonder whether his latest view is any less reductionistic than Skinner's behaviorism. But the real question is whether, given his growth centered basic intent, Rogers could have moved in any other direction (Van Belle, 1980).

We can best appreciate the radical character of the latest development in Rogers' thinking when we compare it with his earliest view. In his early writings respect for individual persons is central; as is evidenced by his conviction that society should free the individual.

But already soon thereafter, as we saw, he began to stress the importance of the growth process and to include individual persons in it. We might formulate his new conviction in this manner: Individuals can only be freely and uniquely themselves insofar as they allow themselves to be changed by the forces of growth operative within them. Change is the central characteristic of uniquely whole persons.

It has always puzzled me how Rogers could hold that individuals can maintain their identity by changing, since the common sense understanding of having an identity is to remain the same over time. This kind of identity or continued-uniqueness-over-time allows people to respect others as persons and also to hold them responsible for their deeds. Thus, an identity which has change as its defining characteristic is an enigma to me. But I was able to follow Rogers in his emphasis on existential living, since he always talked about change and growth in the context of personal uniqueness. For most of his life he continued to see persons as universally unique. That one person's being and becoming is separate from that of another was for him beyond dispute. Thus, change overtime was acceptable because it occurred within separate uniqueness in space.

However, when Rogers became involved in encounter groups, and more fully when he moved to mystical universalism that boundary between people also seems to have been eliminated. Now the separateness of individuals from one another is also gone, together they become part of a larger whole; the group, the life force or cosmic consciousness. I find it difficult to picture what concretely a person who changes all the time and who is no longer separate from others would look like. Thus I fear that by embracing universal wholeness in his later life Rogers has abdicated from his earlier role as the defender of individual persons.

REFERENCES

Bernstein, R.J. (Ed.). (1960). *On experience, nature and freedom, representative selections, John Dewey.* New York: Liberal Art Press.

Bryce, J. (1893). *The American commonwealth: Vol. 2.* New York: MacMillan.

Dewey, J. (1958). *Experience and nature.* New York: Dover Publications.

Dewey, J. (1963). *Reconstruction in philosophy (enlarged edition).* Boston: Beacon Press.

Dewey, J. (1965). *The influence of Darwin on philosophy, and other essays in contemporary thought.* Bloomington: Indiana University Press.

Evans, R.I. (Ed.). (1975). *Carl Rogers, the man and his ideas.* New York: Dutton.

Lipset, S.M. (1967). The unchanging American character. In R.L. Rapson (Ed.), *Individualism and conformity in the American character.* Lexington, MA: Heath & Co.

Potter, D.M. (1967). The quest for the national character. In R.L. Rapson (Ed.).

Richards, F., & Richards, A.C. (1973). Homonovus an emergent image of man. In F. Richards & I.D. Welch (Eds), *Sightings: Essays in humanistic psychology.* Boulder, Col.: Shields.

Riesman, D. (1951). From morality to morale. In H. Stanton & S. Perry (Eds.), *Personality and political crisis.* New York: Free Press.

Rogers, C.R. (1942). *Counseling and psychotherapy.* Boston: Houghton Mifflin.

Rogers, C.R. (1951). *Client-centered therapy.* Boston: Houghton Mifflin.

Rogers, C.R. (1957). The necessary and sufficient conditions of therapeutic personality change. *Journal of Consulting Psychology, 21,* 97-103.

Rogers, C.R. (1959). A theory of therapy, personality and interpersonal relations. In S. Koch (Ed.), *Psychology: A study of a science: Vol. 3* (pp. 184-256). New York: McGraw-Hill.

Rogers, C.R. (1961). *On becoming a person.* Boston: Houghton Mifflin.

Rogers, C.R. (1969). *Freedom to learn.* Columbus, Ohio: Charles E. Merrill.

Rogers, C.R. (1970). *Carl Rogers on encounter groups.* New York: Harper and Row.

Rogers, C.R. (1973). My philosophy of interpersonal relationships and how it grew. *Journal of Humanistic Psychology, 13(2),* 3-15.

Rogers, C.R. (1980). *A way of being.* Boston: Houghton Mifflin.

Toqueville, de. (1845). *Democracy in America, Vol. 2.* New York: Henry G. Langley.

Van Belle, H.A. (1980). *Basic intent and therapeutic approach of Carl R. Rogers.* Redeemer College, Ancaster, Ont., Canada: Wedge Publishing Foundation.

Van Belle, H.A. (1985). Humanistic psychology. In D.G. Benner (Ed.), *Baker encyclopedia of psychology.* Grands Rapids, MI: Baker Book House.

Wilber, K. (1981). *No boundary. Eastern and western approaches to personal growth.* Boulder, Col./London: Shambala Publications.

THE ESSENCE OF CLIENT-CENTERED THERAPY

Jerold D. Bozarth
University of Georgia
Athens, U.S.A.

This paper identifies the essence of CC/PC therapy as a functional theoretical premise. This effort evolved from several of the conclusions reached in the Bower (1986) study, from my recent examination of the evolution of Carl Rogers as a therapist (Bozarth, 1988), from my interaction with co-symposium participants on the *Panel on client-centered therapy* at the 1988 American Psychological Association, and from my understanding of Rogers' theoretical writings. I will state my conclusion of the essence of CC/PC therapy. I will then briefly present the conclusions of the Bower study and summarize my examination of the evolution of Carl Rogers as a therapist. Last, I will consider the implications of the essence of CC/PC therapy.

I use the term "essence" to mean *the* basic nature and *the* basic core of the therapy. I use the terms client-centered/person-centered (CC/PC) therapy together and interchangeable in the way Rogers (1987) used the terms.

The statement: *The essence of CC/PC therapy is the therapist's dedication to going with the client's direction, at the client's pace, and with the client's unique way of being. It is the full committment "to trust in the client's own way of going about dealing with his problems and his life"* (Brodley, 1988).

It is my contention that CC/PC therapy operates within a different paradigm than do other therapies (Bozarth, 1985). It is the essence of this paradigm that differentiates it from other therapies, and, in fact, an essence that appears to be at variance with many of the presentations in the 1988 conference. The next two points summarize findings that contribute to this conclusion.

THE BOWER STUDY

The Bower study is a qualitative study of six notable CC/PC therapists doing therapy. An audio tape of each therapist's therapy sessions was independently reviewed by three listeners. The therapist and client participants responded to questions from the investigator. The emerging concensual data were the following:

1. Therapists had a wide repertoire of non-interfering responses. One therapist responded in a reflective way with near intrusive reflective responses; another rarely commented and then only in a way to clarify his uncertainties; another therapist was described as seductive by the listeners; another used Gestalt type metaphor that emerged from the client; and another therapist periodically "moaned" throughout the session.

2. The clients perceived the therapists as being helpful; the clients overall directed themselves in the process of inquiry. At times, they waited for the therapists to finish responses before continuing with their own explorations. In short, the therapists were experienced as being received by clients as permissable humans whose specific responses did not seem to interfere with the clients' directions.

3. The therapists were perceived by listeners as disappearing in deference to their clients. They were experienced as being a "shadow to the client." Their presence appeared obvious but there was no intervention nor intrusion of the personality of the therapist (Bower & Bozarth, 1988).

The overriding conclusion was that: Client-centered/person-centered therapists were experienced (by clients, listeners, and therapists) as non-interfering individuals who entered the world of the client in such a way as to "disappear" into the client's own process of development (Bower & Bozarth, 1988).

In brief, the study also suggested that: 1. The attitudinal qualities of empathy, unconditional positive regard, and genuineness (described in various ways) were the consistent therapist attitudes that existed; 2. The therapists held a position of total trust in the client's own direction and way; 3. The therapists were active and involved with a total dedication towards understanding the client's world; 4. The therapists had a wide range of response repertoires and personality characteristics but were each intent upon understanding and checking his/her understandings of his/her client; and 5. The therapists did not attempt to intervene in the direction, process, or with the pace of the clients.

The therapists were actively involved and readily dialogued with their clients but "disappeared" into the client's process.

ANALYSIS OF THE EVOLUTION OF CARL ROGERS AS A THERAPIST

My (Bozarth, 1988) examination of Carl Rogers' evolution as a therapist is a qualitative inquiry to two questions. These questions are: 1. *Did Carl Rogers alter his fundamental views of client-centered therapy?* and 2. *Did Carl Rogers change his operational functioning as a psychotherapist?* It was my intent to further ask: What were these alterations? and what changes occurred? My basic thought had been that there was significant alteration of some fundamental views; and that his functioning as a therapist had changed over the years.

My assessment of Rogers' comments in the literature, his demonstration films, and from previous personal communication led me to conclude that *Carl Rogers did not alter his fundamental views of client-centered therapy.* I noted that he was quite consistent in his fundamental views of the importance of the conditions of empathy, unconditional positive regard, and genuineness as attitudinal qualities that therapists needed to experience with their clients, and of his dedication to go with his clients in the direction that the client wanted to go and in the way the client wished to do it. He became somewhat explicit about the importance of being genuine in the relationship. The importance of genuineness as the primary condition to him was expressed in a dialogue with Wood (Rogers & Wood, 1984), and, in an earlier statement when he commented that even when the conditions of unconditional positive regard and empathy were not experienced by the therapist that genuineness alone may be facilitative (Rogers, 1967). He clarified this in an interview shortly before his death saying that "if you have other feelings, other than empathy, then congruence takes preference over everything else" (Hobbs, 1985). His more explicit references to the importance of genuineness in the relationship did not represent any fundamental change in view. He was always dedicated to and intent on going with the client's direction, at the client's pace, and with the client's unique way of being (Bozarth, 1988).

My assessment of Rogers' functioning as a therapist by reviewing demonstration films with Miss Mun (Rogers & Segal, 1955), Gloria (Shostrum, 1964), and Kathy (Rogers, 1975) led me to conclude that *Carl Rogers did not change his operational functioning as a psychotherapist.* He did express a *slightly* wider range of responses over the twenty year period in the demonstration films; and had some spontaneous expressions that "bubbled up," especially, in the Gloria film. A qualitative evaluation of Rogers' response sets in the three films that included a continue frame representing "I am giving you my full attention, please continue;" and a *check frame* meaning "This is what I understand you to be saying" revealed: 100% of the responses in 1955 were check or continue responses (including empathic understanding responses); 90% of the responses in 1965 were continue or check responses (the few declarative responses were the notable responses often referred to); 84% of the responses were continue or check responses in 1975 (Bozarth, 1988).

Dr. Brodley's (1988) examination of eight of Rogers' interviews from the 1940's to late 1985 using a comparable evaluation scheme revealed that in seven of them 92% to 100% of Dr. Rogers' responses were empathic following responses. The session consisting of 100% empathic following responses was the one in late 1985.

My conclusion from this inquiry was the following:

Overall it seems accurate to me to say that Rogers increasingly referred to the importance of genuineness when working with clients and that "realness" of the therapist was increasingly important in his thinking. He responded with slightly more varied comments over the twenty year time span of the demonstration tapes but his preponderent response efforts were clearly geared to the understanding of his clients' worlds - whether in 1955, 1965, 1975, or 1985. Carl Rogers' fundamental views of client-centered/person-centered therapy were not altered. He did not significantly change his operational functioning as a psychotherapist (Bozarth, 1988).

A more holistic viewing of the films and tapes was interpreted as suggesting that Rogers allowed himself to be more expressive over the years. It also seems likely that his varied comments as a therapist over the time periode were more client and situation specific rather than an evolving pattern.

It became clearer to me that whatever Rogers said about CC/PC therapy or did as a therapist was within the context of placing his trust in his clients without doing anything to them or "being up to something" as a therapist.

These two examinations, the one of six notable CC/PC therapists and the other of the evolution of Carl Rogers as a therapist, support Rogers' explicit statements about CC/PC therapy; i.e., that the foundation block of the therapy is the actualizing tendency (Rogers, 1980); that "it is the client who knows what hurts, what directions to go, what problems are crucial. It would do better to rely upon the client for the direction of movement in the process" (Kirschenbaum, 1979, p. 89). He had a profound and unwavering dedication to trusting the client as his/her own best authority.

These reviews lead me to conclude as a functional theoretical premise that: *The essence of CC/PC therapy is the therapist's dedication to going with the client's direction, at the client's pace, and with the client's unique way of being.*

IMPLICATIONS

The implications of the essence of CC/PC therapy are staggering! *It is a functional premise that precludes other therapist intentions.* The therapist goes with the client - goes at the client's pace - goes with the client in his/her own ways of thinking, of experiencing, of processing. *The therapist can not be up to other things, have other intentions without violating the essence of CC/PC therapy.* To be up to other things - whatever they might be - is a "yes, but" reaction to the essence of the approach.

It must mean that when the therapist has intentions of treatment plans, of treatment goals, of interventive strategies to get the client somewhere or for the client to do a certain thing, the therapist violates the essence of CC/PC therapy. This holds true if the therapist is trying to move the client through a certain process, to encourage clients to experience themselves in a certain way, to teach clients to be empathic, or to impose other therapeutic methods on the client.

It is a functional premise that includes wide therapist personality differences, unique ways of doing things, and idiosyncratic ways of responding (Bozarth, 1984) *as far as they are dedicated to the client's direction, the client's pace, and the client's unique way of being.*

It is a functional premise that begets therapists who ascribe to Rogers' principles to test the essence of the approach in a consistent

64

way, over time in order for the therapists to experience the potency of allowing individuals to engage in their own empowerment, in their own ways without their clients being violated by the personal observations and theories of their therapists.

REFERENCES

Bower, D. (1985). *Assumptions and attitudes of the Rogerian person-centered approach to counseling: Implications for pastoral counseling* (Research Project). Atlanta: Columbia Theological Seminary.

Bower, D., & Bozarth, J.D. (1988). *Features of client-centered/person-centered therapists. Paper presented at the International Conference on Client-centered and experiential Psychotherapy. Book of abstracts* (pp. 23-25). Leuven, Belgium, September 12-16, 1988.

Bozarth, J.D. (1984). Beyond reflection: Emergent modes of empathy. In R. Levant & J. Shlien (Eds.), *Client-centered therapy and the person-centered approach: New directions in theory, research, and practice* (pp. 59-75). New York: Praeger.

Bozarth, J.D. (1988, August). The evolution of Carl Rogers as a therapist. In F. Zimring (Chair), *Re-examination of client-centered therapy using Rogers' tapes and films.* Symposium conducted at the meeting of the American Psychological Association, Atlanta.

Brodley, B.T. (1988, August). Panel on client-centered therapy. In F. Zimring (Chair), *Re-examination of client-centered therapy using Rogers' tapes and films.* Symposium conducted at the meeting of the American Psychological Association, Atlanta.

Hobbs, T. (1986). The Rogers interview. *Changes,* 254-258.

Kirschenbaum, H. (1979). *On becoming Carl Rogers.* New York: Delacorte Press.

Rogers, C.R. (1967). Client-centered psychotherapy. In A.M. Freedman & H.I. Kaplan (Eds.), *Comprehensive textbook of psychiatry* (Vol. 2, pp. 1225-1228). Baltimore: Williams & Wilkins.

Rogers, C.R. (1975). *Three approaches to psychotherapy II* (Film). Psychological Films.

Rogers, C.R. (1980). *A way of being.* Boston: Houghton Mifflin.

Rogers, C.R. (1987). Client-centered/person-centered? *Person-Centered Review, 2(1),* 11-13.

Rogers, C.R., & Segel, R.H. (1955). *Psychotherapy in process: The case of Miss Mun* (Film). Pennsylvania State University Psychological Film Register.

Rogers, C.R., & Wood, J.K. (1974). The changing theory of client-centered therapy. In A. Burton (Ed.), *Operational theories of personality* (pp. 211-258). New York: Bruner/Mazel.

Shostrum, E. (Producer). (1964). *Three approaches to psychotherapy* (Film). Santa Anna, CA: Psychological Films.

THE THERAPEUTIC RELATIONSHIP
ACCORDING TO CARL ROGERS,
ONLY A CLIMATE? A DIALOGUE? OR BOTH?

Richard VAN BALEN
Katholieke Universiteit Leuven, Belgium

INTRODUCTION

Rogers' main preoccupation has always been to emphasize the essence of therapeutic practice. For him, this essence is the quality of the relationship, and it must promote growth, in the sense that it has to allow the development of the client's potential. He was afraid that notions of psychopathology, or specific techniques of intervention would push this essence into the background and become objectifying instruments, thus antitherapeutic rather than therapy enhancers. Out of this concern, his almost exclusive emphasis on basis therapy conditions was born, which gave rise to several misconceptions about the simplicity of client-centered therapy, i.e. the assumption that it was limited to stereotyped offering of an ideal therapeutic climate, rather than concrete forms of interaction within the framework of an essential basic attitude.

It seems to me that Rogers himself tended to attribute this apparent simplicity to a lack of understanding of the complexity contained in his clear and simple statements. His impression that the essence of his message was seldom given its full weight by people who quoted his theories and commented on them, can for example be found in his discussion with Evans: "When people try to describe my theories, I find I don't even recognize them" (Evans, 1975, p. 91).

CLOSE-UP VIEW OF THE THERAPEUTIC RELATIONSHIP
ACCORDING TO C. ROGERS

To a certain extent, one could say that Rogers' view of the therapeutic relationship has continuously evolved. This is shown, for example, by his periodic adjustment of terminology according to this evolution. One can however also observe that certain basic assumptions have characterized his views from the start. I will return to this later. I believe that it makes sense to distinguish two periods. Although somewhat arbitrary because we deal in essence with a gradual evolution, and not a sudden change in orientation - we can distinguish the periods before and after 1957. That year, 1957, marks the publication of "The necessary and sufficient conditions of therapeutic personality change" in *The Journal of Consulting Psychology*. And it also marks the Rogers-Buber dialogue, which had in my opinion, not an immediate, but clearly crucial and delayed impact on Rogers' evolution.

THE FIRST PERIOD: THE THERAPIST AS ALTER EGO

In this first phase, the therapist mainly limits himself to exteriorization of his empathic understanding for everything that becomes conscious in the client during his self-exploratory trip.

> "The therapist must concentrate on one purpose only: that of providing deep understanding and acceptance of the attitudes consciously held at this moment by the client as he explores step by step into the dangerous areas which he has been denying to consciousness" (Rogers, 1946, cited in Rogers, 1951, p. 30).

This means that there is really no question of a mutual relationship. In fact, the relationship is so one-sided that "the whole relationship is composed of the client, the counselor being depersonalized for purposes of therapy into being the client's other self." (Rogers, 1951, p. 209).

How does Rogers then see the curative element in such a relationship? I will try to trace, in my own words, Rogers' possible ideas in this regard.

The person who visits a therapist does so, obviously, because he is at odds with himself. In certain circumstances, he has feelings and reactions which do not fit in with what he feels he is, or would like to be. To be confronted with such a contradiction is a threat to him. It erodes his self-esteem.

So when he talks about these feelings and reactions in therapy, he feels threatened. But now, something happens which he does not know from his own experience: The therapist listens attentively, does not behave like an onlooking critic, but tries to let the client's story, with all its nuances, come at him, without distorting it, just as it is for the client. Besides, there is no difference in therapist receptivity between those aspects which the client experiences as unquestionably part of his identity, and those which he experiences as strange and undesirable feelings and reactions. It is exactly this quiet receptivity on the part of the therapist which offers the client "a corrective emotional experience." Indeed, for the first time, the client sees that even these undesirable aspects can be experienced and viewed as something else than a threatening eruption. The experience that the therapist, who is confronted with precisely these same inner contradictions as the client in his role of the client's alter ego, quietly faces the situation without denying or distorting the data, ends up making the client feel calmer himself. And this increased peace allows the client to go a step further than he was capable of before: It is a step further in his attempt to examine more closely his own "incomprehensible feeling" or "strange reaction." He feels encouraged to try to understand this aspect of himself, instead of immediately condemning it. The "healing" action of the relationship follows thus from the therapist's understanding empathy (Rogers, 1951, p. 41).

Thus, "all the therapist has to do" is to listen empathically, and to suggest, by his listening, that there is no reason for panic and self-condemnation. In this way he creates a "growth enhancing" climate, and the client is capable of doing the rest himself.

> "If we can provide understanding of the way the client seems to himself at this moment, he can do the rest..." (Rogers, 1946, cited in Rogers, 1951, p. 30).

Later, when Rogers looked back at this period (Rogers & Hart, 1970, p. 520) he indeed said that research had shown that the therapist limited himself to empathic responses, "and nothing else was permitted to come in." Gendlin, too, refers to this period in a similar way, but adds the critical commentary that this refusal, on the part of the therapist, to offer any personal contribution at all, sometimes led "to the point of complete exasperation and despair of the client" (Gendlin, 1968, p. 226).

THE SECOND PERIOD

Congruence in the service of empathy

The beginning of the second period can, as we said, roughly be set around 1957, with the publication of *The necessary and sufficient conditions.* Alongside the "positive regard" for what the client had to say, and the "empathy" - notions which were central in the first period - we find now "congruence" as added basic attitude. New about this is not really that the two previously emphasized attitudes of the therapist should be "authentic," because this was always self-evident for Rogers. He had stressed already earlier that the client-centered method is only effective inasmuch as it is founded on attitudes which are part and parcel of the therapist as a person (Rogers, 1951, p. 19). Kinget pointed out how, in the Chicago period, it became clear from listening to tapes and interviews and discussing them in groups, "that the therapists whose method failed, applied the non-directive therapy in a consequent enough manner, but did so without any personal conviction. The non-directive character of their intervention was only surface behavior. They had adopted the method because others in their immediate environment had applied it successfully, and not because they accepted the theoretical and philosophical basis of this therapy" (Kinget, 1959, p. 27).

It became increasingly clear that the therapeutic response could not be mere technique, but had to be "flesh and blood." The "reflections" only carried weight inasmuch as they render present an integrated person who is part of the relationship with his whole being. It is thus the absolute priority of certain basic attitudes - in any technique - which Rogers wants to stress.

The therapist's behavior has to be an authentic translation of his conviction. The "client-centered" therapist, who, in his therapeutic activity, approaches any feelings emerging in the client with "understanding empathy," should also carry in himself an equal benevolence towards his own emerging feelings. There should thus be no discrepancy between word and act.

This does not mean, according to Rogers, that the therapist must be, in all aspects of his life, an example of perfect integration. It is enough if he can really be there, during the therapy hour, without restriction. But what if his real feelings during the therapy hour are in conflict with the unconditional empathic attitude? Here too, Rogers is outspoken: The quality of the therapeutic relation demands that now congruence should prevail.

> "It should be clear that this includes being himself even in ways which are not regarded as ideal for psychotherapy" (Rogers, 1957, p. 97).

In other words, the ideal therapist reacts congruently, but the congruent therapist does not only have therapeutically ideal feelings. At such moments, it is not only important to remain congruent inwardly, but also in one's outside communications, in order to continue to conform to the image of a reliable, congruent discussion partner. This does not mean that the therapist should simply communicate his disturbing feelings to the client. Simply allowing oneself to have such feelings, or a discussion about them with a colleague or supervisor, may be sufficient to eliminate their disturbing influence. But if, even then, these feelings remain ("persistent feelings"), and continue to prevent the desired empathic receptivity, a direct mention of them may sometimes be necessary.

> "At times he may need to talk out some of his own feelings (either to the client, or to a colleague or supervisor) if they are standing in the way of the two following conditions" (Rogers, 1957, p. 99).

In a way, one could say that genuineness, in the sense of transparence, is initially still a necessary evil. Hence an inevitable necessity for those moments in which the therapist feels unable to give precedence, without interference, to the real therapeutic activity, i.e. empathic understanding.

The genuineness is at that moment not yet used primarily to confront the client with certain aspects of his disfunction. Even now, Rogers still wants to start from the client's frame of reference. The therapeutic tools are for him still primarily acceptance and empathy. The function of congruence remains, for the time being, limited to preserving the therapeutic efficacy of the other two. This is, in any event, the impression Rogers gives in his dialogue with Buber, also of 1957. We will return to this later.

But soon, Rogers takes a further step to emphasize authenticity as a possible access-road to information, important to the client. In 1961 already, in *A general law of interpersonal relations* - even though he calls this document very tentative - Rogers states clearly the crucial importance of communication of "relevant experience" i.e. of those aspects of the therapist's experience of the situation which are important for the client in order to acquire a clearer view of his own functioning.

> "Very tentatively indeed I would like to set forth one further aspect of this whole matter, an aspect which is frequently very real in the therapeutic relationship, and also in other relationships, though perhaps less sharply noted.
>
> In the actual relationship both the client and the therapist are frequently faced with the existential choice, 'Do I dare communicate the full degree of congruence which I feel? Do I dare match my experience, and my awareness of that experience, with my communication? Do I dare to communicate myself as I am or must my communication be somewhat less than or different from this?' The sharpness of this issue lies in the often vividly foreseen possibility of threat or rejection. To communicate one's full awareness of the relevant experience is a risk in interpersonal relationships. It seems to me that it is the taking or not taking of this risk which determines whether a given relationship becomes more and more mutually therapeutic or whether it leads in a desintegrative direction" (Rogers, 1961, p. 345).

This choice, which he also calls an existential choice, contains a risk, but according to Rogers, a necessary risk to safeguard the bilateral therapeutic character of the relationship. Avoiding this risk, he feels, will not save the situation, but will rather undermine its therapeutic quality.

It is therefore very clear that he abandons, in this period, the notion of "one-way-traffic." The therapist should not try to behave as a pure "alter ego," certainly not at times when he cannot truly feel this way. Thus, attempts on the part of the therapist to give up his personal feelings are now questioned themselves. Indeed, focusing completely and exclusively on the client's world would rather lead the therapist to a belated or lacking conscious recognition of his own empathy-hindering feelings. And an accurate assessment and handling of those feelings seems not only important to preserve one's credibility, and hence therapeutic effectiveness. It now also appears to have become an access-road to a more profound relationship, and could even be vitally important in the survival or decline of its therapeutic character.

The therapist as "companion in the search"

This does, however, not prevent the empathic understanding from remaining central. Communication of empathy remains the "real task" of the therapist. Also essential to this remains that the therapist does not approach the client as an object to be submitted to interpretation from the outside, but as a subject to be helped "in clarifying himself to himself from the inside." Rogers summarizes this as the constant attention to the client's inner frame of reference.

> "I have pointed out that in spite of the changes reflected in client-centered therapy by the development of these three therapeutic conditions, the communication of accurate empathic understanding remains the work of the client-centered therapist. This points to the continued belief among client-centered therapists that understanding the client's world as he sees it is centrally important in effecting therapeutic change. It is this belief which, as Seeman has pointed out, is signified by the term "client-centered"... Many therapeutic systems consider the achievement of an empathic grasp of the client's private world only a preliminary to the real work of the therapist... But the client-centered therapist aims to remain within the phenomenal universe throughout the course of therapy, from the first to the last" (Rogers, 1966, p. 190).

An important difference with statements of the first period is that it is no longer specified that the therapist has to *stay continuously within* the client's inner frame of reference, but rather that he has to remain *directed towards* remaining within this frame of reference. In other words, focusing on the client's frame of reference has to be the therapist's continuous goal.

What now emerges is what L. Rice later (see a.o. Rice, 1980) calls "the companion in search" character. The therapist is no longer the careful "follower" of the client; he does not limit himself any more to reflecting what the client is clearly conscious of. He actively helps searching. Exactly like the client, he concentrates with his whole being on the client's experiential world, but the fact that he "remains in touch with himself" - his parallel attention to his own experience of the situation - permits him now to explore the client's perceptual field "with his own eyes." Hence we have a continuous smooth shift between "how the client experiences the situation" and "how the therapist perceives his client's experiencing." The point is now: "Two see more than one." But, as said, they both try to focus on the same picture: The client's inner experiential world. Remaining faithful to the essence of the client-centered point of departure - i.e. focusing on "the client's world as he sees it" (Rogers, 1966, p. 190) - is now done by checking the therapist's perception against the client's, so that, to quote L. Rice once more, "the client remains the expert of the content" (Rice, 1980). The therapist can, tentatively, present impressions about what he senses to be present "in the hidden corners" of the client's field of perception, but the client has the final say. There lies the criterion: "The client remains the center" (Gendlin, 1968, p. 221).

> "This is not to say, however, that the client-centered therapist responds only to the obvious in the phenomenal world of his client. If that were so, it is doubtful that any movement would ensue in therapy. Indeed, there would be no therapy. Instead, the client-centered therapist aims to dip from the pool of implicit meanings just at the edge of the client's awareness (Rogers, 1966, p. 190).

Starting thus from "his" understanding of the client's world - indeed "starting," because the client's answer will be the access-road to better agreement between two ways of experiencing - the therapist can now allow his own understanding to lead to a "deeper empathy." Indeed, the therapist sometimes succeeds in revealing aspects of the panorama on which both are focusing, which can be enlightening to the client, and which the client may perhaps have overlooked for a long time without the therapist's help. This "contribution" leads to a "renewed" encounter, within the now somewhat modified - but further clarified - "experiential world" of the client. But it remains an encounter "within the world of the client"; i.e. inasmuch as it concerns a "deeper empathy," the point of reference remains the world "as it appears to the client." The therapist may notice some details which shed a slightly different light on this image, but he continues to focus on the "world as the client sees it." One could say that he lends the client his senses for him to take advantage of. However, the therapist does not question the client's set except if he picks up the client's doubt. Only then will he - tentatively - point it out.

But if the therapist can, even carefully, make a small contribution, with the client having always the decisive final say, does he then not remain powerless in front of a client who does not reach fruitful self-exploration? Is it not naive to believe that, with understanding and (even more profound) empathy, everything will get solved? Isn't there a danger, as Buber worded it when facing Rogers in 1957 (Buber & Rogers, 1957, p. 24), that one becomes more and more "individualized," but not "humanized"?

To highlight Rogers' evolution on this point - his attitude towards the question of the therapist's "taking up position" - I feel that a digression into the Buber-Rogers dialogue of 1957 is mandatory.

Rogers and Buber about "encounter"

A term which appears, in this second period, more and more often in Rogers' writings, in his description of what happens in therapy, is "encounter." This notion points indeed to the implication of two real people in the therapy process. The therapist is no longer perceived as an "alter ego" of the client. But when Rogers refers, in his dialogue with Buber, to the therapeutic encounter, he still does so in the sense of an encounter "within" the experiential world of the client. Thus the experiential world of the client remains the meeting place of the two partners[1].

Rogers refers, in this respect, to Buber's "I-thou" relationship (or rather: A relationship-moment within the relationship), where both partners experience both their own and the other's point of view, from a subject-perspective. In client-centered language this would mean that both partners experience simultaneously "both frames of reference."

In therapy, according to Buber, there is no question of reciprocity. On the other hand for Rogers, reciprocity does exist. Not only does the therapist encounter the client (in the client's experiential world), but the client meets the therapist (in the same world). Thus, to speak of encounter means for Rogers also reciprocity: Indeed, there is only encounter when the client, at a given moment, effectively feels the empathic and accepting attitude, which is strongly represented by the therapist.

> "...then I wonder if it isn't reciprocal in the sense that I am able to see this individual as he is in that moment and he really senses my understanding and acceptance of him. And that I think is reciprocal and is perhaps what produces change" (Buber & Rogers, 1957, p. 15).

We are thus looking here at two people who, in spite of their being different, share a common experience. And this it seems, is for Rogers, at the moment, the essence of "I-thou."

> "...a real meeting of persons in which it was experienced the same from both sides" (Buber & Rogers, 1957, p. 12).

Buber replies to this that there may, in this case, be an "I-thou" experience on the part of the therapist, but not on the part of the client.

This is obviously an important restriction. Indeed, the power and humanizing effect of an "I-thou"-experience lies for Buber in the fact that someone suddenly experiences himself in the other person's skin, without loosing contact with himself. Egocentricity is thereby transcended. The other's joy and pain, which I have deeply experienced in myself, can almost no longer be whiped from my skin. My 'self-experience' now also contains the joy and the pain of the other. Thus, for Buber, an encounter in "the experiential world of the client" is not sufficient to describe the therapeutic encounter as an "I-thou" experience for the client.

Let us now briefly see how Buber justifies his reservation. The encounter which you aim for, thus Buber to Rogers, does not break the role distribution for the client. The client experiences the beneficial feeling of being totally accepted, as asker of help, by the provider of this help. An "I-thou" encounter would mean that the client does not only feel what it is like to be understood and accepted as client, but also how it is for a therapist to be totally open to another being. Only if the client experiences, even briefly, this aspect as well, is something basically changed in the setting. Not only being deeply understood, but also understanding deeply, is now part of his experiential world. This is the far-reaching meaning of an "I-thou" encounter. It is an encounter which touches one in the center of one's being, an encounter after which, one could say, one is never the same again, but where one remains, in essence, nevertheless faithful to oneself. One does not become more dependent on others because of this change. On the contrary, one is enriched with an experience which makes one more human. Through such encounters, one transcends being an individual and one becomes a person, one becomes "humanized." The power of human dialogue - and hence the necessity of dialogue in therapy - lies, according to Buber, specifically in this encounter, which opens up the individual, enclosed in himself, to a dimension which will from now on become a full part of his person.

And in therapy this would mean, according to Buber, that the therapist should "lift up" the client, until he does no longer feel only an asker of help, but is capable of breaking through the role difference. Only then will he be capable of incorporating the side of the helper into his own experience. It is exactly the "added value" which the client receives, the ability of learning to see and to use his own potential - thanks to the confirming character of the therapeutic relationship - that will allow him to transcend the role of asker of help. You as therapist, thus Buber, have first handed him something, which makes him capable of this "switch," of this encounter, no longer only in his experiential world, but in the experiential world which contains both poles.

"You see, I, of course, am entirely with you as far as your experience goes, I cannot be with you as far as I have to look on the whole situation. Your experience and his. You see, you give him something in order to make him equal to you. You supplement his need in his relation to you. May I say so personally, out of a certain fullness you give him what he wants in order to be able to be, just for this moment, so to speak, on the same plane with you. But even that is very... It is tangent. It is a tangent which may not last but one moment. It is, as far as I see, not the situation of an hour; it is a situation of minutes. And these minutes are made possible by you. Not at all by him" (Buber & Rogers, 1957, p. 15).

But here, Rogers has again a certain reservation. He is afraid that Buber does not really promote growth of this unique person in this way, but tries to intervene, in a subtle way, in the evolution, so that evolution finally ends up being an imposition of norms from the outside. His fear of foreign influence on a person makes him, for the moment anyway, hear Buber's arguments as a plea for "bestowing," for adding from the outside what is lacking from within.

"... but I do sense some ... real disagreement there, because it seems to me that what I give him is permission to be. Which is a little different from bestowing something on him" (Buber & Rogers, 1957, p. 18).

For the time being, the viewpoints of Rogers and Buber seem irreconcilable. In my opinion it appears as a - temporary - misunderstanding.

For Rogers, it is essential that the therapist does not see the client as someone "who is missing something." The client "has thus everything in himself." The therapist is not a sort of plastic surgeon who improves a bit on nature. He provides someone who has potentially everything in himself already with a chance to blossom.

To Buber, the essence seems to be that man needs other men to become a complete person. What one "adds" to the other is a form of relationship, which "induces" the person to actualize the potential he carries within him.

Buber thus prefers the term "confirm" over "accept." Getting in touch with, and hence developing confidence in latent potentialities, is possible in spite of someone's undeniable dysfunction. It is the eyes of "love" (Buber) - Rogers would say "non-possessive warmth" - which enable someone to see so clearly through illusion. The appeal to these not yet realized potentials, if this can become communicated as an expression of faith and confidence, can, according to Buber, sometimes be decisive for the whether or not actualizing of potentialities. Buber speaks of helping someone to become the "person he has been ...

created to become" (Buber & Rogers, 1957, p. 21).

But precisely this appeal-character appears to Rogers, for the time being, as a normative pressure, as insufficient trust. But when Rogers protests against a "bestowing" attitude, and stresses that, what he wants to contribute, amounts to giving permission to be (to exist, to be oneself), we see Buber agree without reservation ("I'm with you", p. 15). But it seems to me that Rogers, from his side, is not really convinced that they are on the same wavelength, even after Buber agreed, at least for the time being.

Authenticity as independent pole of interaction

a. Self-revelation without imposition

In the years following the discussion with Buber, the "Wisconsin-project" with schizophrenic patients got underway. Here, the use of the therapist's own feelings imposed itself. The therapy with schizophrenics made it clear that "being in contact," which was obviously present with neurotic patients who had come to seek help, was far from self-evident in these circumstances. The less there was to "reflect" on with the client, the more it became necessary to use one's own experiences as access-roads to contact. It became increasingly clear that verbalization of one's own view on the situation, in the perspective of a search for contact, does not have to appear evaluative - and thus alienating - at all. On the contrary, it could become very "process-enhancing." It could create overtures which could not be reached in the "classical" way.

> "Thus, if there was to be a relationship at all, the therapist found it necessary to call upon his own feelings" (Rogers, 1966, p. 189).

This experience with schizophrenic patients, i.e. that it is contact which is in fact basic - more than the frame of reference out of which contact is sought - to make an interaction either self-alienating or self-enhancing, has possibly been crucial for Rogers so as to re-examine his reservations towards Buber[2].

In any event, the recognition of the priority of the notion "contact" during the work with schizophrenics, appears to coincide with Buber's thesis. Indeed, the "I-thou" encounter referred also to the priority of contact, and to the fact that, within the framework of such a mutual self-revelation, the use of one's own feelings about the other does not have to be self-alienating, but can be self-enhancing.

Hence the decisive factor becomes not whether there is influence, but whether it happens within the framework of mutual contact, i.e. contact with oneself as well as contact with the other. A contact which allows the revelation of one's own feelings without it leading to imposition of opinions and value judgments.

> "...in client-centered therapy, there has come to be a greater use of the self of the therapist, of the therapist's feelings, a greater stress on genuineness, but all of this without imposing the views, values or interpretations of the therapist on the client'" (Rogers, 1974, p. 11).

"Imposing" one's own opinion on someone is no longer an absolute danger, but a relative one. Determinant here is prevention of the loss of contact, the not influencing without mutual contact. Hence also the increasing importance of "checking," of repeatedly verifying if one is still (or again) on the common track (see, for example, Gendlin, 1968).

And so, we return to the point where we left the Rogers-Buber dialogue. We advanced our opinion that, in it, Rogers is still not convinced of the reconciliability of Buber's "influencing" with someone "being really himself."

Rogers' wording in "A general law of interpersonal relations" (1961) - which we quoted earlier - implies already the still hesitantly expressed confidence in the possibility of appealing immediately, of taking a clearly divergent stand, not only without self-alienating effect on the client, but rather the opposite. Confrontation therefore emerges as an intermediary step towards a real "I-thou" encounter. And when he later says (Rogers, 1969, p. 236) that he is so pleased when authenticity on his part stimulates authenticity in the other, and leads to something which comes close to an "I-thou" relation, then he does imply the reciprocity in the sense of Buber.

The point is no longer a higher degree of "self-acceptance as a consequence of feeling accepted." No, the point is now, without a doubt: "Being open to the other."

Rightly, and probably more than is often realized, Rogers thus recognizes Buber's decisive influence on his own evolution towards increased "realness."

> "This recognition of the significance of what Buber terms the I-thou relationship is the reason why, in client-centered therapy, there has come to be a greater use of the self of the therapist, of the therapist's feelings, a greater stress on genuineness, but all of this without imposing the views, values or interpretations of the therapist on the client" (Rogers, 1974, p. 11).

The use of one's own experience of the situation should obviously be made carefully. It should not estrange the other from his own feelings, but should precisely bring these feelings "in contact" with another perspective. If that succeeds, there will be an "enrichment" of "experiencing"; and through it also an enlargement of "the real self." The checking with the self is not eliminated. It remains the ultimate criterion, but the boundaries of the self have expanded. The self has incorporated valuable views of others, and these will, from now on, also play a role in checking one's own "organismic feeling."

Later still, Rogers will overtly agree with Buber when he posits the "I-thou" experience(s) as condition for real humanization.

> "In those rare moments where a deep realness in one meets a realness in the other, a memorable "I-thou relationship," as Martin Buber would call it, occurs. Such a deep mutual personal encounter does not happen very often, but I am convinced that unless it happens occasionally, we are not living as human beings" (Rogers, 1980, p.19).

This increasing use of the therapist's feelings found a powerful expression in groupwork, which became increasingly prominent. It was not by chance that these groups were called "encounter groups." And, in part because the therapist could count on the therapeutic power of the group, he began positing himself much more directly. He let it be known more clearly where he, as therapist, stood and what his view on the situation was. But always with an openness to further dialogue, to encounter, and an avoidance of imposition of opinions. But this avoidance does not imply any more that he should be silent. Essential is the "how:" "Do I put someone before a roadblock, or do I search access?" This becomes the new criterion.

> "My feeling of annoyance rose higher and higher until I finally expressed it by simply saying: 'Oh, nuts.' This somehow pricked the bubble. From that time on he was a more real and genuine person, less braggadorio, and our communication improved. It felt good for having let him know my own real angry feeling as it was occurring" (Rogers, 1969, p. 229).

and:

> "I prize it greatly when I am able to move forward in the never ending attempt to be the real me in this moment, whether it is anger or enthusiasm or puzzlement which is real. I am so delighted when a realness in me brings forth more realness in the other, and we come close to a mutual I-thou relationship" (Rogers, 1969, p. 236).

One can say for sure that the phobia of influencing is now a thing of the past (Lietaer, 1983, p. 86). And the reference to the "I-thou" relationship now also has a very different character than in 1957. We have unmistakeably two people who come in close contact, not only with their own feelings, but also with feelings from another perspective about the same situation.

b. Implications for a view of "the fully functioning person"

Thus one could say, a bridge is established between the "end product" (the "fully functioning person") which Rogers had always aimed at as his ideal, and the "unhampered chance to develop." There is now the implicit recognition that healthy development does not happen automatically, once obstacles are removed. In order to become a real human being, a dialogue within the framework of a real mutual encounter is necessary. A person does not only develop fully through the perfecting of functional interactions, but also through self-enhancing encounters. Hence to Rogers individualization is no longer synonym of humanization.

By now it is clear, we hope, that the real self, which Rogers aims at, is a human self. Statements with the implicit message that "The more one is individualized, the more one is humanized" (a.o. Rogers, 1961, pp. 520-522) should therefore be interpreted in the context outlined above. It is not a matter of contenting oneself with a kind of egocentric individualization, which Buber opposes to humanization. What Rogers means is, in my opinion, that "socializing" should not result from restricting the individual, but that it has to originate in an "opening up" of the individual, that it has to be the result of an encounter, of a real "I-thou" experience.

An individual who is thus allowed to be totally himself (which presupposes the positive offering of a loving relationship, of non-possessive relatedness), will develop according to his own abilities, to an "(as) fully (as possible) functioning person." And here it is clear that the kind of person which Rogers envisions, can be described as "the ideal researcher." An open mind, always willing to question present beliefs, whenever such a revision is required to do justice to new evidence. A person who "gives to Caesar what belongs to Caesar" without slavish submission or denial of one's own view. It is also someone whose "courage to be" allows him to "envision the situation as it is" and who, facing a difficulty, is not "overwhelmed" by it, but can take distance from it, take into account all its aspects, and can make an "existential choice."

Precisely this coming to maturity frees him from a rigid and utilitarian form of self-realization, and allows him "a margin of freedom" which permits him, "within the inescapability of fate" (Wijngaarden, 1984, p. 46) to review the form of what appears as self-actualization at the present moment. And Rogers considers clearly "human dignity" to be a better symbol of "self-actualization" than "self-preservation."

Rogers gives an undeniable illustration of this in his publication "Learning to be free" (Rogers & Stevens, 1967, p. 52).

> "I am speaking of the kind of freedom which Frankl vividly describes in his experience of the concentration camp, when everything - possessions, identity, choice - was taken from the prisoners. But even months and years in such an environment showed only that everything can be taken from a man but one thing: The last of the human freedoms - to choose one's own attitude in any given set of circumstances, to choose one's own way. It is this inner, subjective, existential freedom which I have observed. It is the realization that 'I can live myself, here and now, by my own choice.' It is the quality of courage which enables a person to step into the uncertainty of the unknown as he chooses himself. It is the discovery of meaning from within oneself, meaning which comes from listening sensitively and openly to the complexities of what one is experiencing. It is the burden of being responsible for the self one chooses to be, it is the recognition by the person that he is an emerging process, not a static end product."

The realization that I can live myself, here and now, according to "my choice," as Rogers labels this example, is thus far removed from an "individualistic utilitarianism." On the contrary, it points to a certain degree of freedom, which is itself the fruit of "spiritual elaboration."

Rogers' trepidation in front of any estranging influence from outside, made him again and again, emphasize independence, being responsible for oneself only, and the right to "autonomy."

But this does not refer to "auto-nomos," i.e. "someone who creates his own laws"; it refers to the autonomy of a person who transcends effectively his egocentric perspective, in search for the essence, but who never becomes uprooted. He will never defend a view without submitting it to the authority of genuine experience. "A fact" is for him "more important than the Lord Mayor." It is the "irreverence" of him who "in his reverence gives priority to what deserves priority." It is the example of an independent, open mind, of "the man-scientist," in the ideal sense of the world.

CONCLUSION

When I try to summarize Rogers' main focus of preoccupation, throughout these different periods, I can do so very briefly: It is on enhancing, preserving or restoring "the critical function," the critical attitude towards "what is outside" and "what is within."

The critical attitude towards what is "outside" is, in other words, also a "validation of what is within," of one's own "organismic feeling." It evaluates what presents itself - a fact, a norm, an expectation or whatever - in function of one's own person: How does the situation look when I view it from the perspective of personal self-development? Rogers (1961) speaks in this context of personal autonomy, of "internal locus of evaluation."

The critical attitude to what is within or the "validation of what is outside," represents the opposite movement. Does my "sensing" of the situation do sufficiently justice to its totality and complexity? Am I too hasty in my conclusions by reacting to an element of the situation? Do I have a sufficient view of the totality? And do I give proper weight to all its aspects? Rogers speaks in this respect a.o. of undistorted perception, of openness to all relevant information, something which is characteristic of "the fully functioning person," of the way of functioning in personal maturity. In fact, Rogers usually tries to encompass both aspects in a single movement - and this may be the source of misunderstanding. When he speaks of the self-actualizing tendency, which is the motor of the holistic person; when he speaks about "organismic feeling," about the difference between spontaneity and impulsivity, these always imply both aspects of the critical function.

In order not to lose the critical attitude towards "what is within", nor to influence it negatively, a person should not be pushed into a defensive position. Self-exploration can only happen in a sufficiently safe atmosphere. In order not to lose the critical attitude towards "what is outside", one should not be alienated from one's own feelings. Indeed, when "authority" is situated outside of oneself, one cannot critically evaluate it.

The therapeutic relationship therefore means that the therapist has to perform or permit everything which is "process-enhancing," according to these two goals. What contributes to heading in the direction of an optimal combination of the "validation of what is within" and "the validation of what is outside?" (Both Gendlin and Rice emphasize repeatedly, in their own words, the importance of the combination of these two elements.)

Indeed, both these points are essential for a valid "human development." The "wrong" attitude is the one which either cuts someone off from the validation of what is within and leads him to self-alienation, or cuts him off from the validation of what is outside, by cornering him into a defensive position.

The function of the "growth climate" is thus to optimally promote both critical functions. In the first period, Rogers was - as mentioned earlier - so struck by alienation, that he emphasized avoidance of any direct influencing, and expected salvation from a "safe climate which would render defensiveness unnecessary." Later, as he became more and more conscious, not only of the impossibility of not influencing, but also of the necessity to react sometimes from one's own pole, he started, first hesitantly and later more forcefully, to agree. Decisive hereby was his opinion that the proper "process-preservation" - i.e. giving priority to the authenticity of the mutual contact - could guard against "being cut off from one's own feeling" (at least in principle). The mistake was no longer "to make oneself clearly present," and "show how one thought about things," but the "imposition" of views, the insufficient attention to the whether or not safeguarding of the other person's "own center." What has to be avoided is influencing a person uncritically.

The person has to remain "the expert of the content." He should only say yes to what he can accept "out of his own center." But this person (certainly the young person, or the already partly from himself alienated person) is vulnerable in this. Therefore, the therapist now gets an active role: he has to take the process-safeguarding function on his own shoulders. Do I have to style myself a little less prominently because I appear too threatening? Is effecting a decrease in defensiveness the priority? Or do I have to make sure that the client does not take over things too easily? Is the prevention of self-alienation a priority? Do I have to support him in taking his own feelings seriously, because otherwise he would do so too little? How does the client handle the situation in which he finds himself? A defensive self-image on the one hand, and not taking oneself enough into account on the other hand, seem to be the two sides of the coin. The cure lies in the "integration." Rogers also uses the term "wholeness" as a synonym. In this case "organismic feeling" is also a "felt meaning", as it arises in a healthily functioning, thus critical - "towards within and the outside" - human being. And the "self-actualization" of such a human being presupposes the essential "humanization" which numerous critics of Rogers are unable to reconcile (see a.o. Geller, 1982, p. 72).

I hope that it has become sufficiently clear that, as Rogers himself emphasizes, the "growth climate" refers to more than favorable environmental conditions such as air, degree of humidity, temperature, etc.; it refers to psychological attitudes. And that these psychological attitudes are directed towards maintaining or restoring the critical function of "what is within and what is outside." And that basic attitudes imply all interactions which are necessary to reach this goal.

The emphasis which was put here on the evolution in content and function of the notion of authenticity, could potentially lead to misunderstanding. Rogers' conviction that congruence is not only needed to enhance empathy - i.e. to guarantee its authenticity and to promote even deeper empathy - but deserves sometimes, briefly, priority over empathy, does not take away that, for him, "communication of accurate empathic understanding remains the work of the client-centered therapist" (Rogers, 1966, p. 190).

Effectiveness in therapy is unthinkable without "contact." And empathy remains for Rogers the "royal road" that leads to it. But it should not end up in pseudo-contact, and thus in illusion. In instances where expression of "empathic understanding" counters the "real" experience of the therapist who is, nevertheless, with his whole being focused on the client, there "communication of empathy" becomes contact-disturbing, and thus untherapeutic. Resorting to authenticity "as an independent pole of interaction" is then the risk the therapist must take in order to restore contact - or prevent its loss. And if he succeeds, it also implies a "readjustment" of the client's frame of reference. A readjustment on the basis of an "appeal" on the part of the therapist. In crucial moments thus, the client-centered therapist, too, affirms himself as a "real other," as explicitly "conditionally" accepting. This was, in my opinion, as "crucially important" to Rogers as it was "rarely used." Because, in individual therapy, empathic involvement remains largely "the most precious gift one can give to another."

"Then, in my experience, there are other situations in which the empathic way of being has the highest priority. When the other person is hurting, confused, troubled, anxious, alienated, terrified, or when he or she is doubtful of self-worth, uncertain as to identity - then understanding is called for. The gentle and sensitive companionship offered by an empathic person (who must, of course, possess the other two attitudes) provides illumination and healing. In such situations, deep understanding is, I believe, the most precious gift one can give to another" (Rogers, 1975, in: Rogers, 1980, pp.160-161).

Allow me to conclude thus: I am conscious of the fact that this is only a quick sketch, not a finished painting. But if it would become a stimulus for further reflection on the question whether many, even within the client-centered clan, have not all too quickly ascribed a certain simplemindedness to Rogers, I would consider myself amply rewarded. Just as Leboyer, the famous promotor of painless childbirth, never wanted to deny the fact of childbirth, nor wanted to make it superfluous, but he wanted to alleviate the birth-trauma, so, I believe, has Rogers never wanted to deny the necessity of a "specifically human" development. I could well imagine that he would like to be understood and recognized as the "Leboyer of the painless psychic birth." Regrettably, it seems obvious to me that his insufficient explication of the meanings of his terminology has led to misunderstandings. I am afraid that a number of implications were for him so obvious that he became himself a surprised, puzzled onlooker, when he saw how "naively" he was sometimes translated by those who wanted to demonstrate his "naiveté".

NOTES

1. Rogers described in 1951 the term "communication" in a similar way: "Real communication occurs ... when we listen with understanding" (Rogers, 1951, cit. in Rogers, 1961, p. 331), in which the communication aspect is limited to the client's free and unhibited speaking, as a consequence of the receptive and empathic attitude of the therapist.
2. This is of course only a hypothesis. More accurate research would be necessary to know if we can speak here of a cause-effect sequence in this direction.

REFERENCES

Buber, M., & Rogers, C.R. (1957). *Dialogue between Martin Buber and Carl Rogers.* Unpublished pamphlet.

Evans, R.I. (Ed.). (1975). *Carl Rogers: The man and his ideas.* New York: Dutton.

Geller, L. (1982). The failure of self-actualizing theory: A critique of Carl Rogers and Abraham Maslow. *Journal of Humanistic Psychology, 2,* 56-73.

Gendlin, E.T. (1968). The experiential response. In E. Hammer (Ed.), *The use of interpretation in treatment* (pp. 208-227). New York: Grune & Stratton.

Kinget, M. (1959). Deel I. Algemene presentatie. In C.R. Rogers & M. Kinget, *Psychotherapie en menselijke verhoudingen* (pp. 11-171). Utrecht/ Antwerpen: Spectrum & Standaard.

Lietaer, G. (1983). De client-centered benadering in de zeventiger jaren. *Tijdschrift voor Psychotherapie, 9(2),* 76-89.

Rice, L. (1960). A client-centered approach to the supervision of psychotherapy. In A.K. Hess (Ed.), *Psychotherapy supervision* (pp. 136-147). New York: Wiley.

Rogers, C.R. (1946). Significant aspects of client-centered therapy. *American Psychologist, 1,* 415-422.

Rogers, C.R. (1951). *Client-centered therapy.* Boston: Houghton-Mifflin.

Rogers, C.R. (1957). The necessary and sufficient conditions of therapeutic personality change. *Journal of Consulting Psychology, 21,* 97-103.

Rogers, C.R. (1961). *On becoming a person.* Boston: Houghton Mifflin.

Rogers, C.R. (1966). Client-centered therapy. In S. Arieti (Ed.), *American handbook of psychiatry* (Vol. 3, pp. 183-200). New York: Basic Books.

Rogers, C.R. (1969). *Freedom to learn.* Columbus: Merill.

Rogers, C.R. (1970). *Carl Rogers on encounter groups.* New York: Harper & Row.

Rogers, C.R. (1974). Remarks on the future of client-centered therapy. In D. Wexler & L. Rice (Eds.), *Innovations in client-centered therapy* (pp. 7-13). New York: Wiley.

Rogers, C.R. (1980). *A way of being.* Boston: Houghton Mifflin.

Rogers, C.R. et al. (Eds.). (1967). *The therapeutic relationship and its impact. A study of psychotherapy with schizophrenics.* Madison: University of Wisconsin Press.

Rogers, C.R., & Hart, J. (1970). Looking back and ahead: A conversation with Carl Rogers. In J. Hart & T. Tomlinson (Eds.), *New directions in client-centered therapy* (pp. 502-534). Boston: Houghton-Mifflin.

Rogers, C.R., & Stevens, B. (1967). *Person to person.* La Fayette: Real People Press.

Wijngaarden, H. (1984). Client-centered therapie: een eigen identiteit? In G. Lietaer, Ph.H. van Praag, & J.C.A.G. Swildens (Eds.), *Client-centered psychotherapie in beweging* (pp. 41-53). Leuven/Amersfoort: Acco.

CLIENT-CENTERED AND EXPERIENTIAL: TWO DIFFERENT THERAPIES

Barbara T. BRODLEY
Illinois School of Professional Psychology
Chicago, U.S.A.

Experiential psychotherapy (conceptualized by Gendlin, e.g. 1964, 1966) developed, in part, out of client-centered therapy in the 1960s. Through the ensuing years it has been viewed by its proponents as theoretically consistent with and an improvement upon client-centered therapy (e.g. Gendlin, 1974).

One of the arguments supporting the notion that experiential therapy is an improvement upon client-centered rests on the empirical generalization that early-in-therapy experiencing level predicts outcome (e.g. Gendlin, 1969, p. 13). In a recent paper the research that had been considered supportive of the generalization was reviewed (Brodley, 1988). The review showed that the research had been, in fact, inconclusive and cannot be used as a reason for substituting experiential for client-centered therapy. The task remains, however, to clarify the differences in the theories and the differences in the practices of the two therapies in order to show that they are actually two quite different kinds of therapy. This task is the aim in what follows.

The two theories will, first, be described. Second, two fundamental and unique features of client-centered therapy will be explained. Third, the two therapies will be compared to show some major theoretical differences between them. Finally, there will be discussion of the difference between the salient forms of response in the two therapies. The two therapies will not be compared in respect to their effectiveness.

CLIENT-CENTERED THEORY

The primary construct in Rogers' client-centered theory is the "actualizing tendency" (Rogers, 1980, p. 114-123). This axiom or first principle refers to the inherent and immutable tendency of organisms, including human beings, to grow, develop, expand, differentiate, maintain themselves, restore themselves and to realize their natures as best they can under their circumstances. The actualizing tendency is the basic characteristic of organic, including human, life. Quotations from Rogers (1980) which express these ideas are:

> "The actualizing tendency can ... be thwarted or warped, but it cannot be destroyed without destroying the organism" (p. 119). "There is one central source of energy in the human organism. This source is a trustworthy function of the whole system ... it is ... a tendency toward fulfillment, toward actualization, involving not only the maintenance, but also the enhancement of the organism" (p. 123).

Rogers' theory of therapy is logically consistent with the actualizing principle. The therapist does not cause change but, rather, enables change by providing conditions that foster the optimal functioning of the inherent growth tendencies in the person. In Rogers' theory, therapeutic personality change is within the nature of the person. The client-centered therapist, therefore, does not apply treatments but, instead, provides salutary psychological conditions by forming a particular interpersonal environment with the client.

Client-centered therapy theory (Rogers, 1957, 1959) states that a vulnerable or anxious client must be in psychological contact with a therapist who experiences the attitudes of congruence, unconditional positive regard and empathic understanding of the client's internal frame of reference. The theory also states that the conditions of positive regard and empathic understanding must be perceived, at least to a minimum degree, by the client. If these conditions are met, then therapeutic personality change will occur (Rogers, 1959, p. 213). Rogers (1957, p. 100) predicts that the higher the level of the attitudinal conditions that are offered by the therapist in the relationship, and perceived by the client, then the greater the constructive personality change in the client.

This is the theory which was elucidated by Carl Rogers in articles (e.g. Rogers, 1975, 1980), and in demonstrations, films and recordings. From the many illuminating sources it is apparent that the behavior of the client-centered therapist is imbued with and consistently influenced by a non-directive attitude (Raskin, 1947) toward the client and the therapy process.

The non-directive attitude results in the therapist's surrender of control - of the therapy process and content - over to the client. This surrender is in vivid contrast to the standard clinical mandate - that the therapist should maintain control over the therapy and, to the extent it is possible, over the experiences of the client in therapy. The consequence of the therapist's surrender of the usual control is an equalizing of the two persons in the relationship and their partnership in the events of the therapy situation.

EXPERIENTIAL PSYCHOTHERAPY THEORY

Gendlin (1964, 1973, 1974, 1984) and Iberg (1988) have stated that Rogers' therapeutic attitudinal conditions are part of experiential therapy theory. The therapeutic attitudes are viewed as conducive to freeing the actualizing tendency of the individual. Also, the encounter between therapist and client occurring when the conditions are provided is "more a person-to-person than a person-to-professional authority" relationship (Iberg, 1988, p. 1). The explanation of therapeutic change, in experiential theory is, however, attributed to a specific process of experiencing which can occur in the client, called "focusing" or "focused experiencing."

The theory as written and illustrated by Gendlin (e.g. 1982, 1984) makes it clear that the therapist's primary and active responsibility - that is, what the therapist should do in working with the client - is to *direct* the client toward the focused experiencing process (Gendlin, 1966, p. 9; 1974, p. 222) and help the client to maintain a "high experiencing level" (Gendlin, Beebe, Cassens, Klein & Oberlander, 1968).

Theoretically, this view - that there is a particular and necessary client-located process which must occur for therapy to happen, and the corollary view of the therapist's crucial role to influence that process - subordinates the therapeutic attitudes into a supportive role in experiential theory.

The primary role of the therapist in experiential therapy appears to be in his evaluative and directive function in relation to the client's experiencing process, not in his providing the therapeutic attitudes. Gendlin expresses this difference in the two therapies in the following quotes:

"This felt experience is not what people say but what they talk from. And only as they work with this experiencing, and as its felt meanings evolve, does change happen ..." (Gendlin, 1966, p. 9).

"A therapist must strive ... to help the person allow directly felt referents to form, to attend to a bodily felt sense, and to let that live further in words and interactions" (Gendlin, 1974, p. 222).

"We must ... reformulate Rogers' view that personality change depends on the client's perception of the therapist's attitude. The present theory implies that the client may perceive the therapist's attitudes correctly, or he may not. He may be convinced that the therapist must dislike him and cannot possibly understand him. Not these perceptions, but *the manner of process which is actually occurring,* will determine whether personality change results" (Gendlin, 1964, pp. 135-136).

TWO CONTRIBUTIONS OF ROGERS' THEORY OF THERAPY

We return now to Rogers' theory in order to examine two fundamental characteristics of the theory which are unique and important contributions to therapy practice.

The first is *the principle of trust in the client.* The high degree of trust in the client is a unique characteristic of Rogers' therapy. This trust is not a matter of following a rule to be non-directive. But, rather, trust results from the fact that in client-centered therapy the therapist is functioning from a philosophy of persons which leads to certain values and feelings. These particular values and feelings melt into the ubiquitous non-directive attitude. This attitude along with the specific therapeutic attitudes create the interpersonal conditions which enable change in the client. These attitudes express the trust that is felt by the therapist towards the client.

In his relationship with the client, the Rogerian therapist desires to function consistently and constantly from the hypothesis (or from the belief) that the client has the inherent capability to determine his own constructive directions in life and in the therapy. This hypothesis is represented in an attitude of trust in the client's capabilities which is not qualified by preconceptions about the client's status as client or the nature or level of his disturbance. An attitude of paternalism is not justifiable in the context of client-centered theory. Although on rare occasions and under special circumstances the therapist may take responsibility for the client as an expression of congruence.

In practice, with rare exceptions, the client-centered therapist, guided by his non-directive attitude, has no *directive intentions* in relation to the client. The therapist's intentions are distinctly and only to experience and manifest the attitudinal conditions in such a way that unconditional positive regard and emphatic understanding can be perceived by the client.

The second special contribution of client-centered theory is *the idea that therapeutic personality change can be the result of being understood.* In this context, "being understood" means, specifically, that the client perceives and experiences the therapist's empathic understanding and the therapist's acceptance of the client as a whole person. Empathic understanding - deeply experienced by the therapist, coexisting in the therapist along with unconditional positive regard of the client, and embedded in the therapist's wholeness and realness in the relationship - this understanding is the therapist's causal role in the client's change and healing. Nothing else is conceived, by the theory, as needed from the therapist.

To clarify further, Rogers' empathic understanding is a pure empathic *following* of the client. In this *following* the therapist is taken along on an emotive and intellectual journey with the client, under the lead of the client, into the client's world of memories, perceptions, feelings and perspectives. While following empathically, the therapist is sincere, responsive and wholly present - a companion to the client.

An assumption underlying empathic understanding-following, is that the processes and contents experienced and expressed by the client may be of many different kinds, or even unique to a particular client. In Rogers' client-centered therapy there is not an assumption of any specific process nor any particular class of contents being viewed as necessary for therapeutic change to occur.

It should be recognized that Rogers' description of a process development in the course of therapy (Rogers, 1958) - which has been given emphasis in Gendlin's interpretation of client-centered therapy - was meant as a description of the way clients who are experiencing the attitudinal conditions at a high level appeared, to Rogers, to change in their verbal expression as therapy progressed. Rogers interpreted this change in expression to reflect inner change, including change in the experience of self and change in experiencing itself. But *the process theory was not intended as an instruction concerning how the client or therapist should proceed in therapy.*

Rogers felt that his process conception is misunderstood whenever it is translated into goals for therapy that influence the therapist's attitudes and behavior towards the client. He is being particularly misunderstood when a change in attitudes is manifest in trying to influence the client towards goals conceived by the therapist (Rogers, personal communication, 1982).

HOW THE TWO THEORIES ARE DIFFERENT

There are two important theoretical differences between Rogers' client-centered theory and Gendlin's experiential theory to be emphasized here. These differences show up when comparing the two theories in respect to the characteristics of Rogers' theory described above.

The first difference: *In client-centered therapy the therapist functions consistently with trust in the client as a whole person, while in experiential therapy the therapist's trust is in the client's experiencing process.*

In client-centered, the principle of trust manifests in the therapist's non-directive attitude. Consequently the client is free to function in the relationship in his own way as long as he does not violate the therapist's rights. The client's way of relating to the therapist and of expressing himself is accepted. The therapist, if necessary, extends himself to accept and to appreciate - to understand - the client's way (Bozarth, 1990). There is, for example, no client-centered judgement that the client is "just talking" (Gendlin, 1974, p. 221) as there is, sometimes, in experiential therapy.

In client-centered there is no theoretical directive to intervene to change the way the client is talking[1]. The salient client-centered attitude is non-directive and the therapist's trust in the client's capacities for self-direction, growth and self-restoration is, theoretically, consistent and constant.

In experiential theory, the therapist functions from an a-priori assumption that he knows exactly which process of self-expression and interaction is therapeutic. Consequently the experiential therapist is supposed to adopt the attitude of expert in promoting this process.

The experiential therapy client is free to function in the therapy in his own way if he is spontaneously able to function with a high experiencing level or if he is able to choose to resist or refuse the therapist's focusing interventions.

The experiential therapist does not intend to be coercive or insensitive to the client in his directivity. He readily backs off (Gendlin, 1984, p. 92) if the client feels resistant or is disinclined to the therapist's instructions or promptings. But, even when the experiential therapist is not obviously influencing the client to focus he is, indeed, mindful of the client's experiencing level and is trying to increase or sustain the level by the ways he empathically responds. The client may or may not be aware of this directive intention and behavior by the therapist.

This difference - that the client-centered therapist functions from a principle of trust in the person and that the experiential therapist does not - may seem incorrect to the student of experiential because it appears to contradict Gendlin's emphasis on and respect for the focusing process as the basis of personality growth and as the source of personal autonomy.

It should be apparent, however, that trust in the client's high level focusing process, when it occurs spontaneously or is stimulated by the therapist, is not the same as trust in the whole person. In experiential therapy, this qualified trust is especially obvious when the client is functioning with a low experiencing level and the therapist sees it as his responsibility to influence the process to a higher level.

Friedman, an experiential therapist, expresses the difference between Rogers' therapy and experiential therapy in regard to trust and directivity in the following:

> "Rogers put too much faith in (the) self-actualizing tendency. He doesn't offer it enough help ... Clients have to do "felt sense talk" if therapy is to succeed ... Therapists need to be able to help clients learn how to do this ... When a person isn't talking from a felt sense my task is to help him/her do so" (Friedman, 1982, pp. 101-114).

It is important to emphasize for the sake of accuracy and fairness that the experiential therapist tries to do his job of being expert and directive in relation to the client's process in a very gentle, respectful and sensitive way. But this does not obviate the fact that the position of the therapist is theoretically determined to be that of an expert about the client. Gentleness and sensitivity does not obviate the fact that the experiential attitude is directive and is not based on trust in the person as is client-centered.

The second difference: *In client-centered theory the therapist-attributed cause of therapeutic change is in the therapist's attitudinal conditions, while in experiential theory the therapist-attributed cause of change is in the therapist's functions as monitor, director and teacher of focused experiencing* (Gendlin, 1984, p. 82).

Gendlin and Iberg state that Rogers' therapeutic attitudes have a role in experiential therapy. That role, however, is secondary. The Rogerian therapeutic attitudes appear to operate in experiential therapy in two ways: 1. The attitudinal conditions contribute to therapeutic change when or if they have the direct effect of stimulating or sustaining a focused experiencing process at a high level in the client. 2. The attitudinal conditions may create a quality of relationship between therapist and client such that the client feels safe and trusting in relation to the therapist. The trust thus generated may have the result that the client is likely to respond cooperatively to the therapist's impact on focusing level as he makes his interventions.

In contrast, the trust which is stimulated by the client-centered therapist when he provides the attitudinal conditions, is not exploited by any intentions to direct or specifically influence the client. The absence of directivity in client-centered therapy does not imply there is an absence of direction in the client's change. Nor does it imply the therapist has little impact[2].

In fact, the absence of directivity of the therapist along with the remarkable constructive directions of change in client-centered clients gives support to the theory of the actualization tendency and inherent therapeutic powers in the client and tends to justify the client-centered principle of trust in the client.

COMPARISON OF RESPONSES IN CLIENT-CENTERED AND EXPERIENTIAL THERAPIES

The salient forms of therapist response in client-centered and experiential therapy express the difference in the theories and the attitudes of each type.

Responses in client-centered therapy

The "reflection of feeling" (Rogers, 1986) or, as it is called more recently, the "empathic understanding response" (Temaner, 1977; Broadley, 1987) is a form of response identified with client-centered therapy. In fact, however, there is no specific form of response that fully characterizes client-centered work.

Instead there is *a characteristic process which may be called "empathic following" which includes the reflection of feeling but is not limited to that response form.* Reflections, questions for clarification, summarizing responses, figures of speech, vocal gestures and physical gestures and/or any other forms of response may function in empathic following. A therapist's response can be considered to be contributing to the whole experience of the empathic following process if the response has one or both of the following purposes from the therapist's point of view: 1. The response serves to check, in order to validate or correct, the therapist's subjective experience of empathic understanding of the client's present internal frame of reference (Rogers, 1986). 2. The response expresses the therapist's desire to overtly participate in the relationship. In both criteria the therapist's purpose is to follow the client's internal frame of reference insofar as that is being revealed by the client through words, intonations and gestures.

The most articulate and precise form of empathic following response is the reflection of feeling or empathic understanding response. This response is usually present in an empathic following sequence. Empathic following, including some reflection responses, is illustrated in this client-centered therapy interaction that took place a few months ago between the writer (Barbara: B) and her client (Lall: L).

L: "I'm just ... aching to feel more normal. I'm just aching to feel more integrated, you know...

B: You want it so much (L: Yeah) and it's so painful the way it's always been...

L: It's such a waste, you know?

B: Mm-hm. A waste of you.

L: Mhm, a waste of all the gifts I have, and a waste of the relationships that have gone astray (B: Mm-hm) ... (client begins to weep) I'm really sad about that ...

B: Mm-hm ... All that's lost in the stifling of your own growth ... (L: Mm-hm) ... what's missed ... It's something to cry about ... (L: Yeah) ...

L: I cry about it a lot of the time, you know, in and out of therapy ... and where-ever else ... I just feel like ... I've lost a lot of time ... (B: Mm-hm) ... I mean, life is so short ... (B: Hm-hm) and I feel like I've wasted a good chunk of it...

B: Whatever you can do now ... (L: Yeah) you still have lost what you've lost. (L: Yeah) And life isn't long ... So you're just, you're not ...

Whatever you do is not the same as what you could have done if you hadn't had all this ... blockage. (L: Yeah) Mm-hm, and that's a real loss, no matter what ... (L= Uh-huh) ... Mhm ... something to cry about.

L: I'm very afraid that ... it'll be like this for the rest of my life. (B: Mh-hm) ... And I'll die old and lonely like my dad, and be like my mother is ...

B: Unrealized ... so much.

L: Oh, Yeah! ... Never getting to the point where you look back and say, 'I'm comfortable with who I was and the life I've lived.' (B: Mm-hm) And if I just, if I didn't know that that should be one of the things that you should feel when you're old ... (B: Mm-hm) ... it would be easier ... but I'm not headed in the direction where I can say ...

B: Mm-hm ... that you'll be able to say that. (L: yeah) Mhm ... and when you're feeling like you're feeling right now, it's not only the past ... but later, when you're close to death and ... you fear ...

L: Yeah, yeah ..."

In this example, the therapist's empathic following of the client includes communication of several elements of the client's expression. It includes responses which acknowledge situations (e.g. the past, the parents' situations, the imagined future), feelings (e.g. desire, pain, remorse, sadness, fear), perspectives (e.g. "whatever you can do now, you have still lost what you have lost"). It also includes responses which are vocal gestures (Mm-hm, Mhm) and physical gestures (e.g. nods and hand movements).

The therapist's intentions appear clear in the example - to empathically follow and understand the client's complex of meanings and feelings as they unfold in the interaction. Empathic understanding implies the intention to follow in client-centered work. The therapist does not try to get ahead of the client nor to bring particular aspects of the client's experiencing into awareness.

Fully immersed empathic following, however, does sometimes involve the therapist in verbalizing aspects of the client's feelings or meanings that he was not aware of up until the moment they were expressed by the therapist. This happens naturally, but not deliberately, as part of close following. It is an outcome of the therapist's attempt to check the adequacy of his empathic understanding, not because the therapist has intentions such as wanting to enlighten the client.

Another example of empathic following including articulate empathic understanding responses and, also, including what appears to be a verbalization of an element that the client was not aware of, is this excerpt from a demonstration interview by Rogers (Carl: C) with June

97

(J) (1985).

> J: "I'm not *really* in touch with her ... and I think the sense of it is that ....
> It's like that person is not really any good ...no value ...
>
> C: So you're not really well acquainted with that person behind the fence,
> but you do have a sense that she's no good, she's not worth anything
> much.
>
> J: Yes, she's selfish, self-centered, arrogant, wants things for herself ... I
> guess she comes through sometimes, ... but not really, not often, ... it's
> rare.
>
> C: You are sort of ashamed of that selfish arrogant and miserable person
> that's inside. (J: Yes) Even though sometimes she pokes her way out
> through the fence."

Apparently, based on the way June expressed her description of the
hidden aspects of herself, Carl thought she was communicating a
feeling of shame about these qualities of her inner self. Consequently he
checked that out in his second empathic response. This illustrates that
the point in empathic following is not to try to keep behind any more
than to try to get ahead. It is, rather, to engage in trying to understand
the other person, the client. The therapist is following because the
source of the experiences to be understood is in what the client is
expressing. The therapist may grasp some aspect of what the client is
expressing and of which the client is less than fully aware, but what the
therapist is doing is, none the less, following.

The examples, above, of client-centered interactions illustrate the
way in which empathic understanding of the client's internal frame of
reference is an attempt to attend to the whole person (not only the
person's feelings) by trying to absorb and respond to the person's view
of his world including his various reactions and feelings (Zimring,
1988).

Empathic understanding responses and other following responses
communicate the client-centered therapist's empathic understanding,
attention, interest in and acceptance of the client. The constancy of
empathic following and the constant implicit communications of 1.
asking the client to listen to what the therapist thinks he has
understood, and 2. asking the client to let the therapist know if he has
understood or not, and to correct him if he is wrong, along with the
communications 3. that imply "I am here, attentive and interested and
acceptant and truly trying to understand" - all together produce an
effect of respectfulness, valuing and trust in the client and in the client's
perceptions and feelings.

Responses in experiential therapy

In experiential therapy there are two salient response forms. One is a form of responding called "listening" which includes "listening responses" sometimes called "client-centered responding" (Gendlin, 1974, p. 216) or "saying back" responses. The second form of response is a focusing prompt or focusing instruction.

Listening resembles empathic following and listening responses resemble reflections of feeling and other following responses in client-centered therapy. But listening is different from empathic following in having a different purpose.

Listening is empathic, in so far as it attempts to reflect the client's inner experience as the client tries to express it. But listening is more specifically directed toward making the client feel and be aware of his felt sense. Listening is intended by the therapist to help the client refer to his felt sense. And it helps the client learn to attend to his felt sense especially as a bodily felt sensation or a process of sensations from which meanings emerge when attention is given to the felt sense. It also helps the client learn that he can choose to attend to that process from which meanings are created, and heighten the intensity of that process. Some statements that express the experiential viewpoint are:

> "...the experiential dimension in the psychotherapy process defines the core content of therapy and outlines the necessary sequence of tasks (for the client) ... the concrete feeling, personal meaning and experiencing of the patient must be revealed and worked with ... progressively more advanced levels of focusing are essential for progress ... The approach also defines the therapist's work as independent of ... the emotional climate of the relationship. In this light, the therapist is to help the patient expand his experience by supporting the process of focusing by responding to his (the client's) implicit referent ... a step beyond the patient's experiential level, directing him toward the implicit meaning or aspect of his experience, so that the patient can experience it and refer to it more directly" (Klein, Mathieu, Gendlin & Kiesler, 1969, pp. 8-9).

> "It is my claim that only in this physical way does real change occur ... the problem must change in how it literally sets in the body. When that changes, one senses a stirring, a seeping, a physical shift ..." (Gendlin, 1982, pp. 4-6).

A special form of listening response described by Hendricks (1986, p. 155) is called a "focusing reflection." This form of response is consciously used by the experientially aware therapist to direct the client's attention toward the "implicit" by referring directly to the felt experience in the wording of the empathic understanding response. An example of the focusing reflection given by Hendricks is as follows:

> C: "Yeah. I think so. I think so because ... this person feels inaccessible. Yet, not so inaccessible that it's a total impossibility. So it's like I keep trying out my worth ... on him ... and keep coming up against, 'Yeah, I like you, but ...'
> T: O.K. So, how about, 'Yeah, I like you, but ...' Does that fit? Is that exactly right to that whole feeling?
> C: Yeah, it really is. Really is.
> T: 'I like you, but ...'"

It is evident, in the above, that the therapist is trying to focus the client's attention onto the relation between her words and the felt sense (which is pointed to with "that whole feeling") and to heighten awareness of the felt sense. The therapist's responses draw the client's attention to the specific feeling in her body which is stimulated in response to the statement, "I like you but ..."

The experiential therapist's responses in the example show how the client is helped to become aware of her bodily felt experience. They also may help the client discover meanings that arise from attention to the bodily experience. In addition, the focusing reflection helps to teach the client the method of referring to bodily feelings as a generally desirable and healthy procedure.

In contrast, client-centered empathic following might be expressed in response to the initial client statement in the example above in this way:

> T: "You have the sense that he might want you ... so you keep exposing yourself towards him ... then you get that ... 'but' ... that reservation about you, and you feel devalued."

In the client-centered version of the interaction, the therapist is trying to express the complex of perceptions and personal meanings that seem to be conveyed by the client. That is, the response is an attempt to check the correctness of the therapist's empathic understanding of the client's internal frame of reference at the time of expression. This means trying to understand what she is talking about and, crucially for true empathic understanding, *what the client is expressing as her relation to what she is talking about.*

In the example the client is communicating the situation of her attempt to gain intimacy and acceptance from a person who might respond to her in those ways. In her attempt she feels she is risking her "worth." She reports she gets hit with a qualified rather than a whole-hearted feeling from him.

There are three elements in the client-centered response that are intended to check accuracy of empathic understanding. First, the client's perception of the semi-accessibility of the man. Second, the client's attempt to draw him towards her. Finally, the semi-rejection she interpets from his "but ..." and her feeling of being devalued by that qualified response from him.

It is the whole meaning, or at least the most personal and dynamic elements of it, that the client-centered responses are expressing in reaction to the client. In contrast to the experiential therapy response the client-centered one is not deliberately trying to draw the client's attention to her felt sense in order to make her more aware of it or more attuned to it. Although attention to felt sense is often one of the psychological effects of empathic understanding in client-centered therapy, and it might be one of the effects of the client-centered response in this instance.

The second salient form of response in experiential therapy - the focusing prompt or focusing instruction - is illustrated in the following interaction from Gendlin (1982):

> C: "I have all these excuses about why I never do my best, um ...
> T: You come right up to the line and then something holds back.
> C: Yeah ... Well, I think it's ... ah ... that I don't want to test myself. And I'm afraid, ah, the bad things will be confirmed.
> T: Can you feel the pull back, if you imagine yourself going ahead?"

The first experiential therapist response, above, translates the client's meaning (his "excuses") into a dynamic description intended to evoke the felt sense of trying to do something and then stopping or blocking. The second focusing response is a focusing instruction type of response. It ignores the client's explanation of why he does not do his best (the fear of bad things being confirmed) and, instead, asks the client to attend to the feel of the "pull back" in the context of imagining (with feeling) "going ahead." In both responses the therapist is pointing up the inner dynamic of the "go-then-stopped" experience in order to bring the client's attention to it and have the client feel the experience in his body, i.e. to have the felt sense of that situation.

A version of the above interaction showing a possible client-centered way of responding to the same client material is as follows:

> C: "I have all these excuses about why I never do my best, um...
> T: Avoiding trying ...
> C: Yeah ... Well, I think it's ... ah .... that I don't want to test myself. And I'm afraid, ah, the bad things will be confirmed.

T: Afraid you won't measure up, and ... that some bad things about you will really show up ..."

The client-centered intention in this illustration is simply to understand the client's experiences as he brings them out in his communication. This intention is one without a concern for focusing level.

Experiential therapists acknowledge that they direct process. They, truly have, however, no preconceptions about what the client should talk about or what issues need to be explored as is the case in many other therapies. The experiential therapist is committed to openness and receptivity concerning the client's choice of subject matter.

Nevertheless, it should be apparent even from the two short experiential examples above, that experiential work directly influences content as an effect of directing process. This is because content is embedded in process, or vice versa, depending upon one's perspective.

Content is influenced when experiential techniques are used, especially when the therapist explicitly directs the client's process with focusing prompts or focusing instructions. (See the example of experiential work on the next pages.) The influence on the content of client expression is, usually, that the client gives fewer descriptions and expressions coming from his whole self. Examples of the type of self-referring statements which uninfluenced clients make as they express and represent themselves are: "I have all these excuses." "I'm just aching to feel more normal." "I cry about it a lot of the time." "I'm very afraid that ... it'll be like this for the rest of my life." "I'll die lonely." "I'm afraid the bad things will be confirmed." "I keep trying out my worth."

The type of client statement illustrated above becomes less frequent when the experiential therapist uses focusing prompting or instructing techniques. Instead there are statements of the following type: "It's like a heavy wall." "It wants to scream." "Some of me wants to find out..." "Running from the vague thing is sad." The client's subject often changes from "I" referring to the whole self to "they" or "it" referring to feelings, sensations or an aspect of the self. Under the influence of focusing techniques the client tends to describe something he observes in himself or about himself. The client's voice becomes an implicit, passive, novelistic voice rather than the more natural, or spontaneous, active, volitional, self-revealing and self-owning voice that occurs in client-centered interactions.

Another quality of experiential work that often results from the conception of the therapist's task and the techniques that implement the task is the disjunction in the communication situation between therapist and client.

Common purposes of communication are to express oneself and/or to transmit information and feelings. These are often the purposes of the client who has come to the therapist and who begins by discussing his problems, his feelings and situations. What is being said by the client is important to him. His reason for saying what he is saying is, usually, because it has importance to him. He expects, or more often hopes, it will be of interest to the therapist and be an expression of the therapist's interest in him. This expectation appears to be fulfilled by the experiential therapist who gives detailed responses that indicate attention is being given to what the client is saying.

The experiential therapist, however, is not doing what he appears to be doing as he listens to the client. He is not, despite appearance, sharing the client's aim to be understood and of interest. Instead, the experiential therapist is listening closely to what the client is saying primarily in order to monitor the level of experiencing and to help the person engage in the focused experiencing process at a high level. Consequently, unless the experiential client is educated about the therapy, and chooses to actively cooperate in the method, the therapist and the client will tend to be engaged in two different and non-reciprocal activities. They will only have the appearance of shared purpose. Specifically, the therapist will be trying to help the client focus, while the client will be trying to communicate about himself to the therapist and be seeking the therapist's interest in him.

Under the circumstances that the client is familiar with and chooses to cooperate with experiential procedures, the purposes of therapist and client are mutual and not disjunctive. In this kind of experiential partnership the content of the conversation becomes very different from usual conversation and from the conversation of client-centered therapy. The following example of interaction from an experiential therapy session presented by Gendlin (1982) illustrates the distinctiveness of the conversation in experiential therapy when the client is cooperating with the therapist's purpose.

> T: "So we have to go see where your good energy went to.
> (long silence)

C: I have lots of energy there, but it's all tied up.
T: You can feel your energy there, but it's tied up.
C: Yes.
T: Can you sense what's tying it up?
(long silence)
C: It's like a heavy wall in front of it.
It's behind that.
T: You can feel a heavy wall.
C: It's a whole part of me that I keep in. ... Like when I say it's OK when it's not. The way I hold everything in.
(long silence)
There's a part of me that's dead, and a part that isn't.
T: Two parts, one is dead, and one ...ah
C: Survived.
(long silence)
It wants to scream.
T: The dead parts wants to scream and to be let out.
C: To live.
(long silence)
And there's also something vague, I can't get what that is.
T: Make a space for that vague thing, you don't know what it is yet. There's something vague there, but it isn't clear what it is.
C: I feel a lot of tension.
T: OK, Take a break. Just step back a little bit. There's the vague thing, and then, also, there's the tension. Let's talk a little. You've come a lot of steps."

In the interaction above it seems that both therapist and client are in agreement that their task is to talk about the client's inner feelings and bodily experiences and to draw forth from the experiential source more feelings and meanings. At times this appears as if the client were trying to view a film or video showing events that are not entirely clear but trying to report them in as much detail as possible.

The example shows how the experiential therapist is in control of the procedure, directing the client towards the source of what is sensed and towards *what* is sensed. Directivity is also apparent in the instruction "take a break" and "Let's talk a little." The therapist acts as though he knows what the client needs in this procedure pretty much moment to moment. The client seems to accept the therapist's authority and is cooperating in being directed.

Experiential listening and focusing prompts, and focusing instructions are different from client-centered empathic following. The purpose of deliberately focusing the client on the basis that the therapist decides it is desirable does not exist in client-centered therapy. Empathic following, in client-centered therapy often has the effect of focusing the client. But this effect is secondary to its contribution to the client's perception that the therapist is engaged in empathic understanding. The focusing purpose does not exist in client-centered work because such a purpose presumes the therapist knows which kind of experience the client should have in order to change. Client-centered theory does not make that assumption.

CONCLUSION

Client-centered theory and experiential therapy theory are fundamentally different in their views of the therapist's role in constructive personality change. Also, client-centered therapy fundamentally involves the therapist in working with a non-directive attitude whereas experiential involves the therapist in working from a specific directive attitude. These differences, with their many consequences in practice, make it accurate and appropriate to view the two therapies as different kinds of therapy, not ones in an internally consistent continuum of development. Experiential is one of the directive therapies. Client-centered is unique in the arena of psychotherapies - it is distinctly not a directive therapy.

SUMMARY

Rogers' client-centered theory and Gendlin's experiential therapy theory have been described and compared. Differences in the salient forms of response used in the two therapies were discussed and illustrated.

The experiential position involves assumption of a particular therapeutic process - focusing - as necessary for therapeutic change, and posits the view that the therapist's role is to promote this process. These features are different from client-centered therapy and contradict the non-directive essence of client-centered work.

This presentation of the two therapies shows that they are different, and that experiential therapy is not an internally consistent development out of client-centered therapy.

Prior to this writing the real and significant differences between client-centered and experiential attitudes have not been addressed in the literature. Experiential therapy has been viewed simply as an advancement over client-centered therapy. Consequently, people who might be considering these approaches were being confused. Choice about how they might want to work with their clients was obfuscated.

The answer to the important question of which therapy is the most effective remains, at this point in time, a matter of opinion. But it is hoped that this presentation contributes to recognition of the differences between the therapies and, thereby, a clearer choice of approach and, potentially, a clearer comparision of therapies in respect to outcomes.

NOTES

1. Rogers wrote of being selective in his listening and acknowledged he could be viewed as directive (Rogers, 1970, p. 47). Rogers' selectivity, however, has to do with the essence of empathic understanding and is not a directivity. In empathic understanding the listener is attempting to understand/follow not only what the client is talking about. In fact, the crucial understanding concerns the client's expressed relation of *himself to what he is talking about.* Understanding is not empathic until and unless the listener grasps these relations (e.g. reactions, feelings, attitudes, desires, wants, wishes, etc.) in the client's communication.
2. Rogers ventured to describe the process of change occuring in clients when the attitudinal conditions are present in two different ways. One approach was described as "the central or crucial element in change" (Rogers, 1956) and as "the moment of movement." Rogers described movement as having several qualities: Immediate experiencing, without inhibition, with full awareness, and with the feeling of acceptability to the self (of whatever it is the client is talking about). Rogers thought these moments are the change moments which occur more or less frequently whenever there is an overall constructive change in the client. The second approach to change process in the client described by Rogers (1984) was his view that the client gradually adopts the three therapeutic attitudes - congruence, unconditional positive regard and empathic understanding - in himself, towards himself and towards others. In this view the sequence of events in the client's adoption of the therapeutic attitudes varies on the basis of individual differences in personality and problems. These two approaches to change are not contradictory but refer to different levels of analysis of change process.

106

REFERENCES

Bozarth, J.D. (1990). *The essence of client-centered/person-centered therapy.* See this volume.

Brodley, B.T. (1987). *A client-centered psychotherapy practice.* Paper prepared for the Third International Forum on the Person-centered Aproach. La Jolla, CA.

Brodley, B.T. (1988). *Does early-in-therapy experiencing level predict outcome? A review of research.* Paper presented at the Second Annual Conference of the Association for the Development of the Person-Centered Approach. New York.

Friedman, N. (1982). *Experiential therapy and focusing.* New York: Half Court Press.

Gendlin, E.T. (1962). *Experiencing and the creation of meaning.* New York: Free Press of Glencoe.

Gendlin, E.T. (1964). A theory of personality change. In P. Worchel & D. Byrne (Eds.), *Personality change.* New York: Wiley.

Gendlin, E.T. (1966). Research in psychotherapy with schizophrenic patients and the nature of that illness. *American Journal of Psychotherapy, 20,* 4-16.

Gendlin, E.T. (1973). Experiential psychotherapy. In R. Corsini (Ed.), *Current psychotherapies* (pp. 317-352). Itasca, Illinois: Peacock Books.

Gendlin, E.T. (1974). Client-centered and experiential psychotherapy. In D.A. Wexler & L.N. Rice (Eds.), *Innovations in client-centered therapy* (pp. 211-246). New York: Wiley.

Gendlin, E.T. (1982). *Experiential psychotherapy.* Unpublished manuscript .

Gendlin, E.T. (1984). The client's client: The edge of awareness. In R.F. Levant & J.M. Shlien (Eds.), *Client-centered therapy and the person-centered approach (pp. 76-107).* New York: Praeger.

Gendlin, E.T. (1988). *Personal communication.* June.

Gendlin, E.T., Beebe, J., Cassens, J., Klein, M., & Oberlander, R. (1968). Focusing ability in psychotherapy, personality, and creativity. In J.M. Shlien (Ed.), *Research in psychotherapy* (Vol. 3, pp.217-241). Washington D.C.: American Psychological Association.

Hendricks, M.N (1986). Experiencing level as a therapeutic variable, *Person-Centered Review, 1,* 142-161.

Iberg, J. (1988). *Experiential psychotherapy.* Unpublished manuscript.

Klein, M.H., Mathieu, P.L., Gendlin, E.T., & Kiesler, D.J. (1969). *The experiencing scale: A research and training manual,* Vol. 1. Madison: University of Wisconsin.

Raskin, N. (1947). *The non-directive attitude.* Unpublished manuscript.

Rice, L.N. (1984). Client tasks in client-centered therapy. In R.F. Levant & J.M. Shlien (Eds), *Client-centered therapy and the person-centered approach* (pp. 182-202). New York: Praeger.

Rogers, C.R. (1951). *Client-centered therapy: Its current practice, implications, and theory.* Boston: Houghton Mifflin.

Rogers, C.R. (1956). *The essence of psychotherapy: Moments of movement.* Paper given at first meeting of the American Academy of Psychotherapists, New

York.

Rogers, C.R. (1957). The necessary and sufficient conditions of therapeutic personality change. *Journal of Consulting Psychology, 22,* 95-103.

Rogers, C.R. (1958). A process conception of psychotherapy. *American Psychologist, 13,* 142-148.

Rogers, C.R. (1959). A theory of therapy, personality and interpersonal relationships as developed in the client-centered framework. In S. Koch (Ed.), *Psychology: A study of a science. (Vol. 3). Formulations of the person and the social context* (pp. 184-256). New York: McGraw-Hill.

Rogers, C.R. (1961). Persons or science: A philosophical question. In C.R. Rogers, *On becoming a person* (pp. 199-224). Boston: Houghton Mifflin.

Rogers, C.R. (1970). *Carl Rogers on encounter groups.* New York: Harper & Row.

Rogers, C.R. (1975). Empathic: An unappreciated way of being. *Counseling Psychologist, 5(2),* 2-10.

Rogers, C.R. (1980). *A way of being.* Boston: Houghton Mifflin.

Rogers, C.R. (1984). *A conversation with Carl Rogers.* A discussion recorded at the Second International Forum on the Person-Centered Approach. Norwich, England.

Rogers, C.R. (1985). Demonstration interview with June. Recorded Dublin.

Rogers, C.R. (1986). Reflection of feelings. *Person-Centered Review, 1,* 375-377.

Temaner, B. (1977). *The empathic understanding response process.* Chicago Counseling Center Discussion Paper. Chicago.

Wexler, D.A., & Rice, L.N. (1974). *Innovations in client-centered therapy.* New York: Wiley.

Zimring, F. (1988). *A unique characteristic of client-centered therapy.* Unpublished manuscript.

CAN CLIENT-CENTERED THERAPY TRANSCEND ITS MONOCULTURAL ROOTS?

Len HOLDSTOCK
Vrije Universiteit Amsterdam, The Netherlands

Concommitant with an increasing concern about the international face of psychology (Ardilla, 1982; Azuma, 1984; Bernal & Padilla, 1982; Cole, 1984; Ho, 1985; Kennedy, Scheirer, & Rogers, 1984; Kojima, 1984; Pedersen & Inouye, 1984; Rosenzweig, 1984; Russell, 1984; Sexton & Misiak, 1984; Sue, 1983; Torney-Purta, 1984; Triandis & Brislin, 1984; Weis, Rothbaum, & Blackburn, 1984a, 1984b), issues involved in cross-cultural counseling and mental health are coming under renewed scrutiny (e.g. Cox, 1986; Hammond, 1988; LaFromboise, 1988; Sue, 1988; special issues of the *Journal of Consulting and Clinical Psychology,* 1987; the *Counseling Psychologist,* 1985). Among these issues the admonition from therapists has been to be culturally sensitive (Rogler, Malgady, Constantino, & Blumenthal, 1987; Sue & Zane, 1987). While cultural sensitivity is certainly necessary in the context of any cross-cultural therapy, a question which has not received sufficient attention is whether psychotherapy as it is known in the Western world, is really possible and effective in promoting mental health amongst minority cultures?

The issue is of particular relevance for the Person-Centered approach (PCA). Since the PCA has been the therapeutic procedure par excellence to indwell into understanding, accepting and respecting the reality of another person, the approach faces a particular responsibility when it comes to individuals from nonwestern cultures. Is it possible for a theory and psychotherapeutic approach which grew out of midwestern middle-class values, to be transferred to socio-economic strata and cultures distinctly different from those which gave birth to it?

ALL IS NOT WELL WITH THE PCA

Recently, criticism has been directed in the U.S. (Ho, 1985; Sarason, 1981) and in South Africa (Dawes, 1985; Swartz, 1986; Turton, 1986) at the PCA. The essence of the criticism is contained in the fact that the PCA as a major force in the human potential movement, accentuates values which are unique to the U.S. and the Western world. An overemphasis on individualism is considered to be the major stumbling block. Sarason (1981, p. 830) argued that while publication of Rogers' (1947) *Counseling and Psychotherapy* effectively initiated "The age of Psychotherapy ... it defined ... the problems of people in terms of an individual psychology: Problems were personal or narrowly interpersonal and for all practical purposes independent of the nature and structure of the social order."

Ho (1985, p. 1217) described Carl Rogers as one of the major "modern prophets of individualism." Patterson (1986) and others feel strongly that nothing can be further from the truth. Rogers (1979, p. 12) himself, wrote: "We seem as a culture to have made a fetish out of complete individual self-sufficiency, of not needing help, of being completely private except in a very few selected relationships." Although Rogers certainly rejected narcissistic individualism and believed in the interrelatedness of the individual with other people, his point of departure remained firmly embedded in the autonomy of the individual. The origin of control resided inside the person rather than within the larger system or field.

Even the shift in emphasis to person-centered which highlights the social outreach of the theory, does not negate the fact that a "distinctive feature of person-centered theory is and has been its continued stress on the self-actualizing and self-directing quality of people. This apparently simple notion of 'empowering the person,' trusting that he or she can know the proper direction of movement in his or her own actualizing process, is one of the most revolutionary aspects of the theory, cutting it loose from the materialistic determinism of some other systems" (Holdstock & Rogers, 1983, p. 189).

Farson (1974, p. 200), also describes the basic assumption of Person-Centered theory as "Actualizing human potentialities for creativity and growth, regarding the person in the here and now, emphasizing the centrality of the self, and placing significance on experience as well as behavior."

The encounter group movement, of which Rogers was one of the pioneers, can perhaps be regarded as a move away from a narrow individualistic focus. During the last few decades this approach expanded to include as many as 800 people at a time, often from many different nationalities and cultures (Rogers, 1979). Lay and professional people from many different disciplines became involved. Yet, empowering the individual remained the focus through which societal change was to be brought about. If only enough individuals were to change, so it was believed, society would change. Thus, the good of the larger society depended squarely on actualization of the potential of its individual members.

A more determined shift towards larger social issues became apparent during the later stages of Rogers life. During this time his focus shifted from therapy towards such social issues as the nuclear threat and conflict resolution amongst hostile factions in various parts of the world. In 1985 he facilitated a person-centered encounter between leading government officials from Central and Latin America (Rogers, 1986). Perhaps the most prominent example of a political encounter attributed to be in the person-centered mold is the 10-day meeting between Sadat and Begin.

I also consider the reason why Rogers finally accepted an invitation from me to conduct workshops between black and white South Africans in 1982, as an indication of his larger social consciousness. His hope and mine, was to facilitate the process of change in the country through dialogue between blacks and whites. In 1986 he paid a repeat visit. By that time the political situation had deteriorated markedly and I had become sufficiently disillusioned with the traditional way of implementing the PCA in South Africa, not to participate in the second visit.

The 1986 workshops also elicited criticism from other sources. Swartz (1986), somewhat scathingly, called it a "safari." In light of the banning of so many people in the country, she felt that dialogue between people from different groups was not going to solve South Africa's problems. In fact, it served as "little more than a smokescreen for that silence" (Swartz, 1986, p. 140). Rogers and people who work within a person-centered framework, as I still consider myself to do, have also been criticized for not appreciating the implications of the power relations within which discourse is invited (Dawes, 1986; Farson, 1974; Swartz, 1986). Although Farson considered Rogers as "one of the most important social revolutionaries of our time" (p. 197), he pointed out that "Rogers has paid precious little attention to role, power, status, culture, politics, history, systems, technology, and perhaps most significantly to the paradoxical quality of human existence" (p. 201). Few representatives of the PCA, myself included, have. I can still remember reading Farson's words in 1974, without really being able to grasp what he was saying.

Towards the latter part of his career Rogers certainly became more aware of political and status issues, as the conference with leading political figures from Central and South America attests. In *Human dimensions of medical education,* a programme initiated during the 1970s by Orienne Strode, the importance of participation by individuals with high status in the medical professions, was fully appreciated. Attempts were therefore made to elicit the participation of Deans and Heads of departments in medical faculties.

However, although there are indications to the contrary, the point of departure of the PCA has remained embedded in empowering the individual as the ideal means of accomplishing societal change. In addition, despite the fact that he travelled widely, Rogers remained surprisingly uninfluenced by divergent cultural perspectives. The South African situation makes it abundantly clear how much more attention needs to be devoted, not only to issues of political power and socio-economic conditions, but also to the issue of culture.

Turton (1986) attributed the failure of a lay black counseling programme in Soweto to the fact that its aim and methodology were not relevant and appropriate to meet the needs of the people requiring its services. Focusing on actualization needs through nondirective counseling, "obscures and ultimately relegates out the wider social, economic, and political factors involved in the genesis of personal problems" (Turton, 1986, p. 92).

The political situation in South Africa and resultant socio-economic conditions, undoubtedly contribute a great deal to the mental health problems and failure of people to realize their potential. Talking about emotional and interpersonal issues, while basic survival is at stake, raises serious doubt about the relevance of the approach. According to Farson (1974), "It is more the situation which limits and victimizes them that needs fixing, but we will not get to that task if we continue to believe that until we get people straightened out there is little point in trying to make changes in organizations or in society at large" (p. 201).

REVISIONING BASIC ASSUMPTIONS OF THE PCA

Thus, revisioning of the assumptions underlying the PCA seems to be called for. Such a process would be in keeping with the constant modification and refinement which the theory has undergone since its inception (Holdstock, 1978; Holdstock & Rogers, 1983).

The current debate on individualism in American society is of major importance to Person-Centered theory, research, and practice. A recent article, in which Sampson (1988) distinguishes between "self-contained" and "ensembled" individualism, is especially relevant. Self-contained individualism is characterized by firmly drawn self-other boundaries. Personal control is emphasized and social responsibility takes the form of "contractual exchange relationships involving reciprocity" (Sampson, 1988, p. 20). A mundane example of reciprocal self-other relationships would be paying for therapeutic services or for participation in workshops. An example of a higher order of reciprocity is to be found in statements by Nathanial Branden on a lecture tour to promote his book Honouring the self (1988). Branden stated that it was in the interest of every individual to live in a safer, saner, better world, and to try to bring such a world about.

Ensembled individualism, on the other hand, emphasizes more fluidly drawn self-nonself boundaries and field control. Relationships are noncontractual, mutually obligatory and communal, and as such operate by different rules than those which govern a more contractually oriented approach. Assistance is given and received without it being evaluated in material terms or in terms of an infringement on personal freedom.

Calling on Bateson and Lewin, Sampson (1988) points out that although Western culture locates the origin of control inside the person, the actual determination lies within a larger system or field. Similarly, the work of Foucault and Weber demonstrates that the historical process of individualization reflects a change in societal control rather than a freeing of the individual from social authority (Sampson, 1988). Collective and communal loyalties and responsibilities are replaced by bureaucratization of aspects of social life governed by highly abstract, impersonal rules and principles. Thus, the loss of a communal self necessitated the institution of laws to govern the behavior between people. Although the illusion of being more free was created, people actually had less freedom. Failure to adhere to the dictates laid down by bureaucratic institutions, was met by more severe sanction than under a system of communal obligation.

I cannot help but wonder whether development of Client-Centered therapy and the PCA as a formal system to facilitate a sense of respect and empathy for others, is not also a reflection of the bureaucratization of behaving responsibly and caringly towards each other?

Earlier, Sampson (1985) expressed the opinion that it was psychology's focus on the individual as a closed rather than an open system, that was one of the main factors that prevented the discipline from developing meaningfully. He conceptualized the self as a decentralized, nonequilibrium entity that was constantly becoming. A similar notion was expressed by Kohlberg (in Gibbs & Schnell, 1985). Kohlberg maintained that the basic unit of the self was a bipolar self-other relationship, and that the self was born out of the social and sharing process. Gestalt therapists use the concept of the ecological self to distinguish it from the egotistical self. Yet another way in which the difference between self-contained and ensembled individualism has been conceptualized, has been in terms of the egocentric and sociocentric self.

Similar notions of the self exist in the indigenous psychologies of many nonwestern cultures. Among these are both the so-called primitive and the more modern and industrialized societies. Sampson (1988) mentions the Maori, the Chewong of Malaysia, the Oryian (Hindu), the Japanese, the Chinese (Confucian) and the Islamic cultures. For instance, Kojima (1984) states that "the concept of self completely independent from the environment is very foreign to the Japanese ... for the Japanese, self is always in an interdependent relationship with the environment, and neither self nor environment can be defined without reference to the other" (p. 973).

WHAT THE PCA CAN LEARN FROM AFRICA

African culture, too, emphasizes a view of the person that is inextricably interrelated with the larger society, not only of other people, but also of the deceased ancestors, animals, plants and even inanimate objects. Akbar (1984) speaks of "the illusionary being called an individual" (p. 400). Black culture is renowned for its "emphases on groupness ... commonality, corporateness, cooperation, and interdependence" (Baldwin, 1986, p. 244). "The essence of being is 'participation' in which humans are always interlocked with one another" (Setiloane, 1986, p. 14). "I am because we are. We are because I am," is an often heard expression in different parts of Africa, while the Descartian dictum of "I think, therefore I am," becomes "I belong, therefore I am" Even the mythology of creation among the Zulu and Tswana teaches that the first appearance of people was in community. It was as a community of men, women, children and animals that the first beings emerged from a bed of reeds or a hole in the ground (Setiloane, 1986).

The ensembled individualism of Africa extends beyond the concept as discussed by Sampson (1988). It transcends the level of interpersonal relationships and reaches into the realm of the spiritual. Not only humans, but all things are imbued with "seriti" (force, energy, spirit). It is as a vital force, which is part of a larger vital force, that the individual participates in the world. In fact, the human being is not only vital force, but vital force in participation.

It ought to be clear how differently from Africa, the PCA conceptualizes the individual. If the PCA is to become a truly international approach, it has to take cognisance of the spiritually-ensembled manner in which the individual is conceptualized in countries outside the Western world. In doing so, it can set the pace for the psychological profession in the same way that it did in many other respects.

Reorienting its focus towards a spiritually-ensembled individualism, will not only extend the scope of person-centered theory, but also its effectiveness as change agent, in the Western as well as nonwestern world. However, it has to be realized that a dramatic shift in emphasis is required. Indeed, the shift would be so vast that it is debatable whether it will come about within the foreseeable future. What is required is akin to a paradigm shift for the entire Western world. That a start has to be made, is imperative though.

A steady stream of Western thinkers have expressed themselves against the prevailing belief that the locus of control is to be found inside the person and not in the surrounding field. Sampson (1988) is clearly of the opinion that self-contained, or self-sufficient individualism, as I prefer to call it, prevents rather than facilitates the realization of the core values of U.S. society: freedom, responsibility, and achievement. Others have also drawn attention to the limitations of self-contained individualism (see Sampson, 1988). The implications of the new PCA are far-reaching. I will only consider some of the implications with respect to South Africa. First of all, it calls for recognition and acceptance of and respect for the spiritually-ensembled individualism of African culture. I think of the spiritually-ensembled individualism of Africa as the ultimate aim towards which the PCA aspires. Compared to the approach in the West, Africa's person-centeredness is not a circumscribed professional endeavor, but an approach which permeates all aspects of living. I think of it as informal or indigenous person-centeredness. It is an attitude which has been part of the culture for as long as people can remember. Amongst the Nguni and Sotho speaking peoples of southern Africa, person-centeredness manifests as "ubuntu" and "botho" respectively. Having ubuntu or botho means more than anything else. Without ubuntu one lacks an indispensable ingredient to being human and one is regarded as a person deserving pity and sometimes even contempt (Holdstock, 1987). In the words of Nobel laureate Archbishop Desmond Tutu (1981), "The person who had ubuntu was known to be compassionate and gentle, who used his strength on behalf of the weak, who did not take advantage of others, in short he cared, treating others as what they were, human beings" (p. 22).

Even though Africa's person-centeredness has not developed as a formal system of thinking along Western lines, it would be a grave mistake not to regard it as subscribing to similar values as the PCA. The labelling of a theory, system of thinking, or approach, does not mean that the underlying principles have been appropriated, or that exclusive rights to their implementation, have been obtained.

The example of the early, and perhaps even present-day missionaries comes to mind. They believed, and probably still do, that their concept of divinity was the only valid one. It never dawned on them to enquire about the conception of divinity amongst the people of Africa. Similarly, the Person-Centered label does not mean that the principles which it subsumes have only recently been discovered. Person-Centered professionals have to guard against being the missionaries of Western psychology. Other parts of the world have their own indigenous psychologies. It behoves us to learn from these, rather than to perpetuate our own ideology. Listening has been a key component in the context of individual therapy. It can be equally therapeutic in the larger cultural context.

APPLICATION OF THE PCA IN A CULTURAL CONTEXT

Several centuries of negation and disrespect by the various colonial powers have taken its toll on the trust of the continent's people in themselves. South Africa serves as a visible reminder of a process which has been ongoing ever since the first Europeans set foot on African soil. In order to actualize the person-centeredness which is indigenous to the continent, ways have to be found to restore Africa's trust in her own values. It is also imperative that it be done in a manner which is congruent with the continent's indigenous ways of life, not only to avoid taking power away, but to enhance the probability of being facilitative.

Black consciousness leaders like Steve Biko endeavored to raise the awareness of the black population, not only of how socio-economic and political factors affected their lives, but also of their own uniqueness, and ultimately of how they can restore pride in themselves. In this, black consciousness is similar to negritude and Africanicity as it developed in West Africa (Reed & Wake, 1979), and conscientization in Brazil (Freire, 1968). Africentricity (Baldwin, 1988) or Afrocentricity (Asante, 1983) is the logical philosophical heir to concepts like negritude, black consciousness, Africanicity and conscientization.

In accepting and enhancing Africa's person-centeredness in ways congruent with the continent's spiritually-ensembled individualism, the formal approach faces its greatest challenge. It is required to put its money where its mouth is and indwell into a totally different reality, not only of persons individually, but of culture as an abstract, collective and living entity. Another major requirement is that Person-Centered professionals manifest the principles of spiritually-ensembled individualism in their everyday behavior and relationships with others.

Mphahlele (1962) criticized ..."the refusal of the white man to be taught anything by the African" (p. 39) and expressed the opinion that "If the white man shuts his eyes to the good that is in my culture, he is the poorer for it and I am one up on him" (p. 66).

By applying the conditions so necessary for change in the therapeutic and concretely human context to the abstractly cultural, and by taking person-centeredness out of the confines of the therapy hour and workshop format, the PCA has the best chance of facilitating the larger social change that is required in a country like South Africa.

In essence, extension of the boundaries of the approach is in keeping with development of the theory during the past five decades. Since the approach has already undergone several name changes, another may be indicated in order to capture the orientation towards the cultural dimension and spiritually ensembled individualism.

Theorizing about application of the PCA in a context which is widely discrepant from that which gave it birth, is one thing. Implementing such theorizing is another. Without going into a detailed analysis of possible Person-Centered applications, several options are open to us. As already indicated, a major responsibility is to raise awareness of the spiritual and psychological dimensions of African culture. Nadine Gordimer, famous South African author, speaks of a "white-consciousness movement" leading towards "a third culture ... What you can do is to work among your own people to change them; because if white people are to survive in the true sense, which doesn't merely mean saving their necks, it means learning to live in a new way, then they must rethink their values" (Boyers, Vlase, Diggory, & Elgrably, 1984, p. 30).

What is true for South African whites, is also true of Person-Centered psychologists. Awareness needs to be raised within our own profession and in our respective countries and the world at large. We need to become aware of the neglected dimensions of cultures other than our own. This can be done in various ways: By writing, lecturing, conducting workshops and conferences and by doing research. In addition, much can be done to promote African art, music, theatre, healing, mythology, education and business ventures, including trade unionism. A good deal of this is already happening in the country, but Person-Centered and other psychologists are noticeably absent in any of these endeavors. Facilitating social services in the community, such as self-help groups, is another way in which Person-Centered psychologists can work towards the larger good of the community. However, the most important challenge facing us in the cross-cultural domain, is to become actively engaged at a person-to-person level with members of communities other than our own. Since we know about the importance of modeling in shaping behavior, psychologists have to lead the way in exhibiting respect for other cultures by indwelling into and incorporating aspects of those cultures into our own behavior and life-style.

The psychological profession, unfortunately is, or has been impotent in defending what is rightfully its sphere of activity against the power of the government. Most likely our lack of influence in the political arena has been because of our continued absence in this area. The time has arrived for the PCA to decide whether it wants to remain merely a reactive discipline, or whether it wants to become a proactive endeavor (Manicas & Secord, 1983).

REFERENCES

Akbar, N. (1984). Africentric social sciences for human liberation. *Journal of Black Studies, 14*, 395-414.

Ardilla, R. (1982). International psychology. *American Psychologist, 37*, 323-329.

Asante, M.K. (1983). The ideological significance of Afrocentricity in intercultural communication. *Journal of Black Studies, 14*, 3-19.

Azuma, H. (1984). Secondary control as a heterogeneous category. *American Psychologist, 39*, 970-971.

Baldwin, J.A. (1986). African (Black) psychology. Issues and synthesis. *Journal of Black Studies, 16*, 235-249.

Bernal, M.E., & Padilla, A.M. (1982). Status of minority curricula and training in clinical psychology. *American Psychologist, 37*, 780-787.

Boyers, R., Vlase, C., Diggory, T., & Elgrably, J. (1984). A conversation with Nadine Gordimer. *Salmangundi*, Winter, 3-31.

Branden, N. (1988). *Honoring the self. The psychology of confidence and respect.* New York: Boston.

Cole, M. (1984). The world beyond our borders. What might our students need to know about it? *American Psychologist, 39*, 998-1005.

Cox, J.L. (Ed.). (1986). *Transcultural psychiatry.* Beckenham, Kent: Croom Helm.

Dawes, A. (1985). Politics and mental health: The position of clinical psychology in South Africa. *South African Journal of Psychology, 15*, 55-61.

Farson, R. (1974). Carl Rogers, quiet revolutionary. *Education, 95*, 197-203.

Freire, P. (1968). *Pedagogy of the oppressed.* New York: The Seabury Press.

Gibbs, J.C. & Schnell, S.V. (1985). Moral development "versus" socialization. *American Psychologist, 40*, 1071-1080.

Hammond, O.W. (1988). Needs assessment and policy development: Native Hawaiians as native Americans. *American Psychologist, 43*, 383-387.

Ho, D.Y.F. (1985). Cultural values and professional issues in clinical psychology. Implications from the Hong Kong experience. *American Psychologist, 40*, 1212-1218.

Holdstock, T.L. (1978). From client-centered therapy to a person-centered approach. *South African Journal of Psychology, 8*, 20-29.

Holdstock, T.L. (1987). *Education for a new nation.* Johannesburg: ATA.

Holdstock, T.L., & Rogers, C.R. (1983). Person-centered theory. In R.J. Corsini

& A.J. Marsella (Eds.), *Personality theories, research & assessment.* Itasca, IL: Peacock.

Kennedy, S., Scheirer, J., & Rogers, A. (1984). The price of success. Our monocultural science. *American Psychologist, 39,* 996-997.

Kojima, H. (1984). A significant stride toward the comparative study of control. *American Psychologist, 39,* 972-973.

LaFromboise, T.D. (1988). American Indian mental health policy. *American Psychologist, 43,* 388-397.

Manicas, P.T., & Secord, P.F. (1983). Implications for psychology of the new philosophy of science. *American Psychologist, 38,* 399-413.

Mphahlele, E. (1962). *The African image.* London: Faber & Faber.

Patterson, C.H. (1986). Culture and psychology in Hong Kong. *American Psychologist, 41,* 926.

Pedersen, P.B., & Inouye, K. (1984). The international/intercultural perspective of the APA. *American Psychologist, 39,* 560-561.

Reed, J., & Wake, C. (Eds.). (1979). *Senghor. Prose and poetry.* London: Heinemann.

Rogers, C.R. (1942). *Counseling and psychotherapy.* Boston: Houghton, Mifflin.

Rogers, C.R. (1979). Groups in two cultures. *Personnel and Guidance Journal, 38,* 11-15.

Rogers, C.R. (1986). The Rust workshop. A personal overview. *Journal of Humanistic Psychology, 25,* 1-16.

Rogler, L.H., Malgady, R.G., Costantino, G., & Blumenthal, R. (1987). What do culturally sensitive mental health services mean? The case of Hispanics. *American Psychologist, 42,* 565-570.

Rosenzweig, M.R. (1984). U.S. psychology and world psychology. *American Psychologist, 39,* 877-884.

Russell, R.W. (1984). Psychology in its world context. *American Psychologist, 39,* 1017-1025.

Sampson, E.E. (1985). The decentralization of identity. Toward a revised concept of personal and social order. *American Psychologist, 40,* 1203-1211.

Sampson, E.E. (1988). The debate on individualism. Indigenous psychologies of the individual and their role in personal and social functioning. *American Psychologist, 43,* 15-22.

Sarason, S.B.. (1981). An asocial psychology and misdirected clinical psychology. *American Psychologist, 36,* 827-836.

Setiloane, G.M. (1986). *African theology. An introduction.* Johannesburg: Skotaville.

Sexton, V.S., & Misiak, H. (1984). American psychologists and psychology abroad. *American Psychologist, 39,* 1026-1031.

Sue, S. (1983). Ethnic minority issues in psychology. A reexamination. *American Psychologist, 38,* 583-592.

Sue, S. (1988). Psychotherapeutic services for ethnic minorities: Two decades of research findings. *American Psychologist, 43,* 301-308.

Sue, S., & Zane, N. (1987). The role of culture and cultural techniques in psychotherapy. A critique and reformulation. *American Psychologist, 42,* 37-45.

Swartz, L. (1986). Carl Rogers in South Africa: The issue of silence. *Psychology in Society, 5,* 139-143.

Torney-Purta, J. (1984). Annotated bibliography of materials for adding an international dimension to undergraduate courses in developmental and social psychology. *American Psychologist, 39,* 1032-1042.

Triandis, H.C., & Brislin, R.W. (1984) Cross-cultural psychology. *American Psychologist, 39,* 1006-1016.

Turton, R.W. (1986). Bourgeois counseling and working-class clients: Some problems and political implications. *Psychology in Society,* 95-100.

Tutu, D. (1981). My view. *The Star,* August 13, 22.

Weisz, J.R., Rothbaum, F.M., & Blackburn, T.C. (1984a). Swapping recipes for control. *American Psychologist, 39,* 974-975.

Weisz, J.R., Rothbaum, F.M., & Blackburn, T.C. (1984b). Standing out and studying in the psychology of control in America and Japan. *American Psychologist, 39,* 955-969.

THE THERAPY PATHWAY REFORMULATED

Godfrey T. BARRETT-LENNARD
The Centre for Studies in Human Relations
Perth, Australia

The therapeutic conditions model, influential now for 30 years (Rogers, 1957), is concerned with the agency of change, not with its course. While potent in helping to advance knowledge in its own sphere, this model's elegant economy and focus on factors seen as important at any time and throughout a helping engagement, has acted to divert attention from studying the journey or course of therapy where the feature of interest is the change and progression in process from start to conclusion.

No barrier to the last-mentioned focus existed during the emergence of non-directive client-centered therapy. In his founding book, Rogers (1942) suggested that the approach involved a sequence of 12 typical steps. He took care to acknowledge that these steps are not all discrete events, that they shade into each other, and that their stated order is an approximation. After outlining the sequence, Rogers cited an early study not actually flowing from this delineation but supportively consistent with it. Certainly, he concluded, there is foundation for "the hypothesis that skillfully conducted treatment interviews are not a hodge-podge of discrete elements, but that taken as a whole they represent a complete chain in which one element tends to follow another" (Rogers, 1942, p. 47). This chain, and the research which followed, is interesting and instructive still and a useful take-off point for the new perspective which is the centrepiece of this paper.

ROGERS' STEPS OF THERAPY (1942) AND RELATED PROCESS STUDIES

In their main substance, Rogers' array of steps is reduced here to five broader stages, which are easier to grasp in their totality and more readily related to the fresh perspective advanced in this paper. The regrouped stages are based closely on the original author's account in 1942 (pp. 30-45).

Stage 1 is the entry phase (my language), combining steps 1 to 3 of Rogers. It pivots on the client's experience of responsibility and beginning expression of feelings in therapy, both of these specifically assisted and encouraged by the therapist. The client has taken the step of ·coming for help: the counsellor acknowledges this and takes other early opportunity to define or clarify the helping situation. Assisted expression of the client's own feelings begins to gather momentum. In new words, which cannot be far from Rogers' meaning in 1942, there is dawning awareness by the client that "What I feel - what *I* feel and mean - matters here", and is the essential agenda of therapy.

In *Stage 2,* the centrality of feeling-expression is sustained and some movement in the client's feelings - which the therapist has been consistently reflecting and clarifying - becomes visible. This phase spans Rogers' Step 4, where the emphasis typically is on negative feelings, as of anger, despair, fear, pain and hurt, confusion and loneliness, to Step 6, where the balance is depicted as shifting toward positive feelings such as appreciating, liking or loving, feeling self-respect or interest in other people, or having more energy or a sense of growing maturity.

Such movement leads and shades into *Stage 3.* Typically, "insight and self-understanding come bubbling through spontaneously", and there is resulting or interweaving "clarification of possible decisions, possible courses of action" (see Rogers, 1942, steps 6 to 8, pp. 40-41). In a word, this stage involves visibly new self-understanding and insight, and associated exploration of choices.

Stage 4 focally involves new positive (constructive) actions/behaviors in the client's life. These may begin as whispers of things to come; minute, toe-dipping but intentional steps. Gradually, or quite swiftly, firmer choices appear, are expressed concretely or tried out for size, and lead to deeper insights or extended awareness of the bases of life choice and action.

Finally, *Stage 5* - as I cluster the steps - is the termination of therapy, involving and flowing from decreasing felt need for help, acknowledgement that the therapy relationship must end, and a readiness by the client "to go it on his/her own." Desirably, the termination date is set a little ahead of the actual ending and, in any case, positive feelings between client and therapist are seen as a likely and natural feature of the parting phase. There is more reciprocity, between two persons who are now moving beyond their original and distinct purposes in being together, as therapy closes.

Rogers' observations on the course of therapy were soon augmented by now-classical process research. This work literally centred on tracing the patterning of therapy events over time and it forms the richest source of evidence bearing on this early view of the therapy progression. Frequency analyses of particular classes of client or therapist statements occurring in equal intervals of the total interview time were the foundation of most studies.

The pertinent research appearing in the wake of Rogers' book began with William Snyder's ambitious doctoral dissertation. As published two years later (Snyder, 1945), this was forthrightly titled *An investigation of the nature of non-directive psychotherapy*. Snyder's work was based on detailed analysis of 48 interviews drawn from six recorded cases. Direct structuring or therapy-defining responses by T, while never very frequent, were most prominent during the first decile of the interview sequence. This result is thus broadly in accord with Rogers' description (see Stage 1, above). Also most frequent at the start, in Snyder's sample, were clarification of feeling responses. After modest decline, these were still the most prominent category (at about 35% of all therapist responses). A further decline in the last two deciles plausibly reflected distinctive effects of the ending phase.

"Statement of problem" expressions by clients in this study were, as expected, most frequent at the beginning, then settled at a fairly constant level and fell off sharply at the end. Client statements in the "understanding and insight" category rose from a low beginning to a high point of 30% of all client responses at the fourth decile, plausibly approximating stage 3 as distinguished here; then tapering off somewhat, probably as client exploration shifted qualitatively; and finally rising to 30% again in the tenth decile and termination phase, with its component of summing-up (Snyder, 1945, p. 209). Also in keeping with Rogers' perspective, Snyder points out that his data "indicates a marked predominance of negative attitudes in the first interviews with a significant shift toward positive attitudes as treatment proceeds." However, in refinement of this view, "sometimes there is a noticeable relapse after the first insight seems to have been reached and attitudes [may] become negative again when the client is making his choice about the 'way of life' he wants to accept." In what amounts to the termination stage, "there is [as well] often a very noticeable upsurge of positive attitudes toward the counselor" (Snyder, 1945, p. 213).

Within the important "Parallel Studies Project" which followed, Seeman's study (1949) marked a replication and further refinement of Snyder's research, based on a largely post-war (as against a largely pre-war) sample of clients, living in a big city (not a university town) environment. Seeman used the same or equivalent primary categories to those of Snyder, grouping them somewhat differently. Clarification of feeling responses doubled in proportion, from one study to the next, and "restatement of content" replaced simple acceptance as the next most frequent class of response (Seeman, 1949, Table 4). Overall, 85% of therapist responses now fell in the "non-directive" group, as against about 62% in Snyder's study. It seems clear that therapists were now more systematically and consistently reflective than had been true in the very early forties.

Statement of problem responses by clients showed a sequential pattern similar to that previously obtained: Highest in ratio at the start, falling off more evenly than before, and lowest at the end. Understanding-insight and other statements suggestive of positive gain in therapy were of lowest frequency in the first fifth (or, quintile) of the series, rose only slowly until after half-way through the interviews, and were markedly higher in the last two quintiles - broadly in keeping with Rogers' view. Discussion and planning statements, while much lower in percentage terms, followed a similar pattern. In all, the results suggest large areas of overlap and fluidity between the third and fourth stages, as previously outlined, although it would be consistent with the total picture to infer that Stage 3 developments tend to come into view first (Seeman, 1949, Table 6).

Client attitudes classed as negative dominated those viewed as positive, in the first quintile of therapy, the two classes converging to virtually equal frequency by the final fifth of the series. The pattern overall is strongly in keeping with that reported by Snyder, and broadly concordant with the stage schema, except that the latter seems to make insufficient allowance for a spiral-like return to similar issues or emphases arising in a modified context. This sort of complexity is suggested, for example, by Seeman's finding that the proportion of positive attitudes among those expressed in the present tense ("now statements") more than doubled over the course of therapy, while present tense negative feeling-expressions shrank by almost half. In a still more fine-grained result, the frequency of *self-related* positive "now" feelings increased fourfold from the first to final quintile, while negative *self-referent* expressions in the present tense halved (see Seeman, 1949, Tables 9 and 10). Such findings could have led to an explicit refinement of Rogers' schema.

Vargas' study (1954) of "changes in self-awareness in client-centered therapy" also employed ten therapy cases, conducted mainly in the early 1950s and running to a mean of 19 interviews. His process analysis included counting all instances of self description and the incidence of two main classes of "original" self-descriptions. The first kind consisted of self-percepts coming up for the first time in therapy but familiar to the client, and the second "of self-percepts emerging during counseling, or since counseling began, called *emergent original self-descriptions*" (or EOS's) (Vargas, 1954, p. 150). The proportion of EOS's among all self-percepts (S's) was graphed for each fifth of therapy, client-by-client. The results are very interesting:

Ignoring one case whose success rating was at the bottom of the scale, the predominant trend was for very marked increase in the EOS/S ratio, from the first quintile to the third or fourth, followed by a modest decline (in most cases) in the late stages of therapy. This is the only client-centered study I know where expressions of emergent new self-awareness have been identified and charted in their occurrence over the course of therapy. In hindsight, it is in keeping with general expectation, and the stages earlier portrayed, that fresh insights and self-concept shifts *tend* to increase quite strongly until self-exploration in therapy begins to taper off in conjunction with an increased focus on planning and the taking of "new steps in the client's life." Finally, review of therapy gains and consideration of separation/relationship issues mark the ending phase.

There appears to be little subsequent research literature that attempts to track the overall course of individual client-centered therapy or relate process levels to careful generalizations about this total course. More recent descriptions of the therapy life-cycle also are meagre. Some distinct modifications of client-centered therapy, such as that reported by Noel and De Chenne (1974), have introduced certain built-in sequential features. However, steering and management of therapy through a pre-structured sequence of stages runs counter to traditional client-centered philosophy, and seems at odds with the prizing of people in their individuality and uniqueness, and would be unlikely to fit the enabling styles of therapists identified strongly with this approach. Stated otherwise, client-centered therapy is not seen (at least from within) as an orchestrated process, notwithstanding the clear regularities implied in theory and evident from research. A fresh focus on the unfolding progression of events in therapy, which discriminates an inherent order, need not suggest a lock-step approach. It is simply another way in which we can be inquiring, open-eyed and active in our work. I for one want to extend my ability to sense or discern how the therapy enterprise is progressing in a given instance and how it may further unfold. A careful explorer's map of the general route carries this potential.

We commonly regard the therapy enterprise as a means to the end of healing and growthful change, each step building on and reflecting gains already made. Thus, the path or course of events is the enterprise, in basic part. To map this path is to throw further light on the phenomenon and nature of therapy.

THE COURSE OF INDIVIDUAL THERAPY: A PHASIC PROGRESSION

In seeking seriously to characterize the course of client-centered therapy, issues at once spring to view regarding its fundamental nature. Is it, effectively, reeducation? Is it psychic repair and rehabilitation? Is it a matter of discovery and development of undeveloped potentials? Does it centre on emotional growth and interpersonal learning? Is it to transform us from reactive recipients of influence to active agents in our worlds? Is the therapy an approach to redress for the alienating effects of much of contemporary life? With individually varying emphasis, it surely is all of these, and more. Can such a spectrum of purpose in its manifold expressions be pursued through the "same" overall process, or reach fruition through the same kind of journey? This at first sight seems improbable. Yet it is the *process* that largely defines client-centered therapy, and perhaps therapy of any distinctive orientation. And consistency of process, or means, implies a coherence of ends or outcome - a complex singularity to the nature of help in a given approach. Client-centered therapy is a many-sided living whole in which perceived diversity can arise from the distinctive interest of observers, from mixing process or effects that actually represent different stages in the journey, and from the natural variation in relationships between unique pairs of individuals.

It follows that the 'process' of therapy has more than one main dimensional face, as well as many features within each one. A now very familiar face, of course, is the quality of the therapist-client relationship, especially as seen through the lens of the therapy conditions view. For Gendlin and others (Gendlin, 1978) focusing is discerned as also a mainspring of therapy and effectively another primary axis or face of the process. We consider tendencies toward integration, psychic repair, growthful learning and development, higher levels of experiencing and the like (expressions of an actualizing tendency), to be inbuilt and released through the therapeutic relationship. However, although distress may ease quickly, pattern change takes time and determined work. A healing and growthful engagement, unique in kind to the client, does not spring fullblown into being. Working steps in therapy occur within this evolving relationship and contribute to it. Client issues change as progress is made, and these and other features combine to trace a pathway which constitutes the journey or course of therapy and is thus another major face of its process.

Following (finally) is my working view of the pathway of client-centered therapy, drawn and distilled from all of the foregoing, from my own experience as therapist and client, and from reflection and refinement over the time of its incubation. I have again arrived at five main, qualitative phases, each distinct in principle but shading into the next in practice. As described, each phase is like a crest or hilltop from which the view is clearer and the location more discernible than on the slopes and in the valleys between. The phases, together, span the whole therapy route I see, although in practice this may be cut short and end almost anywhere along the way, as further discussed.

A. Beginning: The entry phase

This description assumes that the client is present of his or her own accord, having decided to enter therapy or to try it; and that client and therapist are meeting together in these capacities for the first time. Assuming they are not already in a close personal relationship, whether they are significantly acquainted from other contexts, or meeting as strangers, has no consistent significance[1]. Of greater moment is whether the client has effectively made an informed choice of therapist or has come with little or no knowledge of the particular therapist (T) or of the process and philosophy of helping with which T is identified. In the informed-choice case the Entry Phase generally includes the period from the client's (C's) first approach to the therapist (or contact with T's office, etc.) through whatever preliminaries are involved before the first therapy meeting, to the end of that meeting. What happens, among other effects, would tend to confirm C's choice and add much more specific experiential meaning to it. Where an informed choice was not made, the preliminaries to the first therapy contact may involve greater information exchange than in the first-mentioned case, and the first meetings tend to have a more visibly exploratory character with regard to the therapy medium and enterprise. The Entry Phase, in this case, may well require more than one therapy interview session, and it might not come to fruition at all.

Several elements help to signify and mark that the beginning phase in fact is accomplished, but without implying that therapy need continue through its whole potential course, or that a highly productive course is certain. The proposed signs of advancement through this starting phase are as follows: 1. C in some way shows that he/she feels or distinctly shares responsibility for being there, in the therapy-counseling situation, with T. This may only become quite clear when arrangements are being made for a further interview. 2. C takes some initiatives in accounting for his or her presence, including indication of difficulty, dissatisfaction or distress, either with self, with relationships, and/or with the personal impact of particular life events or crises. There is a message in some form that "I am in trouble, and that's why I'm here", even if largely as victim and little as agent. 3. C has expressed feeling or in some way acknowledged that feelings exist and need be reckoned with, for example, by facing or clarifying them, gaining release from them, developing or transforming them. 4. C has departed as it were, at least part of the time, from a prepared text. Communication is not confined to, or no longer has, a quality of reporting or reciting rehearsed content; and there are episodes in which C is speaking from what is coming now in his/her feelings or thoughts. 5. There is a perceptible (unforced) shift in C's awareness of T, noticed or felt by T. It is a qualitative shift from thinking/feeling aloud to speaking to someone, typically, *from addressing* an invented person, made up from variously based expectations, *to* speaking to or with a person who is coming into view or suddenly *present* in one's first-hand experience of them. 6. There are indications that the client has begun to feel heard by the therapist and to anticipate further personal understanding. 7. What is happening in *this* forming relationship has begun to matter to both participants. The degree and way in which it matters naturally differs widely among clients and varies between therapists. But when this condition applies, neither C nor T could walk away from their association without significant after-thought and/or feeling; and in balance both wish to go on, or to go further[2].

A great deal *can* happen in the first interview in (client-centered) therapy. Usually, it seems, few sessions are as critical, although later on eventfulness may be differently experienced and measured. The following excerpts from the first interview with a woman client in her early or mid-thirties (and whose choice was relatively informed) are thought to illustrate most of the elements and features so far mentioned. The excerpts begin with the first client statement, following an invitation by the therapist to say what brought her into therapy or to share her present feelings; in effect, to begin wherever she chose. She knew that the session was being observed and recorded.

> C 1: "I've been thinking about where to start. There's no really logical place. I guess I'll go from the general to the specific. I've been in therapy a few times and I find each time it helps me but as soon as anything out of the ordinary happens I go back to Stage 1 - so that I find that even though I've gotten some partial help to cope with a specific situation that there hasn't been any - enough change, I find, in my vision or whatever, that makes me feel safe enough for the future, I guess. I always -
>
> T 2: (Interrupting) But you came into this situation, *this* therapy - this prospective therapy experience - with a background of having been in therapy before...
>
> C 2: (Quickly breaking in) Does that invalidate it in any way?
>
> T 3: No, I'm just responding to - making sure I'm catching your meaning - and what I'm hearing is that you have tried therapy; you haven't given up on it or you wouldn't be here, *but it hasn't been of any long range help so far.*
>
> T 3: Right! (Pauses, thinking). Specifically what happened this summer, or last year, when things started to get uncomfortable, was that I was in a dancing class and I suffered some damage to my knees ...[details omitted] One of the doctors seems to think there may be some permanent damage and that my life might possibly be narrowed down, that my activities might be narrowed down, for keeps. That threw me into a pretty severe depression which brought on a lot of

other things kind of tied to it. [T begins to respond, C interrupts and, after a few short exchanges, they return to the same theme.]

C 7: And I guess I was just a little bit weakened to handle them, I was... wasn't ... I was.

T 8: Demoralized?

C 8: Right! I was pretty demoralized. And all of a sudden it just flashed on me how - I think even though this time I'm by now maybe feeling that I could control them again and just push them into a closet, I never know when they'll come out again (T: Yes) under different circumstances. I just don't feel safe any more, I just feel very - er - that I'm just not really handling them (C agitated, moist-eyed, continues speaking) that I'm just repressing them which doesn't help so far (C's voice breaks a little) because they are still very active. And I'm conscious - all of a sudden I've started seeing patterns that I haven't seen before. I always saw every situation apart, and I was sort of wondering how much I did to get myself into these things, how much of it was (pause) was perhaps self-destructive (C pauses, her eyes moist).

T 9: Hmm. Sounds, as I'm hearing what you are saying, it's... you are feeling rather upset as you try and express how it is for you, now, and how it has been recently. And especially this aspect of feeling that you begin to see a pattern where you may have been somehow or another - I'm not quite sure what you mean by self-destructive - but somehow *bringing injury on yourself* (said both with emphasis and a question mark).

[After brief further discussion/clarification of the client's meaning she turns to another side of the same issue]

C12: (More firmly) When I get to the point that I'm functioning well I *add* things. I add too much, and hmm... until everything just topples from the load of it.

T13: Until you just can't cope with it all.

C13: Right, and I find I've been doing this a lot. After my daughter was born, I was just barely coping with having her and studying, and as soon I was just barely able to fit her and my husband and my studies together I started dancing again, and that really got me very rushed, got my husband very rushed because he had to give me rides back and forth, gave me much less time with my daughter. It was like I just... I insisted on it very much, and even after I hurt my leg I went on back dancing two or three times. So, you know, with hindsight, I'm wondering if - (pauses)

T14: If part of your way of being is to push yourself all the time beyond your own limits, somehow?

C14: So then I have a good excuse to fail. I don't know; this is just seeing with hindsight...

[Client adds a bit more context and history, and then returns to the theme of her efforts to understand and explain.]

C17: ... I guess I'd always been *trying* to explain why I got myself in hot water before. And every time I had a different explanation. And I was wondering if I couldn't find one that would fit everything; if it seems to be a habitual pattern ... I was (C clearing her nose) wondering if it had anything to do with, with that particular (C stops).

T18: By the way I'm - .. Oh, there is some Kleenex (pushes it over to client). It sounds as though you - ehr (sighs), you know, you *really* wish you could understand - that you were on top of whatever the hell it is that's going on underneath in you, somehow, that's behind the things, that's driving you or propelling you in the ways that you go.

[Passage omitted until T introduces a question inviting C to focus on the change she is seeking.]

T24: I guess I find myself - er - sort of wondering, wanting to get more of a feeling for *how* you would like to change or what you would like to change, what ways you would like to be different than you are?

C24: (Pause) I suppose self-assurance springs to mind, but that can mean anything. (Slight pause) Yes, I suppose that would cover it (pause, T moves to speak). Do you mind if I put my leg up (slides spare chair a little and rests her leg horizontally).

T25: Having a much more... (aside) is that all right? By self confidence, or self-assurance, I guess you mean a much more positive feeling somehow about being on top of you life, of being able to cope and manage. A sort of expectation that you will - instead of a fear (C: Right) perhaps that you won't.

C25: It's a little bit wider than that though. You used the word 'to be on top of things.' And I would like to feel that I don't *have* to be on top of things - that I can just be, you know, kind of equal to them. (C's voice breaks again, and tears begin to come) Right now I feel I have to be on top of them which I don't think is exactly the way everybody, you know, that it's a realistic expectation.

T26: Somehow that touches a feeling that's close to home for you.

C26: Yes, right (blows nose; pauses)

T27: "On top" is *not* the right word - ehr - you, that suggests pushing yourself and having to be better, maybe other things, I'm not sure. (Gently) I guess I don't want to push you with a question. It's your immediate feeling that I'm -

C27: Well, you did hit home there, but I don't know exactly how - how that works (pause). I mean I would like to feel I don't have to be in control of things in order to survive. It's what I mean about: You can't expect always to be on top of things, and I don't think that one should need that feeling of being on top of things in order to survive. Some people manage quite well without having to feel in complete control, all the time, of what's happening. So, is that realistic or? (T: [softly] I don't know) Do most people feel they have to be on top? I don't know... whether you know either.

T28: I don't really know. But, I'm trying to sense your feeling. I'm not sure how close I am, but it's - and I would like you to correct me - but it's, but you would like to be able to take things more as they come, somehow. Does the expression "rolling with the punches", are you familiar with that?

C28: Yes - Yes, I would like to have that capacity. (T: Yes.)

T29: I guess my sense is that something kind of hurts you about the way - some way - that you push yourself or feel that you have to try to be.

C29: Right. I always feel like - ahm - like if I just (voice quivers and breaks) just forget to try, everything would sort of collapse, and I'm just tired of always trying (takes another cigarette, lights it with the previous one). I ran out of matches.

T30: That if you let go for a minute, that you might lose your grip ... [further mention of matches and client's smoking].

C30: ... Yes I am afraid of losing self-control - but I'm also afraid of circumstances changing and going in a way that I can't handle in some instances. (T: Hmm, Hmm). So it isn't just me, but things outside also. When I'm in a plane I'm convinced when we finally land that it was just me holding it up there. Not really, but emotionally when I'm up there if I'm not just thinking about it staying all the time (voice breaks again), I'm convinced we're going to crash. I am just bringing that up symbolically; I think that holds for just about everything.

T31: That.., I don't know, I just have the image that it must be so *exhausting* for you to carry that load, to carry that weight! (T leans back, involuntarily miming the strained holding or pressing up of a heavy weight)."

The reader may have noted that at C 29 the client - who had been lighting one cigarette with another - mentioned that she had run out of matches. This problem, which T could not help with directly, created opportunity for an episode which undoubtedly brought the client and therapist more distinctly into view to each other, and also provided the lightest moments in the interview.

The episode began with T returning to the client's predicament and mentioning that if they looked outside the door of the interview room shortly, he believed there would be a box of matches there. Only momentarily puzzled, C tuned to the tacit message to the unseen observers. Sure enough the matches were there! T was glad C knew how they had appeared, saying that he did not want her to think he was any kind of magician, either in reference to the matches or to therapy. The 'lesson' was fun; C was alive in her awareness and evident feeling of contact with T. There was increase in her confidence and spontaneity in the therapy situation, linked to a rise in the immediacy of her communication. At the end of the session she planned a series of appointments with T, envisaged as continuing for a number of months (about seven months, in the event). It will be evident, or plausible at least, to the careful reader that each of the suggested criteria for the Entry Phase was met in the course of this interview. The sessions that immediately followed were broadly consistent with the next phase to be described.

B. Forging a personal-working alliance; and the passage from woundedness to hope

Two main streams flowing through the course of therapy can be distinguished. Each feeds and furthers the other, but is distinct. *One stream* is the development of the client-therapist relationship, encompassing each one's evolving perception of the other and the view each has of the kind and quality of their partnership in the enterprise they are engaged in. Since the client is experiencing difficult and troubling adversity, and is struggling or seeking to move beyond present personal boundaries, the client-centered helping association is a form of alliance. And as the relationship between C and T is employed as a means, and the enterprise is both person-focused and demanding, the term "personal-working alliance" is thought usefully appropriate.

In this phase the helping relationship comes strongly into being, although not yet to optimal fruition. As this is happening, the therapist comes to be *experienced* as a resourceful ally in a rather unique sense. (If this does not occur, therapy is likely to be aborted.) In client-centered therapy the client leads the alliance in terms of content issues, and tends to be the junior partner in determining process. C may wish that T would 'take over' more, but this wish recedes as the alliance grows stronger. Such taking-over, in the sense of expanded initiatives on T's part, may on the other hand naturally occur; for example, if C truly seems lost, frozen, stuck, terrified, in an abyss of confusion or despair, or in the grip of extreme anxiety or other emotion seeming to have a life of its own. Gendlin and other exponents of focusing may become active during this phase in working to directly help clients engage and dialogue with their own inner felt sense (Gendlin, 1978).

In effect, this is the make-or-break phase of therapy from the standpoint of therapists. The therapist ally needs to come into view for the client in his/her own likeness as helper-person; and the client likewise becomes not just a string of feelings but an increasingly known whole person to the therapist. The alliance evolves unevenly but overall toward deeper engagement, increasing eventfulness and greater commitment to a (now) sharply real and consequential enterprise. Alternatively, such development never really takes off, or it begins to and then falters and ceases, or is aborted by circumstances. C may never move into a fullfledged therapeutic mode of self-inquiry and discourse with T, perhaps resting instead with modest gain in terms of the immediate crisis or situation that prompted entry to therapy. In the latter case, therapy would stop without the alliance aspect or stream having come to fruition. One might refer to this as a phase B termination.

A related issue to touch on concerns use of the term "forging." To speak of forging the working-personal alliance could evoke imagery of hammering something into shape softened by heat, which is scarcely in keeping with the client-centered approach! However, if quite figurative usage is granted, and given that people can be drawn from within to do strenuous and difficult things, among which therapy surely is a plausible example, the term begins to seem more fitting. Part of the unusual demand of therapy is that clients cannot for long coast through a well-practised repertoire, without the process grinding to a halt or becoming visibly pointless. Add further the feature of a therapist-partner who usually is a stranger and whose way of responding is unfamiliar in its total pattern[3]. Then, it is indeed the case that the alliance is not simply present or given but something produced through strenuous application in a mode of searching dialogue; at once with self and other. However, in a fruitful alliance so forged, the engagement becomes self-propelling, for both partners. As "person-centered" implies, the therapist as person is present too, in such a way that experience or expertise do not diminish the challenge or lessen the personal rewards for the *helper* of a founded personal helping alliance.

The *second stream* in phase B reflects the view that nearly all of us are wounded at times, in a psycho-social sense, and that we carry old wounds that may, under relevant conditions of stress, flare up again. Clients at the beginning of personal therapy may in general be said to be wounded, their varied wounds usually having in common painfully diminished self-esteem or sense of worth, feelings of apprehension or anxiety, a degree of depression or a more existential kind of despair and loss of meaning, and some fresh hurt or disturbing life difficulty in which anger and pain are often fused. Such woundedness from long-term and immediate causes, leaves the person without confidence that "good" can come of his or her efforts, leading to a view of things as through a darkened and narrowing lens - in short, a loss of hope. Persons choosing to enter therapy have not totally lost hope, and the fact of taking this plunge itself typically brings increment.

The client's woundedness may be said to arise from some form of psychic or psycho-social assault. Experientially, it is something which happens to the individual, even if later seen to have been brought on or played into by self. Hope on the other hand arises within the person and is energizing and activating. In a wounded state the individual naturally retreats, or hits out reactively. The hopeful person reaches from within, initiates, takes action. In passing from woundedness to hope the person typically shifts from suffering passivity or reactiveness to a wide-awake, more purposeful and active mode. Such movement may not be large in Phase B but the direction is discernible.

In navigating the passage through Phase B, the client expresses and begins to search into and loosen some of his or her hurt, anger, sorrow or other woundedness, and the helping partnership that meets this test significantly evolves in the process. One outcome is that C ventures, dares now, to actually believe and *feel* that there is a way ahead that is better than the path or track behind. Therapy has begun to ease the burden C has been carrying, it is giving safety to communication and search from the heart and the edge of awareness, and there is promise of further respite, discovery, even new vision. There is, it seems, a route to change in a journey that has actually started. Hope has reawakened. Of course, this transition does not occur for every client, and its completion is a matter of impression and judgement, not of literal and marked discontinuity in the therapy process. Its duration may have been only two or three eventfull meetings, or a three-months saga of hard working therapy sessions. With very deeply disturbed clients, it may take longer still but happen nonetheless, as implied for example in the case of "The silent young man" in the Wisconsin psychotherapy research project (Rogers, 1967, pp. 401-416). Moving to phase C is like rounding a wide, rising curve, distinct at the end (to the alerted driver) both in rearview and in terms of the new vista and detectably changing landscape ahead. It is as though the travellers feel, if they pause to think of it, "Now we are *really* on the way, we have got into our stride and can count on each other. Change *is* possible, but much of the difficult-rewarding journey must still be to come; so let's get on!" Getting on is not either a matter of changing gear or of going on just as before, but of both finding and creating the way through newly central issues in the alliance and in the client's quest.

C. Trust development, and the quest for self: "Who am I?"; "How do I want to be?"

The two streams distinguished earlier continue in modified terrain and flow through Phase C. The recovery or awakening of hope in the client, including many feelings sensed, partly discerned but not yet sharply differentiated, is as individual in specific quality and substance as the client is distinct as a person from others. However, in one form or another, this awakening leads into a new intensity or scope of self-exploration, a more literal questing search for the heart of the individual's identity or for a reconciliation of elements in conflict within the self. By "self" I do not mean to refer solely to the intra-psychic being but also to the self as manifest and related in the world, especially the world of other persons. It is this world which helped to fashion such aspects as the recognized "accepted me", the me I fear, the wanted me and the "not me", and in relation to which change has its primary eventual meaning.

In order for C to deeply open the self to view and review, especially in its normally hidden and most problematic aspects, therapy must be a safe haven and unusual in the authenticity and measure of therapist empathy and other crucial relationship qualities. Put in other terms, in order for C to searchingly disclose unshared thoughts, feelings and actions of the self *and* to work openly at inner dialogue with very indistinct but pressing elements of his or her being (the 'felt sense' in Gendlin's terms), in effect, to search, feel and inquire into the very soul of self, a rare quality of experienced safety and positive trust of T is necessary. This trust, implicitly building in Phase B, is, in its fuller development and significance, advanced as the central feature of the therapeutic relationship and alliance in Phase C.

In his writing on the process conception and scale, Rogers summed up the therapy conditions which need to be met in order for the process scale measures to be valid and comparable by referring to the client as "psychologically received" (Rogers, 1961b, pp. 130-131). Trust in the therapeutic context and sense used here has related, even stronger meaning. Requisite conditions for strong trust include the client having repeatedly experienced being deeply heard, having literally felt T resonating and almost knowing at critical moments "what it is like to *be me.*" It is not necessary that C experiences this quality of empathy continuously, or during every pregnancy and birthing of new awareness. The important element is a founded lack of doubt on C's part that genuine or lived resonation has happened and a confidence that it will recur, especially when C's feelings run very deep and could involve venturing into previously unexplored territory.

Such trust also depends on C having experienced T's caring interest coupled with absence of personal evaluative judgment, especially in contexts where C censures him or herself; and that this experience has happened not just once but over a variety of sensitively difficult areas of self-experience where C or others in C's life have been chronically evaluative. Usually crucial to the quality of trust is C's experience of T as open and revealing of his or her own personhood, not necessarily via informational communication (although at times including this where such sharing occurs spontaneously, or in straightforward response to C's actual interest) but at least through a way of responding that expresses what is immediately present in T's experiencing, with transparent ownership of this experience. Clients themselves may stress the importance of this openness or transparency most convincingly near the close of therapy.

For the therapist to share, even with simple and straightforward brevity, from his or her own life involves an element of risk-taking. At minimum there is likely to be some felt risk of distracting the client or of seeming to invite a shift in content focus from C to T, or (especially during earlier stages of becoming as a therapist) of being "unprofessional", or of behaving in a fashion out-of-keeping with providing a specialized therapeutic service to the client. The positive thesis here is that personal realness and transparency works to *dis*-arm and evoke trust in the other - legitimately, since it cannot of its nature actually be put on (and its mimicry is especially difficult and likely to be seen through). This trust in turn melts away motivation in C to keep up his or her accustomed guard.

In effect, a high level of trust draws to open view self-known secrets which burden the client and much reduces known "musts" and "have-tos" so far as self-presentation in therapy is concerned. Further, such trust founded as described, helps inner walls to become permeable or gradually transparent enough for C to see through. Not only is there safety in this process, in relation to T, but additional confirmation that T is right there, unafraid and unjudging beside C, sharing in awareness of that which is gradually emerging or suddenly erupting into C's felt view. In alternate metaphor, C's trust of T permits them to approach and hear together the first whispers and growing voice of newly released inner dialogue and communication, amplified in volume, clarity and movement by the act of sharing.

Clients very often are struggling with severe and deeply stressful crises in their lives, have not necessarily played a foremost part in precipitating their crises, and *may* be average or above the norm in respect to basic personality integration, or to level of functioning on the process continuum or Gendlin's experiencing scale. However, those who elect or choose to continue in client-centered therapy, in effect hold themselves responsible in significant degree for the pain and needs that bring them to therapy, and have implicitly opted for *self*-change, within the broad meaning of "self" earlier discussed. It would follow that they tend to hold "internal locus of control" attitudes, implying assumed agency in their lives, or at least in the quality of their own experiencing. In practise, it may seem to them that their self influence is at present blocked or impaired, and that a broad purpose of therapy is to restore and develop effective self-propulsion. Effectively, they seek to attain a self or "me" at one with itself, which reaches out capably, vigorously, without fear of wrathful censure from another self within the self, that senses where it is going and knows how to proceed with the journey, and which feels alive and part of lives beyond itself. Persons on the other hand whose orientation is strongly external, whose pervasive feeling and view is that the causes of both trials and joys lie outside *themselves,* would be unlikely to seek client-centered therapy, or at any rate to follow-through in the course outlined here[4].

A major sub-issue or theme in Phase C is likely to be "How do I help to make things go wrong?" or, in more immediately present form "How *am* I helping to make things go wrong?" A more positive counterpart likely also to come up is "I'm better [or stronger, more resourceful, more 'with it'] than I thought. Sometimes I disappoint myself, but overall I'm doing alright in this area of my life"; or "I don't *want* to play that kind of game [or to go on with that activity, struggle, battle, etc.] It's not really me." There is increasing ownership of the self or "I" as the agent of experience as well as where it is happening, and more sense of the ability to make active choices and to discover, learn and change.

The latter can lead readily to the theme: "What do I really *want* to change about myself in ways that I feel or react to situations, to other people, or to a past I carry around all the time?" or, "What are my goals for myself, for the way I want to be, in feeling and action?" Partly because it follows convergently from many elements defining the nature of client-centered therapy, the last questions are almost certain to become prominent in some form, and especially so when the client is working directly and intensively at sorting out and (re)establishing his or her own essential identity[5].

Some of the strands of Rogers' process conception are likely to be directly in focus, in Phase C and are often implied in the client's exploration, new discriminations and altered modes of self-expression. Resulting shifts in the client's process level in the environment of therapy occur, although not in steady progression or over such a wide span as initially implied (Rogers, 1959, 1961a, 1961b and 1967). Rogers originally suggested that "many people who seek psychological help are at approximately the point of stage three", on the 7-stage continuum distinguished. He continued: "They may stay at roughly this point, for a considerable time, describing non-present feelings and exploring the self as an object, before being ready to move on to the next stage" (Rogers, 1961b, pp. 136-137)[6]. When such movement does occur and in terms of stages 4 and 5 of Rogers' portrayal, feelings tend at first to be reported in an objectified way from the past ("It felt"), in the client's life in general ("My feeling has always been ..."), as desirable possibilities ("It would mean a lot to me if ..."), and in other "pointing to" or "arm's length" ways. Then in stage five, "we find many feelings expressed in the moment of their occurrence, ("I'm feeling so nervous and - frightened ..."; "It's so clear - I can *see* ..."), and previously denied feelings really begin to "bubble through" into awareness (Rogers, 1959, p. 99). Hesitantly at first, but increasingly - through process stages 4 and 5 - clients *ascribe meaning* to and from their experience, and reflect awareness that the constructs they use, especially in discriminations regarding the self and others, are not absolute givens but invented lenses that can be modified, replaced, experimented with. Inner discrepancies and incongruence, and sometimes a recognition of self as a complex plurality or system rather than an indivisible monad, are significantly and increasingly in view in processes stages 4 and 5[7].

In its classical operational formulation by Gendlin and others (1967) the (manner of) experiencing scale is depicted as concerned broadly with "the degree to which the client manifests inward reference in his verbalizations." The core feature of stage 4 is that the client "communicates what it is like to *be* him." In further definition of this level, the client is expressively aware of personal feelings and reactions without being "engaged in a struggle to explore himself". But assuming therapy progresses, a major corner is about to be turned. At stage 5, "The client is now using his feelings in a struggle to explore himself" and at this point is seen as "clearly engaged in a process of self-exploration in order to achieve self-understanding", with the effort and uneveness that "struggle" implies.

Phase C of the course of therapy thus encompasses elements and qualities particularly associated with in-therapy client functioning at stages 4 and 5 in Rogers' process conception and the experiencing scale. As seen from a matrix of convergent viewing planes, the client's advance through this phase is made possible by the deepening quality of trust in the relationship, in the meaning described. The association is a recursive one: the trust is "earned" and evolves as the client ventures a cautious step or unexpected leap, is companioned in helping mode, strives again and is confirmed once more in T's response. Within the client, not only are rigid, unchosen older moorings left behind, but any *fixed* anchorages are used in diminishing degree by an increasingly buoyant and mobile, becoming self.

Assuming therapy runs the full course outlined here, Phase C is expected to be the longest in working duration; and in such cases probably the phase in which greatest personal change occurs. A proportion of clients would proceed from phase C directly to termination, or to a termination phase that included foreshortened elements from Phase D. There is no clear-cut boundary between Phase C and D, but a qualitative transition most evident after its occurrence, in the working process of the relationship between C and T and in the ways in which C is proceeding in his or her quest. These two streams tend to be more closely interwoven and less distinct in Phase D than in earlier stages, as implied in my account which follows.

D. Synchronous engagement, and the becoming self in action

In Phase D, feelings and thoughts arising within the client tend to be *recognized* as forming within the context of the relationship with the therapist and often as having reference to it, in its own right or as a particular instance of a more general case. The therapy discourse is synchronous on at least two levels. First, there is an in-phase quality to what is happening from moment to moment in the inner experiencing and exploration of the client and its outward expression to T, as responsive partner and contributor to this experience. (In older terminology, the client is being congruent.) Second, there is generally close coincidence between what each partner is experiencing and meaning or seeking to express and what they are taken to be feeling and meaning by the other. There is a more "sympatico" quality than before, of which simpler expressions are that either partner at times accurately finished the other's words, or "reads" non-verbal signs without distortion of the other's feeling or thought. These aspects of strongly synchronous interaction are substantially founded on the development of trust in Phase C.

The in-phase quality applies now in a further pair of ways. At this stage, much of the client's verbal (and non-verbal) communication is an encoded surfacing of the flow of feeling and experiential meaning *as the latter is occurring.* (In older terms, this implies immediacy.) Very little is said that is planned ahead. While self-exploration may still, at moments, be a difficult struggle, the level and quality of this struggle tends also to be communicated as it occurs; and there is a relatively small and diminishing gap between what is immediately beneath the surface of expression and that which is put into words and/or conveyed in an explicit non-verbal way. The twin to this feature of the process is the interlock and interplay between the client's undifferentiated felt sense and the symbolising meaning-giving level of consciousness. The client now generally can find verbal form and expression for immediately present features of this organic inner sense and substratum of experience.

Whether or not portrayed through Gendlin's powerful language and vision of focusing (e.g. Gendlin, 1968, 1981), a condition of easy interchange or "dialogue" between the symbolizing, conceptualizing, form-giving self and the person's organically present, felt but unformed experiencing (both basic to the working of the human brain-body-mind system) is assumed fundamental to wholeness, or positive wellness. In Phase D, this capacity is both clearly manifest and further developed in the context of the helping relationship mode in its more advanced, synchronous expression. Discernible instances of such inner dialogue generally have occurred before this point but have not become a major inherent feature until the presently identified phase occurs. Either the process is not mastered or else not freely used in the relationship until founded trust is strong and reliable.

As well as moving to a new quality of congruently interactive self-exploration, as so far described, clients now experience or notice new levels of personal change. Often, they are conscious that their values have been shifting and that at minimum there are clarifications and alterations in balance among involvements that are important to them. Their personal priorities, what they most cherish, aspects of the ways they wish to live, have all moved somewhat and are in sharper focus. One's body, visible and internal, tends to become a more integral aspect of self, in this phase; and clients may have a new sense of their own whole presence, of the space they occupy when in motion or still, of their mass and momentum and of their life energy radiating and receiving from the energy of others.

In Phase D the client is likely also to explore, reflect on or notice change in his or her time sense, and of living in time. If such change is only noticed and mentioned after it happens, this may not come up until the next, concluding phase. It may be, for example, that C is now very conscious of being able in a new way to live in the moment, to be interactively in touch, as with the therapist, at the instant things are happening. In addition, C often has a stronger, more differentiated sense of his or her own identity not only in the moment but as a life. There is a new reality to living through and in one's whole life span, to being one's life as well as *being* more nearly one's whole present-becoming self in each step and moment of time.

The use of metaphor and the sharing of literal subjective images - by the client as well as therapist - generally is more prominent and more telling in its expressive-communicative power in Phase D than in other phases. Feelings may be portrayed using space-time metaphor, or as geometric forms, or as though they could be touched and had physical texture, or as being like solid objects or living organisms, and in other ways associated with corporeality. In seeming paradox, such language can help to intensify and give more accurately fitting and less object-like expression to highly personal, felt experience and meaning than more literal expression achieves.

Effectively there is in Phase D more poetry both in the therapy interaction and, probably, in the way the client tends to construe and express his or her experience. Partly because we, most of us, live in a "left-brain" world, stressing rationality, analytical thought and object description, in the course of achieving greater wholeness in therapy the more artistic/poetic/intuitive-expressive side comes forward[8]. "Man" Rogers has argued "is wiser than his intellect" and the spontaneous use of metaphor and subjective images is reflective of this wisdom. As an assimilated part of the person's way of being, it can add to personal effectiveness in real-world contexts. Client-centered therapy sustained at Phase D tends to liberate the creative artist within the client, perhaps literally and at least in terms of the individual increasingly being an architect of self and a more creative builder in relationships with others.

The becoming self in action looks backward largely to enhance or deepen his or her experience in the present, and to see more clearly ahead . Memory of what has gone before is open, not barred, and very strong feelings may come to the fore through this memory. However, memories do not of themselves (any longer) produce deep mourning, intense fears or high exultation. As earlier implied, the person experiences, senses his or her identity in the whole process of becoming, even in the trajectory glimpsed ahead as well as in the "now-being" of the self.

Intensive, personal therapy, in keeping with other (strongly) formative life experiences (Barrett-Lennard, 1978), has some of the elements and qualities of birthing. In the case of client-centered therapy, this does not imply regression or dropping back in order to redo an earlier stage of development but connotes change and emergence in the directions implied, centrally including qualitative shift to a more self-transcending and becoming way of being. As this birthing change occurs it is highly likely that, at some stage in Phase D *and in ways consistent with other mentioned aspects of in-therapy process and wider movement,* that clients will explore the "fit" or lack of it between the becoming self they now experience and the larger context of their life activity and priorities.

Usually, the importance of existing close relationships is affirmed, with a sense of furthered and continuing discovery of what is actual and desired in these relationships. As well, where it has been deeply at issue, a desired-feared separation by now is largely drained of *internal* conflict (and is a matter in and of itself rather than a symbol of something broader), and clients in open dialogue with self can now weigh and choose their course on an organismic basis. Clients may take steps to develop new associations or selectively enhance existing ones, and they may feel less concerned for their standing in casual or public contexts. Major decisions are not necessarily made in the vocational sphere, but active reappraisal typically occurs, the client feels less imprisoned (if this has been an issue) and is more involved in reaching out to express or to further aspects of the becoming self in the context of vocation and avocation.

Transition from Phase D to the concluding Phase E often is influenced by practical considerations that are partly or indirectly a consequence of therapy. These potentially include financial and time/energy/priority considerations on the part of the client, relocation or extended absence by client or therapist, and the existence of fresh or altered situations and relationships in the client's life which are now effective for their continued exploration and growth. The last-mentioned of these may clearly reflect effects of therapy.

Other more intrinsic termination conditions evolving in Phase D include some or all of the following: a. The crises or other conditions precipitating the client's entry to therapy have either receded and become "history", or are now experienced and viewed quite differently by a person whose formerly constricted energies are in flow again and whose resources express a more integrated and in-motion way of being. b. The client has learned or rediscovered how to travel in inner space, knows vividly how it is to be out-of-touch and recover connection, and is applying fruits of his or her journeying and change to outside life contexts. The relationship with the therapist is now enjoyable rather than essential to sustain altered qualities of experiencing and questing. c. When a client has for some time been working in therapy in ways inclusive of Phase D level qualities, the therapist becomes ready for and may begin to expect termination. In the open flow of the relationship, indications of the shifting balance in T's attitude are experienced by C, and in practice form part of the data by which C judges when the time is ripe to conclude therapy. d. A more tentatively advanced condition is that the client becomes ready for a time of psychic relaxation or "letting be", rather than continuing so intensively and directly to question, explore and work at his or her formation and identity. e. The client typically is less vulnerable and much less strained and anxious. This change diminishes one of the posited main conditions of therapy (Rogers, 1957). It also allows for greater sway of conserving, stabilising or homeostatic processes viewed as existing side-by-side with the growth and actualizing tendencies (Barrett-Lennard, 1956). f. Typically, C will raise the topic of termination and explore it with T in accord with the same kind of in phase, inward-outward and forward-moving process as other felt issues. Such exploration, starting in the Phase D context, would herald the transition to Phase E.

E. Termination process: Ending and entry

The explicit termination phase in client-centered therapy, *if following on from phasic mode D*[9], typically is brief in terms of interview duration. It may directly occupy only a single meeting, usually, after being heralded in a previous session. Where the total course of therapy is lengthy, or where the time of ending is governed by external circumstances known in advance, the termination phase may directly include three or four interview meetings.

The ending of client-centered therapy, while it may be uncomplicated in the actual event, contains elements of paradox. It occurs at the point where C and T know each other best as persons, probably value their relationship the most, feel their association merging or capable of merging into a literal friendship relationship and, aside from mixed feelings around their separation, when they are generally most relaxed with one another. Precisely the same features would make it most difficult for C to continue to "buy" T's time or for them to proceed on the basis of an underlying or explicit contract for service.

The last-mentioned aspects contribute in a mixed positive-negative sense to the possibility and meaning of termination of ongoing contact between co-workers, fellow travellers and (would-be) friends. There is no proscription in client-centered therapy against actual friendship or collegial associations continuing after therapy but, often, various features of the personal and life situations of C and T mitigate against such an association. Thus the ending of a deeply meaningful human association is naturally and typically one important issue; an issue involving the way in which the client and therapist feel with and toward each other and the process fluency and synchrony of their inner-outward communication, as each manages a very real separation which in some ways is prototypical of other life partings.

The process of leaving therapy and, usually, the therapist (in terms of active association) naturally includes some sharing of its import and meaning to the participants. Particular, appreciated events, qualities or outcomes are likely to be singled out by the client, if not also by the therapist. Typically also there is reference to current outside projects or forward-reaching plans in the client's life, ones that may sharpen further in their mention, and which express the refreshed or re-awakened becoming self. As the phase continues, images of birthing, of literally growthful unfolding or metamorphosis, quite often occur to the client or therapist. In any case, termination of the journey and course of therapy finally impresses itself as a beginning more than an ending, an entry not to a substitute engagement, not necessarily to any particular new context, but to a way of being and responding: A way which includes an openness to feelings as they are happening, a responsive in-touchness and fluency in speaking from and for differing levels of one's experiencing, a more continuous, regardful and resonant engagement with others, and a quality less of effortful striving and more of spontaneous purposefulness.

There may be moments of sadness in the parting of client and therapist, but termination when the time is ripe, especially following mode D, is such *an affirming* step that there is little or no continuing sense of loss. While there *is* any sharp sense of loss or distinct lack of closure, or while the client is more occupied with departure issues than entry ones, the termination phase is not yet complete and, desirably, one or more further meetings would precede literal parting. As with any significant human association, to a degree the relationship lives on within the participants; but the memories bring no sorrow or regret, in the case of optimal termination. Further, in client-centered therapy, the door is rarely closed permanently. Unless changes in location would make any further contact impractical, the therapist is potentially available in the case of future emergency. And even without such emergency, if C's and T's paths should later cross, each would welcome this contact and easily move to sharing communication[10].

CONCLUSION

I am now conscious that as the thought presented here evolved (through periodic work over several years) plotting the pathway as such became less an end in itself and more a vehicle in the search to further work out and communicate the process nature of client-centered therapy. For me as author many threads have come together, in this search, and I shall be pleased if the result is evocative for the reader. If the view is found useful in training, or if it leads to related statement or research, I hope that these gratifying outcomes are shared and made known to me.

It should be evident now that the "phases" deciphered here are not regarded as uniform steps or rigid markers. They flow from an attempt to catch the essence of a distinct and still unusual quality of association and quest, one which in its specifics is as individual as the participants in the enterprise. Given the requisite resources and commitment, this enterprise and process builds on itself until it becomes evident that another phase, or level, has been reached. No main level can be entirely skipped, for each is a vital part of the foundation for the next. Thus also no mode in full expression can simply be switched into at will, or as an instant product of specific techniques, for its emergence is a growth process and not just a matter of where or how attention is centered.

Therapy of course can come to an end, in practice does end, almost anywhere along the broad continuum. Moreover, the journey is not always as distinctly undirectional as my picture might suggest. In or out of therapy, we are subject to mood swings, biochemical rhythms, ups and downs in relationships and achievement, uneven life stresses. Clients can move ahead strongly in therapy and then seem to slip back, with the process being more like an earlier phase. Oscillating advance and retreat, or spiral-like return to familiar issues tackled on a somewhat different level, complicate identification of where the travellers are on their journey. Nevertheless if therapy is to come to strong fruition, the journey is a progressive one and its underlying direction generally in accord with the sequence discussed. Beyond this, client issues or therapist emphases may in effect stress process and development in one phase more than in another, especially as between phasic modes C and D.

In introducing this perspective, the issue of therapy as recovery and healing, as re-education or growth, or self and interpersonal learning, or social reconnection, etc., was acknowledged. More than difference in language is implied by these alternative and potentially complementary designations. They connote axes and levels of change which appear in differing balance in the phases distinguished. Literal healing and recovery processes are most obvious in Phases B and C. Re-education perhaps, and growth change to new levels of functioning, are most evident in Phase D. Clients may largely heal and recover - with important elements of growth - without going on to Phase D. Development of a person's values and lifestyle would occur more strongly through Phase D process than in other phases. The "person of tomorrow", in Rogers' eloquent description (Rogers, 1971, 1977), would soon be at home in Phase C interaction and be likely to move on to phase D. The person identified as schizophrenic may struggle in therapy (as earlier implied) for a long time before reaching a phase C process. Coming to that stage would represent a great deal of healing movement.

Therapists of most distinctly client-centered approach, especially if trained in the hey-day of self-theory, or for whom Rogers' own work remains a central model and influence, would tend to set much store by Phase C processes, work hard and patiently in facilitating their fruition with clients, and not judge that therapy was failing or faltering if phasic mode D did not appear in any full-fledged way. Therapists particularly influenced by Rogers' later process thinking and, especially, by Gendlin and others of more "experiential" persuasion, may have greatest interest or confidence in therapy that clearly moved to the Phase D level of process in this conception. For therapists of either emphasis working with clients in Phase D probably helps most in the *therapists'* growth.

These last observations are by intent speculative and suggestive. Client-centered therapy and the wider person-centered movement is more pluralistic than in the earlier "school phase" of its development (Barrett-Lennard, 1979). Perhaps it is fitting to end this paper on a note acknowledging that we are not all *closely* of one mind. Time will tell whether the view given here of the pathway of client-centered therapy has a generality which spans most of our variation, contributing both to awareness of our whole cloth and commonality and to further advance.

NOTES

1. There is no proscription in client-centered therapy against C and T knowing each other beforehand, or being in contact on other levels (of a less self-intimate nature than therapy) during the period of therapy. Indeed, since no transference is being cultivated, such contact may further the anchorage between in-therapy experience and outside life experience and behavior. From one significant vantage-point, the aim of therapy is to become unnecessary. For this literally to happen fresh shoots of healing-growthful change need to be exposed and tested in outside life contexts, and then culled and fertilized again in the nutrient laboratory of therapy, perhaps in recurring progression.

2. Another element that seems often, but not always, to mark and reflect the fact that the therapy engagement has actually started is that C's step is a little lighter when he/she leaves the session than when it began; that whatever kind of load C has been carrying and has finally sought help with, is not quite as heavy. The exact sources and forms of this difference are many, but it seems to have fairly consistent physiological counterparts, often visibly including deeper and more even breathing, reduced muscle tension and less noticeable adjustments in circulation.

3. One of these distinctive ways is that certainly there is no contract and usually no implicit collusion to maintain a status quo. The converse - in terms of agreement or understanding to work at change - is the case in some form. Inverting social custom, the emphasis at the start is on what is problematic, difficult and unwanted, in one's own life and self.

4. Internal and external views both seem sound, unless one is held to the exclusion of the other. One potentially can choose to take all external conditions as given and look to oneself as the active agent in varying or changing the quality of one's own life. One may choose alternately to take oneself as given, and look to the influence of environmental conditions on the quality of one's life. Neither stance is invalid, unless used to negate or ignore the other.

5. Many more specific and frequent themes in the overall quest portrayed - broadly, the quest of the self to become more knowingly conversant and at one with itself - could be discerned and illustrated. One example of such a theme is "When/how far can I trust my feelings and intuition as the main guide to what I do?" Another imagined but also real illustration of what a client might actually say is: "I wish, I *want to listen* to my feelings and what I'm sensing, and kind of keep in step on the outside with the me that is inside! I want to learn to somehow keep the inside channel open when I'm occupied with people and tasks outside. I *feel* so much better, and I really *do* better, when this is happening."

6. How "being ready" eventuates, is not indicated. What Rogers posits here appears however to be consistent with Phase B, or at least with a main variant of this phase. How long and difficult a process it is to develop a strong personal/working alliance seems to depend a good deal on the client's process level on entering therapy and on the therapist's versatility in

engaging in the helping mode with persons of varying initial capacity to experientially express, question and explore their own selfhood.

7. Somewhat fresh language is used here, slightly advancing but largely in keeping with Rogers' earlier thought. The aspect of "manner of relating", as richly explicated and rendered in operational form by Gendlin (1967), has more to do with the therapeutic relationship than directly with self-process and self-change. Stage 4 in Gendlin's formulation is headed "Parallel and together: The relationship as a context of therapy" and his finely differentiated account under this heading both complements and is consistent with the view advanced here, as a description of a well-established, personal/working therapeutic alliance. Stage 5 in Gendlin's portrayal builds on stage 4 to include, as well, use of "the relationship as specific therapy" and overlaps with Phase D in the present outline.

8. High trust, as this term is used here, tends to be a prerequisite for the client to relax the guardedness of "left-brain control" and to experiment with and use expressive metaphor and intuitive-imagery. Such expressiveness can seem to leave the self unprotected - even at the risk of ridicule - in a world commonly experienced as demanding a very literal kind of practicality, narrowly logical and rationalistic forms of reasoning, and consistent, predictable behavior.

9. If termination occurs before and without proceeding to mode D, but after a period of Phase C interaction and process, the termination phase is likely to resemble the pattern described here. If it occurs at a still earlier point, therapy per se has not come to fruition and a qualitatively different ending is to be expected.

10. Interested readers are invited to ask the author for an addendum to this paper, containing added illustration from therapy interviews. So far, this focuses on the ending process and includes excerpts from the same therapy partners whose first meeting was drawn on to illustrate the Entry phase.

REFERENCES

Barrett-Lennard, G.T. (1956). Why do clients terminate therapy? *Counseling Center Discussion Papers, 2,* No 18. University of Chicago Library.

Barrett-Lennard, G.T. (1978). *Life crises and formative episodes in adult development.* Unpublished manuscript. Christ's College, University of Cambridge, the NATO Advanced Study Institute on "Environmental stress, life crises and social adaptation."

Barrett-Lennard, G.T. (1979). The client-centered system unfolding. In F.J. Turner (Ed.), *Social work treatment: Interlocking theoretical approaches* (Second ed., pp. 177-242). New York: Free Press.

Barrett-Lennard, G.T. (1985). The helping interview in counselling and psychotherapy. *British Journal of Hospital Medicine, 33,* 287-290.

Gendlin, E.T. (1967). A scale for rating the manner of relating. In C.R. Rogers

(Ed.), *The therapeutic relationship and its impact* (pp. 603-611). Wisconsin: University of Wisconsin Press.

Gendlin, E.T. (1968). The experiential response. In E.F. Hammer (Ed.), *The use of interpretation in treatment: Technique and art* (pp. 208-227). New York: Grune and Stratton.

Gendlin, E.T. (1978). *Focusing.* New York: Everest House.

Gendlin, E.T. (1981). *Focusing (Rev. ed.).* New York: Bantam Books.

Gendlin, E.T., Tomlinson, T.M., Mathieu, P.L., & Klein, M.H. (1967). A scale for the rating of experiencing. In C.R. Rogers (Ed.), *The therapeutic relationship and its impact* (pp. 589-592). Wisconsin: University of Wisconsin Press.

Noel, J.R., & De Chenne, T.K. (1974). Three dimensions of psychotherapy: I-We-You. In D.A. Wexler & L.N. Rice (Eds.), *Innovations in client-centered therapy* (pp. 247-257). New York: Wiley.

Rogers, C.R. (1942). *Counseling and psychotherapy.* Boston: Houghton Mifflin.

Rogers, C.R. (1957). The necessary and sufficient conditions of therapeutic personality change. *Journal of Consulting Psychology, 21,* 95-103.

Rogers, C.R. (1959). A tentative scale for the measurement of process in psychotherapy. In E.A. Rubinstein & M.B. Parloff (Eds.), *Research in Psychotherapy* (pp. 96-107). Washington, D.C.: American Psychological Association.

Rogers, C.R. (1961a). *On becoming a person.* Boston: Houghton Mifflin.

Rogers, C.R. (1961b). The process equation of psychotherapy. *American Journal of Psychotherapy, 15,* 27-45.

Rogers, C.R. (1971). *The person of tomorrow* (phonotape). San Rafael, CA: Big Sur Recordings.

Rogers, C.R. (1977). The emerging person: Spearhead of the quiet revolution. In *Carl Rogers on personal power* (pp. 255-282). New York: Delacorte Press.

Seeman, J. (1949). A study of the process of non-directive therapy. *Journal of Consulting Psychology, 13,* 157-168.

Snyder, W.U. (1945). An investigation of the nature of non-directive psychotherapy. *Journal of General Psychology, 13,* 193-223.

Vargas, M.J. (1954). Changes in self-awareness during client-centered therapy. In C.R. Rogers & R.F. Dymond (Eds.), *Psychotherapy and personality change.* Chicago: University of Chicago Press.

TOWARD A REPRESENTATION OF THE CLIENT'S EXPERIENCE OF THE PSYCHOTHERAPY HOUR[1]

David L. RENNIE
York University, Toronto, Canada

Interpersonal process recall, or "IPR", is a technique of using the replay of either videotape or audiotape to stimulate the recollection of subjective experience during discourse (Kagan, 1975). The technique has been used recently in psychotherapy process research. Thus far, the application of the technique to this domain of inquiry has typically drawn the participant's attention to the subjective experience of particular types of events in a therapy session. Furthermore, the participants have usually been constrained to quantitatively represent their experience through the use of rating scales (see Elliott, 1986).

In the above review, Elliott has indicated that this approach to IPR research may fail to capture some of the more subtle, covert aspects of the experience of therapy. The line of work represented in the present paper addresses this gap left open by mainstream IPR research. Here, no restriction was imposed on clients when reviewing the tape of an entire therapy session, and a grounded theory (Glaser, 1978; Glaser & Strauss, 1967; Rennie, Phillips, & Quartaro, 1988) type of qualitative analysis was applied to the client's accounts.

THE STUDY

This was a field study of 12 clients actively engaged in psychotherapy. They were five men and seven women, ranging in age from the mid-twenties to the mid-forties; all but one were undergraduates in two large universities in Ontario, Canada. Two of these respondents were my clients. At the onset of the study I arranged for the latter to be interviewed about their experience of their sessions with me. Two colleagues of mine (one for each client) conducted these inquiry interviews. I did this as pilot work and then incorporated the findings into the main body of findings resulting from my interviews with the clients of nine other therapists. One of my clients was interviewed about each of two therapy sessions with me, separated by a period of 3 weeks. Furthermore, one of the therapists provided two clients who participated in the study. Hence, the total of 10 therapists produced 12 clients who were engaged in a total of 13 therapy interviews serving as the focus of IPR inquiry.

The clients' therapists were seven Ph.D. psychologists, one social worker, and two graduate students in clinical psychology. With the exception of one of the graduate students, all of the therapists had at least 10 years of experience. Their orientations at the time of the study were as follows: Five were person-centered, one was a Gestalt therapist, one was a transactional analyst, one was a professed radical behaviorist who often displayed a person-centered style, one was an eclectic therapist with a rational-emotive leaning, and one was a relationship-focused therapist who engaged in a lot of self-referencing.

In recruiting research participants, therapists were approached who in turn discussed the matter with selected clients. Because the research pertained to the experiences of clients currently engaged in therapy, participation in it raised the issue of the reactive effects of the research inquiry on the ongoing psychotherapy. A condition of research participation set out to the therapists (and hence to their clients) was that the client should be given the opportunity to determine how, and the extent to which, the information arising from the research inquiry should be conveyed to the therapist. Three alternatives were given: The client could either (a) take the responsibility for the discussion of the implications of the research inquiry for the therapy; or (b) delegate to the interviewer the task of briefing the therapist; or (c) invite the interviewer to join the therapist and client in a discussion of the implications of the inquiry. As it turned out, most of the clients who participated chose the first option.

As arranged, the clients presented either an audiotape or a videotape of a therapy session that had just been completed. In the ensuing IPR session, each client stopped the replay of the tape at points that were recalled as having been meaningful in some way. An inquiry was made of the recalled experience at each of these points. The inquiry interviews lasted an average of 2 hours. The grounded analysis was made on the transcripts of these IPR inquiries.

In this analysis, the disclosures of the clients were broken into "meaning units," or single concepts. For example, "I'm attempting, I think, to get as far away from, uh, the autobiography part as I can. What occurred to me immediately was that - and it's going to come up - is the dream I had the night before, which certainly was significant, but, uh, it became the way out."

As the study currently stands, a total of 944 meaning units have been isolated in the analysis. The portion of the analysis addressed in this paper is based on 713 such units. These units were categorized along the lines prescribed by the grounded theory method (see Rennie, Phillips, & Quartaro, 1988). In this approach, a given meaning unit is assigned to as many categories as are deemed relevant. The basic structure of the analysis, upon which the present paper is based, is illustrated in Table 1.

Table 1

Taxonomy of categories showing number of respondents (Rs) and total number of meaning units (MUs) contributing to each category

CLIENTS' REFLEXIVITY (Core category)

Main Category I: THE CLIENT'S (C's) RELATIONSHIP WITH PERSONAL MEANING	Rs	MUs
(a) *The pursuit of personal meaning*		
C Scrutinizes own processes (C appraises or explains cognitive/ affective/volitional process)	13	230
The Client's track (C's train of thought/path/flow)	13	157
The Client's narrative (telling a story/reviewing past events, with self awareness)	8	78
Insight (C's relationship with heightened awareness)	11	63
C's Contact with Feelings (questing/discovering/assimilating feeling)	9	45
Digestion (coming to terms, over time, with a new awareness)	7	41
Nonverbal communication (description of processes beneath C's nonverbal communication/evaluation of C's/T's non-verbal communication)	9	24
Discriminating use of therapist (controlling the influence of the therapist)	6	22
Client's attentiveness to the therapist (tearing away from self focus to attend to T)	7	22
Catharsis (expressing feeling/the importance of doing so)	5	19
Confessions by client(self-disclosing with embarrassment)	4	16
Root of problem (getting/failing to get to the bottom of the problem)	5	14

(b) *The avoidance of meaning*

Client's defensiveness (defensiveness against self-awareness/ operation/construed perception of C by T)	12	94
Playing for effect (artifice to change perception of C by C and/ or by T)	4	38
Client's resistance (resisting T's response/strategy/plan)	9	27
Willingness to change (mainly C's resistance to change; also C's endorsement of change via intentions/implementation of change via actions)	6	18
Lying to the therapist (lying to T/impact on C's internal processing)	5	17
Negative preparatory set (recalcitrant mood regarding willingness to work in the therapy session)	3	12

Main category II: THE CLIENT'S PERCEPTION OF
THE RELATIONSHIP WITH THE THERAPIST

(a) *"Nonspecific" relationship factors*

Relationship with the therapist (+/- feelings about T; balance of power; caring for T's needs; stability of the relationship)	13	130
Client's perception of the therapeutic task (C's perceptions/ expectancies/evaluations of achievements/roles/goals of both C and T)	11	77
Client's dependence-independence (C's concern about self- reliance vs. reliance on T)	10	77
C's perception of T's evaluation of C (conflict with/uncertainty about/influence on T's perception of C as a person)	10	55
Therapist's manner (comfort/discomfort with T in response to T's facial expression and style)	10	48
Acceptance by the therapist (C's perception of whether or not T accepts/judges/criticizes C)	8	47
Faith in therapy (whether or not C has confidence in the therapy)	10	40
Trust in the therapist (appraisal of whether or not C is in "good hands" in person of T)	7	28
Therapist's care (C's sense of whether or not T has C's interests at heart	9	20

(b) *Client's deference*

Concern about T's approach (conflict with T regarding responses/plans/strategies)	11	112
Fear of criticizing T (expression/justification of fear of criticizing/challenging T)	10	89
C's understanding of T's frame of reference (C's curiosity/ concern about T's intentionality)	10	67
Meeting perceived T's expectations (pressure in C to comply with demands/expectancies of T)	9	29

Metacommunication (impact of/need for communication about communication with T)	9	31
Threatening T's self esteem (C's diffidence about threatening/ indirect challenge to T's self esteem)	4	14
Client's acceptance of T's limitations (C tolerates flaw in T's performance/personality/relationship with C)	6	13
Indebtedness to T (1-way nature of the relationship/ subsidization of the therapy make(s) C feel indebted to T)	4	11

Main Category III: THE CLIENT'S AWARENESS OF
OUTCOMES

Impact of the therapy (effectiveness of C/T operation/ relationship with T regarding thoughts/feelings/behavior regarding therapy moment/session/course)	11	121
Impact of inquiry (different/enriched view of the therapy session as result of IPR)	12	118
		2065

Here it can be seen that there were 2065 assignments to 37 categories. I shall parenthetically refer to these categories throughout the following presentation of findings, as a way of documenting my conceptualization of the client's experience of the process within the psychotherapy hour.

As I have conceived it, the central or *core* category derived in this analysis is *clients' reflexivity* (Rennie, 1984, 1985, 1988). Reflexivity is a "turning back on oneself" (Lawson, 1985, p. 9). The reflexive form of consciousness is self-conscious, the reflexive form of agency is self-mastery, and the reflexive form of self identity is autobiography (Harré, 1984). Clients' reflexivity thus refers to clients' monitoring and evaluation of thinking and feeling, to their enactment of thinking and behavior in response to that monitoring, and to their construction of personal narratives. Harré's interpretation of reflexivity captures more precisely the meaning embodied in the term "agency" as used in philosophy (e.g. Taylor, 1985), in psychoanalytic philosophy (e.g. Schafer, 1976) and in counseling theory (Suarez, 1988)[2]. Although broader in scope, it shares meaning with "metacognition" in cognitive science (e.g. Flavell, 1979).

My analysis reveals that, in the context of their therapy interviews, the clients' reflexivity entailed four main categories of experience: The client's relationship with personal meaning, the client's perception of the relationship with the therapist, the client's experience of the therapist's operations (not in Table 1), and the client's awareness of outcomes. Each of these main categories subsumes lower-order categories. In this chapter, space limitations necessitate that the focus concentrate mainly on the first two main categories (i.e., the Relationship with Personal Meaning, and the Perception of the Relationship with the Therapist), with a minor focus on the "Outcome" main category. Hence, the client's experience of therapeutic operations will not be addressed. Nevertheless, the picture of reflexivity as mediated by a focus on three of the four main categories conveys the basic structure of the client's experience of the therapy hour.

The client's pursuit of personal meaning and his or her perception of the relationship with the therapist are, of course, intertwined and any attempt to address them separately would be artificial. Nevertheless, as an aid to exegesis, the two fields are examined consecutively in the following presentation.

THE REPRESENTATION

The path to meaning

As described by Phillips (1984), therapy gives clients an opportunity to focus on themselves. In focusing, they scan their feelings and locate hitherto dimly perceived zones of tension (Client Evaluates Own Processes). The array of tension zones is evaluated and a given zone is selected. Once this process starts, clients increasingly have a sense of being on a path, or train of thought (Client's track). There is a compellingness to the track: Clients feel that they are on the edge of their experience; there is uncertainty whether words can be found to express what they are sensing and this is associated with feelings of tantalization, and excitement.

When in crescendo along a path, clients are in a state of unreflective, "raw" experience. This state appears to continue until they "catch" themselves with the realization that the particular path they are on is not necessarily the most productive one, or until they encounter a thought or feeling that is threatening, or until the therapist says or does something that disrupts the path. The result of such monitoring is fairly clear: Clients either plunge into the threatening material, or minimize or distort it, or hold it in reserve and proceed with something else. The extent to which clients consciously *elect* these alternatives varies depending on the type of alternative. Clients appear to be more clear-headed and deliberate when either confronting or avoiding threatening material; the extent to which they are fully in control of what they are doing when minimizing or distorting internal experience is more variable. For example, in terms of plunging ahead, one interviewee remarked that she had talked about her immaturity in the session only because she had "built herself up to it;" basically she had not wanted to do it. In a similar vein, the same client indicated that she had stopped herself from getting too emotional in the session because it took her a long time to get over it; this session had occurred on a Friday and she had not wanted to spoil her weekend. On the other hand, she noted in the inquiry that some of the words she had used in the therapy session had "masked" (her word) an inner fear with which she had been contending during the session. At times, during the inquiry, she heard herself saying words which, with the benefit of the hindsight, she realized she had not meant, but there was no indication in her account that she had realized it during the therapy session.

Although the therapist is a shadowy figure when clients are deeply engaged in a meaning vector, the pursuit nevertheless occurs within an awareness of the relationship with the therapist. Clients are supported, strengthened and encouraged by a positive relationship. The categories of awareness comprising this field include: Therapist acceptance, therapist care, faith in the therapist and trust in the therapist. These categories include the so-called "nonspecific factors" of therapy identified by Frank (1961) (Acceptance by therapist; Faith in therapist; Therapist's care; Trust in therapist; Relationship with therapist; Client's perception of the therapeutic task; Client's dependence-independence; Therapist's evaluation of the client; Therapist's manner).

COVERT PATHS TO MEANING

Even when clients experience a positive relationship with the therapist, they do not necessarily say all that they are thinking. Clients in the present study consistently reported in the inquiry that, as busy as they had been verbally with the therapist, they had been even busier in their minds. It seems that the information processing capacities of people are so vast that a dialogue with the self can be carried on while the individual is engaged in a dialogue with another person. There are several advantages to keeping a train of thought private. First, clients can think faster than they can talk, hence they can move faster within their internal experience if they do not feel constrained to share everything with the therapist. Second, thinking without the constraint of verbalizing enables them to think in terms of images which might not be easily expressible in language. Lastly, private thinking enables clients to "play" with their thoughts. Clients do not have to suffer the reification of ideas that sometimes comes about through verbalization; nor do they have to suffer the therapist seizing upon an idea when clients might be ready to commit themselves to it. For example, one client narrated an incident about her work wherein some customers had been demanding and rude. The client had been trying to sort out the extent to which she had been to blame for the incident. Yet, she had been thinking more about it than she had been sharing. As she said in the inquiry, there had been two processes - her talking and what had been going on inside. She had been concerned that her therapist might think her narrative was banal precisely because she either had not wished to or had been unable to convey the richness of meaning in her private thoughts while she had been producing the narrative. She had not shared everything with her therapist because her consideration of blame was occurring in a broader meaning context (Angus & Rennie, 1988). She had been moving toward thinking that she should perhaps quit this job, but this had been a rather new thought. Hence, thinking this thought without verbalizing it had enabled her to play with it at a rapid pace without risking a premature commitment to it (Client's narrative; Client's track; Client's contact with feeling; Insight; Client evaluates own processes).

PLANS AND STRATEGIES

With varying degrees of awareness clients usually have plans for therapy and strategies for achieving them. A plan is an overriding objective, like the resolution of a conflict. A strategy is a particular line of attack that is adopted to fulfil the plan. Plans may be explicated by clients as part of the initial problems presented to therapists; they may also be kept private, as hidden agendas. Furthermore, even though plans may be openly shared with therapists, the strategies clients use to implement such plans may be covert.

To illustrate plans and strategies, one client had planned to use therapy to contend with his deceitfulness, both to himself and others. Unknown to the therapist, he had adopted the strategy of periodically lying to his therapist with the hope that he would be found out, and confronted; he had been relying on the challenge imposed by an indignant therapist to achieve what he had been unable to accomplish on his own (Lying to the therapist; Concern about the therapist's approach; Client evaluates own processes; Client's perception of therapeutic task).

The perception of the relationship with the therapist

The therapist is not always in tune with the client's path. A discordant response by a therapist forces clients out of a nonreflective path into an appraisal of the therapist's response and into an evaluation of the train of thought which they are on versus the path opened up by the therapist.

The extent to which a discordant response is distressing is heavily influenced by the extent to which the response is perceived to emanate from a congruent or dissonant therapeutic plan. Clients who are basically in harmony with the therapist in terms of the overall therapeutic task can be either tolerant of their own behavior if they choose to ignore the therapist, or tolerant of the therapist if they choose to sacrifice their own path for the sake of the therapist. In the first case, clients may feel a twinge of guilt in ignoring or overriding the therapist but can absorb the guilt because they sense the therapist tolerates them. In the second case, clients can be highly tolerant of therapists' foibles if they occur in the context of a good therapeutic relationship. Clients realize that they and the therapist are dealing with a highly ambiguous and complicated subject. Clients do not expect therapists to be highly accurate with every response and charitably write off "dead time" in a session as something that is to be expected (Client's acceptance of therapist's limitations; Indebtedness to the therapist). Furthermore, clients appraise sessions as a whole and tend to be content if one or two highlights can be achieved (Impact of the therapy; Impact of inquiry).

Alternatively, a discordant therapist response can be imbued with negative implications if it occurs in the context of a contentious therapeutic plan. Clients experience such an intervention as the tip of an iceberg; below the surface of the response is the full weight of the contrary set of expectations about the appropriate course of the therapy. They feel constrained, pressured, and engaged in a battle of wills. They may also feel ambivalent about the discordant therapist response if past experience has shown that going in the direction suggested by the therapist actually works, against clients' better judgement. Clients' minds are very busy during such a moment in the transaction. Because of the embedded disagreement about the best way of proceeding in the therapy, it is important for clients to determine whether or not this particular therapist response is another expression of the therapist's contrary plan. Clients thus try to understand the therapist's frame of reference that gave rise to the response (Client understanding the therapist's frame of reference; Concern about the therapist's approach). Mixed up in all of this are memories of the good aspects of the relationship, and realizations that a certain amount of give and take is necessary in order to protect the potential for such positive returns in the future. The main point is that, during such disjunctions within the context of a contentious therapeutic plan, the therapist's intervention is experienced and evaluated in the context of the relationship with the therapist rather than in the context of the clients' relationships with themselves. To the extent that the thoughts and feelings generated by such responses continue to reverberate within clients, the relationship with the therapist can constitute the underlying theme of major portions of the entire therapy session.

CLIENTS' DEFERENCE

As indicated elsewhere (Rennie, 1985), clients have strong tendencies to defer to their therapists when encountering discordant operations. These impulses to defer arise from several sources. First, clients feel like they should give their therapist some "air time", especially when the clients have dominated the session (Relationship with the therapist). Second, they do not necessarily trust the paths they are on, and need to trust the judgement of the therapist who is, after all, the expert (Client's defensiveness; Client evaluates own processes; Faith in therapist; Trust in therapist). Finally, they are afraid of criticizing the therapist because they do not want to hurt the therapist's feelings, and because it could jeopardize the relationship (Fear of criticizing the therapist; Indebtedness to the therapist; Relationship with the therapist). These three sources of inhibition militate against clients' open expression of dissatisfaction with the therapist.

Hence, in addition to covert, self-focused paths of meaning, deferential reactions to the therapist constitute another category of private thoughts among clients. Furthermore, as we have seen, depending on whether or not the discordant response(s) by the therapist occur(s) in the context of a positive relationship, the unexpressed concerns may pertain to the response itself, or to the nature of the relationship. To illustrate deference to a discordant therapist response in the context of a positive relationship with the therapist, one client had an issue around self-pity and had wanted to understand why she pitied herself so much. However, her usually highly accepting therapist in this instance had encouraged her to forget about trying to solve the riddle of "why" and to instead live her life in a more positive manner in the present. In deference to the therapist, the client had tried her utmost to do this but still had been troubled by the nagging need to understand how it had all started. She thus had made a concerted effort to interact with the therapist while inwardly mulling over the "why" question. She concluded in the inquiry that some good things had happened in the session but that she still had been left with the disappointment of not resolving this question (Concern about therapist's approach; Fear of criticizing the therapist; Insight; Meeting perceived therapist expectations; Client evaluates own processes).

Alternatively, unspoken deference to the therapist in response to discordant operations by the therapist in the context of a contentious therapeutic plan is exemplified by another client. This client's therapist had reminded her of mother superior in a Catholic school, of whom she had been terrified. This fear had been catalyzed by the therapist's manner, which had been firm. To complicate matters, in addressing the client's main problem - her family - the therapist had been insistent that the client should deal with her feelings, whereas the client had covertly felt that the therapist should pay more attention to family history because, as it was, the therapist had not seemed to know what the client had been up against. This contentiousness had fed into a deeper issue in the therapeutic relationship. The client had felt that she was a basically normal individual dealing with an abnormal family; in stressing that the client should deal with her feelings, the therapist had been interpreted to mean that the client had not been coping well. She thereby had formed the impression that the therapist had thought of her as a plodding, neurotic individual. At the beginning of the session on which I focussed, the client had been apprehensive that the therapist would ask about a homework assignment which the client had not done. In order to put the therapist off this scent, the client quickly had introduced a dream. The content of this dream had been insignificant in terms of its implication for her understanding of herself. However, it had been highly significant to her in terms of its implications for the relationship with the therapist because it had been light and lively. The client had hoped that the dream would convey that she was basically a normal, light-hearted, creative individual and not the kind of person the therapist had seemed to think she was (Perceived therapist evaluation of the client; Concern about therapist's approach; Fear of criticizing the therapist; Playing for effect; Resistance by the client; Client evaluates own processes; Relationship with therapist). Hence, in this instance, the client had harboured private thoughts about a tactic by the therapist, with the thoughts occurring in the context of ongoing contentiousness about the therapeutic plan. The client had elected to not openly express her dissatisfaction with the relationship, but instead had enacted a privately conceived strategy to influence the relationship.

The representation distilled

Let me summarize this representation of the client's experience of the psychotherapy hour. The client has the capacity to be self aware and operational in response to that self awareness. The client enters a given therapy session with a set of expectations about what to do in it. If the expectations about the relationship with the therapist are positive, then the client intends to address personal concerns; if the relationship is negative, then the client's intention to focus on the self is contaminated by an intention to manage the relationship. In focusing on the self, the client pursues personal meaning defined in terms of contact with feelings, expression of and relief from feelings, insight, and emotional conviction about insights.

The focus on the self is experienced as a path, or track. The client appears to unreflectively pursue a path until encountering negative emotions whereupon, depending on the degree of defensiveness, the client may appraise whether or not to proceed with the line of thinking, and if so, how. Furthermore, the client engages in some covert processing of internal experiencing wherein this processing is sometimes independent of the direction taken by the therapist.

Discordant responses by the therapist snap the client out of nonreflective pursuit of a track and into a state of appraisal. In response to the appraisal, the client may decide to ignore the therapist's response, to challenge it or, as is most frequently the case, to defer to it. Discordant responses by the therapist in the context of a congruent therapeutic plan and associated strategies, even if proving unsuccessful, are philosophically tolerated. Discordant responses by the therapist in the context of a contested therapeutic plan and associated strategies are occasions for a covert and highly thematic preoccupation with the relationship with the therapist.

DISCUSSION

This study raises questions about the validity of the participants' accounts. They were asked to recall what they had been experiencing at a given moment in therapy. When thus engaged, they were interacting with the research interviewers. As we have seen, the interviewees revealed that they had actively monitored their experience and had acted accordingly when interacting with their therapists; it would hardly be surprising if they proved to have done the same thing with the research interviewers. Hence, two questions arise: To what extent were the participants actually recalling their experience during the IPR inquiry, and to what extent was their activity during the IPR procedure influenced by their interaction with the interviewers conducting the research inquiry?

I first shall address the last question. When asked, the interviewees assured me that they had been candid. Nevertheless, a systematic challenge to that assurance would require an inquiry about the inquiry interview, which is a step my research group has yet to take. However, even if this step were taken, it only would be the first step in an infinite regress. Thus we are confronted with the deeper issue of objectivism versus constructionism in human science. Some scholars regard as a myth the notion that human experience exists as a self-contained "monad", accessible without any influence from the researcher (K. Danziger, personal communication, October 20, 1988). Instead, the research participant's representation of experience invariably occurs in a social context and is influenced by it (see Danziger, in press; Gergen, 1982; Reason & Rowan, 1981). From this perspective, the impact of the interviewer in a research interview is not qualitatively distinct from the impact of other research procedures; there is reactivity in all cases. However, this being the case, it does not exclude the possibility that some research procedures are more reactive than others. Furthermore, if this were the case, adequate assessment of the more reactive procedures would have to entail consideration of the necessity of these procedures given the nature of the phenomenon being addressed. In the case of my own work, I have found that, in trying to convey what they were experiencing at a given moment in therapy, the participants sometimes had to grope for the nature of the experience, and for adequate representation of it. During such struggles in the inquiry, I often groped along with them, whence the representation was clearly a co-construction. I felt during such moments in the research interview that a more passive stance on my part only would have served to help curtail the participant's sifting of the internal experience. This is a large issue; full attention to it would require more space than is available in this chapter.

Constructionism was also at play with respect to the first question raised above. Although the respondents were presented with the task of reporting on what they recalled experiencing in the therapy session, their recall sometimes got mixed up with their constructions of what went on in the light of a re-experiencing of the therapy session as they listened to the replay of it. They thus exemplified Spence's distinction between historical and narrative truth (Spence, 1982). There were large individual differences in this tendency toward the one truth or the other. Some clients had a clear sense of what they were up to in therapy and of how the therapist was affecting them; they appeared to be engaging much more in recall than construction during the inquiry. Other interviewees used the inquiry to figure out what went on in the therapy session. During the therapy session these individuals were emotionally reacting more than appraising why they were reacting. The appraisal tended to come later, during the inquiry. Hence, when we "unconfound," as it were, the impact of the inquiry from the interviewees' recall of the therapy session, it would seem that, although every client has the potential to be self-reflective in the therapy interview, anxiety can cause a defensive reaction that inhibits this activity.

When we think of the client's experience of therapy as one in which the client is capable of but does not always engage in self appraisal and executive action, we can see some implications for the practice of therapy. First, therapists can stimulate clients to reveal covert appraisals and intentions when they occur. Second, therapists can encourage clients to engage in appraisals when they are caught up in unreflective emotional and cognitive processes.

The pertinence of stimulated expression of self appraisals reinforces the value of metacommunication (Kiesler, 1982; Rennie, 1988). Metacommunication is defined as communication about communication. It is best stimulated in clients when therapists model the communication of their metacognitions pertaining to their own communications. In accessing the meaning contexts giving rise to responses, metacommunication slows down the progress along a meaning vector. However, this impedence may be precisely what is needed in many instances because it would enable the client and therapist to understand how they are relating to each other in the context of the meaning vector, which in turn could contribute to the negotiation of plans and strategies and culminate in an improved working alliance (Bordin, 1979).

The stimulation of the self-appraisal of cognitive and affective processing may be achieved by either interfering with the client's pursuit of personal meaning, or by inquiries into the basis for a perceived disjunction in the client's experience as mediated by either breaks in the client's processing or by nonverbal cues. The threat of this kind of intervention can be softened if it were made metacommunicatively wherein the therapist reveals to the client the intention laying behind the intervention which in turn enables the client to negotiate the demand.

The stimulation of the client's production and/or reporting of self-reflective processes combined with the therapist's disclosure of his or her own self-reflective processes yields a number of benefits: It provides clients with a tool for objectifying their own processes so that they are in a better position to assume control over them; it clarifies the intentions beneath particular client and therapist responses and nullifies misunderstandings; it exposes each party's plans and strategies for the therapy and opens up the possibility of a negotiated and mutual set of plans and strategies; and it gives the client a heightened sense of equality with the therapist which in turn increases the client's personal sense of power and self esteem.

In closing, I would like to remark on the implications of the study for research into psychotherapy. The study reveals that much of what is salient for the client is covertly experienced. This being the case, we have to be leery of localizing evaluations of therapy in the verbal discourse alone. In order to get a more complete picture, discourse analysts need to access the reflexivity of both the client and the therapist.

Lastly, investigators who prefer an approach to psychotherapy research that is relatively more theory-driven (e.g. Rice and Greenberg, 1984) than the current, descriptive approach are in a better position to hypothesize and study mechanisms of change which are not necessarily within the client's awareness. On the other hand, unless advocates of a theory-driven research strategy are prepared to conduct qualitative analyses of their respondents' accounts, the investigators may lose sight of the role played by clients' reflexivity. Perhaps, somewhere along the line, a unified theory will emerge as a result of the integration of these two perspectives on the client's experience of psychotherapy.

NOTES

1. The author is grateful to the Social Sciences and Humanities Research Council of Canada for financially supporting this research through grants 451-83-3642 and 410-83-1264, to the clients and therapists of the York University Counselling and Development Centre and the University of Waterloo Student Counselling Centre for participating in the study, and to Jeffrey Phillips and Charles Marino for contributing to the interviewing of the participants.
2. In my earlier work I also used the term "agency" to represent both self-awareness and self-control. I have since decided to use "reflexivity" instead of "agency," because I find Harré's terminology is more clear.

REFERENCES

Angus, L.E., & Rennie, D.L. (1988). Therapist participation in metaphor generation: Collaborative and non-collaborative relationships. *Psychotherapy, 25,* 552-560.

Bordin, E. (1979). The generalizability of the psychoanalytic concept of the working alliance. *Psychotherapy: Theory, Research, and Practice, 16,* 252-260.

Danziger, K. (in press). *Constructing the subject: Historical origins of psychological research.* Cambridge: Cambridge University Press.

Elliott, R. (1986). Interpersonal process recall (IPR) as a psychotherapy process research method. In L.S. Greenberg & W.M. Pinsof (Eds.), *The psychotherapeutic process: A research handbook.* New York: Guilford.

Flavell, J.H. (1979). Metacognition and cognitive monitoring: A new area of human inquiry. *American Psychologist, 34,* 906-911.

Frank, J.D. (1961). *Persuasion and healing.* Baltimore: John Hopkins University Press.

Gergen, K. (1982). Toward a transformation in social knowledge. New York: Springer.

Glaser, B.G. (1978). *Theoretical sensitivity: Advances in the methodology of grounded theory.* Mill Valley, CA: The Sociology Press.

Glaser, B.G., & Strauss, A. (1967). *The discovery of grounded theory: Strategies for qualitative research.* Chicago: Aldine.

Harré, R. (1984). *Personal being: A theory for individual psychology.* Cambridge, MA: Harvard University Press.

Kagan, N. (1975). *Interpersonal process recall: A method for influencing human interaction.* Unpublished manuscript (Available from N. Kagan, University of Houston, Farrish Hall, 4800 Cullen Street, Houston, TX, 77004, U.S.A.)

Kiesler, D.J. (1982). Confronting the client-therapist relationship in psychotherapy. In J.C. Anchin & D.J. Kiesler (Eds.), *Handbook of interpersonal psychotherapy.* Toronto: Pergamon.

Lawson, H. (1985). *Reflexivity: A post-modern predicament.* La Salla, IL: Open Court.

Phillips, J.R. (1984). Influences on personal growth as viewed by former psychotherapy patients. *Dissertation Abstracts International, 44,* 441A.

Reason, P., & Rowan, J. (Eds.). (1981). *Human inquiry: A sourcebook of new paradigm research.* Toronto: Wiley.

Rennie, D.L. (1984, May). *Clients' tape-assisted recall of psychotherapy: A qualitative analysis.* Presented at the Canadian Psychological Association Annual Meeting, Ottawa.

Rennie, D.L. (1985, June). Clients' deference in the psychotherapy relationship. In D. Rennie (Chair), *The client's phenomenological experience of psychotherapy.* Symposium conducted at the Society for Psychotherapy Research, Evanston, IL.

Rennie, D.L. (1988, July). Clients' agency in counseling and psychotherapy I: The relationship with personal meaning. In S. Toukmanian (Chair), *The client's development of meaning structure: Cognitive and metacognitive*

172

considerations. Symposium conducted at the First International Conference on Counseling Psychology, Porto, Portugal.

Rennie, D.L., Phillips, J.R., & Quartaro, J.K. (1988). Grounded theory: A promising approach to conceptualization in psychology? *Canadian Psychology, 29,* 139-150.

Rice, L.N., & Greenberg, L.S. (1984). The new research paradigm. In L. Rice & L. Greenberg (Eds.), *Patterns of change: Intensive analysis of psychotherapeutic process.* New York: Guilford.

Schafer, R. (1976). *A new language for psychoanalysis.* New Haven, CT and London: Yale University Press.

Spence, D.P. (1982). *Narrative truth and historical truth: Meaning and interpretation in psychoanalysis.* New York: Norton.

Suarez, E.M. (1988). A neo-cognitive dimension. *The Counseling Psychologist, 16,* 239-244.

Taylor, C. (1985). *Human agency and language: Philosophical papers I.* Cambridge: Cambridge University Press.

MS. C'S FOCUSING AND COGNITIVE FUNCTIONS

James R. IBERG
Illinois School of Professional Psychology, U.S.A.

ABSTRACT

One half hour of videotaped empathic listening to Ms. C by the author was analyzed using five variables. The five variables are all new measures under development and in need of validation studies. Three of the variables purport to indicate the focusing phases through which Ms. C passes in the interview, and the degree to which each utterance involves each phase. The three phases are 1. the story-telling or "pregnant" phase, 2. the direct focusing with a body sense or "parturient" phase, and 3. the relief/insight or "nascent" phase. These variables are meant to be "orientation-free" so that they may be used in psychotherapy process research from any theoretical starting point.

The other two variables are intended to measure the levels of involvement of two classes of cognitive function associated with the two hemispheres of the brain. The cognitive function variables are used to examine differences in the focusing phases. The major finding is that there is statistically significant evidence of a different pattern of participation, by these two modes of cognition, associated with each of the focusing phases. Ms. C's pregnant focusing phase involved more of the "dominant hemisphere" class of cognition, and her parturient focusing phase involved more of the "nondominant hemisphere" class of cognition. Her nascent focusing phase involved more differentiation by utterance between these two classes of cognition: Highly nascent utterances tended to be high in one, but not the other class of cognition, with some utterances mostly dominant mode cognition, and others mostly nondominant mode cognition.

INTRODUCTION

One of my students, to whom I will refer as Ms. C, generously volunteered to work with me while being videotaped. My goal was to demonstrate empathic listening in a very precise way, with frequent responses attempting to be complete and accurate. The resulting session, 35 minutes in length, illustrated focusing movement which was valued highly by Ms. C. She has been kind enough to give me permission to use the videotape for research and presentation of the research.

Starting from Gendlin's definition of focusing (1969) and focusing "movements" (Gendlin, 1978, 1981), used for teaching and guiding focusing, I began looking for the form in which focusing appears in client-centered therapy without explicit prompting from the therapist. In other words, when the therapist is not teaching focusing or explicitly working to produce the focusing movements, what happens? My experience had been that in such cases, focusing still occurred, although not necessarily with the same degree of clear differentiation of movements that Gendlin had worked for so many years to identify. I find the definition of the distinct movements to be immensely helpful for teaching focusing. But after all, focusing was discovered by studying client-centered therapy before focusing had been conceived as a distinct form of introspection. It was by applying some philosophical ideas (Gendlin, 1962, 1964, 1969) to the study of the natural form of client-centered (and other) therapy that Gendlin identified focusing in the first place. To be more specific, in the natural form of focusing, people may not take care to define a "quality handle", or stop talking long enough to "resonate" a handle with the body sense. Nevertheless, the body sense may have formed and the accuracy of symbolization is adequate to produce a shift in the quality of the body sense toward relief, satisfaction and insight.

THREE PHASES OF FOCUSING

When looking for focusing in psychotherapy in this way, it seemed to me more fitting to what I observed to define three phases of focusing[1]. The guiding metaphor which captured my impression of this three phase form of focusing is one of pregnancy, labor, and childbirth.

Quite regularly people seemed to spend some time in a therapy session first in a "story telling" phase in which they spoke about situations and events which had significant meaning and emotion for them. I chose the term *pregnant* for this phase to connote 1. the way in which the person is impregnated with meaning and affect, and 2. the fact that at this point in the process, a clear and full understanding of the reasons for the distress is hidden in the matrix of implicit past experiences and anticipations of future possibilities. During this phase, affect is often talked *about* rather than experienced directly: It may be there, but in the background rather than at the center of the person's attention. On the other hand, sometimes in this phase, affect is overly intense. In that case, to move to the next phase requires attaining *more distance* from the troublesome affect.

The second phase begins when a more direct experience of affect occurs involving both the appearance of *bodily* sensations and manifestations of affect, and a cognitive curiosity and receptivity toward this experiential development. For this phase I chose the term *parturient* which means "in labor," to connote the way in which there is, once this phase begins, an imminent but not yet complete delivery of more meaning to the person's self-understanding. Also true to the analogy of the labor phase of childbirth is the fact that the parturient phase often involves a temporary intensification of the pain of the struggle experienced less directly in the pregnant phase. Typically, this phase occurs in much briefer bursts than the pregnant phase. A way in which the childbirth metaphor does not correspond to a focusing process is that the focusing process is not as much one-way as childbirth - in focusing, one may become parturient, and then return to pregnant for a time, rather than progressing directly to the third phase, which I've labelled "nascent."

The *nascent* phase occurs when new insight or perspective accompanies a change for the better in the bodily experience of affect. The term "nascent" connotes both 1. the birth of the "baby" - now more distinct from the "mother" with corresponding relief, and 2. that the person's feelings and thoughts are in a greater than usual readiness to make new connections and associations as well as to seize interactional opportunities which could not be taken advantage of while in the pregnant phase.

LATERALIZED COGNITIVE FUNCTIONS

Although the focusing phases may be of some interest in and of themselves, they also need validation by bringing them into relationship with variables from a perspective outside of focusing. As a start for this purpose I defined two more variables, based on work which has been done on the cognitive functions associated with the two hemispheres of the brain. Table 1 lists my summary of twelve functions for which Levy (1980) reported evidence of specialization by hemisphere. I have detailed the experimental procedures behind these characterizations elsewhere (Iberg, 1988), and refer the reader there or to Levy for more in-depth discussions of the basis for these two sets of functions.

Table 1

Two sets of cognitive functions

L-mode functions	R-mode functions
A. linguistic processing	I. visuo-spatial construction
	II. recording literal properties of the
B. logic and deduction	physical world (especially those
C. analysis	never previously categorized)
	III. visualizing relationships patterns
D. sequential thought and patterns	of objects in space
	IV. words perceived as unanalyzed
E. naming tasks	wholes
	V. matching tasks
F. identifying distinctive subordinate	VI. extracts critical invariants of form
features that can be verbally labelled	which help identify the stimulus
	as a whole

The appeal of this particular perspective is that it may reveal that successful focusing involves a shift in the balance of the involvement of the two kinds of cognitive functioning. Levy (1980) reviewed some studies in which it was found that certain kinds of severe psychopathology (autism and schizophrenia, e.g.) do involve imbalances of hemispheric functioning, so there is some basis for expecting this may be an important variable for psychotherapy. If we find that this balance is capable of influence by psychotherapy, that would be an important finding indeed, providing evidence regarding precisely what it is, in part, that may be accomplished by psychotherapy.

RESEARCH HYPOTHESES

My first hypothesis is that the focusing phase variables can select out utterances which do represent distinctive forms of expression significant to progress in therapy. Further work must be done in this spirit relating the focusing phase variables to other measures of significant events in therapy such as the "running rating" of the EXP scale (Klein et al., 1986). In what is reported here, I do not attempt this, but only go so far as to achieve reliable ratings of the focusing phase variables. Some of the utterances which receive the highest scores on the variables, which should be most distinctly representative of the three focusing phases, if the variables are doing their intended job, will be presented and discussed. Hopefully, thereby, the reader can form an impression of the clinical meaning of the variables.

The next set of hypotheses has to do with the interrelationships of the cognitive function variables and the focusing phase variables. This represents a limited and preliminary validation effort for the focusing phases. Encouraging results here would warrant additional validation effort, such as identifying other measures related to the cognitive function measures developed here. Eventually, multiple measures (Campbell & Fiske, 1959) applied to these and similar data would build confidence in the interpretation of these variables and findings.

Because of normal communication between the two sides of her brain, I did not expect as large a negative correlation between L-mode and R-mode for Ms. C as would be expected for Levy's "split brain" subjects. But I did expect the correlation to be negative. Levy et al. (1972) found evidence that depending on the definition of the task (e.g. matching for R-mode, and naming for L-mode), one mode tends to "take charge" and stay in charge even for stimuli better recognized and remembered by the other mode. If indeed these two sets of cognitive functions are complementary in this way (competitive), it seemed likely that the utterance bursts which were high on one of the two kinds of cognition would be relatively low on the other, and *vice versa*. Thus my

first formal hypothesis was as follows (the notation I will use is this -
L-mode = "Dom", and R-mode = "NDom"):

$$H_1: r_{Dom.NDom} < 0$$

The basic notion I had for how successful focusing might influence
this association was that the involvement of the two kinds of cognition
would become more balanced. In other words, I thought when the
focuser became highly nascent, that both types of cognitive function
would be involved in thinking and expression, more so than when
highly pregnant or highly parturient.

Clinical impressions of the kind of thinking typical of the phases of
focusing led me to predict that the highly pregnant utterances would be
mostly L-mode, and that highly parturient utterances would be mostly
R-mode. When telling the "story" of their experiences, chronologically
listing events and describing and categorizing other people and
themselves, mostly L-mode thinking seems to be involved (see Table 1).
On the other hand, when a person stops this kind of talking, and is
instead sensing carefully an inner bodily referent, trying to match it
with just the right symbol to express it (seeking a "handle") as in the
parturient phase, this seems more R-mode in character. The difference
between these two focusing phases *is* in part that in the first the person
works with existing ideas to express experiencing, where as in the
second the body sense is felt freshly and symbolized anew, without
searching for existing conceptual categories, but attempting to create
new ones for precise explication. Therefore the next two hypotheses
were these:

$$H_2: \mu_{Dom \mid High\ Pregnant} > \mu_{Dom \mid Low\ Pregnant}$$
$$H_3: \mu_{NDom \mid High\ Parturient} > \mu_{NDom \mid Low\ Parturient}$$

Clinical impressions of the nascent phase led me to predict that both
kinds of cognition would be involved here in a more balanced way than
in either of the first two phases. People often create rich visual
metaphors which capture much meaning in the nascent phase, for
example. But on the other hand, there is often a component of
deductive reasoning as the focuser analyzes again the situation from the
new perspective of the nascent phase. To assess the equality of the
presence of the two kinds of cognitive function, I defined the variable
| Dom-NDom | . The absolute value of the difference between the
two scores, if they are involved equally, will be very low or zero, and for
very unequal involvement, it will be large in value. Thus my fourth and

last hypothesis was this:

$$H_4: \mu_{(\mid Dom\text{-}NDom \mid) \mid High\ Nascent} < \mu_{(\mid Dom\text{-}NDom \mid) \mid Low\ Nascent}$$

METHOD AND OPERATIONALIZATION

In earlier exploratory research with the three-phase conception of focusing, three variables were defined and applied to videotaped therapy sessions. Analysis of these results was used to refine the variables. Whereas I initially sought to define the phases as distinct segments of the therapy session, working with videotapes and ratings led to a different approach. I now define three variables, each with eight items which raters can identify when present. The eight items are summed for each variable, resulting in scores on each variable for each utterance the client makes. Thus a given utterance receives three scores: One for the degree of pregnancy, one for the degree of parturiency, and one for the degree of nascency it manifests. The three sets of items appear in Table 2.

My strategy for using raters is different than that used by Rice (Rice & Kerr, 1986). Where they ask raters to place each audiotape segment into one and only one category, I only ask raters to indicate whichever items are present. Scores on the variables are created by summing over all the judges, basically treating each judge like an independent "item" on a test, with the sum of the items being the variable of interest (like a test score). My hope here is that we simplify the rating task by giving relatively simple items which can be judged only on presence or absence, rather than requiring agreement on clinical judgments regarding which focusing phase the utterance represents.

Table 2
Items defining focusing phase variables

Pregnant
S1. Self or other characterized in trait-type language
S2. Theories put forth to explain behavior or feelings
S3. Comparisons made of self and other
S4. Nonverbal cues of emotion not explicitly said
S5. Awash in emotion or avoidance of emotion
S6. Cognitive grasp of implications expressed

S7. Reporting a pertinent sequence of events
S8. Making interpretations of someone else's feelings or motivations

Parturient

P1. Emotions directly in evidence and referred to as a datum
P2. Process commentary: Noting how one is relating to "it", expressed preferences for how to proceed
P3. Tentative remarks about its meaning
P4. Statements of qualities of emotion in reaction to talking/thinking about the topic
P5. References made to more meaning felt than is understood
P6. Descriptions of changes in the body quality as they occur: "Play by play" narrative
P7. Quiet non-verbal time spent sensing for "it"
P8. Certain words or analogies favored because of their special fit with feelings

Nascent

N1. Statement of perspective that was not there before - relief to better understand
N2. Disentanglement of one's own feelings and values from how someone else feels/is
N3. New clarity regarding what is at issue for one personally
N4. Purer, more refined or complete expression of relationship to the other
N5. Description of emotional developments with perspective and increased equanimity
N6. Emotions that are new and different appear
N7. Discovery of memories relevant to the "same" feelings
N8. Realization of a greater significance to the topic than was formerly appreciated.

The corollary to this approach is that reliability is also handled differently than what is typically seen when judges make ratings. Rather than focusing effort into achieving a high degree of similarity in the ratings of each pair of judges (high inter-rater correlations), I opted for minimal training and maximum freedom of interpretation of the individual items. The intent was to allow each judge to see the clinical data through the items most meaningful to the judge. Individual judge phase scores were then aggregated into a composite score. There is strong evidence that such aggregation *increases* criterion validity compared to the performance of any individual randomly selected judge (Hogarth, 1978), and that the increase in criterion validity is greatest when inter-judge correlations are lower (i.e. there is less inter-judge redundancy). In other words, this approach takes advantage of whatever peculiar sensitivity each judge has to applying the variable to the data, adding that to what the other judges contribute in a like manner.

The reliability (internal consistency) of the individual judge scores and total scores was assessed with coefficient alpha (Nunnally, 1967). Nunnally shows that coefficient alpha "is the expected correlation of one k-item test with other k-item tests drawn from the same domain ... [and] how a highly reliable total test score can be obtained from items that correlate only .25 [e.g.] with one another on the average" (p.193). With this approach we avoid the laborious process of achieving high reliability between each pair of judges, and take advantage of the way that aggregating judgments increases correlation with the underlying (criterion) variable (Hogarth, 1978).

Another difference between this system and Rice's is that she creates nominal categories as the result of the rating process, whereas here interval scales are created: The scores are a count of the number of items that were present in an utterance burst, for which the intervals in scores are meaningful.

The departure from my initial impression that the variables should indicate mutually exclusive sections of an interview has some advantages. Having a score for each phase for each utterance overcomes some problems inherent to the "unit determination" problem which is always an issue in process research (more on this below in this section). There really is no theoretical reason that any given utterance would manifest one and only one focusing phase. The focuser may shift from one phase to another within a given utterance. Scoring each phase separately nicely allows for this, since then such an utterance would receive ratings on each of the phases present. Thus we achieve a bit more sensitivity in tracking the actual process over the interview.

A short training session was given to ten student raters regarding the meaning of these items, which involved reading through and discussing a list of example client utterances for each item in Table 2 (see Appendix A). Then the students watched a videotape of the session, after which they were given a verbatim transcript for rating.They indicated which items were present in each utterance made by Ms. C, writing them in the margin. These ratings were then aggregated by summing the items present for each variable and summing across raters, creating three scores for each utterance unit. The theoretical possible range for each variable is zero to eight times the number of raters (10), or 0-80.

Two variables were created in the same way for the two sets of cognitive functions. The items in Table 1 were described through written examples (Appendix B) which were the basis of a brief discussion. After this, seven student raters (a totally different group) first watched the videotaped therapy with Ms. C, and afterwards received the verbatim transcript for rating. They wrote in the margin the Roman numerals or Arabic letters which corresponded to the items which they believed to be present in each utterance of Ms. C In a fashion similar to the focusing phase variables, these ratings were then aggregated by summing those for each set of items across all the raters to create 1. A score for L-mode, the variable representing the degree of involvement of the cognitive functions associated with the "dominant" hemisphere of the brain; and 2. A score for R-mode, the variable representing the degree of involvement of the cognitive functions associated with the "non-dominant" hemisphere of the brain. The theoretical possible range for these two variables was thus zero to seven raters times six items, or 0-42.

Units for analysis and reliability computations were selected using a combination of the pragmatic and structural dimensions as defined by Russell and Staszewski (1988). Since I wished to analyze aspects of Ms. C's expression across the interview, to create profiles over time, the utterance (what is said between the previous and following speech of the therapist) is a natural choice on the structural dimension. But I am also interested in a form of "illocutionary act" on the pragmatic dimension: what the speaker *intends* to express in uttering what is uttered (Russell and Staszewski, 1988, p. 16). Some utterances (as just defined) do not seem to represent a new illocutionary act. E.g. when Ms. C simply affirms an empathic reflection of her previous utterance, I have considered the affirming utterance part of the previous illocutionary act, rather than a new unit. On the other hand, I want to take advantage of the ease of identification of the structural utterance, so I do not wish to attempt to identify illocutionary acts which are "smaller" than the utterance. Thus my scoring units are what I call *"utterance bursts,"* intended to capture each time when Ms. C *both* starts an utterance *and* initiates the expression of new or additional aspects of what she is trying to say. There were 44 such utterance bursts in the interview.

RESULTS

Reliability

Coefficient alpha (Nunnally, 1967) was computed to assess the reliability of the scores for all five variables (also see preceding section). The results are listed below, indicating acceptable levels of reliability for the five variables.

Pregnant scores: $r_{10.10}$ = .93   Dom scores: $r_{7.7}$ = .78
Parturient scores: $r_{10.10}$ = .77   NDom scores: $r_{7.7}$ = .71
Nascent scores: $r_{10.10}$ = .82

Profiles of focusing phase scores

Figures 1-3 show the profiles of the focusing phase scores across the session. The scores are the total number of items from Table 2 indicated by all ten judges. Dividing these by ten (the number of judges) gives the average number of items per judge for each utterance. From these graphic results, you can see that the scores can be used to break the session into three phases. In the first phase, utterance bursts 1-10, pregnancy scores are relatively high, parturiency scores are moderate but end with a spurt to the most parturient utterance in the interview, and nascency scores are quite low. In the second phase, utterance bursts 11-26, pregnancy scores are moderate to low, parturiency scores are moderate but climbing. In the third phase, utterance bursts 27-44, pregnancy scores are all zero, parturiency scores start high and drop to a relatively low level, and nascency scores are relatively high.

One interesting thing suggested by these profiles is that the parturiency variable seems to mark phase-change events. At the start of the second and the third phase (at the end of the first and second), the parturiency scores are very high. This is consistent with my clinical experience that so much of the success of a session in terms of focusing movement depends on being able to usher in a parturient experience for the focuser/client. If the Rogerian conditions (Rogers, 1957) are effectively created, it can be safe enough for the person to have a direct "welling up" of feeling which the focuser can allow and receive with friendly, curious, respectful attitudes, and which initiates very productive subsequent minutes in the interview.

184

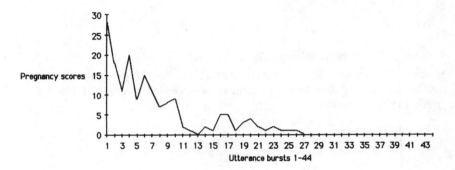

Figure 1: Profile of Pregnancy Scores

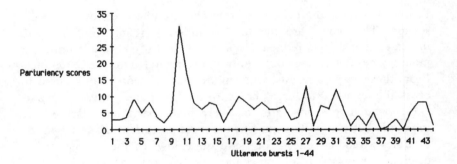

Figure 2: Profile of Parturiency Scores

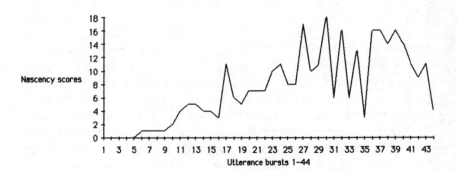

Figure 3: Profile of Nascency Scores

These data are consistent with a clinical impression I mentioned earlier in that parturiency seems to come in shorter bursts than the other two focusing aspects. Whereas both pregnancy and nascency have a more gradual movement and trend over the session, parturiency scores are characterized by three extreme peaks, with the rest of the interview occurring in a more narrow range. This highlights the necessity for the therapist to be alert for signs of parturiency, since if one is distracted or inattentive, one may miss these "doorways to feelings." On the other hand; by the time the highly parturient utterance occurs, there is probably little to do but stay the course, since I think it is the result of effective empathy for what has come before it. It is, however, something that deserves careful handling, since the focuser is especially vulnerable and in a delicate condition as he or she experiences the "unknown" of emotions and experiences not yet mapped out and clear. Thus I do think it is particularly valuable to notice the parturient events, so that especially then one can provide solidly accurate empathy, a gentle and accepting attitude, and confident company for the focuser as he or she proceeds. During these events, the client's attitudes which interfere with productive exploration are likely to be more evident and subject to improvement with the proper interaction with the therapist.

Samples of text scored high from each focusing phase

Here I will include a few of the utterance bursts which were scored highest for each phase, so that the reader can judge the clinical meaningfulness of what the variables measure.

Highly pregnant (utterance bursts 1-4)

> U1a: "...a familiar topic. Well, um, a week ago today, I had an interview about my placement, my diagnostic placement. And at that point, the fact that I'm in the masters program as opposed to the PsyD program was brought up, and I was, I really was quite shaken by it, in that, it was emphasized over and over that it's not automatic for one to go from the masters to the PsyD. Um, she was saying that not everybody does get accepted, and that, it, really the message was coming across that 'there are no certainties, there are no guarantees,' and that has been bothering me, much more than I thought it would. I seem to have had an attitude of 'well, of course I'll get accepted, I mean, why wouldn't I?' and there are all these wonderful qualifications, and yet, ever since that meeting, I'm

having a hard time, it seems like I want to do extremely well in school now; and the more pressure I put on myself to do just par excellence, the harder time I'm having doing it. It's almost as if what I've done before is just put it aside and go about my business and I felt I was doing, I was happy with the way I was doing...

T1 : So, in that meeting it kind of introduced a problem in terms of your feelings about how you're working in school. It reminded you because of repeated references that not all master's students get in, that you can't take that for granted, and you've been more concerned about it since then, about doing well, but if I'm understanding, it sounds like the concern is actually, sort of counter-productive, that it makes you more uptight...

U1b: Very.

T2 : and it's not very helpful. Mmhm.

U2 : Exactly. And, and it seems, before, there was a possibility of that, but it seems because I was able to not dwell on it, that I was able to do the work, and really enjoy it much more. And it seems that from that meeting there wasn't enough encouragement. It seems like it was imbalanced. There was so much emphasis on, well the negativity, and the real possibility of this may be the terminating point. A master's. That, I don't know, I'm just (laughter)

T3 : That, most of the emphasis was on that side, and uh, that wasn't so good for you, to have that emphasized, and no encouragement, in spite of the fact that, it sounds like you've done pretty well in terms of your prior performance and grades, and certainly you felt good in terms of how you were studying and enjoying the material.

U3 : Exactly. Exactly, I'm having a great time in school. And I'm just wondering whether what I consider "good" is not what the school might consider good too, you know, to go on to the PsyD program.

T4 : Uhhuh. It shook your confidence in your own judgment, whether what you feel is good performance, is gonna be, if they'll agree with that, if the administration will agree with that.

U4a: Right, and and, all of a sudden it seems like the rules were changed, and I'm wondering, well maybe I need to find out what they really are. What is the criterion, that I thought that I knew what the criteria were, and, it seems as though...

T5 : I see. It left you with that impression. That maybe you had a misunderstanding about what the criteria are for getting accepted to the PsyD, and you're thinking maybe you should seek clarification of that.

U4b: Yes, and uh (laugh), and perhaps there's just some information that I'm just not taking in. That perhaps I'm kind of living in a fool's paradise. I, I want to know what the truth is. It makes me, I'm not clear on that."

Highly parturient (utterance bursts 10-11)

U10a: "Yeah. Exactly, exactly. And I think I should be. Or for me it is, much more productive. You know I can do the routine stuff. I can do the work part, and yet, still kind of keep, keep the other part, and grow with the other part, and somehow, I don't know, really kind of give it back in a way. Not just grow personally but, thrive, uh, take it on a different level. It seems like the other one is much more superficial and judgmental, and kind of there's a grade and a what have you. And I don't know why I'm doing this [touching her eye]. But it's...

T17: You don't know why you're doing?

U10b: Uh, the eye is just watering. But...

T18: Is that a feeling?

U10c: Uh, I think so. I there's kind of like a, I don't know, kind of a sadness, at not, I don't know, maybe it's the kid in me wanting to play.

T19: You feel a sadness welling up, and think of the kid inside of you.

U11a: Yeah. Yeah, and a kid kind of, you know it's like a little kid in a candy store. That's how I feel in school. It's almost like...

T20: What a nice image.

U11b: That's the way it should be."

Highly nascent (utterance burst 36-43)

U36a: "Right. And, you know this has helped. All of a sudden I feel a little more self-assured. Thinking I was doing just Aine. Sometimes I can take things a little too much to heart and sometimes perhaps I'm misperceiving the message, perhaps I am living in a fool's paradise but if I am it's nice.
(laughter)

T56 : (laughing) You mean if uh, that sounds like there's still a little doubt there about how accurately you perceived the meaning of that meeting. And maybe there's a way you are living in a fool's paradise, but now you're saying 'but if that's true, may be that's not all bad.'

U36b: exactly and...

T57 : You know what you like.

U37 : Right. Right. And the only you know when I will really resolve it is when I apply, and they either accept or reject me. Until then there will always be a little nagging doubt. But there doesn't need to be this, you know this amount that is much more than necessary.

T58 : Mhm. As you are going along. You still recognize that there will come a time when they'll look at what you've done and a decision will be made on that basis, and you can't take that for granted, but it doesn't help to have your, the way you experience the process become so severe that it's not fun. That isn't productive.

U38a: Exactly. It's almost like getting a grip back. Like kind of being able to somehow, I don't know feel diff--feel like I have a hold on things.

T59 : Some of that has happened it sounds like. More of a feeling of having your grip back.

U38b: Yeah.

T60 : It also strikes me, just from what you said about eventually the decision about the PsyD, that you do want that.

U39a: Definitely.

T61 : And that you'd like to have that opportunity open. And that's part of what's made this whole thing difficult, I guess.

U39b: Oh, exactly, because that is my goal, and one way or another I'll get there, it's just that this would be the nicest and the easiest. But uh,

T62 : You mean at this school?

U39c: Exactly. Exactly. And in this program. You know, it's like I'm really enjoying it here, and I hate to think...

T63 : Because of that. Because of how much you're enjoying it.

U40 : Right. Right. And it seems that, well you know, I'll just deal with the rejection if it comes when it comes, and there doesn't have to be this looming worry about that.

T64 : I see. If it comes, the time to deal with that is when it comes, rather than to live with the worry about that possibility so much that it ruins the quality of your enjoyment here.

U41 : Yes, that's it. That made a little difference inside too. It's almost like, 'yeah, go on,' it's like progressively this... (words inaudible) kind of like a little more relaxed. And it is, it's kind of like taking a different perspective on the same situation, and saying 'well it really is half full' (laugh), I mean, I don't have to think of it as half empty.

T65 : Hm. It's nice. It sounds like another little step of feeling better with it.

U42 It is, and sometimes the internal changes, are funny. It, it, there is a definite feeling, and it is inside of my stomach. It seems like it can be really tense, or it can just kind of let go, and mellow out, and...

T6 6: And that's something that's happened. More, just letting go. Hm.

U43 : Yes, exactly. And when it does, it's such a freeing feeling. It's like, (sigh) a breath of fresh air."

I would like to highlight a few things about these segments of the interview. In the pregnant segment, you see a typical report of something that happened, with a kind of chronological order to it. Affect is clearly involved, although not the focus of attention: At the end of U2, for example, Ms.C laughs, but makes no explicit mention of what that is about. Her focus of attention is more on what happened, characterizing that and considering what its implications may be, and what she should do about it.

One key thing about the parturient segment is her reference to a bodily event that is just then occurring, and her accepting, curious, "not-knowing" attitude about that. Also, she finds a phrase which functions like a "focusing handle" for her whole body sense as it is at that point, which is "like a kid in a candy store. That's how I feel in school... that's the way it should be."

There are some clearly nascent things about the segments given above: One is her report of an improved feeling - "all of a sudden I feel a little more self-assured." Also, there is a shift in her perspective with regard to a handle she used earlier: "A fool's paradise." She seems accepting of the same possibility which was threatening her at the beginning of the interview, but now to have more resolve and perspective about it, having become re-grounded in what she likes about her way of doing such things. And there is a report of a change in the bodily experience of feeling about the matter. She refers to this as a "definite feeling... inside of my stomach... such a freeing feeling."

Thus I am quite pleased with the workings of these variables. In my opinion, they successfully indicate the parts of the interview which they were designed to indicate. With this to bolster my confidence in the meaningfulness of these scores, I proceed to examine the relationship of these variables to the other two variables derived from another body of psychological work.

Focusing phases and cognitive functioning

For ease of reference, I repeat here the four research hypotheses stated earlier.

H_1: $r_{Dom.NDom} < 0$

H_2: $\mu_{Dom \mid High\ Pregnant} > \mu_{Dom \mid Low\ Pregnant}$

H_3: $\mu_{NDom \mid High\ Parturient} > \mu_{NDom \mid Low\ Parturient}$

H_4: $\mu_{(\mid NDom-Dom \mid) \mid High\ Nascent} < \mu_{(\mid NDom-Dom \mid) \mid Low\ Nascent}$

H_1. The product moment correlation between Dom and NDom is +.058. This is not supportive of the hypothesis. To explore further what is going on, I dichotomized the variables at their means and constructed a cross-tabulation as follows:

Table 3

Zero order association between L-mode and R-mode scores

		Dom	
		Low	High
NDom	Low	33%(7)	52%(12)
	High	67%(14)	46%(11)
		100%(21)	100%(23)

With the dichitomized variables, we do see a negative association(Yule's Q = -.37), such that when Dom scores are low, 67% of the NDom scores are relatively high, and when Dom scores are high, 52% of the NDom scores are relatively low. A negative association is consistent with the idea that the two kinds of cognitive function tend to compete, but it is not a strong association. In fact, the 95% confidence interval includes zero, so we have little confidence that this association is negative in the larger population of utterances. Perhaps in a normal brain, the communication is good enough so that this effect does not exist.

H_2. Do these data indicate the expected prevalence of L-mode functions in the more pregnant utterances? Table 4 indicates that they do.

H_3. Table 4 shows a significant difference in the mean levels of NDom scores as predicted. The highly parturient utterances involve significantly more R-mode functions than the less parturient utterance bursts.

H_4. To test the hypothesis that successful focusing involves a better balance of the involvement of the two kinds of thinking, R-mode and L-mode, I took the absolute value of the difference on the two scores as an indication of the equality of involvement. If both modes were involved in an utterance burst at equal levels, this difference would be very low or zero. If they were at very different levels, regardless of which was more prevalent, the absolute value of the difference would be high. Thus I predicted that the highly nascent utterances would have a mean on this variable significantly lower than the less nascent utterances. As you can see in Table 4, exactly the opposite was the case.

This finding, dramatically the opposite of what I predicted, calls for some explanation. Close examination of the data do suggest an explanation, and a refinement of my thinking about the way in which greater cognitive "balance" may in fact be a part of high nascency. But it's not the way I expected it to be. As a way of checking for the consistency of this finding across the interview, I examined the absolute value difference scores by the phases suggested from the profiles of the focusing variables. Thus I computed the mean |Dom-NDom| values for utterances 1-26 (Group 1), and compared that to the mean for utterances 27-44 (Group 2). As you can see in Table 4, the finding is the same: The more pregnant and parturient utterances of the first two profile groups have *more equal involvement of L-mode and R-mode functions on this measure than the more nascent utterances of the third profile grouping*[2].

Table 4

Focusing variable dichotomies: t-tests on scores of cognitive variables (splits at the means)

FOCUSING VARIABLE	CATEGORY	n	SCORES ON	MEAN	SD	UNPAIRED t	p
	high	13		8.77	2.62		
Pregnancy			Dom			3.523	0.0005
	low	31		5.52	2.86		(1-tail)
						d.f.=42	
	high	16		9.06	2.24		
Parturiency			NDom			2.12	0.0198
	low	28		7.04	3.42		(1-tail)
						d.f.=42	
	high	19		4.58	2.69		
Nascency			|Dom-NDom|	2.18	0.0349		
	low	25		2.88	2.46		(2-tail)
						d.f.=42	
	Group 2	18		4.67	2.74		
Profile Groups			|Dom-NDom|	2.28	0.0277		
(earlier/later)	Group 1	26		2.89	2.41		(2-tail)
						d.f.=42	

Another way to observe this pattern in the data is to look at three dichotomized variables at a time as in the following table (Table 5).

Table 5

Prevalence of each form of cognition by nascency category and the other type of cognition (all variables split at the means)

	Percent highly NDom Dom category:		Percent highly Dom NDom category:	
	high	low	high	low
Nascency category:				
high	50%	89%*	38%	83%*
	[10]	[9]	[13]	[6]
low	46%	50%	50%	54%
	[13]	[12]	[12]	[13]
Ho: 50% per cell	* z=2.34, p < .05		* z=1.98, p > .05	

Here you can see that for the groups of utterances low on nascency whether high or low on Dom scores, about half the utterances are also high on NDom scores. But for the groups high on nascency, this is true only for the utterances high on Dom scores. For the Highly Nascent, low Dom utterances, a very high proportion (89%) are high on NDom scores. Perhaps the cognitive functions, when Ms. C became nascent, did get more balanced, but not in the same utterances. Rather, we might say that the two modes "found their niches" by *alternating* utterance bursts, or "cooperating," as it were, such that if one mode was high, the other "waited its turn." The right half of Table 5 shows the same pattern highlighting Dom rather than NDom. For the low nascency utterances, regardless of NDom scores, about half the utterances were high on Dom. But for the highly nascent utterances, if Dom was high, only 38% were also high on NDom. If NDom was low for these highly nascent utterances, on the other hand, 83% of the Dom scores were high.

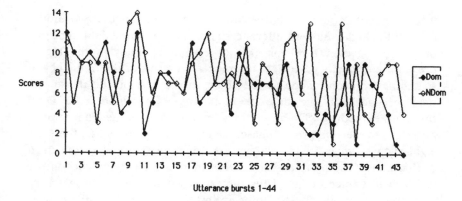

Figure 4 : Dom and NDom over the Interview

Figure 4 shows this effect graphically. Many of the utterances in the first two thirds of the interview have scores on both NDom and Dom at similar or the same levels. But in the last third of the interview, if one of these variables is high, the other tends to be low, and there is a precise alternation of which mode is higher from utterance to utterance for those numbered 34 through 39.

DISCUSSION

To review the findings, then, we found that the utterance bursts which scored high on the Pregnancy variable also scored high on L-mode cognition. The utterances scored high on the Parturiency variable also scored high on R-mode cognition. These two findings are consistent with expectations based on clinical impressions. For the highly nascent utterances, however, we did not find what I predicted. Rather than finding that each utterance had more equal levels of both kinds of cognition involved, we found that highly nascent utterances had a greater *disparity* between the levels of involvement of the two kinds of cognition than those less nascent.

This leads me to re-interpret the kind of "greater balance" which is involved in Ms. C's nascent thinking[3]. Perhaps "balance" is not the most apt metaphor. Rather than both kinds of cognition appearing at high levels in each utterance, we find one or the other taking precedence, with alternation of which mode is dominant from one utterance to the next. Thus the kind of participation the two modes have in the highly nascent utterances appears from these data to be one of greater "cooperation" or ease of turntaking than in the highly pregnant and highly parturient utterances. In terms of the frequency of switching from one mode to the other, in the first profile phase, the most pregnant of the three, there is only one switch from Dom functions exceeding NDom functions (to *vice versa)* in the ten utterance bursts. In the second profile phase, the more parturient phase, there are eight such switches in the sixteen utterance bursts. And in the third profile phase, the most nascent phase, there are eight switches in the eighteen utterance bursts. Thus the increased frequency of switching from mode to mode appears to begin in the second profile phase, with the difference in the level of mode involvements within utterances becoming the greatest in the nascent phase.

What is suggested to be by these findings is that there may be a kind of "psychological crowding" involved in the pregnant and parturient phases, in which the two kinds of cognition are both trying to "have their say" each step of the way on the problem at hand. To the extent that this idea is appropriate, it would not be too surprising that a person, when highly pregnant, is not receptive to "help" from outside. If already crowded internally, additional input may only add to the crowding. Thus we may see here the beginnings of an explanation for the difference I have observed clinically before between pregnant and nascent in readiness for input and ability to take advantage of available help and perspectives from outside. Perhaps the person must first come to an inner cooperation of modes before they can welcome help from outside or be understanding of someone else's perspective.

Additional research is suggested here. Can it be shown that a person is differentially receptive to various kinds of input depending on which focusing phase they are in? Are there some kinds of help to which the person is receptive and others not in each phase? Perhaps, for example, the inconsistency of findings correlating Accurate Empathy to Experiencing (Klein, Mathieu-Coughlan, & Kiesler, 1986) has to do with differential importance of empathy depending on focusing phase.

It would also be valuable to determine if over the course of therapy, the balance of cognitive functions and focusing phases seen in a session can be expected to be different, depending on where in the course one is (initial session, tenth session, pre-termination session, termination session, e.g.). There also may be periods during the therapy that have different proportions than others but not in such a regular way. Perhaps during the beginning of a compulsion to repeat (Freud, 1914; Miller, 1986) we would see a preponderance of the L-mode cognitive functions, or more of the pregnant phase during therapy sessions than after several sessions have been devoted to the vicissitudes of such a re-enactment.

A question that ought to be asked across theoretical orientations is "which therapist responses and activities correlate with subsequent client utterances in each of the focusing phases?" The focusing phase variables have been designed so that they can be applied to therapy process from any orientation. The related question put in a negative way is "which therapist activities and responses correspond to the *failure* to proceed from one focusing phase to the next?" An initial hypothesis is that inadequate empathy to what is said and expressed in the pregnant phase would prevent movement to the parturient phase. A related hypothesis would be that interpretation during the pregnant phase will delay the shift to the parturient phase. Another hypothesis would be that reflection or interpretation during the parturient phase which varies much from the client's wording will be followed by a return to the pregnant phase.

Another cross-orientation question is whether the utterance bursts as here defined, differ or are comparable for different theoretical orientations of therapy. If different, how does this interact with scores on the phase variables and the mode variables?

And additional research is needed to further validate the meaning of the focusing phases. What else correlates to these variables? Here we have begun to see what progressing through the three phases involves cognitively. But what else is involved, and what other variables will corroborate or disprove these findings?

What other variables correspond to the differences found here in the involvement of the cognitive modes? Can it be shown that there are advantages to the more "cooperative" mode involvement we found in the nascent phase? Is it preferred by the client? Does the therapist have preferences or feelings about it? Although Ms. C did not know explicitly about the differences reported here in cognitive functioning, she did have very positive things to say about the effect of this focusing on her mood and her involvement in her school program for several weeks after the session. Do other significant people in the client's life comment on this outcome of therapy if asked? Does it correspond to certain findings on the therapy session report form (Orlinsky & Howard, 1986)?

A final matter I would like to address is what the difference is between the two sets of ideas related to each other in this study. It is not the case that the focusing phases and the two cognitive modes pick up exactly the same things in the client's process in therapy. Although there is a productive overlap that has here generated some interesting questions for further research, there is also at least one difference that I want to emphasize. I noticed this most clearly when working with students who were rating a videotape of a client in therapy with these scales. It became most apparent that the cognitive categories in either mode do not capture the phase-distinct ways that the body carries the experiencing that is being talked about. When Pregnant, the face seems rather fixed or static, and the body and brow appear tense or worried. In the Parturient phase, when a felt sense forms, it is quite evident in the person's body that a special kind of feeling experience is happening. For example, a person's face typically flushes slightly, and there is a sort of fluidity to facial lines and expression that was not present in the Pregnant phase. This gives the impression of a certain tenderness toward their experience that was not present in the Pregnant phase. While Parturient, the person's gaze is generally not engaged with the therapist. In the Nascent phase, the body often appears still relaxed and mobile, with the face frequently "aglow" with energy. But in Nascent, in contrast to Parturient, the expression is more often in relation to the therapist.

These bodily events are not captured in the cognitive categories of Table 1. It is just this difference, in fact, which gets at the special purpose of the focusing phases, which is to capture some of the essential *therapeutic* features of a verbal process. Without such bodily processing of the meaning of what is discussed, even balanced cognition could be entirely intellectualization. What these results suggest for this subject, is that the bodily experience of the meaning that was discussed verbally, when it progressed through the three focusing phases, correlated with a *spontaneous* change in the involvement of the cognitive functions such that the two established a more regular rhythm or higher frequency of alternation from one utterance burst to the next. Will we find the same pattern for other subjects? Will we find systematic differences in the profiles of focusing phases and cognitive modes for different diagnostic categories of people?

In closing, I would like to express my appreciation to Ms. C for allowing me to use the film of her work with me for this research. I believe there is an important contribution made by it to our understanding of what is involved in focusing, and to the extent that these *are* orientation-free measures (Goldfried, 1980), to psychotherapy in general.

NOTES

1. It may be taxing to the reader, but a different formulation of focusing is here necessary and appropriate. The necessity arises from my goal, which is to develop research measures which will be applicable to any form of therapy, not just client-centered. To achieve this, I must identify focusing in the way that it comes without explicit prompting. The appropriateness is based in Gendlin's philosophical work, which is basic to focusing. As long as I maintain functional equality (Gendlin, 1962, p. 214) in relation to the phenomenon we call "focusing," another formulation is *desirable* to further illuminate it, particularly when there is a specific purpose to be served by doing so.
2. The time series plots (profiles) of pregnant and nascent scores are obviously not in statistical control. However, regression modeling confirms that the relationships reported here are not artifacts of autocorrelation or time trends. Contact that author for further statistical details.
3. Until these findings are replicated with other subjects, we can only generalize to the universe of Ms.C's utterances in such interactions, since that is the universe from which we sampled.

REFERENCES

Campbell, D.T., & Fiske, D.W. (1959). Convergent and discriminant validation by the multitrait-multimethod matrix. *Psychological Bulletin, 56,* 81-105.

Freud, S. (1914). Recollection, repetition, and working through. In *Sigmund Freud: Collected papers* (Vol. 2, pp. 366-376). New York: Basic Books.

Gendlin, E.T. (1962). *Experiencing and the creation of meaning.* New York: The Free Press of Glencoe.

Gendlin, E.T. (1964). A theory of personality change. In P. Worchel & D. Byrne (Eds.), *Personality change*. New York: Wiley.

Gendlin, E.T. (1969). Focusing. *Psychotherapy: Theory, Research, and Practice, 6,* 4-15.

Gendlin, E.T. (1978). *Focusing.* New York: Everest House.

Gendlin, E.T. (1981). *Focusing* (revised 2nd ed.). New York: Bantam.

Goldfried, M. (1980). Toward the delineation of therapeutic change principles. *American Psychologist, 35,* 991-999.

Hogarth, R.M. (1978). "A note on aggregating opinions." *Organizational Behavior and Human Performance, 21,* 40-46.

Iberg, J.R. (1988). *Empathy and cognitive functions: A presentation postponed.* Submitted for publication.

Klein, M., Mathieu-Coughlan, P., & Kiesler, D. (1986). The experiencing scales. In L.S. Greenberg & W.M. Pinsof (Eds.), *The psychotherapeutic process: A research handbook.* New York: Guilford.

Levy, J. (1980). Cerebral asymmetry and the psychology of man. In M.C. Wittrock (Ed.), *The brain and psychology.* New York: Academic Press.

Levy, J., Trevarthen, C., & Sperry, R.W. (1972). Perception of bilateral chimeric figures following hemispheric deconnection. *Brain, 95,* 61-78.

Miller, A. (1986). *Thou shalt not be aware: Society's betrayal of the child.* (Trans. by H. & H. Hannum). New York: New American Library.

Nunnally, J. (1967). *Psychometric theory.* New York: McGraw-Hill.

Orlinsky, D.E. & Howard, K.I. (1986). The psychological interior of psychotherapy: Explorations with the therapy session reports. In L.S. Greenberg & W.M. Pinsof (Eds.), *The psychotherapeutic process: A research handbook.* New York: Guilford.

Rice, L.N., & Kerr, G.P. (1986). Measures of client and therapist vocal quality. In L.S. Greenberg & W.M. Pinsof (Eds.), *The psychotherapeutic process: A research handbook.* New York: Guilford.

Rogers, C.R. (1957). The necessary and sufficient conditions of therapeutic personality change. *Journal of Consulting Psychology, 21,* 95-103.

Russell, R.L., & Staszewski, C. (1988). The unit problem: Some systematic distinctions and critical dilemmas for psychotherapy process research. *Psychotherapy, 25,* 191-200.

APPENDIX A. RATING MANUAL OF FOCUSING PHASES

PREGNANT PHASE:
S1. Self or other characterized in trait-type language
   - "they are both emotionally immature."
   - "I do feel heartless and cruel."
S2. Theories put forth to explain behavior or feelings
   - "So when I walk into Madison at any time of the day and no matter what I'm doing, I feel safe because it's a smaller town and I've been there for 4 years and the people are young people because it's a college town - you

know, the majority - and so that anything I do - even if I had a job there - would be easier than New York city and so that's why it's scary."

- "I talk to my parents less than I used to, I guess, cause I'm getting older and I'm more independent and I can do things myself much more easily like you would expect."

S3. Comparisons made of self and other

- "I'm so emotional with my love and expressing my emotion that... my family is very emotional and very open and her family isn't as much and you can definitely see the two upbringings are different."

- "I look at all the other people in school and the working wives in this neighborhood and it's like, well everyone else can do all this stuff and they do it really well, and I can too. I'm just not planning or whatever."

S4. Nonverbal cues of emotion not explicitly said. This may include posture, gestures, facial expression, voice inflection, and rhythm, cadence and volume changes of verbal delivery.

- "And nice presents (grinning)."

- "I could forget about all the past hurts. Ok, I really think I could forgive that. But I don't want a bunch of future hurts (laughing)."

S5. Awash in emotion or avoidance of emotion

- "T: You feel a little bit sad that you don't have that? (face looks very sad) C: Sort of. I must say, though, that I think it's rare that that happens with anybody. It's kind of a drag."

- "T: It's good your mother understands. C: It took her long enough. Finally she understands me a little. (tears) (pause) I'm not supposed to show weakness (crying)."

S6. Cognitive grasp of implications expressed

- "And it's costing me now cause even though I know what I want to do, I'm not as well informed about what I want to do than I would be if I had started a little sooner."

- "I can't talk to the doctor about this because I was pretty upset the last time I visited my therapist and he put me in the hospital, you know. Checked me in."

S7. Reporting a pertinent sequence of events

- "We took this long trip once. It was like a ten hour drive and there were four adults and two kids. Six to fit in the car. Well, I sat in the back with the two kids. And then my brother and his wife and someone else sat in the front seat and for ten straight hours of the trip they said less than three sentences to me sitting in the back seat where the three of them were constantly talking."

- "He's bitching at me because I got this, as he puts it, 'hundred year old goddam thing' out over there. That Chinese temple I have? It's a hundred years old. He wants me to get rid of it, throw it in the garbage. He's complaining that I got too much crap all over the place. All I got left is just a few books. Just a little, not even half the art supplies, most of it is in the garbage. All those paintings I threw out. All the furniture I had is gone. The only thing I took with me was the bed."

S8. Making interpretations of someone else's feelings or motivations

- "He seemed more withdrawn and less available. It was hard for me to make contact with him and I felt it was that he was depressed about his wife's illness."
- "She's pretty closed to a lot of people, and pretty closed to herself."

PARTURIENT PHASE

P1. Emotions directly in evidence and referred to as a datum
- "I feel really trapped - it's a little hard to breathe."
- "I feel sad. There's a lump in my throat right now."

P2. Process commentary: Noting how one is relating to "it," expressed preferences for how to proceed
- "I'm surprised to find this reaction in myself. But it's ok, kind of nice, in a way. I'd like to feel this more often."
- "As bad as that sounds even to me saying it now."

P3. Tentative remarks about its meaning
- "It's easy for me to meet somebody and talk with them right off. But then the thing is, I don't know (pause) I don't know (pause, small laugh) I don't know. I was going to say that, uh, I was going to say that uh, I didn't know if after I get to know somebody, does my friendliness change or does something change where, I don't know. It seems like I don't relate after a while."
- "I don't know if that was because I want to or I did not have a choice."

P4. Statements of qualities of emotion in reaction to talking/thinking about the topic.
- "You know, even though it's very sad, it feels somehow good to be feeling it."
- "It's real comforting to hear you say that. It's amazing. Sitting here listening to myself it's like, what I just said about - why did I say what I just said about my family? It's like even things that come out of my mouth, I just, your mind works so fast you can't even hear as it's coming out."

P5. References made to more meaning felt than is understood
- "Yeah, I do feel sad. I really, really, do. I don't know why but I do. Well, I got a lot to feel sad about."
- "It's hard to explain. I'm not sure why it was an amazing discovery, but it was."

P6. Descriptions of changes in the body quality as they occur: "Play by play" narrative
- "I feel tired about this. This is heavy on my mind."
- "Now that I'm talking about this, it's becoming more hurt than anger."

P7. Quiet non-verbal time spent sensing for "it"
- "I feel (pause) something like regret. But not quite (pause). It's, it's tinged with sorrow."

P8. Certain words or analogies favored because of their special fit with feelings
- "I still get kind of like irritated. No, perturbed about some things that went

on."
- "It's kind of heavy, but it's not like heavy heavy. It's like special heavy. It's like sad heavy. It's like (pause) a part of me says... just sadness for what I've chosen to give up. It's almost like wistfulness, like at the end of a movie."

NASCENT PHASE

N1. Statement of perspective that wasn't there before - relief to better understand
- "Now that you say that back, it's like 'oh, maybe that is his way of getting back at me for getting all the attention when I was a kid. I mean, I was the center of attention. I was the youngest and I did get all the attention from everyone and now maybe that is the way to get back at someone, to not give them the attention now. I never thought of that."

N2. Disentanglement of one's own feelings and values from how someone else feels/is
- "I mean, there's no reciprocity there you know, sharing the good times as well as the bad, and that should be the whole basis of a relationship and that's just not there. I think to myself, I can definitely have something better than this. I'm not sure how important, if at all, this is to him."

N3. New clarity regarding what is at issue for one personally
- "I guess she's hurt me a lot too, and I hadn't really thought about that."

N4. Purer, more refined or complete expressions of relationship to the other
- "Yea. (pause) You never know when (long pause) I don't know, I do feel I like (pause, sigh) I'm afraid that the way I acted at times with him that I didn't (pause), I didn't let him know that I loved him, or, you know, I'm afraid like I ignored him and that he, that I, you know, I just am sorry about that (long pause)."

N5. Description of emotional developments with perspective and increased equanimity
- (after starting out anxious about an audition) "But even if that happened now, it wouldn't be so terrible. I could stand that. I'm not the same as I was then, and it wouldn't be as devastating. I'm older now. Also, I'm young enough so that if that happened consistently, I would know the answer to whether this is what I'm meant to do or not. That's part of what I want to find out, and it's better to find it out now than when I'm forty."

N6 Emotions that are new and different appear
- (following the expression of sadness in example b under P8) "that makes me sad. But in that same area, like sharing that same area with the sadness, is happiness too."

N7. Discovery of memories relevant to the feelings
- "I can still see in my mind, the time I brought home a bad report card, he took his knife out and said he was going to cut my balls off. I think I was in first grade."

N8. Realization of a significance to the topic greater than formerly appreciated
- "Now that I start to think about it, how much this really does affect me! (tears)."

APPENDIX B. RATING MANUAL OF COGNITIVE FUNCTIONS

DOMINANT HEMISPHERE:

A. Linguistic processing: examining the use of words that is involved
- "I used to just categorize them into relationships. I even have my relationships categorized from close friends, good friends, acquaintances."
- "It wouldn't be so bad, but it's the third time it's happened"
B. Logic and deduction: Drawing conclusions based on logical relationships and certain premises.
- "There must be something wrong with me because people just don't go around doing this."
- "I'm sure as a child being taken from its mother, I must have had some separation problems."
C. Analysis: A bit more elaborate than B., but the same in spirit. There is a clear effort to "figure something out" through reasoning.
- "Maybe because I wasn't dealt with about it: At least I can't recall. Probably because I was too young. They probably thought I was too young - 'two years old, what does she know'."
D. Sequential thought and patterns: Linear thinking which follows a step by step pattern, especially chronologically, and/or that identifies sequential patterns in things
- "It was like this pattern with me where I always create distance between people who I really care about."
- "He went out with her first and then me, and then with her again after we discussed how serious we were, so it was obvious who he liked better."
E. Naming tasks: Characterizing the person or thing as a whole with a verbal label or labels.
- "He's a pretty sensitive, nice person."
- "He's a slick mover."
- "I'm not that smart."
F. Identifying distinctive subordinate features: Naming aspects of persons or things with verbal labels. The emphasis is on characterizing various qualities, rather than the person or thing as a whole.
- "He has focus on his goals, and brightness, and a cute sense of humor."
- "It was the mustache I remember."

NON-DOMINANT HEMISPHERE

I. Visuo-spatial construction: Generating a visual image to express a thought or experience

- "it's almost like a boxer who goes out and starts fighting and he wins and wins, but somewhere along the line he's going to face an opponent who's stronger, maybe younger..."
- "We're in the same boat, but we're rowing in opposite direction!"

II. Recording literal properties of the physical world. Features of experience are told with minimum interpretation, and maximum simple description of events and things.
- "We hung out for about 30 minutes, and then we ended up leaving, and going back to my house and partying, having a nice time, and then I went abroad for a few weeks, no, actually for 13 days, and he said he'd call me, and he did."

III. Visualizing relationships of objects in space
- "I didn't want to sit there and watch her glare at me for an hour."
- "I actually have it pictured in my mind how big each of those things are."

IV. Words perceived as unanalyzed wholes. Although analysis may follow these, when introduced, such words are presented as meaningful in themselves.
- "I have that same feeling that I had when I dropped out of high school, which is *'I hate going here, I hate this whole thing!'*."
- "When he did that, it really *bothered* me."

V. Matching tasks. Whenever two things are compared to each other.
- "I think torturing the dog is a little safer than stealing a car."
- "No, it's not quite the same as you said."

VI. Extracting a critical invariant of form. Identifying something that characterizes the essence of the person or object as a whole, but for the first time, rather than placing it in an existing verbal category (as in E. naming tasks).
- "At this point, I can see that I've always been more geared to working full time than going to school."

THE SMALL STEPS OF THE THERAPY PROCESS: HOW THEY COME AND HOW TO HELP THEM COME[1]

Eugene T. GENDLIN
University of Chicago, U.S.A.

THE PRIMACY OF HUMAN PRESENCE

I want to start with the most important thing I have to say: The essence of working with another person is to be present as a living being. And that is lucky, because if we had to be smart, or good, or mature, or wise, then we would probably be in trouble. But, what matters is not that. What matters is to be a human being with another human being, to recognize the other person as another being in there. Even if it is a cat or a bird, if you are trying to help a wounded bird, the first thing you have to know is that there is somebody in there, and that you have to wait for that "person," that being in there, to be in contact with you. That seems to me to be the most important thing.

So, when I sit down with someone, I take my troubles and feelings and I put them over here, on one side, close, because I might need them. I might want to go in there and see something. And I take all the things that I have learnt - client-centered therapy, reflection, focusing, Gestalt, psycho-analytic concepts and everything else (I wish I had even more) - and I put them over here, on my other side, close. Then I am just here, with my eyes, and there is this other being. If they happen to look into my eyes, they will see that I am just a shaky being. I have to tolerate that. They may not look. But if they do, they will see that. They will see the slightly shy, slightly withdrawing, insecure existence that I am, I have learnt that that is O.K. I do not need to be emotionally secure and firmly present. I just need to be present. There are no qualifications for the kind of person I must be. What is wanted for the big therapy process, the big development process is a person who will be present. And so I have gradually become convinced that even I can be that. Even though I have my doubts when I am by myself, in some objective sense I know I am a person.

And then it is true that I reach in for a lot of different things. But when it gets murky and I am not sure I am connected to the other person, then I do not reach in for these things, then I must reflect that person's meanings and stay very close, so that the connection re-establishes. When the client is going around in circles and does not touch down inside, then I might offer a bit of how to do "focusing." And if I see that there is too much focusing, and a sort of "internality" without enough energy coming out, then I might do something like "Gestalt," or I might just express myself, or I might do any number of things. I may express my feeling, but I always know that it is just my feeling. I do not know yet what is coming from that person. The minute something goes wrong I go right back to trying to sense this person; to what is happening. Because this is another being, a different being.

When I think back to the struggle that Carl had with non-directive reflecting, always trying to drop whatever it was he had written, to re-establish the reality of the contact, I feel I am following in his footsteps. He dropped non-directive and he made it client-centered, he dropped client-centered and made it person-centered. First he had the method of reflecting, then he said: "No that is not it, it is the attitudes ..." But we could take his three attitudes and get very technical about them. He would say: "No, no, it is person-centered."

So this is my way of saying that: Do not let focusing, or reflecting, or anything else get in between. Do not use it as an in-between. Do not say: "I can stay here because I have my reflecting-method, I have my ping-pong-paddle, so you cannot get me. You say something? You get it back." There is a sense that we are armed, you see. We have methods; we know focusing; we have credentials; we have doctors. We have all this stuff and so it is easy for us to sit there with stuff in between. Do not let it be in between; put it out of the way. You can have at least as much courage as the client has. If not, I would be ashamed of myself, with all the stuff that I have, if I still cannot really look when this person can. So I want to be there in that same way.

That - I think - is the first job we have. And on the question what we client-centered people need to do now, on this, also, I think the first thing we need to do is to communicate that attitude. That is so necessary in a field that is becoming more and more "professional," which is to say useless and expensive.

CLIENT-CENTERED REFLECTING AS
A BASELINE FOR USING ANY OTHER METHOD

The second thing we need is to communicate the "empathic response," to communicate client-centered reflecting to those who use other methods, and we need to add many other methods to our own. I have always said that client-centered reflecting is a necessary baseline, for using other things. If you do not have that, then you cannot stay in touch with the person. If you do not constantly ask "Oh you did not like that?" or "Oh something funny happened now"; if you do not constantly stop and check, then using any other method is going to be bad. Certainly that includes focusing. I mean, the minute it clouds up and the person looks like: "What are you doing to me?," you have to stop whatever you are doing and you have to say: "You did not like that?" "Something went wrong?" "What just happened?" And then you must listen. Also, as soon as something works, or the moment a step comes in the client, we must stop and listen responsively, just to that. The client-centered reflecting-method is the central thing *with which* to use everything else.

But what I want to tell that you have not heard is that we must add client-centered listening to the other methods. It is unbelieveable that after all these years, we have totally failed to communicate client-centered listening in such a way that the *other* practitioners could have it. How can they go so long without it? How can they be so stupid? But then, I realize, that is largely our fault. We have told them that if one does client-centered listening, then one does nothing else, so, of course, they cannot have it, because they are already doing something else and they know that that is helpful. They are not going to give that up. They cannot "unknow" what they know. It is important to communicate the client-centered reflection method as something that one can *add* to whatever one is doing. We can tell them that *some* of us do nothing else; that is how powerful this thing is. *Some* of us prefer to do nothing but that. Others among us combine many things. So they can add *this* thing to whatever they are doing. *That* is the way to communicate the reflection-method. And if the others try it even a few times, then they will discover what we know.

HUMAN NATURE:
IMPOSED FORM VERSUS AN ORDER OF STEPS

The third job we have, is to communicate how very different our philosophical assumptions are, compared to everything else in the field. I have recently gone into this more and more. Some of the theories I thought I respected, make assumptions that I never realized they did. I see now that this has been the difficulty in communicating with a lot of people, not just *my* difficulty but all of our difficulty.

1. The psychoanalytic concepts assume that the body has no behavioral order at all; that it has a fixed biological machinery, but no behavioral organization. To put it in Freud's terms: The "Id" consists of unorganized drive-energies. In order for that "cauldron" (he also calls it) of drive energies to discharge - that is his term for doing something - the body requires the social patterns. Every human action - he assumes - is patterned by patterns which are imposed from the outside, on the body. We have been arguing with them for years about imposing things on clients, but look deeper. There is nothing but imposed organization in that theory! That is the only kind of order there is. The body is assumed to have no order for behavior, and no interaction from itself.

As most of you know, I am also in philosophy (Gendlin, 1962/1970). In the last ten years or so, my philosophical colleagues have discovered psychotherapy; but the psychotherapy they have discovered is of course psychoanalytic psychotherapy. They love Freud because he comes from the same assumptions that they know. All order - as they think about it - is imposed order. All order consists of patterns which are put on the body. The only kind of order they conceive of is some sort of forms. It used to be relational forms, now it has become social forms. That also makes cultural relativism pervasive. Sometimes it is not even mentioned because it seems so obvious. Obviously, people are different in different cultures. There is no bodily organization of behavior. There is only what the different cultures impose. There are only different forms of "human." There is no "human nature." If we do not think that, then we are not only silly, but unconscious of our own cultural programming. We are unconscious of how controlled we are. We have internalized the social patterns so deeply that we then discover them inside, and think we are free. This is a serious question. If we say that persons and bodies have an internal self-organizing, they will have pity for us. How can we show, how can we even know, when we are externally programmed, and when not?

From Descartes to Heidegger (whom I like a lot) there are only cultural humans; there is no human. Heidegger talks with a Japanese scholar. He tells him: We cannot talk with each other. We have to be very careful because nothing we say is the same. Everything is totally different. It would be all right to say that cultures differ, but he thinks that everything is *totally* different because there is nothing under that: No body, and no person.

Now, the only order is imposed forms. But now, my philosophical colleagues are questioning forms, which for them means that they are questioning everything. Now, they have nothing. They are all saying that there is no human subject. What they are really saying is: They do not know how to think about human subjects. But there are people who can, and that is you. I would like you to take that job on. The philosophical community has not discovered psychotherapy other than psychoanalysis yet. They have not heard from you yet. I think they should. I think you should know that right now they are in a very "open" position to hear you because they have exhausted what they have, and they cannot think about themselves and each other. It is an interesting juncture and I urge you to find some philosophers and talk to them. With Carl Rogers we have been pioneers for thirty years. Now people have caught up almost to the point where they might be able to hear us.

2. Now I want to tell you of my philosophical model. I want to talk about a kind of order that is not "forms." There is another kind of order; persons and bodies have that other kind. It is not forms stamped on, not patterns, shapes, distinct, fixed laws. Instead, it is an "order of steps." Let me say what kind of steps I mean.

There is this rhythm in client-centered therapy: First, the client says something. You say it back and get it wrong. Then they correct it. You accept the correction and they say: "Yes, that is right... but, not completely..." They give you the next tightening. You take that in, too. Then they say, "Yes," with a breath of relief.

And then there is a *characteristic* silence there. And in that silence, the next thing comes. Usually that next thing is deeper, perhaps not every time. You reflect that, again they correct it, you include the correction, they add a specification, you include that too. Again there is a breath, a sigh - and that silence.

That silence is very characteristic. When I teach listening in a round, in class, I point it out. Each student is listened to by the one on the right. Each one talks until - that silence comes. After a very few silent moments, the student says "I am finished, go on to the next person." I tell the class: "Notice the silence that comes there. It is part of what listening is for. What you had ready to say has been heard and responded to. Now you have nothing to say, and yet you sense the problem. It is not all resolved, of course. You have an unclear sense of it - right there - an unclear edge. You sense it physically, without more words.

Here, in class, you do not want to let the others wait, so you say "Go on to the next person." But when you are alone with your therapist-partner, then I hope you will stay in that silence, with that unclear sense, right there, until the next thing comes, from it.

The word "focusing" means to spend time, attending to that inwardly sensed edge. When that happens in the silence, the next thing and the next come gradually from deeper and deeper. Some clients talk all the time, and skip that silence. Some use the silence only to think of something to say. Some feel only the same emotions, over and over. Just talking and expressing does help, and change-steps can come in conversation, and in other ways, inadvertantly, - but often they do not. When the client passes by all the meaningful spots, you might slow the pace, just by reflecting more slowly, perhaps one spot several times. You might sometimes ask clients what they sense, directly, here, in the middle of the body. Also, it is not intrusive to say that we can stay with that unclear edge, there, where the whole thing feels not O.K. I often say: "It's all right to stay here a while, just to sense that." These are bits of focusing-instructions given *during* therapy interviews.

In Belgium I learned that some therapists arrange to teach focusing to each other's clients, *outside* therapy (Leijssen, 1989). In Chicago, too, we have tought focusing to clients in week-end workshops. We found it extremely helpful to the ongoing therapy. There are many ways to teach focusing. I use every method I ever learned on a client-centered base-line. I give bits of focusing-instruction during the sessions. But I can understand that you might be opposed to doing that. On the other hand, I know that you are not against people attending to the sensed edge, where these steps arise. In that sense no one is opposed to focusing. Whether and how to teach it is an issue.

We also need to train our therapists to recognize and respond to focusing, since it often happens naturally. Some therapists do not understand when a client refers to a felt edge. Instead of pointing the response there, these therapists miss that sensed intricacy, which cannot yet be said. They bring everything back only to round, closed, common notions and named feelings. It gets in the way (Hendricks, 1986).

Now I want to turn to the philosophical question about which I am urging you to communicate with philosophers (Gendlin, 1987). They think that when a client says something pathological, seemingly irrational, or exhibit some deficit, you must impose some better pattern. The philosophers think that such steps can only be imposed on experience, by the therapist. You have all listened to such steps. What comes has a characteristic novelty and intricacy. You can tell that neither you nor the client could have invented them. The philosophers think that aside from the socially imposed rationality there is nothing else in people but irrationality. You have often noticed something else: Such steps do not follow by logic, and yet they make sense - we can follow them. They have a certain kind of order, different from logic and from irrationality, something deeper, more exact, more specific, more intricate; maybe not everytime but often.

We are well acquainted with that "order of steps." I call it "carrying forward." It changes as it moves forward. "An order of steps," or you can say: "An order of carrying forward." When you look back from the fourth or the fifth or the seventeenth step, back to where that began, that seemingly silly, wrong or pathological thing or deficit, you will not remember all the turns it took. But, on a tape you can see the steps I am talking about. Those steps have a continuity, but it is not a logical continuity. It is not a continuity of form. If it were a continuity of form, it would be a logical continuity. It would remain silly or pathological or a deficit. If that thing kept its form, we would not get anywhere. Our therapy-method would not work, and I think therapy as a whole would not work.

This content, which has an exact form that we reflect, and strain until we get it exactly, that exact form in some way is also not *just* that exact form, since it gives rise to these steps. That is the order I want to talk about; an order that has very exact forms and yet it is not just those exact forms. It can give rise to a progression, which, looking back, shows that it was more than just those forms, even though it seemed to take those forms. To get the steps, we have to reflect exactly; I am not saying those forms are not there. I am not saying those forms do not matter. I am saying: Something here which is very very exact and formed, is also not just formed but gives rise to steps. That is the kind of order and model I want to talk about.

You have argued with other people. They will say that these steps come from the fact that you as the therapist are in some ways biased. They used to say that Carl Rogers smiled at certain times and that is what made the client go this way or that way. Remember that literature? That he gave unconscious reinforcement. They also say that reflecting exactly is impossible. Nobody can be neutral, as if the words we say brought some new thing to the client. But, the steps do not come from us. They surprise us all the time. We cannot derive the next step.

These people only know an order of forms. So, they say: "If something new happens, you must be sneaking it in somehow, because it can only come from the outside, because there is nothing in there that could make something. And of course the only thing that you could be imposing is some kind of socialization, something that you got from the outside also." That is the only way they can think about it. And, if one thinks about it only in terms of form, then they would be right. In forms there is no human nature, only late twentieth century Dutch nature, or whatever you happen to be. Nobody can come up with a set of forms that are what human beings are. But if you look at the step-process, if you look at the carrying forward, if you are talking about an order where something more keeps happening, then I think we are all the same. And that kind of order is not so silly. And they have not thought of that. But we see that in client-centered therapy all the time.

These steps come in interaction. But interaction, when *they* think about it, is "imposing some kind of pattern." Interaction when we think about it is "carrying forward," picking up on where the person is, making contact with where the person really is. And the very contact changes the form. Now, with focusing, you can prove the point. (I am being cute now.) When you reflect verbally in a client-centered way, they can go on forever saying: "You are bringing in something new." But we find in focusing that when somebody is sitting with you *in total silence,* you can focus much more deeply and much more easily than you can alone. I have conducted thousands of trials on this particular thing with one subject, namely me: I focus by myself. Then I ask the next kind person to keep me company while I focus on the same thing. I always get further. Almost always; if I do not have any trouble with that person. The interaction is a different variable than the content. The interaction continues in silence, the very silence I was talking about. The steps come in an interactional process.

Now I am going to say: The steps *are* an interactional process.

When I worked with Carl Rogers: Either he took on my theoretical things or I took on his and of course I took more of his than he took of mine, but the one wrinkle that I do not remember succeeding in selling him was my argument that the three conditions are sufficient without the proviso that the client has to *perceive* them. He said: Genuineness, empathy and positive regard, *and* that the client perceives those. I do not think that is necessary; I know that perception is not necessary, because many clients are convinced for a year or two that nobody could possibly like them or understand them, and the process works anyway and eventually changes their perception. How would they ever get around to perceiving that the therapist *did* actually understand? That is a change. I know, because I was that kind of client. I always knew that this nice man could not possibly understand my stuff. It took me a long time before I noticed that when I walked into the room, I was already different. The interaction affects you, long before you can think about it. At least sometimes. It is in the interaction or as an interaction, that these steps come.

There is also a special case of interaction, when we respond to ourselves. That is also an interaction. You do not just find out: You are not just a kind of a light that does not change anything. When you give your awareness to something, it is carried forward. That is why it is so powerful to attend inside. It seems like you are doing nothing. Just as the presence of a human being looks like nothing. To be aware directly inside, is a carrying forward process. But the interaction with another person remains more powerful and I have always said that.

The carrying forward order is not always understood. For example, now there is a new theory about "narrative;" people are said to bring meaning into their lives by construing life as a certain story. I think they are perfectly silly writing like that, as if you could put any story on any set of events in your life. I think it *is* true, what they are *trying* to say: That we look back and try to construe the life we had. But the meaning we try to give to it has to carry forward; it has to connect with our bodily experiences, so that we say: "Oh, yes (breath, physical relief), it *can* mean that ..." They do not have the concept of carrying forward, so they write about it as if people were their own fiction writers, as if, with inventiveness, you could make anything out of anything. That is not so.

And that is true also about "cognitive restructuring." You have to ask: When does it work and when not? You try to think in a different way. We do this all the time. When we feel bad about something, we tell ourselves: "Look at it another way, then it is not so hard." But you must not forget to come here to the middle of your body, to see if it made you feel any different. If it did not, you have not "restructured" anything. Then you have to try still another way and another way.

Now what is it actually that is capable of being carried forward? I started by mentioning the common assumption that the body is a fixed piece of biological machinery. The body is like your automobile, they think: Fixed and obeying certain laws.

But, your mind is creative, they think. They do not explain how. Well, let me turn that upside down. How you think and formulate an event, *that* form is fixed. But, the *body-sense* of that form is capable of being carried forward. I want to change the concept of the body altogether. The body is not just a machine. The body is exactly that which is capable of these steps. The content itself, the form alone, is not going to go anywhere. It is going to have certain logical implications but it is not going to change. It is the "body sense" of the form that is capable of being carried forward. Our bodies are such that they absorb all the training, all the language, all the social forms, all the culture, everything we read and then they still imply more... Especially when you have a problem it is like that. You think all the formed facts and still it says: "AAArgghh." It is looking for a solution, or a next step that will intricately take account of all the stuff you think and still go further. It is the body sense, that can go further.

From what someone says, you can go in two different ways: You can take it logically: They said *this.* So this follows, and this follows, and this follows. You can say: "Look, what you are saying implies this and this and this." The other way you can go, the way client-centered therapists will go, is to respond to that which gives steps. We call it "feeling" but that is not a good word. I am saying that the steps come from the "body-sense." Any event, anything anyone says, can be taken in these two ways: Only as formed, or as the body-sense of that formed. I want to argue that the body-sense has all those forms and then it is still always again there, implying more, implying further.

Sometimes we want to respond to the logical form, the event as it happened as form. But as therapists, of course we want to respond to that which will produce the steps.

Now I have to bring that home a little. Every sentence that we utter, prepares the listener for "something." It begins, and then, it unrolls and... Now you do not know how I am going to finish it, but you sense what comes there. The same thing is true of my talk, up to now. You have taken it in with everything you know, and have experienced and read. Now ... you are sitting there ready for ... and I hope I have that.

The body-sense has all the forms in it, all your culture and life. And yet it implies further. It is not just a product of the events and the culture. You can see that in the silences, when therapy works. You can see it even more dramatically when clients say: "I am feeling something, but there are not words for it." They are saying that there are no social forms for it. Words are social forms. We have to wait a while until the language rearranges itself to say it oddly because there are no common phrases for it. You can help this happen if it has not happened. One way you can do that is just by slowing down; by sitting and feeling the clients' feeling when they are not doing so. You can say: "Now wait a minute, I want to feel what you told me." That makes an opportunity for them to come there too. I call that the "body-sense" because to find it, I have to attend to the literal body, here, between the podium and the wall. I have to come in here, into the middle of this body; I have to let go my attention here. I cannot do it too well while I am talking, though I can do it in short pauses. That is the body I am talking about. Now once we get in there, then it is more than what we customarily call "the body." I would want to change that concept so that it would include that.

Any time you talk, unless you are reading or memorized things in advance, how do you find the words? It is your body that talks. I have this prepared, but even so, I open my mouth and I hope the right words come out. It is all I can do. If they do not, I keep talking, hoping they will still come. That which talks is my body. I want the concept of "body" to get much wider than physiology. I am glad they have physiology, when I get sick. I am glad they know what they know. But the concept of body is wider than that, much wider than that. We live every situation with the body. If you try to do it by explicit instructions, you probably trip. Your body has to sense many things at the same time: The floor, the chair, the people, the situation, what happened to you years earlier, and what you are trying to do. You live with what I am calling "your body." The body makes and takes the next step, it wants a solution, a healing, something better, now, than it has had. There are often no words for that, because that has not happened yet. My body is capable of producing steps that have never happened in the history of the world. Isn't that glorious?! Or else you can say that I am in a worse mess than anybody knows how to help me with.

COMMENTS ON TWO THERAPY SEGMENTS

To finish, I would like to read you a couple of therapy segments. I ask you to look at the steps. These are focusing steps. That means that a silence is often felt between one step and the next. The second excerpt I will read is from a person who has done focusing for a long time. It is late in therapy. The first one is "early in therapy" and you can watch me trying to help it happen.

I have written enough about how to find this body-sense, but it is hard to convey the interactional climate around it. That is one thing I would like you to watch for. And then also: Once one knows how to find this inner edge, then it turns out that there is a lot of complexity involved, there. The crudest thing we have always said is: "Do not push and do not run away." But what *do* you do? Well, you keep it company, especially if it is *sore*. You keep *it* company. This "it," it is a funny way of talking. Sometimes when I say these things, someone will say: "You talk funny" and I say: "Yes, I know." You keep it company; I often say: "Let's keep it company."

The client and I, we are going to keep it, in there, company. As you would keep a scared child company. You would not push on it, or argue with it, or pick it up, because it is too sore, too scared or tense. You would just sit there, quietly, I really said it all in the beginning: What that edge needs to produce the steps, is only some kind of unintrusive contact or company. If you will go there with your awareness and stay there or return there, that is all it needs; it will do all the rest for you. If you do not know that awareness is a process in itself, it will seem very mysterious. It needs you there and that is all it needs. That is the sort of thing I would like to illustrate with these two segments.

Segment 1

    C: "I did not want to come today. I do not have anything more to talk about (laughs). Really, there is a level I do not want to touch. I got there once before and I got into crying and I could not get out of it; I could not stop crying. My therapist did not know what to do. She cried too. I looked up and I could see it and I thought: 'Well, she does not know what to do either'."

While she is telling me that, I think: "Well, that is obviously a good therapist." I believe, if it makes me cry, let that be visible. But at that time, it was not so good. So you never know. Or you can say: It was all right, but there should have been something further; hopefully it happens here.

    T: "You do not want to fall in there again that way."
    C: "Right. Usually, I believe in feelings and I think: If you feel it, it gets better. But on this, I don't know."
    T: "So we won't say: Just feel it. You did that and it was not better. Whatever we'll do here, you would like it to be in a different way ..."

(I do not necessarily expect agreement on that, you see, I am doing something, I am preparing some sort of focusing.)

    C: "Right." (And then there is a long silence.)
    "I can feel it right there, just below where I am."

Now that is not my jargon, O.K.? So don't blame me for that. Just think about why a person would say that. That has it all, just that one sentence: "I can feel it right there, just below where I am."

    T: "Let's stay here a long while, just relating to it down there, without going there." Or another way to say it: "If we do anything, let us do it very slowly."
    (Long silence)
    C: "The way the whole thing feels is that I am no good, and I am helpless to do anything about it. And I cannot hardly touch that."
    T: "That is hard to stand. Go slow. It is hard even just to touch that."

Now I am going to stop that excerpt, there.

Segment 2

Here is a different person:
    C: "I want to leave Chicago. The noise outside bothers me."
(Therapist is silent.)

    C: "You do not think that is real. I can tell."

Therapist is mobilizing to give a reflection. He says (I am saying):

T: "The noise is crowding in on you, coming into your 'fire-in place'."

She really knew what she was saying in fact because I have seen her for a very long time.

C: "It is like darts hitting my body. I cannot stand it."
T: "It really hurts."

And now there is one of these silences. I was willing to hear it, so it got heard and now there is the silence. And then she says:

C: "I keep feeling a sense of 'no meaning' in my life." (More silence.) "I just want to leave everything. It is that same spot where I want to die. My wanting to live and to die are so close these days. That is why I have not been able to touch this place. It gets misty there. It is real foggy."

Now I take that to be a step. First she was saying: "I am in this place where the noise hurts me" and now she is saying: "Oh that is my life and death place and when I touch it, it gets foggy." So can you derive that from the other? If I did not read it, would you have known this was coming? I do not see how you could have. I did not.

T: "You can feel wanting to live and also wanting to die, both right there, in the same inside spot and then that gets foggy there."

Now another one of these silences comes. Almost each time, there is this kind of step there.

C: "I do not want to relate with anyone; I wish there were no people to see. They do not mean anything to me. (She has to go to work after this hour.) There is no meaning. When will my life ever have meaning? It feels like it never will and I need meaning right now." (Silence ... Therapist did not respond.)
"I also feel it has to do with my relating to you. I know you are there for me, but it is like I am not allowed to want that."

Now very often in that kind of situation, I will say:"Let us, you and me, be real close and connected around this place; because in it, you do not feel any connection." That has been a real valuable thing to say, very often. "Let us relate all the way around it." It is like saying: "Let us be close," but also acknowledging that right in the center somehow there is no connection, there is an isolation. But I did not do that here. Something else happened. She said: "I also feel it has to do with my relating to you. I know you are there for me, but it is like I am not allowed to want that." So I heard the "not allowed" and it sounded different to me. So I said:

T: "Is that what you said before about your father?"

And I want to notice this therapist's single attempt at a genuine psychoanalytic interpretation. And it turns out to be very helpful also. Notice this: Very helpful. I mean really; but of course wrong, but very helpful. "Is that what you said before about your father?"Now there is this long silence again. Then she says:

> C: "No I can feel that this is not with him. This is different. It is not like with my father."

You see, she has tried it out: "It is not like that." And then, the therapist says:

> T: "It is not about him."

That is the big difference. The big difference is not that we interpret it or do not interpret it. The big difference is that we stay with the person whatever comes there. And anybody working with me knows that I am trying to do that. So they do not even bother about some of the things that I say. But she does bother. She says: "It is not about him. It is not like with my father." And I say: "It is not about him." And then there is another silence.

> C: "I can hardly touch it. There is something and it is right here on the edge, I can hardly touch it; it is ... I cannot want my mother, I can hardly say it."

And I reflect:

> T: "You cannot want her." (Silence.)
> C: "That is where I feel the noise like darts." (More silence.)
> C: "It is real early, real early."
> T: "It feels like a very early experience." (Silence.)
> C: "I cannot want anything."

Silence.

Here come the steps. Silence.

> C: "This needs to rest and it cannot rest. If it lets down and rests, it will die. It needs to keep its guard up."
> T: "There is such a big need and longing to rest and let down and ease; but somehow also this part of you cannot rest. It feels that it will die if it stops being on guard."

Silence. Long silence. What comes is a step.

> C: "Maybe it could, if I could trust something."
> T: "It could rest if you could trust something."
> C: "No, no. MAYBE it could rest if I could trust something."
> T: "It is important to say 'maybe': 'Maybe it could rest if I could trust something'."

(Silence.)

C: "Now, suddenly it feels like a house on stilts, that the stilts go into the earth. All of me on top where the noise is, that is the house. And it is on stilts. It got lifted of this sore place. Now this sore place is like a layer and it can breathe. Do you know those steal posts that they put into the ground to hold up a building? These stilts are like that. All the noise and coming and going is in the house and the house is on stilts, lifted off and the stilts go into the ground."

T: "Those steal stilts go into the ground and you feel them lifting the whole house up off of you and underneath, that sore place can breathe." (Silence.)

C: "Yes, now it is breathing." (More silence.)

C: "It is bathing in warm water."

And then later, she said (these are not exactly her words):

C: "When I was little, I played a lot with stilts. I used to go between the power-wires on them. It was dangerous but it was play. I used to make taller and taller ones and go on them there. Stilts, I have not thought of those for years. Play and danger."

And she is realizing that the themes are related. There was this life and death place here, and stilts have something to do with that and the play is some kind of freeing dimension. So she says:

C: "How does this process do that? It uses all these things to ...."

That is a good place to stop...

QUESTIONS FROM THE AUDIENCE

1. *For what types of clients is this approach most adequate? Do you have any empirical data on outcome and, more specifically, did you compare your approach with the traditional approach of Carl Rogers?* (Reinhard Tausch)

First of all, I would like to be clear: My approach is anything that I can try. If therapy is happening, if the client is moving, or if they do not want me to do something, I would never do it. I do not know if I made that clear enough. I am not saying: "Do not do this," or "Do that." I am not saying that. I am not saying that at all. Apparently I have come across that way, because nowadays sometimes I get clients who say: "I am not going to be able to focus." And I say: "Well, that is fine, there are lots of ways of doing this." And they say: "But you wrote that if I do not focus, I won't get anywhere." I wish I had not written that, if I have written it. O.K.?

I will follow the client wherever the client takes me and if that is doing something for the client, then I am content. And yes, the way I am and the way I respond and the way I talk, they will probably pick focusing up as a side-benefit. But I am not interested in approaching a person with "an approach." I bring focusing in when clients do not seem to have it, and are going around in circles. So I do not know if I am answering the question or avoiding it, but this is the approach that I would counsel. Now I would say - to answer the question - there is a large body of clients who, if you give something like focusing half a chance, who do it immediately. That is the population for whom focusing instructions are indicated, to take the question straight now. I would define the population that the method is appropriate to this way. When you try a little bit of it and it makes a wonderful difference, that is a good thing to do then. At the other extreme there are people whom you would have to push and intrude on, and say: "Look here, stop talking all the time and do this thing that I want you to do." I do not want that. And then there are people who already have it. I am saying: "It is the people between these two extremes for whom this is indicated." But that is not a class of people by present classifications; that includes borderline and psychotic people, including people in the hospital who feel a relief that they can find themselves when they have "been gone"; you know, dissociated sort of experience. We found several times that this is a helpful thing to do with people, right across the continuum of degrees of disturbance. But some other variable is involved and I do not know what it is yet.

As to the second part of your question, I do not think of focusing instructions as an approach to compare to another approach but *within* therapies, both client-centered and some others - though not enough others to brag about -, but within client-centered therapy, I would say we have a string of research studies that show that the people who do this already tend to be successful. Now we do not have anything to show that the people Gendlin teaches are more successful.

We do not have anything to show that teaching this in the context of therapy makes it more successful. That, we do not have. And I would not push it. I would teach it as something that goes along with a more normal response. Like I did here.

2. What is your view of the difference between client-centered and experiential psychotherapy and what is your view of the relation between them? (Barbara Brodley)

I would take client-centered therapy to be the larger thing. First of all, focusing, if that is what we are talking about, focusing to me is a very tiny very important process. What I call focusing is paying attention inwardly to that unclear sense of something there. Now surely therapy and personal development are much bigger things than that. Focusing is a very deliberate way to touch something inside. I have seen that help the bigger process. The bigger process comes from behind you and takes you and expands you, and you do not know what is going to happen. Whereas focusing is this very deliberate thing where an "I" is attending to an "it." I think it is very valuable. But surely, it is not therapy. Therapy is a relationship, therapy is a process of development. These focusing steps I described come in client-centered therapy. That is where I learnt them from, that is where I saw them and if you observe your clients, you will see that they are silent before those steps typically come.

Now the trouble that you are having is not about that process. It is about me *teaching* that process. And it is true that if the therapist teaches that process in some way, there is some problem with that. The therapists need to check their welcome. They need to watch and see whether they intrude; they need to see that the relationship always has precedence. So you do this thing inside the relationship, just like you do when you are in somebody's house. You do not things that they do not want you to do very long.

3. In what you just said, are you not assuming that the process of the steps is the essence of therapeutic change? (Barbara Brodley)

No, no. That is a helpful question. I was trying to straighten that out. I assume that interaction is the broader process. And just about everything interesting is some kind of special case of interaction. And it is only as part of interaction that any of these things works well. So no. I am not assuming that an inner process can be distinguished from interaction. Precisely the opposite. The inner process will give you steps in a context of interaction. And if there is nobody there, then you better interact with it in a friendly way. Otherwise you will not get those steps. You need to interact with yourself, with a certain kind of attitude; as if your inside were a child that you were keeping company. And it is much easier if someone else will be there for you in that kind of silence. So anything interesting about focusing goes on, in the context of relating. The only difference I ever had with that part of the theory was Carl's point about perception. But it is always going to be *"interaction first"* if you ask me.

4. *You emphasized the "body-sense." However, I experience many times with myself and with my clients that there is no body-sense at all, even when I or they have this "it" and can point to it. If this is the case, I think emphasizing the bodily aspect might be more confusing than helpful.* (Rob van Woerden)

I do not want to close down any other channels. I do not think anybody has the right to say: This has got to be this way, for human beings. So if you say that there is a way that they can come differently than from this bodily sense, that is fine with me. I think we need to look and compare, not just which is better, but what the difference is.

I am sure that there is an entry to steps through the literal body. Once you come into this literal body here then you find a space that is much bigger than your literal body. It is quite clear that it is not exactly your literal body, but that is where the entrance is. There might be other entrances.

5. *You have said that you do not agree that the client needs to perceive empathic understanding of the therapist and the other conditions. If you do not perceive the therapist's empathy and so forth, this could mean that it does not exist for the client. Now I make a distinction between "received empathy" and "perceived empathy." Does that make sense to you?* (Godfrey Barrett-Lennard)

Oh yes, we could settle on that completely. That is what it has always meant, also to Carl. It has got to have some impact on the client; and that is what I meant too: Some impact or some kind of effect. The interaction changes the person and *then* they become aware of it. At least some of us. But I would completely agree with you that *re*ceiving it in some way could be one of the conditions. Just *per*ceiving sounds to me like a reflective understanding or a reflected observation that I would have to say: "My therapist understands me." And I would have said: "Nobody can understand *me*. He tries hard, that nice man."

NOTE

1. This chapter is a revised version of the author's plenary address at the Leuven Conference (September 12-16, 1988). Lieve De Wachter made a transcript of the audiotape. The author adapted this first draft and provided it with some comments and clarifications. Germain Lietaer did some further editiorial work and selected from the original dialogue with the audience some parts for inclusion in the text.

REFERENCES

Gendlin, E.T. (1962/1970). *Experiencing and the creation of meaning* (2nd ed.). New York: Free Press.

Gendlin, E.T. (1987). A philosophical critique of the concept of "Narcissism." In D.M. Levin (Ed.), *Pathologies of the modern self: Postmodern studies.* New York: New York University Press.

Hendricks, M.N. (1986). Experiencing level as a therapeutic variable. *Person-centered Review, 1,* 141-162.

Leijssen, M. (1989). *Teaching focusing to "unsuccessful" clients.* Research project in progress, Centrum voor client-centered therapie en counseling, K.U.Leuven.

ON FOCUSING AND THE NECESSARY CONDITIONS OF THERAPEUTIC PERSONALITY CHANGE

Mia LEIJSSEN
Katholieke Universiteit, Leuven, Belgium

"Thus our sharply different therapists achieve good results in quite different ways. For one, an impatient, no-nonsense, let's put-the-cards-on-the-table approach is most effective, because in such an approach he is most openly himself. For another it may be a much more gentle, and more obviously warm approach, because this is the way this therapist is. Our experience has deeply reinforced and extended my own view that the person who is able openly to be himself at that moment, as he is at the deepest levels he is able to be, is the effective therapist. Perhaps nothing else is of any importance" (Rogers, 1967, p. 186).

INTRODUCTION

This article was not presented at the Leuven Conference because, as a member of the Organizing Committee, I was too involved with practical issues at the time to give a presentation. However, the ideas presented here have partly been shaped by my experience during the Conference.

As a result of many misunderstandings, we are in danger of a polarization between those who consider focusing as something strange or ill-fitting within the Rogerian way of working, and those who promote it as a very useful technique. I think that such polarization is useless and even harmful, in that it stops us from deepening and further developing our orientation. I do not consider focusing as a technique nor as ill-fitting, because its practice has helped me to realize the basic therapeutic attitudes more fully. I hope to demonstrate how focusing can be seen as a refinement and extension of the Rogerian basic attitudes.

Rogers has worked out a fairly simple theoretical concept of what a relationship should be like in order to be therapeutically valuable. However, when one tries to trace this concept in therapeutic practice, one encounters it in a great complexity of forms, and one discovers that the practitioner does a lot more than what seems, at first glance, implied in the Rogerian basic attitudes.

Rogers' store of ideas has then been rephrased and further developed by Gendlin, and it is partly thanks to his contribution that the "art" of therapy became a process which can be taught to therapists and clients alike. The kind of process which Gendlin has mainly analyzed was called "focusing." This process involves turning inward and a striving to identify one's momentary felt sense of a problem as well as an attempt to symbolize it by means of words or images. This process leads to a bodily felt sense of relief; new meanings and new possibilities come to the surface.

Rice goes a step further in clarifying the therapeutic process by distinguishing between two separate yet interrelated meanings within the term "relationship": "One group of factors, the 'primary relationship factors' are the aspects of the relationship interactions that can lead directly, in and of themselves, to new experiential learnings in the client. The 'task-relevant relationship factors' on the other hand are important because they help to establish optimal working conditions for the task of therapy" (Rice, 1983, p. 44).

In the present contribution I will try to illustrate how a therapist can specify and deepen Rice's double relationship-offer by integrating "focusing" in her[1] work method. I organized the material of this paper under five headings in which I shall illustrate the following: How focusing specifies and enriches the client-centered fundamental attitudes; how each focusing-step contains a micro-process within psychotherapy; how paying too much attention to a specific work method can endanger the basic attitudes; how the work method used is an expression of the therapist's personality; and how the ability to be in a therapeutic relationship is mainly made up of fundamental attitudes and skills based on them.

FOCUSING AS A PART OF THE FUNDAMENTAL THERAPEUTIC ATTITUDES

Focusing describes an important object of attention in therapy and specifies how it can be approached. On the basis of these two aspects, focusing can be distinguished from other therapeutic activities (Iberg, 1981a).

Rogers (1961) sometimes refers to this specific object of attention, for example in the following statements: "Therapy seems to mean a getting back to basic sensory and visceral experience" (p. 103) - "The client is hit by a feeling - not something named or labelled - but an experience of an unknown something which has to be cautiously explored before it can be named at all" (p. 129) - "The referent of these vague cognitions lies within him, in an organismic event against which he can check his symbolization and his cognitive formulations" (p. 140).

This internal point of reference is further described by Gendlin, at first as "experiencing": "The process of concrete, bodily feeling, which constitutes the basic matter of psychological and personality phenomena" (Gendlin, 1964, p. 111), later as the "felt sense": "The edge of awareness; a sense of more than one says and knows, an unclear, fuzzy, murky sense of a whole situation, that comes in the middle of the body: Throat, chest, stomach, abdomen" (Gendlin, 1984, p. 79). The bodily character of the felt sense is a stumbling-block for many, perhaps because, from a dualistic point of view, "body" is seen as the opposite of "mind." In experiential theory/therapy, however, the body is seen as the total human being, before the split between body and mind, the body as it feels meaning, the body which detects many more nuances in a situation than a person is able to verbalize at that moment, the bodily knowledge which is of a far more complex nature than is rational knowledge. It is on the basis of the bodily feeling that a person speaks and acts. Ideally, words and symbols or actions well up spontaneously from the body. But when the spontaneous stream of experience cannot flow through freely (for example in unsafe conditions), something remains stuck in the body, something remains present which reminds of, or is witness to, the experience which does not evolve further as a whole. One can continue to feel its presence as "something which pinches," a bodily knowing which is at the same time a not-knowing. When the person turns his attention to this bodily sense, then the felt meaning can start moving again. Thus, therapy is restoring contact with the meaning-feeling body in which existence manifests itself, a process in which the arrested experience is touched upon again, so that it can once more start moving and reveal, further unfold, and complete its meaning. (See in this respect the richly illustrated exposé by Depestele [1986] about *The body in psychotherapy.*) However, when the client is imbued with dualistic thinking, the therapist has to take special care that the client is not misled by the term "body." Indeed, he would then search for simple physical sensations and fail to recognize the vague uneasy or budding feeling about a particular situation, which he carries in the middle of his body as the seed of a felt meaning. Iberg (1981a) provides here a usable answer: "There where you feel more than you can say, that is how the felt sense is bodily" (p. 353). This pre-reflective experiencing, which the client feels but cannot express yet, will have to become the object of attention at one time or another in therapy. It is this inner knowing which will open itself in the therapeutic interaction, and from where new meanings will emerge.

The vague, the unformed, the unspeakable can only let itself be known when it is approached in a specific way. The Rogerian basic attitudes will be further specified in the focusing attitude. Dealing with this inner object of attention requires an attitude of waiting, of quietly remaining present with the not yet speakable, being receptive to the not yet formed. To achieve this, it will be necessary to suspend temporarily everything which the person already knows about it, and to be cognitively inactive. This kind of attention can also be found in Zen meditation and Taoism, but in therapy, it is directed towards a specific object, i.e. the felt sense (Iberg, 1981b). This attitude presupposes tolerance for uncertainty, an ability to give up control and to be vulnerable, since neither the therapist nor the client can anticipate what will emerge from the implicit. Not knowing exactly what is going to emerge is very frightening to people who have been used to keeping emotions down and under strict control. It is obvious that a person will only dare to adopt such an attitude if there is already a good deal of intra- and interpersonal security. Hence my reluctance to see focusing as a "skill," I rather believe that it is an attitude which emerges spontaneously in some people in a safe milieu. In others, this way of being occupied inwardly, is not spontaneously used but something which they can nevertheless discover in contact with something (for example the book *Focusing*) or somebody (for example the therapist). However, many clients offer resistance because they experience this inner occupation as threatening. A telling example is that of a client who had been in therapy for three years, and who had recently read the book *Focusing* and followed four teaching sessions on focusing. He said: "What I learned there, I can do it, but I do not dare doing it. I only want to dwell on something when I first know what it is." This client "knows how," but cannot (yet) internalize it, because of inner resistances. Only gradually, in a corrective therapeutic milieu and in interaction with the therapist, who embodies this attitude, will something of this "new" attitude become possible.

Gendlin (1968, 1981, 1984) himself has often described how a therapist can concretely realize a focusing attitude in therapy. Mathieu-Coughlan and Klein (1984) summarized the therapist's experiential response in the following points: "First, the therapist responsively 'listens' to every bit of communication, and also teaches focusing, a little bit at a time, during therapy hours... Second, the therapist's presence and responses as an experiencing person have an inescapable influence on the interaction and thus also on the client's phenomenology" (p. 216). Based on these two aspects of the therapist's experiential functioning is also their "Therapist Experiencing Scale" (Klein, Mathieu-Coughlan, & Kiesler, 1986), in which they make a distinction between "referent" and "manner," referent meaning the aspect of the client's experience which is focused on, and manner the quality of the therapist's experiencing and his manner of conveying it into the interaction.

It is especially this ability to react as an experiencing person which I want to emphasize here as a fundamental quality of a therapist. She keeps experientially in touch with what happens in the client, with what emerges from her own body and with what happens between the two of them. Together these aspects constitute a totality of experiencing from which her words and actions flow. Out of these she gives empathic responses which transcend intellectual understanding. The experiential data also constitute the point of reference against which she can test the authenticity of her words and actions. On the basis thereof, she may experience an aspect of the client's story which the client himself has overlooked. For example with one client I felt very restless at the beginning of each session. After a few sessions, I put this feeling into words, upon which the client told me that he always keeps a watchful eye on the clock in the waiting room, interpreting every minute I start too early or too late with the session as a rejection on my part. Denying or ignoring such feelings by the therapist would lead to a lack of authenticity in the relationship and could lead to persistent incongruence in the client. One of the fundamental attitudes of a therapist is, in my opinion, to remain receptive to one's own bodily experiencing of the whole process; how does it touch and move me, how can I remain with this vague feeling, so that I can express it. To allow this barometer to function in an unbiased and sensitive way, personal therapy and supervision are mandatory. Only when the therapist can approach and express this level of experiencing will she know how to reach that level in the client, and how to help the client deal with it. She can then further use the focusing instructions in such a way that it allows the client to get in touch with his own sense-feeling body, and to make his stream of verbalization more experiential (see also Depestele, 1989).

EACH FOCUSING STEP CONTAINS A MICRO-PROCESS WITHIN PSYCHOTHERAPY

Gendlin (1981, 1984) devided the focusing instructions into six steps, which he describes in much detail. And when teaching focusing, he considered it essential to pay due attention to each step separately. In this part of my exposé, I will cover each of these steps, not for the purpose of teaching them, but in order to describe them as micro-processes or task-relevant processes offered at certain moments in psychotherapy. "They help to establish the working conditions that are optimal for facilitating particular kinds of self-explorations" (Rice, 1984, p. 182). It is important for a therapist to learn when and how specific micro-processes can be used at various moments in therapy. This requires a process diagnosis, in which the therapist recognizes the signals heralding the emergence of a micro-process in need of facilitation. I will describe and illustrate the various micro-processes within focusing, drawing on my own clinical experience and in dialogue with other authors.

1. The therapist lets the client discover which problems are burdening him and helps him to free himself from identification with them

In general, the crux of this first stage concerns making a friendly accepting space where the client can be with a sense of separatedness and where he can feel that he is OK. In particular I have repeatedly found that this is an extremely valuable verbalization of the kind of process in need of facilitation with a client who is overwhelmed by his problems and identifies himself totally with them. For example, a client gets in touch with a lot of "old pain." He says: "It is as if I disappear when I start with this, as if nobody is sitting in this chair any more!" Therapist: "Could you imagine a big box standing between us, in which you put all your old pain, while you yourself remain in your seat? How does it feel when you imagine that?" Upon which the client relaxes and is able to make contact with his pain, without being overwhelmed by it. He discovers that there are many layers in this old pain, which he can now review one by one. This example demonstrates how important it can be for a client to first take distance from his problem, and free himself from identification with it, before he can successfully work on it.

Another example concerns a patient who gets in a state of total panic on account of many difficulties in his present life. Therapist: "Imagine that you sit in a little boat which almost sinks under the heavy load. Each problem in your life is a parcel in your boat. We will now unload all your problems onto the bank. Which heavy parcel will you first unload? Which one do you encounter first?" In this way, all parcels are unloaded. The therapist allows the client each time to feel what it does to his body each time his boat becomes lighter. Next, one of the parcels on the bank is inspected more closely, but it is not allowed to go back in the boat. Every time the client is in danger of being overwhelmed by a problem, the therapist suggests that the parcel remains on the bank, and cannot go back in the boat. This example shows how one should sometimes first inspect all the problems without dealing with any particular one. It permits to establish contact with the person, who is something else than the sum of his problems. It is sometimes very therapeutic when a client experiences that he is still "somebody", when he is free of problems.

McGuire (1982, 1984,) describes how this process can be used successfully in crisis intervention with seriously suicidal patients. Kanter (1982) and Grindler (1982, 1985) show how it helps patients to deal better with cancer and other serious somatic illnesses.

This method almost always demonstrates the effectiveness of the use of images, especially when these are chosen to reflect the client's personal world. In this context, Itoh (1988) mentions an exceptionally powerful image which is used in Japan: The "Tsubo" is a jar in which essentials pertaining to one's life are kept. It may eventually even be used to keep the ashes of the deceased. This symbolic meaning of the "Tsubo" is used in therapy to let the client put away a problem that makes him too anxious or is too overwhelming. Afterwards, one asks the client to formulate a feeling about the "Tsubo."

I have personally experienced the process described in this first focusing stage as different, new and more enriching than what I knew from classical client-centered therapy. Indeed, when the therapist accompanies the client in the creation of a workable distance from an unbearable or overwhelming problem, she posits herself strongly as a process-expert, and often uses suggestions to this effect.

2. The client is asked to direct his attention inwards, and to let a total feeling about the problem arise

This is the most crucial step in experiential psychotherapy. Mathieu-Coughlan and Klein (1984) define the moment when the client can shift his perspective from the outside to the inside (between phases 3 and 4 of the "Patient Experiencing Scale") as a key event in therapy. The therapist can actively contribute to this shift by referring in her answer to the point out of which the client tries to speak, but which is still unclear. For example: "You do not have a reason to suspect your wife, yet there is something going on in you that makes you doubt?"

When a client accepts the invitation to direct his attention inwards, a silence often occurs during which the feeling takes shape. In this phase especially, the above described attitude of waiting and receptive attention is crucial. The formation of a felt experience requires time and silence. Iberg (1981a) says about this: "It is not there immediately, when you turn your attention inward. Emotions may be there but the felt sense is not. It only forms after you begin sensing for it. It comes when you wait quietly to let your sense of the whole come to you" (p. 350).

This step is for many the most difficult one, because the attention is directed to a place where there is often pain, anxiety, confusion and vagueness. Sometimes a lot of work has to be done first in order to achieve basic security. For example: A client told how he was mistreated at home as a child.

> T: "As if you had then behaved very courageously, but now feel something different sitting around?"
> C: "Oh, I took care that they could catch me as little as possible."
> T: "If only they could not catch me ... this is important?"

C: "My father could also be in a good mood."

A few sessions later:

T: "You have told me already a lot about how things were at home; as a child, I would have felt very confused and anxious in such a place. Do you recognize something of that sort when you look into yourself?"
C: "You should never appear weak!"
T: "When you feel anxiety and confusion, are you then weak?"
C: "Only the strong ones survive."
T: "You must have been very strong yourself to stand it there."

There is obviously not yet enough security and trust in this client to turn to his deeper feelings. A year later, there are sporadic changes in this.

C: "I know, my father was mentally disturbed, but that is not enough reason to treat us like that."
T: "Do you still somewhere feel anger towards him?"
C: "He has no right to mistreat me."
T: "He has done you a lot of harm that way."
C: "I cannot explain that to anybody."
T: "You can hardly communicate to anybody else what this has left behind, inside you... but is it maybe also difficult to bear all this by yourself?"
C: "Sometimes I am afraid it will explode."

Here we see a shy first sign of the client's capacity to direct his attention to his inner feelings, and to allow the therapist to share in his inner struggle. While feelings are still threatening for the client, the therapist's presence and listening without making judgments, are particularly important to reassure the client that all feelings are acceptable.

3. One looks for words, images or symbols which express the feeling and which permit holding on to the felt sense

When a client tries to describe his as yet unclear feeling in a word, a sentence, an image or a non-verbal form of expression (see also Leijssen 1984, Leijssen, in press), the therapist should follow attentively and reflect. Especially in this phase, it is important to be very non-directive and to retain loaded words. Indeed, if the therapist changes the client's expression, the client may loose the specific loading connected with the word. Gendlin (1984) calls these words "handles" with which the client can hold on to his whole experience. For example: Therapist: "What is this feeling about your father?... What is the most important quality in it?" (silence). Client: "The most salient is respect." Therapist: "Respect." Client: "But respect from a distance, respect which one could describe as negative." Therapist: "Respect from a distance."

It is remarkable that, in this phase, an image often presents itself as the most vivid expression of this complex experience. Metaphors have the advantage of catching the essentials of the still unspeakable and express it in its full complexity with just a few words. "Metaphorical language seems particularly suited to the task of accurately evoking an experience while leaving open all sorts of possibilities that are not yet clear" (Rice, 1974, p. 309). For example, Rogers' client (1977) expresses his complex painful experience with: "A big lump in my throat," "A goddam tree rammed up my ass."

Sometimes, the image which evokes the whole felt sense comes from the therapist and not from the client. Rice (1974) draws our attention to the fact that the therapist who does not only listen cognitively, but absorbs the client's story with her whole being, can synthesize her own global feeling in an image closer to the client's original feeling than the client's own words. For example, a client has indicated through various examples that he is always careful not to provoke dangerous reactions. The therapist reflects: "It looks as if you were constantly moving about in a mine-field." The client recognizes the image immediately as the exact expression of the totality of his experience, which he had tried to express through all his examples. As illustrated by Santen (1986), the use of an image promotes inward directedness. By its high potency it helps the client to hold on to specific feeling-qualities. The power of the image as "handle" is also illustrated by the fact that the client can often recall the feeling after considerable time has elapsed, via the image. After emergence of the felt sense, it is important for the client to be able to hold on to it in order to test if his expressions reflect it precisely. The capacity to hold on to a felt point of reference (between phases 4 and 5 of the "Patient Experiencing Scale") is seen by Mathieu-Coughlan and Klein (1984) as the next key event in good therapy. When the expression fits exactly the feeling, the client experiences already some relief.

4. There is a back and forth movement between the symbolization and what is felt, whereby the felt sense unfolds itself further, until full relief is experienced

We reflect the expressions which seem correct. The bodily knowledge only accepts precise wording. Other words, even synonyms, do not resonate with the felt sense and are rejected. It is through various precise expressions that the experiencing process will further unfold itself until it is fully expressed. This is accompanied by a bodily sense of relief. This event, which is situated between the stages 5 and 6 on the "Patient Experiencing Scale" has been defined by Mathieu-Coughlan and Klein (1984) as a next key event in therapy. In this process of testing and unfolding, the client will complete his expressions or correct them until a sufficient degree of expression is reached. The therapist keeps listening empathically until the client verbally and non-verbally, says the expression is complete. This can clearly be recognized by a number of signs: As long as words or gestures still betray hesitancy, as facial expression does not radiate peace and contentment, as the client does not yet feel a general bodily sense of relief, the process is not completed. In this case we continue to give the underlying feeling the time it needs to unfold itself further, we check if a particular word expresses the quality of what is felt, and we receive the body's response. When the felt sense is expressed exactly and fully, the client experiences a clear physical relief, a sense of freedom and satisfaction, even if the experience is an unpleasant one. Nothing "presses" any longer inside the client, everything is lying there, clearly expressed, "the child is born." For example, a client questions in the session why she is afraid of coming in contact with others, and hits on the idea that she cannot close her eyes. The therapist asks her what emerges in her with respect to the idea of closing her eyes in contact with others. She answers, haltingly and helped by several interventions from the therapist: "Incredibly tense," "Then, I am lost," "When I get an unexpected reaction, I will be unable to protect myself." When I then ask her what is the worst possible reaction against which she would have to protect herself, a whole story comes to the surface of how, as a fifteen year old, she was raped by the father of a girlfriend at whose house she was staying. I have the feeling that we touched on something important but that not everything is expressed, since I see my client still tense. I ask again: "Do you still feel angry?" And she repeats, again haltingly and with several interventions from me: "Chocked," "Overwhelmed," "Angry at my girlfriend," "Disappointed," "Helpless because I was not allowed to react," "Cowardly because I adapt myself to what others expect from me," "Distaste," "Disgust," "Repulsion." Now the incomplete experience process seems to be sufficiently expressed. She feels relieved, her whole body relaxes. We see here that: "Certain meanings that were not functioning implicitly are reconstituted, regaining their capacity to interact with events" (Iberg, 1981a, p. 350).

5. *The client gets help in protecting the process against the inner critic*

This task can arise at various moments during the previously described micro-processes, because the normative and criticizing voices of the inner critic can prevent the client from getting in touch with the colorful array of feelings, or order him to retreat quickly after a brief venture into their exploration. Besides, an experience-geared process does not unfold according to logic and the thinking processes of a normal adult, so that one cannot determine beforehand the direction which the experiencing process will take. "The initial symbols that fit the felt sense may be primitive, in the sense that they are childish or immature when compared to the normal thought process of the person... Only after the emergence begins with its own just-right symbolization can the material change and become adult and consistent with the rest of the client's explicit conscious content" (Iberg, 1981a, p. 349). Also, we are confronted with a duality between the bodily known, on the one hand, and, on the other hand, the arguments, rationalizations and norms which go against it. Hendricks (1986) points out that clients have a tendency to attack their own emergent experience. We have to help them to recognize this, instead of detaching themselves from their process. The idea here is not so much not to allow anything coming from the outside, but rather giving the blocked process first the time to open itself fully. Gendlin speaks at this stage of "receiving": "One learns to move old voices aside before they crowd out the physical sense of the shift" (1984, p. 88). For example, a thirty-five year old client who lives with his father, and who has arrived in the session at: "I want to get rid of him," immediately adds: "Oh no, that cannot be, after all he has done for me!" Here the therapist comes in: "Could you just allow this feeling of 'I want to get rid of him!' to remain for a moment, without immediately linking it with consequences in reality?" After which the client discovers: "Yes, this gives me peace, and maybe it is not so much that I want to get rid of him but that I cannot accept certain behaviors of him."

The inner criticism can however be very tenacious in some clients, and rationalizations, norms and resistances can stop all feeling. It is as if we first have to dig up the process rather than protect it. I feel that there is still a lot to be learned about this digging up of the process. On the one hand, a stronger communication of the basic attitudes will be required - and it is precisely these clients who make it often the most difficult for the therapist to remain authentic and to follow these attitudes through in a consequent manner - and on the other hand we need to search more intensively for specific facilitating interventions.

6. Further associations, insights, links and new plans emerge, and are integrated

After the felt relief, a new step can be taken: New associations, insights, connections with other experiences and new plans come to the surface. "One's whole map of some trouble changes" (Gendlin, 1984, p. 87). For instance, the previously mentioned "raped" client ends the session with "I have never really received the respect I needed to develop myself as a woman, my whole education was destructive of the feminine ... Now I feel stronger, as if I dare showing myself... I want to take better care of myself, I am going to buy something nice for myself." Mathieu-Coughlan and Klein (1984) situate this experience of new, autonomous and positive feelings between steps 6 and 7 of the "Patient Experiencing Scale," and consider this step as another key event in successful therapy.

In this phase, it may make sense to approach the problem from many different angles, to ask additional questions and to look for connections with other incidents. For example: "What you are confronted with now, how does it fit in with the problems which you encounter lately?" After the felt relief, it may also be useful - after having allowed for some silence first - to consider the steps which will have to be taken in reality. For instance: "What you have discovered now, how could you give it shape in your everyday life?" If there is a moment for giving suggestions or advice in therapy, this is the right one. For example: "In brochure X you will find an interesting choice of group excursions," or "Why not try to discuss it with your father?" In this phase, there is a marked eagerness to make new connections, or to engage in new interactions, or to take steps which one was previously incapable of taking. During these concrete steps in everyday life, the client comes into contact with new aspects of the problem, and this can lead in turn to a new felt meaning. Sometimes the therapist may not agree with the client's new choices but takes care not to let her own value system interfere.

Throughout all these steps the client changes in therapy. But repeatedly we notice the client also learning to use this new way of interacting outside of the sessions, between himself and others. Clients often report that they grasp back at an image (e.g. "unloading the boat") which helps them to create distance when they feel in danger of being overwhelmed by the problems encountered. Or they discover that they have become more sensitive to what presents itself as vague and still undefined. They dismiss their experiences less easily. One could say that the client has learned to become the therapist for his own inner process, something which Gendlin (1984) aptly called "the client's client."

BEING TOO PREOCCUPIED WITH FOLLOWING A SPECIFIC THERAPEUTIC METHOD MAY ENDANGER THE FUNDAMENTAL ATTITUDES

In client-centered circles, care has always been taken not to reduce a fundamental attitude to a technique. Rogers (1980) for example, objected strongly to reducing "the basic attitude of empathy to the technique of reflection" (p. 139). However, in clinical practice, therapists often appear more concerned with technical issues than with the basic attitude itself. I found for example that therapists often offend, with the technique of focusing, not only against the Rogerian basic attitudes, but even against the focusing attitude itself, which ought to be one of receptivity to what is taking shape in the client, in the therapist, and between the two of them. I shall try to make some sort of inventory of difficulties which I have encountered in this regard, in the past years.

A recurrent mistake is that the therapist arrives *too early* with a question about the underlying level; especially when the client would first like to tell more about his whole situation, and feels no need yet of going deeper. The need to go deeper usually only surfaces when the client has "told all," and experiences something like: "What next?", or realizes, in another way, that something in his story is vague, or contains a problem which he would now like to look at (vs. which the therapist thinks he should dwell on). But initially, the client wants to tell his story and wants to be listened to and understood.

The therapist's *use of language* is not always adapted to the client's experience; it mimics too closely the language of the focusing instructions, instead of "How does this feel in your body?", the invitation to focus could for example be worded more specifically according to the client's experience: "Saying things which reveal your knowledge make you feel especially uncomfortable; which sort of discomfort is this?" Also, the word *"body"* is very loaded for some clients; we enter here in a dangerous and forbidden territory, we touch on a taboo, and the client reacts by blocking or closing himself off. It is important to respect this closing-off in such a moment and continue first to establish the safe milieu in which the client can look at his blocking. In women with incestuous and rape experiences, we find this loading of the "body" to an extreme degree.

The global *situational context* and interaction at the time of the presentation of the focusing instructions are sometimes neglected. Usually, this implies an insufficient allowing for the felt meaning to develop, or a denial of it, whether by the client or by the therapist. For example: In the third session, a client told her therapist extensively about her previous relationship with a man. The therapist asks: "Could you remain for a moment with what you now experience about this man? What comes up in you?" The client experiences "tension." When they look closer at this tension, it appears to be related to the here-and-now situation from which the client would like to escape because she knows that she will have to examen this problem more closely in therapy. The way in which this client is affected by the here-and-now in therapy overshadows everything she talks about. The "real" problem of the moment is, initially, not touched upon by the client, nor is the therapist in touch with it. Luckily, in this example, client and therapist do end up touching on the real problem of the moment, even though the focusing instruction was directed elsewhere. But with a client who is very geared to the expectations of others, the invitation to focus on a particular problem may well appear as something which has to be carried out at all cost. This may then distance him further from, say, his uneasiness in the presence of the therapist, and from allowing himself to feel it and deal with it. Gendlin tries to intercept this by providing the client with "split-level instructions": "The moment the instructions seem to do some violence in you, stop, see directly what you have there. On one level 'follow' and on another level 'don't follow' the instructions," "The split-level instruction is to find the individual's process with our diagram and to find where the diagram fails" (Gendlin, 1984, p. 88). Even so, focusing on a specific problem can lead to overlooking something else, something more essential. I became aware of this after an experience with a student who had come to my door with a problem which he wanted to clarify. I felt a little uneasy about the fact that he was always critical of me and felt under some pressure to demonstrate my expertise. Instead of paying attention to that beginning felt sense in me, I immediately followed what the client started to tell me. After the session, the client leaves my office relieved and I am happy that he has been able to work so well on his problem. Some time later, I hear from a colleague that this same student has a lot of negative feelings about me. At that moment, I realized that I had ignored the situational and interactional context in which the student had come with his question, as well as my own beginning felt sense about the event.

At the Conference, Murase (1988) gave some further examples of how being too strongly involved with focusing as a technique detracts from the basic conditions. In his sessions in Japan he primarily met with the problem that clients are sometimes confronted with a mass of terrifying images that make them lose their self-control. Looking back to a similar session, he now claims: "However, truthfully, I was slightly worried and felt some difficulty in empathically understanding her total situation. In retrospect I recognize that I should have stopped the session when she reported these negative images. However in actuality, I relied too much on her responses and not on my 'felt sense.' When I eventually stopped the session she was found to be quite exhausted physically and psychologically. Later she told me that she had tried hard to 'explain' her state of mind whenever she was asked her feelings. What I primarily learned from this experience was that the listener must not continue with a session if he or she has any difficulty in empathizing with the focuser's inner experiences. In this case focusing practice stimulated and developed the focuser's image activity which finally decreased her self-control. Both the focuser and the listener were too eager to practise focusing in a formal way and had ignored the necessary prerequisite, namely, a peaceful relaxed atmosphere, together with the attitude of waiting and 'letting it come' naturally."

The focusing technique lends itself to exploration of intense and crucial life events with someone with whom one does not necessarily have to have a personal relationship, or in instances where one does not have to pay attention to the "mutual relationship," as long as it does not interfere. The therapist does not figure prominently in this technique; there does not have to be a conscious perception of the therapist as a person, her "mere presence" being sufficient for the client to feel secure enough to let the process unfold. The central event is the client's unfolding process, the relationship between client and therapist being secondary as to that unfolding; it is thus not particularly an encounter between two people. But when therapist and/or client consistently give preference to this work method, one may question whether they use it to avoid something else, i.e. the contact or real encounter with the other. This aspect should then really be examined first.

Finally, I would like to mention another problem: On the marketplace of well-being and happiness, focusing can easily conquer a corner as one of the methods with which one can create all sorts of experiences in people. Gendlin's book Focusing (1981) helps to create the illusion that problems are easy to solve if one knows the manual. There are many positive aspects to the fact that insights gained from therapy are translated in principles usable by the public at large. But the danger that focusing will be used here purely as a technique, separated from the basic attitudes, is by no means imaginary. I sometimes have the impression that focusing is engaged in as one of the many "well-being promoting occupations," which people consume, simply for the sake of consuming, to satisfy an experience-hunger, without questioning where this need comes from. In this way, the basic issues are avoided. Therapy is a far more complex and difficult process in which we have to pay special attention to the manner and context in which we give our instructions.

THE METHOD USED IS AN EXPRESSION OF THE THERAPIST'S PERSONALITY

A method in therapy is usually discussed from the standpoint of the client's process. This must remain the main preoccupation. Yet, it is important to realize that the choice of a therapeutic orientation and the method used are also expressions of the therapist's personality. Could it be so that psychoanalytically-oriented therapists have a preference for intellectual understanding? Are behavior therapists people who love to have control? Do family therapists like action and directing? Does Gestalt Therapy find its followers among playful people? And do we, client-centered therapists perhaps have in common an attraction to feeling contact and being understood?

Rogers (1980) tells, in his own straightforward way, something about his own personal affinities: "As I look back, I realize that my interest in therapy certainly grew in part out of my early loneliness. Here was a socially approved way of getting really close to individuals and thus filling some of the hungers I had undoubtedly felt. The therapeutic interview also offered a chance of becoming close without having to go through what was to me a long and painful process of gradual and deepening acquaintance" (p. 34). Consciously or unconsciously, every therapist chooses an orientation consistent with her own personal needs. Everyone's way of expressing the fundamental attitudes is also an expression of her specific "personal characteristics." And it is rightly so, because therapy thus becomes a personal and lively process. If we look at things that way, we can, for example, say that Gendlin has translated the Rogerian basic attitudes into focusing, which is, on the one hand, a new approach to a problem area, and on the other hand, a work method in which Gendlin can be more "himself." I do not feel qualified to analyze Rogers' and Gendlin's personalities in order to confirm this hypothesis; I can only try to look at the issue from my own point of view. I will try to illustrate this by means of a few therapy-dimensions along which each therapist will choose her own position.

First, the dimension of *directivity,* a sensitive issue in Rogerian circles. Initially, I have made an enormous effort to "fit" in "classical" client-centered therapy, in which I thought I had to follow every step of the client. Focusing pleases me a.o. because my active and directive side gets a chance to express itself in a way that seems useful for the client. I would not like to leave my active side out of therapy. Indeed, it contributes an energy and dynamism which, in certain clients, activates again something which has died off or is snowed under. At the same time, the directivity and activity is nicely kept in check when it is used in a process in which silence, waiting for the unspeakable, and continuous checking with the inner referents, take up so much space.

Next, I would like to look at the dimension of *distance-closeness*. Most of the writings on this subject have been caused by concern about establishing a suitable working alliance with the client. In this context, I am struck, for example, by Fuhrmann's remark (1990) about the use of focusing with psychosomatic clients: "There seems to be a third between client and therapist to which both can refer without touching each other directly. That looks like a support to the safety of the client, which enables him to allow more intensity in the therapeutic relation." I believe that, in good therapy, distance is needed to make closeness possible. But I also recognize how this blend between distance and closeness fits me. One of the reasons why focusing appeals to me is that, with my concerned presence, the client can go through an important process; as therapist, I witness an intense and intimate process, which does not always require a feeling of closeness between us, as client and therapist. My need of mutual existential contact is limited to a few people whom I have chosen carefully. In this sense, focusing fits my personality and creates a level of closeness where I feel well with a good number of clients. My sensitivity about not just letting anybody come close to me makes me also sensitive to the space which the client may need to feel safe; I shall not easily sit too close to a client, and shall not easily fuse with him. I seem, as a therapist, to offer a good corrective experience from an invasive, suffocating mother, and schizoid patients blossom in my particular blend of closeness and distance. McConnaughy (1987) remarks about this dimension: "Each therapist needs to determine a comfortable level of intimacy that suits his or her individual character. Appropriate therapeutic strategies are those that are tailored to the therapist's unique interpersonal manner" (p. 306).

Another dimension which I will call *heavyness-lightness* is reflected in one's way of handling a problem. Someone who identifies with problems is "heavy," loaded, burdened, weighed down. Someone who can keep in touch with something else than the problem is "light," open, energetic. This does not mean that problems are pushed away, forgotten or not taken seriously, but only that one does not let oneself be burdened by them. One "has" problems, one "is" not these problems. By means of focusing, we try to establish in the client this "working relationship" with his problem. But I find it also important for me as a therapist that my therapeutic activities are not only characterized by heaviness. I have a need to keep in touch with the "light" side. I want to give the playful, the imaginative, the creative in my personality a place in my therapies. I like to play on words, to use non-verbal means of expression, to mix in humor, and to discover pleasure and meaning in life.

In the preceding paragraphs, I have illustrated some aspects of myself which I can express through focusing. Other therapists may choose similar or different ways of expressing their personal characteristics. And it often appears through all this - as I also illustrated in the dimensions described - that our "weak" side turns out to be our "strong" side as well. Both my strong and my weak side may participate in my working methods, as long as I am conscious of it and am prepared to scrutinize these aspects. The danger is to remain blind to them, or misusing a method in order to avoid difficulties for oneself, and wanting to keep oneself out of the action for one's own personal benefit. Profound self-questioning, honest consideration of my clients' and my colleagues' remarks, and on-going supervision, even after one's training has ended, are, in my opinion, ways of making sure that this does not happen.

THE ABILITY TO BE IN A THERAPEUTIC RELATIONSHIP IMPLIES MAINLY FUNDAMENTAL ATTITUDES AND SKILLS BASED ON THEM

Therapy is, for client and therapist, a search for what the client needs. With an increase of the therapist's ability to be in a relationship, the chance to touch experientially the basic feeling level of the client increases as well, and change and development have a better chance of occurring. In the ability to be in a therapeutic relationship, I distinguish, in a way similar to Rice (1983), between basic attitudes, and skills or techniques. Basic attitudes describe the way of being of the therapist, and determine her behavior. Skills or techniques specify the concrete steps undertaken by the therapist in specific situations, and which give shape to the basic attitudes. Thus I have described focusing as an attitude and a skill or technique, in which several steps can be distinguished. Within client-centered therapy, we arrive at the description of those skills or techniques by analyzing what competent and experienced therapists do in their clinical practice. In this way, something about doing good therapy is laid bare and can be transmitted. Also in this respect, valuable research is being done by Rice and co-workers (Rice & Greenberg, 1984) who study fragments of therapy in order to identify the most facilitating interventions in certain situations, so that one can gain more insight in the processes which make change happen. On the basis of these findings we can sharpen our therapeutic skills and increase our ability to be in a therapeutic relationship.

Apart from this, Rice (1983) underlines the central importance of the primary relationship factors and hopes that we shall learn to see more accurately, precisely when we give these fundamental attitudes a more central place. I want to stress that the basic attitudes come always first, and this is often the only thing we need to meet the client and to touch him in his deeper levels of experience. Gaining more "competence," as a therapist means first: Developing the basic attitudes, and second: Finding, or learning to discover with someone else's help, how these attitudes can find an expression which will allow us to reach specific clients in specific situations. This hypothesis is particularly well illustrated by the person and work of Prouty. Whoever has seen Prouty at work is first struck by his love and empathy for severely withdrawn patients. He longs for contact with them, and gets it too! The behavior that goes along with this can be described as the technique "contact reflections" (Prouty, 1983; Leijssen & Roelens, 1988). His technique can certainly be learned (Hinterkopf & Brunswick, 1981). But Prouty says also that the technique will not work if you do not really want to make the contact. Prouty would never have arrived at his method had he not genuinely been driven by a search for contact. He thus shows here a skill or technique which can make other therapists more capable of being in a therapeutic relationship, on condition that they interiorize the basic attitudes out of which the technique developed, and let their actions be based on them. Out of these attitudes, the therapist searches to make contact, following her own feeling, and following the style which she had developed herself, or has learned from others as being meaningful in specific circumstances.

It has become clearer to me over the years just how far the Rogerian basic attitudes of empathy, authenticity and regard, and the focusing attitude of waiting upon the inexpressible often have to be pursued in order to really be sufficient. With "sufficient" I mean: Until the moment when the fundamental attitudes finally reach the client, and he can internalize them. A client who has internalized the therapist's basic attitudes sufficiently, can remain with his experiences, and in a friendly, accepting manner explore them in various situations, without much further attention from the therapist. It is precisely the clients who have the longest way to go to reach this point, who appeal most strongly to continued maintenance of the basic attitudes in the therapist.

As practitioners, we are often confronted with a painful struggle to get ahead, with the client, through the many obstacles which he presents, through the repetitive scenario of interactions in which we get stuck and through the blind spots of the therapist. If the therapist can maintain her basic attitudes throughout, and/or deepen them, and thus is able to make contact with the essential in the client, then something starts moving. I situate the turning point at the moment where the client really experiences the therapist's basic attitudes, and starts to apply them to himself, even if he still needs the therapist's guidance for it. From this turning point, other developments become possible, and the client's experiential process can further unfold and reorganize itself.

Getting stuck in therapy does not seem due as much to lack of skill as to something in the client which prevents him from internalizing the basic attitudes, or to something which prevents the therapist from fully and consequently realizing the basic attitudes, whereby large areas remain unexplored. The client's resistances can decrease when the fundamental attitudes are more fully realized in the therapist. The therapist can grow in the fundamental attitudes by exploring her own blind spots and sensitivities in personal therapy and in supervision. "Life" too, helps to develop certain qualities further and increase one's ability to be in relationships. For example: Intensive living with a partner, becoming a mother, raising children, various contacts, taking leave of loved ones, etc. have brought me nearer various experiential worlds, stimulated different qualities in me, brought me respect for human peculiarities and confronted me increasingly with the essentials in life.

The therapist's ability to be in relationship can develop, but sometimes a point is reached where it becomes clear that the therapist cannot offer what the client needs, or that it is asking too much of her and that she ceases to make efforts to establish contact. Or the client can feel that the therapist's offer falls short, does not reach him anymore, and he terminates therapy.

CONCLUSION

The client comes to the therapist with an often not yet explicit need. Crucial for therapy will be whether or not the therapist can, on the basis of her ability to be in a therapeutic relationship, get in touch with it and can thus touch the client's deeper layers of experiencing. The fundamental attitudes are the most important feature of the ability to be in a therapeutic relationship. The attitudes of empathy, unconditional regard and authenticity, and the focusing attitude, i.e. directing attention inwards and waiting with the unclear, will eventually be adopted by the client if they are consistently maintained by the therapist. The beginning of this internalization is a first crucial turning point in therapy. From that moment on, the arrested experiencing processes can start moving and new interactions become possible. From that point on also, we can distinguish several key events which reflect the further unfolding of the experiencing process and the reaching of new meanings. How we can concretely facilitate this internalization and further growth can be studied by the analysis of the behavior of clients and therapists in various situations. This permits us to isolate skills or techniques. Thus, within the focusing movement, we were able to distinguish several steps, all of which shed light on a different part of the process. Research may, in the coming years, shed light on yet other processes which experienced clinicians already instinctively know and facilitate. I share Rice's (1983) opinion that discovering signals which invite us to facilitate a particular interaction does not have to be in contradiction with venturing into a real human relationship. As therapists, we can become more skilled by learning specific techniques of intervention by learning to gear our responses better to the client's situation, and by refining our sensitivity about such matters. In this way, we will increase our ability to be in a therapeutic relationship, on condition that these techniques remain embedded in the basic attitudes. Our way of conveying the basic attitudes will always have a personal flavor, typical of the therapist's personality. This contributes to making therapy a personal encounter. However, the therapist has a moral obligation to guard and keep questioning her input, a.o. via supervision and personal therapy. Finally, it seems to me of utmost importance that the therapist keeps searching and remains open to what theory, research and practice can teach her, that she remains fascinated by her work, and delivers her efforts for her clients with dedication and enthusiasm.

NOTE

1. I am a female therapist; hence, my general usage makes the therapist female and, for the sake of clarity, the client is usually male. There are exceptions where case material would otherwise be less valid.

REFERENCES

Depestele, F. (1986). Het lichaam in psychotherapie. In R. Van Balen, M. Leijssen, & G. Lietaer (Eds.), *Droom en werkelijkheid in client-centered psychotherapie* (pp. 87-123). Leuven/Amersfoort: Acco.

Depestele, F. (1989). Experiëntiële psychotherapie: een stap in de praktijk. *Tijdschrift Klinische Psychologie, 19(1 & 2),* 1-15 and 60-81.

Fuhrmann, E. (1990). *Some aspects of combining focusing with person-centered therapy in working with psychosomatic clients.* See this volume.

Gendlin, E.T. (1964). A theory of personality change. In P. Worchel & D. Byrne (Eds.), *Personality change.* New York: Wiley.

Gendlin, E.T. (1968). The experiential response. In E. Hammer (Ed.), *Use of interpretation in therapy* (pp. 208-227). New York: Grune & Stratton.

Gendlin, E.T. (1978). *Focusing.* New York: Everest House.

Gendlin, E.T. (1981). *Focusing* (Rev. ed.). New York: Bantam Books.

Gendlin, E.T. (1984). The client's client: The edge of awareness. In F.R. Levant & J.M. Shlien (Eds.), *Client-centered therapy and the person-centered approach: New directions in theory, research and practice* (pp. 76-107). New York: Praeger.

Grindler, D. (1982-1983). "Clearing a space" with someone who had cancer. *The Focusing Folio, 2(1),* 11-23.

Grindler, D. (1985). Research perspective on "clearing a space" with someone who had cancer. *The Focusing Folio, 4(3),* 98-124.

Hendriks, M.N. (1986). Experiencing level as a therapeutic variable. *Person-centered Review, 1,* 141-162.

Hinterkopf, E., & Brunswick, L. (1981). Teaching mental patients to use client-centered and experiential therapeutic skills with each other. *Psychotherapy: Theory, Research and Practice, 18,* 394-402.

Iberg, J.R. (1981a). Focusing. In R.J. Corsini, *Handbook of innovative psychotherapies* (pp. 344-361). New York: Wiley.

Iberg, J.R. (1981b). *Focusing states rather then traits: A suggested level of abstraction for person perception in psychotherapy.* Unpublished manuscript.

Itoh, K. (1988, September). *The "experiencing" in "Tsubo" image therapy.* Paper presented at the International Conference on Client-centered and Experiential Psychotherapy, Leuven (Belgium).

Kanter, M. (1982-1983). Clearing a space with four cancer patients. *The Focusing Folio, 2(4),* 23-27.

Klein, M.H., Mathieu-Coughlan, Ph., & Kiesler, D.J. (1986). The experiencing scales. In L.S. Greenberg & W.M. Pinsof (Eds.), *The psychotherapeutic process: A research handbook* (pp. 21-71). New York: Guilford.

Leijssen, M. (1984). Focusing in de praktijk van client-centered therapie. In G. Lietaer, Ph.H. van Praag, & J.C.A.G. Swildens (Eds.), *Client-centered psychotherapie in beweging* (pp. 151-179). Leuven/Amersfoort: Acco.

Leijssen, M. (in preparation). Focusing and nonverbal forms of expression. An illustration of a group session, using drawings. *Person-centered Review.*

Leijssen, M., & Roelens, L. (1988). Herstel van contactfuncties bij zwaargestoorde patiënten door middel van Prouty's pre-therapie. *Tijdschrift Klinische Psychologie, 18,* 21-34.

Mathieu-Coughlan, P., & Klein, M.H. (1984). Experiential psychotherapy: Key events in client-centered interactions. In L.N. Rice & L.S. Greenberg (Eds.), *Patterns of change. Intensive analysis of psychotherapy process* (pp. 213-248). New York: Guilford.

McConnaughy, E.A. (1987). The person of the therapist in psychotherapeutic practice. *Psychotherapy, 24,* 303-314.

McGuire, M. (1982-1983). "Clearing a space" with two suicidal clients. *The Focusing Folio, 2(1),* 1-4.

McGuire, M. (1984). Part II of an excerpt from: "Experiential focusing with severely depressed suicidal clients." *The Focusing Folio, 3(3),* 104-119.

Murase, T. (1988, September). *The negative effects of the "focusing" technique.* Paper presented at the International Conference on Client-centered and Experiential Psychotherapy, Leuven (Belgium).

Prouty, G. (1976). Pre-therapy: A method of treating pre-expressive psychotics and retarded patients. *Psychotherapy, Theory, Research and Practice, 13,* 290-294.

Rice, L.N. (1974). The evocative function of the therapist. In D.A. Wexler & L.N. Rice (Eds.), *Innovations in client-centered therapy* (pp. 289-311). New York: Wiley.

Rice, L.N. (1983). The relationship in client-centered therapy. In M.J. Lambert (Ed.), *Psychotherapy and patient relationship.* Homewood: Dow Jones-Irwin.

Rice, L.N. (1984). Client tasks in client-centered therapy. In R.F. Levant & J.M. Shlien (Eds.), *Client-centered therapy and the person-centered approach: New directions in theory, research and practice* (pp. 82-202). New York: Praeger.

Rice, L.N., & Greenberg, L.S. (1984). Patterns of change. *Intensive analysis of psychotherapy process.* New York: Guilford.

Rogers, C.R. (1957). The necessary and sufficient conditions of therapeutic personality change. *Journal of Consulting Psychology, 21,* 97-103.

Rogers, C.R. (1961). *On becoming a person.* Boston: Houghton-Mifflin.

Rogers, C.R. (1967). Some learnings from a study of psychotherapy with schizophrenics. In C.R. Rogers & B. Stevens, *Person to person: The problem of being human* (pp. 181-192). Lafayette, CA: Real People Press.

Rogers, C.R.. (1977). *Carl Rogers counsels an individual II: On hurt and anger.* Washington: APGA video.

Rogers, C.R. (1980). *A way of being.* Boston: Houghton Mifflin.

Santen, B. (1986). Focusing en imaginatie. In R. Van Balen, M. Leijssen, & G. Lietaer (Eds.), *Droom en werkelijkheid in client-centered psychotherapie* (pp. 181-188). Leuven/Amersfoort: Acco.

UNCONDITIONAL CONFIDENCE AS
A FACILITATIVE PRECONDITION

Jan I. HARMAN
Postgraduate Center for Mental Health
New York, U.S.A.

Shunryu Suzuki, the Zen Master whose legacy includes the first Soto Zen monastery in the West, eloquently conveyed the significance of the Japanese phrase "shoshin," or "beginner's mind," which, Suzuki explained, "does not mean a closed mind, but actually an empty mind and a ready mind," (1970, p. 21): "If your mind is empty, it is always ready for anything; it is open to everything. In the beginner's mind there are many possibilities; in the expert's mind there are few" (p. 21).

Carl Rogers seemed to approach the study of helping another to "be that self which one truly is" (1961, p. 163) with a "beginner's mind," and, indeed, seemed to retain his capacity to be "open to everything," as Suzuki put it, throughout his life. For example, in an interview given when he was eighty-two years old, Rogers (1984/1988) spoke of "openness" as "a continuing way of meeting life. This includes openness to the beauty of my fuchsias, as well as to what is going on in me or what is going on in a relationship" (p. 3). Openness to another's experience is central, of course, to the kind of "climate" which Rogers endeavored to provide in psychotherapeutic relationships, one which, he noted, "contains as much of safety, of warmth, of empathic understanding, as I can genuinely find in myself to give" (1961, p. 167). Such openness is implicit in Rogers' description of the empathic process as involving both "entering the private perceptual world of the other and becoming thoroughly at home in it," and looking with "fresh and unfrightened eyes" at that which another fears (1975, p. 4).

Rogers (1961) also observed that movements "toward openness to experience" (p. 173) and "toward trust of self" (p. 175) were among directions taken by those for whom he endeavored to provide a relationship characterized by what have come to be known as the facilitative conditions.

Whether psychotherapy is viewed from the perspective of the therapist or client, then, we recognize that, as Tibetan meditation master Chogyam Trungpa (1985) put it, "any real healing has to come out of some kind of psychological openness" (p. 4). It is therefore important to inquire as to how openness - toward the self as well as toward another - can be developed and sustained.

Trungpa wrote that "openness means we are willing to acknowledge that we are worthy" (p. 5), and pointed out that "there are constant opportunities for such openness, constant gaps in our conceptual and physical structures" (pp. 4-5). The present discussion is intended to examine these latter assertions regarding openness as they may bear upon two questions: 1. How can the facilitative conditions which Rogers (1957) described become fully manifested by the therapist?; and 2. With what understanding did Rogers intend these conditions to be offered to those with whom therapists work? The central thesis of this discussion is that there is a common phenomenological ground from which an approach to answering these two questions emerges. This experiential foundation may be discerned as consisting in an assumptive component of the hypotheses Rogers made in his seminal 1957 paper regarding the role of the facilitative conditions in the process of therapeutic personality change.

Rogers (1957) hypothesized that these conditions, which he noted he had "drawn out" of his clinical experience, are "*necessary* to initiate constructive personality change," and that, taken together, they "appear to be *sufficient* to inaugurate that process" (p. 95). The assumptive basis for these hypotheses would seem to derive from that which Rogers (1961) elsewhere discussed as "one deep learning which is perhaps basic to all of the things I have said thus far," and which, he noted, "has been forced upon me by more than twenty-five years of trying to be helpful to individuals in personal distress. It is simply this. It has been my experience that persons have a basically positive direction" (p. 26). Rogers asserted that "man's tendency to actualize himself, to become his potentialities" constitutes the "curative force in psychotherapy" (pp. 350-351).

One thus has the clear impression that an unwavering confidence in the "basically positive direction" of human beings enabled Rogers to trust that therapeutic personality change would occur if simply allowed to occur. Such trust on the therapist's part would seem to be a context-specific expression of what Trungpa (1984) referred to as the experience of "unconditional confidence," which, he noted, "does not mean that you have confidence *in* something, but it is remaining in the state of confidence.... an unconditional state in which you simply possess an unwavering state of mind that needs no reference point" (pp. 85-86). Rogers (1961) himself referred to the necessity of having "unconditional faith" in another, "no matter what" the other's "present state," (p. 357) if one is to effectively foster another's creativity. Rogers indicated that such unconditional faith is founded upon "accepting the individual as of unconditional worth" (p. 357), adding that the latter "attitude can probably be genuine" only when the "person with a facilitating function .... senses the potentialities of the individual" (p. 357). Phenomenologically, then, the therapist's experience of such unconditional "faith" or confidence may be understood as a facilitative precondition which, as I hope to show, both informs and finds expression through the facilitative conditions originally described by Rogers (1957) as the therapist's congruence or genuineness, and empathic understanding of, and unconditional positive regard for, the client.

It may be argued that confidence in a client's ability to experience therapeutic movement was explicitly conditional in Rogers' view, since he specified six distinct conditions[1] and asserted that "for constructive personality change to occur, it is necessary that these conditions exist and continue over a period of time" (Rogers, 1957, p. 96). Yet what was it that Rogers discovered about the basic nature of human beings such that he would then make so bold an assertion as this: "No other conditions are necessary. If these six conditions exist, and continue over a period of time, this is sufficient. The process of constructive personality change will follow" (p. 96). Although Rogers (1961) was careful to point out that he did not have a "Pollyanna view of human nature," and noted that he was "quite aware that out of defensiveness and inner fear individuals can and do behave in ways which are incredibly cruel," (p. 27), Rogers seemed to address this question in remarking that "one of the most refreshing and invigorating parts of my experience is to work with such individuals and to discover the strongly positive directional tendencies which exist in them, as in all of us, at the deepest levels" (p. 27).

Recognizing that, as Jung (1949/1958) pointed out, "language itself is only a metaphor," and that "even the best attempts at explanation are only more or less successful translations into another metaphorical language" (p. 123), we would expect Rogers' discovery of "strongly positive directional tendencies," if indeed such tendencies exist "in all of us, at the deepest levels" (1961, p. 27), to have been corroborated by the discoveries of others, if perhaps expressed in a somewhat different language. Although rare in the literature of modern psychology, similar discoveries can be found. Heinz Kohut, whom Kahn (1985) regarded as having "succeeded in integrating many of Rogers' concepts of humanistic psychology into his version of psychoanalysis" (p. 893), wrote that "as a depth psychologist I observe regularly that behind the oedipal disturbance lie flawed selfobject responses. And that behind them the primary hope for a normal, self-growth-promoting milieu is still alive" (1982, p. 405). Elsewhere, Kohut (1984) described a patient whose "strength took the form of an innate capacity to maintain a hope for a satisfactory selfobject that would in the future enable him to consolidate the structures he had already formed, however weakly and tentatively, in childhood" (p. 132). Kohut remarked that "we cannot yet fully describe and explain this vigor and the resulting resistiveness to destruction in psychological terms" (p. 132). However, just such a description, in psychological terms, of innate courage and resiliency may be found in Podvoll's (1983) discussion of an "intrinsic instinct toward wakefulness" (p. 14), an instinct Podvoll considers to be "as strong and as omnipresent as any described by Freud and his students, by ethologists, or by cognitive scientists" (p. 15). Podvoll noted that: "While most other instincts appear to involve striving towards personal security, self-justification or pleasure, the instinct toward wakefulness is the urge to penetrate beyond the continuous cycle of ego's self-justification and aggrandizing daydreaming" (1983, p. 15).

Winnicott (1971) would seem to be conveying awareness of an "intrinsic instinct toward wakefulness" in his observation that, "if only we can wait, the patient arrives at understanding creatively and with immense joy .... The principle is that it is the patient and only the patient who has the answers" (pp. 86-87). Guntrip (1969) wrote of a "secret foundation of ... stillness, security, and peace" which "in the deepest unconscious ... is never lost," and which he attributed to "that oneness of the child with the mother, and through her with 'mother-nature'"[2] (p. 269). Searles (1979) hypothesized that "innate among man's most powerful strivings toward his fellow men, beginning in the earliest years and even earliest months of life, is an essentially psychotherapeutic striving" (p. 380), adding that "the tiny percentage of human beings who devote their professional careers to the practice of psychoanalysis or psychotherapy are only giving explicit expression to a therapeutic devotion which all human beings share" (p. 380).

Shainberg (1983) asserted that "the therapist who facilitates healing" has "consistent experience" with a "level of mind" which is "calm and characterized not by thought, but by silence, awareness, emptiness of craving," and that "from this Silence or Source, he sees and feels the inherent goodness of all of his patients, of all men, who when they contact this level of mind, are themselves what they are seeking" (p. 83). Shainberg added that "experience with this level of mind" is "the source of compassionate openness" (p. 83). Trungpa (1983) referred to the "potential that every human being has to express gentleness and warmth in themselves" as a manifestation of what he termed "basic goodness" (pp. 5-6). Trungpa explained that "basic goodness is not necessarily *solid* goodness, but just basic goodness, unconditional goodness" (p. 6). Elsewhere, Trungpa (1984) noted that "it is not just an arbitrary idea that the world is good, but it is good because we can *experience* its goodness. We can experience our world as healthy and straightforward, direct and real, because our basic nature is to go along with the goodness of situations" (p. 31).

MANIFESTATION OF THE FACILITATIVE CONDITIONS AS INFORMED BY UNCONDITIONAL CONFIDENCE

Among those experiences Rogers (1961) observed to be characteristic for clients who have reached what he conceived as the "seventh and final stage" (p. 151) of the process of psychotherapy, two seem particularly reflective of awareness, to some degree at least, of experience of unconditional confidence. One is the client's experience of what Rogers termed "a basic trust in his own process" (p. 151); the other appears to refer to a phenomenological shift such that, as Rogers put it, "the self is much less frequently a perceived object, and much more frequently something confidently felt in process" (p. 153). Jung (1957/1971) emphasized an approach to psychotherapeutic treatment which "presupposes insights which are at least potentially present in the patient and can therefore be made conscious" (p. 279). However, and importantly, Jung observed that "if the analyst knows nothing of these potentialities he cannot help the patient to develop them either"

(p. 279). Similarly, it would seem evident that if therapists have not themselves experienced what Rogers (1961) referred to as a "basic trust" in their own process (p. 151) such that the self ceases to be a "perceived object," but rather becomes "something confidently felt in process" (p.153), they would not be expected to readily, if at all, become "thoroughly at home" (Rogers, 1975, p. 4) with such experiences in another, much less able to provide a climate within which such experiencing could become manifested by another. If, as is posited here, the therapist's experience of unconditional confidence constitutes a phenomenological basis for the fullest manifestation of unconditional positive regard, genuineness, and empathic responsivity, the need for recognition of unconditional confidence as a distinctive component of what Shainberg (1983) has referred to as the "disposition of mind that heals" (p. 83) also becomes evident.

Remarking more than three decades ago that "it troubles me to hold such a radical point of view," Rogers (1957) included among implications of his hypotheses regarding the conditions of therapeutic personality change his conclusion that, if congruence, unconditional positive regard and empathic understanding "are to be acquired" by therapists, "they must," he asserted, "be acquired through an experiential training - which may be, but usually is not, a part of professional training" (p. 101). Although he then indicated that neither training the intellect nor the mere acquisition of information constituted sufficient preparation for becoming a therapist, Rogers (1957) did not suggest any particular form of experiential training as likely to assist one in accomplishing the development of mind he believed necessary. Clearly, then, there is a need to define with greater precision the training of mind which would be sufficient to enable one to shift phenomenologically from mere cognitive understanding of the facilitative conditions to their actual manifestation. Welwood's (1983) description of his own training as a psychotherapist is elucidative in this regard:

> "When I studied Rogerian therapy in graduate school, I felt frustrated because I was never taught how to develop 'unconditional positive regard' for the client. I was told that this was essential, and it sounded good to me, but it was just assumed that I should be able to feel this way toward anyone who walked into my office" (p. xiii).

Rogers was not the first theorist, of course, to emphasize the necessity of experiential training for those who would practice psychotherapy; that distinction, at least in the West, belongs to

Sigmund Freud. In his 1912 "recommendations for physicians on the psychoanalytic method of treatment," Freud (1912/1963) wrote that "years ago I replied to the question of how one becomes an analyst with the answer: By the analysis of one's own dreams" (p. 122); he added, however, that "not everyone is able to interpret his own dreams without the help of another," and credited what was then known as the "Zurich school" (i.e., Carl Jung and his colleagues) with having "laid it down as a requisition that anyone who wishes to practise analysis of others should first submit to be analysed himself by a competent person" (p. 122). Freud advised that "anyone taking up the work seriously should choose this course" (p. 122). A training analysis, however, is a long and expensive endeavor undertaken by relatively few in the helping professions; moreover, it is apparent, as Shainberg (1983) concluded from her experience as a supervisor of psychoanalytic trainees, that "personal psychoanalysis does not always enable the therapist to be consistently empathic with patients who make deep emotional demands on them" (p. 82). Shainberg noted, for example, that she has "seen therapists with long analyses and with a good theoretical grasp unable to work when someone is consistently angry with them" (p. 82).

Shainberg (1983) found in the meditative disciplines of the East "some guidance towards gaining a mind that is able to be and remain open to people" (p. 83). Similarly, Welwood (1983) noted that he eventually "discovered ... that meditation provided a concrete operational method for developing just those ingredients of acceptance and unconditional friendliness that are most essential for successful therapy" (p. xiii), and posited that:

> "A therapist who sits through the subtle, complex twists and turns of his own thoughts and feelings is unlikely to find many of his client's problems all that alien, shocking, or unfamiliar. The more a therapist trusts his own basic goodness underneath his confusion, the more he can help clients find their way between these two aspects of themselves. And the more he can face his own fear, the more fearlessly he can approach his clients' problems as well, which may help them develop greater self-confidence themselves" (p. xiii).

Podvoll (1983) considers the "personal discipline of mindfulness-awareness meditation practice" to be "crucial for the development of the psychotherapist" (p. 14): "Only by studying the nature of our own minds and examining the experience of wakefulness in our own lives," he asserted, "can we recognize and appreciate it in another" (p. 14).

Trungpa (1984) cogently conveyed the direct relationship between meditative practice and the cultivation of both genuineness and unconditional confidence thus:

> "When you have a sense of trusting in your own existence, then what you communicate to other people is genuine and trustworthy. Self-deception often arises because you are afraid of your own intelligence and afraid that you won't be able to deal properly with your life. You are unable to acknowledge your own innate wisdom. Instead, you see wisdom as some monumental thing outside of yourself. That attitude has to be overcome. In order to be without deception, the only reference point you can rely on is the knowledge that basic goodness exists in you already. The certainty of that knowledge can be experienced in the practice of meditation. In meditation, you experience a state of mind that is without second thoughts, free from fear and doubt. That unwavering mind is not swayed by the temporary ups and downs of thoughts and emotions" (pp. 83-84).

By "meditation," Trungpa (1984) explained, he meant to refer to "something very basic and simple that is not tied to any one culture," a "very basic act: Sitting on the ground, assuming a good posture, and developing a sense of our spot, our place on this earth" (pp. 36-37). Importantly, Trungpa added that while the term "meditation" is sometimes employed to refer to "achieving a higher state of mind by entering into a trance or absorption state of some kind," he, rather, meant to refer to "a completely different concept of meditation: Unconditional meditation, without any object or idea in mind," i.e., to "simply training our state of being so that our mind and body can be synchronized" (p. 37).

It may seem odd to imply that body and mind are not by their very nature synchronized, and yet precise examination of our actual experience of ourselves, moment by moment, readily reveals a more or less continual sense of bodily tension attending to ubiquitous, anxiety-laden self-representational mentation. As Tendzin (1987) aptly put it, "generally we don't see anything because we are looking at ourselves all the time. Even when we think we're not, we are" (p. 9). In psychoanalytic terms, one aspect of the lack of inner harmony in this regard may be recognized as a tendency to become transfixed by what could be described as "transferential imperatives" such that, e.g., we find ourselves preoccupied with a struggle to elicit from the world-as-we-experience-it confirmations that we are worthy of self-acceptance. Indeed, Trungpa (1975) discussed the "origin of neurotic mind" as consisting in:

A tendency to identify oneself with desires and conflicts related to a world outside. And the question is immediately there as to whether such conflicts actually exist externally or whether they are internal. This uncertainty solidifies the whole sense that a problem of some kind exists. What is real? What is not real? That is always our biggest problem. It is ego's problem" (p. 7).

It is within the context of the foregoing understandings that the meaning of the first of the earlier-cited statements made by Trungpa (1985) regarding openness can be more clearly discerned. When we become genuinely willing to fully open ourselves to ourselves just as we are, such openness implies that "we are willing to acknowledge that we are worthy" (p. 5). The meaning of the second of the aforementioned statements by Trungpa - that there are "constant opportunities for such openness, constant gaps in our conceptual and physical structures" (pp. 4-5) - emerges from the more precisely differentiated understanding of the nature of ego which mindfulness-awareness meditative discipline yields. Luyten (1985) noted that "ego is neither good nor bad," but rather is "merely a naturally arising sense of self in relation to some context, such as job or family" (p. 44). As such, ego is "inherently conditional, permeable, and subject to change" (p. 44), and "only becomes problematic when we attempt to maintain it" (p. 45). Rogers (1961) seemed to indicate that clients who reach an advanced stage of awareness of themselves approach this very insight; for such individuals, Rogers wrote, "experiencing has lost almost completely its structure-bound aspects" (p. 152), the self "becomes increasingly simply the subjective and reflexive awareness of experiencing" (p. 153), and "personal constructs" come to "be held loosely" (p. 153).

Luyten (1985) observed that "paradoxically, our attempts to maintain ego are based on the inherent awareness that the existence of ego is questionable," and referred to "egolessness" as "simply open awareness" (p. 45). It will be apparent, then, that the "covering and uncovering of this experience of no abiding self" (Luyten, 1985, p. 45) allow for recognition of what Trungpa (1985) referred to as the "constant gaps in our conceptual ... structures," and provide, in turn, "constant opportunities" for openness to ourselves and others.

While Rogers' (1961) process conception of psychotherapy suggests that clients at advanced stages of self-awareness have become more comfortable with the experience of what Luyten (1985) has referred to as "this intermittent, flickering sense of self," clearly for those at less advanced stages this experience, as Luyten notes, "can be very unsettling" (p. 45). It would seem, then, that the critical difference between those who are comfortable with awareness of egolessness and those who find it unsettling consists in the presence, in the former case, or absence, in the latter, of what Rogers (1961) termed the experience of "a basic trust" in one's "own process" (p. 151), or what has been discussed here as the experience of basic, unconditional confidence. When we lack such basic trust or unconditional confidence, we search for something abiding to have confidence in. The search, however, necessarily goes on ad infinitum, as does our dissatisfaction with ourselves, since anywhere we so try to perch our confidence is, as Freud (1923/1960) aptly described ego, "the actual seat of anxiety" (p. 47). Indeed, Luyten (1985) noted that "many symptoms and defenses may be neurotic attempts at controlling the panic that arises with the experience of egolessness" (p. 45).

Curiously then, although, as Tendzin (1987) remarked, "you realize that every moment of your life is vulnerable," and that "there is no point where you can say, 'I am secure'" (p. 9), in the absence of the experience of unconditional confidence we try to pretend to ourselves that this simply is not so. Not surprisingly, ego will even go so far as to try to cleverly construe the notion of egolessness as referring to something abiding in time or space or mind within which it may finally somehow find refuge from anxiety, which is rather amusing, if also sad. In describing just this sort of confusion, the twelfth-century Tibetan physician and scholar Gampopa[3] employed Saraha's exclamation that: "Those who believe in existence are stupid like cattle, but those who believe in non-existence are still more stupid."

With the recognition of egolessness, we may arrive at a clearer conceptual understanding of what is meant by an "unconditional state in which you simply possess an unwavering state of mind that needs no reference point" (Trungpa, 1984, p. 86). However, if we shy away from our immediate, personal experience of the gaps in our sense of self, then unconditional confidence and complete openness remain simply ideas. As Tendzin (1987) remarked, "in this day and age, people talk about psychological awakening and awareness, but the truth of the matter, when you come right down to it, is that fear is your mate" (p. 9); "in order for confidence to become continuous," he noted, "one must understand the nature of fear" (p. 9).

Trungpa (1984) observed that "we know that we are going to die, so we are afraid," and, indeed, "petrified of our death" (p. 47), and asserted that "one's attitude toward death is central to any healing process" (Trungpa, 1985, p. 3). While acknowledging that "no one actually wants to face the possibility of death, or even the idea of death" (p. 3), Trungpa advised that "psychiatrists and physicians, as well as their patients, have to come to terms with their sense of anxiety about the possibility of nonexistence" (p. 9):

"When there is that kind of openness, the healer does not have to solve a person's problem completely. The approach of trying to repair everything has always been a problem in the past, creating a string of successive cures and successive deceptions, which seem to go hand in hand. Once the basic fear is acknowledged, continuing with the treatment becomes very easy .... Of course, it is always easier to look down on your patients and their predicament, thinking how lucky you are that you do not have their diseases. You can feel somewhat superior. But the acknowledgment of your common ground - of your common experience of birth, old age, sickness and death, and the fear which underlies all of those - brings a sense of humility. That is the beginning of the healing process. The rest seems to follow quite easily and naturally, based on one's inherent wisdom and compassion" (p. 9).

While emphasizing the necessity of actually experiencing our fear, Tendzin (1987) noted that this does not mean that the way to become confident is to "constantly terrify oneself" (p. 9); rather, he explained, the "confidence of the discipline of meditation" means that "having had some sense of gentleness in one's own being, it is possible to take the time to actually examine the fear" (p. 9), adding that "when you see that fear and fearlessness are totally interrelated, you begin to have a certain attitude of bravery" (p. 9).

A thorough discussion of how unconditional confidence can be experienced is beyond the scope of this paper.[4] In now considering how unconditional confidence finds expression through each of the three facilitative conditions, however, it will be helpful to bear in mind the following brief description of how such confidence, when experienced, manifests in one's general way of being. Trungpa (1984) noted that "this kind of confidence contains gentleness, because the notion of fear does not arise; sturdiness, because in the state of confidence there is ever-present resourcefulness; and joy, because trusting in the heart brings a greater sense of humor" (p. 86).

THE FACILITATIVE CONDITIONS AS EXPRESSIVE OF
UNCONDITIONAL CONFIDENCE

It is as an experiential component of what Rogers (1957) termed unconditional positive regard that unconditional confidence is perhaps most readily recognizable. In addition to caring genuinely for the client and avoiding "behavior that is overtly or covertly judgmental or evaluative," Gelso and Carter (1985) have understood unconditional positive regard to mean that:

> "The therapist completely trusts the client's resources for self-understanding and positive change. The therapist believes and conveys to the client that he or she, the client, can effectively follow his or her own process of change, can be relied upon to discover him- or herself" (p. 213).

Gelso and Carter added that "presumably, this belief becomes internalized by the client, who learns to trust him- or herself more," (p. 213), an experience analogous to the third phase of Barrett-Lennard's (1981) model of the empathic process, i.e., received empathy, which in this case might be termed "received trust" (i.e., experiencing that one's therapist does indeed trust completely in one's capacity for therapeutic movement). However, when we consider that the basis for trusting completely in another's capacity for self-understanding consists in our recognition of what Podvoll (1983) termed the "intrinsic instinct toward wakefulness" (p. 14), we arrive at an understanding of how it is that clients develop basic trust in themselves which differs somewhat from that of Gelso and Carter (1985). When therapists themselves actually experience that, as Trungpa (1984) put it, "when you are at ease, you find a state of true healthy mind" (p. 171), therapy is not viewed as a matter of persuading clients to take it from us on "blind faith," so to speak, that they can trust their experience, their intelligence, or their inherent resources for development. Although we communicate our trust in their instinct toward wakefulness by the way in which we relate to them, it is not so much that clients "internalize" our "belief" in this regard as that, within a climate characterized by the fullest manifestation of the facilitative conditions, they experience the freedom to arrive at the discovery of their instinct toward wakefulness, and of the trustworthiness of their inherent nature as human beings, for themselves. Trungpa (1983) remarked that in conducting psychotherapy "there are no tricks involved. We are not trying to talk people out of or into anything. We are not trying to talk people out of their insanity, or talk them into sanity" (pp. 6-7); rather, he noted elsewhere, "we do not really change anyone; they simply grow" (Trungpa, 1985, p. 3).

Unconditional positive regard is the manifestation of an appreciative openness; Rogers (1957) referred to this condition as the therapist's experience of "warm acceptance of each aspect of the client's experience" (p. 98). Seguin (1970) wrote of what he termed the "psychotherapeutic eros" as consisting in the "tender, on the part of the therapist, of a gift - the freedom to be - without conditions" (p. 53); "possessing that freedom at last," Seguin noted, "the patient is able to face and accept those parts of himself that he - with or without reason - learned so painfully to reject" (p. 53). Clearly, if the therapist does not experience unconditional confidence, that is, a mind free from fear and doubt, then he or she, knowingly or not, will be unable to warmly accept all aspects of another's experience. That is, therapists experience countertransferential imperatives at the phenomenological boundaries beyond which genuine openness is no longer possible, having encountered self-representational phenomena which effectively entrap and restrain their willingness to acknowledge that they are worthy. The experience of unconditional confidence is thus a precondition for the experience of thoroughly unconditional positive regard. Conditional confidence leads not only to conditional positive regard for the client, but to conditional positive self-regard, which, taken together, become the basis for what Shainberg (1983) referred to as a "collusive way to work: I won't upset you if you won't upset me so much" (p. 82).

Remaining completely genuine in any relationship may also be understood as an expression of unconditional confidence. By fearlessly remaining open to all aspects of themselves, therapists are enabled to be, as Rogers (1957) put it, "freely and deeply" (p. 97) themselves in their relationships with clients. Podvoll (1983) observed that "the therapist's courage ... takes diverse forms," and asserted that "the most comprehensive of all is the ability to be in a relationship beyond memory, repetition, or transference" (p. 30).

Empathic responsivity may be seen as expressive of unconditional confidence in several respects. The most apparent of these concerns the manifestation of what Barrett-Lennard (1981) referred to as an "empathic attentional set" which, he noted, allows for "the possibility of an empathic understanding process" (p. 94).. Attending to another with such perceptual openness, free from what Barrett-Lennard termed a "pre-determined frame of reference" (p. 93), may be understood as expressive of what Trungpa (1984) referred to as an "unconditional state in which you simply possess an unwavering state of mind that needs no reference point" (p. 86).

Beyond this, when empathic discrimination and resonation have been informed by the experience of unconditional confidence, one begins, as Trungpa (1983) put it, to "look into where the patient's health is coming from" (p. 8). It bears reiteration that this is not simply a matter of adopting some new theoretical framework. Trungpa (1984, p. 51) pointed out that "being without doubt has nothing to do with accepting the validity of a philosophy or concept. It is not that you should be converted or subjected to someone's crusade until you have no doubt about your beliefs"; rather, he noted, "absence of doubt is trusting in the heart, trusting yourself" (p. 51). If therapists do not trust themselves in this most fundamental sense, they will find it difficult to completely trust in the inherent health of those with whom they work: one cannot resonate with something one doesn't experience. Podvoll (1983) wrote that "embedded within the history of neurosis is another kind of history whose subtlety and evanescence make it more difficult to explore. It is the history of sanity" (p. 11). While noting that "there are certain signs and landmark events that characterize wakefulness and sanity in another's life," Podvoll emphasized that "they can hardly be noticed until one first experiences and identifies them in oneself" (p. 14).

Finally, and perhaps most interestingly, a new understanding of empathic responsivity emerges when the experience of this condition has been informed by the experience of mind which is free from doubt and needs no reference point. Luyten (1985) employed the term "exchange" to refer to "that process by which we consciously or unconsciously experience another person's state of mind, or they experience ours" (p. 45), and explained that "exchange is not a therapeutic technique, but a constantly recurring moment in which the distinction between self and other flickers" (p. 45). Exchange has "two aspects: Touching and letting go" (Luyten, 1985, p. 45); Luyten described the first aspect, touching, as "the moment of joining another's experience, as well as sharing a common ground of openness" (p. 45).

The capacity for "touching," understood as letting the world fully into one's heart, can be developed through the practice of meditation;

and we have here come full circle, so to speak, for opening our hearts in this way becomes the basis for what Trungpa (1984) referred to as "going beyond fear" (p. 48):

> "When you slouch, you are trying to hide your heart, trying to protect it by slumping over. But when you sit upright but relaxed in the posture of meditation, your heart is naked. Your entire being is exposed - to yourself, first of all, but to others as well. So through the practice of sitting still and following your breath as it goes out and dissolves, you are connecting with your heart. By simply letting yourself be, as you are, you develop genuine sympathy towards yourself. When you awaken your heart in this way, you find, to your surprise, that your heart is empty. You find that you are looking into outer space. What are you, who are you, where is your heart? If you really look, you won't find anything tangible and solid .... If you search for awakened heart, if you put your hand through your rib cage and feel for it, there is nothing there except for tenderness. You feel sore and soft, and if you open your eyes to the rest of the world, you feel tremendous sadness .... this experience of sadness is unconditioned. It occurs because your heart is completely exposed... this experience of sad and tender heart is what gives birth to fearlessness" (pp. 45-46).

When therapists can experience this sadness and tenderness, and the fearlessness which arises from it, the capacity for empathic resonation is especially enhanced: Already thoroughly heartbroken, there is nothing to protect ourselves from, and having become gentle with ourselves, we no longer condemn self-condemnatory thoughts, nor fear fearful thoughts. Having rested the mind, we can afford to relax into the therapeutic relationship completely, and our communication of empathic understanding becomes powerfully genuine. Communication of understanding becomes, as Trungpa (1985) put it, "something more than just mechanically saying 'Yes, I know. It hurts very badly'" (p. 8); rather, when we can "actually feel" another's hurt and "share his anxiety," we "can then say it in a different way: 'Yes, I feel that pain'" (p. 8).

It is important to recognize, at the same time, that, as Luyten (1985) pointed out, the "capacity for touching, or for accurate empathy, is only the first part of exchange," (p. 46), and that without the capacity for "letting go," the second component of exchange, "both client and therapist can get stuck in exchange or 'become fused'," which would be to "grasp the experience of this shared feeling state as an identity" (p. 46). The experience of a state of mind which needs no reference point enables one to let go, for "letting go," Luyten noted, refers to "the capacity of mind to relax fixation" (p. 46). Together, the two aspects of exchange have "direct healing value .... the therapist's relaxation and lack of fixation is directly available to the client" (p. 46).

One has the distinct impression that near the end of his life, Carl Rogers experienced this way of being in the therapeutic relationship. In the interview noted earlier, conducted but a few years before his death, Rogers (1984/1988) said:

> "Recently my view has broadened into a new area that cannot as yet be studied empirically. When I am at my best as a group facilitator or a therapist, when I am closest to my inner intuitive self, or perhaps in a slightly altered state of consciousness, then whatever I do seems to be full of healing. My presence alone is releasing and helpful. I cannot force this experience, but when I can relax and be close to my transcendental core, I may behave in strange and impulsive ways in the relationship - ways I cannot justify rationally and which have nothing to do with my thought processes. But these strange behaviors turn out to be right in some odd way. Profound growth, healing, and energy are present. At those moments, it seems that my inner spirit has reached out and touched the inner spirit of the other. Our relationship transcends itself and becomes part of something larger" (p. 3).

NOTES

1. In addition to the therapist's congruence in the relationship, the experience of unconditional positive regard for and empathic understanding of the client, Rogers hypothesized that three additional conditions were necessary for "constructive personality change to occur": "Two persons are in psychological contact"; the client "is in a state of incongruence, being vulnerable or anxious"; and "communication to the client of the therapist's empathic understanding and unconditional positive regard is to a minimal degree achieved" (Rogers, 1957, p. 96).

2. Erikson (1968) regarded the quality of the mother-infant relationship as the primary determinant of the degree to which the infant develops "a sense of basic trust," which Erikson referred to as "the ontological source of faith and hope" (p. 82). Only when the mother can "feel a certain wholesome relation between her biological role and the values of her community," Erikson asserted, "can she communicate to the baby, in the unmistakable language of somatic interchange, that the baby may trust her, the world, and - himself" (p. 82). Grof's (1976) research with several hundred subjects in more than 2,500 LSD sessions conducted at the Psychiatric Research Institute in Prague and the Maryland Psychiatric Research Center in the United States yielded subjective accounts which would seem to constitute empirical evidence for Guntrip's (1969) hypothesis regarding a "foundation of ... stillness, security, and peace" which "in the deepest unconscious ... is never lost" (p. 269). Grof

found that "transpersonal experiences" were "quite common in advanced sessions" of psycholytic (LSD) psychotherapy (p. 154); in one of the "most profound" of such experiences reported by subjects, Grof noted, the individual "feels that he has reached the reality underlying all realities," wherein "the illusions of matter, space, and time" have been "completely transcended" (p. 203), an experience which, Grof observed, "satisfies the subject's intellectual, philosophical, and spiritual craving" (p. 204). While we may speculate as to whether the nature of "self" which feels it has "reached the reality underlying all realities" (Grof, 1976, p. 203) is not dissimilar to what James (1890) regarded as the "self of all the other selves.... the home of interest.... that within us to which pleasure and pain, the pleasant and the painful, speak" (pp. 297-298), Shunryu Suzuki (1970) cautioned that "Thinking which leaves traces comes out of your relative confused mind. Relative mind is the mind which sets itself in relation to other things, thus limiting itself. It is this small mind which creates gaining ideas and leaves traces of itself" (p. 62).

3. From Gampopa's work entitled *The jewel ornament of liberation,* translated and annotated by Herbert V. Guenther (1959/1971, p. 211; Berkeley: Shambhala).

4. A thorough discussion of the experience of unconditional confidence may be found in Trungpa's (1984) work *Shambhala: The sacred path of the warrior* (chapter 10, "Letting go", pp. 77-86).

REFERENCES

Barrett-Lennard, G.T. (1981). The empathy cycle: Refinement of a nuclear concept. *Journal of Counseling Psychology, 28(2),* 91-100.

Erikson, E.H. (1968). *Identity: Youth and crisis.* New York: Norton.

Freud, S. (1960). *The ego and the id* (J. Riviere, Trans.; J. Strachey, Ed.). New York: Norton. (Original work published 1923).

Freud, S. (1963). Recommendations for physicians on the psychoanalytic method of treatment. In P. Reiff (Ed.), *Freud: Therapy and technique* (pp. 117-126). New York: MacMillan. (Original work published 1912).

Gelso, C.J., & Carter, J.A. (1985). The relationship in counseling and psychotherapy: Components, consequences, and theoretical antecedents. *The Counseling Psychologist, 13,* 155-243.

Grof, S. (1976). *Realms of the human unconscious: Observations from LSD research.* New York: Dutton.

Guntrip, H. (1969). *Schizoid phenomena object relations and the self.* New York: International Universities Press.

James, W. (1890). *The principles of psychology* (Vol. I). New York: Henry Holt.

Jung, C.G. (1958). The psychology of the child archetype. In V.S. de Laszlo (Ed.), *Psyche and symbol: A selection from the writings of C.G. Jung* (pp. 113-131). New York: Doubleday Anchor. (Original work published 1949).

Jung, C.G. (1971). The transcendent function. In J. Campbell (Ed.), *The portable*

268

Jung (pp. 273-300) (R.F.C. Hull, Trans.). New York: Viking Press. (Original work published 1957).

Kahn, E. (1985). Heinz Kohut and Carl Rogers: A timely comparison. *American Psychologist, 40,* 893-904.

Kohut, H. (1982). Introspection, empathy, and the semi-circle of mental health. *International Journal of Psychoanalysis, 63,* 395-407.

Kohut, H. (1984). *How does analysis cure?* (A. Goldberg & P.E. Stepansky, Eds.). Chicago: University of Chicago Press.

Luyten, M.F. (1985). Egolessness and the "borderline" experience. *Naropa Institute Journal of Psychology, 3,* 43-70.

Podvoll, E.M. (1983). The history of sanity in contemplative psychotherapy. *Naropa Institute Journal of Psychology, 2,* 11-32.

Rogers, C.R. (1957). The necessary and sufficient conditions of therapeutic personality change. *Journal of Consulting Psychology, 21,* 95-103.

Rogers, C.R. (1961). *On becoming a person.* Boston: Houghton Mifflin.

Rogers, C.R. (1975). Empathic: An unappreciated way of being. *The Counseling Psychologist, 5,* 2-10.

Rogers, C.R. (1988). An interview with Carl Rogers: A way of meeting. *Laughing man.* San Rafael: Dawn Horse Press. (Originally published Winter, 1984).

Searles, H. (1979). *Countertransference and related subjects.* New York: International Universities Press.

Seguin, C.A. (1970). Beyond instinct, deeper than libido. In A.W.R. Sipe (Ed.), *Hope: Psychiatry's commitment* (pp. 49-56). New York: Brunner Mazel.

Shainberg, D. (1983). *Healing in psychotherapy: The process of holistic change.* New York: Gordon and Breach.

Suzuki, S. (1970). *Zen mind, beginner's mind.* Tokyo: John Weatherhill.

Tendzin, O. (1987). Being without a doubt. *The Vajradhatu Sun, 9(1),* 9, 14.

Trungpa, C. (1975). *Glimpses of abhidharma.* Boulder: Vajradhatu.

Trungpa, C. (1983). Creating an environment of sanity. *Naropa Institute Journal of Psychology, 2,* 1-10.

Trungpa, C. (1984). *Shambhala: The sacred path of the warrior.* Boston: Shambhala (C.R. Gimian, Ed.).

Trungpa, C. (1985). Acknowledging death as the common ground of healing. *Naropa Institute Journal of Psychology, 3,* 3-10.

Welwood, J. (1983). Introduction. In J. Welwood (Ed.), *Awakening the heart: East/West approaches to psychotherapy and the healing relationship* (pp. vii-xiv). Boulder: Shambhala.

Winnicott, D.W. (1971). *Playing and reality.* London: Tavistock.

THE PROCESS OF EMPATHY: HOLDING AND LETTING GO

Greet VANAERSCHOT
Katholieke Universiteit Leuven, Belgium

INTRODUCTION

Empathy is generally considered as an essential skill for a good psychotherapist. This concept has always been regarded as very important, being one of the three core conditions described by Rogers within the client-centered school of thought. But psychoanalysis too has become more interested in the phenomenon "empathy." Proof hereof are the various publications that have appeared on this subject for the last twenty years.

The objective of this article is to elucidate the process of empathic understanding, as it takes place in the very person of the therapist himself. The initial impetus to this quest was the confusion that I had often experienced concerning empathy and congruence. I sometimes felt these basic attitudes to be two completely different and mutually irreconcilable positions which a therapist can take towards his client: Either a receptive, passive, resonant and reflective way of being, in which the person of the therapist himself is practically non-existent, i.e. the empathic position; or, on the other hand, a position in which the therapist exerts his own person in an active way, converting it to the client's process. As such, the therapist becomes very transparent, i.e. the congruent position. Some questions I asked myself in this respect were: Can I ever experience what somebody else experiences or feels, loose and detached from my own being? Shall I ever be able to know one's phenomenological world, without this knowledge referring to my own? What kind of knowledge is meant here? Besides those questions about the nature of this knowledge, I also asked myself about the fundamental attitude as a basis for empathic understanding. Is it really possible to put oneself completely aside? Will the therapist then become a kind of an "empty box" that lets himself fill with the "other"? How do I then "empty" myself? And what does Rogers mean with the "as-if" quality? How am I to understand the moments that I feel I am "merging" with my client, not being conscious of myself as a separate person? In respect to all these questions, I have developed some insight and views, that I shall explain and elucidate by means of some thesis statements. These views are based on the one hand on my own experiences as a therapist and on my experience as a supervisor of graduate students, and on the other hand on literature of both the client-centered and psychoanalytical orientation. These two schools of thought do, in my opinion, very often stand for rather similar views and experiences, and I feel that an open dialogue between them can only contribute to our knowledge of therapeutic work.

A. EMPATHY AS THE ROYAL PATHWAY TO "KNOWLEDGE" OF THE CLIENT'S WORLD

Empathy is in both the client-centered and psychoanalytical orientation considered as a way of knowing equivalent to any other form of knowing.

Rogers (1959) discerns empathy from two other ways of knowing, i.e. introspection and science. Each of these ways of knowing is essentially a formulation of hypotheses. It is the frame of reference one takes as well as the way of checking those hypotheses which distinguish those three ways of knowing. With regard to introspection, one perceives oneself from one's own frame of reference, and the checking is realized by further focusing on one's own experience. The scientist however will perceive the object of concern from his own frame of reference, and as such the newly formulated hypotheses will be checked through the internal frames of reference of his colleagues. With empathy finally, one perceives from the internal frame of reference of the subject of concern and the new hypotheses will be checked with the subject itself. Thus, Rogers considers empathy to be a special way of knowing, which is indeed different, but equivalent to other modes of knowing.

Kohut too argues that empathy is indeed a different, but in no respect an inferior mode of observation. In his opinion, empathy is essentially "vicarious introspection," and "only a phenomenon that we can attempt to observe by introspection or by empathy with another's introspection may be called psychological" (Kohut, 1959, p. 452).

So, empathy essentially means knowing the subjective inner world of the other. This knowledge originates from an attempt to perceive from the subject's internal frame of reference, and not from one's own subjective viewpoint. To put it with Rogers:

> "The state of empathy, or being empathic, is to perceive the internal frame of reference of another with accuracy, and with the emotional components and meanings which pertain thereto, as if one were the other person, but without ever losing the 'as if' condition. Thus it means to sense the hurt or the pleasure of another as he senses it, and to perceive the causes thereof as he perceives them, but without ever losing the recognition that it is as if I were hurt or pleased etc. If this 'as if' quality is lost, then the state is one of identification" (Rogers, 1959, p. 210-211).

Rogers' definition clarifies the kind of knowledge that is meant here: The knowledge of the other's inner subjective world namely consists of both emotional and cognitive elements. The therapist tries not only to know, but also to feel what the client feels and experiences.

An important aspect, especially emphasized in psychoanalytical literature, is the fact that empathy is an intrapsychic phenomenon, a capacity proper to mankind. This idea stresses the process in the therapist himself. This aspect is elucidated by Buie's definition (1981), which is in fact a summary of all the different elements that are thought of by different analysts as being more or less essential for the concept of empathy. "One could say that empathy occurs in an interpersonal setting between persons who remain aware of their separateness, yet in essence it is an intrapsychic phenomenon based in a human capacity to know another person's inner experience from moment to moment" (Buie, 1981, p. 282).

B. EMPATHIC UNDERSTANDING WILL NEVER LEAD TO A DIRECT KNOWLEDGE OF THE PHENOMENOLOGICAL WORLD OF THE OTHER. OUR KNOWLEDGE IS ALWAYS INFERENTIAL: THE PROCESS OF EMPATHY IS ONE OF COMPARISON AND "TUNING IN TO"

Here, the question can be asked: How can a therapist get to know the other's inner subjective world? What is this "process of entering the other's world?" What kind of process takes place in the therapist? How is perception from the subject's internal frame of reference possible?

Many consider empathy to be an innate capacity, a kind of sixth sense, an intuitive apprehending, a special way of knowing that has nothing to do with the "normal" sensory perception. This is, in my opinion, a misapprehension which is still heard in both the psycho-analytical and client-centered circles. Breeding ground for this point of view is, I think, the sudden and at first sight inexplicable way the empathic therapist comes into contact with parts of the client's phenomenological world.

First, I would like to illustrate this sudden understanding by means of an example from my own practice. Secondly, I shall elaborate on this empathic process, and in a third part I shall discuss the limitations, characteristic to this process.

1. Illustration

The clinical example I have chosen is the case of a young woman, whom I have been seeing for about a year and a half. Until recently, therapy merely consisted of building up a relationship of mutual trust, which was extremely difficult for her. Gradually, she has started to show me something of what she is experiencing inside and she has begun to utter some of her feelings. Until then, her inner world was completely blocked. Therefore, I could hardly share the client's inner experience. I had to imagine what she felt, but no matter how hard I tried, it remained a merely cognitive understanding, I could not really empathize with her.

Recently, she has come to tell me something about an enormous anxiety, arisen by a certain coincidence which gave her the feeling that there was no place for her. All of a sudden, I could apprehend a part of her inner world; I could suddenly understand and feel what she was going through. All of a sudden the image of me and my little daughter came to me: The way I take her on my lap and comfort her when something frightening happens; how I hold, cuddle and reassure her, telling her: "Calm down, baby, tell mummy what's wrong!" At that very moment I had that similar intense feeling of motherly care towards my client, and at the same time, I realized that she had never experienced this. Through this intense apprehending I came to a deep understanding of her inner experiences. From then on, I continuously switched from exploring her enormous anxiety on the one hand, to trying to find an actual solution on the other hand so that her situation would become less frightening to her. Exactly this switching made it possible for her to express her fear and explore it further. In later sessions, it became clear that my apprehending had been correct: Her mother had indeed never been able or never wanted to protect her daughter from outer aggression.

On the one hand, I was puzzled that my experience had been so intense and that I could, all of a sudden, be so sure about things she had lived through during her childhood. She had, after all, not yet mentioned the lack of protection and safety from her mother's side. Moreover, I even presumed that these experiences in their very concrete forms had again become accessible to her, exactly because of what had happened in this session. Besides, this experience was unfamiliar to me, because in its actual form, it does not refer to my own past, since I have never experienced such a lack of basic security.

On the other hand, it is no wonder that I came to that sudden knowledge. I do indeed know anxiety as a universal experience and the yearning for comfort that is not fulfilled. The experience of an anxious person looking for comfort is also familiar to me, namely in relation with my children. Furthermore, the idea that basic trust and the feeling of security develop in early childhood, in relation with the parents, and especially with the mother, is no theory to me, but very tangible in everyday life.

2. Empathizing is "tuning in to"

A direct knowledge of the other's phenomenological world is not possible. Our knowledge of the other's experiences is built on our perception of that other person. We do then take for granted that the other's experiences are similar to our own, from which we do have a direct knowledge. Bebout elucidates this idea. He puts: "One can choose to believe that another's subjective experience can never be exactly the same as one's own; it can equally well be argued that one's experience is never entirely different from someone else's" (Bebout, 1974, p. 384). This implicit assumption that the experiences of man are to a great extent similar is the basis for any conclusion about the experiences of the other. Our knowledge of the other's inner world will always be a deduction. Empathic comprehension includes the inference of certain perceptions, meanings and emotions on the basis of our perception of the other. For example: We deduce somebody's sadness on the basis of signals, relayed by that person and which we experience within ourselves as utterances of sadness, like weeping, a sad look or expression, etc. We can, however, never directly know and feel the other's sadness.

Rogers (1959) also refers to the importance of inference in order to know somebody else's experiential world. "The internal frame of reference is the subjective world of the individual. Only he knows it fully. It can never be known to another except through empathic inference and then can never be perfectly known" (Rogers, 1959, p. 210).

I found a further elaboration of this idea in an article of Buie's (1981). He puts that any deduction on someone else's inner feelings is the result of a range of comparisons between signals that one perceives from the other with the inner referents one has. From early childhood, every person develops a range of internal resources which are available for this process of comparison. These referents and this process can be either unconscious, pre-conscious or conscious. It is often so that originally only the final conclusion of this process will be consciously experienced, whereas some parts of that what took place on the pre- or unconscious level only become conscious after a while, as in retrospective self-analysis, for example in supervision.

Buie distinguishes four kinds of internal resources, which he links to four kinds of empathy. This is, of course, a theoretical distinction; in practice, those four internal resources are drawn on at the same time, and as such, they contribute to a global empathic understanding. I will briefly discuss those forms, and I shall try to translate Buie's formulations into the client-centered terminology.

In a first form, "Conceptual empathy," a cognitive understanding is meant. To Buie, this form means obviously more than a mere cognitive understanding of the client's personality, based on theoretical knowledge. He refers here to Greenson (1960, 1967) who puts that the therapist develops a "working model" of the client. This model consists of the client's physical appearance, affects, ways of behaving, experiences, attitudes, defences, phantasies, etc. The better the therapist gets to know the client, the more extensive, accurate, and as such the more workable this model becomes. Empathic listening means then that the therapist listens through this working model.

Greenson (1960) chooses an example from his own practice, that illustrates the use of this working model. It is the case of a woman, whom he had been treating for several years. The client is telling him about a party she went to, and all of a sudden, she starts crying.

"Suddenly she began to cry. I was puzzled. I was not 'with it' - the crying left me cold - I could not understand it. I realized that I had been partially distracted by something she had said. At the party she mentioned a certain analyst and I had become sidetracked, wondering why he was present. Quickly reviewing the events she had recounted, I found no clues. I then shifted from listening from the 'outside' to participant listening. I went to the party as if I were the patient. Now something clicked - an 'aha' experience" (Greenson, 1960, p. 421).

The client had told about a woman who had served her that evening. This evoked in her the image of her kind, big-breasted nursemaid; hence she was moved. Discussing this example, Greenson puts:

"I shifted - from listening and observing from the outside to listening and feeling from the inside. ... As I worked with this patient day by day, I had slowly built up within me a working model of the patient. ... It is this working model which I now shifted into the foreground of my listening. I listened through this model" (Greenson, 1960, p. 421).

Buie mentions this working model as an example of a conceptual referent.

As a client-centered therapist, I would translate the use of this working model as: "To get to know the private meaning world more and more, making myself familiar with it, and becoming thoroughly at home in it." In my opinion, we do refer to the evocation of such a working model when we talk, for instance, about the client getting completely present in us before the session starts. The inner image we have of our client is in this conceptual form appealed to in a rather cognitive way.

In the second form, "Self-experiential empathy," the therapist uses his own experiences and memories. Something in the therapist is touched by the client's story. Important here is that the therapist is not overwhelmed with the memories that are evoked in him. If this were the case, it would not only mean that what is touched in the therapist is not coped with, but it would, moreover, not contribute to a better understanding of the client. Essential to these referents is exactly that they are neither overwhelming, nor exhausting. On the contrary, they help the therapist to build a more accurate image of the client's meaning and emotional world, both on the cognitive and emotional level. This form emphasizes the importance of similarity as a basis for empathic understanding. This does, however, also imply that the therapist must be present as a congruent person, accessible to himself.

When the therapist does not dispose of the necessary referents in himself, he must appeal to his imagination. This is the third form: "Imaginative imitation empathy." It is an active imaginative process, by which one immerses oneself completely in the other. This form is pre-eminently active: In one's imagination, one puts oneself into the world of the other. Through this imagining and imitating in phantasy, the knowledge of human emotional experiencing can be extended. The therapist's empathic ability is as such not restricted to his own experiences. This "putting oneself into the other's world" is indeed also an important aspect of empathic understanding in Greenson's example (Greenson, 1960). This makes clear that in reality, several referents are appealed to at the same time.

These three forms concur with Rogers' view. Especially the third form, the imagining of the other's phenomenological world, is an important aspect of Rogers' definition of empathy, which is, in my opinion, often overlooked. Still too often the empathic listening of the client-centered therapist is considered as "passive, resonant," as well within as outside of client-centered circles.

The fourth form, "Resonant empathy" refers to an intense resonance. It is a kind of contamination, a primitive form of emotional communication, in which a strong feeling within one person evokes that same feeling within the other. Buie calls this a primitive form insofar as it developmentally precedes other forms of affective communication. This form does not imply cognitive understanding. For example: An at first calm and laughing baby will start crying, incited by the baby next to him.

Little attention is paid to this resonant form in client-centered circles, and it is mostly considered to be rather negative, namely as a loss of the "as if" condition. I think, however, that this form of emotional communication can positively contribute to a better empathic understanding. As such, this form can be helpful to get more in touch with the sorrow, anxiety, anger, etc. that the client experiences. When this resonant form does not occur - for example: A client is crying and the therapist is not affected by it - it can be a signal to the therapist: Either that the client is not really in touch with his sorrow at that moment, or that the therapist cut himself off from the client's sadness. The danger, however, that the therapist would forget that client and therapist are two different persons, and that as such, he cannot make a clear distinction anymore between the client's phenomenological world and his own, is not unreal. But then, this risk is just as real with the other forms of empathy, especially with the second form.

Comparable to Buie's classification is the distinction Bebout (1974) makes between "vicarious," "physiognomic" and "cognitive" empathy. As Bebout defines "vicarious empathy," it highly resembles "self-experiential," and especially "imaginative imitation empathy." He stresses that this form of empathy means taking the place of another person through imagined participation in another's experience. He puts that this form does in fact correspond to Rogers' view on empathy. The second form as described by Bebout," Physiognomic empathy" comes close to "Resonant empathy." But Bebout thinks this form to be more than communication of strong affects. He calls it a form of "body language," which also includes simple physical responses: Yawning, laughing, coughing, postural mimicry, etc. For instance: When perceiving some danger, a passenger in a car presses his foot against the floorboard as if applying the brakes, although he knows that this can have no effect whatsoever. Finally, there seems to be a similarity between "Cognitive empathy," Bebout's third form, and Buie's conceptual form.

As such, a first step in empathy is a "comparing" process, in which the therapist appeals completely to his knowledge and to his own person in order to come to a cognitive and emotional understanding of the client's phenomenological world. In this stage, however, the therapist's understanding is still a hypothesis, which must be checked with the client's inner frame of reference. The therapist tries to tune in to the client, using the inner referents at his disposal, and by means of the empathic answer. In other words: He tries to create a state of mind for himself, which resembles as much as possible the client's. The formulation "tune in to" is used by both Barrett-Lennard (1981) and Rogers (1986) in respect to the empathic process. Rogers uses this term, dealing with the function of communication of empathic understanding: " I would be testing to see if I was deeply in tune with my client, because this 'intune-ness' is in itself healing, confirming, growth-promoting" (Rogers, 1986, p. 130). The "empathic answer," the "reflection of feeling" has as such a central position in this process of "getting in tune to." It is a means of checking, and thus a necessary step in this process. This "intune-ness" is also in Gendlin's opinion a necessity. The empathic answer is to therapy what watching the road is to a driver. Therapy without this continuously tuning in to is blind therapy (Gendlin, 1974).

So, the empathic process is essentially one of comparing and tuning in to. The first step being a comparing process brings us to the simple, but so often forgotten truth that every understanding is in the end always based on a certain uniformity of human experience. In order to use these collective similarities as the basis for understanding, the therapist must be present as a congruent person. Congruence is then not contradictory to empathy, but on the contrary, a necessity. Congruence remains the basis for each of the four empathic forms. The more congruent the therapist is, in other words, the more available he is to himself, the richer the inner referents[1] available for the process of comparing and tuning in to, will be. The relationship between congruence and empathy will be dealt with more explicitly under D.

3. The limitations of empathy

The definition of the therapist's empathic understanding as a process of comparing and tuning in to allows us to explicate a few generally accepted, but nevertheless seldom described limitations proper to this process.

First of all, the therapist's empathic understanding depends on his sensory perception of the signals the client relays. These signals are supposed to be an expression of what is going on in the client. In reality, this does not always seem to be the case. Clients have been found to give incomplete or incorrect signals, or they do not succeed in expressing what is on their minds. The more closed a client is, the less he shows and communicates of his own inner world, the more difficult it becomes for the therapist to get under the skin of his client.

A second limitation has to do with the inner referents the therapist has at his disposal. The therapist can, as far as possible, try to develop and make these referents accessible to himself, (through, for instance, own therapy, by reading novels that bring him into contact with new kinds of worlds, through clinical-psychological literature, greater life experience, etc.), but not to such an extent that he can find a similarity in himself with each experience a client can have. In other words, one can never be "whole." Barrett-Lennard too refers to these limitations.

"The extent to which this (empathic understanding) process then does happen depends also on B's (= client's) expressiveness in regard to his or her own experiencing and on A's (= therapist's) actual capacity to responsively tune in to the particular qualities and content of his experiencing, thus, at best, to know experientially what it is like to be the other person at the time. A's actual empathy will vary partly as a result (figuratively) of having a finite range of natural frequencies, such that there are aspects of B's experiencing to which he/she can resonate readily, clearly, and strongly and other aspects where such reverberation occurs lightly or incompletely or that are sensed only in a partial and effortful way" (Barrett-Lennard, 1981, p. 93).

A third, and also the most fundamental limitation is the fact that a therapist can never directly know the client's inner world, but that this knowledge is always a deduction. The therapist assumes that there is, at a given moment, a similarity between the client's inner experiences and his own inner referent. This, however, is apparently not always so. Sometimes, a number of referents have been found to fit in with certain signals, and it is only by carefully checking that it becomes clear which hypothesis it is that must be kept on.

When making these limitations more explicit, the importance of checking the similarity the therapist believes to see and feel between the client's experience and his own, is stressed once more. Rogers too emphasizes the importance of this checking in his definition: "It means frequently checking with the person as to the accuracy of your sensings, and being guided by the responses you receive" (Rogers, 1975, p. 4). So, in empathy, the client's inner experience remains the criterion on which the therapist can confirm or, when necessary, correct his hypothesis. "Knowledge which has any 'certainty' in the social sense, involves the use of empathic inference as a means of checking... When the experience of empathic understanding is used as a source of knowledge, one checks one's empathic inference with the subject, thus verifying or disapproving the inferences and hypotheses implicit in such empathy. It is this way of knowing which we have found so fruitful in therapy" (Rogers, 1959, p. 211-212). Gendlin too stresses the importance of checking. He formulates this as the fourth rule for an experiential response: "We follow the client's experiential track." According to him, sensitivity is no magic source upon which the therapist can draw to find the right answer; "rather, it consists in carefully noticing the client's next reaction to what the therapist says" (Gendlin, 1968, p. 212-213).

C. TUNING IN TO THE CLIENT, AND AS SUCH ACQUIRING "KNOWLEDGE" OF THE CLIENT'S PHENOMENOLOGICAL WORLD PRE-SUPPOSES A LISTENING ATTITUDE, CHARACTERIZED BY OPENNESS

Empathic listening (the process of making oneself familiar with the other's phenomenological world) demands from the therapist a great openness (= receptivity, susceptibility) to anything that comes from the client. Rombauts (1984) calls this "the deepest breeding ground" of empathy. He also emphasizes that this receptivity is not restricted to the therapeutic setting, but that it is rather a way of living. Meant here is an openness to anything that presents itself as well from outside as from the own inner world.

Rogers (1975) refers to this specific listening attitude, when he writes:

> "To be with another in this way means that for the time being, you lay aside your own views and values in order to enter another's world without prejudice. In some sense it means that you lay aside yourself; this can only be done by a person who is secure enough in himself that he knows he will not get lost in what may turn out to be the strange or bizarre world of the other, and can comfortably return to his own world when he wishes" (Rogers, 1975, p. 4).

This statement seems to contradict the content of B, namely that the empathizing therapist must appeal to and use his whole person. It does at least give rise to the question: How is one to understand this "putting oneself aside"?

First of all, I will try to elucidate this listening attitude, called openness. Very clarifying in this respect are Margulies' ideas about empathy as a creative process. Then, I will deal with some related concepts in psychoanalytical literature, trying to point out some similarities and differences with the client-centered viewpoint. Finally, I'll discuss the relation between the attitude of openness on the one hand, and on the other hand the "being in process" as described by Rogers as a fundamental feature of the "fully functioning person".

1. Openness: Letting go again and again

Margulies (1984) puts that the empathic listening attitude, which will here, following Rombauts, be called openness, is of crucial importance to enable the active, imaginative process of absorbing oneself completely into the other: Buie's "Imaginative imitation empathy" and also the form that is focused on in the client-centered orientation. Margulies has come to this thesis from a comparison of two introspective methods of investigation, namely, the phenomenological and the psycho-analytical. Both methods are comparable: "Both techniques prepare the subject to put aside the usual biases to observation" (Margulies, 1984, p. 1026). Both Husserl and Freud found out that people sometimes resist certain explorations. Freud calls these "denial mechanisms." The phenomenologists put that our perception is distorted by our knowledge. Artists too are intuitively aware of the enslavement knowledge can have on perception and expression. Both methods are comparable: They both lead to a suspension of knowledge; as such it becomes possible to discover what one had not seen before.

Margulies has studied this suspending process more in detail, and describes two steps in it. A first step is the negative capability: This is the capacity to go against the need of knowing, the capability to bear uncertainty and confusion. This concept comes from John Keats. A fundamental feature of the human mind is the organizing and synthetic function of perception: We organize our experiences spontaneously. Husserl's and Freud's recommendations go against this natural synthetic inclination, in other words: The subject is asked not to organize his experience immediately. This "negative capability" does furthermore mean that one does not only go against the own inclination to structure and organize new experience data, but it also means the negation of what is known: To make fluid what is fixed, to undo existing structures. It is an act of will and even an aggressive one.

Avoiding immediate conclusions and suspending knowledge is also proper to the therapeutic work. It is, in my opinion, precisely the essence of openness. The therapist too submits to this "not-knowing." It means that he puts his (theoretical) knowledge aside while listening to his client and that he avoids to draw conclusions prematurely. In this respect, Berger (1987) very rightly remarks that the negative capability does not mean that it is possible to approach the client's story as a "tabula rasa," " a mind emptied of its contents" (Berger, 1987, p. 86). The mind, possessed by negative capability is not empty, but actively open. Information and hypotheses are suspended, and the investigator avoids "applying closure too quickly" (Berger, 1987, p. 86). This suspending of "applying closure" enables several experience data to be present at the same time; precisely the fact that the structuring and organizing (that takes place after the closure) now happens on more and other experience data than usual, makes new structures and new knowledge possible. It is, after all, the presence of a "large body of knowledge," that creates an opening for new possibilities (Berger, 1987, p. 86). It is the source for creativity and renewal. Wexler (1974) develops an analogous idea in the elaboration of his cognitive theory, looking for a connection with the "information processing theory." And so does Rice's (1974) contribution on the therapist's evocative function also imply this same basic idea. She describes the listening attitude of the evocative therapist: "Although the therapist tries to grasp each new attempt of the client toward more adequate construction, he avoids any attempt of his own toward closure."And further: "I am assuming here that it is important for the therapist to avoid closure of his own, leaving the client free to explore his total reaction in the situation and to reconstruct it for himself" (Rice, 1974, p. 301). She too relates this attitude to creativity and renewal. "In fact, when evocative reflection is functioning well, and the client's experience is unfolding, many aspects of it will come as a surprise to the therapist" (Rice, 1974, p. 301).

Margulies puts that the negative capability does not only mean that the therapist must suspend his knowledge, but that he also denies his own "self." "Perhaps it is one component of the sometimes exhausting nature of therapeutic work - the therapist not only bears intense affects but also denies the self in the pursuit of the other" (Margulies, 1984, p. 1030). In my opinion, this idea contributes to a better understanding of the therapist's total focus on the client, which is so typical for empathy. The therapist does not only focus his attention on the client, listening to him and being committed to what he or she is telling, but he puts himself "in brackets." This, however, does not mean that the therapist loses himself, does not exist anymore, completely becomes "the other." But it does mean that he lets his own consistency and definite structures run. The self-concept will also (that is, more or less) be abandoned in the empathic experience. The therapist as a structured and organized entity is almost non-existent. In this respect, Margulies quotes Rogers (1965), who describes the therapist as a "pane of glass," as almost "non-existing."

The concept of "negative capability" as described by Margulies seems to fit in better with my experience with empathy than the notion openness, although the two notions are basically similar. But openness does not, in my opinion, suggest the therapist's struggle against his craving to know, to organize, summarize and structure his experience. The therapist does not only lay aside his theoretical knowledge, his opinions and expectations, but he also suspends his own structuring, organizing, knowledge-creating functions as long as he thinks this is necessary or advisable.

The negative capability is, however, only a preliminary step in the process of looking for the reality, the truth about the other. The second step is "Einfühlung," empathy, "the feeling himself into the reality of the other, as if to illuminate the object contemplated from within," as Keats defines it (in Margulies, 1984, p. 1031). This is undoubtedly also the therapist's goal: Entering the world of the other, trying to live for a moment in the other's world. Very striking here is the similarity with Rogers' (1975) definition of empathy:

> "It means entering the private perceptual world of the other and becoming thoroughly at home in it. It involves being sensitive, moment by moment, to the changing felt meanings which flow in this other person, to the fear or rage or tenderness or confusion or whatever that he or she is experiencing. It means temporarily living in the other's life, moving about in it delicately without making judgments; ..." (Rogers, 1975, p. 4).

This focusing on the other, which is so typical for empathy, implies that the therapist does not apply his structuring, knowledge-gaining capacities on his own experiences, but that he puts them at the disposal of his client and his flow of experiencing. So, it is always the client's phenomenological world that the therapist is trying to know. The experiences the therapist makes himself familiar with, always originate in the client.

So, when one is pursuing the goal of sharing the other's (phenomenological) world, there are always two important steps to be taken. The first step is a proscription, namely, the negative capability. The second step is empathy, the imaginative projection of one's own consciousness into the other, the sympathetic and creative imagination. This imagined participation in another's experience is only possible when one gives way to one's own structuring and applies one's own structuring capacities to what is evoked in oneself by the other.

When one really wants to get within, and to feel at home in the other's world, one must consider all knowledge and all empathizing as temporary. This does also mean that one must give way to this knowledge over and over again. The therapist must then constantly strive for a position of tension between knowing and not-knowing, between holding and letting go. And it is exactly this "letting go again" which is so typical for what is called "openness." In this respect, openness is no passive state, but an activity. Empathy is "active receptivity" (Rombauts, 1984).

2. Some related concepts

In the psychoanalytical literature, I have found a number of classic concepts that, I think, come very close to the above mentioned listening attitude of openness. I do not aspire to completeness, but I will try to pass on to the reader something of the similarity that has struck me.

Fliess (1942), for example, refers to an "altered state" of the therapist during the empathic experience (in Berger, 1987, p. 22). He proposes that this points to a regression of the superego and ego of the therapist. As such, the hold of the superego and the ego on the therapist's unconsciousness is relaxed, and the therapist's unconsciousness can resonate freely with the patient's. Such a regression is useful because it enables the therapist to experience the patient's inner world from within. Fliess thinks this useful regression to be the counterpart of the therapeutic "regression in the service of the ego" on the part of the patient. Margulies (1984) calls the definition "regression in the service of the ego" a semantic attempt to capture the reversal of the cognitive synthetic function, introduced by the creative imaginative process. But he does question the notion "regression" in this context. Regression refers to the archaic and not-new. Creativity is indeed linked up to an unconscious way of thinking, but it also demands an increase of possibilities.

Olinick (1969) uses the notion "regression in the service of the other," and refers as such to the "temporary and partial suspension of the usual forms of reality orientation in favor of an access to one's own subliminal, or preconscious, functioning" (Olinick, 1969, p. 42-43). Olinick clearly relates this regressive state of the therapist to openness. "This partially regressive openness and receptivity of the analyst render him permeable, even vulnerable at times, to certain processes within the patient" (Olinick, 1969, p. 42). Like Margulies, Olinick stresses the difference between this therapeutic form of regression and regression in the psycho-pathological sense; he also connects it to creativity:

> "I do not imply that the analyst is regressed as we use this term in psychopathology. The presence of his observing ego, and the fact that this openness to what is within himself and the patient is thereby controlled and partial, make for a different effect, more in accord with what we see

in creative work and problem-solving. During this controlled regression, the analyst gains a more direct knowledge of the other person than is otherwise within his scope" (Olinick, 1969, p. 43).

The therapist's regressive state, as discussed by Fliess and Olinick, also reminds one of Freud's "evenly hovering attention." Supporting this idea, Isakower proposes that the therapist's state is slightly less regressed than, but complementary to the patient's. The more the patient regresses, the more difficult the therapist's task becomes.

> "During these periods it is easier to listen as an observer or outsider to the patient's associations than it is to listen as if from within the patient. Listening as if from within requires paying attention imaginatively and actively, as well as passively, to one's own personal imagery, inner feelings, and visceral sensations" (Isakower, quotation in Berger, 1987, p. 28).

So, the more a patient regresses, the more the therapist's capacity to openness will be appealed to. Isakower, by the way, seems to argue strongly in favor of listening to and keeping contact with the own "felt sense" that is evoked by the client's story. In my opinion, the focusing-instructions can be seen as an attempt to help the client speak from a less fixed and structured state; not talking "about" himself, but from "within" himself.

3. Openness and process

The suspending of structures and the capacity of bearing confusion can also be called the capability of "being in process." And this brings us to Rogers' "fully functioning person." In my opinion, this "being in process" should not be understood as the absence of any structure, but as a continuous capability of letting go. This "fully functioning person" is someone who possesses the negative capability, who is capable of openness and who can continuously and smoothly move between knowing and not-knowing. The "fully functioning person" is someone who is empathic to himself.

At the Conference, Jan Harman (1990) also referred to this special "state of mind" that openness really is, with the notions "egolessness" (Luyten 1985, in Harman, 1990), and "unwavering state of mind that needs no reference point" (Trungpa, 1984, in Harman, 1990). Harman points out that there is a relation between whether or not the therapist is capable of allowing and bearing this experience of "egolessness" on the one hand and whether or not he is experiencing a basic trust in his own process on the other hand. Rogers (1961) describes the latter as an important characteristic of clients who have reached the seventh and last stage in the psychotherapeutic process. Harman calls this the experience of unconditional confidence. He also puts that this openness is an essential feature of the fully functioning person, and that the tendency towards self-actualization must really be understood as a capacity to openness, and not as a development of innate capacities.

Berger, from a psychoanalytical viewpoint, also proposes that "the sense of hopefulness that sooner or later a surprising, unexpected or unconventional solution will emerge" is an essential condition for the capacity of allowing a state of confusion. "A therapist's repeatedly interpreting a theme or a pattern despite the interpretation's having been shown to have had no useful effect is often a sign that the therapist has consciously or unconsciously fallen into a state of hopelessness" (Berger, 1987, p. 87).

D. EMPATHY AND CONGRUENCE ARE NO OPPOSITE POSITIONS. CONGRUENCE WITHIN EMPATHY ON THE ONE HAND AND TRANSPARANCE ON THE OTHER CAN BE CONSIDERED AS THE TWO ENDS OF A CONTINUUM

The concept of congruence was introduced by Rogers (1957) as one of the six necessary and sufficient conditions of therapeutic personality change. This means that the therapist is in touch with his own flow of experiencing and does not deny any experiences or feelings relevant to the client to his awareness. He theoretically elaborated on this concept in 1959. As he defines it here, this concept refers to a continuous revising, correcting and reorganizing of the self-concept on the basis of accurately symbolized self-experiences. This revising of the self-concept presupposes the individual to be open to his experience. Concerning the uttering of these feelings, Rogers states that it is certainly not the aim for the therapist to express his own feelings. This, however, might be necessary, if those feelings are standing in the way of the therapist's unconditional positive regard and empathy (Rogers, 1957). But this does not mean that the therapist should talk out these feelings to the client; expressing those either to a colleague or supervisor might be just as effective. In his articles of 1959 Rogers still makes the difference between the expressing of persistent feelings, called transparance, and the inner congruence.

Rogers initially clearly considers the therapeutic value of congruence in the service of both the other core conditions. Congruence is important for the therapist's empathy and unconditional positive regard to be "real." The therapist's transparency is important when the relationship threatens to deteriorate. Meant here is in the first place the uttering of negative feelings that may harm a relationship; feelings that are a barrier between client and therapist.

In my opinion, Rogers distinguishes two levels in congruence: A "process level," namely keeping in touch with one's own flow of experiencing; and a product level, namely, articulating and, if so desired, the expressing of one's own feelings. On the "product level," empathy and congruence seem contradictory to each other: In empathy, it are the client's feelings that are focused upon, whereas in congruence the therapist's feelings are concerned. This, however, only seems a contradiction: Actually it is one and the same process. Gendlin (1970) expresses this same idea:

> "As verbal content, congruence seems contradictory to empathy (in empathy we tell only exactly about the client, while in congruence we tell about ourselves). As experiential processes, empathy and congruence are exactly the same thing, the direct expression of what we are now going through with the client, in response to him" (Gendlin, 1970, p. 459).

In my opinion, it is not only so that empathy and congruence are not contradictory, but I even think that congruence is in some way necessary in empathy. The more congruent the therapist is, the more accessible he is to himself and the more he can dispose of inner referents that help him to tune in to the client. On the other hand, in the empathic process it is the client's phenomenological world that the therapist tries to get to know. He is not present as a person who wants to be the center of attention, who wants to focus on his own opinion and feelings.

Following the above mentioned distinction between "process" and "product-level," I think we can then distinguish two forms of congruence, which we can consider as the two ends of a continuum. I would call the first the unstructured or fluid form. This is how the empathizing therapist is congruent, namely listening with his whole being. I would call the second the structured or fixed form. When the therapist is congruent in this way, he is in touch with his own viewpoint, his own explicit opinions and his own personal experiences. He is in touch with himself within his own frame of reference. This form of congruence is proper to the therapist who faces the client as a separate and distinct person. It is out of this structured form of congruence that the therapist gives, for instance, feedback to the client, or that he mentions elements that are relevant to his relation with the client. It is out of this way of "looking at" the client that the therapist presents alternative viewpoints to the client, etc.

So, the question is not: "Is the therapist congruent or not while listening empathically?," or: "Are the congruent and the empathic positions opposite to each other?" The therapist is ideally always congruent. What distinguishes the empathic from the transparent position is the way in which the therapist is congruently present, namely, letting go or holding his own flow of experiencing; process- or product-oriented; focusing on the client's or his own frame of reference.

The therapist only indirectly knows the client's phenomenological world, namely through his own experiencing of this world. By means of the empathic answer, he tries to tune his own experience in to the client's. Sometimes, this does not seem to work. This has possibly to do with, for instance, a resistance of the therapist against entering into a certain phenomenological world or against certain experience data; a resistance that has to do with his own conflicting contents that are obviously not coped with. It can, however, also have to do with a feeling like: There is "something wrong" in the client's story, I cannot get within because "something does not seem right." A further exploration then could show that the client denies important information, that he suppresses important aspects which the therapist does, (very vaguely in the beginning, more explicitly later on) indeed notice. A congruent therapist is sensitive to this almost physically experienced signal that "something is wrong," and he tries to focus on it. The therapist should not withhold "That what is wrong" from his client because this can in fact contain information that can "open" something to the client. In my opinion, it is exactly the experiencing of such a signal in himself that brings the therapist to shifting his attention from the client's frame of reference to his own. The therapist's sensing of such an incongruence in the client's phenomenological world (that can be known by the therapist through his own experience of it), is as a matter of fact the signal for the therapist to switch from the fluid form of congruence, proper to the empathic position, to the structured or fixed form.

E. "AS IF" DOES NOT REFER TO THE SUBJECTIVE FEELING OF KEEPING DISTANCE, BUT TO THE CONTINUOUS AWARENESS OF THE CLIENT BEING THE SOURCE OF EXPERIENCES AND TO THE THERAPIST MAINTAINING OPENNESS TOWARD THE CLIENT'S FRAME OF REFERENCE

1. Empathy and merging

The degree of self-other differentiation between the therapist's and the client's experiences is an important aspect in most definitions of empathy. Rogers (1959 and 1975) stresses the importance of a clear distinction between the therapist's and client's experiencing (the as-if condition). But then again, many therapists, me included, feel, at moments of very strong empathic involvement, that they happen to merge with the client and that they lose every feeling of distance. In this respect, Buie writes:

> "The central quality of empathy, ... is that of feeling a state of mind which seems quantitatively to match and be held in common with the patient. This seems just to happen instantaneously, and subjectively the analyst feels he simply is 'identified with' or is 'sharing' the patient's inner experience" (Buie, 1981, p. 283).

How then can such experiences be understood? According to me, it would be erroneous to evaluate all these moments of empathic involvement in which the "as-if" condition is not experienced by the therapist (in such a sense that he is not feeling any distance between himself and the client) as "empathizing wrongly."

Corcoran (1982) tried to find out about the relation between empathy and the maintaining of the self-other differentiation. He concluded that there is a negative relation between empathy and the maintenance of emotional separation. His findings do also induce to the hypothesis that there is a critical point in empathy above which, when empathizing with more intensity, the emotional self-other differentiation gets lost. So, high levels of empathy would go together with a loss of emotional separation. On the basis of these findings, one can ask oneself whether deep empathy is indeed possible when this self-other differentiation must be maintained at any moment. Considering all the previous, I think one might say that "deep" empathy means that the feelings and experiences of the therapist resemble more and more those of the client; that the difference between the therapist's subjective feelings and those of the client becomes minimal, or even completely fades away for an instant. Corcoran's conclusions would then mean that the therapist experiences a feeling of merging when he creates in himself a state of mind that comes close to the client's.

Hence the question to be asked is: How is the "as if" condition, as mentioned by Rogers, then actually to be understood? Does Rogers mean that the therapist can tune in to the client no further than to the point where this emotional self-other differentiation threatens to fade? Or can we understand this "as if" quality in another way?

2. *"As if" refers to the continuous awareness of the client as the source of experience, and to the maintenance of the therapist's openness towards the client's frame of reference*

In my opinion, the "as if" condition as Rogers proposes it in his 1959 definition of empathy, must in the first place be understood as the stressing of the necessity of being continuously aware that the experiences and feelings that the therapist is trying to live into, do originate in the client, and not in the therapist. Barrett-Lennard makes this aspect more explicit in his 1962 operational definition (that is based on Rogers' 1959 statement) "with continuous awareness that this consciousness is originating and proceeding in the other" (Barrett-Lennard, 1962, p. 3). So, the therapist may indeed at some moments have a feeling of merging with the client, without this implying a loss of the "as if" condition. For it is indeed important that the therapist remains aware of the fact that what he is experiencing now, originally comes from and belongs to the client, and not from and to himself. The maintaining of this awareness is only possible if the therapist keeps up towards the client's frame of reference the attitude of openness, that he has towards his own (phenomenological world, entire knowledge, himself, etc.). Also as far as the client's frame of reference is concerned, the therapist must continuously as well as smoothly shift from knowing to not-knowing; and, he must constantly be able to let go again.

On the Leuven Conference, Jan Harman (1990) expressed a very analogous idea. He refers to Luyten's notion of "exchange" (Luyten 1985) which alludes to the process through which we experience, consciously or unconsciously, someone else's state of mind. This exchange is not a "therapeutic technique, but a constantly recurring moment in which the distinction between self and other flickers" (Luyten 1985, In Harman, 1990). According to Luyten, this exchange has two aspects: "Touching" and "letting go." "Touching" means: "The moment of joining another's experience as well as sharing a common ground of openness" (Luyten 1985, In Harman, 1990). Letting go refers to "the capacity of mind to relax fixation" (Harman, 1990). This capability of "touching" or of accurate empathy, is as such only the first part in this exchange. Without the capacity of "letting go," therapist and client can get stuck in this exchange or fuse. These formulations also make clear that it is important to move continuously and smoothly between holding and letting go; Luyten too considers this capacity of letting go as essential in order to avoid to get stuck in fusion, or - to put it with Rogers - to maintain the "as if" condition.

CONCLUSION

Openness is, in my opinion, the most essential feature in the empathic attitude. Only the person who can remain actively open, can tune in to the other. Only the person who can allow confusion and fluidity in himself, who can feel at ease with it, and knows (has experienced) that this is not destructive, can foster this way of being for the client, and stay comfortable with it. Only the person who knows from within what it means "to be in process," and to let go over and over again, can continuously sense an "other level" in the client, and help to get fluid and smooth again what was blocked and frozen. This does not only demand courage, but also, and especially, lots of confidence. The trust that confusion and disorder will not last, but that from them, new order will grow.

NOTE

1. These inner referents can both consist of certain contents (forms 1 and 2) as well as of certain capacities the therapist has developed (forms 3 and 4).

REFERENCES

Balter, L., Lothane, Z., & Spencer, J.H. Jr., (1980). On the analyzing instrument. *Psychoanalytic Quarterly, 49,* 474-504.

Barrett-Lennard, G.T. (1962). Dimensions of therapist response as causal factors in therapeutic change. *Psychological Monographs, 76,* No. 562.

Barrett-Lennard, G.T. (1981). The empathy cycle: Refinement of a nuclear concept. *Journal of Counseling Psychology, 28,* 91-100.

Bebout, J. (1974). It takes one to know one: Existential-Rogerian concepts in Encounter Groups. In D.A. Wexler & L.N. Rice (Eds.), *Innovations in client-centered therapy* (pp. 367-419). New York: J. Wiley & Sons.

Berger, D.M. (1987). *Clinical Empathy.* London: Jason Aronson.

Buie, D.H. (1981). Empathy: Its nature and limitations. *Journal of the American Psychoanalytic Association, 29,* 281-307.

Corcoran, K.J. (1981). Experiential Empathy: A theory of felt-level experience. *Journal of Humanistic Psychology, 21(1),* 29-38.

Corcoran, K.J. (1982). An exploratory investigation into self-other differentiation: Empirical evidence for a monistic perspective on empathy. *Psychotherapy: Theory, Research and Practice, 19,* 63-88.

Fliess, R. (1942). The metapsychology of the analyst. *Psychoanalytic Quarterly, 11,* 211-227.

Freud, S. (1912). Recommendations to physicians practising psychoanalysis. *Standard Edition, 12,* 109-120.

Gendlin, E.T. (1968). The experiential response. In E. Hammer (Ed.), *Use of interpretation in therapy* (pp. 208-227). New York: Grune & Stratton.

Gendlin, E.T. (1970). A short summary and some long predictions. In J.T. Hart & T.M. Tomlinson (Eds.), *New directions in client-centered therapy* (pp. 544-562). Boston: Houghton-Mifflin.

Gendlin, E.T. (1974). Client-centered and experiential psychotherapy. In D.A. Wexler, & L.N. Rice (Eds.), *o.c.* (pp. 211-246).

Goldberg, A. (1983). On the scientific status of empathy. *Annual of Psychoanalysis, 11,* 155-169.

Greenson, R.R. (1960). Empathy and its vicissitudes. *International Journal of Psychoanalysis, 41,* 418-424.

Greenson, R.R. (1967). *The Technique and practice of psychoanalysis.* New York: International Universities Press.

Harman, J.I. (1990). *Unconditional confidence as a facilitative precondition.* See this volume.

Kohut, H. (1959). Introspection, empathy and psychoanalysis: An examination of the relationship between mode of observation and theory. *Journal of the American Psychoanalytic Association, 7,* 459-483.

Levy, S.T. (1985). Empathy and psychoanalytic technique. *Journal of the American Psychoanalytic Association, 33,* 353-378.

Luyten, M.F. (1985). Egolessness and the "borderline" experience. *Naropa Institute Journal of Psychology, 3,* 43-70.

Margulies, A. (1984). Toward empathy: The uses of wonder. *American Journal of Psychiatry, 141,* 1025-1033.

Olinick, S.L. (1969). On empathy, and regression in service of the other. *British Journal of Medical Psychology, 42,* 41-49.

Rice, L.N. (1974). The evocative function of the therapist. In D.A. Wexler & L.N. Rice (Eds.), *Innovations in client-centered therapy* (pp. 289-311). New York: J. Wiley & Sons.

Rogers, C.R. (1957). The necessary and sufficient conditions of therapeutic personality change. *Journal of Consulting Psychology, 21,* 96-103.

Rogers, C.R. (1959a). A theory of therapy, personality, and interpersonal relationships, as developed in the client-centered framework. In S. Koch, (Ed.), *Psychology: A study of a science* (Vol. 3, pp. 184-256). New York: McGraw Hill.

Rogers, C.R. (1959b). Client-centered therapy. In S. Arieti (Ed.), *American Handbook of Psychiatry* (Vol. 3, pp. 183-200). New York: Basic Books.

Rogers, C.R. (1961). *On becoming a person.* Boston: Houghton Mifflin.

Rogers, C.R. (1975). Empathic: An unappreciated way of being. *The Counseling Psychologist, 5(2),* 2-10.

Rogers, C.R. (1986). Rogers, Kohut and Erickson: A personal perspective on some similarities and differences. *Person-centered Review, 1,* 125-140.

Rombauts, J. (1984). Empathie: actieve ontvankelijkheid. In G. Lietaer, Ph. van Praag, & J. Swildens (Eds.), *Client-centered psychotherapie in beweging* (pp. 167-176). Leuven: Acco.

Trungpa, C. (1984). In C.R. Gimian (Ed.), *Shambhala: The sacred path of the warrior.* Boston: Shambhala Publications.

Wexler, D.A. (1974). A cognitive theory of experiencing, self-actualisation, and therapeutic process. In D.A. Wexler & L. N. Rice (Eds.), *Innovations in client-centered therapy* (pp. 49-116). New York: J. Wiley & Sons.

Wexler, D.A., & Rice, L.N. (Eds.). (1974). *Innovations in client-centered therapy.* New York: Wiley.

CONCRETE INTERVENTIONS ARE CRUCIAL: THE INFLUENCE OF THE THERAPIST'S PROCESSING PROPOSALS ON THE CLIENT'S INTRAPERSONAL EXPLORATION IN CLIENT-CENTERED THERAPY

Rainer SACHSE
Ruhr Universität, Bochum, F.R.Germany

INTRODUCTION

In our studies of process research in client-centered therapy we examined:
- The influence therapists have with their concrete verbal behavior on the client's self-explorative behavior (intra-personal exploration), or as we prefer to say, the client's explication process.
- How therapists can stimulate this process and what they by no means should do to interfere with this process.
- Whether it becomes more difficult for the client to "deepen" the explication level further depending on the depth of explication a client has attained.
- Whether therapeutic interventions become more important depending on how deep a client is in the explication process.

THE EXPLICATION PROCESS: THE CLIENT'S PROCESSING MODE AND THE THERAPIST'S PROCESSING PROPOSALS

In our conception of client-centered therapy we assume that the essential goal of therapy involves the explication of the client's internal frame of reference in regard to his relevant problems. This goal is already implicit in the scale of "intrapersonal exploration" (Truax, 1961; see also Sachse, 1984, 1986a, 1986b, 1987, 1988a, 1988b; Sachse & Maus, 1987, 1989). The essential aspects of the internal frame of reference are considered as "personal relevant meaning structures or schemata" (see Herrmann, 1972, 1982; Crocker et al., 1984; Schank & Abelson, 1977; Kuhl, 1983; Sachse, 1989) which contain evaluations or emotions. Their activation leads to feelings or felt meanings (Bower, 1981).

A clarification or explication process requires a client to face the relevant parts of his meaning structures by putting forward relevant questions. These questions first aim at describing a problem, but later aim at clarifying the client's feelings and the felt meanings determined by aspects of the problem. Eventually, these questions aim at explication of the problem-determined meaning structures (Sachse, 1986a, 1986b, 1988a, 1988b).

These questions, whether explicitly or implicitly mentioned by the client, are described as the client's processing modes. A processing scale with eight levels has been suggested; a client can go through it in the explication of his meaning structures (Sachse, 1986a, 1988a, 1988b, Sachse & Maus, 1987).

The scale differentiates eight processing stages or levels, which range from "shallow processing" to "explication of relevant structures of meaning", so-called "deep processing."

Levels are determined by the asking of specific questions, which the client tries to answer implicitly or explicitly:

Level 1:		*No discernible processing of relevant contents*
		The client asks no relevant questions.
Level 2:		*Intellectualizing*
	Question:	How do I explain that ? Which theory can I use?
	Answer:	Using "knowledge" without reference to own feelings or personal data.
Level 3:		*Report*
	Question:	What actually happened? What was the concrete situation or behavior?
	Answer:	Concrete description without explicit reference to opinions, evaluations and feelings.
Level 4:		*Assessment/Evaluation*
	Question:	How is the content assessed?
	Answer:	By assessment labeling (for example: "A is stupid" or "behavior B is bad.") The assessment is seen as a characteristic of the content.

Level 5:   *Personal assessment*

Question: How do I assess the content?

Answer: The client assesses the content and recognizes that it is a part of his own frame of reference.

Level 6:   *Personal meaning*

Question: Which feelings or felt meanings does the content arouse in me?

Answer: The client senses a feeling or felt meaning about the content and says so explicitly.

Level 7:   *Explication of relevant structures of meaning*

Question: What makes me feel like this in this context?

Answer: The client explicates (verbalizes) aspects of meaning which he recognizes in himself with regard to the content being processed.

Level 8:   *Integration*

Question: Can I find any connections with other aspects of meaning?

Answer: The client draws connections between the explicated aspects of meaning and other aspects. He finds similarities or contradictions.

The *changes* in the client's processing mode are above all of relevance here. We have analyzed so-called "triplets." A triplet is a unit which consists of a client's (complex) statement, a therapist's intervention and then again a client's resulting statement:

THERAPY PROCESS...	→ Client Statement	→ Therapist Statement	→ Client Statement	→ ...
RATING	Processing mode (PM)1	Processing proposal (PP)	Processing mode (PM)2	

If one considers the changes in the processing level of the client from the first to the second statement of the triplet, there are three possible cases:

- *constant level:* The client's processing mode does not change.
- *deepening:* The client's processing mode is of a higher level (is deeper) in the second statement than in the first.

- flattening:	The processing mode in the client's second statement is flatter (is of a lower level) than in the first.

CHANGES IN THE PROCESSING MODE (example):

Processing   Processing
mode 1   mode 2

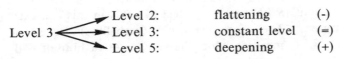

Level 3	Level 2:	flattening	(-)
	Level 3:	constant level	(=)
	Level 5:	deepening	(+)

The therapist can support the client's explication process by raising questions in his interventions either explicitly or implicitly. By doing so, he gives the client hints on how this process can be carried on.

If a client is willing to accept these offers, he will proceed in the direction of the activated questioning. In order to determine which proposal a therapist gives with each statement - bound to certain contents - we developed a scale for processing proposals (Sachse & Maus, 1987, 1989). This scale is parallel to the client's processing scale. The parallelism of these two scales allows an interactional analysis (see Pfeiffer, 1976) on a microlevel of psychotherapy (Baumann & Von Wedel, 1981; Baumann et al., 1984).

The absolute processing proposal is not as important as the relative proposal in regard to the support given to a client's explication process. This means: How does the therapist's proposal relate to the mode of processing the client realizes in the directly preceeding sequence.

The relation between the processing level of the client and the therapeutic offer may be:

- constant level:	The therapist matches the client's processing mode.
- deepening:	The therapist exceeds the client's processing level (for example: stimulating personal assessment whereas the client is still on the level of reporting events).
- flattening:	The therapist's proposal keeps a lower level in

comparison to the client's just realized level
(e.g. stimulation to report whereas the client
has already reached a level of personal
assessment).

Let us have a look now at the effects of the therapist's proposal on the
client's processing in terms of what modifications can be observed
between the statements before and after the therapist's intervention:
The effects on the client's processing mode can therefore be constant,
deepening or flattening.

EFFECTS OF PROCESS PROPOSALS ON THE CLIENT

The therapeutic process must be examined in its psycholinguistic
aspects in order to explain the effects of processing proposals on the
client.

Both therapist and client take turns in speaking and listening. They
alternately have to translate what they mean into language and to work
out the partner's verbal communication in order to understand one
another (see Hörmann, 1976, 1983; Herrmann, 1985; Engelkamp,
1984). An essential assumption in linguistic psychology is that a
speaker potentially always exerts influence on his listener with what he
says. In Hörmann's (1976) terms, the speaker directs the awareness of a
listener. The speaker changes what a listener is conscious or aware of
and thus changes what he can do, experience, and think, on the basis of
that awareness.

The effect of language as an agent capable of directing consciousness
at least in the short-term, has often been validated (see Bransford et al.,
1972; Barclay et al., 1974; Loftus & Palmer, 1974; Jörg, 1974).
However this is not always the case: A listener can quite possibly
"defend" himself against control, for example by just ignoring the
speaker's statement (Jörg, 1984). Nonetheless, there should be a high
probability of this effect, which means that the listener accepts the
speaker's proposals. If we transfer this onto the therapist's relative
processing proposals for the client, we are led to make the assumption
that there is a strong control-effect on the client's explication process: A
therapist is supposed to direct the client's consciousness at least for a
short period. He directs the consciousness of the client to the questions,

the proposals he had raised. That is, constant-level, deepening or flattening processing proposals should be accepted by the client at a very high rate.

We called this assumption the "directional hypothesis."

TESTING THE DIRECTIONAL HYPOTHESIS

We analyzed sessions from the middle phase of therapy of 152 clients (91 female and 61 male). 56 Therapists (28 male and 28 female) contributed a maximum of three tapes. From each tape, ten non-overlapping triplets were selected (C-statement, T-statement, C-statement), starting after the first five minutes of the session. In this way, a total of 1.520 triplets were analyzed. Table 1 shows the results.

Table 1

Results concerning the directional hypothesis; based on figures of the first Sachse and Maus study (1987)

Relation between T's proposal and C's level	Effects on the client's explication level			
	+	=	-	Sum
+	127	38	16	181
%	70,2	21	8,8	
=	411	560	235	1206
%	34,1	46,4	19,5	
-	15	20	98	133
%	11,3	15,0	73,7	
Sum	553	618	349	1520
%	36,4	40,7	22,9	

The directional hypothesis can be directly tested with the help of DEL-analyses (Hildebrand et al., 1977a, 1977b).

The DEL-coefficient of this analysis shows the "quality of prediction" of a certain hypothesis (a DEL-coefficient of 1 means an optimal prediction: All data observed correspond to the hypothesis). In this case, the DEL-coefficient can be considered as "a measure of the directional effect": The higher the DEL- coefficient, the stronger the directional effect of processing proposals on the client's mode of processing.

If we apply this analysis on our data (Sachse & Maus, 1989) we get a DEL-result of 0.212 (p < .001). The hypothesis is confirmed: The directing effect of a therapist's processing proposal on the explication level of the client is demonstrated. In addition to this a further differential reflection of these effects with a Chi-square comparison allows further statements (for details, see Sachse & Maus, 1987):

1. The majority of deepening processing proposals have deepening effects: A client who is offered a deepening processing proposal will most probably accept this and, at least for a short time, move further in the direction of a deeper explication level. Therefore, a therapist can purposely facilitate the client's process with proposals that have a deepening effect. The risk of causing a contrary effect, meaning a flattening effect, is small.

2. Flattening proposals predominantly cause flattening effects. As for deepening proposals, these offers are most often accepted. This shows that a therapist can impair a client's process, at least for a short time, with his proposals. Directing a client's processing mode can therefore also have a negative effect.

3. The therapist's directing effect is minimal for constant-level processing proposals: The constant-level effects here are actually more frequent than deepening or flattening effects; nevertheless, on the whole, these proposals are more often not accepted than accepted.

   Constant-level processing proposals seem to allow a client much greater freedom to realize constant level, deepening or flattening processing modes.

Looking at the strong directing effect of the therapist's processing proposals on the client's process, especially the risk of impeding the explication process, it seems clear that a therapist must be a "process expert" (Gerl, 1981). What a therapist actually does is not at all irrelevant; quite the contrary: It is of great significance. Therefore, a therapist must carefully consider his actions and his processing proposals to the client in order to adequately adapt to the client's prevailing processing level. The therapist must therefore not only understand the contents of what the clients say, but also understand the achieved processing level of these contents and must adapt his interventions flexibly (Sachse, 1985). For this, he needs intervention rules that indicate which proposals have a high probability of leading to what effects.

This study concerning the hypothesis of directional influence has been replicated in a second study (Sachse & Maus, 1989) on a sample of 800 triplets, stemming from 80 clients and 30 therapists (see Table 2).

Table 2
Results of the second study of Sachse and Maus, 1989

| Relation between T's proposal and C's level | Effects on the client's explication level | | | |
	+	=	-	Sum
+	245	44	23	312
%	78,5	14,1	7,4	
=	157	222	53	432
%	36,3	51,4	12,3	
-	2	5	49	56
%	3,6	8,9	87,5	
Sum	404	271	125	800
%	50,5	33,9	15,6	

A DEL-analysis of these data yields a DEL of .417 (p < .001). According to these data the directing effect is even more pronounced than in our first study.

This result led us to the hypothesis that the "directing effect" will be stronger when the client's level of "intrapersonal exploration" is higher; this hypothesis has been confirmed in a study we just completed.

It is interesting, too, that flattening proposals are accepted to a greater extent than deepening ones; deepening in 78,5% and flattening in 87,5% of the cases.

CHANGE AS A FUNCTION OF CLIENT'S PROCESSING LEVEL

A second question was whether keeping or enhancing the quality of the explication process presents different degrees of difficulty for clients in various sections of the processing mode (Sachse & Maus, 1989). In raising this question, we can divide the whole spectrum of the explication process, the eight levels of the processing mode, into three processing sections:
- the "flat section": levels 1 and 2
- the "middle section": levels 3, 4 and 5
- the "deep section": levels 6, 7 and 8.

The question then arises: Are there different degrees of difficulty for clients in deepening, or in avoiding a flattening of the processing mode, depending on the circumstances - whether they happen to be in the "flat section" (1 and 2), in the "middle section" (3, 4 and 5) or in the "deep section" (6, 7 and 8)?

On the basis of our data (see Table 3) we were able to confirm the following hypotheses (Consider that the following data result from the splitting of the total data from Table 2 into the three levels):

1.1 Acceptance of deepening processing proposals decreases from the "flat" to the "deep" sections: Whereas in the "flat" section 88,5% of the deepening proposals are accepted and 70,8% in the middle section, in the deep section only 42,9% are accepted.

1.2 Similarly, the deepening arising from the client's own initiative, i.e. following a constant-level proposal of a therapist, decreases in correspondence to the depth of the achieved level: Whereas clients deepen their explication level on their own following constant-level proposals at a rate of 88,6% in the "flat" section, 34,2% achieve this in the "middle" section and only 4,9% do so in the "deep" section (these differences are highly significant). This indicates that the deeper the level at which clients are already working, the more difficult it is for them to deepen the explication process further.

2.1 Clients tend to accept more flattening proposals if they are working at a deeper level: they accept flattening proposals in 63,2% of cases in the "middle" section (in the "flat" section no flattening proposals were found); in the "deep" section, 93% of these proposals were accepted.

2.2 The clients' tendency to flatten the processing level on their own increases the deeper the processing section they are in: Thus clients flatten in spite of constant-level proposals at a rate of 1,0% in the "flat" section, 15,5% in the "middle" section and 37,4% in the "deep" section.

These results indicate that clients in the "deep processing" sections are very irritable: Inadequate interventions, especially in these sections, have a strong effect. It is also difficult for clients to remain in the "deep processing" section. It is interesting to see that clients leave the "deep" level of their own initiative only in 37,4% of cases, whereas they accept 93% of the therapist's flattening proposals: The tendency to leave the "deep" level of intrapersonal exploration cannot simply be interpreted as a "bottom-effect." (It must also be considered that leaving the deep level at times may be useful for the therapy process on the whole).

DIRECTING EFFECT IN THE VARIOUS PROCESSING SECTIONS

We assumed the directing effect of the therapist's proposals as more pronounced when the client's actual explication level is deeper: The more difficult the explication process is for clients, the more therapist prompting and support will deepen the process (Sachse & Maus, 1989).

In testing the directing hypothesis (see Table 3) we applied separate DEL-analyses for the three processing sections and found broad confirmation supporting the hypothesis: A DEL of -.005 (n.s.) is found in the "flat" section, whereas the "middle" section shows a DEL of .189 (p < .001); in the "deep" section, the DEL-value equals .326 (p < .001).

The directing effect thus clearly increases: The deeper the clients happen to work, the more their explication process is influenced by the therapist's proposals. In other words, the relevance of the therapist's concrete intervention increases the deeper the client already has progressed in the explication process.

Table 3
Number and percentage of deepening effects (first value)
in relation to the number of deepening and non-deepening proposals
(second value), separately for the three starting levels;
same for flattening effects

Starting level	Deepening effects following deepening proposals	Deepening effects following other proposals	Flattening effects following flattening proposals	Flattening effects following other proposals
1/2	23/26	62/70	0/0	1/96
%	88,5	88,6	0	1,0
3/4/5	102/144	353/1033	55/87	168/1090
%	70,8	34,2	63,2	15,5
6/7/8	3/7	11/223	40/43	70/187
%	42,9	4,9	93	37,4

Differences between the deepening effects of deepening and non-deepening proposals are significant in the "middle" and "deep" sections (for the "middle" section: Chi-square = 44.5, df = 1, p < .001; for the "deep" section: Chi-square = 17.4, df = 1, p < .001).

Looking at flattening effects (Table 3), we can see that the acceptance of flattening proposals strongly increases from the "middle" to the "deep" sections; spontaneous flattening also increases but flattening effects appear significantly more often in the "middle" and "deep" sections following flattening proposals than they do spontaneously (for the "middle" section: Chi-square = 29.1, df = 1, p < .001; in the "deep" section: Chi-square = 20.1, df = 1, p < .001).

This makes it quite clear that therapists, at this specific point, exert strongly destructive directing effects. They can easily get the client out of constructive process sections.

CONCLUSIONS

Our studies allow us to state the following conclusions:

1. Therapists' verbal interventions direct the clients' explication process to a high degree. It is therefore important that the therapist aims his interventions well. His concrete interventions are not at all unimportant; on the contrary, they have a crucial influence.

2. The deeper a client already is in his explicating process the more difficult it will be for him to stay at this level: Clients are more vulnerable to influence when they are deeper in their explicating process.

   This clearly shows that a therapist must carefully try to keep a client on a deep explication level and that interventions at this point must be chosen with special care. Therapists must have effective therapeutic rules at their disposal, allowing appropriate interventions. General attitudes are not sufficient.

3. Unfavorable interventions have a stronger effect then constructive interventions. This highlights the degree of responsibility of therapists in the explication process.

These results support a concept of action-oriented client-centered therapy in which processing rules and processing aims are of great significance.

REFERENCES

Barclay, J.R., Bransford, J.D., Franks, J.J., McCarrell, N.S., & Nitsch, K. (1974). Comprehension and semantic flexibility. *Journal of Verbal Learning and Verbal Behavior, 13,* 471-481.

Baumann, U., Hecht, Ch., & Mackinger, H. (1984). Psychotherapieforschung: Unterschiedliche Perspektiven. In U. Baumann (Ed.), *Makro-Mikroperspektive* (pp. 3-28). Göttingen: Hogrefe.

Baumann, U., & Wedel, B.V. (1981). Stellenwert der Indikationsfrage im Psychotherapiebereich. In U. Baumann (Ed.), *Indikation zur Psychotherapie* (pp. 1-36). München: Urban & Schwarzenberg.

Bower, G.H. (1981). Mood and memory. *American Psychologist, 36,* 129-148.

Bransford, J.D., Barclay, J.R., & Franks, J.J. (1972). Sentence memory: A constructive versus interpretative approach. *Cognitive Psychology, 3,* 193-202.

Crocker, J., Fiske, S.T., & Taylor, S.E. (1984). Schematic bases of belief change. In J.R. Eiser (Ed.), *Attitudinal judgment.* New York: Springer.

Engelkamp, J. (1984). Verstehen als Informationsverarbeitung. In J. Engelkamp (Ed.), *Psychologische Aspekte des Verstehens* (pp. 31-53). Berlin: Springer.

Gerl, W. (1981). Zum Aspekt der "Lenkung" in der psychotherapeutischen

Kommunikation. *GwG-Info, no. 44,* 15-22.

Herrmann, Th. (1972). *Einführung in die Psychologie: Sprache.* Frankfurt: Akademische Verlagsgesellschaft.

Herrmann, Th. (1982). *Sprechen und Situation.* Berlin: Springer.

Herrmann, Th. (1984). "Sprachverstehen" und das Verstehen von Sprechern. In J. Engelkamp (Ed.), *Psychologische Aspekte des Verstehens* (pp. 15-30). Berlin: Springer.

Herrmann, Th. (1985). *Allgemeine Sprachpsychologie. Grundlagen und Probleme.* München: Urban & Schwarzenberg.

Hildebrand, D.K., Laing, J.D., & Rosenthal, H. (1977a). *Analysis of ordinal data.* Beverly Hills: Sage.

Hildebrand, D.K., Laing, J.D., & Rosenthal, H. (1977b). *Prediction analysis of cross classifications.* New York: Wiley.

Hörmann, H. (1976). Meinen und Verstehen,. *Grundzüge einer sprachpsychologischen Semantik.* Frankfurt: Suhrkamp.

Hörmann, H. (1983). *Was tun die Wörter miteinander im Satz? oder: wieviele sind einige, mehrere und ein paar?* Göttingen: Hogrefe.

Jörg, S. (1984). Möglichkeiten und Grenzen der Bewusstseinslenkung beim Hörer. In J. Engelkamp (Ed.), *Psychologische Aspekte des Verstehens* (pp. 91-109). Berlin: Springer.

Kuhl, J. (1983). *Motivation, Konflikt und Handlungskontrolle.* Berlin: Springer.

Loftus, E.F., & Palmer, J.C. (1974). Reconstruction of automobile destruction: An example of the interaction between language and memory. *Journal of Verbal Learning and Verbal behavior, 13,* 585-589.

Pfeiffer, W.M. (1976). Zur Erfassung des therapeutischen Prozesses mit Hilfe komplexer Skalen. In Gesellschaft für wissenschaftliche Gesprächspsychotherapie (Ed.), *Die klientenzentrierte Gesprächspsychotherapie* (pp. 155-161). Frankfurt: Fischer.

Sachse, R. (1984). Vertiefende Interventionen in der klientenzentrierten Psychotherapie. *Partnerberatung, 2,* 106-113.

Sachse, R. (1986a). Gesprächspsychotherapie. Hagen: Fernuniversität Hagen. *Kurseinheit zum Kurs "Formen der Psychotherapie" im Projekt "Wege zum Menschen."*

Sachse, R. (1986b). Selbstentfaltung in der Gesprächspsychotherapie mit vertiefenden Interventionen. *Zeitschrift für Personenzentrierte Psychologie und Psychotherapie, 5,* 183-193.

Sachse, R. (1987). Wat betekent "zelfexploratie" en hoe kan een therapeut het zelfexploratie-proces van de cliënt bevorderen? *Psychotherapeutisch Paspoort, 4,* 71-93.

Sachse, R. (1988a). Das Konzept des empathischen Verstehens: Versuch einer sprachpsychologischen Klärung und Konsequenzen für das therapeutische Handeln (23). In Gesellschaft für wissenschaftliche Gesprächspsychotherapie (Ed.), *Orientierung an der Person: Diesseits und Jenseits von Psychotherapie* (Vol. 2, pp. 162-174). Köln: GwG.

Sachse, R. (1988b). From attitude to action: On the necessity of an action-oriented approach in client-centered therapy. Bochum: Ruhr Universität.

308

Berichte aus der Arbeitseinheit Klinische Psychologie, Fakultät für Psychologie, no 64.

Sachse, R. (1989). Zur allgemeinpsychologischen Fundierung von Klientenzentrierter Therapie: Die Theorie zur "Konzeptgesteuerten Informationsverarbeitung" und ihre Bedeutung für den Verstehensprozess. In R. Sachse & J. Howe (Eds.), *Zukunft der Klientenzentrierten Psychotherapie* (pp. 76-101). Heidelberg: Asanger.

Sachse, R., & Maus, C. (1987). Einfluss differentieller Bearbeitungsangebote auf den Explizierungsprozess von Klienten in der Klientenzentrierten Psychotherapie, *Zeitschrift für Personenzentrierte Psychologie und Psychotherapie, 6,* 75-86.

Sachse, R., & Maus, C. (1989). Zielorientiertes Handeln in der Gesprächspsychotherapie. *Versuch einer Neukonzeption klientenzentrierter Psychotherapie* (in press).

Schank, P.C., & Abelson, R.P. (1977). *Scripts, plans, goals and understanding.* Hillsdale: Erlbaum.

Truax, C.B. (1961). *A tentative scale for the measurement of depth of intrapersonal exploration.* Wisconsin University: Psychiatric Institute Discussion Papers.

A SCHEMA-BASED INFORMATION PROCESSING PERSPECTIVE ON CLIENT CHANGE IN EXPERIENTIAL PSYCHOTHERAPY

Shaké G. Toukmanian
York University, Toronto, Canada

Clients seek therapy for a variety of psychological problems that differ widely in complexity, symptomatology and thematic content. They also differ extensively in their level of motivation, sensitivity to and awareness of issues and in the quality and quantity of their verbal output. However, an examination of *how* clients express themselves in therapy (i.e. the way in which they formulate their experiences, thoughts and feelings) reveals that, despite their apparent diversity, they share a common processing characteristic. In other words, their manner of communicating, particularly in the early stages of therapy, suggests that they are running a "perceptual treadmill." They seem to look at the same information, draw the same inference, attribute the same meaning, and reconfirm the existence of the same experience over and over again, unaware of *how* they may structure the elements of their experience differently and in ways that potentially may lead them to deal with their problems more effectively.

As therapy progresses, however, the quality of clients' discourse changes considerably. When relating their thoughts and feelings, clients often tend to be more reflective and tentative in their judgements, less general and more focused and personal in their explorations. Furthermore, their view of self becomes gradually anchored within their own experience of the "I" and "ME." Their acceptance of self increases and their perceptions and appraisals of others and relationships become more "realistic" in the sense that they become personally more meaningful and satisfying. Clients also seem to be able to recognize and differentiate aspects of an experience, which may have never been part of their perceptual field before, and integrate these into diverse and more flexible perspectives.

By and large, these observations are consistent with the proposed therapeutic goals of client-centered and experiential therapies. They do, however, suggest that there is more to these orientations than the facilitative quality of the therapeutic relationship (C. Rogers, 1959). In other words, whatever it is that clients accomplish in therapy appears to be mediated by their *active involvement* in certain kinds of perceptual processing strategies that they themselves *learn* to generate and utilize over the course of therapy (Neisser, 1967).

It would seem, therefore, that if we are to understand how experiential treatments actually work, we need to go beyond their broad perceptual formulations and delineate (a) the nature of inferential processes that mediate change in clients' perceptions; and (b) the kinds of therapeutic interventions that optimize clients' engagement in these processes at different points in therapy. This, I believe, can best be achieved by advancing a framework for experiential therapy that is rooted in an explicit model of perceptual organization and change rather than by describing or reformulating the processes and procedures of an existing system of psychotherapy in the language and concepts of cognitive psychology (cf. Goldfried & Robins, 1983; Wexler & Rice, 1974). The short-term experiential treatment method presented in this chapter represents an approach that is derived from a schema-based perceptual model of cognitive affective functioning.

BACKGROUND AND ASSUMPTIONS

My approach to conceptualizing and evaluating the process of psycotherapeutic change (Toukmanian, 1983, 1986) is based on a schematic developmental view of mental activity that assigns a central role to perception in human functioning. Within this context, perception is broadly defined as the act of construing and representing one's own view of "reality." It is conceived of as a schema-driven and experientially-based developmental process that, at any given moment in time, reflects the perceiver's capability to detect, organize and give meaning to environmental and internal information on the basis of his or her past transactions with the world (e.g. J.R. Anderson, 1981; Fiske & Taylor, 1984; Hayes-Roth, 1977; Leventhal, 1982; Neisser, 1976; Weimer, 1977).

Guided by this schematic processing view of perception, the treatment method described below is based on four important assumptions. The first assumption is that clients have the ability to perceive and become aware of the elements of their experiences, differentiate between conflicting or incomparable constructions, and resolve these discrepancies in personally meaningful and satisfying ways (C. Rogers, 1959). Second, it is assumed that the manner in which clients talk about their experiences in therapy is the most immediate and perhaps the only available index of *how* they process or organize and make sense of information regarding self and self in relation to certain classes of events in their environment.

The third assumption underlying the approach is that clients' experienced difficulties with self, others and situations reflect an underlying perceptual system that is developmentally arrested or restricted in the kind of information that it can accept and the way in which this information is processed. This assumption is based on the notion that when people are repeatedly exposed to highly familiar and redundant information (e.g. emotions, subjective reactions, etc.), they learn, for the sake of efficiency, to subject this information to an "automated mode of processing" (Shiffrin & Schneider, 1977) and base their constructions on the rapid scanning of a few readily recognizable cues which are processed without conscious intent and without interfering with other mental activity (Bargh, 1982; Posner, 1978).

The fourth and final assumption is that such automated or invariant constructions are very difficult to modify unless the processing is deliberately interrupted or "deautomatized" *and* followed through by interventions that engage clients in the reprocessing of these experiences in a "controlled" fashion (Shiffrin & Schneider, 1977). In other words, it is assumed that when clients are given the opportunity to focus on and explore a given experience in a slow and reflective way, they learn to apply different kinds of perceptual operations to the elements of an experience and subsequently analyze the experience in more depth (Craik & Lockhart, 1972). The contention here is that engaging clients in a controlled mode of processing enhances their schematic development which in turn enables them to reorganize and reconstruct their experiences in more comprehensive and flexible ways.

TREATMENT STRATEGIES AND PROCEDURES

It is important to recognize from the outset that the focus of the perceptual-processing treatment approach is not on what clients perceive but on *how* they perceive or formulate their problematic impressions of self and events in their environment. The approach is, thus, a content free, client-process oriented treatment method that aims at helping clients change or modify the manner with which they habitually go about construing certain classes of intra- and interpersonal events, and generate new and potentially more functional processing strategies that have adaptive consequences for them.[1]

Therapists working from this orientation perform two important functions. First, through their empathic, nonjudgmental and accepting way of relating to clients, they are instrumental in developing and maintaining a safe and trusting therapeutic environment. This is an essential component of therapy but necessary only as a *first step* or a prerequisite and not as a "be all or end all" condition for therapeutic improvement. The therapist's second and most vital function, however, is to catalyze the process of clients' perceptual skills development. This is achieved through therapeutic interventions that systematically focus on particular kinds of client "process markers" (Rice & Greenberg, 1984), or dysfunctional patterns of perceptual operations, that are discernible from the differential quality of clients' moment-to-moment verbal participation in therapy. These markers essentially serve to inform the therapist as to "where the client is at" with respect to his or her level of perceptual functioning, i.e. they help establish a differential "process diagnosis" (Toukmanian, 1983).

The identification of process markers requires that therapists be constantly alert to the nature of processing dysfunctions that are contributing to clients' failure to perceive (and by implication to deal with) certain classes of life events more fully. When listening to clients talk, therapists need to become aware of, for example, how elaborate is the client's representation of such events? Is the client's construction superficial, stereotypic, and abstract or detailed, personalized and idiosyncratic? Is the source of validating information regarding the particular experience internal or external to the client? Are there particular types or classes of information that are nearly never picked up? Is this client capable of generating alternative interpretations of a given event? Is he or she capable of "suspending judgment" and engaging in a propositional mode of information processing to allow several alternative interpretations of an event to coexist? These and similar other questions, addressing the kind of information that clients detect (or fail to detect) and the processing operations that they utilize, function as diagnostic guides for the formulation of therapeutic interventions that are specific to clients' existing perceptual dysfunctions (see Appendix).

Marker specification involves singling out expressions that suggest the presence of an automated and constricted pattern of schematic processing (Shiffrin & Schneider, 1977). Indicators of such constructions are found when clients describe a complex experience in a packaged or condensed fashion (e.g. "...I kind of fear being... I still have to watch *being vulnerable...*") which when tested for differentiation or elaboration does not yield readily to the therapist's intervention, i.e. gives only a fleeting sense of the extent and intensity of the experience. Other markers are connotative expressions that are rich in subjective meanings not easily understandable to the therapist (e.g. "...I think in some ways *I am incidental...*") and stereotypic qualifiers of the ought and should variety (e.g. "...I'm feeling that *I should have a different reaction...* it does not sound like the right kind of filial loyalty...").

Interventions at these process markers requires that therapists focus on or reallocate clients' attention (W. Anderson, 1974) to such expressions using paraphrases, reflections or bids for clarification. In the present context, the intent of this deliberate deployment of attention is to help clients "slow down," scan and become aware of the elements contained in their experience.

Although a necessary condition for change, deautomatization by itself is not sufficient to "stretch the limits" of clients' perceptual system vis à vis a given event. To help clients explore the experience in more depth, therapists need to respond to their clients in ways that will engage them in a variety of controlled processing operations (Shiffrin & Schneider, 1977). This entails the use of process oriented interventions that facilitate clients' (a) recall of information associated with different facets of an experience; (b) differentiation of implied meanings in the information being processed; and (c) reschematization and reconstruction of the experience from a more complete and internally discerned data base.

Facilitating clients' recall of past experiences

Clients' accounts or recollections of their past experiences provide the grist that runs the therapeutic mill of most treatment orientations. While the majority of clients have little difficulty remembering factual information of the who, what, where and when variety (i.e. information that is external to them), their recall of "subjective reactions" contained in these experiences is often poorly articulated and sketchy. An essential aspect of the therapeutic task, therefore, is to facilitate clients' reconstruction of the subjective elements or facets of the "problem."

From a processing standpoint, this activity serves two important purposes. First, it helps clients generate a more complete data base to further their explorations; and second, it provides therapists with the opportunity to identify those components in clients' experiences that were inadequately processed in the past for their reprocessing in a controlled fashion in the present.

To help clients reconstruct past experiences, in as complete a fashion as possible, therapists need to use interventions that function as effective retrieval cues, i.e. that activate patterns of perceptual operations compatible with those carried out at the initial encoding of the event (e.g. Moscovitch & Craik, 1976; Tulving & Thomson, 1973). This process is often facilitated through interventions that engage clients in a "guided" search for the elements contained in their original construals to concretize the experience. Thus, to the extent that an intervention is "accurate" in general terms (i.e. is successful in reinstating some processes that are germane to the initial construal of the experience), further reconstructions of the same type are encouraged, each approximation serving as the new and more complete data base for subsequent analyses. "Evocative reflections" or interventions that make use of imagery, metaphor and vivid language (Rice, 1974) are particularly effective as mnemonic aids in this regard. The following excerpt illustrates this reconstructive recall process.

> C1: "I give a lot to people ... I enjoy it... I guess... in times when I need help *they should be able to help me out* [Marker]... they should be able to say... maybe that's why I do... maybe I don't know what to expect when I do something for somebody.
>
> T1: I'm not sure what you mean when you say 'they should be able to help me out'
> [Therapist focuses client's attention on marker].
>
> C2: Well... whenever I see anybody in trouble... I go and help... they don't

need to ask... I just do it... but I don't like to go and ask for favours... [Client attempts to elaborate].

T2: They should be able to somehow read your mind... and know what you want [Focus still on marker].

C3: They can't read my mind... that's for sure... (laugh)... it's not as if I expect a medal or a big favour... although...

T3: No, I guess not... but I guess you don't want to be a beggar, hat in hand either.
[Therapist uses a metaphor to concretize the experiential quality of client's conflict].

C4: Yeah... Maybe that's it... because a lot of times I get reasons like my brother gave me... like I get excuses... that they are busy that they don't have the time...da.. da... da... like they don't even bother...

T4: You sound as if this kind of experience happens to you often... [Therapist attempts to cue client to recall other experiences of the same kind for further exploration].

C5: When I think back... not just with my brother... like the time I had that job... and I had to prepare that report... yeah... and (reflective) when... a few months ago I needed someone to take care of the kids when I was gone... [Client is engaged in a memory search].

T5: And when you think back... the thing that stands out most in your mind is... [Therapist deliberately stops and does not finish the sentence to encourage client to search for specific elements of her experience].

C6: Anger... I get really mad... oh yes I can fly off the handle... very easily... but I don't... I don't make waves... I just feel angry and frustrated... [Client is able to identify the subjective elements in her experience].

T6: What else do you experience? Anything else that stands out for you?

C7: I don't know... (voice drops to a whisper) I feel... I guess a little bit hurt too... that after all I do for these people... they don't bother... thinking really that nobody cares... nobody will ever care!!"

In the above excerpt, the client's use of a stereotypic expression, "they should be able to help me," to qualify her need for attention served as marker. In T1 the therapist focused the client's attention on the expression for clarification. As C2 did not yield much information, in that the client's elaborations were somewhat vague, the therapist continued to hold her attention to the marker using an intervention that deliberately exaggerated what the therapist thought might be one of the implicit meanings of the marker expression.

The client's struggle to articulate her rather poor image of herself was captured by the therapist's "beggar" metaphor (T3). This served to concretize the two elements of her conflict in interpersonal contexts: Her desire to be viewed as a nice, helpful but strong individual and the anxiety associated with her extreme neediness for others. The therapist was then able to engage the client in a series of guided recall operations (T4 to T6) which served to cue her to some of the elements of her subjective reactions to people across a variety of interpersonal situations.

Differentiation of meaning

As a complex, person specific and central attitudinal cognitive structure, the "self" exerts a strong influence on how people perceive and make judgments about events occurring within themselves and in their environment (e.g. Kuiper, Derry, & MacDonald, 1982; Greenwald & Praktanis, 1984; Linville, 1985; Markus & Sentis, 1982; T.B. Rogers, 1981). As such, engaging clients in a "controlled mode of processing" also entails getting them to focus on and explore their "felt sense" of an experience or the meaning that a particular experience has for them. Thus, the therapists' main intent here is to assist clients to become aware of the "perceptual roadmap" (Toukmanian, 1984) that they habitually use as a guide to making inferences about self and self in relation to others and events in their environment.

As this is one of the more difficult but crucial steps in therapy, therapists need to be particularly systematic and tenacious in repeatedly following through clients' "markers" for an in-depth analysis of the target event. This requires that interventions not only engage clients in the differentiation of implicit meanings contained in their view of an experience (Wexler, 1974), but more importantly, encourage them to relate these "discovered" facets of meanings to their self-referenced perceptions and judgments. To facilitate this process, therapists need to use reflections of perceived affect and probes for perceived meanings and meaning associations to introduce a "beneficial uncertainty" (Beier, 1966) in clients' evaluations of the situation thus giving them an opportunity to reconsider reconstructing their experiences differently. In other words, what this intervention strategy essentially does is that it helps clients, over the course of their explorations, to generate a new "blueprint" or a modified "roadmap" of perceptual operations with which to reformulate an experience.

The following transaction, is an illustration of this process.

C1: "If my sister had started with this thing about how burdensome it was for her to do things without me I would have ended up with a long dialogue... explaining... there would have been an *emotional penalty...* [Marker].

T1: And what's the nature of this emotional penalty?

C2: Well, that she would make an effort to let me feel that I wasn't doing what she would like me to do...

T2: Emotional penalty... I'm still not sure what that means to you. [Focus still on marker in C1].

C3: I guess that... it means that I have the anxiety of trying to fix things for others... for family... on top of hoping of being me... and taking care of things here...

T3: Being there for your mother *and* for your sister *and* for your kids... and somehow trying... [Therapist concretizes for the client the extent of her expectations of herself with respect to family].

C4: Ye'ah... trying to um... *be perfect for other people* and I'm not... I feel I'm burned out from all the years before... It's like I feel I gave it and it's in a bank... so I'd sort of like to cash in on what I gave already and not give any more... to *stay detached... uninvolved...* [markers that were focused on and explored earlier on in therapy].

T4: I guess you're saying "Lay off... I like to have my own space for a change"... but somehow... [Therapist encourages the client to give a more personalized meaning to the marker expression in C1].

C5: Yeah... I just feel very... umm... tenacious about me... but I still feel bad when I feel the necessity of shutting off...

T5: Even though you have accumulated enough in the bank... there still is that feeling that...'I cannot cash in... my credit is not good enough.' [Therapist uses the client's own metaphor to concretize and juxtapose the incongruent elements of her conflict].

C6: I think it's the feeling that I'm not big enough to do for more than me... You know... that I'm not two adults... I'm only one. A lot of people have spent a lot of time trying to get me to be more than one... I think umm... the penalty is that I sometimes fight this feeling that... [Client recognizes the nature of the conflict].

T6: That you really are not one adult, but two.

C7: Or... ought to be!

T7: Ought to be... I'm not sure where this "ought" comes from. [Therapist engages the client in a focused exploration].

C8: It comes through... messages from other people... but it comes from me too... probably... it has to... [An awareness of source of conflict emerging].

T8: "I'm not big enough if I'm not two people."

C9: (Long pause)... And I'm not big enough if I'm only *one* adult giving to people... Oh boy!! I don't know where I got that one! (laughs) It doesn't even sound reasonable! (laughs). [Client recognizes the basic source of conflict]."

In the above example, the client's idiosyncratic way of characterizing her difficulty in communicating with her sister was portrayed in her use of the expression "there would have been an emotional penalty." In T1 and T2, the therapist focused on this marker to get the client to clarify the meaning that the expression had for her. As the client struggled with this bid for clarification, she was able to identify two internal states; feeling "burned out" from trying to be "perfect" for others and anxious about her being lost in the shuffle. An interpretation to this effect would probably have been true to the actual content of what the client said - but it would have hindered her from recognizing how she came to formulate or arrive at the inference. Instead, the therapist used interventions (T3 through T5) that served to cue the client to some of the contradictory elements of her conflictual experience. In other words, these interventions helped the client to engage in certain kinds of perceptual operations that allowed her to identify the nature of the contradictory information contained in her emotional difficulty (C6). And when the client was further encouraged to focus on and integrate these elements into her construction of the experience (T6 through T8) she was able to recognize the role that her own negative view of self had played into creating her strained relationships with others.

Reschematization

The availability of new and internally discerned information on a given experience, necessitates a reorganization in the clients' system of self- and other-relevant schemata. In other words, it requires that clients attend to this rich pool of differentiated information, integrate some of its elements into their existing network of schemata and, on the basis of these, develop a new internal representation(s) of the experience. This is a rather complex activity wherein the integration of previously differentiated facets of meaning into a superordinate meaning structure for the experience (Wexler, 1974) is an important component of the overall process.

The term reschematization, in the present context, refers specifically to the process of *developing,* through the application of a variety of perceptual operations, *new links* or associations among qualitatively different schematic structures and *generating diverse perspectives* on a given experience. In this sense, reschematization may be thought of as a "flexible networking" activity which, at any given moment in time, brings a range of differentiated and well developed schemata to bear on the processing of the experience.

Some clients engage in this process quite spontaneously or with minimum therapist involvement. This was the case with the client in the previous example. The excerpt that follows demonstrates this phenomenon.

> C9 : "(long pause)... And if I'm not big enough if I'm only one adult giving to people... Oh boy! I don't know where I got that one! (laughs). It doesn't even sound reasonable! (laughs). But somehow it's not the same as giving to friends. And that's what I've been thinking about too. That... there is no emotional penalty with friends... I'm realizing now... I can choose to give it to friends... or family... But the dependency has a... long standing... I still try to fix things for other people... sometimes at my own expense. (Therapist: Mm...Hmmm)... And I need to let go of that stuff... say that it's okay...
> T9 : Because?
> C10: Because I'm entitled to!
> T10: Entitled to what?
> C11: To live my own life and do it well... Do it as well as I can."

It can be seen from this brief interaction that as soon as the client became aware of how her own negative construal of self contributed to her strained relationships with others, she was able to immediately and quite spontaneously (a) test the validity of this view of self across other interpersonal situations; (b) realize that there was no "emotional penalty" in giving to friends - meaning that her feelings of vulnerability were related specifically to family situations; and (c) recognize, somewhat tenuously, that she had to "let go off the stuff," i.e. of her tendency to ignore her own needs by putting the needs of her family before her own. The therapist's subsequent interventions helped the client to incorporate this previously ignored aspect of self into her self-structure. This in turn led the client to generate and become aware of other perspectives, i.e. that she indeed was entitled to her own needs and to her desire to carry on with her life and responsibilities to the best of her capabilities.

Unlike the client described above, the majority of clients require that therapists be more active in guiding them to reschematize their construals. In other words, prior to the resolution of a conflict, most clients' network of schemata may be well differentiated and rich in personal meaning but still be vulnerable or subject to automated processing. Automatization on this level is often reflected in clients' highly individualized and idiosyncratic but rather loose manner of communicating which, when tested, does not lead to the formulation of a new perspective(s). Intervention at such "process markers" requires, therefore, that therapists (a) focus clients' attention to previously evoked and differentiated information (e.g. Anderson, 1974; Wexler, 1974); (b) prompt clients to reexamine and reorganize this information in different ways and become aware of the range of possible perceptual options that is available to them; and (c) encourage them to use this processing "know-how" to redintegrate the experience in a new internal representation that offers them a fuller and personally more meaningful resolution for the experienced conflict. This process is illustrated in the following excerpt.

C1: "...when I think about all this (referring to her very strained relationship with parents)... I can sort of do *flip flops* [Marker]... think about it this way and that way... and I get myself confused...

T1 And when you're thinking straight about it? [Therapist encourages the client to focus on previously differentiated elements of the positive component in her conflict].

C2: Well, I guess that the situation at home is unfortunate... a sad and difficult thing to deal with but it's just something that happened... reflecting on it... it is a sad situation but it is not the only way to live... You know there was a time when I sort of felt trapped in there and I'm not trapped... I don't feel trapped any more.

T2: I wonder what it was that was making you feel trapped. [Therapist encourages the client to focus on previously differentiated elements of the negative component in her conflict].

C3: I guess... feeling the sadness, the hurt, the loneliness... or thinking that my parents are feeling these things... and wanting to improve the situation for them because they couldn't. But I guess I can't do that... and... having a sense that I wasn't getting the love that I wanted and... perhaps if I stayed and tried to help out... that miraculously all this love would be directed my way but... I guess what I wanted isn't going to happen... everybody loves in a different way... and in their own way... my parents care about me... It's just not, you know, my particular conception of what I would like but... [Client generates new perceptual options].

T3: So it's not really a matter that you have to change your parents or... [Therapist engages the client in the process of redintegration].

C4: Or change myself...

T4: It's just a matter of living with the way things are... within you and the situation... [Therapist reflects the client's redintegrated view of self].

C5: Yeah... and I guess accepting my family situation... and my parents as they are... They are part of life but they are not my whole life... and my goals, values are different from theirs... and, you know, all along I've been waiting them to somehow conform to my needs... my image of Mom and Dad... and in that mess I sort of felt I had to conform to what they thought I should be... (a deep sigh). [Client generates new perspective from old "data"].

T5: *Their* image of a loving daughter... [Therapist helps the client to consolidate her awareness of self, independent of parents].

C6: Yeah... I don't know if that's exactly it but... I'm not going to change for them or for their world... to do my own thing doesn't mean that I have to totally eh... separate from my family. I don't feel that way... No... (reflectively). It's O.K.... like my wall is secure... It's just an acceptance... it doesn't feel like defeat. Not at all. It just means I can start building now... [Client arrives at a resolution]."

In this transaction, T1 and T2 served to direct the client's attention to the differentiated components of her conflict - her strong need for parental approval on the one hand and her desire to break away from this extreme dependency on the other. By encouraging the client to "review" her perceptions of the situation, the therapist was able to engage the client in a comparative analysis of her past and present construals of self and self in relation to parents. Once the process of "reappraisal" was set in motion, she was able to question the accuracy of her past inferences, generate new and more flexible perceptual options, and entertain the possibility of reconstructing her previously held view of this experience differently. In other words, she was able to shift from a tight, undifferentiated and categorical manner of processing to a less rigid and more reflective and deliberate mode of perceptual analysis that allowed her to reorganize and reinterpret the elements contained in her conflictual experience differently.

The intent of the three subsequent therapist interventions was to get the client to impose some structure on the fluid state of her perceptual system. By encouraging the client to take a closer look at her new options, the therapist was able to stimulate the client to reprocess relevant aspects of her new constructions and redintegrate these into a differentiated view of self that was separate from that of her parents. Once the client was able to untangle her own perceptions of self from those she had introjected from family, she also came to appreciate the degree of compatibility between her own views and those of her family. This in turn led her to diffuse the conflict and arrive at her own resolution of the problem based ostensibly on information that she herself had generated. In other words, she was able to put the circumstances of her situation in a new perspective, recognize her own separateness as an individual, and redefine self *in relation to parents* rather than in terms of conditions and expectations set for her *by parents.*

To summarize, this short term experiential treatment approach involves the systematic application of a series of client process oriented interventions to identifiable client markers which recur on a number of occasions and at different points over the course of therapy. The main thrust of these interventions is to engage clients in different kinds of perceptual operations and to get them to reanalyze and restructure the elements contained in their problematic experiences in more comprehensive and meaningful ways. Thus, when clients are repeatedly called upon to perform these operations on information in a variety of content areas, they gradually and systematically break away from their habitual patterns of perceptual analyses and acquire new ways of processing their experiences. And as clients become aware of the possibilities of their own perceptual resources, they develop new and more flexible processing strategies that lead to fundamental changes in the manner with which they go about formulating their perspectives on self, others and everyday social contacts and relationships.

NOTE

1. This therapeutic goal is similar to some information processing-based formulations of client-centered therapy (e.g. W. Anderson, 1974; Wexler, 1974; Zimring, 1974). However, as it will be seen below, the way in which this treatment method goes about achieving this goal and the intervention strategies that it advocates differ in several important ways. As a conceptually-driven method of therapy, the perceptual-processing approach offers a *moment-to-moment* specification of (a) the nature of clients' dysfunctional modes of processing that need to be attended to and modified at different points over the course of therapy (i.e. the targets for therapeutic interventions); (b) factors involved in the identification of these targets from clients' verbalizations that reflect the presence of these model-specified client processing dysfunctions (i.e. client process markers); and (c) intervention strategies that need to be used at different markers to facilitate change in clients' manner of processing and construing an experience.

REFERENCES

Anderson, J.R. (1981). Concepts, propositions, and schemata: What are the cognitive units? *Nebraska symposium on motivation.* Lincoln: University of Nebraska Press.

Anderson, W. (1974). Personal growth and client-centered therapy: An information processing view. In D.A. Wexler & L.N. Rice (Eds.), *Innovations in client-centered therapy* (pp. 21-48). New York: Wiley.

Bargh, J.A. (1982). Attention and automaticity in the processing of self-relevant information. *Journal of Personality and Social Psychology, 43,* 425-436.

Beier, E. (1966). *The silent language of psychotherapy.* Chicago: Aldine.

Craik, F.I.M., & Lockhart, R.S. (1972). Levels of processing: A framework for memory research. *Journal of Verbal Learning and Verbal Behavior, 11,* 671-684.

Fiske, S.T., & Taylor, S.E. (1984). *Social cognition.* New York: Random House.

Goldfried, M., & Robins, C. (1983). Self-schemas, cognitive bias and the processing of therapeutic experiences. In P.C. Kendall (Ed.), *Advances in cognitive behavioral research and therapy* (Vol. 2, pp. 33-80). New York: Academic press.

Greenwald, A.G., & Praktanis, A.R. (1984). The self. In R.S. Wyer & T.R. Srull (Eds.), *Handbook of social cognition* (pp. 129-178). Hillsdale, NJ: Erlbaum.

Hayes-Roth, B. (1977). Evolution of cognitive structure and processes. *Psychological Review, 84,* 260-278.

Kuiper, N.A., Derry, P.A., & McDonald, M.R. (1982). Self reference in person perception in depression: A social cognition perspective. In G. Weary & H.L. Mirels (Eds.), *Integrations of clinical and social psychology* (pp. 79-103). New York: Oxford University Press.

Leventhal, H. (1982). The integration of emotion and cognition: A view from a perceptual-motor theory of emotion. In M.S. Clarke & S.T. Fiske (Eds.), *Affect and cognition* (pp. 121-156). Hillsdale, NJ: Erlbaum.

Linville, P.W. (1985). Self complexity and affective extremity. Don't put all your eggs in one cognitive basket. *Social Cognition, 3,* 94-120.

Markus, H., & Sentis, K. (1982). The self in social information processing. In J. Suls (Ed.), *Psychological perspectives on the self* (pp. 41-70). Hillsdale, NJ: Erlbaum.

Moskovitch, M., & Craik, F. (1976). Depth of processing, retrieval cues and uniqueness of encoding as factors of recall. *Journal of Verbal Learning and Verbal behavior, 15,* 447-458.

Neisser, U. (1976). Cognitive psychology. New York: Appleton-Century-Crofts.

Posner, M.I. (1978). *Chronometric explorations of mind.* Hillsdale, NJ: Erlbaum.

Rice, L.N. (1974). The evocative function of the therapist. In D.A. Wexler & L.N. Rice (Eds.), *Innovations in client-centered therapy* (pp. 289-318). New York: Wiley.

Rice, L.N., & Greenberg, L.S. (1984). *Patterns of change.* New York: Guilford Press.

Rogers, C.R. (1959). A theory of therapy, personality and interpersonal relationships, as developed in the client-centered framework. In S. Koch (Ed.), *Psychology: A study of a science. Vol. 3: Formulations of the person and the social context* (pp. 184-256). New York: McGraw Hill.

Rogers, T.B. (1981). A model of the self as an aspect of the human information

324

processing system. In N. Cantor & J.F. Kihlstrom (Eds.), *Personality, cognition, and social interaction* (pp. 193-214). Hillsdale, NJ: Erlbaum.

Shiffrin, R.M., & Schneider, W. (1977). Controlled and automated human information processing: II. Perceptual learning, automatic attending, and a general theory. *Psychological Review, 84,* 127-130.

Toukmanian, S.G. (1983). *A perceptual-cognitive model for counselling and psychotherapy* (Tech. Rep. No. 138). North York, Ontario: York University, Department of Psychology.

Toukmanian, S.G. (1984). *Therapist manual: Perceptual-cognitive method of therapy.* Unpublished manuscript. North York: York University, Department of Psychology.

Toukmanian, S.G. (1986). A measure of client perceptual processing. In L.S. Greenberg & W.M. Pinsof (Eds.), *The psychotherapeutic process: A research handbook* (pp. 107-130). New York: Guilford Press.

Tulving, E., & Thomson, D.M. (1973). Encoding specificity and retrieval processes in episodic memory. *Psychological Review, 80,* 352-373.

Weimer, W.B. (1977). A conceptual framework for cognitive psychology: Motor theories of the mind. In R. Shaw & J. Bransford (Eds.), *Perceiving, acting, and knowing: Toward an ecological psychology* (pp. 267-311). Hillsdale, NJ: Erlbaum.

Wexler, D.A. (1974). A cognitive theory of experiencing, self actualization and therapeutic process. In D.A. Wexler & L.N. Rice (Eds.), *Innovations in client-centered therapy* (pp. 49-116). New York: Wiley.

Wexler, D.A., & Rice, L.N. (1974). *Innovations in client-centered therapy.* New York: Wiley.

Zimring, F.M. (1974). Theory and practice of client-centered therapy: A cognitive view. In D.A. Wexler & L.N. Rice (Eds.), *Innovations in client-centered therapy* (pp. 117-138). New York: Wiley.

APPENDIX
A SPECIFICATION OF CLIENT PROCESS MARKERS AND THERAPEUTIC STRATEGIES

C1 . Client uses an expression which stands out as a packaged, undifferentiated and static characterization of a feeling and thinking state, i.e. reflects an automated mode of perceptual activity (e.g. "...my world is falling apart..." "...I don't seem to have self-confidence anymore...").

T1 . Therapist recognizes the expression as a "marker" and deploys client's attention to the expression by using simple probes, minimal encourages, etc. (i.e. disrupting the automated process).

C2. Client responds to the demands of the therapeutic task, attempts to elaborate, clarify and/or expand on the meaning of expressions

C2a. Client scans areas of experience for possible relevance; elaborations rely heavily on factual information of who, what, where and when of an experience (e.g. "my marks are not so good... my teenage son is in trouble again with the law... I don't seem to have enough money to live on... and my social life is a disaster...").

T2a. Therapist brings client's locus of attention to the implicit meanings (internal source of information) attributed to the stimulus situation by using open-ended questions, probes, interrogative reflections, etc.

C2b. Client differentiates and recognizes aspects of experience from an external frame of reference; uses other generated standards, "shoulds" or pat and stereotypic qualifiers to characterize an internal state; self is implied but not recognized (e.g. "...I should be able to provide a better home for my kids... for my husband..." "I guess I haven't got what it takes... my parents were right all along....").

T2b. Therapist recognizes externality of client's construal; qualifiers serve as "markers"; reflections of perceived affect, probes of perceived meanings and meaning associations used to introduce uncertainty in client's assertions, unconditional interpretations and evaluations of self (i.e. engages client in controlled self-explorations).

C3 . Client discriminates different aspects of subjective reactions to a given situation; construals recognized to have an internal base; manner of communicating is reflective but tight and analytical (e.g. "...I suppose it links up with self-image... not being able to or at least not being able to competently say what I want to say... and then feeling badly about it later... going through some subterfuge...").

T3 . Client's logical "if then" style of self exploration serves as marker; interventions use metaphoric/imagistic language to capture and concretize the experiential quality of client's response, i.e. serve to access new dimensions of implied meanings or significances attached to the view of the experience.

C4 . Client discerns and explores facets of implied meanings of experience, interrelates differentiated meanings and construes the experience in a

T4 . Therapist recognizes client's unusual and idiosyncratic expression as marker; maintains client's focus on own internally uniquely personal way; an emerging new and fuller perspective on self and experience; highly personalized and idiosyncratic manner of communicating (e.g. "...it feels as if I am constantly looking for a lost childhood"; "...it's like quick sand... the more I try to please... the more I lose ground... myself... get buried...").

differentiated and discerned meanings; interventions engage client to reexamine and review past and present perceptions of self and self with regard to different interpersonal situations.

C5 . Client recognizes the possibility of construing an experience differently; actively engages in generating and appraising alternative perspectives based on recognized new self perceptions (i.e. needs, values, strengths, etc.); explorations focused internally; manner of communicating reflective and tentative (e.g. "I'm not sure... but it would seem that... I need this relationship but I also have the right to be me").

T5 . Internally based and propositional nature of client's construals serves as marker; interventions engage the client to focus on and explore own perceptual options (i.e. to reschematize and redintegrate aspects of self and the situation into alternative perspectives).

C6. Client generates a more comprehensive and individualized view of experience; communication reflects an integrated perspective based on a richer and more differentiated view of self.

Client recognizes new perspective as potentially more meaningful; uses his/her articulated and more flexible processing system to explore and validate new perceptions of self in other life situations.

Note: Although there is a general progression from C1 to C6 in the client's manner of processing over the course of therapy, any one or a combination of these processing modes may occur at any point during or across therapy sessions.

CONFRONTATION AND NON-CONFRONTATION AS DIFFERENTIAL TECHNIQUES IN DIFFERENTIAL CLIENT-CENTERED THERAPY

Dieter TSCHEULIN[1]
Universität Würzburg, F.R.Germany

The topic of this chapter builds on the hypothesis of client-therapist complementarity which was shortly mentioned in former studies of the author (Tscheulin, 1983a, 1983b). Complementarity in the therapeutic relationship can be explored empirically by means of interpersonal assessment tools, such as the "Structured Analysis of Social Behavior" (SASB) of Benjamin (e.g. 1974, 1982). During the last years, this has attracted growing interest, for example in the studies of Brokaw (1983), Henry, Schacht and Strupp (1986), or Kiesler and Goldston (1988).

This chapter refers to the hypothesis of complementarity, because it enables to trace therapeutic effectiveness back to a main principle which is not only found in basic therapeutic behavior ("therapeutic bond"), but also in differential therapy ("therapeutic interventions", cf. Orlinsky & Howard, 1987; Tscheulin, 1980, 1988).

THE HYPOTHESIS OF COMPLEMENTARITY

According to this hypothesis, a constructive change of personality is only possible if the participating persons in the therapeutic contact have a complementary relationship. Their characteristics are reciprocal and complementary. This statement applies as much to the field of basic therapeutic behavior, where relationship factors are mainly considered, as to the field of differential therapy, which deals with the use of specific techniques for each individual case.

One example of complementarity in the field of basic therapeutic behavior is the encounter of a self-incongruent client with a therapist, who is highly self-congruent in his relationship with this client and who is able to remain so, independently of the client's behavior.

In the field of differential psychotherapy, complementarity can be seen, for example, in the heterogeneity of groups which involves the "very Norm" as Foulkes (1948) says (see Appendix). In individual therapy, one aspect of complementarity can be seen in the differentiation between self-centered and action-centered clients and their respectively limited resources (cf. Tscheulin, 1976, 1983a, 1988; Duval & Wicklund, 1972, for details). This way of differentiating clients guides the use of confrontation and non-confrontation as differential techniques.

The self-awareness of self-centered clients is directed towards their inner self. They experience themselves for considerable periods of time as a "person-object" and are thus more likely to become aware of inner discrepancies. They are at risk of developing symptoms such as phobic anxiety, lack of self-confidence, and negative self-regard.

Action-centered clients are spontaneously less capable of self-reflection. They often involve themselves in action and are absorbed by the action. So they direct their attention to the outside, towards the goals of their actions. Consequently, they are at risk of not "seeing" possible discrepancies between their desired and their real behavior. Their problems will not be expressed through anxiety but through "blind action-taking", through "flight into activity" and through hysterical, addicted or delinquent behavior. They are often considered to be rather difficult clients, who profit only little or not at all from psychotherapy.

A differential approach for these different types of clients can theoretically be derived from the hypothesis of complementarity as follows:

The extremely self-centered clients (thus hindered in their activities) are met by therapists who use action-activating techniques. For example, by assigning tasks ("homework assignments") and by encouraging concrete actions, or by consistently talking about real life elements (using "nonjudgemental dialogue"). The action-centered clients, who have difficulties experiencing themselves (thus overlooking many aspects, especially contradictions within themselves), are met by therapists, who place their experiencing at the client's disposal and help them by experience-activating techniques.

CONFRONTATION

A central and also essential experience-activating technique is confrontation.

Bastine and Kommer (1979, p. 423) define it as a "picking up of discrepant messages, which the client perceives and evaluates incompletely or incorrectly. Thus it is not possible for the client to avoid facing these discrepant messages."

This definition is to a large extent identical with those of Anderson (1968) or Berenson, Mitchell and Laney (1968). The studies presented here, are based on this definition. It is important, however, to know the *conditions* for constructive confrontation as well. These conditions consist of the ability of the therapist to accept and to accurately understand the client. Therefore, the instructions in the experiments reported below always call attention to the fact that a confronting procedure has to be carried out only within the presence of basic therapeutic behavior. In all the studies, it has been checked whether these conditions were fulfilled or not.

CONFRONTATION AND ACCURATE EMPATHY

The term confrontation can be specified in the following way: When a therapist confronts, he offers the client his own perception, which differs from that of the client. He calls the client's attention to behaviors, beliefs and emotions, which he perceives as either discrepant within the client or discrepant to his own experiencing.

This specification illustrates both the closeness and the distinction from "accurate empathy". According to Egan (1975, p. 58): "Confrontation at its best is an extension of advanced accurate empathy."

To put it precisely: Accurate empathy results from the client's inner frame of reference alone, while confrontation requires the inner frame of reference of the therapist as well. Confrontation consists of putting the therapist's inner frame of reference next to that of the client. But is it correct to use confrontation in the encounter with every client?

INDICATION OF CONFRONTATION

An answer to the question of indication can be derived from what was said before: Confrontation as a differential strategy is recommended for action-centered clients, but not for self-centered clients. This was empirically verified as well in ex-post-facto comparisons as in quasi-experiments.

A comparison of ten successfully completed client-centered therapies with both extremely action-centered and extremely self-centered clients shows e.g. that the psychotherapies with the difficult action-centered clients last four times longer - or, put differently: The therapist is four times more available to the action-centered client than to the self-centered client.

This, however, is not the only difference between psychotherapies with action-centered and with self-centered clients. The therapist also confronts action-centered clients significantly more often during a therapeutic session (about four times as often; cf. Tscheulin, 1983a, p. 249, for details). If one considers one of the essential determinating aspects of confrontation, one can also say that the therapist offers the client both his experiencing, and his view of the client more frequently.

Experimentally, the indication for a differential procedure was demonstrated by systematically applying and avoiding confrontation in a quasi-experimental design with sixteen clients and four experienced therapists. The clients were graduate students in time-limited personal therapy of six therapeutic hours. They were selected from a larger group of psychotherapy trainees because they were either extremely self-centered or extremely action-centered. For each therapist, two self-centered as well as two action-centered clients were randomly assigned to either the "confrontation" or the "non-confrontation" approach. So, the design had four "groups" (conditions) with four clients each.

According to the hypothesis of complementarity, the correct differential procedure for the therapist is to not confront self-centered clients and to confront action-centered clients (two conditions). Clients in these two conditions should experience positive changes and helpful verbal interactions are expected to occur for both types of clients. This, however, should not be the case when self-centered clients are confronted and action-centered clients are not (the other two conditions).

The predicted differences were produced (cf. Tscheulin, 1983a,

1983b). Five years later, these results were validated by replication (cf. Tscheulin, 1988).

In both experimental studies, the dependent variable was mainly the client's judgment of success. This was estimated by means of a questionnaire called "Veränderungsfragebogen des Erlebens und Verhaltens - VEV" (Zielke & Kopf-Mehnert, 1978). This questionnaire contains items such as "I feel less rushed" or "I have less self-confidence". Using this kind of data, the two favorable and the two unfavorable conditions (groups) were found to be significantly different ($U = 8,5$; $p = .005$). In all but 3 out of 16 cases of the first study, the experienced changes corresponded to the prediction.

It is important to emphasize one point: These effects of confrontation (and non-confrontation) have been proved and verified using an instruction which permits therapist confrontation and non-confrontation only as far as basic therapeutic behavior is maintained. This was expressed by the empirically verified fact that all the clients in each of the four conditions experienced their therapists as being comparably empathic, esteeming and self-congruent.But what about the criteria for "discrepant messages?"

CRITERIA FOR A SCIENTIFICALLY-BASED PRACTICE AND TRAINING

The publications mentioned above illustrate the level of sophistication of this kind of research: The value of confrontation (as a differential procedure to overcome the difficulties with the action-centered clients) is either proved ex-post-facto or produced in a quasi-experiment with the help of experienced therapists who are instructed "to always confront when they detect a discrepancy within the client." This approach thus relies on the correct intuition of the experienced therapist. And this assumes that the experienced therapist somehow already knows the criteria to decide whether a confrontation is appropriate or not.

This is doubly unsatisfying. Scientifically, it remains unclear which characteristics of the client's process-behavior actually are used by the therapist as criteria for a confronting procedure. At a practical level, the unexperienced beginner risks "arbitrary action" and a diagnostic attitude, which are both incompatible with basic therapeutic behavior.

In two recent studies, this problem was investigated in two different ways. The leading question was: What are the critical characteristics of client's speech behavior which have to be taken into consideration as a cue for using confrontation?

This question can be pursued examining the categories of client speech behavior, to which the therapist refers when confronting or deciding not to confront: What are the characteristics of the *clients' statements prior to confrontation?*

A category system was tested in order to allow content analyses. The system holds six categories into which the client's statements can be reliably classified. The categories are (cf. Tscheulin, 1988, p. 280): A. Client contradictions e.g. between verbal and non-verbal behavior or present and earlier statements. B. Limitations in the client's statements. C. The search for reasons and explanations ("brain-work" ignoring the experience). D. Description of problems as being beyond one's own control and feasability. E. Generalizations. And F. Statements which do not fit categories A through E (without any cues that experience is ignored).

In successful individual, partner, and group therapies (with one therapist), 95% of clients' statements prior to confrontation fell into categories A through E, and only 5% into category F. However, of the clients' statements prior to non-confrontations, 94% feel into this contrasting category F and the remaining 6% into categories B, C and D.

A similar pattern also emerges in another study, limited to individual therapies by six different therapists.

Categories A through E all characterize in very different ways discrepant statements given by the client, which he himself, however, does not experience. One can say that it is with the help of the confrontation that an unperceived discrepancy is made accessible to the client. Such categories of client statements can be used as a basis for a confronting procedure, as well in practical work as in training.

THE SPEECH BEHAVIOR OF ACTION-CENTERED AND SELF-CENTERED PERSONS

Confrontation as a differential procedure can, however, also be founded by setting out criteria for the content and form of speech behavior which action-centered and self-centered persons tend to show. This makes it possible to react adequately during the therapy process without previously having to make psychodiagnostic decisions (which, in this case, are particularly problematic). This means that, on the basis of theory, it is possible to proceed rather confrontingly or rather non-confrontingly.

For the purpose, a catalogue was developed with criteria concerning the content and form of dialogues, starting from theoretical reflections as well as from practical experience. Then the catalogue was used in content analysis of the whole second contact of two pairs of extremely action-centered vs. self-centered clients (cf. Tscheulin, 1988, p. 182).

The results found by content analysis with this catalogue show that:
- Self-centered persons make longer pauses.
- They leave out words more frequently and produce unfinished sentences (anakoluthes).
- They also use more "filling-in words" and superfluous phrases.
- In the client-therapist interaction, action-centered persons show a higher relative amount of speaking (more than twice as high).
- The statement "I do not know" (or statements of similar content) is frequent.

Regarding the content of statements, we found that:
- Self-centered as opposed to action-centered persons show an "adjustment of their behavior to their own personal values".
- "To behave in a non-conforming way" is a topic discussed by action-centered clients: Self-centered clients do not speak about this point.
- Self-centered clients search within themselves; in contrast, action-centered clients very frequently search elsewhere for the cause of events.
- Contrary to self-centered people, action-centered people are more likely to speak about dominant behavior and not to consider submissive behavior.
- The statements of action-centered clients give more evidence of activity and initiative, omitting passivity and waiting.
- Action-centered clients talk about and evaluate other people much more often than do self-centered clients.

CONCLUSION

The reported studies and results are based on reliable data. They show internal validity. External validity of the studies, however, which allows generalization, remains relatively uncertain. This limited generalizability is primarily due to the fact that the number of therapists participating in the quasi-experiments is relatively small, and that experimental verification with a series of unlimited and extensive dialogues has not been possible so far. Regardless of the fact that validation has to be continued, one can say that the hypotheses, formulated and verified, give sufficient indications that it is worth studying factors concerning techniques in addition to those concerning relationship, also in "relationship therapies" such as client-centered therapy; in other words, studying the "specific therapist interventions" as well as the "relational climate" (Lietaer & Neirinck, 1986; Roelens, 1984). For example, the study of confrontation as a differential technique in client-centered therapy can help to find ways of optimizing the effectiveness of these types of therapies. At the same time, it can provide important information concerning the differential indication of psychotherapeutic approaches, some being more confronting and others more non-directive.

NOTE

1. With acknowledgements to Luc Roelens for his valuable comments and suggestions.

APPENDIX

Mente and Spittler (1988 , Vol. 2, p. 75) cite Foulkes: "The deepest reason why these patients (psycho-neurotics) can reinforce each other's normal reactions and wear and correct each other's neurotic reactions, is that collectively they constitute the very Norm, from which, individually, they deviate." They discuss the topic from a practical point of view.

REFERENCES

Anderson, S.C. (1968). Effects of confrontation by high- and low-functioning therapists. *Journal of Counseling Psychology, 15,* 411-416.

Bastine, R., & Kommer, D. (1979). Konfrontation als Strategie psychotherapeutischen Handelns. In L.H. Eckensberger (Ed.), *Bericht über den 31. Kongress der DGfPs in Mannheim 1978. Vol. 2. Praxisfelder der Psychologie* (pp. 412-416). Göttingen: Hogrefe.

Benjamin, L.S. (1974). Structural analysis of social behavior. *Psychological Review, 81,* 392-425.

Benjamin, L.S. (1982). Use of structural analysis of social behavior (SASB) to guide intervention in psychotherapy. In J.C. Anchin & D.J. Kiesler (Eds.), *Handbook of interpersonal psychotherapy* (pp. 190-212). New York: Pergamon.

Berenson, B.G., Mitchell, K.M., & Laney, R.C. (1968). Levels of therapists functioning, types of confrontation and type of patient. *Journal of Clinical Psychology, 24,* 111-113.

Brokaw, D.W. (1983a). Markow chains and master therapists: An interpersonal analysis of psychotherapy. *Dissertation Abstracts International, 44(5),* 1585-B.

Brokaw, D.W. (1983b). *Markow chains and master therapists: An interpersonal analysis of psychotherapy.* Unpublished dissertation, University Microfilm International, Ann Arbor.

Duval, S., & Wicklund, R.A. (1972). *A theory of objective self-awareness.* New York: Academic Press.

Egan, G. (1975). *The skilled helper.* Belmont: Wadsworth.

Foulkes, S.H. (1948). *Introduction to group-analytic psychotherapy.* London: Heinemann Medical Books (1949 in New York).

Henry, W.P., Schacht, Th.E.,& Strupp, H.H. (1986). Structural analysis of social behavior: An application to a study of interpersonal process in differential psychotherapeutic outcome. *Journal of Consulting and Clinical Psychology, 54,* 27-31.

Kiesler, D.J., & Goldston, C.S. (1988). Client-therapist complementarity: An analysis of the Gloria films. *Journal of Counseling Psychology, 35,* 127-133.

Lietaer, G., & Neirinck, M. (1986). Client and therapist perceptions of helping processes in client-centered/experiential psychotherapy. *Person-Centered Review, 1,* 436-455.

Mente, A., & Spittler, H.-D. (1980). *Erlebnisorientierte Gruppenpsychotherapie (2 Vols.).* Paderborn: Junfermann.

Orlinsky, D.E., & Howard, K.I. (1987). A generic model of process in psychotherapy. In W. Huber (Ed.), *Progress in psychotherapy research. Selected papers from the 2nd European Conference on Psychotherapy Research* (pp. 445-458). Louvain-la-Neuve: Presses Universitaires.

Roelens, L. (1984). In het verlengde van empathie: psychotechnologie in het kader van client- en ervaringsgerichte psychotherapie. In G. Lietaer, Ph. van Praag & J. Swildens (Eds.), *Client-centered psychotherapie in beweging* (pp. 429-446). Leuven: Acco.

Tscheulin, D. (1976). Ein Ansatz zu einer differentiellen Gesprächspsychotherapie als Beitrag zur Theorienbildung in der klientenzentrierten Psychotherapie. In P. Jankowski, D. Tscheulin, H.-J. Fietkau, & F. Mann (Eds.), *Klientenzentrierte Psychotherapie heute* (pp. 98-109). Göttingen: Hogrefe.

Tscheulin, D. (1980). Lernziel Therapeutisches Basisverhalten. In V. Birtsch & D. Tscheulin (Eds.), *Ausbildung in Klinischer Psychologie und Psychotherapie. Ziele, Inhalte und Methoden in Lehre und Studium* (pp. 109-128). Weinheim: Beltz.

Tscheulin, D. (1983a). Differentielle Gesprächspsychotherapie. Kontradiktion oder Innovation? In G. Bittner (Ed.), *Personale Psychologie. Festschrift für L.J. Pongratz* (pp. 241-257). Göttingen: Hogrefe.

Tscheulin, D. (1983b). Ueber differentielles therapeutisches Vorgehen in der klientenzentrierten Therapie. Ein empirischer Beitrag zu einer differentiellen Gesprächspsychotherapie. In D. Tscheulin (Ed.), *Beziehung und Technik in der klientenzentrierten Therapie* (pp. 53-64). Weinheim: Beltz.

Tscheulin, D. (1988). *Wirkfaktoren psychotherapeutischer Intervention. Ein heuristisches Modell zur einheitlichen Betrachtung psychotherapeutischer Intervention aus klientenzentrierter Perspektive.* Unpublished Habilitations thesis, Philosophische Fakultät III der Universität Würzburg.

Zielke, M., & Kopf-Mehnert, C. (1978). *Veränderungsfragebogen des Erlebens und Verhaltens* (Manual). Weinheim: Beltz.

TOWARD A SPECIFIC ILLNESS CONCEPT OF CLIENT-CENTERED THERAPY

Gert-Walter SPEIERER
Universität Regensburg, F.R.Germany

THE STATUS QUO AND PERSPECTIVES OF CLIENT-CENTERED THERAPY

In my opinion, person-oriented, necessarily differential, psychotherapeutic treatment of neuroses and psychosomatic disorders on the basis of a single theory is, if not an illusion, futuristic as a single theory of human behavior.

Therefore, for now and the near future, it seems that several competing concepts of illness and related therapies are useful for individually optimal psychotherapy. Amongst them, psychoanalytic, behavior, and - last but not least - client-centered therapy concepts are the best known on account of the number of scientific publications they have led to.

However, there are marked differences in the degree of recognition of these forms of therapy for the professional psychotherapeutic treatment of persons suffering from psychoreactive, neurotic and psychosomatic disorders. Client-centered therapy is disadvantaged especially in the Federal Republic of Germany. This is not due to CCT being less effective. Beyond an explanation in terms of the professional power of psychoanalytic and behavior therapy societies in this country, the situation is also the result of the poor compatibility of CCT with the scientific positions of the medical model of treatment that are still valid and the requirements of the public health system. For example, in a public health service system, diagnostic procedures are a necessary basis for a positive indication of CCT and as a basis of decision of refunding. Also diagnostic assessment is necessary and should include differential diagnosis leading to options such as non-indication, or indication of further diagnostic procedures or different therapeutic options.

The relative absence of such diagnostic procedures among client-centered therapists is due, in part, to the fact that a general accepted CCT-specific concept of illness has not yet been sufficiently elucidated. Such a concept must allow a similary specific indication of CCT, since indications can be set by psychoanalysis and behavior therapy, two competitors of CCT for the treatment of similar groups of patients. CCT research, published in English and German, only shows a few contributions to catalogue of phenomenologically, symptomatologically, and psychodynamically specific criteria for the indication of CCT (Speierer, 1979, 1980, 1982; Zielke, 1979, 1982; Biermann-Ratjen, 1979).

Therefore, first of all, a theory of illness specific to CCT is needed, which will lead to a specific indication of CCT. Secondly, comparative studies of CCT versus psychoanalytic and behavior--modification techniques are necessary, with clearly defined groups of patients using DSM-III or ICD-9.

My contribution aims at demonstrating that a CCT-specific concept of illness is possible. It is person-oriented and meets the clinical reality. It shows where and how Rogers' theoretical and metapsychological positions are still valid, and where they have to be abandoned or modified taking into account clinical reality and recent results of CCT-research, of developmental psychology, of clinical psychology, and of research on the genesis and forms of neuroses and psychosomatic disorders.

INCONGRUENCE AS THE CENTRAL CONSTRUCT OF THE CCT ILLNESS CONCEPT

The client-centered concept of illness is, like current psychiatric nosology of neuroses and psychosomatic disorders, phenomenologically oriented and focused on observable and communicable conscious phenomena.

In the CCT concept of illness, the phenomenon of incongruence and its equivalents are the focus of interest. Therefore, Rogers (1959) himself did not describe traditional diagnostic entities. Instead, Rogers showed the social conditions of the beginning, the onset, the compensatory manifestations, the course and the therapeutic amelioration of pathological incongruences and symptoms of incongruence in their dynamic interdependencies, and with the self-subject as the representative of personality.

Empirical research has demonstrated that in the first three to five sessions of CCT-treatments that are assessed as successful, there regularly are incongruences of which patients are conscious or at least nearly aware. A phenomenological presentation of these incongruences according to Rogers (1959) and Speierer (1986) follows later in this article. These incongruences are accompanied by subjective suffering and, mostly, by physical symptoms related to neurotic and psychosomatic disturbances.

The course of successful CCT also regularly shows that, if accompanied by the experiences of diminishing incongruence, feelings of illness and psychological as well as physical symptoms fade or lose their meaning as illness indicators (Speierer, 1986).

Incongruence in CCT is not only an intrapsychic phenomenon. Often, it is only in the CCT-dialogue that incongruence can come to awareness. In other words: incongruence can become apparent through CCT interaction, yet it is not thereby generated by this interaction. If this were the case, the clients' experiencing process would be blocked. The client would no longer feel understood by the therapist. There would be increased risk of failure or of premature termination of therapy.

THE DEFINITION OF INCONGRUENCE AND THE SELF

Incongruence is subjectively experienced as, at least dimly, conscious. Incongruence is generated by experiences which put the self or parts of it into question. Incongruence is experienced as unpleasant. It is stressful, hurtful and threatens of destruction of the self. The self(concept) encloses the concepts, values, memories, rules of conduct, i.e. the cognitions and attitudes which a person owns and which form his self-identity and his self-respect. This includes individual conceptions of the quality of life, life satisfaction, and life-plan.

The central thesis of the CCT-illness concept is: There are no neuroses nor psychosomatic disorders without incongruence. Yet it is not postulated that every incongruence is psychopathogenic. On the contrary, it is assumed that awareness of incongruence is much more frequently followed by coping free of neurotic and psychosomatic consequences, if one refers to a representative sample of the population. Additionnally it is postulated that only some of the psychopathogenic incongruences will be affected by psychotherapeutic treatment. Therefore, we introduce the concept of "not socially conditioned incongruence." The proposed CCT illness concept refers to those psychoreactive, neurotic and psychosomatic disorders which have their causes in socially conditioned and therefore psychotherapeutically treatable incongruence. This dismisses all claims of omnipotence (explaining and treating all disorders which may be caused by incongruence).

THE GENESIS OF INCONGRUENCE

Rogers (1959) postulated incongruence as being based on "conditions of worth" which are incompatible to the "organismic valuing process." Conditions of worth emerge from the needs of positive regard and self-regard. These needs are fulfilled to a large extent by the evaluations of significant others. If others value only parts of the behaviors of the person, the person will, in turn, positively regard only some parts of his behavior and of himself. The other parts of behavior and of the self are negatively valued by the other, contrary to the problem-person's own former valuing. The person takes the negative evaluations as conditions of worth and rejects parts of his or her own behavior. These become incongruent in the self. The problem-person's self-regard will be split or will decrease in a generalized way. If these negative experiences cannot be avoided, they will produce incongruence. Bringing incongruence into awareness is experienced as a threat to the self. Reactions to this threat are, on the one hand, psychological coping strategies, aimed at reducing dangerous incongruence or at terminating it. On the other hand, if such strategies are not successful, psychogenetic symptoms of illness will arise.

INCONGRUENCE AS DIFFERENT FROM CONCEPTS OF CONFLICT THEORY AND FROM PSYCHOANALYTIC CONCEPTS OF CONFLICT

Evaluation of a behavioral experience as positive for the valuing process of the organismic self and as negative for the conditions of worth of the socialized self can be conceptualized in a conflict theory framework as an appetence-aversion conflict. Therefore, some authors have defined incongruence as a mere intrapsychic conflict, and CCT as a therapy of internal conflict.

This definition of incongruence as an intrapsychic conflict within the self-concept which stems from incompatible innate organismic values and acquired socialized or introjected values used to evaluate behaviors (i.e. the actualization), is only one way to define the CCT concept of illness in the frame of an experimental or social psychological conflict model. The experience of a behavior actualizes an internal appetence-aversion-conflict. This conflict is elicited by a behavior and becomes conscious as an incongruence, for example in the form of the experience of an inner disruption. It has to be pointed out that the behavior itself is not conflictual per se.

Occasionally, psychoanalytic critics of CCT have, in my opinion, erroneously interpreted incongruence as an ambivalence conflict between the "Id" and the "Super-ego." They have therefore criticized CCT-theory as a kind of simplified copy of the psychoanalytic theory without Eigenvalue. But the organismic valuing process and the actualization tendency is not identical to Freud's "Id." CCT does not separate "Id," "Ego," and "Super-ego." The organismic self is more than the "Id." Within the organismic valuing process is, at least, a limited autonomous self, the organism's survival program. It can be free of conflict and still include incongruence in the form of experiences evaluated as disruptive. In support of this CCT-theory is the observation that psychosomatic disorders are successfully treated by reducing conscious incongruence. CCT treats disturbances which, in reference to analytic concepts are caused before the psychoanalytic structural model of personality becomes valid, i.e. before intrapsychic Id-Superego conflicts can emerge. The incongruence concept of CCT exceeds by far conflict theory incongruences (Rogers & Sandford, 1985). Incongruence includes, in addition to the concept of conflict, the incongruence between the organismic self - or the combination of the organismic self and the socialized self - on the one hand, and new individual, social, and non-social experiences on the other. There are experiences which do not stress the self by actualizing a conflict within the self, but which put into question the actual self-concept in a very direct way. The causes of this second sort of incongruence can be recognized in recent findings of developmental psychology (Peters,

1986). They have confirmed the client-centered position of a primal autonomy of the self and of its three basic conditions for normal growth. These causes of non-conflictual incongruence are early socialization deficits as well as later deficiencies in interpersonal relations concerning unconditional positive regard, congruence and empathy from significant others. They cause psychopathogenic deficits of self-empathy in the form of rigidity and lack of flexibility in thinking, experiencing and behaving. Furthermore, they are accompanied by reduced coping strategies for incongruence, poor and preferredly negative self-communications, inaccurate symbolizations, an intentional and generalizing structure of perception, emphasis on external values and diminished self-responsibility. They constitute low congruence, low ability of congruence or incongruence-intolerance. Such persons are, to a high degree, prone to experience incongruence after very different kinds of social and non-social stressors, not in a conflict-like way, but in many other ways which are a strain to the status quo of the person's weak self.

Compared to people with average incongruence-tolerance, they experience incongruence in so many situations of everyday life that it is not possible for them to reduce nor to compensate incongruence by avoidance behavior nor by any other psychological coping strategy. So beyond a conflict model, psychoreactive, neurotic and psychosomatic disorders can arise.

THE LATENCY OR COMPENSATORY STATE OF INCONGRUENCE

The main psychological coping strategies to compensate incongruence are: 1. Selectivity of perception. 2. Masking out experiences that are unacceptable for the self. Masking can be total or partial. In the last case, inaccurate symbolizations result. 3. Avoidance behavior. Complete masking or avoidance of incongruent experiences does not result in psychological suffering. The person experiences himself as normally healthy, but pays the price of diminished self-actualisation and/or so-called blind spots in his perception. This should be called the latency or compensatory state of incongruence.

Looking at the above-mentioned coping strategies of incongruence being out of the awareness of the person concerned, it becomes clear, in comparison with the psychoanalytic concepts of defense or resistance mechanisms, that, in the CCT view, defense is less a sign of neurotic illness requiring psychotherapy than a healthy compensation and coping process. Within the CCT framework, treatable illness symptoms are only accompanied by subjective suffering if incongruence as such becomes conscious. Therefore Rogers has not developed any techniques to work on unconscious defense and resistance. Regular use of the CCT offer, i.e. client-centered empathy used as explained below, and restricting the indication of CCT to volunteer patients with psychoreactive, neurotic, and psychosomatic disturbances uncomplicated by overlapping or underlying psychosis, has led me to believe that it is not necessary nor adequate to introduce the concept of resistance in the CCT model, neither as an explanatory construct nor as a treatment goal.

If one considered that empathically adressing the patient's frame of reference on the latent emotional components of his actual experience were equivalent to working through resistance, this would lead to introduce the psychoanalytic construct of the unconscious in CCT. In doing so, the therapist would be empowered with the expertise of exclusively knowing about the patient's unknown meanings and connotations. In my opinion, this is incompatible with the CCT model of the therapeutic relationship. Instead, I view resistance as an error of empathy on the therapist's side. The criterion of empathy in CCT should not be set by the therapist, but be defined by the client. If the client works through his incongruence in such a way that he experiences he is getting along better with himself, this means that the therapeutic behavior was empathic. This can be expressed methodologically: Empathy is indicated by a movement of the client's response to the right of Klein et al.'s (1969) experiencing scale, or Rogers' (1959) process scale. This movement is apparent during the therapeutic dialogue and is achieved with the help of the therapist, whatever behavior variables involved.

In other words, what is considered by a therapist as resistance to his empathy or as resistance of the client to his own empathy is in my sense, an artifact due to temporarily lack of empathy on the part of the therapist. I personally view psychoses as considerably more difficult to treat with psychotherapy (alone or in combination with antipsychotic drugs) than neuroses and psychosomatic disorders. However, I will concede to those working with psychotic and borderline patients that these patients' "resistances" may be conceptualized differently from what I just pointed out and may be handled differently in the sense of a disturbance-specific modification of CCT-treatment. I shall mention here the early results of Rogers et al. (1967), Truax (1970) and recent results of Teusch (1986).

THE SYMPTOMS OF NON-COMPENSATED PSYCHOPATHOGENIC INCONGRUENCE

Within the CCT concept, treatable illness-symptoms are accompanied by subjective suffering only when incongruence is at least dimly conscious. The main symptoms of non-compensated psychopathogenic incongruence are: 1. Feelings of psychophysical stress, vulnerability and hurt. 2. Feelings of inferiority, dejection, discouragement, hopelessness and depression. 3. Anxiety, phobic and compulsive behaviors to avoid vaguely felt and non concrete dangers. 4. Abrupt realizations of self-incongruent behaviors, which are experienced as not belonging to oneself. Sense of unity of personality may be falling apart. At times, incongruent experiences become autonomous; at other times, behavior oscillates between self-congruent and self-incongruent parts. This causes anxiety, strain, disturbance, and corresponding physical symptoms. Patients often refer to this state as "no longer being the master in their own house," "no longer being in control." Empirical reevaluation of this phenomenology of incongruence, already described in detail by Rogers (1959), was undertaken by content analysis of transcripts from the first three sessions of 4 ICD-diagnosed CCT-patients, selected as examples (Speierer, 1986). The following range of symptoms and ways of experiencing illness was found: 1. Poor control of self and behavior, and overwhelming as well as excessive reactions. 2. Subjective illness-concept with self-related pathogenic hypotheses, in contrast to external hypotheses of causation. 3. Conscious incongruence between experience and self-concept. 4. Negative self-evaluation, poor self-confidence, and self-pity. 5. Experience of insufficiency, achievement-failure, and stress-intolerance. 6. Generalized negative self- and symptom-experiences. 7. Experienced or feared misunderstanding of critique of significant others and of the majority of strangers. 8. Restriction of behaviors, experiences, and perceptions. 9. Unattainable ideals of being (perfect). 10. Strain through alien or unorganismic conditions of worth.

FIVE RISK FACTORS OF PSYCHOLOGICAL ILLNESS

1. Non-socially caused capacity for congruence and incongruence

A non-socially caused inability to reach congruence between self-concept and experience must be built into the CCT illness concept beyond Rogers' position.

Such a concept can explain the presence of disturbances which are not treatable by psychotherapy, neither by therapy in general nor specifically by CCT. Though these disturbances may be seen as psychogenic, my position takes into account results of epidemiologic, genetic, and constitutional studies of neuroses and of psychosomatic disorders (Schepank, 1986). Non-socially caused inability to be congruent can explain that congruence between individual experiences within the organismic evaluation by significant others is not possible. Therefore, social mediation of congruence fails, even in optimal conditions for development. It takes into account the fact that, sometimes compensatory abilities are lacking and cannot be effectively offered. If this factor dominates, neurotic and psychosomatic disorders have to be taken as fateful. They are not treatable by psychotherapy. In traditional terminology, they are labeled as character-disorders. If this factor is strong within malignant forms of hypochondria, compulsive disorders, and anorexia nervosa, it explains why even optimal therapeutic endeavors are insufficient.

This factor also has to be taken into account in somatopsychic disturbances following organic diseases. Psychotherapeutic response is also limited by the treatability of the organic disorder.

2. Incongruence between societal and organismic values

This explains the occurrence, the incidence, and the phenomenology of neuroses and psychosomatic disturbances of the members of certain subpopulations, for example ecclesiogenic neuroses. It can be reduced by following psychohygienic and psychoprophylactic measures: Tolerance for organismic values, socialization of values in accordance with organismic ones, education respectful of vital human needs, training in coping strategies to compensate incongruence.

3. Psychopathogenic relationships between children and their significant others as well as relationships between all persons in relations of dependency

From an ontogenetical point of view, early relationships which do not respect the basic needs of the human organism (Rogers, 1959), constitute a risk of pathological development. Recent findings of developmental psychology (Peters, 1986) and on the psychophysiology of psychosomatic patients (Lynch, 1987) support the idea that an early relationship between children and patients which meets the criteria of CCT is a pre-requisite for healthy personality development. Clinical evidence stemming from children's psychological and psychosomatic reactions shows that children's disturbances can arise when disturbed relationships between reference persons and child are actualized and can either fade away when the relationship improves or take a chronic course if the disturbed relation persists.

4. Poor ability to compensate and poor possibilities of compensation of incongruence

This can explain, in relation to the three risk factors mentioned above, the chronification of early neurotic and psychosomatic symptoms and an eventually malignant generalization and course. This may develop if psychohygienic or psychologically helpful extra-therapeutical offers of communication and communicative relationships are lacking, and if psychotherapeutic aids are not considered or rejected. Existing possibilities of compensation can lead to an apparently spontaneous and durable remission of neurotic and psychosomatic symptoms despite pathogenetic interpersonal relations (according to CCT). This risk factor explains how pathogenic incongruence can be compensated without subjective suffering nor feelings of illness, in spite of the presence of the characteristic compensation-symptoms mentioned above. These states of compensated or latent neuroses should not be subjected to psychotherapy. Psychotherapy only has a chance when subjective suffering shows the break-down of coping strategies for compensating incongruence.

The main compensation symptoms are: Selective perception, distortion of certain experiences, denying of experiences, rigidity of thinking, feeling, and acting, memory defects, blind spots, overgeneralization, avoidance of certain experiences. Incongruence and compensation symptoms are more often observed in different areas of actualization, than within the same area. If they are experienced as separate from the self, alien, and autonomous - in short incongruent - then they become conscious. They can cause so much suffering, that, in extremis, psychotic or psychosis-like episodes can occur. More often, awareness of these symptoms causes such an intolerable feeling of "disease" that the patient seeks a therapist.

5. Life-change events

These explain the often abrupt psychological and/or physical breakdown and the onset of illness of seemingly healthy and compensated persons. Live-change events often seem to occur before the onset of psychosomatic illness (v. Uexküll et al., 1986).

As to choice of organ, psychosomatic diseases, i.e. incongruence accompanied by bodily symptoms, CCT accepts the present valid scientific knowledge. For example, the individual specifity of reactions and the non-specificity of stimuli is acknowledged within the frame of stress-reactions. Also, the phases-model of stress-sequela is used as a bridge-concept for the pathogenic effects of incongruence as a psychological stressor. This is justified by the empirically demonstrated effectiveness of CCT for different psychosomatic disorders which are accompanied by conscious experiencing of incongruence.

According to recent hypotheses about disturbance specificity or symptom specificity in relation to psychosocial experiences, one cannot expect psychotherapy to bring attributions of meaning, nor progress in certain specific symptoms or syndroms. Recent results instead seem to support innate and socialized identification- and imitation processes. It is hardly possible to differentiate innate and social sources of illness-behavior or to know if there may be a common disposition. Twin-studies of neuroses show that the symptomatology is apparently more genetically determined than was thought (Schepank, 1986). I tried to account for these results by the first risk factor in this illness-concept of CCT. Accepting the idea of non-socially caused and unchangeable incongruence allows to give up inadequate psychotherapeutic strivings for omnipotence. Rogers in his metapsychology of CCT, has not considered this aspect. The limits of Rogers' views of self-alienation as the ultimate cause of neuroses, with self-actualization always tending towards health, and with the three variables being the sufficient condition of every psychotherapy, have to be considered and modified.

DIFFERENTIATION OF NEUROSES, CHARACTER NEUROSES, AND PSYCHOSES

The border between neuroses and the so-called character-neuroses is marked in the latter group, by the lack of conscious incongruence, suffering caused by the symptoms, and by the lack of typically psychotic disturbances of thoughts, feelings, and behaviors in the latter group. The border between neuroses and psychoses is in neurotic patients usually marked by the awareness of incongruence, the insight into the existence of a disturbance, the ability to take a distant position, and the lack of the characteristic disturbances of formal thinking, feeling, and behavior, though in some cases these differences may not be very clear.

SPECIAL FEATURES OF TRADITIONALLY DIAGNOSED DISTURBANCES (ICD-9) FROM THE VIEWPOINT OF CLIENT-CENTERED THERAPY

Empirical and clinical studies on the indication of CCT (Speierer, 1979, 1980, 1982) and its efficiency (for an overview, see Finke & Teusch, 1986; Bommert, 1986) now cover the entire field of disturbances amenable to psychotherapy. They include in- and out-patient forms of application, single therapy, therapy of pairs (Auckenthaler, 1983), and group therapy (Mente & Spittler, 1980; Eckert & Biermann-Ratjen, 1985).

The disorder-specific dynamics of incongruence in accordance with this CCT-illness concept have not yet been worked out in such a comprehensive manner. In this section, therefore, it will be shown, with an example, that some of the traditionally labeled neurotic and psychosomatic disturbances can already be described at least partly in the CCT-terminology, because of significant incongruences that go beyond the individual case.

As the traditionally labeled disturbances need not be exhaustively determined by the incongruence concept in every single case of CCT-practice, three consequences have to be considered.1. There has to be a test-phase of therapy to correctly diagnose the impact of conscious incongruence on the pathology of every single patient. 2. There has to be a diagnosis and differentiation of the different origins of incongruence and the assessment of the risk factors. 3. The CCT basic and additional variables for optimal therapy have to be used, centered on the individual. Criteria of diagnostic and therapeutic action are, as has been pointed out, the client's self-exploration, self-empathy, and its movement on the process-scale.

1. Hysterical neuroses

The most striking incongruence of hysterical patients from a phenomenological point of view is that they want to appear as more than they really are. Grandioze fantasies in the self-image, especially in the ideal self, are incompatible with experienced importance and inferiority in the range of personal, intrapersonal, sexual, and vocational abilities. The patients complain, though there is no apparent deficit. They often appear indifferent, mainly towards bodily symptoms. Nowadays, symptoms rarely are the formerly well-known psycho-motor and fainting fits, but more often consist of headaches, vomiting, nausea, and, less frequently, loss of sensitivity, numbness, paralysis, blindness, deafness, aphonia, artifacts and signs of simulation.

The indifference of hysterical patients concerning their symptoms contrasts with the attitude of hypochondriac patients. The latter's main incongruence is between the magnitude of their concern and the objective insignificance of their symptoms. The incongruence of "belle indifférence" has to be distinguished from the incongruence between the subjective experience and the physical symptoms of psychosomatic patients, for example of high-blood-pressure patients. As investigations by Lynch (1987) show, high-blood-pressure patients are not able to subjectively perceive even abrupt rises of heart rate and blood-pressure. With feedback, however, they are not only capable of experiencing adequately, i.e. congruently, the strain, but of accurately symbolizing it. CCT ameliorates or terminates hysterical symptoms, if the dialogue is successful (a) in reducing unrealistic and unattainable self-concepts and ideals of being; (b) in letting the patients experience that if they do not dramatize their suffering they are still positively regarded by the therapist and also by others; (c) CCT helps hysterical patients, if they come to reduce their feelings of inadequacy, weakness and inferiority, to differentiate them, and reduce their generalizing effect.

Here is a casuistic example: One of these patients, 57 years of age, carpenter, psychogenic fits of fainting which begun 8 months before therapy. Additional symptoms: Sleep disturbances, self-distrust, discontentment with his life-situation. CCT individual treatment of 16 one-hour sessions once a week. In the beginning of therapy, the patient showed the following psychodynamic pattern: He experienced poor control of self and of behaviors, overwhelming and exaggerated reactions mainly in situations in which he felt put down by others. Additionally, he showed feelings of inadequacy, poor competence in various areas and intolerance to stress. Besides, he felt misunderstood by his wife and boss. He feared being misunderstood and criticized by the majority of others. These experiences formed a constellation of intolerable incongruence with his self-concept of being a strong man. At the end of therapy, the patient experienced trust in himself, autonomy, confidence, and self-realization. He could accept himself better, show contentment and imperturbability. He extended his behavior and his experiencing, and made new experiences. He felt more power, and became able to stand stress. He had gained greater acceptance of his own faults. He developed a more positive image of his relationships to others and of others to himself.

The patient expressed it with the following sentences:

In the beginning of therapy: "For the sake of peace, I give in." This sentence shows his self-concept. "Quarreling puts an enormous strain on me afterwards, I am very irritated, because I get out of control, and I do not find the right words." This sentence expresses the felt incongruence between his self-concept (to give in for the sake of peace) and his experience of engaging in quarreling. Also the phrase expresses the self-devaluation, the turmoil and the feeling of loss of control. The patient also experiences his fainting fits as confusing and no longer understands himself. "I cannot understand that one breaks down all of a sudden."

The same patient at the end of therapy: "And I always looked for causes everywhere else, but not in me... I feel very much better ... I can enjoy my work, it runs even better ... Yes, above all courage and self-confidence, and I can sleep at night, this is a big thing ... And I am now able to tell someone else, what he should do better ... Yes, and everyday problems no longer worry me much. I look at things as if I were somebody else, and I can tolerate them. If I cannot do it now, I can do it after a while. Before therapy, the smallest thing drove me mad... And above all, what makes me happy is that I must not take as many pills any longer."

The work with several handicapped hysterical patients is impeded, especially in the beginning of therapy, by unrealistic expectations about the therapist's power, hopes in and prizing of the therapist which can switch after some sessions to disappointment and criticism. Because of this, many therapists are not able to build up and maintain positive regard, congruence and empathy. Another obstacle to the therapeutic process may be the patient's attitude of dependency and his demands of support from the therapist. If this attitude does not change significantly during therapy, the therapist feels less and less of a facilitator of the patient's developing autonomy, but more and more of a supplying agent, who is being exploited. So it can be understood that hysterical patients who have been successfully treated by CCT contribute only 9% to a sample of 155 successful CCT therapies (Speierer, 1979).

2. Neurotic depression

In psychogenously depressed patients the main phenomenological incongruence is that their symptoms of "feeling depressed and oppressed, listlessness, vertigo, unhappiness, imbalance, their wish to cry, sadness and melancholy, and bursts of weeping are most often not associated with specific situations and behaviors" (Zielke, 1979, p. 108). The patients experience and suffer from the paradox that their psychological and physical irritation does not originate from a causal factor, although they make some vaguely conscious personal attribution of causes. The second source of the depressed patient's incongruence are his requirements for perfection, dictated by his conscience and which go unquestioned. In the light of these perfectionistic requirements, their own behavior seems to them as worth nothing, in spite of exhausting efforts. They feel worthless, they lack imperturbability. The future has no (positive) prospect. Small negligences or criticisms from others can lead to long-lasting ruminations and can be accompanied by raving against the self. Fantasies of self-destruction lead to risk of suicide and to suicidal attempts. Fantasies of exterminating a potential agressor occur much more often than the acting out of violent impulses against others. Outbursts of verbal aggression occur frequently and "vandalism" occasionally. This is experienced as loss of control and overwhelming reactions. Such experiences are accompanied by feelings of guilt. So aggressiveness is the third source of incongruence. Unfullfilled wishes of being understood, valued, and passive expectations of support are a fourth source of incongruence in these patients.

According to the above-mentioned results of Speierer (1979) neurotic depressive patients are the largest group of successfully treated CCT-clients. They represent 41% of Speierer's sample. In Zielke (1979), they also have the best prognosis with CCT.

Therapeutic success for these patients already shows, under certain conditions, after a few sessions. Using the three basic variables of CCT and additionally the variable "Forming (cognitive) constructs and strategies" CCT can be recommended for crisis intervention within a frame of 5 sessions (Speierer, 1986b).

Content analysis of therapy transcripts shows that patients' improvement of mood is accompanied by new insights. They often occur in the form of gestalt-like "Aha" experiences within or after therapy sessions. They consist in a change of cognitions. Examples of this are: 1. Insight that symptoms and problems are self-generated, in a context of new experiences in which symptoms and problems are ameliorated and overcome by autonomous activities; 2. More differentiated and enlarged experiencing in the context of stronger motivation for more practizing of new experiences; 3. Adaption and respect of organismic values which suit the patient's own wishes and abilities (Speierer, 1986). Here is an example of a patient of this group: Male patient, 52 years old, civil service employee, suspicion of a psychotic episode when he was 18, later on several phases of depressive reactions, which were exclusively treated by antidepressant drugs. During a year before CCT, again depressed, unsuccessfully treated by tranquillizers and antidepressants. About 8 weeks before CCT, additional anxiety of a non-phobic type, feelings of pressure in the chest, and difficulty in concentrating. His CCT-treatment was set up as a crisis intervention. It consisted of two sessions of 30 minutes each, the second one 10 weeks after the first. The patient was referred to CCT by his psychiatrist as well as by the consultant cardiologist. He expresses the above-described psychodynamics as follows: "Right now,

I do not realize a connection (between the depression) and personally meaningful events ... I do not assume that ... the causes which then led to the depression, that these causes still play a role ... With regard to my work in the civil service I have no problems ... After the first treatment ... for years I have worked on myself. Let us say (I have) completely repressed this time; strange, this came to my mind only after many years ... Now I feel terrible, I feel physically exhausted, I have had ever so many physical examinations, blood-tests, there was nothing ... I get up in the morning and I am groggy, smashed, not only physically, but also psychologically ... I feel a very limited capacity of performance, my ability to concentrate is miserable..."

The same patient during the second session: "I can tell, I am pleased... I put ... too much demands on me. I wanted to do everything in a 100% or 150% way. It is a sort of habit of being perfect ... I work against this habit and since then, I feel better ... I feel too, that the fear of failing is a cause ... I realize that sometimes I am still struggling, but then I am able to stop it by consciously thinking it over. Then I can control it ... Last time, I told you, I often stand in front of a wall, a mountain when I ... then you said, why not simply walk around. I thought about it too, why not. But I feel, before, I could not do it, because of my wanting to be 100% ... Now I think, if there is a wall, let it be and I wave my hand at it. I mean, after having talked with you, I thought you have often read about these things, but I did not become aware of them, it became clear to me only when we talked... Now I feel much more active... I do things again, I started some sport jogging and riding the bicycle ... And I would like to tell something, which recently happened to me during holidays when I struggled. We were in a restaurant and I noticed the bill wasn't okay, but I was not 100% sure. So I did not ask the correct price. Instead I payed. Later it became clear that the waitress had cheated me, since I had studied the list once again. The difference was only 2 Deutschmarks, but somehow I was very upset. I argued against myself: 'You should have asked,' and so on and then it started again. It was a continuous spinning of thoughts for hours. I could not stop it. The next day, it was the same. Only when it came to my mind, 'stop, you are again going in that old direction, again this urge to be perfect, you feel you were not perfect enough.'.. When this became conscious, the spinning of thoughts went away ... I feel like I am somebody else since, I do not feel so trapped anymore, so stuck ... I still take medicine, but at a reduced dose of 50%. I will start gradually reducing it..."

3. Psychosomatic disorders

In spite of the different physical aspects of psychosomatic patients in relation to the CCT-model of illness, a common psychodynamic pattern can be postulated.

Recent empirical and experimental, as well as clinical, psychophysiological and psychotherapeutic research converge to confirm this thesis in many ways.

For example, the psychophysiologist Lynch names the following components of the psychogenesis of psychosomatic disorders: 1. A genetic constitution to react to stress with certain organ-systems; 2. The inability to realize how these body-systems react to psychological stress; 3. The therefore resulting inability to connect their changes with different states of feeling; and 4. The most important fact that these reactions are not noticed and understood by significant others, so that serious emotional misunderstanding can result (Lynch, 1987, p. 304, retranslated from German).

In psychosomatic patients, most prominent incongruence from a phenomenological point of view is the seemingly functional autonomy of their physical symptoms, i.e. their impression independence of that signs of illness are virtually independent of what they experience. Their inability to feel how their own body reacts to individual, social and material experiences - in client-centered terminology, the lack of organismic evaluation- blocks the formation of an autonomous organismic self-concept and, instead, leads to a self-substitute, which is extremely dependent on the self of other persons and their values, i.e. dependent on internalized conditions of worth.

Consequently, psychosomatic patients have a narrow, negative and/ or distorted self-image. The narrowing is often rigidly restricted to a single area of experience. Its relation to the patient's main symptom(s) is often easily noticed; for example the relation to body, figure, and weight in anorexia nervosa patients (Grimm, 1987). However, the relation of self-image distortion and body systems, may not be apparent in the first instance, with essential hypertonia patients or different forms of headaches.

Parallel to the negative self-image are problems of self-worth, self-confidence, feelings of inferiority, failing, and inadequacy as well as cognitions of being uninteresting to others, not lovable, and feeling helpless in social and intimate relationships. Patients' disordered self-concepts can extend to questioning and doubting who they are. Because of the lack of self-confidence - in other words an unconscious or only vaguely conscious organismic self and its orientation in organismic values - patients try to live up to the expression of their relatives, reference groups, and society. They introject conditions of worth and build pseudo-self-concepts. Their only source of self-respect is an extremely conformistic, otherdirected behavior which eventually takes the form of ritualized schemas. These persons try to gain or maintain their own worth by conformity, intellectual achievement, caring for others, and by their symptoms.

Patients are afraid to trust their impulses and feelings. They are even more afraid of acting them out. They often cannot communicate their needs to others. Sometimes, they cannot even express them to themselves. Because of imagined disappointments, they refrain from social contacts as well as from other corrective experiences. They give more weight to the possible and fantasized negative consequences of new experiences, especially interpersonal ones, than to the positive changes that would lead to fulfillment of their wish to be unconditionally loved for their own sake, to be understood, and to gain allowance.

Besides these emotional needs, there often are equally important meta-needs (Maslow, 1980), for example the wish to find a meaning to life.

Striving for autonomy and self-assertion often seems to be for patients a wish for autonomous functioning of the psychological personality from the physiological body, i.e. a separation of the self from the body. The body has to function. In this context there is a more or less marked inability to register physical, sensory signals and feelings, and an inability to use the body consciously as an instrument of self-representation, self-expression, self-development, and inter-personal communication.

In contrast to this desire for control or freedom from the own body, psychosomatic patients often suffer, in the beginning of treatment, from a lack or break-up of a close and positively valued interpersonal relationship, in which the partner has served as a substitute for the self. Patients are often depressed or even in despair because they experience the lost partnership as vital to them. Only through therapy do they eventually recognize the dangers for their own self-development of such a symbiotic conception of relationships. They may later approach the concept of the fully functioning person: "More open and free relationships on the basis of direct experiencing and with realistic perception" (Rogers, 1959).

I have observed the first stage of this symbiotic ideal of relationships not only in psychosomatic patients, but also in persons with alcohol- and drug problems. As long as the patients transfer this relational concept onto the therapeutic relationship, progress by means of an exclusively CCT-offer of the three basic variables is limited and often impossible. In that case, additional therapeutic variables like self-disclosure of the therapist, the building of constructs and strategies, focusing, and other means of activating the patients' actualizations in areas other than the experiencing seem indicated. To the extent that CCT aims at helping patients to sense the relations between their experiences and their body reactions, to differentiate and accurately symbolize them as well as to restore or build a new and organismic evaluation and, consecutively, an organismic self-concept, patients can integrate a more autonomous concept of relationships into their self-concept and reduce or give up their former symbiotic ideal of personal relations. The CCT-offer has proved to help psychosomatic patients very effectively. They form the third largest group of successful patients in the above-mentioned patient sample (21%) (Speierer, 1979).

From case-studies and empirical research, the same author (Speierer, 1986a) has shown that psychosomatic patients treated successfully by CCT, experience, in the beginning of therapy, incongruence together with external hypotheses of causation and poor control of self and behaviors, with overwhelming and excessive reactions. At the end of therapy, patients show insight into how they themselves produce symptoms and problems, they show reduction or allienation of symptoms, an expanded range of behaviors, new experiences, as well as self-confidence, autonomy, optimism for the future, self-realization, self-acceptance, contentment, and imperturbability. Furthermore coping strategies such as differentiation, limiting, and relativation were apparent and showed movement in the direction of the fully functioning person.

Here is again an example of a patient showing significant parts of this psychodynamic structure in the beginning, and her psychological development towards the concept of the fully functioning person at the end of CCT: This is a 17-year-old female patient, highschool student. Symptomatology has included, for more than a year, artificially induced vomiting, fear of failing, problems with her father, insecurity, fear of other people, and fear of close friendships. She received individual CCT of 11 sessions of 50 minutes, once a week. In the beginning of therapy she said: "I am very ambitious ... I know, I can make it." (These sentences show her self-concept.) "...When I do very normal things, the anxiety and the insecurity arise, so that I think I fail. Then I let the others do it." (This shows the patient's experience.) "This hits me terribly." (This demonstrates the incongruence of experiences and self-concept.) "And then the feeling, you are not capable of doing anything." (This shows her generalized self-devaluation.) "It is really sometimes completely undetermined. Formerly I had the power to control myself, but now ..." (the sentence shows the low self-empathy in the form of no longer understanding herself and no more being in control.)

The same patient at the end of treatment: "Always the fear of being disappointed, it does not do any good. I always had the attitude to put them aside, the difficulties ... To a large extent it is my own fault, the whole anxiety, I believe, I often talked myself into it ... Well, however, I can stand it ... Even if I am disappointed sometimes, I will no longer resign to such an extent. This is my insight... I even got headaches, because I keyed myself up. And so I always took pills, I no longer do it that much. I do what I feel is right. I always asked whether I was right or wrong. I did what people said. But I will not do so any more. I still listen to them, but in the end I do what I believe is right. So I feel more secure. I can say that I no longer feel so anxious and I can talk more quietly ... I can work more again, and my grades are getting better again. This contributes to my feeling more secure."

REFERENCES

Auckenthaler, A. (1983). *Klientenzentrierte Psychotherapie mit Paaren.* Stuttgart: Kohlhammer.

Biermann-Ratjen, E.-M., Eckert, J., & Schwartz, H.-J. (1979). *Gesprächspsychotherapie.* Stuttgart: Kohlhammer.

Bommert, H. (1986). Gesprächspsychotherapie, psychiatrische Aspekte. In K.P. Kisker et al. (Eds.), *Psychiatrie der Gegenwart. Vol. 1: Neurosen, Psychosomatische Erkrankungen, Psychotherapie* (pp. 307-329). Berlin: Springer.

358

Eckert, J., & Biermann-Ratjen, E.-M. (1985). *Stationäre Gruppenpsychotherapie.* Berlin: Springer.

Finke, J., & Teusch, L. (Eds.). (1986). Klientenzentrierte Psychotherapie in der Psychiatrie. *Zeitschrift für Personenzentrierte Psychologie und Psychotherapie, 4,* 361-366.

Grimm, K.H. (1987). *Klientenzentrierte, stationäre Psychotherapie bei Anorexia und Bulimia nervosa.* Paper presented at the "Kongress Gestörtes Essverhalten," Göttingen.

Klein, M.H., Mathieu, Ph.L., Gendlin, E.T., & Kiesler, D.J. (1969). *The experiencing scale. A research and training manual (Vols. 1 & 2).* Madison: Wisconsin Psychiatric Institute.

Lynch, J.J. (1987). *Die Sprache des Herzens. Wie unser Körper im Gespräch reagiert.* Paderborn: Junfermann.

Maslow, A. (1980). Eine Theorie der Metamotivation. In F. Capra, St. Grof, A. Maslow, Ch. Tart, K. Wilber et al. (Eds.), *Psychologie in der Wende* (pp. 143-152). Bern: Scherz.

Mente, A., & Spittler, H.-D. (1980). *Erlebnisorientierte Gruppenpsychotherapie.* Paderborn: Junfermann.

Peters, M. (1986). Frühe Mutter-Kind-Interaktion und klientenzentrierter Ansatz. *Zeitschrift für Personenzentrierte Psychologie und Psychotherapie, 2,* 233-242.

Rogers, C.R. (1959). A theory of therapy, personality, and interpersonal relationships, as developed in the client-centered framework. In S. Koch (Ed.), *Psychology, a study of a science* (Vol. 3, pp. 185-252). New York: McGraw-Hill.

Rogers, C.R., Gendlin, E.T., Kiesler, D.J., & Truax, C.B. (1967). *The therapeutic relationship and its impact: A study of psychotherapy with schizophrenics.* Madison: University of Wisconsin Press.

Rogers, C.R., & Sandford, R. (1985). Client-centered psychotherapy. In H.J. Kaplan & B. Sadock (Eds.), *Comprehensive textbook of psychiatry* (Vol. 2, pp. 1374-1388). Baltimore: Williams & Wilkins.

Schepank, H. (1974). Erb- und Umweltfaktoren bei Neurosen. Tiefenpsychologische Untersuchungen an 50 Zwillingspaaren. In *Monographien aus dem Gesamtgebiet der Psychiatrie* (Vol. 11). Berlin: Springer.

Speierer, G.-W. (1979). Ergebnisse der ambulanten Gesprächspsychotherapie. *Fortschritte der Medizin, 35,* 1527-1533.

Speierer, G.-W. (1980). Diagnose und Indikation in der Gesprächspsychotherapie. In J.C. Brengelmann (Ed.) *Entwicklung der Verhaltenstherapie in der Praxis* (pp. 408-433). IFT-Texte 3. München: Röttger.

Speierer, G.-W. (1982). Diagnostik in der klientenzentrierten Gruppenpsychotherapie. In M. Zielke (Ed.), *Diagnostik in der Psychotherapie* (pp. 78-106). Stuttgart: Kohlhammer.

Speierer, G.-W. (1986a). Selbstentfaltung in der Gesprächspsychotherapie. *Zeitschrift für Personenzentrierte Psychologie und Psychotherapie, 2,* 165-181.

Speierer, G.-W. (1986b). Selbstentfaltung entsprechend der Theorie der Gesprächspsychotherapie unter den Bedingungen ambulanter psychiatrisch-psychotherapeutischer Krisenintervention. *Zeitschrift für Personenzentrierte Psychologie und Psychotherapie, 4,* 435-445.

Teusch, L. (1986). Gesprächspsychotherapie schizophrener Patienten. *Zeitschrift für Personenzentrierte Psychologie und Psychotherapie, 4,* 391-398.

Truax, C.B. (1970). Effects of client-centered psychotherapy with schizophrenic patients: Nine years pretherapy and nine years posttherapy hospitalization. *Journal of Consulting and Clinical Psychology, 3,* 417-422.

Uexküll, T.von., Adler, R., Herrmann, J.M., Köhle, K., Schonecke, O.W., & Wesiack, W. (Eds.). (1986). *Psychosomatische Medizin.* Stuttgart: Kohlhammer.

Zielke, M. (1979). *Indikation zur Gesprächspsychotherapie.* Stuttgart: Kohlhammer.

Zielke, M. (1982). Diagnostik in der klientenzentrierten Psychotherapie (Einzeltherapie). In M. Zielke (Ed.), *Diagnostik in der Psychotherapie* (pp. 106-127). Stuttgart: Kohlhammer.

COGNITIVE PROCESSES AS A CAUSE OF PSYCHOTHERAPEUTIC CHANGE: SELF-INITIATED PROCESSES

Fred ZIMRING

Case Western Reserve University, Cleveland, U.S.A.

This chapter had two roots. The first was the inadequacy of explanations for client-centered therapy, the other was some research findings about the effect of examining our feelings. The questions about the explanations arose when I began doing client-centered therapy. The usual assumptions about why people changed as a result of psychotherapy did not apply to client-centered psychotherapy. The research about the effect of examining feelings gave rise to an explanation which can be substituted for the usual, inadequate assumptions for change after client-centered psychotherapy.

Most verbal psychotherapies rest on the assumption that change takes place as the result of uncovering or discovery of some hidden, underlying feelings or meanings which are causing the person's problems. The client-centered therapist works in a unique manner, one that does not fit with the usual assumption. Rogers (1957) described how the client-centered therapist should function when he described the necessary and sufficient conditions for therapeutic change. He said that it is sufficient for therapeutic change if a congruent therapist with unconditional positive regard empathically understands the internal frame of reference of the anxious client. It is not necessary for the therapist to understand underlying feelings or meanings. Indeed, for the therapist to understand these feelings and meanings would be an error, if these are not in the client's frame of reference at the moment.

Rogers' methods have been demonstrated to bring change (Rogers & Dymond, 1954). If change occurs without the client-centered therapist having to aid the client's uncovering of the hidden cause of their problems, the question becomes one of explaining the cause of this change.

The explanation for the change caused by client-centered therapy, discussed in this paper, grew from research, the other root of this paper.

Some years ago it seemed to me that clients thought more clearly after successful client-centered psychotherapy. This observation led to a number of studies (Zimring, 1983, 1985, 1988) which described the effect of examining our feelings on cognitive processes. In these studies, changes in cognitive performance after people examined their feelings were assessed. These studies revealed the processes involved in the examination of feelings which were causing change in cognitive performance. It is possible that these causal processes are responsible for some of the changes which occur as a result of client-centered therapy. To consider this possibility, it will be necessary to describe the research findings and the nature of the causal processes that they revealed. After these causal processes - which are part of our examining our feelings - are described, the argument will be made that these are some of the processes responsible for the effect of client-centered therapy.

THE COGNITIVE EFFECTS OF THE FOCUSING INSTRUCTION

In order to have an experimental procedure for examining our feelings, part of a procedure originated by Eugene Gendlin was used. In 1978, Gendlin published a set of instructions for focusing which asks the listener to turn inward and consider feelings in a series of stages or "movements." In the research described below, the instructions for the first movement is used. In that movement subjects are asked to relax and "see how you are now." They are asked to "pay attention to that part where you usually feel feelings like sad or glad or scared." They are instructed to stand back from and not to get involved in these feelings. They are to examine these feelings and describe whatever other feelings are present.

A series of studies was done to find what cognitive processes are affected by these focusing instructions. If a particular cognitive process was thought likely to be one affected, a task which involved that process was chosen. The effect of focusing on performance on that task was measured and compared to performance without focusing. For example, in several studies the performance of a cognitive task after the focusing instructions and after naming the color of dots was compared.

As to what cognitive processes might be affected by these focusing instructions, attentional processes were the most obvious candidates. It seemed reasonable to assume that the focusing instruction orients the person to internally, self produced stimuli such as feelings and sensations. If people are more oriented to internal stimuli, they should be better able to ignore irrelevant external stimuli. The Stroop test is one in which subjects are presented with a sheet of one hundred words composed of the names of colors printed in ink of colors other then the colors named. The task of the subject is to name, as fast as possible, the color of the ink in which the name of the color is printed. Thus, the word "red" is printed in green ink and the subject's task is to say "green." If the feeling-focus caused by the focusing instruction enables us to avoid irrelevant stimuli, than it should enable us to ignore the color named by the word and name the color of the ink more rapidly. Such proved to be the case. Subjects named the color of the ink more rapidly after the first focusing movement.

To find whether focusing on feelings affects complex performance, its affect on mental addition was tested. When, after the focusing instruction people were given a fairly simple and automatic task to do, adding 222 and 444 mentally, for example, their performance was no better. When however, people were asked to do more complex mental addition, adding 746 and 385, for example, their performance was better after the focusing instruction. This instruction aids complex performance, but does not help automatic performance.

Focusing on feelings may also increase the orientation of the person to self-produced information. If so, then feeling-focus should have more effect on cognitive tasks which involve self-produced information and less effect on tasks in which externally supplied information predominates. This prediction was tested in several experiments. In one experiment, the effect of feeling-focus on remembering a digit span in the order given by the experimenter was measured. Here, the digit-span task of the Wechsler-Bellevue was used. At the start, three digits were read at the rate of one per second and the person was asked to recall them in the order given. A second trial of three digits was given, and again the person tried to remember them in the order given. Four digits were then read and the procedure was continued until both trials of a series of digits were missed. The score was the longest series remembered. In the other part of this experiment, subjects were asked to remember spans of digits in the reverse order.

If the focusing instruction has a greater effect on self-generated information, then, after focusing, when the person has to reverse the order of the digits and so generate the span of digits that is to be remembered, more digits should be remembered than when what is to be remembered is supplied by the experimenter. This proved to be the case. When people had to remember digits in reverse order, they remembered significantly more after the focusing instructions. When they had to remember the digits in the given order, people did not remember more after the focusing instructions.

There were similar findings in another experiment. People were read eight digits and asked to form the last six into three pairs. They were to decide whether each pair was even or odd and above or below fifty. Thus, if the sequence was "1 3 9 7 4 6 3 8" the last three pairs are "97", "46", "38", the last two pairs are even and below fifty and the first pair is odd and above fifty. After the focusing instructions for the first movement, people were significantly more likely to remember their classifications of the pairs of digits. These focusing instructions did not increase their memory for the digits. Again, as in the previous experiment, examining one's feelings aided the memory for material that was self-generated, but not the memory for material provided by the experimenter.

This conclusion that the focusing instruction affects self-generated material was additionally supported in further studies. When people classified objects (as either expensive, moderate or cheap in one study and either hot, tepid or cold in another) the focusing instructions increased the memory of the person's classifications. That is, these instructions increased the memory for whether the object was either hot, tepid or cold, in one study, but did not affect the memory for the names of the objects as supplied by the experimenter.

In the above experiments the focusing instruction affected recall memory. In a further experiment, this instruction was found to increase recognition memory. In one session, people originated some words and heard others from the experimenter. A week later the people were presented with the words and asked to recognize the source. People were significantly better at recognizing the source if they had been given the focusing instruction the previous week.

As to why this focusing instruction affects memory, a hypothesis was drawn from the work of George Mandler (1969, 1980). He found that when people formed a relationship between items by sorting the items into categories long term recognition memory for these items was improved. He called this relationship between items, inter-item organization. The next study was done to find if the focusing instruction increased inter-item organization. For this purpose a famous experimental task which tests inter-item organization was used. Bransford and Franks (1971) used a group of propositions that were related in meaning. They thought that people would automatically integrate these propositions. They expected that this automatic integration of meaning would result in people mistakenly identifying an integrated sentence as one they had seen previously, although they had only encountered related propositions that were constituents of the integrated sentence.

To test this expectation, Bransford and Franks (1971) gave subjects a series of propositions such as "The rock rolled down the mountain," "The tiny hut was at the edge of the woods," "The rock crushed the hut." Recognition was tested by showing subjects both propositions that had been previously seen and some that had not been presented. People were also shown novel sentences which combined the propositions that they had seen before. For example, people were shown, for the first time, the combined sentence "The rock which rolled down the hill crushed the tiny hut at the edge of the woods." The experimenters found, as predicted, that people automatically combined propositions and mistakenly identified combined sentences that they had not seen before. Thus, in terms of the above example, people said they had seen the combined sentence, although they had, in fact, not seen that sentence.

If the focusing instruction increases the use of inter-item organization, it should increase the false recognition of the Bransford and Franks task. In a study testing this hypothesis, it was found, as predicted, that the false recognition of the combined sentences was significantly greater after the focusing instruction.

To find whether the focusing instruction increased the effects of the inter-item relations formed in recall memory, another study was done. People were given a list of words to remember. Some of the words, when first read to the person, were accompanied by questions which were answered with either a "yes" or "no." These questions had to do with incidental, rather than defining properties of the words. For example, after the word "sheep," the question was asked "Is it needed?" Recall was tested in two ways. First by free recall where the person was asked to recall as many words as possible, in any order. Then, recall was cued with questions like: "Do you recall what was needed?" Cued recall was significantly improved after the focusing instructions. Examining feelings in this way improved the use of item organization formed in the experimental situation.

In summary, the focusing instruction:

a. Enhances complex, effortful performance but not automatic performance.

b. Increases attention to internally generated rather than to externally supplied material.

c. Increases the relating we do of this internally generated material.

The purpose of this chapter was to present an alternative explanation for the effects of the focusing instruction based on the cognitive functioning involved in examining our feelings. One way to do this, which structured the above discussion, was to look at the cognitive effects of these instructions. Another way of understanding the functioning of these instructions is to look at the instructions themselves.

THE PROCESSES INVOLVED IN THE FOCUSING INSTRUCTION

The focusing instruction, in the modification used, was: "This is an exercise to look at your feelings. I won't ask you specifically about your feelings. You can do this exercise silently... to yourself, I'll just guide you through it. What I'd like you to do is to see how much you can relax your body. (Relax own body... (30 s). I realize this is hard to do in a strange situation... (10 s). What I will ask you to do will be silent just to yourself. Take another moment just to relax... (20 s). All right now, inside you I would like you to pay attention to that part where you usually feel feelings like sad or glad or scared... (20 s). Pay attention to that area in you and see how you are now... (10 s). See what comes when you ask yourself, 'How am I now?,' 'How do I feel?,' 'What is the main thing for me right now?' ... (10 s). Sense how you feel. Let the answers come slowly from the sensing... (5 s). When something comes, do not go inside it... Stand back, say 'Yes that's there. I can feel that there.' Let there be a little space between you and that... (5 s). Wait again and sense... (5 s). Usually there are several things... (30 s)."

In order to understand the processes that are started by having a person follow this instruction, it will be necessary to analyze it in detail, to understand what each phrase in the instruction asks the person to do. This instruction asks the person to do a number of quite different things. In detail:

1. When the instruction tells the person to attend "inside you" it says that the task involves internally generated material, that the person listening, and not the experimenter is going to supply the relevant material. In addition, when this sentence asks the person to pay attention to that part "where you usually feel feelings like sad or glad or scared," it specifies the type of information that is relevant for the task, i.e. internally generated information in the form of emotional reactions.

2. Asking the person to pay attention to that area and to see how they are now, does several things. It tells the person that it is their state (which in terms of the previous sentence should be an emotion) at the present moment which is relevant to the task. The instruction begins to tell the person that they are to examine, not express, the feeling.

3. This instruction then asks ("see how you are now") for an initial formulation or description of the feeling.

4. The next sentence asks the person to answer the question "How I am right now" and then goes on to define the "am" in terms of feeling ("how do I feel"). This confirms that the task requires formulation of a description of the internally generated data. This sentence is also asking that the initial formulation of how the person is feeling be further defined.

5. When the instruction then asks the person "what is the main thing right now?," it introduces a new element. That is, the sentence says that it is the most important, central emotion which should be formulated and described.

6. The next sentence, in asking the person to "sense," again is asking for an orientation to internally generated data. It is asking the person to try to describe that data to themselves. When the person is told to let the answers come slowly from this sensing, he is being told that a process of attaining knowledge (here about the nature of the present feeling) is taking place. In addition, the instruction to sense and describe an internal object assumes that there is a configuration, a grouping of internal data to which the person should direct his attention.

7. This emphasis on attending to the configuration of internal data, is confirmed repeatedly in the successive sentences. When the person is told "not to go inside it" and to "stand back," the person is told not to experience the feeling, not to get involved in a sequence of emotional behaviors, but rather to continue to perceive and organize the internal data.

8. When the instructions for the first movement conclude by "Then ask what else you feel. Wait again and sense. Usually there are several things," the person is being asked to go through this process of generation again.

At a general level, these instructions lead the person through a series of activities.

a. They ask the person to attend to internal data.

b. They ask the person to generate an initial formulation, or hypothesis, about a particular kind of organization of this internal data.

c. The instruction then asks that this formulation be checked against relevant, internal data and changed when necessary. These instructions ask the person to observe rather then express the feeling.

CONTROL STUDIES ABOUT THE EFFECTIVE ASPECTS OF THE INSTRUCTIONS

Studies were done to find what aspects of the focusing instruction affected cognitive performance. These studies used cognitive tasks that had been found to be affected by the focusing instruction. These studies then measured whether another instruction or condition, which had particular aspects of the focusing instruction, had similar effects on that cognitive task. For example, because in several studies it had been found that the focusing instruction affected the Stroop task which involved naming the color of the ink, the effect of various aspects of the focusing instruction on Stroop performance was measured. Because the focusing instruction starts with a request for the person to relax, the effect of the relaxation part of the instruction upon the Stroop task was tested. Having the person relax, by itself, had no effect on the Stroop task.

In addition to asking the person to relax, the focusing instruction asks the person to examine inner content, not only for the feeling at the moment, but to examine various aspects of the present feeling. Perhaps relaxation and this scanning of internal content is responsible for the change in cognitive processing that occurs after the focusing instruction. Several studies tested this possibility. In one, people were told that they would be asked to decide whether words that would be said by the experimenter fit easily into categories held by the person. After being given the focusing instruction to relax, the person sat with eyes closed. People were asked to think of the categories of animal, vegetable, and mineral. When the experimenter said the names of common nouns such as "duck," "tree," or "justice," the person was to nod affirmatively if the noun fit easily into the person's animal, vegetable and mineral categories and shake his or her head negatively, if it did not. People were not asked about their categories. Their only response was to move their head. The people then did the Stroop task. The combination of relaxation and scanning did not effect the Stroop task. Evidently, these are not the aspects of the focusing instruction responsible for the cognitive effect. The focusing instruction requires attending to present feeling. Is it the activity of attending to inner material which is responsible for the effect of the focusing instruction? Would the activity of attending to any inner material have this effect? Or is it necessary that it is feeling material to which the person is attending? As discussed previously, the focusing instruction leads the person through a series of activities. It asks the person to attend to internal data and to generate an initial formulation, or hypothesis, about a particular kind of organization of this internal data, a feeling. The instruction then asks that this formulation be checked against relevant, internal data, and changed when necessary. Is it these activities by themselves that cause the cognitive effect?

To answer these questions, an instruction was constructed which required the same activities as the focusing instruction, but did not involve feeling content. This new instruction asks the person to attend to physical sensation as the internal data. The sensation instruction asks that the person produce and attend to particular physical sensations. This instruction also asks that the person compare the sensations and generate a hypothesis. This hypothesis is then checked against relevant data.

Two forms of the sensation instruction were found to be equivalent and were combined in later studies. In these sensation instructions people were asked to produce and contrast four sensations on the back of their hands. They were told "I would like you to contrast four sensations on the back of your hand. These are a pinch, a rub, a press and a squeeze." At this point the experimenter demonstrated each on the back of his hand. The instruction continued. "Please contrast these sensations finding how they are similar and how they are different from each other. See if you can find some ways of describing them which would convey what is happening to someone who has not experienced them."

In the other version of the sensation instruction, which was later combined with the above, people were told, as in the last instruction, that four sensations on the back of the hand were involved, and the motions of producing the sensations were demonstrated. Then people were told "You will notice, when you produce sensations on the back of your hand, that the fingers that are doing this pinching, rubbing, etc., sometimes feels the texture of your skin before you feel the sensation on the back of your hand. Sometimes however, you may feel these sensations on the back of your hand first. Also, you will notice some of these sensations on the back of your hands fade more rapid then others. Which fades most rapidly, which next most rapidly and which most slowly? Please contrast the sensations in these ways."

The effect of this sensation-focus instruction and of the usual focusing instruction was compared to the effect of an "external focus" condition. In this latter condition, people crossed out the letter "e" whenever it occurred on a page of typescript. Both the sensation-focus instruction and the usual feeling-focus instruction significantly improved the performance on the Stroop task more than did the external-focus condition. People named the color of the ink in which the names of colors were printed. There was no difference between the effect of sensation-focusing and the feeling-focusing instruction.

The effect of both of these instructions on mental addition was also measured. After two, three digit numbers were read to the person, the answers given and the time taken to answer was recorded. People did five mental addition problems after each instruction. Again, performance after the sensation-focusing and feeling-focusing was significantly better than performance after crossing out "e"s. That is, after each of the two focusing instructions, arithmetic problems were added significantly faster then after the external-focus condition. There was no difference between the feeling-focusing and sensation-focusing instruction.

Thus, at least in terms of the cognitive effects, the sensation instruction is similar to the usual focusing instruction. The feeling content of the usual focusing instruction is evidently not critical for the cognitive effects. Rather, the critical feature is the activities involved in these instructions. These activities are, to repeat: 1. First, that something is internally generated by the person. With the feeling-focusing instruction this was either the generation of feelings or the generation of sensations that one considers in deciding what is being felt at the moment. With the sensation-focus instruction, physical sensations were generated on the back of one's hand. 2. Then, these generated elements have to be organized and compared. With the feeling-focus instruction, this comparison was of the elements that make up the feeling and the comparison of successive formulations of what is being felt. The sensation-focus instruction required the comparison of self produced physical sensation. 3. Next, both instructions required a hypothesis or formulation from the person. The feeling-focus instruction required a formulation of the present feeling. The other instruction asked for a formulation about which sensation faded most rapidly etc. 4. Both instructions asked that the formulations be checked against relevant data and changed where necessary. Thus, the feeling-focus instruction asked both that the person examine the present feeling several times, that other aspects of the feeling be described and that other feelings be formulated.

"COMMON" PROCESSES

So far we have examined both the processes involved in the focusing instruction and those characteristics of the cognitive performances which are affected by this instruction. These two groups of processes have similar characteristics. Both involve the generation of internal data. Both involve interrelating and comparing this internal data in the form of hypotheses and then testing these hypotheses against the relevant internal data. However, even assuming that these are the processes used in the focusing instruction, why do these processes affect what comes afterward?

REASONS FOR THE COGNITIVE CONSEQUENCES OF THE "COMMON" PROCESSES

Possible explanations for the effect of the focusing instruction upon subsequent cognitive activity can be drawn from the work of Fergus Craik (1983). He has been interested in memory processes and has been suspicious of the assumption that long term memory results from transfer from temporary to permanent storage. Instead, he proposed that the durability of memory is a function of the depth and elaboration of the initial encoding and the compatibility of the retrieval processes with the initial encoding.

Craik (1983) also has an interest in the memory processes of the elderly. There are large age differences in some memory tasks and no differences in others. For example, young subjects do better at free recall tasks, but are no better at recognition memory tasks. Similarly, when the memory for a list of words is tested, there is little difference between the young and old for the most recently given words, but considerable difference in the memory for words given earlier on the list.

These findings have been taken as evidence for two different stores or systems underlying the two tasks. The memory of words early on the list has been thought to be drawn from one store and the memory for words late on a list has been taken as evidence for a different store. A transitory, short term store has been thought responsible for the memory of the words early on a list, and a long term, permanent, memory store as responsible for the words later on the list.

Craik's explanation is based on the encoding and retrieval differences in the two types of tasks. Some encoding operations are so well practised, or the stimuli are so compatible with the relevant processing mechanism, that the operations are carried out automatically, without conscious effort or awareness. This type of encoding is so automatic that it takes place when cues are presented by the environment. This kind of processing is termed "environmental driven."

Other encoding operations, for example, understanding a complex sentence, require much more attention and effort. These encoding operations are not cued by the environment. Instead, they require self-initiated activity.

Retrieval operations are similar. In some tasks, like looking at a word and deciding if it was in a list of words you had seen previously, the operations are automatic and are cued by the material given. These processes can be described as environmentally driven. In other tasks, like recalling a word some time after you have seen it, retrieval has much less environmental support and requires more self-initiated activities. These activities include reconstructing the original word without environmental help. The memory tasks that involve automatic, environmentally supported encoding are also the tasks that use environmentally supported retrieval. Similarly, tasks requiring self-initiated processing, also require self-initiated processing on retrieval.

Craik examined the cognitive tasks in which the young and the elderly performed similarly and those tasks in which they performed differently. Those tasks in which they performed similarly, tasks like recognition memory, were tasks in which there were automatic processes of encoding and retrieval that were cued by the environment. Those tasks in which the cognitive performance of the young and the elderly were different were those in which there was less environmental support and in which more self-initiating tasks were required. Craik proposed that the difference in the performance in these types of tasks did not require the assumption that the elderly were deficient in long term store. Instead, he concluded that the elderly do not have difficulty with tasks requiring automatic, environmentally aided processes. They do have difficulty with tasks in which there is less environmental support and where more self-initiated processes are required.

It will be remembered that some cognitive tasks were aided by feeling and sensation-focus and some were not. Those that were aided were tasks, like complex mental addition or the classification of objects or numbers, which required effortful activity that had to be initiated, planned and executed by the person involved. The tasks that were not aided were tasks, like memory for digits, that involved automatic processing. Thus the tasks that were aided were those using processes that Craik called self-initiated processes. The tasks that utilize the automatic environmentally driven processes were not aided.

The "common processes" utilized in the feeling and sensation focus instructions are intensive self-initiating processes. The processes of generating and comparing internal material and then forming and checking hypotheses involving this material, involve many self-initiating processes. Working with internally, self generated material may start processes of self-generation which then continue. The person may be more ready to use self-initiating processes after the "common processes" resulting from the feeling and sensation-focusing instruction. When this happens, and the task that follows these instructions, like complex mental addition, utilizes these self-initiated processes, performance is helped. Tasks which do not use self-initiated processes, like remembering a span of digits, are not aided by these instructions.

THE "COMMON PROCESSES" AND CHANGE OF FEELINGS

To understand how these common processes of generating and testing internal data and hypotheses change and affect feelings, the functioning of these processes in psychotherapy will be examined. Assume, as an example, that a male client says "Darn her. Last month I told her to do it and she didn't, and last week I told her to do it and she didn't, and yesterday I told her to do it and she still didn't." Assume the therapist responds "It's very annoying that she won't do what you ask." The client would then generate a hypothesis about how he feels and use it to check the therapist's description of his emotion, "annoying." The client might then say "It was more than annoying, it was infuriating." This is a process of generating and testing internal data and hypotheses that is similar to those brought about by the feeling-focus and the sensation-focusing instruction.

The therapist's response in the above example caused the client to attend to and process information about his internal reactions. If the therapist had instead said "Did she understand what you wanted?," the client would have processed information about "her" and her understanding, about what he had said in the situation and how she responded, etc. The therapist's response influences whether information about external or internal events are processed by the client.

Similarly, in our daily thinking we process information about external and internal events. Thus, in replaying, in my mind, a conversation I had with a friend a few minutes ago, I am processing data about an external circumstance. If I am thinking about how I felt about the conversation, data about internal reactions is being processed. When data is processed, new learning frequently results. What is learned depends upon the type of data processed. If I am thinking about the conversation with my friend and think of other conversations I have had with him recently, I may notice a commonality to them. This common theme may tell me something of a major concern of his that seems to underly much of what he has talked about recently. If, however, I am thinking about how I feel about the conversation, I may find that I feel rejected by his inability to attend to anything I say about my life. If I then thought about how I felt about other conversations I had with other people, a common theme to the feelings might emerge. I might, from this, learn something about my feelings of rejection.

An assumption of many types of psychotherapies, including the focusing instructions, is that it is desirable to stimulate consideration of internal data. This seems to be necessary because much of our thinking is concerned with the external world. A reason for this can be drawn from the theories of George Herbert Mead (1934). According to Mead, the self is not something we are born with. Instead, the self comes from social experience and begins with the infant's interactions with parents and other significant individuals. The child perceives, and eventually incorporates, the attitudes of these "significant others." The self consists of these attitudes. When the child enters school and interacts with groups, the attitudes of the groups become, for the child, the attitude of the community. These attitudes become part of the self and are responded to, within the self, as the child responded to the group.

Conversations and interactions with others are incorporated by the child as part of the self. Thinking is the mental occurrance of these conversations and interactions. This constellation of attitudes, conversations and interactions with others is termed the "me" by Mead. The "me" is a recipient self, which, although busily interactive, is passive in its lack of initiating. The passivity is reflected in our language. When one is an object, one talks about "what happened to me."

The "me" incorporates only past learnings and does not allow for innovative action. That we spend much of our time in the "me" mode is apparent. Much of our mental activity is spent in imaginary interactions. It is interesting that much of this mental activity is started by what happens in our external world. Thus, we begin a mental interaction with someone when something in our environment reminds us of that person. This mentation, these "me" state interactions, resemble the environmentally driven cognitive functioning that was described above. Thus, to automatically go through a series of mental interactions after being reminded of someone is much like going through a series of automatic processes when asked whether a word that is presented to you was seen before.

Mead postulated another aspect of the self, the "I", as the source for creative action and for the ability of the self to behave independently. He had little to say about how the "I" develops. The "I" reacts to the attitudes and interactions with others that make up the "me." The "I" changes the response of the self from being the attitudes of others to something more idiosynchratic. This mode of the self is less automatic and more self-initiating than is the "me" mode. In its lack of dependence upon external cues, its lack of automaticity and its dependence on the self for guidance, the "I" mode resembles the self-initiated cognitive processing that was described above when recall memory was discussed.

Client-centered therapy moves us from this "me" mode. The client-centered therapist responds to and "reflects" the persons' attitudes about themselves and their world. This was done in the previous example wherein the therapist responded to the client's "annoyance" that "she" didn't do what she was told. This type of response helps to move the client from the "me" mode where he or she is considering others to the "I" mode consideration of self. When people are in the "I" mode they respond in new ways, ways more appropriate to the moment.

What was termed the "common processes" may be the processes responsible for moving the person from the "me" state. These "common processes" may move the person from the "me" state for the same reason that these "common processes" changed the cognitive performances that followed the focusing or sensation instruction. As the self-initiating cognitive processes were stimulated in the cognitive performances which followed the focusing instruction so might stimulating these processes change the mode of the self. That is, the self-initiating processes, the processes of generation, comparison and test, which took place as part of the focusing or sensation instruction might stimulate self-initiating processes in the person and move the person from the "me" state. The person in the "me" state is imagining interactions with others and is processing information about people and interactions. When the feeling-focus or the sensation-focusing instruction, or the client-centered interview starts self-initiating processes which result in the person considering and judging information about internal reactions, the person is no longer in a "me" state.

To repeat: In the "me" state the person is reacting to the world. When a stimulus impinges, when the person, for example, sees something that reminds him or her of an incident with his or her spouse, the incident and interaction occurs mentally. This is automatic and is environmentally driven, similar to the automatic remembering of a span of digits. When in an "I" state and the same stimulus occurs, the person will not respond automatically. Instead, the person may find himself choosing not to think about the incident but rather choosing to continue with what he was doing when the incident occurred. Choosing to continue with what he was doing is a use of self-initiated processing as was complex cognitive performance. The focus or sensation instruction or the client-centered therapy interview in stimulating the use of the self-initiated processes decreases the automatic responses the person makes after the instruction or interview and increases the amount of choices made. The person changes from reacting to considering.

THEORETICAL CONSIDERATIONS

The explanation for the effect of the focusing instructions offered above, that these instructions start a series of processes, is, of course, different from the explanation offered by Gendlin. He postulates that there is a continual series of experiential reactions occurring within the person and that psychological trouble occurs when we do not attend to these reactions. The focusing instructions are a way of increasing the person's attention to these reactions. The process explanation offered above should be amplified. What results from the operation of a process is the result of both the nature of the process and the nature of the material that is entering into the process. Thus the result of the growth process is an interaction of the particular stage of the growth process that is present and also of the particular material that is growing. This interaction of process with the material being processed could be seen most clearly in the experiments reported above. The same processes that resulted in the report of feelings when the focusing instruction asked for feeling material, resulted in cognitive performance when cognitive materials were involved.

Psychotherapies differ in both the processes they use and in the material involved in those processes. Some psychotherapies may have roughly similar processes, but in directing the client's attention to different material, result in different products.

The focusing instruction directs attention to feelings. What will result, at best, is increased knowledge of feelings. There will be a different result with client-centered therapy because different material is thought important. It will be recalled that Rogers specified that it was both necessary and sufficient that the therapist empathically understand the internal frame of reference of the client. This concern with understanding the client's internal frame of reference is of critical importance. The emphasis is not on understanding feelings or meanings, unless these are in the client's internal frame of reference at the moment. Rather than understanding any particular content, the therapist is to try to see the client's world in the way the client sees it.

When the therapist indicates an understanding of the client's internal frame of reference, with how the client sees his or her world, this understanding may enter into the processing that the client is doing at the moment. Rogers was a master at stating the client's feeling or reaction in the context of the client's frame of reference. That is, Rogers frequently stated the client's present reaction to his or her feeling or meaning. For example, take the following exchange, taken from the middle of the fourth interview with Mrs. Ett (Rogers, 1947).

> Ett: "That's right. Then there is this strong feeling of not wanting to be identified with the mob, shall we say? Sounds very snobbish, but I find myself doing things or dressing or thinking, ultimately it will end up that I dress and wear my hair and put on make-up just the way that everyone does, but it's with great - ah - well, I try great effort, but it adds up that I do. I choose my handkerchief first, you can see I spend a lot of time looking for odd design, they please me, but primarily because I know nobody else will have them. Ah - I have this feeling that, when I shop for a dress, I get very weary to myself and I think 'Oh what the hell is the use, this dress is only one dress, or supposing that I did pay $50 or $60 for it, so this is the same dress that has been copied maybe a thousand times for other people.' What's the use of putting on lipstick or make-up? Everybody else does it. I mean I have that feeling - conscious feeling all the time of not wanting to do something because everybody else does it.
>
> Rogers: It means a great deal to you to be different, not just one of the gang, one of the mob."

It should be noted that Rogers does not just note or comment on her feelings of wanting to be different. Instead he frames this comment in terms of her present reaction, to this feeling: "It means a great deal to you to be different." In presenting this material to her, material having to do with her present perspective on her feeling, he is offering this material to be processed. What will be compared and processed is this material about her present perspective. What may result is the client's consideration of her own frame of reference, not just consideration of the feeling of "not wanting to do something because everybody else does it." If the therapist's response had focused Mrs. Ett only on this feeling, she might have explored the feeling, finding other situations in which she did not want to be like other people. The aspect of Rogers' response that has to do with Mrs. Ett's framework may cause her to explore how much being different matters and why it matters, very different topics than those topics which would have resulted from exploring the feeling.

What is being proposed in this chapter is that what results from psychotherapy is a function both of the processes started by the therapist's response and also of the material that is involved in the processing. This explanation for the effect of psychotherapy is very different from the explanation given for most verbal psychotherapy. There it is assumed that the client or patient changes because he, or she, learns about those aspects of their being which were hidden or repressed. In the explanation given here, it is asserted that the source of what is learned is quite different. Instead of finding what was hidden, the combination of particular processes and material produces the new material, the new feeling or realization. The oak tree is not in the acorn. It develops from the acorn as particular processes interact with particular material. Psychotherapy theory has emphasized on the formative processes that produce new material. It is no coincidence that Rogers continually saw psychotherapy as a growth process.

REFERENCES

Bransford, J.D., & Franks, J.J. (1971). The abstraction of linguistic ideas. *Cognitive Psychology, 2,* 331-350.

Craik, F. (1983). *On the transfer of information from temporary to permanent memory.* Trans. Royal Society London, B302, 103-420.

Gendlin, E.T. (1978). *Focusing.* New York: Everest House.

380

Mandler, G. (1980). Recognizing: The judgment of previous occurrence. *Psychological Review, 88*, 252-271.

Mandler, G., Pearlstone, Z., & Koopmans, H.J. (1969). Effects of organization and semantic similarity on recall and recognition. *Journal of Verbal Learning and Verbal Behavior, 8*, 410-423.

Mead, G.H. (1934). *Mind, self, and society.* Chicago: University of Chicago Press.

Rogers, C.R. (1947). *The case of Mrs. Ett.* Unpublished manuscript, University of Chicago Counseling Center.

Rogers, C.R. (1957). The necessary and sufficient conditions of therapeutic personality change. *Journal of Consulting Psychology, 21*, 95-103.

Rogers, C.R., & Dymond, R. (1954). *Psychotherapy and personality change.* Chicago: University of Chicago Press.

Zimring, F.M. (1983). Attending to feelings and cognitive performance. *Journal of Research in Personality, 17*, 288-299.

Zimring, F.M. (1985). The effect of attending to feelings on memory for internally generated stimuli. *Journal of Research in Personality, 19*, 170-184.

Zimring, F.M. (1988). Self-focus and relational knowledge. *Journal of Research in Personality, 22*, 273-289.

IN SEARCH OF UNIVERSAL CONCEPTS IN PSYCHOPATHOLOGY AND PSYCHOTHERAPY

Martin A. Van Kalmthout & Floris A. Pelgrim
Universiteit Nijmegen   Universiteit Leiden
The Netherlands   The Netherlands

INTRODUCTION

The proliferation and refinement of diagnostic categories in psychopathology reflects on the one hand a tendency towards scientific objectivity and precision, but on the other hand, it also holds the danger of increasing fragmentation that inevitably results from the never ending process of information gathering and analysis. Consider, for example, the authorative DSM categorization which according to Kazdin (1986) has increased the number of recognized mental disorders from about 100 diagnostic categories in his first edition to over 180 in his second. In the third edition more than 260 diagnostic categories were included (APA, 1980, 1987). The same trend has been noticed in psychotherapy where about 60 approaches were identified in the early 1960s (Garfield, 1982) and recently over 250 techniques were counted (Herink, 1980).

This state of the art poses serious problems to the practicing psychotherapist as well as to the psychotherapy-researcher and theoretician: Fragmentation not only is an impediment to straightforward and focused action, but also to empirical research and theoretical reflection. Take for example the very often cited "ultimate question" in psychotherapy-research: "*What* treatment, by *whom,* is most effective for *this* individual with *that* specific problem, under *which* set of circumstances?" (Paul, 1967, p. 111). At this moment, it seems unconceivable for researchers to point out how 250 techniques should be linked to 260 diagnostic categories. We believe, however, that this is not merely a practical problem but a fundamental one as well. In our view, these developments also reflect fragmented thinking in psychopathology and psychotherapy and we are of the opinion that they must be counterbalanced by some kind of integrative effort. In this chapter we want to make a contribution to that aim. Our purpose in this chapter is therefore to promote an alternative approach which will hopefully lead to a more comprehensive way of thinking in psychopathology and psychotherapy. As far as psychopathology is concerned, this approach implies that the search is directed at core human problems, instead of at ever finer distinctions in psychopathology. As far as psychotherapy is concerned, our approach implies that our search is directed at the change process itself, not at finding and distinguishing ever newer techniques and "methods." We assume that the variety of psychopathological categories and psychotherapeutic approaches and techniques first of all reflect culturally, historically and socially determined idiosyncracies, not substances per se like diseases and therapeutics in medicine (Ellenberger, 1970; Szasz, 1965, 1979; Van Kalmthout & Van der Ven, 1985).

In this chapter, we explore this alternative approach to psychopathology and psychotherapy by referring to the notion of a common conflict basic to all the psychoneuroses (the "universal conflict") and, consequently, a common therapy (the "universal therapy"). We do not wish to declare, however, at the end of our chapter the ultimate truth about human problems and their solution (see Osbourne & Baldwin, 1982). Our aim is rather to explore the fruitfulness of an approach which is directed at searching the core of psychoneurotic problems and at fundamental change. We hope that this will contribute to unifying conceptualizations in psychopathology and psychotherapy, but also give the clinician an anchorage for meaningful therapeutic action.

The importance of integrative thinking in psychopathology and psychotherapy has been formulated also by Dietz where he describes the work of Jerome Frank as "a unified theory of suffering and healing." Elaborating on Frank's contribution he writes:

> "The reader of the papers collected here will agree that this has remained a hallmark of Frank's writings, for he has a *synthetic touch*. I am inclined to believe that the tendency of so many of us to subdivide, to classify, and to polarize is the source of much bigotry and despair. We are indeed fortunate that there are some among us who, like Frank, maintain the broader vision and link us together" (Dietz in: Frank, 1978, pp. X-XIII).

It is in this spirit that we undertake our search for the possible universal elements in psychopathology and psychotherapy.

The concept of the universal may evoke quite a number of prejudices and misunderstandings in clinicians as well as in psychotherapy researchers. One of these certainly is that the concept of the universal promotes thinking in terms of abstractions and metaphysical concepts and therefore leads away from concrete problems and symptoms. We want to point out from the beginning that we take this critique very seriously and strive for an approach which is concrete and of practical help to the clinician. If we did not succeed in this respect we certainly would feel that our approach has a serious drawback. So our starting point is the concrete symptom or problem and we certainly do not despise the concrete materials on symptomatology which have been collected, for example, in DSM III and other categorizations. But our search has to go through these concrete manifestations to the basic common problems possibly underlying them. The same is true for psychotherapy. We do not intend to put aside the rich variety of methods and approaches in psychotherapy, but rather to consider them as different ways to fundamental change processes. This implies that we take the individual client and his concrete symptoms very seriously as well as his unique needs and possibilities. But at the same time, we would like to help him or her to look for the core of his problem, which may be a problem common to many people and, in that sense, could be called universal. Carl Rogers seems to have sensed this notion, as is demonstrated in the next citation from *A way of being* (1980, p. 8):

> "There is another peculiar satisfaction in really hearing someone: It is like listening to the music of the spheres, because beyond the immediate message of the person, no matter what that might be, there is the universal. Hidden in all of the personal communications which I really hear there seem to be orderly psychological laws, aspects of the same order we find in the universe as a whole. So there is both the satisfaction of hearing this person and also the satisfaction of feeling one's self in touch with what is universally true."

Our study has been much stimulated by the work of Hellmuth Kaiser and in this chapter we begin by summarizing his view on the concept of the universal. Next, we will mention some other authors, but will give special attention to Rogers and Skinner. The reason for this selection is that they both are authorities on conceptions of a universal psychopathology and psychotherapy, the former exemplifying a universal content, the latter a formal view of universal problems and therapies. To carry our study a little further, we next present Mahrer's view on this problem, because he discussed it at length in his writings.

After this review, we will undertake a more difficult task which is to explore the question of how the different conceptualizations of universality in psychopathology and psychotherapy are interrelated. To conclude, we will give some suggestions as to how this approach can be furthered by theoretical and empirical research.

THE CONTRIBUTION OF HELLMUTH KAISER TO THE SEARCH FOR UNIVERSAL CONCEPTS

Hellmuth Kaiser (1893-1961) spent a lifetime searching for the conditions of effective psychotherapy (Fierman, 1965)1. At one point in this search, he became fascinated by the question of whether all psychoneurotic patients, with all their different symptoms and problems, nevertheless have some basic problem in common. After testing out (and rejecting) several hypotheses, he became more and more convinced that all neurotic patients (Kaiser wanted to limit his work explicitly to that category) had a common symptom, which for that reason he named the universal symptom. After this discovery, he went on to find out whether this universal symptom was a manifestation of a universal conflict, and little by little he defined such a conflict. The last step was to formulate a universal therapy, that is a therapy that would be effective for all psychoneurotic patients, assuming that they were all suffering from the universal conflict and the universal symptom.

Kaiser can thus be considered the first one who seriously explored the concept of the universal in psychopathology and psychotherapy, because he developed a "triad of universals" (Fierman, 1965), namely *the universal psychopathology, the universal symptom* and *the universal therapy.* By universal is meant in this context: "...an observation or concept applicable to all people with psychological disorder which is to say all people, since no one is entirely free of neurosis" (Fierman, 1965, p. 207).

The content of the universal psychopathology is described by Kaiser as follows: "It is the thought that, perhaps, really every neurotic disturbance might center around the patient's effort to obviate the inner experience of being an individual or, in plain English, of being alone" (Fierman, p. 133).

These efforts to weaken the boundaries of his being an individual take the form of delusional devices to fuse with something or someone else. In interpersonal relationships, this is apparent in double communication. This can be seen for example when somebody starts saying something and, halfway in his statement, begins to deny or weaken it. It sounds as if he does not dare to take full responsibility for this opinion. This is referred to by Kaiser as the concept of *duplicity*, which he considers the universal symptom,, that is the core of all psychoneurotic symptoms. Duplicity is described by Kaiser as follows: "Patients did not talk straight. They were never completely, never wholeheartedly behind their words. Listening to them caused some inner struggle, almost as if one had to listen to two speakers talking simultaneously. There was a strange duplicity about their communications" (Fierman, p. 36-37).

The universal therapy according to Kaiser follows his conception of the universal symptom of duplicity. If the latter is the core of neurosis, then the universal therapy should consist of breaking through the pattern of double communication, by communicating directly and straightforwardly instead of leaving the patient alone, which in the end most people will do because they cannot bear this duplicity any longer. By staying with the patient, the therapist breaks the vicious circle of duplicity: "'Not to withdraw physically' from the patient is necessary for treating this condition; however, this condition is easy to fulfill and creates no problems at all. The crucial condition which makes all the difference between psychotherapy which helps, and alleged psychotherapy which does not, is that the therapist does not withdraw psychologically" (Fierman, p. 154).

This conception of the universal therapy implies that Kaiser rejects the notion that methods or techniques are the effective ingredients of psychotherapy and postulates a number of therapist qualities as the crucial variables: "My main point is that the conditions for effective psychotherapy can be expressed only in terms of personality characteristics of the therapist, and not in rules of what he should do" (Fierman, pp. 159-160).

Among the requirements of the therapist are: 1. A genuine interest in people, and more specifically, an interest in establishing straightforward communication. 2. The absence of theoretical conviction as well as 3. The absence of neurotic protective patterns in the therapist which interfere with such communications. 4. And, most important, the mental condition in the therapist of receptiveness for or sensitivity towards the noncommunicative elements in the patient's behavior (this is his duplicity).

In fact, Kaiser was of the opinion that the absence of any structure in such a therapy activates the universal conflict and consequently enhances the patient's duplicity, which gives rise to an excellent opportunity for therapeutic work.

Kaiser remained always sceptical and critical about his own ideas and admonished his readers to be so too: "Indeed, there is no lack of questions to answer and problems to solve" (Fierman, p. 136).

In our discussion of this chapter, we will deal with some of the questions which Kaiser's work raises. Here, we will just list four questions which Kaiser himself raised in regard to his own conceptualizations (Fierman, pp. 136-141):

1. How is the universal conflict connected with the universal symptom of duplicity?
2. If the universal conflict is not only common to all psychoneurotic patients but to all humanity, what then distinguishes the neurotic from the reasonably healthy person?
3. What is the relation between the universal conflict and all the other symptoms, apart from the universal symptom of duplicity? Or: what is the relation between all the other symptoms and the universal symptom of duplicity?
4. Assuming that most of humanity is counteracting the universal conflict by delusion formation in a rather healthy way, one has to answer the question of whether delusion is compatible with mental health.

So much for Kaiser's contribution. We limit here our presentation to his concept of the universal and its three modes. We shall not go into the discussion of the content of his concepts; we first ask whether other theoreticians of psychotherapy have similar concepts in their systems. We are convinced that many important figures in the history of psychotherapy indeed have such concepts; e.g.: Freud, Jung, Rank, Rogers, Skinner and many other thinkers in the psychodynamic and existential-humanistic tradition could be studied from this point of view (see: Beck, 1973; Yalom, 1980). However, presenting all these great thinkers here exceeds the scope of this chapter and, as said before, we limit ourselves to Rogers and Skinner as authorities representing two different approaches with respect to universality in psychopathology and psychotherapy.

ROGERS' CONCEPTUALIZATION OF THE UNIVERSAL IN PSYCHOPATHOLOGY AND PSYCHOTHERAPY

Rogers can be considered one of the best examples of a proponent of a universal psychopathology and psychotherapy. The following quotation indicates this in regard to the former:

> "I have however come to believe that in spite of this bewildering horizontal multiplicity, and the layer upon layer of vertical complexity, there is perhaps only one problem. As I follow the experience of many clients in the therapeutic relationship which we endeavor to create for them, it seems to me that each one is raising the same question. Below the level of the problem situation about which the individual is complaining - behind the trouble with studies, or wife, or employer, or with his own uncontrollable or bizarre behavior, or with his frightening feelings - , lies one central search. It seems to me that at bottom each person is asking, "Who am I, really? How can I get in touch with this real self, underlying all my surface behavior? How can I become myself?" (Rogers, 1977 [1961], p. 108).

In terms of "incongruence" or dissociation the same is said in the following: "The satisfaction or fulfillment of the actualizing tendency has become bifurcated into incompatible behavior systems. This dissociation which exists in most of us is the pattern and basis of all psychological pathology in man" (Rogers, 1963, p. 24).

Incongruence insofar as it manifests itself in behavior (see: "incompatible behavior systems") can be considered an example of what Kaiser called a universal symptom.

The following quotation shows Rogers' view on the universal therapy. Talking about his well-known necessary and sufficient conditions for personality change to take place, he states:

> "It is not stated that these six conditions are the essential conditions for client-centered therapy, and that other conditions are essential for other types of psychotherapy. I certainly am heavily influenced by my own experience, and that experience has led me to a viewpoint which is termed "client-centered." Nevertheless my aim in stating this theory is to state the conditions which apply to any situation in which constructive personality change occurs, whether we are thinking of classical psychoanalysis, or any of its modern offshoots, or Adlerian psychotherapy, or any other" (Rogers, 1957, pp. 100-101).

From the above quotations it may be clear that, like Kaiser, Rogers is convinced of the fact that there is a universal psychopathology (namely the search for who I really am), a universal symptom (namely incongruence) and a universal therapy (the six conditions). This formal agreement does not imply, however, that the content of their conceptualizations is similar. So one interesting question is: What are the similarities (if any) and differences between Kaiser and Rogers in the content of their conceptualizations of the universal? We won't go into this question at this moment however, but will pay attention to it in our general discussion.

SKINNER'S FORMAL CONCEPTUALIZATION OF THE UNIVERSAL IN PSYCHOPATHOLOGY AND PSYCHOTHERAPY

In contrast to Kaiser and Rogers (and also to Freud, Jung, Rank and the existentialists), Skinner has a formal conceptualization of the universal in psychopathology and psychotherapy, that is, he does not give a certain content to the universal (like: "Incapacity to be alone;" "not being able to see who I am;" the Oedipus-complex; etc.) but gives a formal description in terms of his system of principles of operant conditioning. Skinner formulates the universal psychopathology as follows:

> "The control exercised by the group and by religious and governmental agencies, as well as by parents, employers, associates, and so on, restricts the selfish, primarily reinforced behavior of the individual. It is exercised for just that reason. Certain by-products, however, are not to the advantage of the controller and are often harmful both to the individual and to the group. These are especially likely to be encountered when the control is excessive or inconsistent" (Skinner, 1953, p. 359).

In other words: Excessive control or punishment is the main cause of psychoneurotic problems. If this is considered the universal psychopathology, then the universal therapy has to counteract that process. That is why Skinner introduces the concept of "nonpunishing audience," which in certain respects reminds us of Rogers' necessary and sufficient conditions:

> "...the therapist constitutes himself a nonpunishing audience. The process through which he does this may take time. From the point of view of the patient, the therapist is at first only one more member of a society which has exerted excessive control. It is the task of the therapist to establish himself in a different position. He therefore consistently avoids the use of punishment. He does not criticize his patient nor object to his behavior in any way, ... In particular, he avoids any sign of counter-aggression when the patient criticizes or otherwise injures him. ... As the therapist gradually establishes himself as a nonpunishing audience, behavior which

has hitherto been repressed begins to appear in the repertoire of the patient" (Skinner, 1953, p. 371).

So it can be said that Skinner considers the nonpunishing audience as the principal technique of all forms of psychotherapy, that is the universal therapy. In contrast to Rogers he does not consider the nonpunishing audience sufficient under all circumstances, but other techniques may be necessary, especially the instruction of an effective repertoire of new behaviors, for example self-control techniques.

Also the circumscription of the universal symptom is formal. Skinner talks about maladaptive behaviors and considers these the universal object of all therapies, not inner causes, etc.

MAHRER'S CRITIQUE OF THE UNIVERSALITY CONCEPT

Most existential-humanistic thinking is expressed in terms of universals as far as psychopathology is concerned. That is, in existential-humanistic thinking there is extensive speculation about the fundamentals of the "human condition" like fear of death, responsibility, loneliness, meaninglessness etc. (Yalom, 1980). In sharp contrast, Mahrer, although himself a representative of existential-humanistic thinking, has vehemently criticized and even rejected the universality concept in psychopathology and psychotherapy:

> "It is an error to elevate to a universal characteristic of human beings some special kind of human quality about which many of us can feel awful. For example, at one time or another many of us might have bad feelings as we come to experience the possibility of our inevitable death. By the same token, we might feel terrible about experiencing failure, impotence, physical ailment, old age, or loneliness. It is, I believe, an error to describe all human beings as vulnerable to all of that as a kind of unhappy fateful "humanness." I do not consider, for example, loneliness as some inevitable, inescapable condition of human life (cf. Moustakas, 1961). It is neither necessary nor universal. I see loneliness as a particular potentiality for experiencing found in some persons and not necessarily in all persons, and like any other potential, capable of being accompanied with bad feelings under the right conditions" (Mahrer, 1978, p. 63).

This stand on the usefulness of the concept of the universal does not imply, however, that Mahrer is a proponent of psychiatric categories. Like most humanists, he rejects the usual diagnostic categorizations as being irrelevant to "humanistic theory" (as he calls his system). Where he is opposed to is the postulation of basic motivations, basic needs, basic tendencies, intrinsic human nature or basic drives.

On the other hand, Mahrer agrees with what we have called a *formal* conceptualization of universality. That is to say that like Skinner, he has a formal system in which universals are described in the sense of the concept as it is used here. In his case what is universal is "the relation between potentials," not the content of the potentials (By potentials Mahrer means: "Potentials for experiencing"). Relationships between potentials can either be "integrative (loving)" or "disintegrative (fearful, hateful)":

> "Our theory asserts that these relationships are best described as varying from integrative to disintegrative, and that the universal characteristics of all infants consist only of relationships between potentials, relationships of either an integrative or a disintegrative nature. Except for this, we eschew all other statements about supposedly universal human conflicts. We reject the thesis that the universal human conflict is between the expression and control of aggressive and sexual instincts. We reject that our universal human conflict is between needs for belongingness, security, and closeness, and needs for independence, separation, freedom ... What is necessary, and therefore universal, is the existence of integrative or disintegrative relationships among potentials, regardless of their nature or content" (Mahrer, 1978, pp. 624-625).

So we can conclude that Mahrer joins us in promoting an approach away from fragmentation; however, like Skinner, he prefers a formal definition of the universal instead of a definition of specific contents. There seems to be one exception: Love (integrative relationships) and hate/fear (disintegrative relationships). Love and hate are not formal descriptions, but contents. One question arising here is whether at a certain point the content and the formal meet.

We come back to this and to a number of other questions in the following discussion.

DISCUSSION

We have explored the utility of maintaining the notion of a common conflict and a common therapy. This search was triggered by our discontentment with the ever-increasing fragmentation in psychopathology and psychotherapy. The work of Hellmuth Kaiser presented us with the concepts of the universal symptom, the universal psychopathology and the universal therapy, and also a number of questions regarding these concepts. We next investigated whether there were other theoreticians who used similar concepts. First of all, we discussed Rogers and concluded that he is one of the most clear-cut representatives of the universal triad and that, like Kaiser, he gives specific contents to the universals. Next we discussed Skinner, because he turned out to be a clear representative of a formal conceptualization of the universal. Lastly, we paid attention to Mahrer's critique of the concept of the universal and we concluded that, contrary to almost all his existential-humanistic colleagues, he gives a formal conceptualization of the universal.

In the present discussion we would like to go briefly into a number of questions which have been raised by our search for the usefulness of the concept of the universal.

1. There are different conceptualizations of the universal conflict (and thus the universal therapy). We paid attention to Kaiser's formulation (the basic conflict between individuation and loneliness), to Rogers' conviction (the estrangement of conscious man from his directional organismic processes), to Skinner's view (the conflict between the selfish behavior of the individual and outside control) and to Mahrer's concepts (integration versus disintegration of potentials). Apart from these four conceptualizations, there are many others. For example, there is Freud's contention, of the Oedipus-complex as the universal human condition. Frank (1974) has nominated *demoralization* as the common denominator of all psychopathological conditions (and hope as its antidote). In Buddhist thinking, *dukkha* (that is the universal human experience of pain and suffering and the experience of the imperfection and impermanence of all existence) has been considered the universal essence of all human problems. In the West, the concept of the universal has flowered especially in existential-humanistic thinking (see for example, Yalom, 1980; Becker, 1973). Fear of death, fear of loneliness, fear of responsibility and lack of meaning have been described as fundamental to the human condition, that is common to all mankind. In our exposé the question now arises how all these conceptualizations of the universal conflict and therapy (and many others not mentioned here) are interrelated. Do they refer to different basic conflicts or are they just diverse conceptualizations of one and the same fundamental conflict?

First of all we do not find it necessary for our purposes to infer one (or two) fundamental conflict(s) from the many possible conceptualizations, because our intention is to promote integrative rather than fragmented thinking in psychopathology and psychotherapy. This implies that the search for universal conflicts and therapies as such already serves our purposes, and it is of less importance to determine the universal problem or therapy. We do not even feel urged to choose between a content-approach and a formal conceptualization. From our point of view both approaches are interesting and certainly quite compatible.

Secondly, we take the different conceptualizations very seriously though, because we think they mostly really refer to fundamental human problems. This implies that we are interested in asking how the different conceptualizations are interrelated. We agree with Mahrer, however, that not all human beings necessarily experience all these fundamental conditions. What is true is that all human beings have the potential of experiencing, for example, fundamental human isolation, death anxiety, anxiety of being nothing or nobody, etc. This does not imply that there are no fundamental human problems and that these cannot be described. On the contrary, they have been described from the beginning of human history and these descriptions are worth studying because they represent the "body of knowledge" on these problems. Although not all humans, nor all clients, experience or want to experience these fundamental problems (and that is their good right and freedom), we think it important to consider in all clients the relation of the actually experienced conflict to conceptualizations of the universal conflict and find out what effective therapeutic insight and action this could bring.

2. We emphasized in the introduction that the concept of the universal is not meant to promote abstraction and metaphysical thinking. On the contrary, it is meant to help people experience the essence of their problems instead of only the various manifestations of it. This poses the question of the relation between the universal and the particular (Bohm, 1987). Human beings have concrete problems and symptoms and every approach which takes people seriously has to start there and not elsewhere (for example through "reformulating" the patient's problem). In this respect, Kaiser made an important distinction between the universal conflict and the universal symptom. The latter refers to the concrete behavior of the patient. Maybe one of the reasons why existential-phenomenological thinking in psychiatry and clinical

psychology has not had the impact it deserves is that it was lacking in concreteness. Rogers has indicated (see the quotation in the introduction) that starting from the concrete individual patient one can meet the universal if there is the willingness to go to the core of the problem and to fundamental change rather than superficial modifications. In order to be concrete, a high level of empathy, respect and genuineness is necessary (Rogers, 1957). To get to the core of the problem and to fundamental change, a therapist also needs a feeling of what in general are the basic core-conflicts of human life. This prevents him from following all kinds of fashionable approaches, "methods" and "techniques," which are just incidental, limited and time-bound myths and illusions (Van Kalmthout & Van der Ven, 1985). So on the one hand we respect the concrete form in which the everlasting human problems present themselves, but on the other hand emphasize the importance of experiencing the basic forms human problems tend to take, which are of all time and all cultures. Kaiser has formulated a good balance between the universal symptom and the universal conflict, the first being the expression of the latter. In his theory there is also a causal link between the two, and also between these two and the third universal, namely the universal therapy. This also is a necessary requisite for any theory about the universal.

3. The concept of the universal implies the idea that human "core" problems and "therapies" which are of all times, of all cultures, and thus of all humankind can be formulated. This is not to say that there are no variable, historically and culturally determined forms of psychopathology and psychotherapy. Rather our thesis proposes that there are perennial constants in human problems and their solutions: These constants are called here universals. This also implies that for every person there is the same condition to *experience,* aside from all the different historically and culturally determined forms. This is, in our opinion, the basis for the science and practice of experiential psychotherapy. Such therapy is directed at helping people to see *what is* (Gendlin, 1962; Mahrer, 1978; Osbourne & Baldwin, 1982; Rogers, 1980; Wagner et al., 1984). This "seeing" of course implies a lot of things, like accepting one's fundamental loneliness, one's inevitable death, one's individual responsibility, etc. Experiencing in this sense is contrary to "illusions", myths, etc., about reality, but directed at experiencing reality as it is (inside and out) and thus promoting

integration, which is equivalent to dissolving conflicts.

4. We stressed the importance of being concrete instead of abstract and metaphysical, which is sometimes the case when people talk about *the* universal. Experiential psychotherapy is in our opinion a good vehicle to combine the existentialists' interest in the most fundamental questions of life and the concreteness of humanistic and other therapies. One special field now emerging in our circles seems especially apt for studying the universal, namely the experiential study of dream therapy (see, Gendlin, 1986; Vossen, 1986). In dreams, universal human symbols representing universal human conflicts, as well as fundamental personality changes, manifest themselves in the most concrete unique form of the particular person in the stage of his development. Another interesting field of research here is the study of so-called critical moments in therapy (Mahrer & Nadler, 1986). These critical moments also seem to contain deep fundamental universal conflicts and changes, again in a very concrete and personal form.

In the introduction we formulated our concern regarding the increasing fragmentation in psychopathology and psychotherapy. In our conclusion we place even more stress on the importance of exploring alternative routes in psychopathology and psychotherapy which counteract this fragmentation and promote a more integrative approach. There is one other important argument for undertaking such an endeavor: Behind the fashionable DSM-III approach and psychotherapeutic eclecticism is the old medical model of diagnosis and therapy (Buttler & Strupp, 1986). Existential-humanistic thinking, and other approaches too, have always had good arguments not to follow that line in the field of human suffering and healing (Rogers, 1957; Mahrer, 1978). The contemporary, renewed fashion of psychiatric categorization and "treatment" challenges those opposed to that view to further an approach which seems more respectful of human beings. We are aware that our article is just a modest contribution to that undertaking and that many serious questions remain in the search for universal concepts. Hopefully, our preliminary search will stimulate others to join us in this difficult, but worthwhile undertaking.

NOTE

1. The collected works of Kaiser were edited after his death by some of his friends: Fierman (1965).

REFERENCES

American Psychiatric Association (1980). *Diagnostic and statistical manual of mental disorders (DSM-III)* (3rd ed.). Washington, DC: American Psychiatric Association.

American Psychiatric Association (1987). *Diagnostic and statistical manual of mental disorders (DSM-III-R)* (3rd revised ed.). Washington, DC: American Psychiatric Association.

Becker, A. (1973). *The denial of death.* New York: The Free Press.

Bohm, D. (1987). *Unfolding meaning. A weekend dialogue with David Bohm.* London: Routledge & Kegan.

Butler, S., & Strupp, H.H. (1986). Specific and nonspecific factors in psychotherapy: A problematic paradigm for psychotherapy research. *Psychotherapy, 23,* 30-40.

Ellenberger, H.F. (1970). *The discovery of the unconscious. The history and evolution of dynamic psychiatry.* New York: Basic Books.

Fierman, L.B. (1965). *Effective psychotherapy. The contribution of Hellmuth Kaiser.* New York: The Free Press.

Frank, J.D. (1974). *Persuasion and healing. A comparative study of psychotherapy* (rev. ed.). New York: Schocken Books.

Frank, J.D. (1978). *Psychotherapy and the human predicament.* New York: Schocken Books.

Garfield, S.L. (1982). Eclecticism and integration in psychotherapy. *Behavior Therapy, 13,* 610-623.

Gendlin, E.T. (1962). *Experiencing and the creation of meaning.* New York: The Free Press.

Gendlin, E.T. (1986). *Let your body interpret your dreams.* Wilmette, IL: Chiron Publications.

Herink, R. (Ed.) (1980). *The psychotherapy handbook.* New York: New American Library.

Kazdin, A.E. (1986). The evaluation of psychotherapy: Research design and methodology. In S.L. Garfield & A.E. Bergin (Eds.), *Handbook of psychotherapy and behavior change* (3rd ed., pp. 23-68). New York: Wiley.

Mahrer, A.R. (1978). *Experiencing: A humanistic theory of psychology and psychiatry.* New York: Brunner/Mazel.

Mahrer, A.R., & Nadler, W.P. (1986). Good moments in psychotherapy: A preliminary review, a list, and some promising research avenues. *Journal of Consulting and Clinical Psychology, 54,* 10-15.

396

Osbourne, J.W., & Baldwin, J.R. (1982). Psychotherapy: From one state of illusion to another? *Psychotherapy: Theory, Research, and Practice, 19,* 266-275.

Paul, G.L. (1967). Outcome research in psychotherapy. *Journal of Consulting Psychology, 31,* 109-118.

Rogers, C.R. (1957). The necessary and sufficient conditions of therapeutic personality change. *Journal of Consulting and Clinical Psychology, 21,* 95-103.

Rogers, C.R. (1963). The actualizing tendency in relation to "motives" and to consciousness. In M. Jones (Ed.), *Nebraska symposium on motivation* (pp. 1-24) Lincoln: University of Nebraska Press.

Rogers, C.R. (1977) [1961]. *On becoming a person.* London: Constable.

Rogers, C.R. (1980a). *A way of being.* Boston: Houghton Mifflin.

Rogers, C.R. (1980b). Empathic: An unappreciated way of being. In C.R. Rogers, *A way of being* (pp. 137-163). Boston: Houghton Mifflin.

Skinner, B.F. (1953). *Science and human behavior.* New York: McMillan.

Szasz, Th. (1961). *Myth of mental illness.* New York: Harper and Row.

Szasz, Th. (1979). *The myth of psychotherapy. Mental healing as religion, rhetoric, and repression.* New York: Anchor.

Van Kalmthout, M.A., & Van der Ven, A.H.G.S. (1985). The basic structure of psychotherapy as exemplified in hypnotherapy. In M.A. Van Kalmthout, C.P.F. Schaap, & F. Wojciechowski (Eds.), *Common factors in psychotherapy.* Lisse, The Netherlands: Swets & Zeitlinger.

Vossen, A.J.M. (1986). Rogeriaanse droomtherapie. In R. Van Balen, M. Leijssen & G. Lietaer (Eds.), *Droom en werkelijkheid in client-centered psychotherapie* (pp. 23-48). Leuven/Amersfoort: Acco.

Wagner, A.C., Barz, M., Maier-Störmer, S., Uttendorfer-Marek, I., & Weidle, R. (1984). *Bewusstseinskonflikte im Schulalltag. Denkknoten bei Lehrern und Schülern erkennen und lösen* (Chap. 1 and 7). Weinheim & Basel: Beltz Verlag.

Yalom, I.D. (1980). *Existential psychotherapy.* New York: Basic Books.

FUNDAMENTAL DIMENSIONS IN EXPERIENTIAL THERAPY: NEW DIRECTIONS IN RESEARCH

Laura N. RICE & Leslie S. GREENBERG
York University, Toronto, Canada

In this chapter we will describe a research program in which we have been engaged for a number of years. We will discuss some of the conclusions we have reached and some of the directions that we plan to follow in the future.

The central goal of this research program is to identify and attempt to understand the in-therapy client processes that lead to therapeutic change in client-centered and other experiential therapies. Although ultimately we need to study the cumulative change processes over the whole course of therapy, our main focus has been on the classes of identifiable change events in which some important shift takes place within a single session. These are events in which there has been some crucial shift in the way the client experiences self and self-in-the-world. While the essential focus is on identifying client processes, we also focused on the ways in which these processes could best be facilitated by the therapist.

This research direction was initially guided by our own clinical observations and by conclusions based on earlier process research (Rice, 1973; Rice & Wagstaff, 1967). One important conclusion was that client process needs to be studied within the context in which it takes place. A given type of client process might be highly productive in the context of one kind of event and quite unproductive in the context of another. Although some client process measures summed across an interview do yield suggestive relationships with outcome, such relationships may be weak even when it is a potentially important process, because this process has different significance in different contexts (Rice & Greenberg, 1984).

Our second key conclusion was that there are sequences of client-therapist interchanges that form recognizable "events" within a therapy, events that seem to recur often within and across clients. The specific content in these events will be different for different clients or for the same client at different times, but there are structural similarities that characterize the different classes of events.

Although a successful therapy has a wholeness that is crucially important and is unique to each client-therapist team, our view is that it can also be viewed as involving the client's engagement in the resolution of a series of affective-cognitive processing tasks. Such potential change events begin with a "marker" that signifies that the client is currently motivated to explore some area of functioning. These change events also involve a set of interactions between client and therapist that have a particular structure. When resolution is successfully reached there is a sense that something important has been resolved. Experienced therapists often intuitively recognize such opportunities for change and develop a feel for the ways in which the process can be facilitated. The goal of our research program has been to build on such clinical recognition in a way that will yield explicit understanding of the processes in which the client needs to engage, and some knowledge of how these processes can best be facilitated by the therapist at each stage. Some client-centered therapists would disagree with the proposal that therapists should respond selectively to different kinds of client markers in order to facilitate particular kinds of client process at particular times. They not only view it as unnecessary to be selective if the Rogerian relationship conditions are truly present, but they also consider that the therapist's engagement in purposive and selective responding would interfere with the spontaneity and genuineness of the relationship (Brodley, 1990).

Our view is that the approach that we are proposing is quite consistent with the basic Rogerian assumptions about human functioning that underlie client-centered therapy. The most basic assumption of client-centered therapy, and most other experiential therapies, is that human beings are fundamentally motivated toward growth and wholeness, toward developing their full potential (Rogers, 1959). A closely related Rogerian assumption is that people are informed by their own organismic reactions to situations. Under favorable conditions these experiences can be symbolized accurately in awareness and can provide the most trustworthy guide available for personal growth (Rogers, 1959).

Restated in our terms, the implication is that growth can be blocked for many people by the way in which they have learned to process some of their own organismic experience. But if these processing blocks can be overcome, and the person can become more open to internal and external experience, growth can proceed. Therefore a crucial function of the therapist is to try to facilitate the client's accurate access to this experiential level by selectively responding at times when the client is experiencing particular kinds of processing blocks.

One further point needs to be clarified here. We make a distinction between the "primary relationship conditions" and the "task-relevant relationship conditions" (Rice, 1983). The primary relationship conditions are the conditions viewed by Rogers (1957) as necessary and sufficient for therapeutic change. In our view these lead *directly* to crucial new experiential learning for the client. The task-relevant relationship conditions are those that establish optimal working conditions that enable the client to engage in the different kinds of processes needed for particular kinds of change tasks. Although the task-relevant conditions will be somewhat different for each of the different change tasks, they are consistent with the primary relationship conditions.

THE RATIONAL-EMPIRICAL APPROACH

To engage in the type of research program described above we needed a discovery-oriented methodological approach that would allow us to remain close to the clinical data and retain a freshness of observation, but that would also provide rigorous cumulative results from our intensive observations of therapeutic process. In addition we believed it was important to move beyond purely naturalistic observation and to allow theoretical considerations to guide our observations.

We therefore adopted a rational-empirical approach adapted from the study of problem solving (Greenberg, 1984b). This allowed us in the rational phase to tap the rich source of ideas drawn from theory and clinical experience in experiential therapy. In the empirical phase it allowed us to engage in a process of increasingly rigorous observation against which to compare our rational conjectures. This approach, which involves moving back and forth between theory (explicit or implicit) and observation of concrete phenomena in order to describe more accurately the phenomena under study, is described in *Patterns of change* (Rice & Greenberg, 1984) and has become the foundation of our investigative approach. It results in the progressive construction of models to capture the continued discoveries and refinements that result from oscillating between ideas and data, and between reflections on invariance in the data back to observations of the data. This process continues in order to confirm or disconfirm one's earlier models until such time as further observation no longer yields further discoveries, and one's model is believed to capture the phenomenon under study. We utilized this approach to identify and understand key classes of change events that seemed to recur within and across clients and to map out the client paths to resolution, and then to identify the ways in which they could best be facilitated by the therapist.

PROCESS DIAGNOSIS

As we mentioned earlier, we view therapy as involving not only the crucially important primary relationship conditions but also involving task-relevant conditions that enable the client to engage in a whole series of cognitive-affective processing tasks (Rice, 1984). We assume that if there are processing difficulties that interfere with accurate access to one's own inner experience, then growth and satisfying functioning are blocked to some extent. Therefore psychotherapy is designed to facilitate the client's reprocessing of experience that has previously been incompletely processed or even distorted. Our further assumption is that the presence of different types of current processing difficulties is indicated by different classes of client markers. Each class of marker is an indication that the client is currently experiencing a particular kind of processing difficulty, and that he/she is currently motivated to explore it.

Therefore one of the principles that characterize our whole approach is the importance of what we call "process diagnosis." The therapist is listening and responding empathically to the client's internal frame of reference. But he/she is also listening for markers that indicate the presence at this moment of a particular kind of processing difficulty, and responds selectively to these markers. Since a marker usually also indicates the client's readiness to explore the issue, this selective responding is not felt by the client to be too influencing or non-empathic. We are not drawing any diagnostic conclusions about the person as a whole, and we are not making any assumptions about the particular content that needs to emerge. We are making the diagnosis that, if the therapist can enable the client to engage successfully in a sequence of particular kinds of processes, the client will be able to reprocess and resolve some important area of experience in a more satisfying and growth-producing way.

Our second basic principle is that the therapist is *process-directive* but not usually content-directive. The therapist is process-directive in the sense of trying to enable the person to engage in a sequence of processes that could lead to successful resolution. The therapist has a map of the type and sequences of processes which are likely to be productive, and an awareness of how these processes can best be facilitated.

The therapist is seldom content-directive, and does not make assumptions about the content that the client needs to access. The content involved in a particular processing difficulty is likely to be idiosyncratic, and thus any attempt to pre-judge an optimal product of processing would interfere with the client's accurate processing of his/ her own organismic experience. Our assumption is that only the client has privileged access to the crucial experiential data needed for resuming growth, and that any content assumptions on the part of the therapist might interfere with the person's discovery of the particular flavor of his/her own inner experience.

Our experience has been that selective, process-directive responding at different markers does not need to interfere with the spontaneity and genuineness of the relationship. Furthermore the client is still the judge of the extent to which he/she wants to engage in the processes suggested by the therapist. The therapist typically makes suggestions and selective reflections. If the client chooses not to follow them, the therapist usually returns to the mode of empathic reflection.

IDENTIFICATION OF CHANGE EVENTS

The evocative unfolding of problematic reactions

Rice (1974) identified a particular kind of change event which involved clients' describing and exploring some incident in which they reacted in a way that seemed unexpected, inappropriate, or otherwise problematic. When clients were encouraged to explore the incident in a live and vivid way, they were often able to reprocess the experience more completely and to discover the nature of their own idiosyncratic construal of some features of the stimulus situation, and to recognize this construal as leading to their own problematic reaction. This seemed to fit well with the basic Rogerian assumption that one's inner and outer reactions depend on the way in which stimulus situations are perceived (Rogers, 1959). Thus it seemed that these problematic reactions were triggered because some feature of the situation activated some important self-relevant schema rather than the schema that would have been appropriate to that situation. When the experience was re-evoked in therapy, clients were amazingly well able to remember stimulus aspects and internal reactions that had not been fully processed in awareness at the time. They were able to recognize the link between such construals and their own problematic reaction. In some cases they also spontaneously recognized this kind of reaction as an example of a much broader style of functioning.

Following our rational-empirical approach, the "marker" that signaled clients' readiness for this kind of search was specified, and the different stages that seemed to lead to resolution and change were identified (Rice & Saperia, 1984). A preliminary empirical test of the effectiveness of this approach was conducted, comparing the "evocative unfolding" approach with the more usual client-centered reflections at a similar marker, yielding a significant difference in client satisfaction in favor of the interview using the evocative approach. Perceived empathy on the Barrett-Lennard Relationship Inventory (Barrett-Lennard, 1986) was equal in the two treatments.

Later empirical studies, improved and extended the model and provided evidence for the effectiveness of the specified therapist interventions (Lowenstein 1984; Wiseman, 1986; Wiseman & Rice, 1989). The evocative unfolding of problematic reactions is described in detail in Rice and Greenberg (1984).

Two-chair dialogues

Greenberg (1979, 1984) identified a change event involving the Gestalt therapy intervention of promoting a dialogue between two different aspects of experience. This dialogue seemed to be particularly effective when people were currently experiencing an internal conflict in which two tendencies or aspects of the self were in opposition. This type of dialogue often led to the recognition or owning of certain aspects of experience, and resulted in conflict resolution. By bringing the conflict between the two aspects fully into awareness and by having the two parts make contact with each other, the differences were reduced and the probability of an integration between the two opposing views was enhanced. Thus if the client was able to identify with, and speak from, each aspect to the other, a process of internal listening emerged.

Using our rational-empirical approach we identified the client marker that signalled a readiness for two chair dialogue (Greenberg, 1979, 1984). This marker, which we called a "conflict-split," signalled client's readiness to engage in a self-evaluation dialogue involving a critic and an experiencer. Intensive analysis of a number of resolution dialogues revealed that clients followed an identifiable performance pattern involving a sequential set of steps. A key step in the resolution process was the softening of the previously harsh critic. The resolution of conflict splits by two chair dialogue is described in detail in Rice and Greenberg (1984).

Having specified the marker and the intervention, we compared the use of this intervention at a split with reflection of feeling at a split, in both analogue (Greenberg & Clarke, 1979), and clinical studies (Greenberg & Dompierre, 1981), and found significant effects on in-session process and post-session outcomes in favor of two-chair dialogue. It is important to note that in all instances the therapists using the two-chair dialogue were perceived as equally empathic on the Barrett-Lennard Relationship Inventory. In further empirical studies we demonstrated that two-chair dialogue was more effective than cognitive problem solving in helping to resolve decisional conflict (Clarke & Greenberg, 1986), and finally were able to relate certain steps of the resolution process depicted in the model to treatment outcome (Greenberg & Webster,1982).

We have also begun to investigate a further type of change event using dialogue. In this event the client, rather than engaging in an intrapsychic dialogue between parts of the self, engages in an interpersonal dialogue with an imagined significant other in the other chair in order to resolve unfinished business (Greenberg & Safran, 1987). In a recent analogue study we found that this form of empty chair dialogue with a significant other led to greater tolerance toward the other and a greater sense of personal optimism than did empathic reflection alone (King, 1988).

THE PROCESS-EXPERIENTIAL APPROACH

Our initial interest in identifying and studying change events centered around the goal of improving the effectiveness of particular orientations, such as client-centered and Gestalt. Then as we gained more understanding of the client processes that were necessary for resolution of each class of change events, it seemed intuitively clear that the different kinds of change events could supplement each other, contributing different kinds of change processes and different effects.

We also concluded that both evocative unfolding and two-chair dialogue could be included within a basically client-centered relationship in a way that would be consistent with the primary relationship conditions and the basic underlying assumptions. In both of these kinds of events the therapist relates to the client with empathy, respect, and genuineness. Both can be integrated into a single treatment because they share general assumptions about client change. Both of these kinds of change tasks are oriented toward facilitating people in making their own discoveries rather than having therapists implementing their own assumptions about the content that needs to be recognized. In both kinds of event the client is viewed as the only one with privileged access to his/her own experience, while the therapist is viewed as possessing knowledge about how to facilitate *processes* that are likely to be productive.

We concluded that this "process-experiential" therapy, based on process-diagnosis and combining a variety of interventions for specific processing difficulties, included within the primary relationship conditions, was a potentially powerful approach.

DIMENSIONALITY

Then we started asking ourselves why we felt that these different events would supplement each other. As clinicians we had observed that they seemed to address successfully quite different kinds of experienced problems, but it seemed important to examine these differences from a more theoretical perspective. In attempting to understand the psychotherapeutic change processes in terms of basic psychological theory, we have felt that the most relevant concepts were those of cognitive-affective information processing. The importance of cognitive psychology as a theoretical framework had been shared by a number of the contributors to the book *Innovations in client-centered therapy* (Wexler & Rice, 1974). Since then, the increasing emphasis in theoretical psychology on affective processing (Greenberg & Safran, 1987; Zajonc, 1980) has increased the relevance of information processing for understanding experiential therapies, enabling us not only to think of dysfunction in terms of cognitive-affective processing difficulties, but also to think about the modes of processing that are needed in order to overcome these difficulties.

In thinking about the kinds of cognitive-affective processing involved in the different classes of change events, and the ways in which these led to change, it seemed clear that different client modes of engagement were mobilized in the different events, and that these different performances addressed different processing needs in the different events. Our conclusion was that these different kinds of client engagement accessed schematic structures in different ways in promoting resolution.

We concluded that the different modes of client engagement necessary for resolving the different change tasks seemed to cluster along different dimensions. These modes involved different in-session client styles of affective information processing. When clients were engaged in unfolding problematic reactions they were processing information in such a way as to re-experience the situation to some extent, and their attentional energy was turned inward, toward accessing their own immediate inner experience and trying to symbolize it in awareness. We decided to call this dimension "experiential search." We concluded that Gendlin's "focusing" (Gendlin, 1981, 1984) also belonged to this dimension. Although the focusing process is facilitated by the therapist in quite different ways, and might be maximally useful at different kinds of markers, both focusing and evocative unfolding involve this kind of experiential search process.

The mode of engagement in the two-chair approach to conflict-splits is very different. Although there is some experiential search, the client's energy is invested in actively and spontaneously expressing his/her own immediate experiential reactions. This is a process of discovering and acknowledging through doing, and involves a particular type of information processing. In this process the client is asked to enact certain aspects of experience in order to recognize from what is expressed what is being felt, and to own it as his/her own. The process of expressing appears to activate a certain experience which emerges vividly into awareness, demanding attention. In addition, in this event, change is facilitated by expression from one part of the self toward another part of self, promoting contact and confrontation between the two conflicting aspects of the experience. This produces a differentiation and integration of the two aspects.

We decided to call this dimension "active expression." Although the markers and processing difficulties addressed are somewhat different in the different Gestalt experiments, clearly the two-chair experiment at a split and the empty-chair dialogue for unfinished business utilize a similar type of active expression and belong on this same dimension.

We feel that thinking in terms of dimensionality of client engagement can be an important direction. The different dimensions of client mode of engagement are the visible signs of the different kinds of cognitive-affective processes required to access and modify certain kinds of schematic processing involved in the different processing difficulties.

THE INTERPERSONAL EXPERIENTIAL LEARNING DIMENSION

We have recently begun to describe and study a third dimension, involving the experiential learning that takes place in the relationship with the therapist. The therapeutic conditions specified by Rogers do much more than facilitate the "work" of therapy. They have a direct cumulative impact, in and of themselves. For instance empathy as defined by Rogers (1957) conveys to clients that the therapist has a very basic trust in their inner experience as a source of information for guiding their own lives, enabling clients to feel and act on this trust. Unconditional positive regard, when truly experienced by the therapist, conveys to clients that they are valued and respected just as they are, not as someone valued for particular qualities, or as someone to be shaped up. This is extremely affirming, enabling them to respect themselves. They can thus begin to let go of artificially imposed criteria, and make their own unique changes. True therapist congruence provides a unique experience with a real person, in which each one can respond to their own feeling safely and responsibly.

Although the consistency of this relationship over the course of therapy is important, there do seem to be recognizable and powerful relationship events that take place within a single session. Identifying and selectively facilitating them could increase the cumulative effects of the primary relationship. We call this third dimension "interpersonal experiential learning."

We have identified and studied one such event which we call "empathic prizing at a vulnerability marker" (Rice & Greenberg, in press). As clinicians we had encountered moments when a client was starting to express, often with great difficulty, some intense present emotional experience such as fear of the future or despair about his/her live. These moments had a special quality that suggested to us that this was not a time to try to facilitate experiential search nor to instigate what we have called "active expression." This seemed to be a time for the therapist to resonate empathically with the client's feelings, and to reflect them in their full intensity, without being scared, clearly and genuinely respecting and prizing the client. We found that when we were truly able to respond in this way at such times, clients were able to go deeper and deeper into the feeling until they seemed to "touch bottom" and were able to start up again. Clients seemed to experience a sense of relief and wholeness. The effect seemed to be much more than catharsis. The client had taken the risk of entering deeply into a feared experience, and the therapist, rather than being shocked or frightened, was clearly resonating to it as a shared human experience. This seems to break the sense of isolation and fragmentation.

ILLUSTRATIONS OF DIMENSIONS

In order to convey some feel for the three dimensions of client involvement, a brief excerpt from an event from each dimension is given below. The full events were, of course more complicated.

Experiential search

The problematic reaction that this client reported involved the intense anxiety she had experienced in walking down an empty hotel corridor. After the scene was re-evoked and re-experienced to some extent, she began the intensive experiential search process. Her attention was turned inward, searching for the particular impact the situation had on her. With a continued internal focus she began to differentiate the meaning of the experience for her.

> C1: "The thing that gets me is those closed doors - that long row of doors - that's what got to me.
> T1: Something about that long row of closed doors -?
> C2: Yeah - I get a kind of spooky feeling - if there's music or voices - it's o.k. But if it's just silent - I don't know -
> T2: There's just something about that silence - something creepy -?
> C3: Yeah. There could be anything behind there.
> T3: Something lurking right behind that door -
> C4: But I feel that the room might be empty, and somehow that would be even worse.
> T4: Something about an echoing, empty room -
> C5: Yes. I'm all alone. Everybody has left."

This kind of internal search continues, and a new meaning is reached when she realizes that she had construed this corridor of empty rooms as total isolation. She was alone in an empty space. As the session continued she broadened her search and examined her fear of isolation, or even desertion, in other kinds of situations, and recognized that this had prevented her from seeking a kind of independence that she really wanted.

Active expression

A client involved in a two-chair dialogue expresses some of her harsh criticisms toward herself and continues with the expression of the other part in response.

> C1 : "You're useless, awful
> T1 : Do this some more -
> C2 : You're terrible, no good, just useless. You'll fail whatever you try. You're just no good at anything!
> T2 : Change. What happens for you when she says this to you. 'You're terrible, useless, no good.'
> C3 : I feel so overwhelmed - shattered like - what's the use of -
> T3 : Uhhuh shattered like - no use - even trying.
> C4 : (Client partially curls up in chair). Sighs.
> T4 : Uh huh I hear you sigh. What is your sigh saying as you curl up.
> C5 : Oh just I've had enough I'd like to go away somewhere nice and safe.
> T5 : Yeah just get away from all this, this barrage. Just far away nice and protected, safe.
> C6 : Yeah just nice and protected, away from all these attacks.
> T6 : Uh huh, can you speak from this position, actually curl up into a

ball and tell me what it's like?

C7 : (Curls up in her chair) Well I feel all warm and cozy, kind of safe, safe from all the demands and criticisms, protected; here I'm safe.

T7 : Just safe and protected from the attacks, protecting yourself from your attacker.

C8 : Yeah, I wish she would lay off.T8: Tell her this.

C9 : Yeah just lay off, leave me alone, let me be.

T9 : Tell her what you need from her.

C10: I just need you to let me be. I need some peace and quiet... and just some time - yeah - just time and space to be me."

The client in this segment actively expresses different aspects of her experience. First she actually attacks and criticizes herself. Then she moves her position and expresses what it feels like to be attacked. She then actually takes on a physical posture and speaks from that position. Here the active expression leads to a discovery and recognition of what she is expressing and finally to an assertion of need to the other side. This expression establishes contact between different aspects of experience and toward the creation of the context for a new synthesis out of the dialectical process.

Interpersonal experience

This woman had lost her husband and her brother in the last three years. She continued to function adequately in her job, but was experiencing avoidance anxiety and depression.

C1: "Just now I was thinking of someone at work mentioning a woman who took her own life. She just couldn't take it any more. I can understand that ... the pressure. It's the pressure that eventually can get to you. I just thought - there is so much going on - the pressure - it doesn't quit. Then I think 'I just have to keep going.'

T1: So there's pressure - day after day. But you just have to keep going.

C2: I'm dealing with it on the outside. But inside I don't feel very strong. It's like I don't have anything left. It's like I'm pulling from something but I don't feel like there's much there.

T2: Uh huh. So it's like pulling from an empty well. And there just isn't anything left right now."

In the context of the therapist's empathic responses the client arrives at her inner despair - that there is little strength left. When the therapist responds to her inner despair in its full intensity - that the well is empty - in an empathic, prizing manner, this has an important impact. She begins to cry, and expresses the intensity of her despair.

> C3: (Cries) "Yeah. The well is empty. It's been too long - just too long.
> T3: It's been a long, long struggle.
> C4: Like I don't want to go on.
> T5: If they are gone, it's like I don't want to carry on any more."

She continues, revealing her fear of going mad and her sense of hopelessness. Then, after she seemed to "touch bottom," she started to pull upward a bit. She begins to talk about her frustration at the new opportunities she is missing - a new, interesting job she could have had.

> C6: "I'm so aware of what I clamp off - all that excitement - the possibilities of what I could do.
> T6: Yeah, and you really want to live and enjoy things.
> C7: Yeah, I really do. (long pause) It's been important for me to be able to talk like this - because it's me."

RESEARCH PROGRAM

We are currently planning a research program in which the effects of a marker-driven experiential therapy, which we are calling "process-experiential" therapy, will be examined in detail. Although the efficacy of each of the separate tasks incorporated in this approach has been studied to some extent, we want to study the effects of an integrated, marker-driven approach.

Robert Elliott, who has worked with us, is currently studying the efficacy of a marker-driven approach with a depressed population, with an emphasis on understanding the client's view of the change process (Elliott, Clark, Kemeny, Wexler, Mack, & Brinkerhoff, 1990).

The population in our study will be adults suffering from a combination of high anxiety, moderate depression, and interpersonal and identity problems. The therapy offered will be time-limited, involving approximately 16 weekly sessions. Half of the clients will receive the process-experiential, marker-driven therapy, which will involve the primary relationship conditions plus the inclusion of two kinds of events from the experiential search dimension - focusing when the person is on the surface of his/her experience or is confused, and evocative unfolding at problematic reactions - and three kinds of events from the active expression dimension - two-chair dialogue at conflict splits, two-chair dialogue at subject-object splits, and empty-chair work on unfinished business. Each of these events will be instigated and facilitated by the therapist at the appropriate markers. The other half of the clients will receive a therapy involving the primary relationship conditions from well-trained and experienced client-centered therapists who have not been trained in the marker-driven approach.

Although our chief interest is in studying the change processes in the marker-driven process-experiential therapy, the comparison with client-centered therapy as it is usually practiced will enable us to ask three important questions. The first question is whether or not the marker-driven component adds to the effectiveness of usual client-centered therapy, conducted by experienced therapists. The second question we are asking is whether or not the relationship will be perceived on the Barrett-Lennard Inventory as positively in the process-experiential therapy as it is by clients in the client-centered therapy. The third and most detailed kind of analysis will involve studying the whole process of change. For instance we will be making detailed analyses of the effects of each kind of marker-driven task on: 1. The level and kind of process in that session as assessed by the Experiencing Scale (Klein, Mathieu-Coughlan, & Kiesler, 1986), and Client Vocal Quality (Rice & Wagstaff, 1967; Rice & Kerr, 1986) and 2. The effects on session change as assessed by newly constructed, task-relevant post-session and inter-session measures completed by the clients. Each of these measures will be related to final outcome and follow-up.

FUTURE DIRECTIONS

We would like to conclude by mentioning some developments in experiential therapy that we hope will take place.

Experienced therapists have a rich store of process hypotheses, based on their experiences at particular points in therapy. As clinician-investigators they are in a position to try out some of these ideas in their therapy practice, and to observe the effects that follows. They would also be able to use a rational-empirical approach to constructing a model of the change processes involved in successful resolution. This is a creative and exciting process for the clinician-investigator, enriching the way one trains and supervises therapists as well as enriching one's own practice.

We hope that some of them will be interested in identifying and studying new kinds of change events from the above three dimensions or from new dimensions, and sharing them with the field. Events from the relationship dimension might be especially interesting to study further. For instance in Lietaer's (1984) chapter on unconditional positive regard, he raises several issues that might lead to the identification of interesting markers. For example an interesting marker might be identified at a time when unconditional positive regard is seemingly in conflict with the congruence of the therapist. It could then be profitable to study the ensuing client-therapist interactions that lead to a positive outcome in such encounters.

In any kind of process-experiential approach two questions need to be asked before incorporating new tasks from these three dimensions or form new dimensions. 1. Would they supplement the process-experiential approach by addressing different kinds of processing difficulties or even by drawing on different dimensions of client engagement? 2. Would they violate the basic assumptions about human functioning that underlie client-centered and most other experiential therapies?

We feel strongly that programs of systematic rational-empirical research in experiential therapies of the type we have suggested could make important contributions to the psychotherapy literature on research and practice. Clinician-investigators are in a position to conduct change-process research that could clarify and enrich the change processes in client-centered and other experiential therapies.

REFERENCES

Barrett-Lennard, G.T. (1986). The Relationship Inventory now: Issues and advances in theory, method, and use. In L.S. Greenberg & W.M. Pinsof (Eds.), *The psychotherapy process: A research handbook* (pp. 439-476). New York: Guilford.

Brodley, B.T. (1990). Client-centered and experiential - Two different therapies. See this volume.

Clarke, K., & Greenberg, L. (1986). The differential effects of Gestalt two-chair and cognitive problem solving in resolving decisional conflict. *Journal of Counseling Psychology, 33,* 11-15.

Elliott, R., Clarke, C., Kemeny, V., Wexler, M.M., Mack, C., & Brinkerhoff, J. (1990). *The impact of experiential therapy on depression.* See this volume.

Gendlin, E.T. (1981). *Focusing.* New York: Bantam.

Gendlin, E.T. (1984). The client's client: The edge of awareness. In R.L. Levant & J.M. Shlien (Eds.), *Client-centered therapy and the person-centered approach* (pp. 76-107). New York: Praeger.

Greenberg, L.S. (1979). Resolving splits: The two-chair technique. *Psychotherapy: Theory, Research, and Practice, 16,* 310-318.

Greenberg, L.S. (1980). The intensive analysis of recurring events from the practice of Gestalt therapy. *Psychotherapy, Theory, Research & Practice, 17,* 143-152.

Greenberg, L.S. (1984a). Task analysis of intrapersonal conflict. In L.N. Rice & L.S. Greenberg (Eds.), *Patterns of change: Intensive analysis of psychotherapy process* (pp. 67-123). New York: Guilford.

Greenberg, L.S. (1984b). Task analysis: The general approach. In L.N. Rice & L.S. Greenberg (Eds.), *Patterns of change: Intensive analysis of psychotherapy process* (pp. 124-148). New York: Guilford.

Greenberg, L.S., & Clarke, K.M. (1979). The differential effects of Gestalt two-chair dialogue and empathic reflections at a conflict marker. *Journal of Counseling Psychology, 26,* 1-8.

Greenberg, L.S., & Dompierre, L. (1981). The specific effects of Gestalt two-chair dialogue on intrapsychic conflict in counselling. *Journal of Counseling Psychology, 24,* 288-294.

Greenberg, L.S., & Safran, J.D. (1987). *Emotion in psychotherapy.* New York: Guilford.

Greenberg, L.S., & Webster, M. (1982). Resolving decisional conflict: Relating process to outcome. *Journal of Counseling Psychology, 29,* 468-477.

King, S. (1988). *The differential effects of empty chair dialogue and empathic reflection for unfinished business.* Unpublished master's thesis. University of British Columbia, Vancouver, B.C.

Klein, M.H., Mathieu-Coughlan, P., & Kiesler, D.J. (1986). The experiencing scales. In L.S. Greenberg & W. Pinsof (Eds.), *The psychotherapeutic process: A research handbook* (pp. 21-73). New York: Guilford.

Lietaer, G. (1984). Unconditional positive regard: A controversial basic attitude in client-centered therapy. In R.L. Levant & J.M. Shlien (Eds.), *Client-centered therapy and the person-centered approach* (pp. 41-58). New York: Praeger.

Lowenstein, J. (1985). *A test of a performance model of problematic reaction points and an examination of differential client performance in therapy.* Unpublished M.A. thesis. York University, Toronto.

Rice, L.N. (1973). Client behavior as a function of therapist style and client resources. *Journal of Counseling Psychology, 20,* 306-311.

Rice, L.N. (1974). The evocative function of the therapist. In D.A. Wexler & L.N. Rice (Eds.), *Innovations in client-centered therapy* (pp. 289-311). New York: Wiley.

Rice, L.N. (1983). The relationship in client-centered therapy. In M.J. Lambert (Ed.), *Psychotherapy and patient relationships* (pp. 36-60). Homewood, IL: Dow-Jones Irwin.

Rice, L.N. (1984). Client tasks in client-centered therapy. In R.L. Levant & J.M.

414

Shlien (Eds.), *Client-centered therapy and the person-centered approach* (pp. 261-277). New York: Praeger.

Rice, L.N., & Greenberg, L.S. (1984). The new research paradigm. In L.N. Rice & L.S. Greenberg (Eds.), *Patterns of change: Intensive analysis of psychotherapy process* (pp. 7-26). New York: Guilford.

Rice, L.N., & Greenberg, L.S. (in press). Two affective change events in client-centered therapy. In J. Safran & L.S. Greenberg (Eds.), *Affective change events in psychotherapy*. New York: Academic Press.

Rice, L.N., & Kerr, G. (1986). Measures of client and therapist vocal quality. In L.S. Greenberg & W. Pinsof (Eds.), *The psychotherapeutic process: A research handbook* (pp. 73-106). New York: Guilford.

Rice, L.N., & Saperia, E.P. (1984). Resolution of problematic reactions. In L.N. Rice & L.S. Greenberg (Eds.), *Patterns of change* (pp. 29-66). New York: Guilford.

Rice, L.N., & Wagstaff, A.K. (1967). Client voice quality and expressive style as indexes of productive psychotherapy. *Journal of Consulting Psychology, 31,* 557-563.

Rogers, C.R. (1957). The necessary and sufficient conditions of therapeutic personality change. *Journal of Consulting Psychology, 21,* 95-103.

Rogers, C.R. (1959). A theory of therapy, personality and interpersonal relationships as developed in the client-centered framework. In S. Koch (Ed.), *Psychology: A study of a science. Vol. 3. Formulations of the person and the social context* (pp. 184-256). New York: McGraw-Hill.

Wexler, D.A., & Rice, L.N. (1974). *Innovations in client-centered therapy.* New York: Wiley.

Wiseman, H. (1986). *Single-case studies of the resolution of problematic reactions in short-term client-centered therapy: A task-focused approach.* Unpublished doctoral dissertation. York University, Toronto.

Wiseman, H., & Rice, L.N. (1989). Sequential analyses of therapist-client interaction during change events: A task-focused approach. *Journal of Consulting and Clinical Psychology, 57,* 281-286.

Zajonc, R.B. (1980). Feeling and thinking: Preferences need no inferences. *American Psychologist, 35,* 151-175.

THE NECESSARY CONDITIONS FOR EVALUATING CLIENT-CENTERED THERAPY

Duncan CRAMER
Loughborough University, United Kingdom

More than 30 years have passed since Rogers (1957) propounded his bold hypothesis that the only conditions necessary for therapeutic improvement are that the client should experience a certain minimal level of all three facilitative qualities of unconditional acceptance, empathy, and congruence from the therapist. The relationship between these facilitative conditions and therapeutic outcome is postulated to be a direct linear one in which higher levels produce greater improvement. This idea has stimulated considerable research (e.g., Gurman, 1977; Mitchell, Bozarth, & Krauft, 1977), some of which has provided support consistent with it (e.g., Barrett-Lennard, 1962; Rudolph, Langer, & Tausch, 1980). However, to date no single study has adequately tested this influential proposition, as has been recognized (e.g., Gurman, 1977; Watson, 1984).

As a first step towards rectifying this situation, the main conceptual and methodological conditions which need to be met will be briefly outlined and discussed in this chapter. Without agreement on what these are, future research may continue to remain inconclusive. One issue in particular receiving insufficient attention in the past is the problem of determining the causal nature of this hypothesis. While a true experimental design is the ideal way of doing this, its use raises various questions which have to be resolved before such a study should be attempted.

CLIENT PERCEPTION OF FACILITATIVE CONDITIONS

Rogers (1957) explicitly stated that for therapeutic improvement to occur it is the client who must perceive the therapist as providing the three facilitative conditions since it is this perception which initiates and brings about psychological change. For example, for the client to accept her or himself, she/he has to feel accepted by the therapist. In other words, it is not sufficient for these qualities simply to be present. They need to be conveyed to the client. In addition, since Rogers proposed that all three facilitative qualities are necessary for therapeutic improvement, all three should be assessed to determine if minimal levels have been experienced.

However, since the accuracy of the client's perception of these qualities has been questioned (Truax & Carkhuff, 1967), some studies have used trained outside observers to judge them, typically from a few 2- to 4-minute segments of tape-recorded therapy sessions (e.g., Bozarth, Mitchell, & Krauft, 1976; Garfield & Bergin, 1971). Any failure to find a significant relationship between therapeutic outcome and facilitativeness assessed in this way cannot be taken as evidence against Rogers' hypothesis since the qualities were not judged by the clients themselves. This argument is strengthened by the fact that one person's perception of these qualities is not always highly related to that of others in either clinical (e.g., Barrett-Lennard, 1962; Rogers, Gendlin, Kiesler, & Truax, 1967/1976) or nonclinical samples (e.g., Burstein & Carkhuff, 1968; McWhirter, 1973). This latter finding suggests the lack of agreement may not be due to the client's emotional disturbance. The client measure most frequently used to assess these qualities is the original Relationship Inventory (Barrett-Lennard, 1962), which was subsequently refined (Barrett-Lennard, 1964). This questionnaire distinguishes level of regard from its unconditionality, thereby forming four rather than three facilitative conditions. Items are worded to control for response set and the internal reliability of the test (as measured by split-half and alpha coefficients) is high for clinical samples (Gurman, 1977). The only study to factor analyse the interitem correlations in clients found some support for the factorial validity of its four scales (Lietaer, 1976). Further evidence for their validity comes from nonclinical studies where subjects described a current close relationship (Cramer, 1986a, 1986b).

While it is appropriate to separate unconditionality from level of regard, the affective value of unconditionality needs to be determined since unconditional negative regard is presumably less facilitative than conditional negative regard (Cramer, 1989). No study assessing unconditionality of regard in clients has done this (e.g., Barrett-Lennard, 1962; Rogers et al., 1967/1976). In addition, Rogers clearly proposed all three qualities need to be perceived to some minimal degree, which has been defined as their just noticeable presence (e.g., Mitchell et al., 1977; Rogers et al., 1967/1976). Consequently, it is essential to determine whether this proposition is true and if so to ensure that this condition is met (Cramer, 1986c). Once again, this has not been done in client studies.

Another client measure occasionally used (e.g., Sloane, Staples, Cristol, Yorkston, & Whipple, 1975) to assess these qualities is the Relationship Questionnaire (Truax & Carkhuff, 1967), although this is less satisfactory than the Relationship Inventory for the following three reasons. Very little information on its reliability and validity is available. It assesses the three facilitative qualities of accurate empathy, nonpossessive warmth, and genuineness, and so does not distinguish unconditionality from level of regard. Since some items tap two or all three of these conditions, the three scales are not independent.

INDIVIDUAL THERAPY

Rogers' hypothesis has been studied in both individual and group therapy. However, one problem in exploring this issue in group therapy is determining who the major therapeutic agent is and deciding what to do if some other person takes on this role during the period of investigation. Some studies of group therapy have assumed this agent to be the therapist (e.g., Truax, 1966) while others have given equal importance to every relationship in the group (e.g., Culbert, 1968). If neither assumption is wholly appropriate, the size of the relationship between the facilitative conditions and therapeutic outcome will be reduced. Consequently, it is simpler and more satisfactory to test this hypothesis in individual rather than in group therapy.

Indices of therapeutic outcome

These facilitative conditions bring about numerous changes in the client which have been specified (Rogers, 1959, 1961). Although acknowledging its arbitrariness, Rogers (1958) distinguishes the process of therapy from its outcome. Changes in the therapeutic process are not necessarily apparent outside it and are usually assessed by trained judges from short segments of tape-recorded sessions (e.g., Walker, Rablen, & Rogers, 1960) in terms of the following seven aspects of the client's behavior: 1. Relationship to feelings and personal meanings; 2. Manner of experiencing; 3. Incongruence; 4. Communication of self; 5. Personal constructs; 6. Relationship to problems; and 7. Manner of relating.

Indices of outcome reflecting more general and enduring changes include some of the following characteristics: 1. Self: Experience congruence; 2. Self: Ideal-Self congruence; 3. Anxiety; 4. Positive self-regard; 5. Locus of evaluation; 6. Acceptance of others; and 7. Locus of control. Although not stated as part of the central tenet of client-centered therapy but in keeping with its phenomenological framework, assessment of these variables from the client's perspective seems preferable. Various reliable measures of them are readily available such as the Rosenberg (1965) Self-Esteem Scale and the Zung (1974) Self-Rating Anxiety Scale. While more objective tests of therapeutic improvement and assessments from more viewpoints are desirable, this is often not practicable. Evidence suggesting substantial consensus between different observers (e.g., Mintz, Luborsky, & Cristoph, 1979) also make them less necessary.

Experimental designs and causal inference

TRUE EXPERIMENTAL DESIGNS

The ideal design for determining a causal relationship between therapeutic change and the facilitative conditions is a true experimental one (Campbell & Stanley, 1963), where clients are randomly assigned to treatments which only vary in the extent to which these facilitative conditions are seen as being provided. In such a design, the facilitative conditions need to be manipulated. It is not sufficient to simply create, for example, two post hoc groups one in which the therapists are perceived as showing more of these qualities than those in the other. This is, in fact, a quasi-experimental design in which any observed effect may be due to the clients, the therapists, and/or to some interaction of the two.

One problem in implementing this design is determining how the facilitative qualities should be manipulated. Before this is done, further information on a number of related issues is desirable. Since the facilitative conditions are thought to be interdependent, manipulating one of them may also automatically affect the others. If so, it would be only necessary and simpler to change one of them. Indeed, it would be of interest to find out if the facilitative qualities are dependent on each other. The first condition to be manipulated should be the one which is least likely to inadvertently modify other variables not necessarily related to the facilitative conditions.

It could be argued that the act of manipulation is by its very nature one of incongruence and will be seen as such. If altering either unconditional positive regard or empathy also results in lower congruence, than a decrease in either of these two conditions would be more appropriate than an increase since change in congruence would be in the same direction. Although, Truax and Carkhuff (1965) showed that a therapist could lower for 20 minutes the degree of unconditional acceptance and empathy expressed without affecting congruence, the presence of these qualities was assessed by independent raters and not by the three clients themselves. The clients might, therefore, have experienced a reduction in congruence which was not noticed by the raters. If, on the other hand, the facilitative conditions are found to be independent, then manipulating only one of them may be a rather stringent test of a theory which postulates that all three are necessary. In this case it may be more appropriate to modify all of them.

Ethically, an increase in facilitativeness is preferable to a decrease, provided that firstly room for such improvement exists and secondly relatively experienced therapists could show this. With respect to the first point, data from Barrett-Lennard (1962) on 12 therapists with a mean of five years experience revealed that clients perceived them as providing 79 per cent of their maximum score on their least facilitative quality. The corresponding figure (on a different measure) for the six therapists in the study by Sloane et al. (1975), who had an average of 17 years experience, was about 70 per cent. Whether these figures represent the highest level of these conditions which can be realistically expected is not known. If so, less experienced therapists may have to be used since they have been found to receive lower scores on these qualities (Barrett-Lennard, 1962).

Turning to the second point, although a number of different methods for teaching interpersonal helping skills are available (e.g., Marshall & Kurtz, 1982), their effectiveness has been largely evaluated on students and lay helpers and not on qualified therapists. As the scope for improvement for experienced therapists is lower, the effectiveness of these methods is also likely to be less. The extent to which the previous level of these conditions could be readily reverted to when necessary is also not known. If a relationship between therapeutic outcome and these facilitative conditions exists, then the size of that effect will depend on the difference between the two levels. A smaller difference will produce a smaller effect and so will require a larger number of subjects to be statistically significant.

To control for differences between therapists, it is preferable that the same therapists should show both higher and lower levels of these conditions and that clients should be randomly assigned to these two treatments. If this is not possible, then random allocation of the therapists to the two treatments would be necessary and a larger number of therapists would be required to control for therapist variability. Needless to say, the success with which these conditions had been manipulated would have to be checked via the clients' perception. While control for the effects of no treatment and nonspecific factors in the evaluation of different therapies is desirable, this is less important here provided that greater than minimal levels of these conditions has been shown in at least one of the two treatments. Without this last proviso being satisfied, no difference in effectiveness can be expected. However, any failure to find the expected differences in outcome when it is met would strongly suggest that the facilitative conditions do not determine therapeutic improvement.

QUASI-EXPERIMENTAL DESIGN

In view of some of these difficulties, it is perhaps not surprising that no one has tried to test Rogers' theory with a true experimental design. However, alternative quasi-experimental designs exist which allow greater causal inference to be drawn than the designs used hitherto. They have four main advantages: 1. They do not require the facilitative conditions to be experimentally manipulated; 2. The relative importance of the different facilitative conditions can be compared; 3. The effect of therapeutic status on the perception of these qualities can be assessed as well as their effect on therapeutic status; and 4. Any bias arising from the fact that both the facilitative conditions and therapeutic outcome are measured from the same perspective is controlled. Consequently, as a further step towards testing this theory, this type of design may be more appropriate. This has already been done in terms of ongoing close personal relationships but not as yet those involving professional therapists (Cramer, 1987a, 1987b, 1988).

This design involves assessing both therapeutic status and the facilitative conditions at the same time and at least at two different points separated by a period during which some therapeutic change can be assumed to have occurred. The period the two variables of therapeutic status and facilitative conditions refer to should be the same so that one does not come before the other. If the two variables are measured at more than two points, then the results from any two points can be compared with those from others to determine the similarity of the findings. The two main ways in which the data from this longitudinal or panel design can be analyzed are cross-lagged panel correlation analysis (Kenny, 1975) and linear structural relationships analysis (Jöreskog & Sörbom, 1986). Both methods require relatively large samples of subjects to be tested.

In the first method the two cross-lagged correlations are compared. That is, the correlation between the facilitative conditions at time 1 and therapeutic status at time 2 is compared with that between therapeutic status at time 1 and the facilitative conditions at time 2. If the first correlation is significantly more positive than the second one, it suggests that the facilitative conditions are a stronger determinant of therapeutic status than the other way round. However, to interpret a significant difference like that, the data need to fulfil the following four criteria: 1. The two measures are assessed at the same time and refer to the same time period; 2. The internal reliabilities of the measures are similar; 3. Their test-retest reliabilities are equal; 4. The correlations between the two variables at the same point in time are similar. This last criterion is important because it suggests that other factors affecting the relationship between the two variables remain the same at the two points. In other words, it eliminates the influence of other spurious factors influencing the cross-lagged correlations.

This method, however, has the following four disadvantages. Firstly, the four criteria are rather stringent and might not always be met, thereby ruling out its use. Secondly, only two variables at a time can be investigated. Thirdly, it provides no indication of the strength of the influence of a variable. And fourthly, the absence of a significant cross-lagged difference may indicate, amongst other things, either reciprocal causation or the influence of spurious other factors. These problems may be overcome by linear structural relationships analysis. This method can be used to compare the appropriateness or statistical fit of four competing models in this case. The first model assumes that both the variables at time 2 are influenced by those at time 1. In other words, it posits lagged reciprocal causation between the two different variables. The second and third models assume that only one of the two variables at time 1 (either the facilitative conditions or therapeutic status) affects the other at time 2. That is to say, these two models postulate that the facilitative conditions either determine therapeutic status or are determined by it. The fourth model asserts that only the same variables influence each other, so that the facilitative conditions at time 2 are only affected by the facilitative conditions at time 1 and that therapeutic status at time 2 is also only determined by therapeutic status at time 1. The model which provides the best fit to the data is accepted as being the most appropriate one. Further details of these methods can be found elsewhere (e.g., Cramer, 1987a, 1987b, 1988).

Although many of the previous studies of individual therapy have used a longitudinal design (e.g., Barrett-Lennard, 1962; Rogers et al., 1967/1976), only one of them (Fretz, 1966) has collected information on both the facilitative conditions and therapeutic outcome at the same times. However, the published data are insufficient and the number of clients (17) is too small to conduct the analyses advocated here. Needless to say, findings such as those of Barrett-Lennard (1962), which show that clients who perceive their therapist early on in therapy as providing more of these facilitative conditions are later judged by their therapists as having improved more, do not preclude the possibility that this is due to the client's therapeutic status rather than to the facilitative conditions provided, or to some interaction between these two factors.

Number of sessions and timing of assessment

Clients should receive a sufficient number of therapy sessions to show a significant amount of improvement. In a probit analysis of fifteen sets of data from 2,431 outpatients in individual therapy (Howard, Kopta, Krause, & Orlinsky, 1986), the greatest improvement was estimated to have taken place within the first 13 sessions after which 62 per cent of them had improved. After one, two, and four sessions respectively, 24, 30, and 41 per cent of clients had improved. Since, for whatever reason, many clients do not receive more than five sessions (Garfield, 1986) and since considerable improvement occurs within that period, assessment of therapeutic outcome primarily within the first few sessions of therapy is more economical when fewer of them will have left. More importantly, the results will be more representative of what occurs in therapy generally.

Although Barrett-Lennard (1962) has suggested that a number of sessions should elapse before clients judge the therapist's facilitativeness, assessments made shortly after the start of therapy have been found to correlate very highly with those made at the end of therapy some months later (Rogers et al., 1767/1976). This implies that initial impressions may be fairly stable. The mean score taken at several different points in therapy also shows little change over time (Barrett-Lennard, 1962). In addition, since a positive view of the therapist early on in therapy is positively related to continuing treatment (Bottari & Rappaport, 1983; Ford, 1978; Saltzman, Luetgert, Roth, Creaser, & Howard, 1976), the failure to include clients who only attend a few sessions may reduce the variability in the facilitative conditions which is naturally found, thereby decreasing the possibility of obtaining the hypothesized relationship.

There are three additional advantages of using a smaller rather than a larger number of therapy sessions if a true experimental design is to be employed. Firstly, any ill effects due to the experimental manipulation will not last as long. Secondly, therapists will use a less preferred approach for a shorter period. This will most probably mean that they are less likely to lapse into their normal way of working. And thirdly, the shorter the treatment period the greater the chances that any observed effect is due to the treatment itself and not to any other extraneous events which may have occurred in the meantime.

For the quasi-experimental design outlined above, both therapeutic status and the facilitative conditions are required to be assessed at least at two points in time. For the true experimental design, however, both these need only be assessed following the manipulation of the facilitative conditions. Measurement of therapeutic status prior to manipulation, however, is necessary to see if there are any pretreatment differences and to be able to control them statistically through residual gain scores or analysis of covariance. While follow-up assessment may be desirable, it is not essential for two reasons. Firstly, to interpret this information, clients should receive no further treatment during that period. This is difficult and unethical to ensure, particularly if the number of sessions for observation have been limited in the first place.

If this cannot be done, then the follow-up data will be misleading if differences in the effectiveness of treatment are related to differences in seeking further therapy. For example, clients who see their therapists as being less facilitative and who remain in therapy may have more sessions than those perceiving them as being more facilitative. This additional therapy may compensate for the lower facilitative conditions received and so result in no differences in therapeutic status being observed at follow-up. Determining how much additional therapy was received may also be problematical since some clients are not always willing to admit to this (Paul, 1967). And secondly, little change in improvement seems to occur between the end of therapy and some time later (Nicholson & Berman, 1983).

Clients and therapists

To generalize the findings to the wider client population, a large heterogeneous sample of typical clients should participate. The more disturbed these clients are, the greater the room for showing improvement. Since clinical diagnosis or severity seems to be unrelated to degree of improvement within a specified period, more seriously disturbed clients need not be excluded from taking part. For example, Howard et al. (1986) found that in terms of client ratings of outcome, little difference existed between groups diagnosed as depressed, anxious, and borderline-psychotic in the amount of improvement shown within the first few sessions.

To control for differences between therapists, a number of them should be involved. Since the extent to which the provision of these facilitative qualities is a function of the therapist rather than the client or the therapist-client relationship is not known, this could be partly determined by ensuring that each therapist in the nonexperimental design treats at least two clients. Sufficient variability of the facilitative conditions should exist to enable any relationship between these conditions and therapeutic outcome to be demonstrated. Although the theoretical approach of the therapist with each client may be easily recorded, no control for this is needed since Rogers believes that these facilitative qualities are not related to any particular therapeutic technique. This is surprising since a directive approach is judged as being less unconditionally accepting and empathic than a nondirective one according to the Truax rating scales used by Rogers et al. (1967/

1976). However, although behavior therapists have been independently observed to be more directive than psychoanalytic therapists, clients did not perceive them as being less accepting or empathic than the psychoanalytic ones (Sloane et al., 1975).

CONCLUSION

Despite the considerable research that the hypothesis on the facilitative conditions has stimulated, there is still no adequate experimental evidence to show that therapeutic improvement depends on the client's experience of the therapist as being unconditionally accepting, empathic, and congruent. Such evidence would involve, among other things, the facilitative conditions being successfully manipulated as judged by the participating clients rather than outside observers. Although a number of naturalistic studies of individual therapy have assessed these facilitative conditions from the client's perspective and have provided some tentative support for their effectiveness, none of them have tried to control for the two equally plausible possibilities that the facilitative conditions are a function of either the client (rather than the therapist) or both the client and the therapist. While these alternative interpretations are best investigated using a true experimental design, the potential practical and ethical difficulties of doing this suggest that it may be more convenient initially to explore these explanations using a quasi-experimental one. Here both therapeutic status and the facilitative conditions would be measured at the same time at a minimum of two points early on in therapy and the data would be interpreted using cross-lagged panel correlation and linear structural relationship analysis. Until this is done, the evidence in support of Rogers' views on what constitute the facilitative factors in therapy will be less than sufficient and efforts to teach these qualities may prove to be misguided.

426

REFERENCES

Barrett-Lennard, G.T. (1962). Dimensions of therapist response as causal factors in therapeutic change. *Psychological Monographs: General and Applied, 76,* (43, Whole number 562).

Barrett-Lennard, G.T. (1964). *The Relationship Inventory: Forms OS-M-64, OS-F-64, and MO-M-64 plus MO-F-64.* Unpublished manuscript. University of New England, Australia.

Bottari, M.A., & Rappaport, H. (1983). The relationship of patient and therapist-reported experiences of the initial session to outcome: An initial investigation. *Psychotherapy: Theory, Research and Practice, 20,* 355-358.

Bozarth, J.D., Mitchell, K.M., & Krauft, C.C. (1976). Empirical observations of antecedents to psychotherapeutic outcome: Some implications. *Rehabilitation Counseling Bulletin, 20,* 28-36.

Burstein, J.W., & Carkhuff, R.R. (1968). Objective, therapist and client ratings of therapist-offered facilitative conditions of moderate to low functioning therapists. *Journal of Clinical Psychology, 24,* 240-241.

Campbell, D.T., & Stanley, J.C. (1963). *Experimental and quasi-experimental designs for research.* Chicago: Rand McNally.

Cramer, D. (1986a). An item factor analysis of the original Relationship Inventory. *Journal of Personal and Social Relationships, 3,* 121-127.

Cramer, D. (1986b). An item factor analysis of the revised Barrett-Lennard Relationship Inventory. *British Journal of Guidance and Counseling, 14,* 314-325.

Cramer, D. (1987a). *Facilitative friendships: A manifest variable path analysis of panel data.* Manuscript submitted for publication.

Cramer, D. (1987b). *Facilitative friendship and self-esteem: A latent variable path analysis of panel data.* Manuscript submitted for publication.

Cramer, D. (1988). Self-esteem and facilitative close relationships: A cross-lagged panel correlation analysis. *British Journal of Social Psychology, 27,* 115-126.

Cramer, D. (1989). Self-esteem and the facilitativeness of parents and close friends. *Person-Centered Review, 4,* 61-76.

Culbert, S.A. (1968). Trainer self-disclosure and member growth in two T groups. *Journal of Applied Behavioral Science, 4,* 47-73.

Ford, J.D. (1978). Therapeutic relationship in behavior therapy: An empirical analysis. *Journal of Consulting and Clinical Psychology, 46,* 1302-1314.

Fretz, B.R. (1966). Postural movements in a counseling dyad. *Journal of Counseling Psychology, 13,* 335-343.

Garfield, S.L. (1986). Research on client variables in psychotherapy. In S.L. Garfield & A.E. Bergin (Eds.), *Handbook of psychotherapy and behavior change* (3rd ed., pp. 213-256). New York: Wiley.

Garfield, S.L., & Bergin, A.E. (1971). Therapeutic conditions and outcome. *Journal of Abnormal Psychology, 77,* 108-114.

Gurman, A.S. (1977). The patient's perception of the therapeutic relationship. In A.S. Gurman & A.M. Razin (Eds.), *Effective psychotherapy: A handbook of research* (pp. 503-543). New York: Pergamon.

Howard, K.I., Kopta, S.M., Krause, M.S., & Orlinsky, D.E. (1986). The dose-effect relationship in psychotherapy. *American Psychologist, 41,* 159-164.
Jöreskog, K.G., & Sörbom, D. (1986). *LISREL-VI: Analysis of linear structural relationships by maximum likelihood, instrumental variables, and least squares methods.* Mooresville, IN: Scientific Software, Inc.
Kenny, D.A. (1975). Cross-lagged panel correlation: A test for spuriousness. *Psychological Bulletin, 82,* 887-903.
Lietaer, G. (1976). Nederlandstalige revisie van Barrett-Lennards Relationship Inventory voor individueel-terapeutische relaties (Dutch revision of the Barrett-Lennard Relationship Inventory for individual therapeutic relationships). *Psychologica Belgica, 16,* 73-94.
Marshall, E.K., & Kurtz, P.D. (Eds.). (1982). *Interpersonal helping skills: A guide to training methods, programs, and resources.* San Francisco: Josey-Bass.
McWhirter, J.J. (1973). Two measures of the facilitative conditions: A correlation study. *Journal of Counseling Psychology, 20,* 317-320.
Mintz, J., Luborsky, L., & Christoph, P. (1979). Measuring the outcomes of psychotherapy: Findings of the Penn Psychotherapy Project. *Journal of Consulting and Clinical Psychology, 47,* 319-334.
Mitchell, K.M., Bozarth, J.D., & Krauft, C.C. (1977). A reappraisal of the therapeutic effectiveness of accurate empathy, nonpossessive warmth, and genuineness. In A.S. Gurman & A.M. Razin (Eds.), *Effective psychotherapy: A handbook of research* (pp. 482-502). New York: Pergamon.
Nicholson, R.A., & Berman, J.S. (1983). Is follow-up necessary in evaluating psychotherapy? *Psychological Bulletin, 93,* 261-278.
Paul, G.L. (1967). Insight versus desensitization, in psychotherapy two years after termination. *Journal of Consulting Psychology, 31,* 333-348.
Rogers, C.R. (1957). A theory of therapy, personality, and interpersonal relationships, as developed in the client-centered framework. In S. Koch (Ed.), *Psychology: A study of a science: Vol. 3: Formulations of the person and the social context* (pp. 184-256). New York: McGraw-Hill.
Rogers, C.R. (1961). The process equation of psychotherapy. *American Journal of Psychotherapy, 15,* 27-45.
Rogers, C.R., Gendlin, E.T., Kiesler, D.J., & Truax, C.B. (Eds.), *The therapeutic relationship and its impact: A study of psychotherapy with schizophrenics.* Westport, CT: Greenwood (Original work published in 1967).
Rosenberg, M. (1965). *Society and the adolescent self-image.* Princeton, NJ: Princeton University Press.
Rudolph, J., Langer, I., & Tausch, R. (1980). Prüfung der psychischen Auswirkungen und Bedingungen von personenzentrierter Einzel-Psychotherapie (A test of the psychological effects and conditions of person-centered individual therapy): *Zeitschrift für Klinische Psychologie, 9,* 23-33.
Saltzman, C., Luetgert, M.J., Roth, C.H., Creaser, I., & Howard, L. (1976). Formation of a therapeutic relationship: Experiences during the initial phase of psychotherapy as predictors of treatment duration and outcome. *Journal of Consulting and Clinical Psychology, 44,* 546-555.
Sloane, R.B., Staples, F.R., Cristol, A.H., Yorkston, N.J., & Whipple, K. (1975).

428

Psychotherapy versus behavior therapy. Cambridge, MA: Harvard University Press.

Truax, C.B. (1966). Therapist empathy, warmth, and genuineness and patient personality change in group psychotherapy: A comparison between interaction unit measures, time sample measures, patient perception measures. *Journal of Clinical Psychology, 22,* 225-229.

Truax, C.B., & Carkhuff, R.R. (1965). Experimental manipulation of therapeutic conditions. *Journal of Counseling Psychology, 29,* 119-124.

Truax, C.B., & Carkhuff, R.R. (1967). *Toward effective counseling and psychotherapy: Training and practice.* Chicago: Aldine.

Walker, A.M., Rablen, R.A., & Rogers, C.R. (1960). Development of a scale to measure process changes in psychotherapy. *Journal of Clinical Psychology, 16,* 79-85.

Watson, N. (1984). The empirical status of Rogers' hypotheses of the necessary and sufficient conditions for effective psychotherapy. In R.F. Levant & J.M. Shlien (Eds.), *Client-centered therapy and the person-centered approach: New directions in theory, research and practice* (pp. 17-40). New York: Praeger.

Zung, W.W.K. (1974). The measurement of affects: Depression and anxiety. In P. Pichot (Ed.), *Psychological measurements in psychopharmacology: Modern problems in pharmacopsychiatry* (Vol. 7, pp. 170-188).

EXPLORATORY THERAPY IN TWO-PLUS-ONE SESSIONS: A RESEARCH MODEL FOR STUDYING THE PROCESS OF CHANGE

Michael BARKHAM & David A. SHAPIRO
University of Sheffield, United Kingdom

INTRODUCTION

Within client-centered and experiential psychotherapies, a single paradox is evident, namely that while Rogers was a prime instigator in advocating the need for, and initiating the practice of psychotherapy research, this enterprise within both client-centered and experiential psychotherapies has never been at a lower ebb. The "third force" in psychology has, in effect, been relegated from the "research league." This chapter addresses this issue by providing a cost-efficient generic model for investigating the process of client change while also providing a cost-effective delivery service to clients. This approach, while espousing the integrating of the three central facets of theory, research, and practice, also adopts the Rogerian emphasis on the client's perception of the therapeutic process. Accordingly, the data reported in this chapter reflect the client's perspective of process variables within the course of a very brief model of psychotherapy.

Considerable interest exists in brief psychotherapies. While centres for psychotherapy research traditionally espouse time-limits of eight, twelve, sixteen and twenty sessions, there has recently been considerable enthusiasm by clinical-researchers for therapies in which clients are seen for very brief durations. One particular rationale for implementing these very brief therapeutic interventions, apart from the needs of psychotherapeutic service delivery systems (Howard, 1988), is that they provide a context in which the therapeutic techniques are effectively heightened, thereby providing a unique window into the process of change.

Research model

The traditional model of psychotherapy research applies research methods to already existing models of psychotherapy. These include studies of naturally occuring therapy or traditionally brief therapies undertaken in research settings. The common factor among these approaches is that the research enterprise is applied to established therapeutic deliveries. In contrast to this approach, a research model for brief psychotherapeutic interventions, termed "two-plus-one" therapy, has been developed (Barkham, 1989; Barkham & Hobson, 1989), based upon findings derived from the psychotherapy literature. The generic two-plus-one model comprises two one-hour sessions one week apart followed by a third one-hour session three months later: Hence the term, two-plus-one therapy.

The rationale for this model comprises three elements. First, the dose-effect literature (Howard, Kopta, Krause, & Orlinsky, 1986) attests to the negatively accelerating curve when percentage of clients showing measurable improvement is plotted as a function of the number of weekly sessions received by clients. For example, prior to the first session, 14% (ë 4%) of clients show measurable improvement, with 30% (ë 5%) of clients attaining this criterion after two sessions. After four sessions the figure is 41% (ë5%), and after eight sessions 53% (ë5%). This suggests an initial treatment block of two sessions to be cost efficient in terms of resources and improvement rates. Second, the psychotherapy literature (e.g. Frank, 1959) attests to the view that two major components contributing towards change are: 1. expectancy of relief, and 2. relearning as a function of time, independent of time spent in therapy. For example, Frank (1981) has argued that what occurs between sessions may be as important as what occurs in the sessions themselves. This suggests that the incorporation of time within a very brief therapy model would heighten its effectiveness. Third, reviews of time-limited therapies (Johnson & Gelso, 1980) have suggested that all therapies should include a follow-up session, and that initial sessions should begin on a weekly basis. These suggestions have led to the development of the two-plus-one model as a research-derived model for psychotherapeutic service delivery systems and a quasi-analogue of the psychotherapeutic process.

A characteristic of this model is that it has been developed in a research context. In effect, the model has been developed as a cost-efficient method for investigating process-impact-outcome links. Because of the brevity of the duration of any therapy presented within this model, the use of the specific techniques characteristic of the therapy will be emphasized. Accordingly, any therapy employing this model must be technique driven. It is hypothesized that this will result in a lessening of the influence of non-specific factors (e.g. the therapeutic alliance) and thereby enable researchers to address the question of whether the outcomes of therapies are equivalent when technical differences are heightened. A central aim of this model, however, is not to achieve the briefest therapy: ultimately this could be regressed to the solitary single-utterance intervention (e.g. "No!" or "Don't!"). This tells us little about the process of therapy. While the two-plus-one model *is* brief, its research rationale determines that it comprises the essential components of the psychotherapeutic process, thereby enabling researchers to study the process of outcome.

This model is, perhaps, unique in attempting to combine the advantage of analogue studies with that of clinical relevance. Psychotherapy research has traditionally allowed itself to be constrained by psychotherapy delivery. For example, the high cost of service delivery and research analysis has lead to psychotherapy research becoming a costly and selective activity, thereby creating a gap between practitioner and researcher. There is a need in the psychotherapy research enterprise for delivery models which reflect common practice in psychotherapeutic service delivery systems, and which derive from a research rationale which enables cost-efficient research to address central theoretical questions.

Exploratory therapy

The generic model of two-plus-one therapy has been implemented within a relationship-oriented therapy, termed Exploratory therapy (Barkham, 1989; Barkham & Hobson, 1989). The general characteristics of Exploratory therapy are derived from Hobson's (1985) Conversational model. The Exploratory model draws heavily on features of experiential therapy due to its emphasis on process, particularly as it occurs in the "here-and-now" in the relationship between client and therapist. Key features of this treatment include the following: 1. the assumption that the client's present problems arise from disturbances of significant personal relationships; 2. the creation within the therapy situation itself of a relationship in which the client's interpersonal problems are revealed, explored, understood, and modified by the testing-out of possible solutions which are generated in the dialogue; 3. to promote this process, various conversational strategies are adopted, including negotiation, a language of mutuality, the use of metaphor to enhance the immediacy and "wholeness" of experienced affect, and focusing on the here and now experience of the client in the session; and 4. various levels of hypotheses are presented: understanding hypotheses in which the therapist expresses their view of the client's experience, linking hypotheses suggesting connections between different experiences of the client, and explanatory hypotheses suggesting causes or reasons for behaviour and experience.

A model of psychotherapeutic change

Research, having shown psychotherapy to be effective (Lambert, Shapiro, & Bergin, 1986), now faces the challenge of providing accounts of how change has taken place; that is, providing a theoretical model of change which can be tested empirically. A model of change proposed by Stiles, Elliott, Llewelyn, Firth-Cozens, Margison, Shapiro, and Hardy (in press) suggests hypothesized processes through which clients assimilate problematic experiences (e.g. memories, feelings, wishes, ideas, intentions, or attitudes) which are threatening or psychologically painful. Conceptually, attitudes comprise three components: Thoughts, feelings, and behaviours. Traditionally, these three components have been crudely "matched" with differing psychotherapeutic modalities: Thoughts with dynamic, feelings with experiential, and behaviours with behavioural therapies. However, conceptions of the "integrated" or "whole" person - a meta-aspiration for all therapies - would suggest that each of these three attitudinal components would be present in any single psychotherapeutic delivery.

A feature of the assimilation model (Stiles et al., in press) is that it incorporates the affective, cognitive, and behavioural components of clients' adaptive functioning. Accordingly, the model does not espouse one psychotherapeutic process at the cost of another, but rather posits a sequencing of processes through which change occurs. Briefly, the assimilation model posits a sequence of affective reactions to experiences from "warded off," through "painful," "problematic," "puzzling," towards "understood" and finally "mastered." These affective reactions are associated, loosely, with five therapeutic impacts derived from the work of Elliott, James, Reimschuessel, Cislo, and Sack (1985): 1. unwanted thoughts, 2. awareness, 3. insight, 4. problem definition, and 5. problem solution.

Change mechanisms

Exploratory therapy comprises specific characteristics which enable mechanisms of change to occur. This chapter focuses on three areas: 1. session dimensions, 2. session impacts, and 3. the client-therapist relationship. The Exploratory two-plus-one model would lead to various predictions concerning these three process variables.

First, regarding session dimensions, the underpining theory would lead to the prediction that effective sessions should be characterized as deep rather than shallow, and rough rather than smooth. Second, for session impacts, the initial two sessions should involve the client becoming more aware of feelings through focusing on their feelings, leading to change by way of the client gaining new insight into the self. By the close of the second session clients should have gained a sense of the definition of work to be carried out, thereby moving from awareness and self-understanding towards a sense of action. The third session, being a review, would not be expected to address new material. It might, however, be characterized by a more active, solution-based approach. Third, concerning the client-therapist relationship, the heightening of technique within a therapeutic duration in which the main treatment block (i.e. the two-session block) is less than the optimal number of sessions necessary to achieve a client-therapist relationship (O'Malley, Suh, & Strupp, 1983; Sachs, 1983), would lead to the prediction that comparatively low ratings should pertain across the three sessions on any sampled relationship variable.

Research strategy

In order to test these hypothesized mechanisms, a single case analysis of the relation between process and outcome in one selected case was adopted. Outcome data from a small data set is initially presented in which evaluation of outcome is derived from procedures advocated by Jacobson and Revenstorf (1988). The adoption of the single case strategy for discussion of process was employed in order that the data arising could be closely related to clinical descriptions from the case. Accordingly, this account functions as a test of the ability of this generic model of psychotherapy to provide an informative description of the therapeutic process. The measurement of psychotherapy process is characterized by the completion of a comprehensive battery of pre- and post-session process measures by the client and therapist.

METHOD

Sample

The client was one of a sample comprising eight clients referred to the psychological clinic who met the threshold level for inclusion in the pilot sample. The threshold was defined as scoring below 16 on the Beck Depression Inventory (BDI: Beck, Ward, Mendelson, Mock, & Erbaugh, 1961). Clients were offered two sessions of Exploratory therapy on consecutive weeks, followed by a third session three months later. All clients were white-collar employees and were currently in employment and attending work. They were referred by general practitioners, occupational health officers, or by themselves.

Therapists

The therapists were both qualified clinical psychologists with 18 months (M.B.) and 16 years (D.A.S.) post-doctoral clinical experience respectively at the initiation of the pilot study. The therapist in the case reported here was the first author (M.B.).

Procedure

Clients were assigned to one of two therapists according to their availability, with one therapist seeing five and the other seeing three clients. All eight clients who began therapy completed the programme. All sessions were audiotaped while the sessions of cases five to eight were also videotaped.

Outcome measures

Clients completed the BDI on three occasions prior to their first therapy session: Initial screening (T1), two weeks later (T2), and immediately prior to their first therapy session two weeks later (T3). Clients then completed the BDI two weeks after the second session (T4), two weeks prior to the third session (T5), and six months after beginning therapy (T6).

Process measures

Three process measures were completed: the Session Evaluation Questionnaire (SEQ: Stiles, 1980), client and therapist post-session impact form (Elliott, 1986), and the Agnew Relationship Measure (Agnew & Shapiro, 1988). Two indices were derived from the SEQ which comprises 24 bipolar statements. First, smoothness of session was derived from the mean of four items: safe-dangerous, difficult-easy, unpleasant-pleasant, and rough-smooth. Second, depth of session was derived from the mean of four items: valuable-worthless, shallow-deep, full-empty, and special-ordinary. Session impacts were derived from Elliott's (1986) form in which clients evaluate the impact from the session on 21 items. Five task items are pertinent to this study: 1. insight into self, 2. insight into others, 3. awareness of feelings, 4. definition of problem to work on, and 5. knowing what to do about problems. Items were rated on a 5-point scale with anchor points of 1 ("not at all present") and 5 ("greatly present"). Client ratings of 4 ("very much present") and 5 ("greatly present") were selected as denoting a sufficiently salient status of these impacts. Three relationship factors were derived from the 35-item Agnew Relationship Measure (ARM: Agnew & Shapiro, 1988): 1. therapist and client involvement in the therapeutic proces (seven items), 2. confidence in the therapist (seven items), and 3. the empowered client (three items). Both client and therapist ratings are considered.

Measuring reliable and clinically significant improvement

Statistical and clinical improvement were determined by procedures advocated by Jacobson and Revenstorf (1988). These procedures require two criteria to be met before being confident that both reliable and clinically significant change has occurred. First, the change score must show reliable change: that is, the change in the score is not attributable to the measurement error of the difference between the pre- and post-scores. Second, the change in the score must attain a criterion level showing it to represent a different population: that is, the change score places the individual in a different population (i.e. functional/psychologically healthy) from that at intake (i.e. dysfunctional/distressed). The most stringent criterion would be two standard deviations beyond the intake mean. However, because a one standard deviation change would place the "average" client from the present sample within the normal range for the BDI (i.e. 0-9), and because initial interest is on change to a clinically improved status rather than movement within degrees of clinical improvement, a liberal criterion level of one standard deviation from the intake mean was selected.

OUTCOMES

The outcome data for the eight cases are presented in Table 1. The mean BDI scores attained at the three pre-therapy assessments suggest a relatively stable level of depressive symptomatology prior to the first therapy session. Only a single client (case 4) met both improvement criteria (i.e. reliant change and clinically significant improvement defined as 1 SD) prior to therapy (i.e. at T3). Although the data set comprizes only a small sample, this single case, representing 12.5% of the group, is within the range expected to show measurable improvement prior to therapy (14% ± 4%). At T4, three clients (cases, 6, 7, and 8), met both improvement criteria. This represents 37.5% of the total sample and slightly exceeds the expected range (i.e. 30% ± 5%). At T5, six clients (cases 1, 2, 3, 6, 7, and 8) met the criteria, representing 75% of clients in the sample, a level maintained at T6 (i.e. six months after therapy).

For the single case selected, case 7, the BDI scores at the three pre-therapy assessments place this client in the range of mild depression while BDI scores after the initial two sessions place the client in the normal range. Further, this client shows both stable pre-therapy BDI scores together with the highest change score from T3 to T4, thereby identifying it as an exemplar of immediate change. Although a slight deterioration in the BDI scores does occur between T5 and T6, this latter score is still within the one standard deviation range.

Table 1
Reliable and clinically significant change on the Beck Depression Inventory across therapy for eight clients receiving two-plus-one Exploratory therapy

		Pre therapy		Post 2nd session	Pre 3rd session	Post 3rd session
Client	T1	T2	T3	T4	T5	T6
1	11	4	5*	6	2**	1**
2	7	11	7	6	0**	0**
3	10	7	10	10	6*	6*
4	13	-	9	7*	9	9
5	14	13	11	9	11	8
6	7	5	7	4**	0**	0**
7	15	12	14	4**	4**	7*
8	10	14	10	2**	2**	0**
Mean	10.88	9.42	9.13	6.00	4.25	3.88
Sd	3.00	4.04	2.80	2.67	4.10	3.98

T1, T2... T6 : Assessment times
Bold figures   = Reliable change: reliable change index = 3.11 BDI points.
        * = Clinically significant change: 1 Sd = 7.88 on BDI.
      ** = Clinically significant change: 2 Sd = 4.88 on BDI.

A SINGLE CASE

Stephen was married with two children both of whom had recently left home. At work he had recently experienced a re-organization in which a team structure had been replaced by a matrix comprising upwards of 70 people. Stephen felt desperately alone and "fragmented", at times feeling as if he were a child having to hang on to a parent. A central dynamic for Stephen was his need to work for the "common good", being able to invest in those people close to him, be it at work (team) or at home (family). His father had been particularly demanding and Stephen had attempted to please him and felt he was "repaying" something, feeling he had to show he was worthy of the things that people had entrusted in him. He was concerned not to let people down but, although relatively successful, felt he had not performed as well as he might. In the therapeutic interactions, he continually undermined what he said, devaluing his views.

A significant moment in the first session occurred when he was challenged about his inability to do something for himself. He responded, without thinking, that this was wrong: "I don't think I've got that right." It was almost "sinful" for him to respond to his needs. Therapy focussed on his feelings of loss (i.e. team structure and children leaving home). He no longer had others to invest in: he was, in effect "homeless", describing the flux of the matrix structure at work as being like moving from foster family to foster family. In the second session, he described leaving the first session "with a sense of shock, having said things I've not said before." He was clearer about his sense of "bereavement." In the past, bereavements (i.e. in the family) had been shared, but he had been unable to share the feeling of being bereft at work.

After the second session he wrote "If I can learn to value myself then I will be able to function more effectively in the new 'unstructured' environment in which I work." His initial statement in the third session reflected his progress: "In many ways, things are quite a lot better." He had been offered local promotion and felt he had received something back from the organization rather than being lost in it: "I've been much more integrated: the sense of fragmentation is far less." He felt able to verbalize things more freely. In the organization, he felt he could pick up working relationships and work with them for the necessary time and then "put them down" at the end. Therapy had enabled him to re-establish one-to-one relationships at work, and he made reference to the "blinding revelation" from the first session that he felt it almost sinful to do anything for himself. However, he recognized a sense of seeing things through "rose-coloured spectacles."

THE PROCESS OF OUTCOME

This section considers the hypothesized changes in session dimensions, impacts, and client-therapist relationship which occurred in the above case study. Effective therapy was predicted to be characterized by sessions which were deep (rather than shallow) and rough (rather than smooth), and to feature session impacts defined as "awareness," "insight into self," and "definition of problem to work on" during the initial two sessions, with "problem solution" defining the third session. The client-therapist relationship was hypothesized to be defined by comparatively low factor scores compared with normative data due to the very brief duration restricting the development of the therapeutic relationship.

Session dimensions

We compared this case with the normative data arising from the first Sheffield Psychotherapy Project (Stiles, Shapiro, & Firth-Cozens, 1988). Results showed the first session to be relatively deep and rough, a finding tempered at the second session when the client, immediately prior to the second session, rated the first session again. He perceived the session as being deep and rough but less intensely so than experienced at the time of the actual session itself. The rating of depth and roughness of the second session approximated the normative data, while the third session was rated as deep and smooth. Accordingly, these data provide support for the hypothesized session dimensions at the first session, while those at the second are within the range of the normative data, with the final session showing the effects of positive improvement. Positive mood rated immediately after sessions one and two was stable and approximated the norm, although there was an increase in positive mood at the third session.

Session impacts

Session one was characterized by "awareness" and "insight into self," with session two being characterized by "insight into self" and "definition of a problem." Session three was characterized by "awareness," "definition of problem" and "knowing what to do." The data suggests a sequencing towards greater assimilation of problematic experiences from awareness, through insight, towards a definition of a problem to work on by the end of the second session, and then, at the third session, knowing what to do about a problem.

Client-therapist relationship

We compared client and therapist scores respectively for the single case with normative data from the Second Sheffield Psychotherapy Project (Agnew & Shapiro, 1988). The client's ratings on all three factors exceeded the mean of the normative data. Factors 1 ("involvement") and 3·("empowerment") were rated higher at session two than session one, while factor 2 ("confidence") remained constant. At session three, factor 1 ("involvement") was rated lower while factor 2 ("confidence") increased, and factor 3 ("empowerment") remained constant. Therapist's ratings showed a global pattern, with session two being rated as a "poorer" session than session one on all three factors. Session three was rated higher than session one on factors 1 ("involvement") and 2 ("confidence"), while factor 3 ("empowerment"), although decreasing at session two, and again very slightly at session three, consistently remained one standard deviation above the normative mean. These data counter the predicted low factor scores, showing that relationship factors are present in a very brief duration therapy with a good outcome.

DISCUSSION

This chapter has presented the rationale for developing and implementing a research model of psychotherapy, and has presented a single client's perception of the therapeutic process in a very brief therapy model. The purpose of this chapter has been as much to stimulate the adoption of more cost-efficient research strategies across a wide range of differing therapeutic modalities as it has been to present specific findings. The aim has been to address a central question. Can a very brief therapy model, driven by the needs of psychotherapy researchers to address theoretical questions about the psychotherapeutic process, be implemented which is viable to both practitioners and clients as a delivery service (i.e. produces reliable and clinically significant improvement in clients)? The latter is a prerequisite for enabling the model to be adopted as a research strategy.

This prerequisite is most directly addressed by comparing the group data with the dose-effect literature (Howard et al., 1986). Although the sample size is small, the percentage of clients showing both reliable and clinically significant improvement (to one standard deviation) is within the dose-effect range at pre-therapy and marginally in excess at two-sessions. Prior to the third session, equivalent to 13 weeks in the dose-effect curve, the finding that 75% of clients met both criteria exceeds the dose-effect curve based on 13 weekly sessions, and is consistent with the predicted percentage after 26 weekly sessions. The small sample size precludes making statements about the two-plus-one model being more effective than weekly sessions. However, the comparative data do suggest that clients receiving the two-plus-one Exploratory model are not disadvantaged as reflected in the rates of reliable and clinically significant improvement for clients receiving weekly sessions over a similar time-span. This data can, therefore, be used to satisfy the prerequisite that the model should be viable to both clients and practitioners prior to its psychotherapeutic research utility. However it should be emphasized that the model has, as yet, only been implemented with clients presenting with mild depression. As a treatment model, rather than as a research model, it remains an empirical question whether this delivery model would be sufficient for clients presenting with more severe symptomatology. Similarly, the robustness of the generic model will only be apparent when alternative therapy modes have been adapted and implemented within the model.

The data relating to session dimensions provides support for the expected process of change through therapy. In particular, the finding that the initial session is characterized as deep is consistent with findings from the first Sheffield Psychotherapy Project (Stiles, et al., 1988) in which clients rated Exploratory sessions as deep. However, in that comparative outcome study, comparing Exploratory with Prescriptive (cognitive-behavioural) therapy, clients did not rate Exploratory sessions as significantly deeper than Prescriptive sessions. Accordingly, depth of session appears to be a common session dimension. By contrast, clients rated Prescriptive sessions as significantly smoother (i.e. less rough) than Exploratory sessions, suggesting it to be a mode-specific feature of Exploratory therapy.

The data from the single case presented here provide an exemplar of the relationship between these two session dimensions, and suggest a possible mechanism of change by which improvement occurs as a function of the impact arising from the perceived "roughness" but which is contained by the clients due to their perceiving the session as deep. This combination of roughness and depth provides the basis for a different mechanism from that occurring in a session rated as rough but not deep. This latter combination would be indicative of a persecutory style (Meares & Hobson, 1977) in which the therapeutic process was largely determined by the agenda and needs of the therapist.

The progression through therapy, as represented by the two session dimensions and session mood are suggestive of a process by which at the second session the ratings are broadly equivalent with normative data. This suggests that by the second session of the two-plus-one model, the ratings of these three session dimensions are equivalent to those obtained across therapies of longer duration. The finding that the third session was rated as deeper than the first session can be explained when considered in conjunction with the smoothness rating which is important. The third session is deep but smooth, suggesting that important issues have been addressed and that while these are meaningful, and therefore deep, they are addressed in a "rounding off" manner rather than the earlier "rougher" and deeper work.

The findings from the session impacts provide some initial evidence for the congruence of processes within the two-plus-one model with theoretical models of change. In particular, these session impacts provide initial data for testing the assimilation process (Stiles et al., in press). However, the session impacts do not map directly onto the assimilation model. Indeed, the session impact "awareness" more closely approximates the assimilation stage termed "problem clarification," denoting a clearer state of awareness than that denoting the stage "vague awareness." Further, "problem clarification" may be more appropriately termed "problem recognition". According to the assimilation model, therefore, session one is characterized by "problem recognition" and "personal insight."

Findings from the second session provide support for a linking of "personal insight" and "definition of a problem to work on," leaving the client with a clear sense of the area of application within which they have to work. By the third session, the client-rated impacts are located towards the assimilated end of the continuum, with the single case client rating "definition of a problem to work on" and "knowing what to do" as most salient. However, the progression is not simply linear. The client also rated "awareness," redefined here as "problem recognition." This rating may suggest a feedback loop in which the working through of problems redefines the initial problem for the client, thereby making it a more salient impact. These data are indicators of the need for further research efforts into making the assimilation scale compatible with self-report inventories of session impacts.

The findings relating to the client-therapist relationship showed the client's perception of their empowerment and the therapist's and client's involvement in therapy to increase at session two compared with session one. Thus, the second session being smoother and less deep, and being characterized by a move towards greater assimilation of problematic experiences, was associated with the client feeling more empowered as well as being more involved in therapy. By contrast, the therapist perceived the second session less favorably, perhaps reflecting the comparative lessening of depth and roughness. By the third session, the finding that client-rated involvement in the therapeutic process declined is congruent with the model: the three-month interval increasing the client's sense of autonomy, thereby enabling the client not to be dependent upon the therapist. Similarly, the client's experience of success during this interval perhaps enables him to feel more confident in the therapist (although it may reflect the client's own increase in self-confidence).

The association between relationship factors and session dimensions and impacts requires systematic research in order to understand more fully the process of outcome. For example, one account of change which would be congruent with the generic two-plus-one model might predict a deep and rough initial session (session dimensions) enabling the client to become aware of experiences and feelings (session impacts), thereby enhancing the client's openess to experience (akin to client self-relatedness: Orlinsky & Howard, 1986). In turn, this "experiencing" leads the client to feel, and to perceive the therapist, as more involved in the therapy as well as the client feeling more personally empowered (relationship factors). Rather than the building of a trusting therapeutic relationship early in therapy providing the basis for later therapeutic interventions, the generic two-plus-one model might hypothesize that good technique delivered early (i.e. at session one) and facilitating the assimilation of problematic experiences, drives the therapeutic relationship. The data from this single case require extensive clinical replication.

CONCLUSION

In conclusion, the approach adopted in this chapter is argued to be one which is both cost-effective for client and practitioner, as well as effective for the psychotherapy researcher. The investigation of process variables (in this case, session dimensions, impacts, and relationship factors), provide the basis for accounts of change in psychotherapy which are available to the individual practitioner as well as to researchers. The present predominance of cognitive and behavioural therapies arose largely from the combined effects of their emphasis on briefer therapy duration (compared with psychodynamic therapies) and a high priority placed on evaluation and research. The upsurgence of behavioural and cognitive therapies has been paralleled by the decline of both client-centered and experiential therapies. Where these latter therapies do exist, they do so largely in private practice rather than within service delivery systems, which, in itself, hinders the endeavour towards systematic research into the processes and outcomes of these therapies. The generic model presented in this chapter is offered as a means for practitioners and researchers within client-centered and experiential therapies to redress this imbalance.

REFERENCES

Agnew, R.M., & Shapiro, D.A. (1988). *Therapist-client relationships: The development of a measure. SAPU Memo 765.* Department of Psychology, University of Sheffield.

Barkham, M. (1989). Exploratory therapy in two-plus-one sessions: I. Rationale for a brief psychotherapy model. *British Journal of Psychotherapy, 6,* 81-88.

Barkham, M., & Hobson, R.F. (1989). Exploratory therapy in two-plus-one sessions: II. A single case study. *British Journal of Psychotherapy, 6,* 89-100.

Beck, A.T., Ward, C.H., Mendelson, M., Mock, J., & Erbaugh, J. (1961). An inventory for measuring depression. *Archives of General Psychiatry, 4,* 561-571.

Elliott, R. (1986). *Client/therapist post session questionnaire.* Unpublished manuscript, Department of Psychology, University of Toledo.

Elliott, R., James, E., Reimschuessel, C., Cislo, D., & Sack, N. (1985). Significant events and the analysis of immediate therapeutic impacts. *Psychotherapy, 22,* 620-630.

Frank, J.D. (1959). The dynamics of the psychotherapeutic relationship. *Psychiatry, 22,* 17-39.

Frank, J.D. (1981). Therapeutic components shared by all psychotherapies. In

J.H. Harvey & M.M. Parkes, *The master lecture series. Vol. 1: Psychotherapy research and behavior change* (pp. 9-37). Washington, DC: American Psychological Association.

Hobson, R.F. (1985). *Forms of feeling: The heart of psychotherapy.* London: Tavistock Press.

Howard, K.I. (1988). *The psychotherapeutic service delivery system. Keynote address at the 19th Annual Meeting of the Society for Psychotherapy Research.* Santa Fe, Mexico, 16 June 1988.

Howard, K.I., Kopta, S.M., Krause, M.S., & Orlinsky, D.K. (1986). The dose-response relationship in psychotherapy. *American Psychologist, 41,* 159-164.

Jacobson, N.S., & Revenstorf, D. (1988). Statistics for assessing the clinical significance of psychotherapy techniques: Issues, problems, and new developments. *Behavioral Assessment, 10,* 133-145.

Johnson, D.H., & Gelso, C.J. (1980). The effectiveness of time limits in counseling and psychotherapy: A critical review. *The Counseling Psychologist, 9,* 70-83.

Lambert, M.J., Shapiro, D.A., & Bergin, A.E. (1986). The effectiveness of psychotherapy. In S.L. Garfield & A.E. Bergin (Eds.), *Handbook of psychotherapy and behavior change* (3rd ed., pp. 157-211). New York: Wiley.

Meares, R., & Hobson, R.F. (1977). The persecutory therapist. *British Journal of Medical Psychology, 50,* 349-359.

O'Malley, S.S., Suh, C.S., & Strupp, H.M. (1983). The Vanderbilt psychotherapy process scale: A report of the scale development and a process-outcome study. *Journal of Consulting and Clinical Psychology, 51,* 581-586.

Orlinsky, D.E., & Howard, K.I. (1987). A generic model of psychotherapy. *Journal of Integrative and Eclective Psychotherapy, 6,* 6-27.

Sachs, J.S. (1983). Negative factors in brief psychotherapy: An empirical assessment. *Journal of Consulting and Clinical Psychology, 51,* 581-586.

Stiles, W.B. (1980). Measurement of the impact of psychotherapy sessions. *Journal of Consulting and Clinical Psychology, 48,* 176-185.

Stiles, W.B., Elliott, R., Llewelyn, S.P., Firth-Cozens, J.A., Margison, F., Shapiro, D.A., & Hardy, G.E. (in press). Assimilation of problematic experiences by clients in psychotherapy. *Psychotherapy.*

Stiles, W.B., Shapiro, D.A., & Firth-Cozens, J.A. (1988). Do sessions of different treatments have different impacts? *Journal of Counseling Psychology, 35,* 391-396.

THE SUPPLEMENTATION OF CLIENT-CENTERED COMMUNICATION THERAPY WITH OTHER VALIDATED THERAPEUTIC METHODS: A CLIENT-CENTERED NECESSITY

Reinhard TAUSCH
Universität Hamburg, F.R.Germany

The effectiveness of client-centered psychotherapy, originated by Carl Rogers (1951, 1954), has been demonstrated in numerous empirical studies both in the USA and in Europe. Researchers were able to show that this relatively brief therapy has very positive effects. However, I have come to consider that a supplementation of client-centered therapy by other, equally validated psychotherapeutic methods has become necessary for *some* of the clients. This is the central theme of my chapter. First, I want to answer the following question:

WHY IS A SUPPLEMENTATION NECESSARY?

1. It is obvious from daily practical experience that we as client-centered psychotherapists help some of our clients only insufficiently. This is in agreement with our empirical results from ten doctoral theses of a research project on individual therapies with approximately 200 clients, and on group-psychotherapy with 350 clients (e.g. Rudolph, Langer, & Tausch, 1980; Bruhn, Schwab, & Tausch, 1980; Schäfer, 1982; Dirks, Grimm, Tausch, & Wittern, 1982; Westermann, Schwab, & Tausch, 1983). In these studies, the percentage of therapies resulting in little or no change of clients' psychological health is apparent (ca. 20%). In follow-up studies one year after psychotherapy (Pomrehn, Tausch, & Tönnies, 1986) as well as through lasting friendships with a number of clients, it became clear to me that client-centered psychotherapy was a valuable experience in which many people changed significantly. However, some of the clients experienced little or no lasting changes towards greater emotional health.

To a certain extent, the reasons for clients' limited changes are the following: a. Psychotherapists do not possess a high degree of the three qualities that are important for therapy: Empathy, warmthcaring, and congruence. b. In their empathic understanding, psychotherapists mainly attend to clients' emotions. Carl Rogers however mainly attended to person-related cognitions as far as they are related to emotions (Tausch, 1988b). c. Client-centered psychotherapists are probably hardly aware that clients are occasionally looking for a stimulating facilitation of their self-explorative activities, cognitive restructuring, information about possibilities of alternative behaviors etc. Clients may experience this as a very helpful support (Lietaer & Neirinck, 1986). d. There is no possibility for clients to choose their psychotherapists or to choose between individual and group-psychotherapy, although this free choice is very significant (Schäfer, 1982).

2. As a fact, some other psychotherapeutic approaches have proved very effective also, like some relaxation techniques or some forms of cognitive-behavioral therapy. If we are open and congruent rather than negligent, we may accept these documented results and use them for the well-being of our clients.

3. In part, clinical psychology, psychiatry and general psychology have progressed during the last decade, for example with respect to the genesis and maintenance of emotional disturbances. It is now widely accepted that the basis of emotional disturbances is multicausal: Biochemical processes, psychological processes, social environment, and their interactions. When these various conditions accumulate and there is little social support, the individual's ability to cope may be greatly reduced. These multiple causes of emotional disturbances and their effects on many cognitive, emotional and behavioral processes imply a multimodal approach.

Further, Richard Lazarus (Lazarus & Folkman, 1984) was able to demonstrate that emotional and behavioral disturbances are mainly the consequence of person-related cognitions (appraisals). These cognitions may be changed (reappraisal) in the therapeutic communication; yet changes may also be induced by other experiences.

Also, emotional disturbances are related to everyday stressors (Folkman & Lazarus, 1986). The consequence of experiencing continuous stress is often a negative self-concept; and, in turn, a negative self-concept produces further stressful experiences. A negative self-concept may have its origin in childhood, which was also the view of Carl Rogers. Yet it may also develop during adulthood, through continuous daily stressors and through the stress of difficult life-events (divorce, separation from partner, or illness). Therefore it seems reasonable to diminish stress reactions.

These theoretical results suggest that client-centered communication psychotherapy may be supplemented in the case of clients with psychoneurotic or psychiatric complaints who *do not* change significantly or who do not show lasting changes after psychotherapy.

This supplementation does not reduce the fact that client-centered communication psychotherapy, according to Carl Rogers' concept, may produce very positive and effective changes: Particularly a reappraisal of the self, which in turn influences emotions as well as behavior. It is also my view that if the therapist lives the three qualities of empathy, warmthcaring and congruence to a high degree, these are, on the side of the therapist, sufficient conditions for constructive changes in the psychotherapeutic communication. However, some clients do not perceive a high degree of these qualities of their therapists and/or they do not change. For them, communication therapy on its own is not a sufficient condition.

WHAT ARE THE CRITERIA OF THE CLIENT-CENTERED CONCEPT FOR THE CHOICE OF SUPPLEMENTATION?

In my view, the therapist's empathic and caring attitude towards the client has the following consequences for the therapist-client contact:
1. The decision concerning the kind of supplementation which may be helpful for the client will be made with each client *individually*. In an empathic way, we must ask: What is helpful for *this* client? What does *he* need to facilitate his emotional health? Which supplementation is accessible to *this* client? In this way, we are acting in a client-centered manner and not in a therapist-centered manner by offering our standard therapy or choosing methods which we prefer.
2. The supplementations may produce changes which we may not achieve in communication therapy alone, or only in a limited sense.
3. The supplementations should not be directive, i.e. the client should not be led to accept alternative appraisals of self or decisions from his

therapist. Instead, these supplementations should constitute experiences in a situation which is transparent for the client, and which facilitates the cognitive and behavioral changes the client is striving for. The supplementations respect the phenomenal world of the client, his experiences and desires. The *client* determines his behavior, during as well as after therapy.

4. Respect and caring are the presuppositions for any therapist-client contact. Therefore, a therapist must offer his client only the supplementations which have been validated by empirical research. This is one of Carl Rogers major principles in all of his work and it contributed to his wide recognition.

5. The supplementations and their effects should facilitate and not be a barrier to communication in therapy.

6. These supplementations facilitate the client's independent activity and also make him more independent from the therapist. They have a positive influence on his self-efficacy and a healthy life-style after therapy.

CONSEQUENCES FOR THE PRACTICAL PSYCHOTHERAPEUTIC WORK

Which therapeutic options follow these client-centered criteria? What are desirable supplementations? In my view, the following methods are particularly valuable:

1. Relaxation techniques, especially progressive muscle relaxation (Jacobson, 1938), autogenic training (Schultz, 1950), in some cases Hatha-yoga, breathing-exercices, physical training, meditation. Positive effects of these therapeutic options have been demonstrated in numerous empirical studies, for example with regard to a more positive self-concept. The above-mentioned therapeutic approaches are transparent, non-directive and non-judgemental. Also, physical training, meditation and Hatha-yoga are helpful options even though their empirical validation is not as extensive.

The effects of relaxation can be explained theoretically in the following way: Anxiety, fears and emotional stress are usually related to muscle-tension which can become chronic. Because of these and further physiological processes, emotional tension rises, perception is narrowed and cognitive processes (appraisal, imaginations, memories) are of a rather negative nature. When the muscles are relaxed and, at the same time the activity of the sympathic nervous system is diminished, the self and personal situation is perceived in a less negative way, the emotional-physiological reactions of the individual are less excitable in relation to stressful events. Moreover, the client himself creates the positive experience of being able to reach calmness and to react in a more relaxed way (self-efficacy). If the therapist acts in a client-centered way throughout these exercises, takes the client's experiences seriously and helps the client to clarify them, this in turn increases the positive effects of these exercises.

2. Reduction of fears and emotional stress by client-centered group-communications and non-systematic desensitization (Wolpe, 1958). Clients may talk about their emotionally disturbing experiences in groups. Afterwards, they imagine the stressful situation in a relaxed state. In this way, they make a positive experience of the stressful situation. They then talk about their experiences; this contributes to clarification and intensifies the experience.

We looked at this combination of client-centered and behavior therapy in the following empirical studies: a. 362 persons participated in a study on the reduction of their fear of dying and death (Lohmann, Tausch, Langer, & Tausch, 1987; Tausch, 1988a), and another 122 persons for their fear of the death of a partner or a parent (Tausch, 1987). b. Further we offered so-called neurotics a seminar on the reduction of serious daily stress (Plön et al., 1988). c. We helped clients to cope better with the stress resulting from separation/divorce from a partner (Ruwwe & Tausch, 1988). - In all of these empirical studies non-systematic desensitization and client-centered communication in groups have proved to be very helpful possibilities.

3. Behavioral counseling is another supplementation, for example giving important information to the client on healthier living, on various coping strategies with respect to loneliness, too much pondering, planning one's time-schedule, self-help groups, changing inadequate subjective theories (for example the idea that cancer is the result of suppressed aggresiveness and can be healed by letting out one's aggressiveness). The therapist may communicate these informations directly and/or in writing or through books, and may thereby support the client's reappraisal process if this is what the client wants to achieve.

4. Other supplementations are the methods of behavior therapy, such

as problem-analysis and clarification, mental training of desirable behavior, training in vivo, facilitation of increased self-control (for example with eating-problems or smoking).

5. One important non-psychological supplementation is the medical treatment of bio-chemical disturbances of cerebral metabolism which are closely related to some emotional disturbances. If we are truly caring for the client, we cannot disregard these facts and the biological processes.

6. Philosophical, religious, spiritual cognitions may be significant for cognitions of the self and for the personal situation and life-style. However, I do not yet have any experience facilitating clients' clarifications in this respect, with the exception of recommending books.

PRACTICAL PROGRAMMING OF CLIENT-CENTERED PSYCHOTHERAPY, WITH SUPPLEMENTATIONS OR IN COMBINATION WITH OTHER THERAPIES

- Usually, client-centered communication therapy (individual or group) will be offered first, and, in most cases, continued throughout the supplemented therapeutic meetings. The major effect of communication is to help the client clarify and change his self (reappraisal), to develop more selfrespect and motivate the client to care for himself by becoming active.

- If the therapist notices during the first ten contacts that the client suffers from emotional disturbances (for example serious muscle-tension, everyday or life stress, wrong naive theories, e.g. concerning life-style, nutrition or illness) which will probably not change through client-centered communications, or if there is no progress in the client's well-being, then the therapist calls the client's attention to this and offers him information on additional therapeutic options which the client may accept or reject.

- Supplementary therapies (for example relaxation, reduction of fears, behavioral training) are usually offered as separate units from the client-centered communications, either with the same or another therapist.

However, in some cases it is helpful to offer short supplementary sequences *during* the communication (for example a brief relaxation, a brief non-systematic desensitization). This is particularly helpful if the client is making little progress due to little flexibility and rigid cognitions.

- Another type of combination is also possible. The client may come for 1-3 meetings in which he may be counseled and find an orientation himself. During these meetings, both therapist and client may plan the therapeutic programme, including client-centered communications and supplementations. Tests which are sensitive to the client's phenomenal world and behavior may be useful at this planning stage. As therapist, I sometimes gain better insight into the client's world when I include the data.

- One further possibility is the following: The client may be offered to participate in a 5 to 7-day client-centered workshop, possibly during the holidays. At the heart of the therapeutic programme are client-centered group-communications. Additionally, there are daily workshops in mental training, reduction of everyday and life stress, and workshops in which relaxation-techniques and physical training can be learned. This is a way for the client to start experimenting - with the support of his group - and to find out which option is most accessible to him.

SOME FINAL REMARKS

You may wonder what has remained of client-centered psychotherapy as we have known it so far?

Client-centered psychotherapeutic communications, individually or in a group, remain the way they were conceived and skilfully conducted by Carl Rogers.

For clients who need or wish, we offer a psychotherapeutic programme. It consists of client-centered communications and the additional elements which are significant for the individual client's change in cognitions, emotional mood, behavior and motivation. With communication therapy alone, these changes might not be achieved.

The word "client-centered" therefore stands for a certain quality of communication therapy between therapist and client, and also for the offer of the additional therapeutic possibilities which are suited to the individual client's needs. These therapeutic supplementations are the consequence of the therapist's empathic understanding, his warm

454

caring for the client and his openness.

For client-centered *psychotherapists,* the work with a supplementary psychotherapy programme will be facilitating: They will gain insight into other scientifically validated psychotherapeutic approaches and cognitive-phenomonological theories of general and clinical psychology. Their therapeutic activities will go beyond communication. This will also include structured situations in order to facilitate the client's experiences.

The *clients* gain a greater choice amongst several therapeutic options: Quicker and deeper changes in cognitions, well-being and behavior, reduced risk of developing too much self-directed attention without changing their coping abilities, better outcome/involvement ratio, greater self-help abilities and therefore greater independence from the psychotherapist.

Some readers may feel uneasy and resist this client-centered therapy; others may welcome it or may already be working along these lines. In presenting this therapeutic approach, my intention is not to criticize. Instead, my motivation is to improve our option in helping clients in the true, *client*-centered sense: This means including all the scientifically validated options which can help the individual client change his cognitions, emotional-physical reactions and behavior.

REFERENCES

Bruhn, M., Schwab, R., & Tausch, R. (1980). Die Auswirkungen intensiver personenzentrierter Gesprächsgruppen bei Klienten mit seelischen Beeinträchtigungen. *Zeitschriftt für Klinische Psychologie, 3,* 266-280.

Dircks, P., Grimm, F., Tausch, A., & Wittern, O. (1982). Förderung der seelischen Lebensqualität von Krebspatienten durch personenzentrierte Gruppengespräche. *Zeitschrift für Klinische Psychologie, 9,* 241-251.

Folkman, S., & Lazarus, R.S. (1986). Stress processes and depressive symptomatology. *Journal of Abnormal Psychology, 95,* 107-113.

Jacobson, W. (1938). Progressive relaxation. Chicago: University of Chicago Press.

Lazarus, R.S., & Folkman, S. (1984). *Stress, appraisal and coping.* New York: Springer.

Lietaer, G., & Neirinck, M. (1986). Client and therapist perceptions of helping processes in client-centered/experiential psychotherapy. *Person-centered Review, 1,* 436-455.

Lohmann, M., Tausch, A., Langer, I., & Tausch, R. (1987). Die Vorstellung des eigenen Sterbens im entspannten Zustand und personenzentrierte Gespräche. *Zeitschrift für Personenzentrierte Psychologie und Psychotherapie, 6,* 59-71.

Plön, S., Berbalk, H., & Tausch, R. (1988). *Ein kombiniertes Therapieangebot bei 75 Klienten mit seelischen Beeinträchtigungen.* Unpublished manuscript.

Pomrehn, G., Tausch, R., & Tönnies, S. (1986). Personenzentrierte Gruppenpsychotherapie: Prozesse und Auswirkungen nach 1 Jahr bei 87 Klienten. *Zeitschrift für Personenzentrierte Psychologie und Psychotherapie, 5,* 19-31.

Rogers, C.R. (1951). *Client-centered therapy.* Boston: Houghton Mifflin.

Rogers, C.R., & Dymond, R.F. (Eds.). (1954). *Psychotherapy and personality change.* Chicago: University Press.

Rudolph, J., Langer, I., & Tausch, R. (1980). Prüfung der psychischen Auswirkungen und Bedingungen von personenzentrierter Einzel-Psychotherapie. *Zeitschrift für Klinische Psychologie, 9,* 23-33.

Ruwwe, F., & Tausch, R. (1988). *Klientenzentrierte Gruppengespräche und kognitiv-verhaltenstherapeutische Desensibilisierung bei Klienten nach Trennung vom Partner.* Unpublished manuscript.

Schäfer, H. (1982). *Erleben und Auswirkungen psychotherapeutischer Einzelgespräche.* Unpublished doctoral dissertation, Universität Hamburg, Fachbereich Psychologie.

Schultz, I.H. (1950). *Das autogene Training* (6th ed.). Stuttgart: Thieme.

Tausch, D. (1987). *Die Vorstellung des möglichen Sterbens einer nahestehenden Person, eine empirische Untersuchung einer psychotherapeutischen Möglichkeit.* Frankfurt: Lang.

Tausch, R. (1988a). Reappraisal of death and dying after a person-centered behavioral workshop. *Person-centered Review, 3,* 213-228.

Tausch, R. (1988b). The relationship between emotions and cognitions: Implications for therapist empathy. *Person-centered Review, 3,* 277-291.

Westermann, B., Schwab, R., & Tausch, R. (1983). Auswirkungen und Prozesse personenzentrierter Gruppenpsychotherapie bei 164 Klienten einer Psychotherapeutischen Beratungsstelle. *Zeitschrift für Klinische Psychologie, 9,* 241-252.

Wolpe, J. (1958). *Psychotherapy by reciprocal inhibition.* Stanford, CA: University Press.

CLIENT-CENTERED THERAPY VERSUS PSYCHOANALYTIC PSYCHOTHERAPY: REFLECTIONS FOLLOWING A COMPARATIVE STUDY

Jochen ECKERT & Eva-Maria BIERMANN-RATJEN
Universitätsklinik Hamburg, F.R.Germany

INTRODUCTION

There is considerable evidence, that the era of comparative psychotherapy studies is past and, with it, the hope of gaining fundamental knowledge from such studies. For some time now, rather than examining and discussing the results of individual studies, dominant academic opinion has regarded the results of various overview studies and meta-analyses as the final state of knowledge on the subject.

This state of knowledge of empirical psychotherapy research can be reduced to two main points:

1. Psychotherapy is an effective form of treatment, i.e. as a method it works better than no psychotherapy, or than placebo treatment; in the long term, its effects are greater than the results of spontaneous remissions.

2. There is no essential difference between the effectiveness of the various therapy methods.

These statements are based on very carefully conducted, methodologically faultless single studies (e.g. Sloane, Staples, Cristol, Yorkston, & Wipple, 1975), on overview studies, by which the results of the available comparative investigations were compared with one another (e.g. Luborsky, Singer, & Luborsky, 1975), and on the comparative examination of numerous controlled studies of the various therapy methods by the technique of meta-analysis, which was introduced by Smith, Glass and Miller in 1980.

Although, on the one hand, we can be glad that Eysenck's theory of the ineffectiveness of psychotherapy (1952) finally seems to be refuted, it is, on the other hand, impossible to overlook the slight insult implied by the conclusion that all forms of therapy are equally successful.

As a prospective psychotherapist, one could conclude from this that it makes virtually no difference which method of therapy one were to be trained in, and that a discriminating attitude to differential therapy indications is superfluous.

This conclusion has been drawn not only by many of those engaged in therapy research, but also by practitioners (compare Hambrecht & Norcross, 1984; Karasu, 1986; Bozok & Bühler, 1988; Herschbach, 1988). They appear to presume that different therapy methods can be compared with one another in the same way as different drugs competing on the open market: All contain the same basic active ingredient, and differ otherwise only in color and in form, and of course in price. For this reason, the protagonists of this viewpoint suggest the following: Research should concentrate on this basic active ingredient of psychotherapy, which they refer to, strangely enough as "unspecific factors," and in practical situations one should proceed eclectically - after all, sometimes a pink pill does work better than a white one!

In the wake of this new trend, books are appearing with titles such as "Psychotherapy, an eclectic approach" (Garfield, 1980); the "Common component model" (Frank, 1982) is favored as an explanation for the effectiveness of psychotherapy, and "integrative psychotherapy" is increasingly being taught at the Institutes of Psychology. Dieter E. Zimmer's article "Für alle ein Preis und ein Dämpfer" in one of the leading German weeklies (*Die Zeit,* 1988) has also made the educated German layman conversant with this viewpoint and state of knowledge.

HYPOTHESES AND EVIDENCE FOR THE QUALITATIVELY DIFFERENT EFFECTIVENESS OF THE VARIOUS THERAPY METHODS

We consider the conclusion on which this trend is based to be inadequate, because it disregards two facts, which have since been empirically verified:

1. Each therapy method offers a particular therapeutic relationship, which in turn leads to qualitatively different changes in the patient's state, and
2. not every patient is able to respond equally well to every form of

therapeutic relationship offered, as is perhaps shown by the failure rate of 20-30% common to all therapy methods: This quota includes those patients, who either do not benefit from a completed course of treatment, or whose condition even deteriorates. It does not include those patients who break off the treatment prematurely, the so-called drop-outs.

Grawe's (1976) and Plog's (1976) comparison of the effectiveness of client-centered therapy (CCT) and behavioral therapy, in the treatment of patients suffering from severe phobias, provide one of the first pieces of empirical evidence for the theory that the various methods of psychotherapy offer different therapeutic relationships, leading to qualitatively different results. From a quantitative viewpoint, both therapy methods brought about comparable changes in the symptoms and general condition of the patients. However, a positive evaluation of the success of the treatment on the part of the patients who underwent behavioral therapy was closely correlated with the reduction of the phobic symptoms. This was not the case with the CCT-patients.

An interpretation of these results suggests itself: Patients who have undergone behavioral therapy judge the success of this therapy on the basis of the extent to which their phobic symptoms have disappeared; they thereby adopt the therapeutic paradigm of those who are treating them, who are primarily concerned with symptoms, and how to get rid of them.

CCT-therapists are more concerned with the patient as a person, with his existential experience. It is therefore not particularly surprising that the association between symptomatic change and therapeutic success, found in patients in behavioral therapy, does not occur here.

A further piece of empirical evidence for the supposition that patients react to the basic assumptions specific to each school of therapy concerning what makes that method therapeutic, is to be found in the results of the short-term therapy project conducted by Meyer (1981, 1986). This project compared the effects and processes of psychodynamic therapy (PT) with those of CCT. Without going into details of the methods used, the following table indicates the results.

Table 1

*The Hamburg Short Psychotherapy Comparison experiment
(Meyer, 1981, 1986): Clusters of clients,
type of outcome and psychotherapy orientation*

CLUSTER No	PATIENTS n/cluster			OUTCOME CRITERIA	
	PA	CCT	Sum	Improvement	Insight
1	4	4	8	-	-
2	7	9	16	+	+
4	3	10	13	+	-
6	7	0	7	-	+

Table 1 shows four of the six so-called "clusters" of patients. A cluster is composed of those patients exhibiting maximum similarity with one another on a series of 21 outcome criteria and at the same time maximum differences from the patients in other clusters.

For our purpose, only clusters 4 and 6 are of interest. The general condition of the thirteen patients in cluster 4 can be described as "improved", but with regard to the criterion "insight" they are classified as "not improved." In the case of the seven patients in cluster 6, however, things are the other way around.

This becomes interesting when we consider the treatment methods to which these patients were subjected: the CCT-patients tended to show improvement in their general condition, but did not gain insight into the psychodynamic forces which characterized their illness. On the other hand, all patients exhibiting more insight, but less improvement, were treated by psychoanalysts (PA).

50% of all patients treated fall under this constellation of results, which seems to reinforce the mutual predjudices of both schools of therapy: The psychoanalysts can come to the conclusion that the CCT-therapists as a rule only achieve transference cures, i.e. recovery without insight; and the CCT-therapists see their suspicions confirmed, that although psychoanalysts can help their patients gain insight into their condition, that alone is not sufficient to bring about any further changes in their condition.

We are not presenting these results in order to strengthen old prejudices. In combination with our own reflections, they rather offer a further confirmation of the assumption that the basic convictions of the therapist, with regard to the origin, perpetuation and conditions of change of psychic phenomena and symptoms, are transferred within every psychotherapeutic treatment.

To exaggerate a little, the psychoanalyst sees no other way to a permanent cure than that of making the patient aware of unconscious or preconscious conflicts, and their defence mechanisms, a process which he calls "insight."

The CCT-therapist assumes that the way to a healing process can be opened by encouraging the patient to adopt with himself the relationship which the CCT-therapist is offering him: self-empathy, congruence and a sense of his own intrinsic value (Biermann-Ratjen, Eckert & Schwartz, 1979). In the course of this process, the incongruence between self and experience, or, more exactly, between organismic experience and self-experience, diminishes. Whether insight is developed at all, and if so, to what extent, is not expressively postulated in CCT theory. The Meyer data show that it is not impossible to attain insight under these circumstances (see Table 1, cluster 2).

RESULTS OF THE COMPARISON BETWEEN CLIENT-CENTERED AND PSYCHOANALYTIC GROUP PSYCHOTHERAPY

Our purpose in presenting now our own comparative therapy study is primarily to provide further evidence for our hypothesis that the individual therapy methods offer qualitatively different therapeutic relationships, which lead to qualitatively different therapeutic processes and effects. As this study has already been published in full elsewhere (Eckert & Biermann-Ratjen, 1985), we will dispense with an exact description of the experimental conditions in the present account.

We compared the processes and effects of in-patient group psychotherapies, which were conducted in a psychiatric ward run on psychotherapeutic principles, based on the client-centered (CCT) and on the psychoanalytic (PA) concepts of therapy.

A total of 209 patients (CCT: 117, PA: 91) took part in our investigations. As a rule, subjects were treated for three months as in-patients, and participated in approximately fifty group sessions of 90 minutes duration in the course of this time. The average age of the patients was

27, and the proportion of men and women was about equal.

From the diagnostic viewpoint, the majority of the patients were suffering from neuroses and personality disturbances. The most conspicuous clinical characteristics were attempted suicide or a preoccupation with suicide.

The patients were examined on three separate occasions: before starting the treatment (pre), immediately following the end of the treatment (post 1), and two years after their discharge (post 2 = follow up). In order to measure the effect of the therapy, we used personality questionnaires and standardized interviews; the analysis of the therapy process was based on tape-recordings (ratings), process questionnaires, and a Q-sort.

Before we come to the results of our investigation, we would like to draw attention to three facts, which lend these results considerable significance:

1. The patients undergoing the two forms of treatment being compared lived for a period of three months in the same therapeutic milieu: A psychotherapy ward in a university psychiatric clinic. Apart from the psychotherapy, they all took part in the most varied therapeutic activities: Group dynamics exercises, sports (primarily swimming), excursions, visits to theatre and cinema, ward parties etc.

2. The treatment took the form of group therapy, in which in addition to the therapist, the group itself represents an important therapeutic factor.

3. The data, which illustrate most clearly the differences between patients who underwent client-centered therapy, and those who underwent psychoanalytic therapy were gathered by neutral investigators, two years after the treatment was concluded.

What this means is that the factor "therapist" seems to be of almost negligible influence in the face of the large number of long-term "unspecific factors", which singly or in combination, were in a position to affect the patients.

The results, which apply to both groups, are: The in-patient group psychotherapy which we investigated led in general to desirable changes in the self-experience of the patients in various different personality areas. These changes (pre- and post 1 differences in the "Freiburger" personality questionnaire and the "Giessen-test") - for example decrease in introversion, increase in "social potency", or fewer depressions - did not occur when the patients received no treatment at all, or when they were only treated within the framework of the usual standard psychiatric care (results of a comparison with a control group).

The positive changes in the self-experience of the patients still persisted two years after the end of the treatment (results of the 2 year follow-up investigation), i.e. the positive effect of the therapy remains, and can even lead to further positive developments in some areas of personality (e.g. depressions).

At the time of the follow-up survey we also enquired into the concrete circumstances of the patients, i.e. we asked about changes in the following areas of life: Home, work, partner relationship, sexuality, and leisure. On average, the patients indicated significant positive changes in all those areas.

With a few exceptions, there was little difference in the average extent of these changes between PA- and CCT-patients.

We are thus able to furnish proof of the long-term effectiveness of in-patient group psychotherapy, but at the same time we duplicated the "sickening" result of so many other studies: Namely that client-centered therapy and psychoanalytic psychotherapy are, on average, equally successful.

The comparison of mean changes in relation to a particular characteristic is a quantitative comparison. In our efforts to discover qualitative differences in the effects of these two forms of treatment, we followed various methodological paths; principally, we analysed the intercorrelations of the changes which had been measured. In the course of this procedure, we arrived at the definite conclusion that two years after the end of the treatment distinct differences exist between the two groups in the nature of the points of reference, on the basis of which the patients assess themselves and their environment.

The point of reference for the PA-patients appears to be the sense of internal and external autonomy which they perceive in themselves; the point of reference for CCT-patients is their ability to enter into relationships, and make contact with others.

We interpret this difference as being an expression of the fundamentally different views which these two therapy methods have of the development of psychological disturbances, and of the different therapeutic procedures they generate. PA-patients learn to observe the influence of the id and the super-ego on the ego, whereas CCT-patients learn to observe their emotions in interaction with their environment, primarily in relation to the people to whom they personally relate most closely.

DISCUSSION OF THE RESULTS

As already indicated, the results presented above provide empirical support for our thesis that each therapy method offers its own particular therapeutic relationship, thus leading to qualitatively different experiential changes in the people being treated. If this is the case, then our second thesis, the validity of which has yet to be verified, gains in importance when considering which therapy to recommend to which patient: "Not every patient is able to respond equally well to every form of therapeutic relationship."

Amongst the elements of the therapeutic relationship offered by each therapy method are the so-called "therapy process variables," e.g. the nature and quality of the rapport between therapist and patient.

The importance of the therapy process variables for the success of the therapy was first proved by client-centered therapists in the course of numerous empirical investigations (e.g. Garfield, 1971). Since then, a number of empirical studies in behavior therapy and psychoanalysis have also been reported - especially in the fields of short-term psychodynamic therapy (Gomes-Schwartz, 1976; Malan, 1980; Strupp, 1980; Buckley, Conte, Plutchik, Wild, & Karasu, 1984; Leuzinger-Bohleber, 1985).

Summarizing the results of these studies, we are led to the following conclusions:

1. It is important for the course and the results of the therapy that the therapy process variables of a particular patient, considered by a given therapeutic theory to be significant for the course of the therapy are sufficiently present in the concrete therapeutic situation. Examples of process variables are the "self-exploration" of a patient in CCT, the "transference capability" of a patient in psychoanalysis, or the "visualization capability" of a patient undergoing systematic desensitization.

2. It is important for the course and the results of the therapy that the patient-therapist interaction takes a form regarded by the school of therapy as favorable for the course of the therapy. In a psychoanalytically oriented therapy, for example, the transference

feelings perceived by the therapist are incorporated into the therapeutic dialogue in a way which has emotional significance for the patient; in CCT, the degree of self-exploration shown by the client varies with the degree of empathy exhibited by the therapist.

3. On the basis of our investigations (Eckert, Schwartz, & Tausch, 1977; Eckert, Belz, & Pfuhlmann, 1979; Eckert, Biermann-Ratjen, Blonski, & Peters, 1979) into the reactions of the patients to the concrete events of the therapy, we arrived at the following abstract formulation of these connections, the validity of which appears to be independent of the person of the therapist, and of the therapy method applied:

In order that a therapy may take a favorable course - and therefore have a favorable chance of success - a decisive factor seems to be that the patient is able to perceive and accept the therapeutic relationship offered to him by the therapist in a way which allows him to relate to it on an emotional level, so that in his reaction to it he can experience a change in his emotional and/or cognitive state. We have termed this process characteristic the "Responsiveness of the patient to the therapeutic relationship being offered."

We were also able to prove the significance of this process variable for our in-patient group: The measurement of this variable by means of a group process questionnaire during the initial stage of therapeutic contact allowed prediction, on average, of 25% of the variance of change on various personality assessment scales (Eckert & Biermann-Ratjen, 1985, pp. 91 & 117 onwards).

Summing up, we would like to emphasize the following:

It is evident that the various therapy methods offer (the patient) different therapeutic relationships.

Patients who later turn out as successfully treated apparently perceive this specific offer of a therapeutic relationship as being right for them, and thereby adopt the "theory" of their therapist. Whether, and to what extent, this takes place can be determined by observing the process variable "Responsiveness of the patient to the therapeutic relationship being offered." This variable can not only be observed clinically, but can also be measured objectively by means of process questionnaires.

CONSEQUENCES

Following from our previous considerations, we think it is possible that those patients whose treatment was unsuccessful were unable to respond to the concrete therapeutic relationship which was offered to them. The question therefore arises, whether these patients would have benefited more from a different therapy, i.e. from the offer of a different therapeutic relationship.

We suppose, also in accordance with our clinical observations, that this question can be answered in the affirmative. We thereby start with the premise that the responsiveness of a patient to the offer of a particular therapeutic relationship cannot be independent of the way in which the patient has experienced, judged and coped (or failed to cope) with both the outside world and himself up to this point or to put it in terms of Mahoney (1980), his "willingness to experience" or his "schemata."

The less contradiction between the concrete therapeutic relationship being offered and the patient's "willingness to experience" the more favorable the chances for a promising therapy process and thereby for successful outcome.

This assumption could provide a useful guideline for thinking about differential therapy indications. We have no further points to make at this stage, except for the final observation that the therapeutic relationship being offered is not defined by the therapy method alone. The various possible settings, such as individual or group therapy, offer different relationships in each case, and of course, the person of the therapist does too.

There is, therefore, plenty more thinking and research to be done, in order to determine the parameters of the "personal equation between patient and therapist" (Strupp, 1987, pp. 541).

REFERENCES

Biermann-Ratjen, E.-M., Eckert, J., & Schwartz, H.-J. (1979). *Gesprächspsychotherapie. Verändern durch Verstehen.* Stuttgart: Kohlhammer.
Bozok B., & Bühler, K.-E. (1988). Wirkfaktoren in der Psychotherapie: spezifische und unspezifische Einflüsse. *Fortschritte Neurologie und Psychiatrie, 56,* 119-132.

Buckley, P., Conte, H.R., Plutchik, R., Wild, K.V., & Karasu, T.B. (1984). Psychodynamic variables as predictors of psychotherapy outcome. *American Journal of Psychiatry, 141,* 742-748.

Eckert, J., Schwartz, H.-J., & Tausch, R. (1977). Klientenerfahrungen im Zusammenhang mit psychischen Aenderungen in personenzentrierter Psychotherapie. *Zeitschrift Klinische Psychologie, 6,* 177-184.

Eckert, J., Bolz, W., & Pfuhlmann, K. (1979). Ueberprüfung der Vorhersagbarkeit von psychotherapeutischen Effekten aufgrund der "Ansprechbarkeit" des Klienten bei Gesprächspsychotherapie und psychodynamischer Kurztherapie. *Zeitschrift Klinische Psychologie, 8,* 169-180.

Eckert, J., Biermann-Ratjen, E.-M., Blonski, D., & Peters, W. (1979). Zur Prädiktion der Effekte einer Gesprächspsychotherapie anhand eines Indikationsinterviews. *Zeitschrift Klinische Psychologie und Psychotherapie, 27,* 22-29.

Eckert, J., & Biermann-Ratjen, E.-M. (1985). *Stationäre Gruppenpsychotherapie: Prozesse, Effekte, Vergleiche.* Berlin: Springer.

Eysenck, H.-J. (1952). The effects of psychotherapy. An evaluation. *Journal of Consulting Psychology, 16,* 319-324.

Frank, J.D. (1982). Therapeutic components shared by all psychotherapies. In J.H. Harrey & M.H. Parks (Eds.), *The master lecture series* (Vol. 1). Washington, DC: American Psychological Association.

Garfield, S.L. (1971). Research on client variables in psychotherapy. In A.E. Berlyne & S.L. Garfield (Eds.), *Handbook of psychotherapy and behavior change.* New York: Wiley.

Garfield, S.L. (1980). *Psychotherapy. An eclectic approach.* New York: Wiley.

Gomes-Schwartz, B. (1978). Effective ingredients in psychotherapy: Prediction of outcome from process variables. *Journal of Consulting Psychology, 46,* 1023-1035.

Grawe, K. (1976). *Differentielle Psychotherapie I. Indikation und spezifische Wirkung von Verhaltenstherapie und Gesprächspsychotherapie.* Bern: Huber.

Hambrecht, M., & Norcross, J.C. (1984). Aktuelle Trends in der Psychotherapie in den USA. *Nervenarzt, 55,* 230-235.

Herschbach, P. (1988). Psychotherapieforschung in der Krise. Was können wir von den primitiven Heilern lernen? *GwG-Zeitschrift, 70,* 33-37.

Karasu, T.B. (1986). The specificity versus nonspecificity dilemma: Toward identifying therapeutic change agents. *American Journal of Psychiatry, 143,* 687-695.

Leuzinger-Bohleber, M. (1985). *Psychoanalytische Kurztherapien. Zur Psychoanalyse in Institutionen.* Opladen: Westdeutscher Verlag.

Luborsky, L., Singer, B., & Luborsky, L. (1975). Comparative studies of psychotherapy. Is it true that "everybody has won, and all must have prizes"? *Archives of General Psychiatry, 32,* 995-1008.

Mahoney, M. (1980). Psychotherapieerfolg: Implikationen kognitiver Konstrukte. In W. Schulz & M. Hautzinger (Eds.), *Klinische Psychologie und Psychotherapie* (Vol. 1). Berlin: DGVT & GwG.

Malan, D.H. (1980). *Toward the validation of dynamic psychotherapy.* New

468

York: Plenum Press.

Marzali, E.A. (1984). Prediction of outcome of brief psychotherapy from therapist interpretive interventions. *Archives of General Psychiatry, 41,* 301-304.

Meyer, A.-E. et al. (1981). The Hamburg short psychotherapy comparison experiment. *Psychotherapy and Psychosomatics, 35(2-3),* 81-207.

Meyer, A.-E. (1986). *Wodurch wirkt Psychotherapie?* Unpublished manuscript. Available from: Abtlg. für Psychosomatik und Psychotherapie, Universitätskrankenhaus Hamburg, Martinistrasse 52, D-2000 Hamburg 20, W.-Germany.

Plog, U. (1976). *Differentielle Psychotherapie. II. Der Zusammenhang zwischen Lebensbedingungen und spezifischen Therapieeffekten im Vergleich von Gesprächspsychotherapie und Verhaltenstherapie.* Bern: Huber.

Sloane, R.B., Staples, F.R., Cristol, A.H., Yorkstone, N.J., & Whipple, K. (1975). *Psychotherapy versus behavior therapy.* Cambridge, MA: Harvard University Press.

Smith, M.L., Glass, V., & Miller, T.J. (1980). *The benefits of psychotherapy.* Baltimore: John Hopkins University Press.

Strupp, H.H. (1980). Success and failure in time-limited psychotherapy (Comparison 1, 2, 3, 4). *Archives of General Psychiatry, 37,* 595-603, 708-716, 834-841, 947-954.

Strupp, H.H. (1986). Psychotherapie: Einige Bemerkungen zu Forschung, Ausbildung und Praxis. In M. Amelang (Ed.), *Bericht über den 35. Kongress der DGfPs,* Heidelberg, 1986 (Vol. 2, pp. 535-543). Göttingen: Hogrefe.

Zimmer, D. (Ed.). (1983). *Die therapeutische Beziehung.* Weinheim: Edition Psychologie.

Zimmer, D.E. (1988). Für alle ein Preis und ein Dämpfer. *Die Zeit, 30.*

CARL ROGERS, CARL JUNG AND CLIENT-CENTERED THERAPY

Henk R. Wijngaarden
Vrije Universiteit Amsterdam, The Netherlands

A SCHEME OF THE HUMAN PERSON

I will start in the style of Jung by presenting a scheme of the human person. I emphasize only one scheme, an expression of one point of view from which the person can be considered (Jacobi, a student of Jung, gives in her introduction to his theory 13 different schemes to illustrate his vision [Jacobi, 1945]). Such a scheme is an attempt to bring order into the phenomena; it is a part of Jung's thinking, but it is, at the same time, a reduction.

The scheme I present tries to illustrate the degree of consciousness of the person. This scheme does not use the metaphor of descending into the depth (depth-psychology) but, instead, tries to describe steps on the way to individuation, to becoming a person.

1. body-awareness
2. conscious awareness
3. judging
4. decision-making

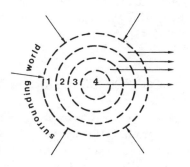

action, behavior

The person lives in a world that surrounds him and exerts an influence on him from all sides. In a manner consistent with Lewin's thinking, the boundary between the person and the world is seen as a permeable one, as indicated by the dotted line. When does the piece of bread I eat become part of me? When I have it, in my mouth? When it is in my stomach? When I have digested it? Till when is my hair or are my nails part of me? Till I cut them? Till when are my excrements part of me? The concept of permeability is an indication of an insoluble problem.

The world around us is mainly a world of people, especially of important others. We cannot exist without them; we are not autonomous but interdependent. Men need men. To become a person we will have to give our personal answer to all the emotions and experiences that are evoked in us by the world in which we live.

BODY-AWARENESS

When we pass the permeable boundary between the surrounding world and the person, we come to realm 1: The body with its qualities and attributes, its genetic dispositions, its Id, its collective unconscious and so on, the realm of experiences of which the person has no awareness ("realm" is a metaphor again; in dept psychology, the metaphor "layer" would be used). Here is the domain we share in common with the higher species of animals, a domain where pain and fear, rage and pleasure occur and where the person is identical to such moods or emotions, without being aware of them. Many psychotherapies, including client-centered therapy, deal with the difficulty of bringing emotions from this realm through the permeable boundary into the next one.

CONSCIOUS AWARENESS

Realm 2 is the one where we can be aware of our experiences. Here we are on firm Rogerian ground. We are all well aware of the importance of recognizing: "That's me." The conditions of the therapist are aimed at that experiencing, as well as many techniques in focusing, in Gestalttherapy and in body-therapies. Here Rogers' theory stops because of his trust, I might say his faith, in the power of an innate tendency in the human being to maintain and enhance itself towards a fully functioning person. When one is aware of one's experiences and experiencing process, one will, according to Rogers, make one's choices in a direction of expanding or intensifying one's life. Not that this is an easy development: "I would not want to give the impression that my clients move blithely or confidently in this direction. No indeed - Freedom to be oneself is a frightening responsible freedom, and an individual moves toward it cautiously, fearfully, and with almost no confidence at first" (Rogers, 1961, p. 171). Rogers' trust and experience is however, that once one is going in that direction, the process will go on. He describes a process of *maturation.*

I shall not repeat here my criticism of Rogers' theory; I have done that elsewhere (Wijngaarden, 1988). But many therapists who consider themselves to be client-centered do not agree with Rogers on this point. Let me quote Pfeiffer as an example: "The human being does not only have a constructive potential, but also a destructive one, that cannot be explained only by the denial of fundamentally positive impulses" (Pfeiffer, 1986, p. 370). This is a basic difference with Rogers' view of man, but it is in accordance with Jung. It appears that Rogers hardly knew the work of Jung, but many of his ideas can be found in Jung's writings. Rogers speaks about the importance of acknowledging and accepting denied or distorted aspects of ourselves as "that's me"; Jung writes about the shadow as being part of ourselves, as "that's me too," and he stresses the necessity to recognize and acknowledge our feelings and experiences as expressions of ourselves, for "one cannot change what one does not accept" (Jung, 1932, p. 25). Jung speaks about the trustworthiness of the collective unconscious; and Rogers writes that the organism of the person "can be wiser and often is wiser than his consciousness" (Rogers & Kinget, 1960, p. 282). Jung considers the psyche as a self-regulating system (Jung, 1934, p. 90), and Rogers speaks about the self-regulating functions of the organism (Rogers & Kinget, 1960, p. 287). Despite all these agreements, Jung and Rogers start from different basic views of man. For Jung, the forces of the human psyche can work out positively as well as negatively. We can turn them into positive or negative forces, as individuals, or as mankind in general. The development of the human being is not a matter of natural maturation like that of plants or animals, provided that this process is not hampered by outer influences, but of *individuation,* a matter of ethical decisions (Jacobi, 1945, pp. 166, 178, 204), and that is a curse as well as a blessing, for it is inevitably attended by loneliness; one cannot give a more comforting word for it (Jung, 1934, p. 190).

JUDGING

Here we pass the boundaries to realm 3 of my scheme. We not only have our feelings, we also can judge them, decide whether we agree with them, want to take them as guidelines for our actions, or not. This is a common experience. Often we shrink back from something we have to do, out of fear or timidity, or because of the heaviness or tiresomeness of the job; nevertheless we do it. Of course, this can be the effect of a lack of inner freedom, but it can also be the effect of inner freedom.

We are all familiar with those clients for whom it is so difficult to feel what they feel and to recognize that as "that's me!". In my experience, the next difficult step is usually to look at those feelings, i.e. to take some distance from them instead of only being them. Sometimes a client does not understand the question: "What do you think of that feeling?" because he has no notion of the possibility of judging his own emotions in the same way as some clients do not know they can own their feelings. Judging here is not an intellectual manoeuvre; it is a rationally and emotionally satisfying answer, in which one is not internally divided but has an experience of wholeness, of being in accordance with oneself - Jung would say an experience of being "true to one's own law" (Jung, 1934, p. 190). We all have our jealousies, anxieties, vanities, hatreds and so on; we cannot help it, they are there. We are not responsible for their existence, but we are responsible for what they do to us, for in how far we let them influence our behavior. Rogers' "that's me" is not enough. Coming to awareness also means that we judge all those aspects that belong to "me," and decide how we want to live with them.

DECISION-MAKING

This leads us to the boundary of realm 4, the domain of conscious choice, where decisions are made. We can do something, knowing and feeling that it is wrong. Of course, this can be the result again of what we have been taught, of being weighed down by internalized commands from outside, but it can also be the result of weakness or unwillingness to stand for our conviction or our conscience. It is well expressed in the confession of St. Paul: "I discover this principle then: That when I want to do the right, only the wrong is within my reach" (Rom. 7: 21). Even with full consciousness we can betray ourselves. It is often a difficult and heavy decision to be true to our own law. My attention has been called to Otto Rank by an article by Pfeiffer (1980). Like Jung, Otto Rank is a forerunner of humanistic psychology and, consequently, of client-centered therapy. He stresses the importance of will, the act of conscious judging and decision-making (Rank, 1936). In my views it is necessary to make a clear distinction between judging and decision-making as different psychological activities, but I think client-centered therapy could gain from considering Rank's concept of will seriously.

To do justice to Rogers, I will quote his description of the aim of life: "To use Kierkegaard's more aesthetically satisfying terms, it means, to be that self which one truly is. I trust I have made it evident that this is not an easy direction to move, nor one which is ever completed. It is a continuing way of life" (Rogers, 1961, p. 181). Nevertheless, as a consequence of his optimistic view of man, he did not pay much attention to the human struggle that is inherent in judging and decision-making. Looking back on what I have said till now, I realize that I have described grades in awareness and in the freedom that is made possible by this awareness. This approach is in accordance with Swildens' characterization of neurosis as an illness of freedom (Swildens, 1986, p. 68), and with Rank's emphasis on what happens in the conscious ego.

I have to stress the permeability of the boundaries. It is an act of decision-making to look seriously at one's vague feelings; that is already a deed of freedom aiming at expanding freedom. But freedom is a difficult and heavy good. The price of freedom is the struggle to be undivided within oneself, to be true to one's own law, to be whole. Courage is needed when we are afraid of the consequences of what we really are - see Luther: "Here I stand, I have no choice." Unselfishness is needed when our self-love is at stake. This is not a natural process of maturation, but often a matter of self-conquest. Decision-making is the nucleus of human freedom; consciousness is not the cause but the prerequisite for the measure of freedom that is possible. About these experiencings, we can learn more from Jung and from Rank than from Rogers.

Our motor behavior, what we do, how we act, can be derived from the four different realms of consciousness and freedom, of ego-strength, that I have described. In psychotherapy we try to help our clients to have the courage to feel what they feel (from realm 1 to realm 2), to form their own judgment of those feelings (from realm 2 to realm 3) and to choose their own inner conviction (from realm 3 to realm 4). We have to listen carefully as to how the disturbances of inner freedom and consciousness are felt . This means that we, as therapists, address the elements of freedom in our clients, trying with them to find where their problems and inhibitions are lying. If there are no traces of freedom left, as in some cases of psychosis, this approach will have no success.

What is always fundamental is the conscious experiencing of our feelings, our judgments, our decisions. We have to be careful not to mistake emotionality or spontaneity for this experiencing - it was Klages who saw emotionality as the result of the ratio between the liveliness of human feelings and their depth (very lively emotions can be very superficial).

FREEDOM AND ITS LIMITATIONS

The question whether human beings have a margin of freedom is a philosophical one. But it cannot be denied that experiencing freedom does exist, and that is the phenomenon with which I am dealing here. In any case, as the behaviorist Krasner writes, "for all practical purposes" (Krasner, 1965, p. 23), we cannot omit this concept.

On the other hand, people have their limitations. Rogers has stressed the necessity for the therapist to understand his clients within their own frame of reference, to be able to feel like they feel, to share their experiencing, albeit with the "as-if quality" to prevent identification. I could not agree more; but in order to do this, we have to reckon with the limitations of each individual. People are different; if we want to understand them, we need a thorough knowledge of those differences. We need a diagnosis, not to play the god-like role, as Rogers feared (Rogers, 1951, p. 221), but to intensify our understanding of our clients.

Thinking about the present lecture, I remembered that before the war and during the first years following it, characterology was in high esteem in psychology. Personality-theories generally stress one or another aspect of the person. Characterologies like that of Klages (1926) try to develop a system in which all the aspects of the person will be described. Such a broad spectrum of human aspects helps to understand what is going on in our clients. One of Klages topics, for example, is the *attitude* of the person. Many psychologists have written about this subject. Klages himself, makes a distinction between the tendency towards self-preservation versus the tendency towards self-dedication. Jung made the well-known distinction between extraversion and introversion (Jung, 1921). Others distinguish inner-, other-, and outer-directedness of the person (Riesman, 1950), field-dependency and field-independency (Witkin, 1962), external and internal control (Rotter, 1966). De Haas writes about the different attitudes of opening versus secluding oneself, and of adjusting oneself versus exerting an influence (De Haas, 1982). These are all different attitudes towards life, of which therapists and especially client-centered therapists must have a notion in order to understand their clients.

Next to the attitudes of the person, we have to understand his *qualities* or capacities. This is the field of many typologies (f.i. Kretschmer, Freud, Jung, Heymans, Eysenck). Think of a rationalist. He can be approached with rational arguments, because they have emotional value for him. To him, they feel good. (He himself would say: They do not *feel* good, they *are* good.) As therapists, we have to understand this is honestly what he experiences and we have to meet him within that frame of reference. Otherwise, we shall not start where the client is. The consequence for client-centered therapy is that this leads to different approaches of people with different disturbances, as Swildens has very clearly demonstrated (Swildens, 1988). But this also leads to the acknowledgement that other therapies can be better suited than the client-centered approach. For very inhibited people, a body therapy can be more helpful for loosening up, unfreezing, than a talking therapy, provided that such catharsis will be followed by a further working through of the problems.

Another aspect of human functioning - I still follow Klages' train of thought - is *motivation*. Rogers' theory presents one overruling force: The tendency towards growth. Adler also postulates one fundamental tendency: The "Gemeinschaftsgefühl." Freud describes two basic drives: Eros and Thanatos. In Jung's theory, archetypes are the sources of energy. (He does not enumerate them but there are about twenty.) Murray speaks of need-fulfillment as the motivating force; he gives a taxonomy of 41 of those needs. Lewin calls the psychological forces vectors; their number is countless. Fromm's fear of freedom could be such a vector.

So we can see that psychologists have looked at motivation in many different ways, each with good reason. The schools to which we feel ourselves attracted decide which motivation will be at the foreground of our awareness, but we can be influenced by other ideas as well. After having read Karen Horney's writings on the pride-system, I usually recognize a pride-system in my clients more often than when I have not thought of her work for a long time; then her ideas fall out of my current awareness.

IMPLICATIONS FOR THE CLIENT-CENTERED THERAPIES

I will now try to speak of the implications of these lines of thought for the client-centered therapies.

1. The personality model

What we have in common is a *personality model* in which a tendency towards growth as well as a tendency towards avoiding growth (in the same sense as Fromm's fear of freedom) are struggling to have the upper hand. In this struggle we accept a margin of freedom, with all its ethical implications. I quote Jung: "Ethics have not been brought down from Sinaï but are a function of the human soul" (Jung, 1943, p. 49). Consciousness-raising, which our therapies are aiming at, is a prerequisite for the possible measure of freedom, but not its source. In decision-making lies the ethical responsibility of the human being - this seems to me a fundamental trait of humanistic psychology and, consequently, of client-centered therapies.

For a long time I have looked for a firm client-centered *personality theory*. I have come to the conclusion that each personality theory inevitably is a reduction of the human being, because it cannot avoid looking at its object from a specific point of view, clarifying and explaining some aspects, omitting others. All those theories have their relative adequacy, insofar as the human being is a drive-reduction system, a reinforcement machine, a computer, and so on. I do not believe in one all-embracing personality theory; they all have their relative value. The same restriction is valid for a specific client-centered personality theory, contrary to the idea of keeping the whole person in perspective. The consequence of this premise is, that we need to acknowledge the relative values of these theories and use them as heuristic starting-points in our phenomenological approach of the person, trying to understand which vision best describes what is going on in this individual client or client-system at this moment. Our anti-dogmatism (Wijngaarden, 1984, p. 48) requires a broad expertise in the field of psychology. That is the reason why I fall back on the ideas of Klages. In my opinion when we deal with motivation, we can very well use the archetypical forces of Jung, because they are, by nature, biological as well as psychological, not reductible, and typical of the human species. Studying the process of decision-making, we can learn a lot from Rank's concept of will. Transference and countertransference are psychoanalytic concepts which we have to consider seriously. We have to respect all those contributions, but we highly value the possibility of growth of the person and try in therapy to create the circumstances that will enhance that growth.

2. Striving for a person-to-person relationship

We have in common the fact that we strive for a person-to-person relationship in therapy, and we therefore emphasize the conditions worked out by Rogers; however, not as he thought because they are sufficient, but because they are important for providing a climate of freedom that promotes growth. We know that the relationship is not one of equals: We, as therapists, are the helpers, our clients are the helpees. We earn our money on the basis of this cast. But we try to stand next to our clients, expecting that this will stimulate their independence. Hence the difference with psychoanalysis in handling transference phenomena.

3. The emphasis on the experiencing of our clients

In the third place we have in common our emphasis on the experiencing of our clients as the main way to their self-understanding and self-knowledge, to their possibilities for change and growth. We do not deny the importance of insight, nor of learning-processes that lead to behavioral changes as well as to habit formation. However, our interest and attention is primarily directed at experiencing - that is our *choice,* and that is where we have developed our greatest sensitivity and expertise. Our use of interventions and techniques (including listening to dreams, active imagination, focusing, hot seat, bioenergetics) will have to depend on their probability of enhancing the experiencing process in this client at *this* moment. Intuition will play an important role here, but this intuition can only florish adequately if it is based on a solid knowledge of psychology.

CONCLUSION

I have to stress the fact that I do *not* advocate some form of eclecticism. I fear that would lead to an unsystematic trial and error approach of our clients, even if it were supported by research findings. The three points I have described, especially the attitude of focusing on the experiencing-process, are typical of the client-centered style of psychotherapy and give us an easily recognizable identity in comparison with other psychotherapy currents, as shown by Eijmael (1987). It is also possible to focus on insight or on behavior, with the same aim of influencing the feeling-process of the clients or patients. Sometimes, these points of view will match best with a client. That is a matter of diagnosis. As I have often done, I gladly quote Barendregt again: "If people have qualities, maybe it can do no harm to bear that in mind" (Barendregt, 1982, p. 37).

I fear my presentation might be seen as a weakening of the position of the client-centered therapies among other therapies. That is not my opinion. I admire the edifice of psychoanalytic theory, but, at the same time, I feel shut in when I enter that building. Client-centered therapy has its place in the open field and is therefore vulnerable. The landscape has not been explored minutely and laid out exactly on a map. We have the compass of our humanistic starting point and of the conditions that results from it. The focus on experiencing is our hallmark. In addition to that, we need a thorough knowledge of what is going on in people, in the ways they are influenced, but not ultimately determined by their personal dispositions and their social life circumstances. Consequently, we need thorough knowledge of the different psychological and therapeutic theories with their relative values. Gendlin's book on dreams offers an illustration of this process (Gendlin, 1986). Gendlin does not give a theory but, within the typical client-centered approach of concentrating on the experiencing process, he makes a critical use of different dream theories. This knowledge and recognition of the work and insight of colleagues in other currents of therapy will not weaken but strengthen client-centered therapy.

REFERENCES

Barendregt, J.T. (1982). *De zielenmarkt.* Meppel: Boom.

Eijmael, J. (1987). *Gedragstherapie en client-centered therapie vergeleken.* Amersfoort/Leuven: Acco.

Gendlin, E.T. (1986). *Let your body interpret your dreams.* Wilmette, IL: Chiron.

Haas, O. de. (1982) Individuele procesgerichte gesprekstherapie. In H.M. van der Ploeg (Ed.), *Psychotherapie.* Alphen aan de Rijn: Stafleu.

Jacobi, J. (1945). *Die Psychologie von C.G. Jung.* Zürich: Rascher.

Jung, C.G. (1921). *Psychologische Typen.* Zürich: Rascher.

Jung, C.G. (1932). *Die Beziehungen der Psychotherapie zur Seelsorge.* Zürich: Rascher.

Jung, C.G. (1934). *Wirklichkeit der Seele.* Zürich: Rascher.

Jung, C.G. (1943). *Ueber die Psychologie des Unbewussten.* Zürich: Rascher.

Klages, L. (1926). *Die Grundlagen der Charakterkunde.* Leipzig: Barth.

Krasner, L. (1965). The behavioral scientist and social responsability. *Journal of Social Issues, 21(2),* 9-30.

Pfeiffer, W.M. (1980). Otto Rank. Wegbereiter personenzentrierter Psychotherapie. In W. Schulz & N. Holzinger (Eds.), *Klinische Psychologie und Psychotherapie* (pp. 93-102). Berlin: DGTV & GwG.

Pfeiffer, W.M. (1986). Ist das Rogers'sche Persönlichkeits- und Therapiekonzept im Hinblick auf psychiatrische Erkrankungen angemessen? *Zeitschrift für Personenzentrierte Psychologie und Psychotherapie, 5,* 367-377.

Rank, O. (1936). *Will therapy.* New York: Knopf.

Riesman, D. (1950). *The lonely crowd.* New Haven: Yale University Press.

Rogers, C.R. (1961). *Client-centered therapy.* Boston: Houghton Mifflin.

Rogers, C.R., & Kinget, G.M. (1960). *Psychotherapie en menselijke verhoudingen.* Utrecht: Spectrum.

Rotter, J.B. (1966). Generalized expectancies for internal versus external control of reinforcement. *Psychological Monographs, 80* (whole number 609), 1-28.

Swildens, J.C.A.G. (1986). Over psychopathologie en haar belang voor de client-centered psychotherapie. In R. Van Balen, M. Leijssen, & G. Lietaer (Eds.), *Droom en werkelijkheid in client-centered psychotherapie.* Leuven: Acco.

Swildens, J.C.A.G. (1988). *Procesgerichte gesprekstherapie.* Amersfoort/Leuven: Acco.

Witkin, H.A. (1962). *Psychological differentiation.* New York: Wiley.

Wijngaarden, H.R. (1984). Client-centered therapie: een eigen identiteit? In G. Lietaer, Ph.H. van Praag, & J.C.A.G. Swildens (Eds.), *Client-centered therapie in beweging.* Leuven: Acco.

Wijngaarden, H.R. (1988). De theorie van Rogers. *Mededelingenblad VRT, 2,* 51-57.

PSYCHOTHERAPY INTEGRATION FROM
A CLIENT-CENTERED PERSPECTIVE

Arthur C. BOHART
California State University
Dominguez Hills, U.S.A.

There has been a growing interest in eclectic and integrative approaches to psychotherapy, as well as in commonalities among differing approaches (Bohart & Todd, 1988; Frank, 1982; Goldfried, 1980; Guidano, 1987; Marmor, 1987; Norcross, 1986; Ryle, 1982). I will examine certain common underlying factors and how they relate to client-centered therapy. In the first section I will argue that the "process orientation" of client-centered therapy is in various forms a goal of all psychotherapies. In the second section I will discuss common factors in the processes of change in psychotherapy.

A PROCESS ORIENTATION IS
THE GOAL OF ALL PSYCHOTHERAPY

One aspect of a client-centered approach is its process orientation. The person is seen as an ongoing process, and to be a process is seen as being fully functional. Process is primary, structure is secondary (Gendlin, 1964; Bohart, see this volume).

This orientation implies that living systems are interactive processes. They are continually in "dialogue" with their environments, responding to them, integrating information from them, and feeding forward that integration into behavioral change.

In humans, the capacity to adapt or modify responses to fit an ever changing environment appears to be greater than in other species. Not only can they modify their behavior within certain "programs," but they can "stand back" and modify the "programs." Thus a key feature of humans is their capacity for truly *creative adaptation,* to operate in the "I (intelligent) mode" of functioning rather than the "M

482

(mechanical) mode" (Hofstader, 1979). I will call the use of this capacity "effective self-monitoring."

Self-monitoring

To suggest that the goal of therapy is to make people more process-oriented is to say that most therapists wish to maximize people's ability to accurately identify what is going on in here and now situations, note whether past learning is a help or a hindrance in dealing with these situations, and creatively alter and modify behaviors and schemas if necessary. I define effective self monitoring as this capacity. From a client-centered perspective, the self monitoring activity which leads to creative adaptation is that of listening to and focusing on one's felt meanings.

All of us occasionally "distort reality" - we operate on mistaken or nonviable beliefs. Similarly, from time to time we attempt to cope with some situation in a nonadaptive or nonviable way. What is dysfunctional is if we are unable to recognize when our beliefs or behaviors are nonviable and change them; or if we can recognize their nonviability, but are unable to change them anyway.

Therefore it is our failure to *recognize and/or change* maladaptive beliefs or coping responses that is the crux of psychopathology, leading to the repetition of dysfunctional behavior. Following from this it can be said that the goal of all therapies is to *restore* effective self monitoring (however each therapy defines it).

Client-centered therapy

Client-centered theory has particularly emphasized the human's ability to creatively interact with a changing environment. One of the major goals of Rogers' therapy was to help a person reflexively live in her feelings, be open to all information in the here and now situation, and hold constructs tentatively. Psychopathology occurs when a person tries to "force" reality into preconceived, rigidly held constructs. When this happens the person is unable to apprehend relevant here and now information. This forces the person to respond in rigid, stereotypic ways. This means that the person will be "stuck" in repeating old ways of coping with the world, whether these are currently "organismically wise" or not. Functionally, the person will not be "present centered."

In contrast, a fully functioning person who holds constructs tentatively is able to continually differentiate new meanings out from her interactive experience with the world. She moves away from simplistic, global, and rigid either/or constructs. In order to do this she is open to all information in the moment; most importantly, internal information from her own felt meanings. The effective self monitoring, creative listening/focusing process is an inner dialogue between the experiential, felt meaning level of the person, and the more conceptual, self-observational, "verbal" or "symbolizing" level of the person. Via the process of inwardly referring a "felt shift" often takes place - a new integration or reorganization of experience. I believe this is akin to Watzlawick's (1987) "second order change." It is through such a process that a person is able to creatively alter her "own programming."

Implications for other approaches

Rigidly held beliefs, cognitions, percepts, or action patterns, are therefore contradictory to effective self-monitoring. Effective self-monitoring leads to a kind of unfolding of more differentiated and integrated ways of dealing with the world. In order to do this, one must adopt an hypothesis testing attitude towards life. Finally, people act dysfunctionally because they are stuck. That is, they are using constructs or coping devices that are not working, but are unable to change. We shall see that these ideas appear in other theories as well.

1. PSYCHOANALYSIS

Psychoanalysis is the most "structure-oriented" of all approaches to psychotherapy. According to classical Freudian theory people develop a fixed personality in early childhood and that stays relatively unchanged throughout life. Modern object relations theorists similarly believe that fixed self and ego structures are developed within the first three years of life and persist in a linear causal way into adulthood.

Psychoanalytic models do not emphasize fluidity and change in personality. Nevertheless, the goal of psychoanalytic therapy is to free the person from the rigid constraints of the past so that he or she can effectively function in the here and now. This includes making the person aware of infantile impulses and wishes and the repressions and defenses used to disguise them. This allows the conscious ego to separate present reality from the shadows of the past, and to respond to the here and now in its own terms. What is seen as "increased ego functioning" by psychoanalysis is an increase in the ability to effectively self monitor. For object relations theory, overcoming splitting and becoming separated and individuated allows more flexible differentiated perception of the here and now.

Self-monitoring for analysis, however, seems to be more of a "top down" process than it is for client-centered therapy. The "observing ego" rules and controls the bodily impulses. Nevertheless psychoanalysis also is striving for a process oriented way of living: An hypothesis testing attitude, a "present-centered" orientation, more differentiated and integrated constructs about the world in contrast to rigid either/or constructs, and the potential for new, creative adaptation.

2. COGNITIVE APPROACHES

Ineffective self monitoring appears to be the central idea in cognitive therapies, such as that of Beck (Beck et al., 1979). His "cognitive triad," "cognitive errors," and "primitive schemas" are examples of dysfunctional ways of evaluating self, events, and the probability of future occurrances. For Beck primitive self schemas represent rigid global undifferentiated either/or thinking. Beck's therapy focuses on creating more differentiated ways of interpreting events, countering, for instance, overgeneralization and selective abstraction. And the major goal is to develop a flexible hypothesis testing attitude towards life, not to substitute positive cognitions for negative ones. In other words, the goal is to adopt a process orientation towards life.

3. SOCIAL LEARNING THEORY

Generally behavioral theories do not fit under the concept of process. Since traditional behavioral theories see all behavior as either conditioned or random, there is no room for a concept of creative adaptation. Behavior therapy aims to replace one set of rigid conditioned responses that are dysfunctional, with another set of functional conditioned responses.

However, Bandura's social learning theory, which is really a cognitive theory, has placed a central emphasis on self monitoring. Bandura (1986) presents a thorough analysis of effective and ineffective self-monitoring and self regulation. He spells out specific ways of effectively living in the here and now. He emphasizes such process ideas as focusing on immediate goals and behaviors, instead of on dystal, global outcomes.

Social learning theory sees effective functioning as flexible and differentiated. Mischel and Peake (1982) have demonstrated that generally behavior is quite variable from one situation to the next, except when a person is acting dysfunctionally. Findings reported by Mischel (1984) showed that rigidity occurred only when individuals were unable to effectively cope.

4. STRATEGIC FAMILY SYSTEMS VIEWS

Milton Erickson (Leva, 1987; O'Hanlon, 1987) thought humans possessed an enormous capacity for creative change. Watzlawick (1985) has asserted that change happens all the time in everyday life. De Shazer (1985) believes the goal of psychotherapy is to release the person from being "stuck" in blocks to her creativity so that she can "move" and evolve new, unique solutions to problems. Thus therapy aims to create "second order change" (Watzlawick, 1987).

These theorists are in agreement with client-centered theory in seeing the human as a process (an "open system") under normal circumstances. Psychopathology happens when the person gets "stuck" in rigid, repetitive ways of coping.

These are strategies or "solutions" that once worked, but no longer work. However, because the person believes that what she is doing is the "right and proper" thing to do, environmental feedback that the "solutions" are no longer working is not taken as information that something new and different needs to be done. Instead it is taken as a sign that one must strive even harder to do "more of the same." This leads to redoubled efforts on what is not working, and the person-situation system spirals out of control. Being stuck often involves rigid, global either/or ways of construing the situation. Interventions are designed to create the awareness that things are not *always* "the same" (increase differentiation, De Shazer, 1985).

Dysfunctions in self-monitoring are inadvertent

A multitude of possible reasons have been proposed to explain dysfunctions in self-monitoring. What is common to them is the implication that the person *inadvertently* or *unknowingly* repeats noncreative and noninteractive ways of dealing with situations, either because of unconscious reasons, or because the person is unaware that these ways are not viable. For social learning theory dysfunctional strategies are learned through modeling and reinforcement. For client-centered theory rigid constructs are reinforced by parents, and children are not taught how to focus experientially. For psychoanalysis rigid dysfunctional self monitoring ("poor ego functioning") rests on the repression and denial of infantile wishes. For object relations theory the failure to separate from the mother leads to impaired ego functioning. For Beck's cognitive theory children think in global either/or constructs, but need positive learning experience or they do not develop flexible differentiated hypothesis-testing ways of dealing with the world. For strategic approaches the person is acting in "good faith" by doing what he believes is "right and proper," but unknowingly is not engaging in flexible hypothesis testing.

Problems are attempts at solutions

A commonality related to the above discussion is that problems are actually attempts at solutions. This has clearly been explicated by Gendlin (1968), who argues that there is a positive thrust underlying dysfunctional behavior. My paper on "borderline personality disorder" (Bohart, this volume) is based on this idea. I have already indicated how strategic therapists operate on this assumption. From a social learning perspective dysfunctional self-monitoring strategies have been learned either through modeling or because they once brought reinforcement. In either case it could be argued that the person is continuing to use them because of an expectation that they will "work." Beck's cognitive approach holds that the person is legitimately trying to solve life problems when utilizing dysfunctional cognitive strategies. Finally psychoanalytic approaches are based on the idea that "solutions" in early childhood (repression, defenses) become dysfunctional when carried unchanged into adulthood.

THE PROCESS OF CHANGE

How does one create a flexible, hypothesis-testing, process orientation in a person who is stuck in rigid, dysfunctional ways of self-monitoring? The problem is two-fold. First, even if the individual is aware of how he is stuck, he may not know *how* to change. Second, dysfunctional self-monitoring includes ways the individual processes information. Therefore "corrective" information may get dysfunctionally processed by the very system the information is designed to change. As an example, consider a depressive who is told that he is creating his depression by thinking depressively. This bit of information may be taken by the depressive as *further evidence* of his inadequacy. The information is *used* to think depressively.

These two difficulties amount to the proposition that *simple corrective information* is usually inadequate to create therapeutic change. Typically people try to change themselves by 1. trying to analyze and understand the causes of their problems, and 2. by trying to self-engineer change, usually through commandments and advice (Gendlin, 1964). These two modalities are also the typical ways others try to change a person's behavior. Yet from Freud on it has been recognized that such simple "intellectual" information has not been therapeutic. Even "correct" insights and advice often fail to cause change. The ineffectiveness of corrective information has been termed the "access" problem (Bohart & Todd, 1988), and it has frequently been noted previously (Freud, 1910/1963; Gendlin, 1964; Watzlawick, 1978).

If a person is stuck in a vicious circle of dysfunctional self-monitoring, then the ways he is seeing the world are not working. How does one break into this vicious circle? There are two general ways. First, from a strategic perspective Watzlawick (1987) has argued that "if you desire to see, learn how to act." The implication of his view is that we change our ways of "seeing" through *new experience.* Reframing this I would argue that therapeutic change must involve *learning from experience,* or "experiential learning." This means that the therapeutic learning situation must either provide the context for new learning experiences, or, provide *new ways of looking at old experience.* Second, one must create a *context* in which this new learning can occur. In order to do that one must either suspend or circumvent the ways the person's dysfunctionally self monitors.

A change in "Know How" - Experiential learning

Gendlin (1964, 1968, 1969) has been on the forefront of advocating the necessity for an experiential component to psychotherapy. Based on his work I believe that virtually *all* therapy approaches include experiential components. My set of experiential components includes: Tuning into felt meanings, emotional catharsis techniques, use of batakas, roleplaying, encounter group exercises, guided imagery, systematic desensitization, assertion training, learning through vicarious experience (modeling), direct behavioral practice of coping skills, emotional reliving in psychoanalysis, immediacy and authenticity in existential and humanistic therapies, homework assignments in cognitive therapies, Aaron Beck's daily record of dysfunctional thoughts, body oriented techniques such as in bioenergetics, Milton Erickson's use of teaching stories, and other strategic exercises designed to provide new experience.

In discussing the role of the experiential in psychotherapy I wish to draw a distinction between *experiential* and *affective*. The experiential is often considered as a kind of "affective" event in psychotherapy. I believe such an equation is confusing. The real key to changing in psychotherapy is not *affective* learning, but *experiential* learning, and they are not one and the same. In fact, I construe the affective as a *subset* of the experiential. Therefore the key distinction is not intellectual learning versus an affective or emotional process. Rather it is *sheer intellectual or cognitive understanding* versus a *kind* of learning that *impacts* at or flows from the experiential level ("experiential understanding").

I suggest that most everyday behavior is "perceptual - motor" in nature. It involves "know how" that occurs rapidly; often without the mediation of conscious verbally encoded thought. Driving, dressing, and even engaging in complex social behaviors are examples of the complex "know how" we are able to enact automatically. Other examples of "know how" include all the skills of craftspersons, expert surgeons, therapists, athletes, musicians, auto mechanics, and even mathematicians.

Know how also includes "knowing how to perceive situations" - including the immediate perception of meanings in everyday events. An example is of a chess expert who can immediately "see" what is happening on the board, without laborious conscious thought and interpretation. This is not to say that there may not be an interpretive - constructive process going on at some level, as many information processing theorists would postulate. However even if such activity is going on, it is much more rapid and at a different level (the "tacit") than conscious, intellectual thought.

The acquisition of perceptual - motor knowledge is what I call experiential learning (learning through living, learning through doing). It may often *include* cognitive, verbally encoded aspects (as when skills are acquired through verbal instruction *and* practice). Following a distinction made by cognitive psychologists I have been calling this "knowing how" in contrast to "knowing that" or "knowing about" (abstract, cognitive knowledge).

With this in mind we can frame one part of the access problem as: How do we as therapists turn abstract, cognitive understandings ("knowing about") into bodily learned, concretely experienced knowledge ("knowing how")?

It follows that there is more to experiential know how than "affect." Emotions and affects are one kind of thing that is experienced. But far more is experienced than simply emotions or affects. We experience how a painting looks (visual experience), we experience the touch of clothing on our skin, and we directly experience the meaning of shouted words. We also directly experience a person's tone of voice as threatening, another's soft look as a romantic come-on, or still another's behavior as "caring." All these experiences may include affective responses as a component. But experiencing someone as caring is a way of apprehending or "sensing," and is not itself specifically "affective" (though one may feel "good" in response to the caring). Another example: Einstein is reported to have said that he was "guided by a feeling" in developing relativity theory. But surely "feeling" here refers to a "sensing" (perceiving) rather than to an affect or emotion.

The experiential level of knowing involves a "learning from living," and includes a vast store of bodily processed information, including thoughts and emotions. Consistent with Gendlin, there is therefore far more information available at this level of knowing than can ever be put into words. This point is congruent with recent cognitive views of nonconscious information processing and "tacit knowledge" (Guidano, 1987; Lewicki, 1986; Shevrin & Dickman, 1980).

Further, this level is capable of reacting quickly in a highly complex, flexible, and creative way. Professional athletes often spontaneously improvise in ways that are too rapid to have been guided by conscious planning. Many athletes say they play better when they are too tired to think.

However experientially based "know how" is not always adaptive or accurate. Growing up in a dysfunctional family may lead to quick rapid perceptions and actions that make sense in that family context but are maladaptive elsewhere. Often the person may intellectually understand his maladaptiveness, yet be puzzled by why he still *perceives* someone as threatening when she is not, or why he still reacts defensively when it is not necessary. Even more puzzling is that these reactions often "feel right" even when the person intellectually knows they are dysfunctional. This makes sense if we understand such reactions as bodily based perceptions.

Therapy therefore needs to impact at the experiential level. Because emotions are a significant component of experience, they can often provide "doors into" this level. The presence of an emotion may signal the availability of the whole set of "perceptual motor knowings" (felt meanings) that are relevant. Working with emotions may alter the correlated felt, perceived or experienced meaning of events (Greenberg & Safran, 1987). Therefore, dealing with emotion may be a particularly important way of evoking change.

Following from this discussion, there are two general reasons why intellectual knowing often fails to create change. Neither intellectual understanding (insight) nor intellectual self-instruction (advice) usually has any immediate impact on how one actually experiences and behaves. This is not surprising if one draws an analogy to classroom situations - one does not learn how to be a therapist from abstract intellectual understanding gained from textbooks or lectures. Such understanding needs to be fleshed out and modified by experience. This means abstractions need to acquire the concrete bodily referents of "know how" in order to affect behavior and perception. When one really "sees" the focusing process work for oneself the words one has read about it acquire a more rich and elaborated sense of meaning. In fact, once one has gotten an experiential understanding of focusing it will reach beyond and be more complex than the words used to acquire it! The words guiding learning will come to be seen as crude approximations to what is now experientially known.

Abstract understandings in therapy must work the same way. In psychoanalysis it is not useful to intellectually deduce that one "must have" hated one's father. It is useful to recover vivid memories of feeling angry at one's father, so that one "knows" one hated him. A good example of how therapy needs to "unpack" abstractions and return the client to the concrete data of experience can be found in the work of Rice and Saperia (1984).

Abstract understandings are also usually too general to concretely guide behavior. For one of my clients, it was one thing for her to know intellectually that her anxiety is based on trying to control everything in her life. It was another to know how, in a bodily sense, to not try to control, or to "let be." Telling a client that she needs to "let things flow" for instance, is too vague and abstract to tell her body how to do it.

In sum, therapies need to create change at the experiential level. Gendlin (1964, 1984) sees this level as a richly textured and complex network of "felt meanings." The process of listening and attending to the bodily "sense" of things leads to the elaboration of that felt sense in words or symbols. This elaboration creates a "felt shift" at the experiential level. This shift is a more differentiated experienced understanding. For Gendlin, therefore, experiential change can occur through a process of inwardly referring and elaborating or articulating. However Gendlin has frequently noted that experiential change can be effected via other therapeutic methodologies.

I have previously noted four sets of experiential interventions (Bohart & Todd, 1988). These include: Direct experiential learning, experiential articulation, experiential evocation, and acquisition through habit and practice. Direct experiential learning includes learning through active practice of behaviors or skills, as in behavior therapy. However it also takes place in client-centered therapy in the form of learnings that occur through the experience of the relationship itself. Gendlin (1968) has pointed out that how the therapist is with the client is a more potent form of learning than what is said. Learning through direct experience also occurs in self psychological and object relations therapies, Gestalt, cognitive, and strategic approaches, in differing ways.

Experiential evocation involves the deliberate evocation of experiential reactions in therapy. This is most characteristic of Gestalt, body therapies such as bioenergetics, encounter activities, and "cathartic" therapies that evoke emotion. It also includes the use of guided imagery.

I wish to treat experiential articulation in more detail. Behavioral and strategic therapists have discounted the value of insight in psychotherapy. However it is clear to those of us who do verbal psychotherapy that there *are* conditions under which inward, verbally based self exploration and/or insight can lead to meaningful change at the experiential level.

For client-centered therapy "insights" are not meaningful unless they are anchored in and acquired from "getting in touch with" one's experience of self, situations, and the world. Rice and Saperia (1984) ask the client to suspend her judgments of the situation, both in terms of her feelings and internal reactions, and in terms of her perceptions of the situation itself. By suspending prejudgements and returning to the "experiential data base," the client is able to induce (gain insight into) meanings implicit in perceptions and reactions in that situation. This contrasts to an abstract "intellectual deduction" process where she might *conclude* that the meanings *must* be there.

For Gendlin (1969, 1981) the focusing procedure is one in which intellectual analytic activities are suspended, and the client tries to "listen to" her experience. Suspending preconceptions can be said to create a "new look" at one's experiencing, and leads to articulations emerging from that experience. The verbal (or symbolic) formulation of the "felt meanings" involved is not so much a cause of the change as it is a product of the change, or perhaps more accurately, a concomittent part of the change process.

Gendlin (1968) has suggested that the change process in psychoanalysis operates in a similar manner. Client-centered therapy and psychoanalysis are probably the two "paradigm" examples of how referring to experience (in the form of "feelings," images, and memories) and then letting insights or articulations emerge from that experience, can create experiential change. However experiential articulation occurs in other psychotherapies.

For Bandura (1986) putting into words what one is observing during therapeutic modeling facilitates the learning process. For Beck's cognitive therapy clients learn to flesh out cognitive abstractions by keeping a concrete record of daily experience - when and where the client thinks dysfunctionally. The two-chair technique in Gestalt (Greenberg, 1984) includes experiential articulation.

A final note on experiential articulation: for Gendlin the process of articulating felt meanings not only can alter one's experiential "sense" of things, but is the essence of creativity. From his perspective there is something gained from experiential change occurring through the internal articulation process (focusing) that is more rich than experiential change brought about by simple behavioral practice.

The final set of experiential interventions involves the use of habit and practice. It overlaps with the other three sets. I have argued that sheer intellectual understanding is not therapeutic. Yet there are clients who take an insight or piece of advice from a therapist and use it to change. In everyday life athletic coaches and other teachers of skilled performances often give advice that seems to be effective in changing behavior. Finally, cognitive therapists such as Beck and Ellis believe that cognitive change can lead to behavior change. How can this be so?

First, in cognitive therapies the insight or advice *by itself* does not usually cause change. I have already mentioned that cognitive therapies employ homework assignments. They also have clients keep daily records of specific experiences they have had, and sometimes employ imagery.

More importantly, there are ways in which cognitive insights can lead to experiential change. This can occur where the insight or formulation is used as a guideline for experiential *practice.* For instance, a baseball player may be told to keep his eye on the ball. This piece of advice by itself will not magically facilitate keeping the eye on the ball. However if the person practices doing this, then he alters the perceptual-motor know how involved. In a similar manner for therapy, if one practices saying positive things to oneself as one lives through or imagines specific situations one may essentially alter perceptions and behaviors in those situations (Zilbergeld & Lazarus, 1987). Practice gradually guides both an alteration in attentional focus (perception), and the acquisition of new behavior.

Practice implies a *step by step* acquisition process, until one finally "gets it." I am not aware of any direct form of this in client-centered therapy. However the focusing procedure (Gendlin, 1974) is a step-by-step process which results in small moments of experiential adjustment or change. One rarely focuses and creates mammoth change all in one session. Rather, each step of focusing creates change which makes further experiential change possible through repeated applications of focusing. This process may have much in common with the acquisition of experiential understanding of abstract cognitions through practice. For instance, one may abstractly learn the principles of assertion and then practice them. With each practice attempt a closer and closer approximation to full experiential acquisition or understanding of what it means to be effectively assertive is achieved.

Circumventing dysfunctional self monitoring

I have suggested that direct help-intended communications may be ineffective because they get misinterpreted by the client *through* his dysfunctional monitoring system. One reason the client may be stuck is that he may be overlooking, ignoring, avoiding, or misinterpreting potentially corrective information feeding back from everyday interactions.

Dysfunctional self-monitoring can be loosely equated with the "internal critic" described by many writers (eg., Gendlin, 1984; Greenberg, 1984). There are two ways therapies have tried to "circumvent" the dysfunctional self-monitoring system in order to get information "through." The first involves the "phenomenological method," and the second "indirect suggestion." Both may work by shifting the client's attentional focus.

The phenomenological method

As a depressed person observes the flow of experience, his depressive assumptions focus him on its negative aspects. His depressive assumptions become a self-fulfilling prophecy. Positive (or even neutral) aspects are either not attended to, or misinterpreted by the depressive schemas. How can the therapist get this person to focus on other, more positive aspects of experience and to challenge his depressive interpretations?

In the phenomenological method the client is encouraged to suspend the ways he has of selecting what aspects of experience to focus on, and the ways of formulating interpretations of that experience. I call it the phenomenological method because it is akin to the work of Husserl (1964). The purest form of this in psychotherapy is found in receptive meditation (Washburn, 1978), where the meditator attempts to allow the flow of experience to simply be noted and observed. This is also encouraged by many therapies.

Through suspending judgments and allowing experience to simply flow and be observed, a certain act of "distancing" takes place so that the observer feels separate from the observed contents of consciousness. This allows new perspectives to be gained, aspects of experience never before noticed to surface, and ultimately, reorganizations of experience to take place. As an example, the depressive may overfocus on the one thing he did wrong in a conversation. Letting go of preconceptions so that he does not overfocus on that one thing will result in a "standing back" and a gaining of perspective so that the one thing may no longer be seen as "bad," or will take its proper place in the relationship of things.

Letting go of preconceptions and gaining perspective should encourage "bottom up" processing, where generalizations are formed by *inducing* them from experiential data. In contrast, the dysfunctional pattern is often a *deductive* one (or "top down" process). The person notices certain experiences, combines those experiences with preconceptions, and *deduces* things about the self. Thus the depressive might notice a conversational mishap, combine that with a general proposition that "good conversationalists are smooth," and deduce that "I must not be a good conversationalist."

Of course the idea that one can suspend all one's preconceptions is an ideal. The idea of experience free from *any* conceptual organization is questionable (Wexler, 1974). Nevertheless the effort to suspend preconceptions may be therapeutic nonetheless, if the goal is to "free up" the self-monitoring system so that new input can get in.

In client-centered/experiential therapy the phenomenological method appears in the focusing technique. Focusing "clears a space" and the client is able to get distance and realize that "I am not my problems," (Gendlin, 1981). In addition, the "stance" of the client-centered therapist in general is to be "phenomenological" (Shlien, 1970). For instance, Lietaer (1984), writing on unconditional positive regard, says that "...unconditionality implies, among other things, no judgment from the outside and no approval or disapproval stemming from the frame of reference of the therapist" (p. 43). It has been suggested elsewhere (Bohart & Todd, 1988) that the client-centered therapist plays the role of a "surrogate receptive meditator," helping the client "track" the flow of experience in a nonjudgmental way.

Other therapies also utilize the phenomenological method in varying degrees. In psychoanalysis it appears in the form of free association. In cognitive therapy clients are encouraged to keep a "daily record" of dysfunctional thoughts. They write down the event and their interpretation of that event. Then they practice developing alternative interpretations. This teaches by implication the idea that one's preconceptions are preconceptions, and that there are alternative interpretations available.

The phenomenological method has the following consequences: Creation of "distance," "space," and "perspective;" learning that concepts are concepts; and developing of more of an hypothesis testing attitude towards constructs. In addition self acceptance, as considered by many therapists, involves adopting a relatively phenomenological attitude towards the self.

Self acceptance as phenomenological. For client-centered therapy self acceptance is neither having high self esteem nor self approval. It includes separating the "whole self" from behavior (Lietaer, 1984), and generally liking or prizing the self while not necessarily liking or prizing all of one's behavior. In that sense it involves taking a nonevaluative, nonjudgmental attitude towards the self (one can like or prize oneself without *judging* it as either good or bad). This formulation of self acceptance is shared by the cognitive therapies of Beck and Ellis. One could argue that psychoanalysis fits in also. For psychoanalysis self acceptance means acknowledging the present of repressed and disowned aspects of the self. This implies that one needs to learn not to identify oneself with some *particular* aspect of one's experience.

Indirect suggestion

The second major way of circumventing the dysfunctional self monitoring system is to use indirect techniques. This set of procedures is largely used by therapists who have been influenced by Milton Erickson (O'Hanlon, 1987). Techniques include the use of paradox, reframing ("positive connotation"), hypnosis, suggestion, teaching stories, and so on. Since this is a set of procedures relatively limited to this therapeutic approach, I shall not explore them here, though I believe client-centered therapists "reframe" just because they believe in a "positive thrust" (Gendlin, 1968).

Shift in attentional focus

I believe that both the phenomenological method and indirect methods work by shifting the attentional focus of the client. This attentional shift allows new aspects (including more positive) of the experiential field to get noticed. Also shifting attentional focus can bring the context of a problem into clearer perspective, and this context may lead to a change in interpretation of the problem. Strategic interventions such as the use of paradox often involve having the client engage in the "same" problem behaviors, but in a different context than before (De Shazer, 1985).

Client-centered experiential responding causes a shift in attentional focus (Wexler, 1974). First it does this by focusing the client's attention at a relatively neglected part of the experiential field ("felt meanings"). Second it does it by focusing attention, on the *positive thrust* and *process* oriented aspects of one's experience. In cognitive therapy, having clients practice alternative interpretations of events shifts attentional focus.

Focusing attention on the future. Several therapy approaches focus the client's attention more on the future than on the past. Shlien (1988) has commented on the importance of the future from a client-centered perspective. Other approaches include the behavioral perspective of Zilbergeld and Lazarus (1987), Bandura's (1986) social learning approach, and the strategic approach of De Shazer (1985).

In therapy both De Shazer, and Zilbergeld and Lazarus have a client practice concretely imagining how she wishes to be in the future. Such imagining may refocus the client's attention away from what is stuck and wrong and onto what is possible and moveable.

Examination of a transcript by Rogers (1986) reveals how many of his reponses capture the future-oriented focus of the client's fears, as well as the future-oriented thrust of where she wants to go. For instance, Rogers says: "Part of your fear is: 'Look what happened to my mother, and am I following in the same path ... and will I feel that same fruitlessness, perhaps?'" (p. 201). Elsewhere he says: "...if you were a better friend of the little girl inside of you, would that make you less fearful of the risk of marriage?" (p. 206).

CONCLUSION

Several of the concepts and constructs in client-centered therapy can be found (in different and altered forms) in other therapy systems. There are further similarities between client-centered and other therapies which I shall not review here (see Bohart, 1982, and Leva, 1987, for other examples). What the existence of these similarities suggests is that, beyond the many differences, there may be common processes and goals at work in different approaches. It further suggests the potential for developing a common "generic" model of how therapy operates and what its goals are. In that many of these generic concepts are so central to client-centered therapy, I believe that client-centered therapy provides one good basis for an integrative approach to psychotherapy.

REFERENCES

Bandura, A. (1986). *Social foundations of thought and action: A social cognitive analysis.* Englewood Cliffs, NJ: Prentice-Hall.

Beck, A.T., Rush, A.J., Shaw, B.F., & Emery, G. (1979). *Cognitive therapy of depression.* New York: Guilford.

Bohart, A. (1982). Similarities between cognitive and humanistic approaches to psychotherapy. *Cognitive Therapy and Research, 6,* 245-250.

Bohart, A. (1990). *A cognitive client-centered perspective on borderline personality development.* (This volume).

Bohart, A., & Todd, J. (1988). *Foundations of clinical and counseling psychology.* New York: Harper & Row.

De Shazer, S. (1985). *Keys to solution in brief therapy.* New York: Norton.

Frank, J.D. (1982). Therapeutic components shared by all psychotherapies. In J.H. Harvey & M.M. Parks (Eds.), *Psychotherapy research and behavior change.* Washington, DC: American Psychological Association.

Freud, S. (1963). Observations on "wild" psychoanalysis. In P. Rieff (Ed.), *Sigmund Freud: Therapy and technique.* New York: Crowell-Collier. (Original work published 1910.)

Gendlin, E.T. (1964). A theory of personality change. In P. Worchel & D. Byrne (Eds.), *Personality change.* New York: Wiley.

Gendlin, E.T. (1968). The experiential response. In E. Hammer (Ed.), *Use of interpretation in treatment.* New York: Grune & Stratton.

Gendlin, E.T. (1969). Focusing. *Psychotherapy: Theory, Research and Practice, 6,* 4-15.

Gendlin, E.T. (1974). Client-centered and experiential psychotherapy. In D.A.

Wexler & L.N. Rice (Eds), *Innovations in client-centered therapy.* New York: Wiley.

Gendlin, E.T. (1981). *Focusing.* New York: Bantam.

Gendlin, E.T. (1984). The client's client: The edge of awareness. In R.F. Levant & J.M. Shlien (Eds.), *Client-centered therapy and the person-centered approach: New directions in theory, research, and practice.* New York: Praeger.

Goldfried, M.R. (1980). Toward the delineation of therapeutic change principles. *American Psychologist, 35,* 991-999.

Greenberg, L.S. (1984). A task analysis of intrapersonal conflict resolution. In L.N. Rice & L.S. Greenberg (Eds.), *Patterns of change.* New York: Guilford.

Greenberg, L.S., & Safran, J.D. (1987). *Emotion in psychotherapy.* New York: Guilford.

Guidano, V.T. (1987). *Complexity of the self.* New York: Guilford.

Hofstader, D. (1979). *Godel, Escher, Bach: An eternal golden braid.* New York: Random House.

Husserl, E. (1964). *Cartesian meditations: An introduction to phenomenology.* The Hague: Martinus Nijhoff.

Leva, R.A. (1987). *Psychotherapy - The listening voice - Rogers and Erickson.* Muncie, IN: Accelerated Development.

Lewicki, P. (1986). *Nonconscious social information processing.* New York: Academic Press.

Lietaer, G. (1984). Unconditional positive regard: A controversial basic attitude in client-centered therapy. In R.F. Levant & J.M. Shlien (Eds.), *Client-centered therapy and the person-centered approach: New directions in theory, research, and practice.* New York: Praeger.

Marmor, J. (1987). The psychotherapeutic process: Common denominators in diverse approaches. In J. Zeig (Ed.), *The evolution of psychotherapy.* New York: Brunner/Mazel.

Mischel, W. (1984) Convergences and challenges in the search for cross-situational consistency. *American Psychologist, 39,* 351-364.

Mischel, W., & Peake, P.K. (1982). Beyond déjà vu in the search for cross-situational consistency. *Psychological Review, 89,* 730-755.

Norcross, J.E. (1986). *Handbook of eclectic psychotherapy.* New York: Brunner/Mazel.

O'Hanlon, W.H. (1987). *Taproots: Underlying principles of Milton Erickson's therapy and hypnosis.* New York: Norton.

Rice, L.N., & Saperia, E.P. (1984). Task analysis of the resolution of problematic reactions. In L.N. Rice & L.S. Greenberg (Eds.), *Patterns of change: Intensive analysis of psychotherapy process.* New York: Guilford.

Rogers, C.R. (1986). Client-centered therapy. In I.L. Kutash & A. Wolf (Eds.), *Psychotherapist's casebook.* San Francisco: Jossey-Bass.

Ryle, A. (1982). *Psychotherapy: A cognitive integration of theory and practice.* New York: Grune & Stratton.

Shevrin, H., & Dickman, S. (1980). The psychological unconscious: A necessary assumption for all psychological theory? *American Psychologist, 35,* 421-434.

500

Shlien, J.M. (1970). Phenomenology and personality. In J.T. Hart & T.M. Tomlinson (Eds.), *New directions in client-centered therapy.* Boston: Houghton Mifflin.

Shlien, J.M. (1988, September). *The future is more important than the past in determining present behavior.* Paper presented at the International Conference on Client-Centered and Experiential Psychotherapy, Leuven, Belgium.

Washburn, M. (1978). Observations relevant to a unified theory of meditation. *Journal of Transpersonal Psychology, 10,* 45-65.

Watzlawick, P. (1978). *The language of change.* New York: Basic Books.

Watzlawick, P. (1985, December). *Brief therapeutic interventions.* Paper presented at the Evolution of Psychotherapy Conference, Phoenix, AZ.

Watzlawick, P. (1987). If you desire to see, learn how to act. In J. Zeig (Ed.), *The evolution of psychotherapy.* New York: Brunner/Mazel.

Wexler, D.A. (1974). A cognitive theory of experiencing, self-actualization, and therapeutic process. In D.A. Wexler & L.N. Rice (Eds.), *Innovation in client-centered therapy.* New York: Wiley.

Zilbergeld, B., & Lazarus, A.A. (1987). *Mind power.* Boston: Little, Brown.

PART II
SPECIFIC PROBLEMS AND SETTINGS

DREAM WORK IN CLIENT-CENTERED PSYCHOTHERAPY

Jobst FINKE

Rhein. Landes- und Hochschulklinik Essen, F.R.Germany

It is well known that, up to now, client-centered psychotherapy has attached only minor importance to dreams and to therapeutic work with dreams. Only in recent years can a growing trend towards a change in this attitude be observed. Books on dreams were published in 1985 (Wijngaarden) and 1986 (Gendlin). Notable contributions to this subject were made by the paper presented by Vossen (1986) and the essay written by Jennings (1986). In the German-speaking countries, Pfeiffer, in particular, has been making significant contributions on this subject, starting as early as 1980.

One of the most important reasons for this rather late interest taken by client-centered therapists in the dreams of their clients is surely the principle of non-directedness. This principle seems to forbid client-centered therapists to question their clients about dreams unless they recount them spontaneously, which is less frequently the case. In the context of this question, however, attention must be drawn, in particular, to the specific abstinence from understanding and interpreting. The client-centered therapists tend to just "look at" the statements of their clients instead of seeing through them in order to discern a meaning. Dreams, however, with their enigmatic quality and apparent opacity, represent a phenomenon that seemingly demands to be understood and interpreted. The reawakened interest of client-centered therapy on the phenomenon of dreams, on the other hand, can be taken as a sign that this therapy school no longer adheres quite as strictly to its historically well-founded reservation about interpretation and the wish to "see through."

The objective of this paper is to describe the characteristic features of client-centered dream work. In this connection two questions present themselves:

1. What is the difference between client-centered dream work and other types of dream therapy, i.e. what are the essential elements of client-centered dream work?

2. Which positions of the different dream theories of depth psychology can be reconciled with the client-centered theory of personality and neuroses? These are namely the positions that could become axioms of a client-centered theory of dreams.

This paper will deal primarily with the second question. The first question will then be answered in a somewhat condensed form.

THE CLIENT-CENTERED DREAM CONCEPT

Therapeutic work with dreams presupposes a basic view, a preliminary understanding, of the nature of dreams and what can be demonstrated by them. Empirical dream research has proved the importance of dreaming for mental health: Depriving a person of dreams by interupting the REM phases (e.g. by waking him or her during these phases) can lead to psychotic disorders. From an empirical point of view, however, the importance of the dream contents for the dreamer in his waking hours is still unclear. The advocates of client-centered psychotherapy who are greatly influenced by the spirit of empirical-reductive research are, for this reason also, very reticent to interpret dream contents. Dream work could be justified, however, even from this point of view. In this case, the dream account would not be examined to find its meaning; rather, it would be seen solely as a universal symbol, similar to a TAT board or screen on which the individual problems of the client can be projected and illustrated.

Thus nothing would be said here about the meaning of the dream account; rather, the reaction of the client to this account in the therapeutic situation would be decisive. However, advocates of client-centered psychotherapy who empatically take up positions within the realm of humanistic psychology would tend more to regard dream contents as an expression of productions of the self. According to this view, this expression is basically comprehensible and can contribute towards throwing light on the self with all its problems, its contradictions and its striving towards actualization. The dream would thus be viewed as a structure which, being the product of the dreaming client, is related to his or her waking hours and provides insights into his or her "inner world." This latter position will be defended and discussed in detail in this paper.

Three basic patterns for determining the meaning of the dream account will be presented. To a certain extent, these patterns provide guidelines for an interpretative working through of the dream contents, i.e. interpretation schemes. These interpretation schemes represent basic axioms for understanding dreams. They constitute the preliminary understanding or theoretical scope of reference with which the therapist approaches his client.

The representation of the opposite

Gendlin (1986) recommends that the first question to be asked during dream work is whether the dream possibly represents the opposite of what the dream account at first seems to express.

Outrage at an act of violence, for example, could indicate the wish for dominance and agression. This "transformation into the opposite" could correspond to the defense mechanism "reaction formation" already described by A. Freud (1946). C.G. Jung (1982) described a similar phenomenon in his discussion of the compensatory function of dreams. According to Jung, the split-off side of the psyche, the "shadow," asserts itself in a compensatory manner in dreams.

This view, which is to a certain extent the product of classical depth psychology, can also be reconciled with the client-centered theory of neuroses, for a dualistic tendency is not alien to this theory neither, as expressed by the concept of incongruence. According to Rogers, neurotic disorders are caused by the incongruence between the self concept and the organismic tendency. The dream thus represents the appropriate symbolization of the organismic tendency denied by the self-concept during its waking hours. However, feelings of shock, feeling afraid and hesitating, which often occur in dreams, lead to the opposite suspicion that the self-concept, with its fending off tendencies, finds its expression here. Dreams would therefore represent the result of the incongruence between self-concept and organismic perception. They have the function of illustrating - and therefore enabling expression of - tendencies that are not symbolized in waking consciousness. Dreams could thus be viewed as a kind of "test behavior" in which the self-concept is forced to confront its organismic tendency and, during this confrontation, to change and expand itself. Aspects of this organismic tendency that have not yet been symbolized, a willingness to act that has not yet been perceived, could thus be integrated into the self-concept.

From a psychoanalytic point of view, Fromm (1951) and, more recently, Lüders (1982) have in principle already called attention to the problem-solving function of dreams.

The progressive tendency

Dream interpreters of the pre-psychological era believed that they could predict the future from dreams. As early as 1900, Freud, in the name of "scientific" dream interpretation, refuted the idea that it was possible to predict future events by studying dreams. For him, dreams represented firstly a repetition of the past and secondly a reenactment of childhood wishes. Quite a few authors hold the opinion that dreams can deal with the future, nonetheless, even if not in the future-predicting manner described above.

In direct opposition to the position of Freud, who saw in dreams primarily an expression of the past and of regressive ideas, Ernst Bloch (1982) emphasized the progressive character of dreams, and especially of day-dreams, which he felt were concerned with the future and with the setting of goals. For Jung, too, dreams had what he called a prospective function. This kind of future-directed concept of dreams is also in keeping with the spirit of humanistic psychology. The creative future-directedness, the "futureness" (Heidegger), the unpredictable process of becoming (Rogers), the open horizon of possibilities - and not the state of being chained in compulsive repetition to the past - is their credo. Client-centered therapists therefore examine dreams to determine to what extent they shed light on the forward-looking fantasies, the hardly admitted intentions and the future actions of clients, actions which have so far only taken place in dreams.

In designing his or her own possibilities, a person is shed of himself or herself (Heidegger 1963). This design is often expressed more clearly in dreams than during waking consciousness. The effect of self-actualizing tendencies can be observed in dream activities, which are an expression of what the future-directed self could be and would like to become. The urge to become whole, i.e. to complete the design, is fulfilled in dreams.

Rogers (1961) sees mankind as being involved in a never-ending process of changing and becoming; this becoming often expresses itself more empathically in dreams than in conscious experience. Contradictions also manifest themselves in dreams however, such as the factors inhibiting self-actualization and becoming; the incongruence between regressive clinging and progressive tendencies is often symbolized in dreams in an impressive manner.

The dream figures as parts of the self

The different, often divergent parts of the self are represented by the various characters or figures appearing on the dream scene. It is known that Jung (1982) referred to this kind of dream interpretation as dream work on the subject stage. In Freud's writing, one can already find references to the idea that the person of the dreamer is represented by various dream figures (Thomä and Kächele, 1986). Gendlin (1986) also states that one of the questions to be asked about the dream is which parts of the dreamer reveal themselves in the various characters in the dream. This interpretation scheme is therefore especially suited to the client-centered approach, since the concept of self-actualization suggests that psychic processes can be understood as the differentiation and balancing out of various parts of the self.

Existential philosophy, an important cornerstone of humanistic psychology, describes the nature of man as a struggle of self-definition, in which the world in its various manifestations serves as a moment of self-confirmation. In an original experiencing of the world, things do not appear in a distant scientific objectification, but rather invariably as reflections of the own self. For this reason it is legitimate, with this approach as well, to view dreams as manifestations of this natural experience of the world and to interpret the various dream figures as parts of the self.

In so far as the different dream figures, which are often numerous, correspond to various aspects of the self-concept as well as of the actualization tendency, dreaming also represents a differentiation of this moment. The self-concept and the actualization tendency do not reveal themselves in dreams as self-containing entities, but rather represent in turn various aspects. The task of client-centered dream work is to elicit the relationships - but also the contradictions - between these aspects.

DREAM WORK

Up to now we have looked at basic schemes for understanding dreams in client-centered psychotherapy. These schemes can be used to establish guidelines for the interpretation of clients' accounts of dreams. It must be noted, however, that suggesting interpretations on the basis of insights gained in therapy does not exactly represent a client-centered approach. The therapeutic benefit lies especially in the opportunity for intensive experiencing of emotions, strivings and fantasies. Interpretations, i.e. significant insights into the meaning of the dreams, should be worked out by the client himself as far as possible. However, since the therapist is supposed to give the client encouragement and assistance in this work, he or she must have a kind of premonition, a preliminary understanding of the possible dimension of these interpretations or of the direction they might take. For this purpose, he or she will need the interpretation scheme described in this chapter.

Notwithstanding these remarks, client-centered dream therapy is characterized, both in theory and in practice, by features distinguishing it from many other forms of therapy. Features that are necessary for client-centered dream work will be presented here as hypotheses:

- Client-centered empathic understanding involves step-by-step interpretation (Finke, 1985). An interpretation, in the sense of comprehension of a whole complex of interrelationships, is not given by the therapist in one step. Instead, insight is gained gradually in many small therapeutic steps.

- Understanding of interrelationships is only of therapeutic significance when it takes place within the context of the client's actual experience. This is why client-centered dream work has to activate experiences in a special manner and help the client to discover his or her own feelings.

- The manifest dream content has a value of its own and is not just a surrogate for a concealed layer of meaning. For this reason the dream account should be looked at in as concrete and vivid a manner as possible, one close to experience. To a certain extent, the client should dream his or her dream once again, this time in the presence of the therapist.

This reexperiencing of the dream content is often more important than its interpretation.

- The attempt to understand the individual details of the dream, i.e. to interpret its symbols, is client-centered only if the reference system of the client is taken into consideration. In this context, the therapist should assume a phenomenological position, i.e. he should interpret the subjects of the dream on the basis of the most obvious comprehension.

The strategies to be employed in client-centered dream therapy are mainly those normally used in everyday client-centered therapy. Reference is made here first to the three basic features of client-centered work and then to the so-called additional features (Truax & Carkhuff, 1967, Carkhuff & Berenson, 1967). The following therapeutic strategies[1] can be distinguished:

Empathic understanding of the dream experience: The therapist verbalizes the emotional content of the dreamer's experience. The patient should reexperience the moods and feelings present in the dream, e.g.: "In this situation you were paralyzed by fear."

Concretization: The therapist tries to elicit details of the dream episode or dream landscape: "This strange room you came into - what did it look like exactly? Try to remember which objects you recognized."

Structuring of the dream subjects: The therapist attempts to sum up details of the dream episode in a central category or as part of a coherent experience. In this way, the patient may be motivated to establish the relationship between the dream and his or her life situation: "Time and time again you had this feeling of being humiliated by a big overbearing man."

Empathic understanding of the dream reaction: The therapist verbalizes the emotional or cognitive reaction of the client to his or her dream episode. The client should be encouraged to grapple with the feelings and judgments evoked by the dream report: "The way you behaved there, it now seems rather strange to you." "That this old crooked house keeps cropping up gives you something to think about."

Empathic understanding of dream actions: The therapist encourages the client (without imperative emphasis) to enter into a dialogue with the figures in the dream in order to achieve a greater closeness to the experience: "If you could approach the big man, what would you say to him?" The therapist then attempts to summarize the experience of the dream in actions. "You just felt correctly the way you had to summon up all your courage to say that to him." The reaction to the experience of the dream actions can also be verbalized: "You can hardly understand any more that that cost you so much effort." These strategies should be employed in a changing order; focusing alternatively on the dream experience and the real experience has proved to be a useful technique.

NOTE

1. Interpretation is not discussed as a method in its own right, as it is the result of the methods described.

REFERENCES

Bloch, E. (1982). *Das Prinzip Hoffnung* (Vol. 1, 8th ed.). Frankfurt: Suhrkamp.
Carkhuff, R.R., & Berenson, B.G. (1967). *Beyond counseling and therapy.* New York: Rinehart and Winston.
Finke, J. (1985). Verstehen und Einsicht in der klientenzentrierten Gesprächspsychotherapie. *Zeitschrift für Personenzentrierte Psychologie und Psychotherapie, 4,* 327-337.
Freud, A. (1946). *The ego and the mechanisms of defense.* New York: International Universities Press.
Freud, S. (1969). *Die Traumdeutung. Studienausgabe* (Vol. 2). Frankfurt: Fischer. (Original work published in 1900).
Fromm, E. (1951). *An introduction to the understanding of dreams.* New York: Rinehart and Co.
Gendlin, E.T. (1986). *Let your body interpet your dreams.* Wilmette, IL: Chiron.
Heidegger, M. (1963). *Sein und Zeit* (8th ed.). Tübingen: Niemeyer.
Jennings, J.L. (1986). The dream is the dream is the dream. *Person-centered Review, 1,* 310-333.
Jung, C.G. (1982). *Vom Wesen der Träume.* G.W., Vol. 8. Olten: Walter.
Lüders, W. (1982). Traum und Selbst. *Psyche, 36,* 813-829.
Pfeiffer, W.M. (1980). *Klientenzentrierte Traumtherapie.* Vortrag GwG-Kongress Berlin & AGAe-Symposion Essen.
Rogers, C.R. (1961). *On becoming a person.* Boston: Houghton Mifflin.
Thomä, H., & Kächele, H. (1986). *Lehrbuch der psychoanalytischen Therapie.* Berlin: Springer.
Truax, C.B., & Carkhuff, R.R. (1967). *Toward effective counseling and psychotherapy.* Chicago: Aldine.
Vossen, T. (1986). Rogeriaanse droomtherapie. In R. Van Balen, M. Leijssen, & G. Lietaer (Eds.), *Droom en werkelijkheid in client-centered psychotherapie.* Leuven/Amersfoort: Acco.
Wijngaarden, H.R. (1985). *Luisteren naar dromen.* Meppel: Boom.

CLIENT-CENTERED DREAM THERAPY

Toine J. Vossen
Katholieke Universiteit Nijmegen, The Netherlands

INTRODUCTION

Dealing with dreams in a therapeutical way has always had a special place in psychoanalysis, this entirely in the tradition of Freud, the designer of the dream therapy. Jung even went one step further and gave the dream a completely central place in his therapies, and his followers did the same.

Thus the dream has always been generally accepted in these two great therapeutical schools. In the client-centered orientation, however, the dream has always been noticeably absent: Either the dream was just not discussed or it hardly got any attention. Because of the specific nature of the Rogerian approach, dealing with dreams was hardly imaginable and, in fact, has been impossible for a long time (see among others Jennings, 1986).

With this contribution, I will now try to create a place for the dream within this orientation, as a rich source which can be used for client-centered aims and for treating it in a therapeutical way as a fruitful addition to the existing way of working.

I will try to explain, both from a personal and a historical point of view, why it has taken so long for this orientation to do this and why it was not until now that some representatives of this orientation have developed a way of dealing with dreams. I will also briefly discuss Gendlin's approach and compare it to my own.

I shall look at the dream through Rogerian eyes, as it were, in order to discuss its special nature and its therapeutical fruitfulness, and also to elucidate its clues for a client-centered approach. Next I shall describe the form of the client-centered dream therapy which I have developed and illustrate it with several examples, and I shall add theoretical and methodological comments to this account.

PROLOGUE

My own development in this respect can best be described with a dream. For seven or eight years, I had been dreaming the same dream at regular times. I dreamed that, as a Dutchman, I was wandering through a Flemish town. It was Antwerp, but it looked like Leuven too, in a way: I was wandering around in circles. Then, on the way back, about half way down, I lost the way, again and again. Despite all my searching and asking, I never succeeded in getting back to the point where I had started.

At the time, I could never understand this recurring dream, nor could I connect it with anything in my life. What it did tell me was that there was something unfinished in my life; something important, something I just could not round off.

Then what happened? In 1985, I was asked to deliver a speech on dreams in Antwerp, Belgium, and when I was considering this request, I suddenly realized what this dream meant and, at the same time, I knew that I would never dream it again; and soon I dreamed again that I was walking through a Flemish city, but now I reached my destination without any difficulty whatsoever.

What was happening in this dream that kept repeating itself to me? Well, one should know that about forty years ago something began which would be very important to me, exactly there in Antwerp, the city where I would later deliver that speech. Every Monday for more than a year, I went to the staff meeting of the children's psychiatric clinic of Professor Dellaert in Antwerp, as part of my studies in psychology at Leuven University just after the war. What struck me most while I was there was how this man could look at his subjects. What that man had seen after he had been watching a child for half an hour was unbelievable. I also tried to learn how to look at things but I soon found that I could not do it his way. I had to think of a way of my own. And I started by looking at trees and at what they felt like from the inside.

And thus I wandered through the parks and over the boulevards of Antwerp and Leuven and, by doing so, discovered basic things about projection phenomena, on which I then wrote my dissertation with Dellaert.

Thus, I learned to look at the individual images of trees, and at what they contained emotionally, and later I learned to look at all sorts of things in nature and, from there, at forms of behavior, attitude and experience of children and adults. From that moment on, I have always been fascinated by *images,* whatever their nature: Images of fantasy, images of children's games, and especially of drawings made by children, and how they expressed very precisely and succinctly what was going on in their minds. The *diagnostic* approach (and especially that of empathic diagnostics), became an important thread in my life.

At the same time, we students discovered, though unofficially, Rogers' publications and came in touch with something completely different, namely his unequalled way of encountering people empathically. This slowly became a second important thread in my life: That of *client-centered therapy.*

These two things, however, cannot easily be combined. Diagnosis, for example, is performed completely separately from psychotherapy sessions. Moreover, diagnosis is basically an isolated event: In the act of diagnosing, there is only you and the image, while therapy mainly consists of communicating with another human being, especially in the way Rogers did it. In fact, he reversed everything. Rogers, after all, cast off the rational view of the Freudian tradition of his time and dedicated himself unconditionally to plain empathy: Away with observing and judging in contact, away with diagnosis!

Therefore, these two threads in my life remained separate for a long time, and even wide apart, exactly like the pavements in the Flemish town in my dreams. I did try to bring these two threads closer together, for example in the children's therapies I did (Vossen & Vossen-Felix, 1971) but that was still not explicit enough. I also tried to do so in the development theory which I developed and which could be used to test concrete behavior and experience in therapies, but this was too much after the actual contact (Vossen, 1967). These two lines, therefore, were not easily joined. Everything becomes even more complicated if one considers the fact that Rogers kept his eyes closed, as it were, in his therapies, and in this I was very much alike. That is why there were many things he just did not see; nor did we, his followers, for quite some time. For example, he did not see the large discrepancy between his warm broad solidarity and the stereotyped intervention technique which kept us Rogerians in conflict and in doubt for a long time. His theory was also - as Wijngaarden puts it (1984, p. 44) - more *mythological* than scientific, more naive than realistic, and our way of working was always very difficult to explain to others. Rogers has not actually been able to integrate observation into his therapeutical approach. It became clear to me that this *gap* between observation and contact, diagnosis and therapy, was the hole in the circle of my journey through that Flemish town, it was the hole in my mandala.

At the same time, this personal problem between Rogers and myself was a problem of cultural development. Feeling and communication were breaking through: "Away with the pressure of norms and consequences, away with the controlling and manipulating rationality," as one could permit oneself to cry out in those times of luxury and economical as well as cultural growth. This was actually an antithesis. The time we live in now, however, with world recession and the big cultural revolution, calls for a different attitude; among other things, they call for viewing while being watchful but at the same time retaining the contactual achievements. Is this going to be the beginning of a new synthesis?

Without my actually realizing it, this gap in my work with dreams was being filled: The integration of the thread of encounter with that of observation, looking at images as a way to unlock feelings, alternatively combining intensive viewing and empathic encounter. It was not until I was asked to present this in Antwerp that it suddenly became clear to me that I could use this for the completion of my way of working, so as to close the "Antwerp gap."

DEVELOPMENTS WITHIN THE ROGERIAN APPROACH

Until recently, it was virtually inconceivable to use dreams in the client-centered approach. There was no room for anything like that because one had to stick to the fixed technique of reflection. Moreover, experiencing in the here and now had a sacred and central place. I can still remember, as if it were only yesterday, how at the time Gendlin meant to dismiss fantasy and images together with hallucinations as being "no experiencing" (1970, p. 164, 165). But fortunately, things changed. Although the "in der Beschränkung zeigt sich der Meister" (selfrestraint reveals mastery) could be clearly applied to Rogers and his talent, his followers, ourselves included, started to feel too restricted: We felt too much incapacitated and our unquestioning faith, though very strong, led us often to make mistakes. So we started longing for something new.

It started off very slowly. Six years ago, Lietaer (1983) put everything into a nice and systematic order, and recently De Haas (1985) did the same: At first people began to concentrate on *self-exploration* in a more selective way, a first more active focus (Truax & Carkhuff, 1967). After that, Carkhuff and Berenson (1977) introduced the use of concreteness and *confrontation,* the latter requiring introducing the dimension of observation, be it momentarily. Gendlin (1970a, 547 ff.) broke through the restrictions of non-directiveness and prepared the way for *active intervention* and declared: "You can do something actively as long as you have an eye for ..." Active conduct therefore requires that you open your eyes and start to observe. Kiesler in the United States (1982), Van Kessel (1975) and others in my own country developed an orientation of continuous observation to get to grips with *interaction.* Rice (1974) went for vivid images and *evocation.* And thus, more and more nuances of looking at behavior appeared: Viewing while being watchful so that one could get a survey, could assess and direct, could refer to reality. People started to point out motives and themes, oppositions and contradictions; they started to draw the client's attention to aspects the therapists thought important; and also to judge and direct the course of the communication and process, etc.

Thus the client-centered orientation gradually developed into a form of therapy in which the therapist, in addition to affective empathy, actively and directively influences communication and process in an estimating, assessing and differentiated way, without losing the strength of the empathic encounter; a *continuously alternating combination, therefore, of viewing and "feeling,"* a subtle integration of both.

With this development, the time was finally ripe for the inclusion of dreams in this orientation; these strange "visual things." This was impossible before.

DREAM CHARACTERISTICS SEEN FROM A ROGERIAN POINT OF VIEW

In order to deal with dreams and to understand the client in his dream, it is necessary to develop a greater insight into the dream as a phenomenon, into the characteristics of the dream. This is the reason why I want to take a closer look at the dream, independently of Freud, Jung or anyone else, completely separately from any theory, purely by

516

stating simple facts as they present themselves directly in people's - and in the reader's - experience, and also how they appeal to us in our experience.

This is a simple form of phenomenology which fits the Rogerian approach perfectly, right from the start. We could also say: Lets look at dreams through "Rogerian eyes." My intention is mainly to get a little closer to the *uniqueness* and the *special character* of dreams as *a form of human experience.* I will do this with a very short example of a dream, a flash. of a strange meeting which, however small, contains many valuable moments of experience and could be an example of almost any dream.

As part of a clinical pastoral training in Germany (Klinische Seelsorge Ausbildung, Pastor Ostermann, Waldbröl), I had been working with the participants and their dreams for a day. The next day, we celebrated our leave-taking with a meal of hot wafers and cherries. The participants' partners were also there. People were merry and chatting pleasantly. On my left were two participants who were having a profound discussion on dreams, on my right was a woman in her early thirties, unknown to me, the partner of one of the participants. She had hardly taken any part in the discussion, but at a certain moment she interrupted them saying: "I don't have very much confidence in working with dreams!" "Why not?" I asked. She said: "For the last few years I have been dreaming this recurring dream; I once presented it to a psychoanalyst, and later on to another and they both came up with explanations which were useless to me." This roused my curiosity, so I asked: "What was your dream?" She hesitated, looked at me and apparently overcame her hesitation, for she replied: "In this dream of mine, I am at a fair: I am holding on to a merry-go-round which is turning round. Then, all of a sudden, it starts to go faster and faster. I cannot hold on any longer and I am hurled away into nothingness. Then I wake up, drenched with sweat."

My first reaction was to try and place myself in her position: "It is as if you are hanging on to something ("an etwas hängen" - here one should think of the metaphorical meaning) and you feel cheerful and comfortable; and then it seems as if things are speeding up and are taking a direction impossible for you to follow; and then you are lost; lost and lonely."

Her face turned pale, ashen, then she stammered: "Could it be then that I still have not got over my mother's death?" After a while, she recovered and started to talk, at first very quietly, but soon flushed with excitement: When she was five years old, her mother died rather suddenly. She herself was the oldest child in a large family and, as a matter of course, had taken charge of the household. Her father was ever so proud! "But I managed very well," she continued, "and still do: At the moment, I am reading Germanic studies together with educational science in University. I am also helping my husband with social activities." Then she said: "I am very sorry, but I have got to go to the ladies'." She disappeared into the ladies' room and at that very moment a taxi arrived to pick me up and take me to the station. I never saw her again; I do not even know her name. I asked my table companions to explain the situation to her and give her my regards: I have felt rotten about it for a long time afterwards.

If one lets this event sink in, one will soon find out that it contains an abundance of moments of experience. It impresses one immediately: This did not happen in therapy but in a normal social situation, not in any serious context, just relaxing and enjoying ourselves. The first person uses only one sentence. The other responds with one sentence, even using almost the same words. And the result is that both persons find themselves deeply involved in someone's life, right in the middle of it... It makes you wonder how this is possible, and from clients and students from the dream therapy seminars you keep hearing this cry of *amazement:* "How can this be possible!" Well, all I can say is that it is possible with dreams!... This already tells you something about the strangeness and uniqueness of dreams. And it cannot fail to make a lasting impression! Despite the many things that are known about dreams now, also due to neuropsychological research (Coenen, 1985), despite all one's experience, it still goes beyond one's understanding and imagination.

What further observations can we make? The dream is a series of images which together form a *story.* And a story wants to be told, requires an understanding ear, a listener. And the funny thing is: However strange, confusing or foolish the dream story may be, it always has a plot and that plot is always neat and clear and completely equal to that of a classic tragedy. Jung (1947, p. 253) had already pointed this out. There is always an exposition, secondly a plot, then a culmination and it ends in the denouement, the solution. What is amazing is that we are not consciously there but that without knowing it we subconsciously create a product of a higher order, as clear and differentiated in its formal structure as a *cristal;* even the short dream of our example gives evidence of this.

Apart from that, the story is an event, one in which we take part ourselves, but dreaming in itself is also an *event* that happens to us. This double event therefore undoubtedly affects us; thus we arrive at a second characteristic: Apparently, a dream has an *emotional charge.* The images are not neutral: They mean something to the dreamer: It is as though they wanted to draw his attention to something, although he might not know to what: Actually, there is no way he can escape from it. It has a threatening aspect as well, but it does not let go.

I have already said that a story wants to be told, especially if the contents of the dream happen to yourself and have an emotional charge. In this the dream fits the therapeutical situation automatically: You can talk about it in therapy, there is a listener. This seems to me to be predominantly applicable to Rogerian therapy.

There is however another aspect: There is also an inhibition of the will to talk; there always seems to be a shivering fear, an *ambivalence,* that is also the case in our example; the thing which apparently was so important to that woman, announces itself as something obscure, something inconceivable, as an enigma, with the threatening aspect that "one will never know what else it entails." And this double aspect is always present in dreams, that is why we all have these contradictory tendencies inside of us, which we never seem to get rid of: Because of the threatening aspect, we tend to forget, the dream as quickly as possible, never to dream it again, or to dismiss it as funny, unreal, foolish or nonsense. But at the same time, there is always this charge; it won't let go, it sticks to you, it arouses your curiosity. *Resistance and attraction* are always present, either *simultaneously* or alternately. Or, to put it more strongly: There is something contradictory and problematic in the structure of the dream itself; after all, it seems to be very important to us, but it presents itself as an enigma. We do not understand a single bit of it; but then again it is we who are dreaming it. It is so familiar, but it happens completely out of our control. That is why people always feel a bit put out as far as dreams are concerned and why they are bothered by them. Because of this, the *dream* is, *structurally* speaking, *problematic* and makes one *dependent.* This is why dreams are so much in need of a person who can explain them, and this has been so in all times and cultures. With this basic structure of a natural dependency on an event which is so natural in itself, the dream automatically fits into the therapeutical relation. Fortunately there is a good balance: The therapist himself is reminded every morning of the fact that he is just as small in this as his client.

What else can we find? The dream clearly has a *personal* character which is clearly connected with the uniqueness of a person, and also in terms of privacy, intimacy, it requires trust; when one talks about one's dreams, one gives someone else permission, as it were, to look behind the scenes, even though one does not know oneself what is going on there: This is a delicate matter which requires special *consideration*. The therapist who does not take this delicate aspect into account will soon be punished; but if he is respectful, he will find that his client's trust will increase: This will deepen the relationship and the process.

Aspects such as ambivalence, overcoming fear and trust reveal themselves in several ways. The client's confidence to talk about dreams will gradually grow when talking to beginner dream therapists, and it will grow simultaneously with the therapist's confidence in his own increasing competence. I have often seen clients not talk about their first dreams until the leavetaking after a therapy contact, or write them down and have the letter delivered by post in between two contacts, so that there was no possibility of work on them instantly. Often the first dreams are brief, sometimes just a single flash. This is because of a need for safety, related to the degree of *trust*.

We can see another very specific aspect of the dream in our example: Apart from an emotional charge, the dream also has a *dynamic charge;* it carries a therapeutically operating power which immediately gets a process going or gives it a boost; thus it can lead to a breakthrough or to a new layer. And the nice thing is that this power often can be elicited from the dream fairly easily. In our example, this was possible even with just one touch.

Another striking feature in our example is something else which is very strange about dreams: This charge can be *stored* and *kept* in the dream for many years - as in an uranium compound - and released after all that time in its *full strength,* as a vivid experience of the here and now. Time after time I have seen examples of this. It was once exemplified in a curious way: A therapist in training started his first supervision contact with a fear for his clients. I pointed this out to him, and his reaction was to relate two dreams which he had had in primary school when he was eight years old. The effect of these dreams was fertile and the experiences were tangibly present; for a long time, these two old dreams kept turning up in the contacts as two glowing active threads.

The phenomenon of the *recurring* dream is strange as well, the same dream which keeps turning up at regular times. We have mentioned this both in my dream about the Flemish town and in the dreams of the German woman. It is as if the same kind of experiences presented themselves time after time, if they pushed and could not find their way so that the emotional and dynamic charge could not be released. If someone who has recurrent dreams is taken care of, the charges will be released and the dream will not come back anymore: There is no longer a "need" to this dream. My dream about the Flemish town did not come back after I had realized what it meant.

Once a dream has been worked through and the charges have been released, people will remember the images for a long time as being private, meaningful and profound. The situation is even that when experiences are reflected in psychotherapy using the client's own dream images, the effect will be much clearer than if the therapist uses ordinary images and phrases. After all, what could be more client-centered?

Let us go back to the example. There is yet another striking aspect which is specific of all dreams: It sounds a little more complex and phenomenological: In our experience we continually transform dreams into things; a dream with an emotional charge is not easy to carry around, certainly not for months or years. However if we *transform* the dream *into a thing,* things will be different; after all, a thing can be put away, put aside or, if necessary, in one's pocket; if we do this with a dream, the charge, the tension will be pushed back, be smoothed, and it will become more bearable; we can then go on living with it in a more comfortable way. It is possible with a dream to transform it into a thing. Again, the striking aspect of the dream is that this thing - as opposed to other experience transformations - can be easily *de-transformed* to be reformed into the vivid reality of our inner self. We have this in our example.

Once this thingaspect came up in a somewhat humorous way in the following example: Recently, a colleague supervisor told me that a client started the supervision contact with the following words: "Let's first relate a dream." And she proceeded to do so. According to my colleague, the content of the dream was dramatic and sinister, but she had said at the end of her story, "well, that's it then!" and she had cheerfully started her supervision. The supervisor, however, just could not do a thing, completely stunned by the horrors he had gone through while listening to her story: She had taken it with her as a thing and had handed it over as such.

This thing-aspect can be observed in another way as well: We are not conscious when we are dreaming. All we are left with is a reminder, a memory of a series of images, of a kind of comic strip; apparently, the basic sensitivity is *condensed,* expressed as a *conglomeration* in this comic strip, in this closedup thing or, if you like, it is *cristallized* in it. In that way, we can carry it around with us for a long time. The cristals can be brought back to active experiencing at any moment, simply by *dissolving* them again in the hot bath of the affective contact. This seems interesting, especially for Rogerians!

Apparently, it is this thing-aspect which Gendlin (1970b, p. 165) misjudged. He considered dream images together with hallucinations as "decomposed pieces" of which the "felt meanings are not functioning." Obviously he only saw this side of the matter, how they seem to be "Fremdkörper" (strange bodies). At the time, he did not see how these "things" are connected to the person by way of a thin but warm umbilical cord as it were. Clients also experience this thing-aspect very clearly. At first the dream is remote and closed, it cannot be looked into nor looked through it, nor crept into; in a therapeutical contact, it suddenly opens up to become a very vividly experienced living reality. This release happens mainly in therapeutical contacts and forms the root of dream therapy.

Furthermore these images are such clearcut "visual things" that they automatically require being looked at with someone else, being studied and considered in depth. It is strange that when you look at your own dream images, they usually remain what they are: Just things, closed and impenetrable. But if somebody else joins in, looks at them and asks for example: "What kind of thing is that, just look at it?" the thing, the image usually immediately starts working. It opens up and becomes related to the person. A client once said: "They bloom, just like flowers." Obviously someone else's attention is essential to the openingup. So I believe that our "person to person" therapy automatically fits in with this.

Another important aspect is specific to dreams; dreams make matters distinct and clear. The vague complaints which clients often have when they are conscious, are presented in *a clear and differentiated* way in the dream, moreover with a depth and structure which I find beautiful and touching and which motivates me to commitment. We can see this in our short example: The short dream consists of two parts (the merry-go-round and the nothingness) and of an additional third part (her actual life). These three parts form three structures of life which added together display coherence and interrelation. First of all, there is a *genetic coherence*. The order is correct: Firstly, the affective connection with the mother, next the crude separation and finally her present life. But these structures are also like superimposed *layers* in active *interrelation* which form a vivid entity of experience and behavior for her. In this case her current life is the top layer; this layer is always the most conscious one. In ordinary client-centered therapy, the client is speaking from this layer. If we then follow Rogers' example and make a continual contact with the "silent stream below," we shall slowly go lower and deeper. The dream however immediately presents us with a set of deeper layers. It immediately *refers to* and *gives access to* layers which are *below* that of "the silent stream below." The woman in our example says, from the top layer, that she manages to carry on; the top layer is used as a way of escaping and surviving, in order to stay away from the layer below the nothingness. The reason for her being so active and always running from one place to another is simply to prevent herself from being engulfed by the underlying depression. She keeps herself very busy in order not to feel this emptiness deep down inside her. This middle layer, the layer of loneliness, rests in its turn on the basis, the foundation of everything: Here one can find the affectionate band and dependency which was cut off so crudely, but which is still present and did not start working and pushing inside her until a couple of years ago. This basis, the root of the dream, always appears in the beginning, in the first opening of the dream, therefore in the first words and sometimes even in the very first word.

One can see how differentiation, form and structure are *reflected* in a clear and profound way. This is the case in every dream. Recognizing this is empathic viewing or empathic *client-centered diagnosis;* in ordinary words, it means seeing how the aspects that are enclosed in the images have their place and function in human life. If one can see these orders, one will perceive them differently. Empathy will become more sensitive, deeper, broader, and greater and will enable the therapist to help the client more specifically and adequately (see also Hamelinck and Swildens, 1985).

This reflection of the problems in dreams is also mentioned, among others, by Wijngaarden (1985).

Let us take a last look at our example. I like the parallel between the contents of the dream and the *interaction,* probably relevant to people who practise interactional psychotherapy; the dream is about approaching something and hanging on to it, it is about surrendering and separation; and this is also reflected in her behavior: She approached me and so I more or less became the merry-go-round; if there had been more time, a warm connection would have rapidly developed and then I really would have become the merry-go-round. Unfortunately, the rest of the dream is repeated in a similar way: She has to pull out (to the ladies' room) and the merry-go-round was gone, another abandonment. But the other side of the interaction is true as well: I felt rotten for several reasons, among other things because I was pulled out as well and was thrown into some sort of nothingness. So much for our example.

POSSIBILITIES FOR THE ROGERIAN APPROACH

It is clear that even a short flash of a dream encounter can be very rich. Apparently dreams are rich, condensed, *special sources of experience* with a very specific dynamic power, with their own possibilities. Furthermore their nature makes them automatically fit a therapeutical contact, especially if this contact is of a Rogerian nature. Why should Rogerians neglect this rich source? Including dreams in this approach seems very obvious to me, whatever the school within this orientation; each therapist will find his own *clues.*

I think Rogerian therapy is originally a *translating therapy.* We have seen that the dream, as far as structure is concerned, requires translation. Translation follows automatically. My "translating" reaction when the German woman mentioned her dream is a clear example.

We still think that *empathy* is important and fruitful; we have seen that placing oneself in someone else's dream leads to active and intense empathy which reaches the deeper layers.

Whoever is of the opinion that *self-exploration* is important will be quite satisfied. Dreams express this in their structure: After all, dreams continually put a question mark with respect to our inner self.

If one sees *confrontation* as powerful, this possibility remains here, not only from the outside but from deep down inside. We saw it in the example: One sentence was a real bombshell. The danger of confrontation is that it can have a threatening effect and create dependency when it does not result in a link with a person's own experience. In the above case, the confrontation will naturally go through that experience.

It must be clear now to the *interactionalist* that dreams are a set of interactions which the dreamer continually tries to realize in real life and in the therapy situation. These basic attitudes of the interaction are easier to pick up from the dream than from the client's behavior, as they are continually being presented in a well-delineated way.

For those who like to work with *evocation* and vivid images, the deep experience is continually being evoked via vivid images and it is the client himself who gives abundant examples of these.

If one wants to go fast and deep, wants to break through the tough layers of behavior and experience, one will find easy reference and access to the layered reflection of the dream.

So the dream seems to fit the client-centered approach in a natural way and its clues are easy to grasp. Therefore I believe that if we Rogerians launch into dream therapy, we can enrich it, compared to other forms of dream therapy (Freud, Jung, and others), with the strength of the very specific assets of the client-centered approach. I have experienced that whoever starts to work with dreams is soon fascinated by them and cannot stop anymore. This has happened to me and apparently to Gendlin as well (1986).

The time seems to have arrived to include the dream in the client-centered orientation. The standard method has finally evolved in such a way that this has become possible. Some representatives of this client-centered therapy have initiated the handling of dreams in a client-centered way, simultaneously but completely independently of each other and from completely different startingpoints.

It can therefore be expected that more client-centered therapists will make use of these possibilities. This will be the beginning of a new development within this orientation.

GENDLIN'S APPROACH

Now that the father of the experiential school has thoroughly changed his opinion on dreams and duly recognizes the special nature and value of the dream and has even worked out his own way of dealing with dreams (1986), it seems important to me to have a closer look at this approach. Because it is a valuable approach in itself, and additionally, as being an example of its possibility of integrating dream therapy within our orientation. I would also like to clarify the method which I have developed by comparing it to Gendlin's.

As far as I know, no author has ever worked out his way of working with dreams and their backgrounds in such an extensive, far-reaching and detailed way as Gendlin: He presents an exceedingly differentiated, well-structured, step by step methodology, which is very clear and concrete from a didactic point of view. This is very praiseworthy. Gendlin's book is not a description of exactly how he works himself, but a didactic book (instructions with clarifications, background visions and examples). This will, in a way, complicate the comparison between our two ways of working.

What strikes me as being distinctive, to put it shortly, is this:

As the originator of the experiental approach, he postulates that the core of everything, and the test for everything, is in what he calls *"the body,"* as is the title "Let your body interpret your dreams." And in the silence of *focusing* - as he masterfully demonstrates in several examples, meaningful, rich, and unique interpretations come into existence in the "body" of the dreamer himself. Gendlin has a deep respect and a "saintly esteem" for a client's own experience. In this sense, he is totally client-centered. He explicitly states his opinion on this point, which explains statements like "Only the dreamer can interpret the dream," and nobody else; each therapist will have his own interpretation; "your (therapist's) associations don't matter much"; "giving your view (would) close everything" and "don't mix in your own stuff." This seems to be a fair point of view and it prevents a lot of "desecrations" of the dreamer by therapists. However, there is also another side to this matter: In doing this, he disregards a wide world of possibilities. We shall see that with my approach, the opposite of all these propositions is true as well.

Furthermore, one of the striking aspects of dreams is that focusing in itself will not completely settle things. Not even with Gendlin. Other things are also needed. In this sense the title does not cover the charge.

Gendlin has however revealed the origins of his position: In an eclectic way, from all existing knowledge and theories on dreams. This is why it is such a modest method, as he puts it himself. From this knowledge he distils a fixed *set of 16 questions* (part of which are instructions), which he asks the dreamer to focus on. This forms the *second pillar* of his method.

Everyone who has experience working with dreams will say that these are nice and useful questions concerning important things which always play a part in dreams, but I do wonder about certain other aspects.

Gendlin does not explain why he needs these questions; he does not need them in his ordinary focusing either; why can he not focus purely on the images themselves? Do dreams require more? Why and how? This is left unanswered. Not accounting for this makes his method seem somewhat dualistic. There are more objections attached to this set of questions. The questions are preestablished, presented a priori and from the outside; therefore they do not arise from the dreamer's experience in the here and now. Furthermore, they do not spring from the client's frame of reference but from that of the therapist, who thus comes up with unfamiliar material, which he thinks is important. In this way, he will induce and prescribe, which is contrary to his own explicit position of respecting the client's experiencing and which is inconsistent with client-centered principles. It is acceptable that Gendlin works in such a practical way, but he has to allow for it in his methodology. So this is also a strange duality. I am convinced however, that he himself uses these questions in such a way that they will fit in the here-and-now; unfortunately, he does not show this, nor the importance of it.

Gendlin gives a lot of examples which I think bring out many fine and valuable things. I believe that the result is similar to what I accomplish, but that Gendlin achieves this in a very different way. I will point this out occasionally in the description of my way of working.

Gendlin is practical and concrete in many respects. He also knows how to imply and clearly translate complicated issues like personal aspects that are projected away, contradictory experiences, Jung's shadow person, Perl's identification with the opposite, and to offer these translations in a plausible way. He is also very careful in his way of working. He checks again and again the dreamer's re-actions with hypotheses and counter-hypotheses. In order to get new moments of growth in a responsible way - by breaking through the limited interpretation of the dreamer - he works out an extensive method which is obviously very dear to him, namely the "bias control." This method is extremely complicated but I suspect Gendlin has to do this in such a complex way because he officially heads only for the experiencing of the dreamer; he does not dare to draw on the firm basis of the objectivity of the structures of the images. In the way I work, this checking and breaking through can happen at any moment, directly, through the structures of the images, as we shall see later on. In other words, what I think Gendlin's method lacks - despite all his carefulness regarding experiencing - is the precise and exact justification for every detail of the image. Furthermore, there is a discounting of the function of the beginning of the dream, which I will extensively return to later on. I also think that the genetic effect is too limited; consequently, among other things, the identifications with the oppositional aspects remain rather linear; my experience is that they become much deeper if they have first been worked through genetically.

So much for the two important pillars which Gendlin depicts. I can however see a *third pillar* in his way of working which I even think may be the most important one, but which he strangely enough does not mention nor explicitly includes in his methodology. So this is not accurate and gives a distorted picture of the theoretical structure. This pillar remains implicit. It is the pillar of the active and constructive influence of his own person, in more than one respect.

So he is continually busy with stimulating his client, putting him at ease, reducing his fear, helping him to cross thresholds, presenting things in a plausible way, paraphrasing actions in dreams - without scruples - i.e. interpreting them. He sometimes does all this by way of sharpwitted reactions in the here-and-now, sometimes by using his profound insight and experience with people and their dreams, also by way of his own views on personality which he presents in a clear and simple way, then again by way of bright ideas. He does this in a very sensitive and creative way. I enjoyed it very much when I read it. I recognize a lot of myself in it and I find reactions which are sometimes literally the same. He also departs openmindedly from his perception of human beings, of personality construction, of the place of oppositional aspects in this, etc. A lot of this boils down to well-experienced and professional diagnoses and this is the very aspect which he thinks he has to reject. With all these actions, Gendlin constantly influences the client indirectly, but also directly (with respect to content). But he acts as if he were unconscious of this. All these things, including the oppositions, are no sin to a practical man, on the contrary; they express flexibility, spontaneous creativity and truthfulness. I appreciate this very much. But the methodology requires that everything is taken in an explicit way and that it is justified. At this point Gendlin also has to revise his theory and to refine it.

There is a second personal aspect: From the above and also from the examples and the explanation in his book, it is clear for whoever wants to see it that Gendlin realizes the client-centered principles frequently and extensively. But strangely enough, he does not mention this fundamentally active inheritance from Rogers with which he is so familiar. Nor does he include it as an active factor, let alone as a bigger pillar on which his way of working would be based. At the Leuven Conference, however, he explicitly stated that his way of working in psychotherapy and focusing are subordinated to the client-centered principles, and he elaborated on some aspects in a more integrated way (Gendlin, 1990, this volume). I am curious to know whether and to what extent he will concretely extend this to dealing with dreams.

MY METHOD

From a methodological point of view, my starting-point is different from that of Gendlin. Furthermore, there is no formalized methodology or technique. One can however indicate two main tendencies which form the basis of my way of working. They are the following:

1. As a client-centered therapist convinced of the use of Rogers' core conditions, I make an enormous effort to realize these basic conditions with regard to the client and his dream. As already mentioned I shall only complete these at one point by calling in the dimension of viewing - a dimension which was avoided by Rogers. If the dream is considered as a "visual thing," this is of course a necessity. But it is also the exactness of the empathy which forces me to pay attention to *all* the aspects which I see as expressing the client's experiences. Furthermore, I would not be congruent if I did not take into account everything which I think I see in the dream and the client.

2. If I want to be able to understand the client and his dream, and if I

want to deal with them in an adequate way, it seems natural to follow the characteristics of the dream which I have already described, and to take them into account when working with them.

These two outlines characterize my way of working. This is why it does not seem to be an eclectic method but a development of the traditional client-centered approach regarding the treatment of the client and his dream.

The limited scope of this chapter does not allow to mention again all the dream characteristics or to add the links in a systematic way. The reader will easily recognize them in a further description. I will, however, mention one aspect because it clearly has a methodical consequence. It is the following: The dream appears to be a precipitate, the decristallization of basic experiences and, so, it is the exact expression of what is really going on in a client's mind. While Gendlin is heading for the dreamer's reactions and also realizes his responsibility, his "bias control," by way of experiences, I shall proceed via the precise nature and structure of every detail of image and action, via the exactness of every moment in succession and the genetic structures that are linked to it. Together, we shall then have a look at every single element, go into it in depth. My questions will arise in the here and now, out of the interaction of the nature and structure of the image, the client's experience and my experience. Thus I arrive at the "method" of "walking" through a dream, a method which I will describe later on. This also means that a "felt sense" alone does not satisfy me, it is not enough, all the structural elements have to fit in, they have to be completely right at every moment.

To put it more clearly I react differently in every dream, I pick up different things and I pick them up in a different way and I use them in the conversation. The personal and specific qualities of this client, with this dream, now, at this moment of our conversation, and many imponderable aspects will then determine my method. However, I will systematically be intent on placing myself deeper and deeper in my client's position and on helping him get closer to the basic feelings of his own dream. This, in fact, is the main aim and method.

I work in a more *systematic* way with people whom I do not know very well, or who are still far distanced from their inner selves, like clients who are only at the beginning of a therapy or students who have only just started a course in dream therapy. In other terms, I start by letting the other person relate his dream in every detail. This in itself is already important. After all, we have seen that the dream is a story and a double event. It has to be told. By being told the dream will get a bit closer to the client. Because of fear, most people try to read on my face what kind of effect everything they tell me has on me, how I experience it and rate it. This is a very important aspect. In *no way,* therefore, will I remain "neutral," at a distance. I do not adopt a pose of whatever nature, I just could not do a thing like that. My attitude has to be real. After they have told me their entire dream I usually ask what kind of experience they get from it.

Then I start again, right from the beginning, and I go over the dream with the client. I take him by the hand for a walk through his own dream, through the series of images and the course of the action. At every image and every detail, we stop and *linger,* and I help him to unlock the emotions that are enclosed in his own dream product, I help him to release the feelings that are locked up in it, or to put it differently: I help him to get the *experiential process* going. I help him with many stimuli and little questions such as: "Just look at it! What exactly do you see? What does it evoke in you? What are you doing now?" etc. By lingering on the images with the other person and looking at them together, the images will get a chance to start to work, as I have already indicated. And they actually do. This is my first attempt at bringing the client a little closer to the emotions and experiences that were decristallized in the images.

Stopping and lingering form an experiential and fundamental aspect of my work; all the approaches I will describe below will fit in with this and are aimed to promote them. However, I shall not isolate them as a separate technique, as Gendlin does.

Experience shows that every client wants to *run ahead,* to the next subject and especially to the climax, the denouement or the catastrophe. I keep pulling the client back, and continually force him to go over every detail as to give the experiential process a chance. As I adhere so much to the exactness of the dream to express specific basic experiences, I want to take into account all the structural elements as precisely as possible; that is the reason why this stopping and questioning is almost always a matter of confrontation. If one starts in this way, meaningful aspects always quickly appear to the dreamer into which he can then find his way a bit further. But sometimes this is clearly not the case. Some aspects manifest themselves as insignificant, dense, meaningless, secondary, and the client tends to skip them, to walk past them, to avoid them. These aspects still seem to be far removed from his conscious world. They seem to be *impenetrable* or they give him a sense of *unwantedness* or; "Whew! Let's get out of here," or often a vague but strong sense of threat, and the process takes a direction in which he just does not want to go. I know this feeling very well from working with my own dreams, this sudden emergence of revolt and sometimes it is intense inner resistance one gets at such moments.

The next step is to *raise* in the client the *specific* characteristic of every image. If the images represent things, this will be facilitated by asking what their *function* is, i.e. their general function when considered out of the dream context; for example, when there is a car in a dream: "Yes, what is a car for?" It is not until this general-specific element has been raised that we can place it in the concrete context, so that a new meaning comes into existence which in turn evokes new emotions. I still find this an amazing event. I will give a few more examples later on. Afterwards, we elicit further details with the help of questions like: "What kind of car is it? What does it look like?," so we can get closer to what this car personifies.

People in dreams are, of course, very important. With them I work in a similar way. With a thing it is its function which expresses its specific nature, but when, for example, there is an unknown man in a dream, it is the fact that he is a man and not a child or a woman, and furthermore his social and physical role or the meaning in life which express his specific nature. This is completed with questions like: "What kind of man is he? What aspect of him strikes most?" That is first his *outward appearance,* next what he represents as far as *intention* and *feeling* are concerned. Here is a short example. A woman dreamt that she had a baby and she wanted to show it to an acquaintance. He was gay. Her response to the questions was that she was trying to find recognition for this new part of her life. The question was raised: "And why do you try to find it with a gay person in your dream? What does a gay person mean to you, and especially this one?" And successively we got: "An acquaintance, a fighter for recognition, a man who in fact represents emotionality to me." She was actually trying to find a mother, but her disturbed relation with her own mother would not allow to present a real mother figure. That was too dangerous, therefore this compromise. When I asked: "What does he look like?," we got successively: "Blond hair, blue eyes, ...yes, he looks like me ...blimey! He is a fighter for recognition and so am I ... his character is like mine too... I think he represents something inside of myself; that I am trying to find recognition in myself for this new part of my life ... in the motherly feelings inside of me. In earlier days I would have refused this fiercely in myself."

I also work in a similar way with animals, with images of nature, with activities or events, with spacial categories and categories of time; I linger on all these things and I try to evoke their specific nature. I continually direct the client's view. I make him watch and I ask what he sees and experiences. The *raising* of this awareness is what I am interested in, and more specifically the consciousness of the exactness and precision of every image. This requires *continuous, very active intervention.* For example, if someone says about a helmet in a dream: "It is used for protection," the answer is too global. I shall not ask: "Protection for what?," since I have experienced that that does not arouse a lot; I shall say for example: "You did not dream that you were wearing shinpads!" That is likely to arouse a reaction like: "Gosh, apparently it is my head I want to protect." Or when it concerns a car and I feel that the outcome is too limited, I shall say: "Yes, but you did not go by bike! What is the difference?" Thus, I often work by contrasts to raise the precise and specific important aspects. Then the basis of the experience will come up more quickly.

As to the specific structure of the images, I shall also often point out aspects which the client ignores and add to these, expand them, study them in depth or even correct them, if the nature and the structure of the image and action ask for it. All this happens in many different ways, spontaneously and creatively, but always through the nature and the structure of the image. I want it all to be precise and sound. A felt sense in itself is not enough. After all, it is easy to arouse a lot of different emotional reactions from a dream. The felt sense has to contain all the structural elements.

I also keep a very close eye on the *order* of everything, which appears to be extremely important, and on the function of the image as a whole. Therefore people often think I am a fusspot, tough and persevering but, later, they are thankful because it was through this they gained access to a concealed and impenetrable aspect of themselves which would otherwise have been lost to them.

This type of active intervention seems, from a superficial point of view to go against the client, and not to be client-centered. But it really only aims at deeper experiencing of the client which would otherwise be neglected.

Naturally, this method encounters more resistance than Gendlin's method, but one continually breaks through all the things that the client fails to notice, neglects or avoids. Afterwards, however, he will always be grateful that by being tough and persevering you did not keep this piece of individuality from him, but rather saved it for him.

While raising the awareness concerning the specific nature of every image, *personal and general human* moments get involved. The generally human moments let themselves easily be explored in the way just mentioned. In my experience, complicated theoretical constructions, such as Jung's collective unconscious are not at all needed.

Another contribution to this approach is made with the help of questions such as: "What does it make you think of, of what does it remind you?," i.e. the *associations* of Freud (1922). However, I do not experience these questions as rational-associative, but as dimensions of empathic deepening; they do however have another function: They give the client an excellent opportunity to experience events and emotions again and, consequently, to give his opinion on them; they especially feed the "Rogerian" conversation.

We then arrive at another important part, which often forms a kind of conclusion; this is approached with questions like: "Do you recognize this in your life? Can you connect it with something in your life? With what you said earlier this morning?," etc. This evokes links with other experiences, in the present and the past, with other situations in the client's life, with his behavior in therapy etc. These links and the detailed interrelation with the reality of one's life is experienced as very important. At this stage, to a large extent, the client immediately recognizes these links. They partly involve analogous moments or patterns of experience, behavior, attitude, parts for which it is necessary that the therapist himself notices them and signals them. The genetically and psychodynamically developed frame of reference of the therapist or, to put it simply, his view on the meanings of life, in whatever form they appear, is also important in this part.

All the questions just described are only aimed at helping the client. Their order is not systematic. Their place and order are determined, as I have already indicated, by the individual moment of *this* dream image in *this* dream, *now,* of *this* dreamer and his way of reacting. The questions will overlap and melt into one another; one thing will lead to the next; thus it will become an "organic" tissue, a natural entity which is individual and flexible at any moment. Therefore the questions are only *aids* to help the client and myself at a specific very moment to get closer to his basic feelings.

Furthermore, I am constantly concerned with *empathic translation* and paraphrasing. This is a very essential thread and, to my mind, a true Rogerian one. I reflect a lot of the client's utterances, I mirror back feelings and thoughts as I understand and experience them in my world and in relation to what is happening; I translate a lot into vivid and expressive images, and into sayings and expressions that our language abounds in. I also translate the client's images in this way if he is not capable of doing so himself. My restatement of the dream of the German woman was already an illustration of this and the strength of its effect was clear. I hand over words in a responding way, words of which clients say that "they are words which arouse"; "words which from beneath help me to get through very deep things inside of me." This is considered to be a beneficial experience.

This constitutes a very clear difference between Gendlin's method and mine in Rogers' line. Gendlin transforms everything he sees - and he sees a lot - into questions and instructions, and he makes his client focus on them. Out of consideration for his client, he keeps a distance and does not venture further. From what I see, I keep touching the client, as it were, in an empathic way and in a participating solidarity.

Here are some more examples:

A student in a group related that he had dreamed that there was a rope coming out of his mouth; the dream remained *concrete* and *closed* to him. It opened up with the obvious translation of another member of the group who suggested that it was "a connection, a relation he was sick and tired of, which he was fed up with." He became painfully aware of the situation that relation was in.

A client dreamed that he arrived at his parents' home which was being pulled down; then he turned round and walked away feeling good. In this case, the experience was also limited by the concrete aspect to the physically turning around; when this was translated into: "And then you were finally able to turn your back on it," he all of a sudden realized what was going on.

What happens there is already strange and difficult to describe. It is something very essential but still contains many questions. Let me, for the moment, carefully put it like this. In those moments it is as if the closed dark image is being *lit up* and opens up, as if a link with the person is created. Something gradually *reveals* itself to the client so that things come to light which were previously concealed but which existed deeper down, therefore only in one part of his person. This suddenly breaks through into his more conscious spheres and consequently becomes a part of his entire person. Thus the client becomes whole and the hidden aspect becomes his in his experience as well.

Usually, clients can convey this more clearly and succintly. Thus the client on the video I made (Vossen, 1986), simply expresses this fact by saying: "It will become mine, it will become me!"

These revelations often go hand in hand with profound aha-experiences. A client described this very nicely in a questionnaire as: "Being stunned, incredulous, and at the same time knowing that it is true!" Somebody else said: "It is so miraculous, as if lots of different pieces out of the sky are falling into place deep down inside me!" Some more clients said:

- "As if a dike has broken through and a waterfall has been released."
- "As if I was touched by a magic wand."
- "Being touched by a healing hand."
- "Being reconnected to the source of life."

This whole contains numerous other *specific aspects*, too many to describe within the scope of this chapter. I will however mention a couple of these. Several examples have already shown how reflection on the contents of a dream can arouse an intense reaction and evoke more reactions and emotions than a reflection of a statement in an ordinary therapeutical conversation. I have confirmed this continually. Why would this be? I think this fact is closely connected with the two aspects of the dream which we have already mentioned: The content of the dream has a special emotional and dynamic charge. It involves an experience which is pushing out at that moment and which is still concealed and impenetrable - this intensifies the emotional meaning - while this concealment is what is wanted so badly. It is the reflection which often brings about the unlocking and the release.

There is another practical point. When raising people's awareness to the meanings of the contents of dreams, one often meets with what I would call the *discoloration* of the dream by the dreamer, afterwards, in a state of wakefulness. The dreamer nearly always takes a certain position towards his dream after he has dreamed it; positive, negative, important, meaningless, etc. These standpoints which he takes after the dream often lead to a distortion of the basic emotions and, if they are fixed and rigid, will make it more difficult to call up the pure basic experiences.

I shall give a few examples. *Traumatic fear* can cause people to take such a fixed standpoint. I am thinking of a client who dreamed that she was going to the market to buy some food but was very careful that it was not too much; at first she associated this "scantiness" with a traumatic time she had about ten years earlier when she had anorexia. It is important that the dream therapist recognizes these distortions and is not put off, but it requires special interventions to release a client from such a standpoint. Sometimes, this is easily done by raising the client's consciousness for the specific and current aspects of the dream and the facts of its context, so that his standpoint does not fit anymore. In this example, it was easy to make the client conscious of the meaning of "going to the market"; it was really "going out" and, as such, was something completely new in her life and totally out of place in her life as an anorectic. Afterwards it was not very difficult to let her find a much more subtle meaning for the "scantiness."

A strong and *rigid standpoint* taken afterwards occurs with contents of dreams which are linked to fixed and strong standpoints in a state of wakefulness. For example, a vegetarian is worried about meat in his dream. I have seen this twice. It occurs, among other things, in the illustration of a detailed dream which I will describe later on. At first the vegetarian *has* to smooth down the expressiveness of the meat as a symbol, to deny it or discolor it; he then needs help to release himself from this standpoint; sometimes the revelation is in no way welcome at this moment and his resistance can be strong.

Another example: If someone with an antiracist attitude has a dream in which a black person has evil intentions, he will automatically get into a situational conflict; in our subconscious, we Westerners often think of the Negro in terms of a strong, primitive strength, sometimes of a sexual nature, which we cannot recognize because of a sense of guilt which we reject. This causes oppositions, which are most of the time at the root of the problem, to flare up and therefore it would be fruitful if they were resolved.

I shall conclude the description of the method with a final and very important factor which is generally very effective and which in a very special way determines the Rogerian nature of the method. The feedback which we get from clients and students in observation reports and questionnaires shows that the contactual and *personal contribution* of the therapist is extremely important; and - according to the old Rogerian rule - the client has to experience this very strongly. When indicating which aspects are effective and which are not, people mention among others as effective contributions of the therapist: His attention, interest, commitment, seriousness, his fascination, being moved, inviting, his calmness, strength, humor and genuineness; apparently, it is important to clients to be able to read the therapist as an open book; this evidently makes them continually aware of their position, of how the therapist experiences everything and also evaluates it; from this they experience that seemingly foolish, silly and embarrassing things in a dream express many profound and personal elements. They can start to appreciate themselves again. This will have a vital and contagious effect, so they say. It is also important that gruesome and embarrassing elements are not avoided; the therapist must always lead when descending into the darkness, into the threatening or guiltridden hole; all this seems to be very useful in recognizing, facing, resuming and accepting many different aspects of their lives which did not get a chance before.

Thus people often notice the therapist's confidence and so become confident in themselves and in the process they are undergoing. This increases trust and dissolves fear. This process will also dissolve the fear of nightmares. The outcome, people say, will always be positive, even if this takes the form of a fierce confrontation.

As a therapist, I am an intermediary, I restore links. This wonderful event can be elicited again and again through concern and a genuine warm and personal touch. This touch brings the closedup dream thing which was so far away closer again. It opens it up and lights it up and it turns it again into the vivid emotional reality of which the person finds himself to be the centre again.

It is not difficult to recognize *Rogers' core conditions* in these aspects which are experienced as very effective. Another striking aspect of these observation reports is that, when describing the method, people hardly explicitly describe methodological or technical aspects, but mainly these core conditions in a rich diversity.

The process which is thus created often automatically happens within a "natural" conversation. Sometimes, however, it looks like hard work and toil. Often the matter gets stuck somewhere but this is frequently resolved in a following contact or even by the client himself in a spontaneous way independently of me and of our contacts. Sometimes however, the problem is just not resolved.

With Gendlin, as he himself indicates, this process will happen in little steps. I think this is a necessary consequence, as his focusing continually isolates the process into little steps. As a result of this way of working, the process will at first seem to be more of a melting, a releasing, than a moving and the consequent flowing which often gains momentum, running extremely smoothly also outside the sessions. It seems to me that this is caused by the continuity of contact and interaction.

ILLUSTRATIONS, WITH SOME THEORETICAL AND METHODOLOGICAL COMMENTS

I will now illustrate some aspects of this method further and add some theoretical and methodological comments. (Illustrations were recorded with the permission of the people involved). Firstly, a short domestic example: Our daughter-in-law, an English speaking South African woman by birth living in Holland, far away from her home country, suddenly lost her father. They had been very close; she was 25 years old at the time. After a couple of months, my wife and I slowly began to worry; apparently she could not talk, could not mourn her great loss. One morning, when she was visiting us for the weekend and we were having breakfast, she said: "Dad, I had this funny dream; I was sitting on a large bed and I was feeling very bad; my wisdom teeth were extracted and lots and lots of different people, mothers, brothers and other members of the family walked past in a queue and they put presents at my feet; it was like a funeral! I just don't understand it." I reacted with the question: "What was the firm and wise support in your life which apparently you have so painfully lost?" For one moment she looked surprised, then she burst into tears and she cried and talked a lot that day about her sadness. The stagnating mourning process finally got started and this was caused by the dynamic power of the dream. Again, it is amazing that such an essential process as the mourning process which did not get a chance along ordinary paths, pushed its way up and expressed itself in the vivid image of the extracted wisdom teeth with the enclosed dynamic possibility of being processed again.

Another example is that of a participant in a sixweeks clinical-pastoral training in Germany. This participant, who had a difficult position in the group, told us in the fifth week of the training about a dream he had on the evening of the beginning of the training. The dream started like this: "I turned up for the beginning of the training, but it had already started. When I came in, I saw that they were doing some sort of musical chairs on that song." Then followed the extensive account of his dream. When he was finished, I naturally started with the beginning of his dream. What the dreamer virtually pushed away was that song; the game was played to a certain song. I did not know this song, as I am Dutch; so I curiously asked what it was. "Well, that common song," was the answer (clearly wanting to go no further). "Yes, but what is the name of that song?" Finally he said "Reise nach Jerusalem!" "What does Jerusalem mean to you?" "The capital of Israel," unmistakingly pushing it aside. I was thinking to myself: "Well, well, Jerusalem for a theologist and a whole company of them together! ". And with small questions, I led him to the bible and from there to the new Jerusalem. While asking some more questions, I tried to figure out what that new Jerusalem meant to him and when something like the great longing for bliss started to leak through, he suddenly got emotional for the first time. Then everything opened up inside of him and, stammering, he told me how he had been intensely looking forward to this training, how much it meant to him personally, how much depended on it for him, his great expectations and on the other hand the enormous fear that he would be excluded from the group (the musical chairs). This was one of the reasons he was in such a difficult position in the group. He had not really realized all this in a conscious way and he had not been able to express himself in the group. The carryover of this dream made his reentery into the group possible. This made his problem clear, distinct and acceptable to the other members of the group. It is no longer very difficult to react constructively to someone's initially difficult and obscure behavior if the background is revealed so dramatically.

For many therapists and clients, the link between exclusion and musical chairs in the dream will be easy to grasp. This should draw their attention to the fact that the unconspicuous and seemingly meaningless "that song" may go unnoticed, whereas it is in fact the key to the most important detail.

The fact that meanings of dreams are easily grasped is often a danger to both parties because it may cause them to neglect essential aspects which seem to be accidental or meaningless.

This example also illustrates something I have already mentioned before; that both the exactness of the empathy and the congruence, the authenticity, each in their own way, demand that one does not neglect nor disguise anything of what one sees.

Here is another short example with several theoretical comments: A client once said at the end of a session: "I dreamed that I was knitting a jumper at my mother's; it was partly finished. Then I and my husband and children came to collect it; but my mother gave me the brushoff: She did not understand what had got into me! She had long before given the jumper to my youngest sister. I cleared off, feeling terribly ashamed."

As there was not much time left, I asked her: "What do you think was the most important part of the dream?". "The end, of course," she said. To her that was a matter of course; she had been talking for months in therapy about the terrible rejection by her mother. I said: "I think the beginning is the most important part." "Why?" she curiously asked. I said: "Have you ever knitted together with your mother?". "No, never." "Do you ever knit with somebody else?" "Yes, with my oldest daughter." Thus we talked about the cosiness and the happy atmosphere of knitting together. "But now you are dreaming that you were knitting with your mother, just try to fit that in!" Her eyes filled with tears. The longing for this connection with her mother was finally released. So far, she had not had the faintest idea that it existed, but it apparently was still living deep and hidden inside of her. The charge of the dream stuck to her memory for weeks. Later she could inwardly say goodbye to her mother and free herself from her.

Again I think it is striking that the last part, the rejection, forms the conscious top layer; the first part, the longing, the veiled lower layer is the root of the dream.

From a methodological point of view these two last examples clearly illustrate how viewing, but also watching and *guarding* and even *correcting* go together in this method with *feeling* and *meeting* and how all these dimensions reinforce each other to move further.

For Rogers himself, and for the majority of his followers, this was not possible in the past. Therefore, this method not only enriches the traditional method by including a new and rich source (the dream), but also by introducing a methodological addition: By restoring the link between watching and feeling in our methodology - precisely what we aim at with our clients.

NATURE AND FUNCTION OF THE DREAM

These illustrations also shed more light on the nature and function of the dream. One could say that the two women - the German woman and the one of the last illustration - show a child-like dependency which is something from the past. Yet they had not dreamt about it at the time, but they had been dreaming about it recently, in the present. This is very strange and fascinating. Apparently the dream always concerns the *present*. It is in this present moment that the experience of dependency starts to work its way through, to push. My dream about the Flemish town also appeared when my desire to close the gap started to work. This dynamic working of the root can nearly always be found in the beginning of the dream. Therefore, my experience is that if one is not able to open up the beginning of the dream in an essential way, little will come out of it. However, I have always been surprised that there is no mention of this in the literature.

What we have seen so far about dreams allows us to state the following about the *function* of dreams: Dreams are continually related and elaborate on what is living inside of us at the present moment, on what *occupies* us now, what is working inside of us, what is going on and wants to bud, wants to break through, on what we - even though we may not be clearly conscious of this - are elaborating on, what we are dealing with. Furthermore, the dream reflects all this in a series of images, making them become visible to the eye.

I often think of water plants. Sometimes I walk to our pond and then I see a new water plant. "Gosh, I did not know that," I sometimes say, very surprised; but I will not be able to make that discovery until the plant is visible and sticking out of the water. This corresponds to our consciousness. But, of course, the plant was there long before and it needed quite a while to bud and to develop. But to me, it had been invisible all that time, in the darkness of the water.

With dreams, we are now able to see in the night, to see in the darkness underneath the water and to see things grow, before they finally stick out of the waters and become visible in the daylight of our consciousness.

Therefore, dreams are always one step ahead of our consciousness and of our conscious actions. A big change in life or in therapy is always reflected in dreams, as any change in our inner selves before it is actualized in deeds in our waking life. All the movements in a therapy, breakthroughs and even relapses, are reflected in dreams. This aspect of dreams gives us a *diagnostic hold*, a support for both therapist and client. For obvious reasons, it is also effective as an *evaluation*. This "diagnostic aspect" is very obvious to me in every dream, but Gendlin only rarely takes it for granted (in the "sounding dreams") and this is completely in keeping with his fundamental attitude.

SOME FURTHER ILLUSTRATIONS AND CLARIFICATIONS

I will give a few other illustrations to clarify the importance of the beginning of dreams: Someone from a dream class dreamed that he went to his brother's house to celebrate his birthday. Next, he related an elaborate and fascinating dream on which we worked very hard and which appeared to contain quite a few important things for him. This dream had been occupying my thoughts for days and I kept thinking of that birthday, when something started to dawn on me. In a next contact, I asked him: "What is the English word for the Dutch 'verjaardag'?" (NB: The Dutch word for "birthday" is semantically only connected with a person's anniversary but absolutely not with a person's birth.) "Birthday." "What does it mean?" "Day of your birth." "Now say that in relation to your brother." "The day of my brother's birth." I made him repeat this one more time and then it was as if something inside of him broke down, and the whole tragedy of his brother's birth, of his mother's illness and of her reactions came out. He could still remember all these things, but now they came out filled with emotions. He could now feel how this tragedy had determined his whole life profoundly and it became accessible to his experiencing. The basic moment of the beginning of the dream had been released.

Here also it is obvious that if one is not able to open up the beginning of the dream there is a lot which will not come out.

I am also thinking of someone who had an elaborate dream which started however when he found himself in a site hut; it is not until it became clear from that that he was altering his whole life, that it became possible to set the rest and subsequently open it up.

Another example: A thirteen-year-old girl was dreaming that she suddenly had to sail with her physical education class; she was standing at the bow; an extensive account then followed which did not have any sense nor meaning until one understood the beginning. Here it clearly involved a change in her, her puberty and her period and everything it entailed. Most of the time, the therapist has to feel this or, to put it differently, he has to see through this in a diagnostic way in order to be able to help the client. If one leaves these things to the client on the basis of a socalled non-directive principle, these things do not get a chance.

A last short example: "I was at the Post Office; in little groups we were working with clay in front of the counter." A lot of other things were happening. The client associated the clay with "excrement," her own filthiness and aggression, which she tried to put into shape. She found it more difficult to get a closer understanding of the Post Office. It appeared to depict an essential part of what she had told me that morning. She had discovered that, even though she was conscious of her frustrations with other people, she kept running away from them. In doing so, she locked away the uneasiness, dissatisfaction and dislike for these people and she repressed these feelings for them. What was left was the physical uneasiness and the many physical complaints she had, which therefore seemed to belong to both herself and her weak physical constitution and did not have anything to do with the outside world. The Post Office made her realize what she was doing: Not dealing with her reactions in her own body but "directing" them to the people involved and "sending" her emotions to the receiver, to the correct address.

Therefore, we can state the following about the *importance of the beginning of the dream:* The beginning, the exposition, is much more than simply the startingpoint of the dream; it is always the atmosphere and the framework in which further contents will happen. Furthermore, it is usually the *key* to the understanding of what will follow. Finally, it is in many cases even the genetic and psychodynamic root or matrix of the whole. It is the new moment of growth which is budding, the "what it is all about." The rest is more the "how": How people try to realize this new aspect and what they encounter in doing this (cf. development theory, Vossen, 1976).

I shall conclude with a brief account of a dream which has been workedout thoroughly (an exact registration of a complete dream session, "live," with a feedback of the client afterwards can be found on the video "Client-centered dream therapy," Vossen, 1986).

An intelligent engineer of just over forty talks in the first contact vaguely and in very abstract terms about the great fears he has of other people and how isolated he lives. In the second contact, he comes up with a dream: "I am sitting at a long bare table with a lot of people; I get my food, but there is an empty space on my plate, there is no meat. I look around and climb onto the table to get a bit higher and, with great effort, I creep through a hatch onto the loft; there is a lot of hay lying on the floor. When I try to take my chance, a little brown man turns up with a whip in his hand and hits me on the head. I wake up with a dream." (Here also there are three layers. The bottom layer, the beginning - the empty space - is the root of the dream). Working on the dream, I start at the beginning. The bare tables evoke in him the cold atmosphere of the period when he was at the seminary; the sense he has of its sadness and loneliness starts to become stronger. When he comes to the empty space on his plate he says: "Meat, it does not mean anything to me, nor does lacking it; I am more or less a vegetarian." It shocks me to hear how he has rationalized the abstinence of the basic needs in his life in such a way. It needs time and more active intervention to detach his vegetarian attitude, which holds up the process, and consequently to give the experience of the function of meat a chance, first cognitively, then actively. Through a lot of questions and exhortations and through confrontation with the fact that all the rest of the dream and also the disaster in the story are exactly about this lack, it slowly gains meaning: Meat is the powerful means which one needs to live and to grow, and it is being withheld from him. The cold atmosphere and the part his mother played, which now, appears through his associations, slowly make his abstinence more essential, namely as an abstinence of love. This has a profound and painful effect.

Climbing gives him the delightful experience, of being capable of taking initiatives and starting to fill up the deficiency. But then he also starts feeling the drawback which lies on top of it. After all it is a forbidden,illegal, criminal road which can only be travelled in secret, with guilt. Then I have him take a thorough look at the loft; he fairly soon responds with: "Apparently there is enough in stock." And then something inside of him is torn apart, and he fiercely and bitterly talks about his experience: "Well, there was a large store of everything at the time at home, but I did not get it." Now everything goes back to the basic feeder, his mother, the main person who is responsible for the cruelty of obviously and consciously withholding love; he starts to see very emotionally how this has marked his life.

At first, he experiences the whipping of the little man just as some sort of punishment for his forbidden deeds, for his guilt. Looking a bit further into the matter he sees a connection between this little man and a teacher from primary school, who has had great influence on his life. Something to do with that teacher has happened, but he cannot exactly remember what; what he does get is an image of when he walked home from school as a little boy, all on his own with his little schoolbag, his face turned to the ground. This image starts to have a stronger and stronger effect on him. Then the emotion of loneliness and defeat breaks through, and also how this was symbolical for much of his life. It is not until the following contact when we continue to work on that dream that he remembers something of the experience with the beloved teacher; at the time, he was caught doing something, totally unexpected and he can still hear his teacher's cry: "Caught you there, a thousand lines!" He now feels how deeply traumatic this has been for him. It has been the cause of a change in his life. This was the whiplash in the dream.

Next, he can connect this with his present life. The basis of his fears and isolation becomes clear to him. He, the guilty person, is in constant danger of being caught, of falling short. This is actually how he still experiences his life: Never safe, never sure, marked, as it were, an outcast! With these experiences, his life started to move. It even gained momentum. In the following weeks, he had to cry a lot and he often talked to his wife, for the first time really. The grief over what had been withheld from him - the root of the dream - started to release itself; the mourning for this basic lack in his life had started. In most cases this is the first stage in therapy for such problems.

Again one can see how, on the one hand, the dream, as opposed to our consciousness, reflects a whole life in different layers of its total structure, in a clear and differentiated way; the client does not realize this on a conscious level. But additionally, the dream offers the possibility of access to and disclosure of these thick layers; the twisted and frozen life starts to flow again. This would not have been possible without the dream - certainly not in a man functioning in such an abstract way.

CONCLUSION

In conclusion we can say the following. Now that the Rogerian orientation has developed into an orientation which, in active and specific ways, can mobilize, influence and develop a client's process of experience, it also offers the possibility of including the dealing with dreams. Dreams appear to be a rich, condensed and special force of experiencing, with a specific nature and possibilities which are completely and specifically their own. When one starts to look at dreams with "Rogerian eyes," one can very naturally start, in different ways, to make use of this rich source of experience for client-centered aims. The links with the client-centered aproach seem numerous and easy to grasp.

Gendlin (1986) has elaborated on one possibility of client-centered dream therapy; this in keeping with his experiential psychotherapy, with an eclectic use of everything that seems useful to him. He says himself that this is only one of the many possible methods.

In my work, this experiential aspect can also be largely recognized. It is a basic aspect which is woven into the whole in various ways. If one wants to classify my way of working, the best thing one can do is to say that it is a continuation of the traditional client-centered approach, completed however with the introduction of a dimension which was not developed but rather avoided in our orientation; this is the dimension of looking at images in an empathic way as a means to disclose feelings, alternately combining viewing and feeling, and integrating this into other dimensions. Therefore, it in no way involves the eclectic recuperation of a means from another orientation. It aims at introducing in our methodology the neglected dimension of viewing and at restoring the integration of viewing and feeling - our aim with our clients. In this, it is an addition to the traditional client-centered dimensions of methodology.

Gendlin's way of working and mine have a lot in common despite different starting-points which are determined historically and personally. It seems to me that they complement each other.

If one looks at dreams in a client-centered way, each according to his own nature and potential, then other approaches can definitely be developed. Again, why would Rogerians neglect this rich source of dreams? I am of the opinion that anyone who includes dreams in his work, whatever school they represent within this orientation, will soon be fruitfully, creatively and fascinatingly occupied. I think that if client-centered psychotherapists launch into dream therapy, they will enrich other traditional forms of dream therapy with the uniqueness of the client-centered approach.

REFERENCES

Carkhuff, R.R., & Berenson, G.B. (1977). *Beyond counseling and therapy.* New York: Holt, Rinehart & Winston.
Coenen, A.M.L. (1985). *In Morpheus' armen: over slaap en slaapstoornissen.* Assen: van Gorcum.
Freud, S. (1922). Die Traumdeutung. In: *Gesammelte Werke. Vol. 7.* Leipzig: Dieticke.
Gendlin, E.T. (1970a). A short summary and some long predictions. In: J.T. Hart & T.M. Tomlinson, *New directions in client-centered therapy* (pp. 554-562). Boston: Houghton Mifflin.
Gendlin, E.T. (1970b). A theory of personality change. In: J.T. Hart & T.M. Tomlinson, *New directions in client-centered therapy* (pp. 120-174). Boston: Houghton Mifflin.
Gendlin, E.T. (1982). *Experiential psychotherapy.* Unpublished manuscript.
Gendlin, E.T. (1986). *Focussen.* Haarlem: De Toorts.
Gendlin, E.T. (1986). *Let your body interpret your dreams.* Wilmette, IL: Chiron.
Gendlin, E.T. (1990). *The small steps of the therapy process: How they come and how to help them come.* (This volume).
Haas, O.P. de (1985). Van Rogeriaanse therapie naar procesgerichte gesprekstherapie. *Tijdschrift voor Psychotherapie, 2,* 83-93.
Hamelinck, L., & Swildens, J.C.A.G. (1985). *Diagnostiek vanuit een client-centered kader.* Paper presented at the Colloquium of the Dutch and Flemish Societies of client-centered therapy, Antwerp, April 1985.
Jennings, J.L. (1986). The dream is the dream is the dream. A person-centered approach to dream analysis. *Person-centered Review, 1,* 310-333.
Jung, C.G. (1947). *Ueber Psycho-Energetik und das Wesen der Träume.* Zürich: Walter.
Kessel, W. van (1975). Van reflektie tot interventie. *Tijdschrift voor Psychiatrie, 17,* 342-354.
Kiesler, D.J. (1982). Interpersonal theory of personality and psychotherapy. In: J.C. Anchin & D.J. Kiesler, *Handbook of interpersonal psychotherapy.* New York: Pergamon.
Lietaer, G. (1983). De client-centered benadering in de zeventiger jaren. *Tijdschrift voor Psychotherapie, 2,* 76-89.
Truax, C.B., & Carkhuff, R.R. (1967). *Toward effective counseling and psychotherapy.* Chicago: Aldine.
Vossen, A.J.M. (1976). *Zichzelf worden in menselijke relatie.* Haarlem: De Toorts.

548

Vossen, A.J.M. (1986). *Client-centered droomtherapie.* Video (Memo, Postbus 9822, 3506 GU Utrecht, The Netherlands).
Vossen, A.J.M., & Vossen-Felix, E.G. (1971). Communicatie met het kind als persoon. In: J. de Wit et al., *Psychologen over het kind* (Vol. 2, pp. 217-242). Groningen: Tjeenk Willink.
Wexler, D.A., & Rice, L.N. (1974). *Innovations in client-centered therapy.* New York: Wiley.
Wijngaarden, H.R. (1984). Client-centered therapy: een eigen identiteit? In: G. Lietaer, et al., *Client-centered psychotherapie in beweging* (pp. 41-54). Leuven: Acco.
Wijngaarden, H.R. (1985). *Luisteren naar dromen.* Meppel: Boom.

THE IMPACT OF EXPERIENTIAL THERAPY ON DEPRESSION: THE FIRST TEN CASES

Robert ELLIOTT, Claudia CLARK, Vivian KEMENY
M. Mark WEXLER, Carol MACK, & John BRINKERHOFF
University of Toledo, U.S.A.

INTRODUCTION

Experiential therapy encompasses a broad class of humanistic and phenomenological therapies which emerged in the 1940's as alternatives to psychoanalytic and (later) behavioral approaches to psychotherapy. The two best-known examples of this approach are client-centered therapy (Rogers, 1951, 1961, 1980) and gestalt therapy (Perls, 1969; Perls, Hefferline & Goodman, 1951). In general, experiential therapies emphasize (a) the client's current feelings, perceptions and bodily sensations; (b) the need to allow the client freedom to create his or her own unique meanings and decisions; (c) the creation of an accepting and empathic person-to-person relationship between client and therapist; and (d) the importance of fostering awareness and integration of disowned or conflicted aspects of the person (Gendlin, 1979; Goldenberg, 1983; Mahrer, 1983). Consistent with these emphases, the therapist typically refrains from giving advice or making interpretations. Instead, she or he works actively to help the client develop his or her own insights and solutions to problems, sometimes using special techniques to enhance awareness and expression of emotion-laden experiences.

The subject of this paper is a form of experiential therapy which synthesizes client-centered and gestalt approaches around a set of important therapeutic "tasks" (e.g. resolving internal conflicts) (Rice & Greenberg, 1984, 1990). The therapy shares with other experiential therapies an emphasis on primary relationship conditions (e.g. empathy), but has two features which set it apart from others: First, and perhaps most important, it is explicitly "marker-guided," meaning that the therapist's interventions are guided by immediate process markers (or "process diagnoses"). These markers indicate that the client is ready to work toward resolving a particular problematic experience and needs therapist help in processing the emotional information involved. Second, it emphasizes change in cognitive-affective representations (schemata) of self and others; it is not principally a cathartic or expressive therapy. Emotional arousal is a means to the end of accessing and changing central representations of self and others, rather than an end in itself.

A number of recent developments make this an opportune time for researching experiential therapy. One of these is Greenberg and Safran's (1987) formulation of the nature of human emotion and its role in the process of therapeutic change. In this view, emotion is a complex multilevel phenomenon with intimate connections to both cognition (in the form of "hot cognitions") and behavior (in the form of "action tendencies"). Furthermore, a number of specific techniques which extend the range and power of experiential therapy have been described and are now being researched. These include (a) Gendlin's (1978) Focusing technique for helping clients identify, describe, and "shift" feelings; (b) Greenberg's (1984) work on the Gestalt two chair method for resolving internal conflicts; and (c) Rice's (Rice & Sapiera, 1984) use of "Systematic Evocative Unfolding" for resolving painful or puzzling personal reactions. These and other techniques provide clients with methods for coping with specific distressing experiences. All employ a process of separating and "playing off" different parts (e.g. states, wishes, values) of the person, thereby accessing important beliefs about self and others. Further, all address the issue of translating therapeutic experiences into extratherapy behavior change or definition of problems for further work. Our version of experiential therapy integrates the above-mentioned techniques. A draft treatment manual has been prepared (Elliott, Greenberg, Rice, & Clark, 1987), with a more extensive version under development.

Despite this recent progress, experiential therapies in general have been under-researched (Wolfe, Waskow, Lowery, & Docherty, 1984). More research is needed, especially systematic examinations of change in integrated (multitechnique) experiential treatments that focus on specific clinical disorders.

Theory of depression

Because they center around emotion, the problems of living covered by the psychiatric label "Major depression" seem highly appropriate for experiential therapy. Experiential therapy assumes that depressive emotion and the clinical syndrome of major depression have a variety of causes, including those stemming from biological, cognitive, interpersonal, and environmental conditions. Nevertheless, the following general points can be made about the origins of depression from the experiential perspective (Greenberg, Elliott, & Foerster, in press):

1. Experiential therapy assumes that the depressive reaction ultimately derives from a biologically adaptive withdrawal-conservation response to physical injury or inhospitable/intractable environmental circumstances (Greenberg, Elliott, & Foerster, in press). Clinical depression (as opposed to adaptive "depression") occurs when a person reacts with withdrawal-conservation to perceived *emotional* injuries or to situations incorrectly assumed to be hopeless.

2. Experiential theory also holds that previous hostile or critical interactions with significant others (including physical and emotional abuse) lead the person to introject two things: (a) a "vulnerable" self experienced as weak (fragile, powerless) and/or bad (mean, unworthy) (Rogers, 1959), and (b) an angry internal "critic" as part of the self (Perls, Hefferline, & Goodman, 1951). While the overly-harsh internal critic is symptomatic of depression, it further contributes to the internalized sense of the weak or bad self and blocks other adaptive ways of coping with the environment, especially anger. The weak/bad self and the critic constitute an experiential vulnerability to depression.

3. A major depressive episode occurs when the person experiences a current stressful situation which evokes critical, weak or bad aspects of self. Such situations include real or perceived interpersonal loss (e.g. through divorce or death), personal failure (e.g. job loss), physical illness, moral transgression, or emotional or physical abuse. The combination of stressor and activated weak/bad self schema leads the person to fall back on unadaptive withdrawal/conservation.

Theory of therapy

The theory of what brings about change in experiential therapy of depression can be summarized as follows: The therapy begins by working within the depressed client's phenomenology, rather than trying to dispute it. This enhances the development of the therapeutic relationship, an important factor leading to client change. Next, the therapist's attitude of acceptance and empathy plays an important role in experiential therapy with depression. As the client experiences this attitude, he or she comes to internalize the therapist's optimistic and accepting view as an alternative to the self-rejection (Rogers, 1959). In addition, the therapist fosters client autonomy by offering choices about the therapeutic process (e.g. whether to approach or avoid painful material) and by refraining from directive interventions. This makes it more likely that the client will attribute progress to his or her own efforts, increasing the likelihood that treatment gains will be maintained (cf. Brehm & Smith, 1986).

Furthermore, in contrast to cognitive therapy (e.g. Beck, Rush, Shaw, & Emery, 1979), experiential therapy posits a bidirectional link between cognitive and affective elements of depression. This interactive position is in line with recent theories of emotion (e.g. Greenberg & Safran, 1987; Zajonc, 1980). Finally, the techniques used in experiential therapy are targeted at specific important depressive experiences, including lingering grief and anger toward significant others, the client's internal critic, and difficulties with making decisions (Greenberg & Webster, 1982).

Evidence for effectiveness

Despite the obvious fit between depression and experiential therapy, at present, there is little direct evidence of its effectiveness with depressed clients. This is largely an accident of history. Early researchers used the now-defunct diagnostic category of "neurotic" to describe their client populations. The sucess of client-centered therapy with "neurotic" clients suggests that experiential therapy is likely to be effective with so-called major depressive disorder, formerly subsumed under the "neurosis" label (Rogers & Dymond, 1954; Shlien, Mosak & Dreikurs, 1962; Smith, Glass & Miller, 1980). In addition, there is already some adventitiously-obtained evidence from two studies from the cognitive therapy literature which suggest that experiential therapy can be an effective treatment for depression (Fuchs & Rehm, 1977; Shaw, 1977). In both studies, weak forms of client-centered therapy groups, used as so-called "attention placebo" controls, outperformed wait-list controls.

In this paper, we provide data on the impact of short-term experiential therapy on clients diagnosed with clinical depression. We will report data on the impact of both entire treatments (i.e. outcome) and sessions and important events within sessions; we will also review data collected using both standardized, structured measures and open-ended qualitative approaches. Four main types of data will be reported: (a) outcome measured before, during, after treatment and at 6-month follow-up, (b) personal changes described by clients at the end of treatment, (c) client and therapist ratings of the impacts of sessions, and (d) clients' free descriptions of the most helpful and hindering events in each session.

METHOD

Sample and treatment characteristics

CLIENTS

At this writing, ten clinically depressed clients (out of a planned sample of 20) have completed treatment. These clients were recruited through advertisements in local newspapers. After an initial telephone interview to determine appropriateness and willingness to participate, prospective clients were given the Hamilton Depression Scale (Hamilton, 1960), the Millon Clinical Multiaxial Inventory (MCMI; Millon, 1983), the Beck Depression Inventory (BDI; Beck, Steer & Garbin, 1988), the Symptom Checklist-90 (SCL-90; Derogatis, 1977), and the Diagnostic Interview Schedule (DIS; Robins et al., 1981). Inclusion criteria required the presence of two of the following three: (a) Hamilton > 13 (using the original 17 item version); (b) BDI > 10; (c) DSM III diagnosis (based on DIS) of Major Depressive Episode.

Prospective clients were excluded if they (a) had recently (within the past 6 months) been in psychotherapy (4+ sessions) or psychiatrically hospitalized; (b) had a DIS lifetime diagnosis of bipolar, schizophrenic, schizophreniform or antisocial personality disorders; (c) had a DIS recent (within previous three months) diagnosis of Anorexia, Bulimia, Drug or Alcohol Abuse or Dependence; (d) were actively suicidal; or (e) had another psychiatric or medical disorder judged by evaluator and principal investigator to be clinically predominant over depression.

Table 1 presents some descriptive data for clients, showing them to be evenly divided between males and females. The typical client was married, in his or her 30's, had completed some college, and worked at a clerical or accounting job. Most clients had experienced two or more episodes of major depression, and were also diagnosed with a concomitant anxiety disorder. Clients who completed at least 12 sessions were counted as "completers". (Four other clients who received more than 3 and less than 12 sessions were considered "drop-outs.")

Table 1
Descriptive information on clients

Gender		Education	
Female	5	Did not finish High School	3
Male	5	High School, plus some	
Diagnosis		college	4
Major depressive disorder		Bachelor's degree	3
Current	10	Marital Status	
With previous episodes	9	Married	5
Additional diagnoses		Single	
Generalized anxiety disorder	5	Never married	2
Dysthymia	3	Divorced	3
Social phobia	2	Occupation	
Age		Clerical/Accounting	5
30-39	7	Professional/Managerial	2
40-49	2	Self-employed	1
50-59	1	Unemployed	2

THERAPISTS

The therapists were two advanced graduate students in clinical psychology and the first author (RE). The graduate student therapists had several years' experience at the university of Toledo; the first author had approximately eight years' previous experience doing experiential therapy. In addition to their previous experience, therapists went through six months of training primarily with undergraduate volunteer "clients."

EXPERIENTIAL THERAPY OF DEPRESSION

Clients were generally seen for 16 sessions of experiential therapy (range: 12-20 sessions). The general features of experiential therapy of depression were outlined earlier; the treatment is described in more detail in a manual (Elliott, Greenberg, Rice, & Clark, 1987) and related materials (Gendlin, 1978; Greenberg, 1984; Rice & Sapiera, 1984). As it applies to depression, experiential therapy starts with investigating the client's mood disorder and the nature of his or her depressive experiences. The probing begins by examining what the depression is about (e.g. the sense that one is doomed to be driven into destructive relationships). This work of exploring the depressive feelings is carried out by using the "Basic Mode" in which the therapist reflects (paraphrases) what the client says and asks open questions about feelings and meanings in order to foster client self-exploration. As exploration continues, the therapist listens for and reflects client statements which imply growth, desire for change, or newly emerging ways of feeling, thinking or acting (Rice & Greenberg, 1990).

Beyond this, the treatment is "marker-guided" in the sense described by Rice and Greenberg (1984); that is, the therapist is particularly sensitive to "depressive markers," or indications that the client is ready to work at resolving an important depressive experience. The most common of these is the expression of lingering regret or "if only" which signals that the client is ready to work on leftover anger or hurt ("unfinished business") involving a significant other (e.g. an alcoholic parent). When this marker occurs, the therapist helps the client to engage in an imaginary dialogue with the significant other, often playing both self and other (the empty chair technique). In this dialogue, the client is encouraged to express the unresolved feelings, to imagine how the other would respond, and to work with the feelings and memories evoked to the point of forgiveness or at least understanding of the other (Greenberg & Safran, 1987).

A second important marker in depression is strong self-criticism, indicative of an inner split between a harsh internal "critic" and a weak/bad self. This marker signals the therapist to encourage the client to enact a conversation between the two sides, in order to empower the weak/bad self and to integrate the conflicting aspects of self (Greenberg, Elliott & Foerster, in press). A related marker is client expression of apathy, feeling stuck, or suppressed emotion, revealing the operation of a self-interruption process (Perls et al., 1951); a two-chair dialogue is also used at this marker, again with the goal of client self-empowerment (Greenberg et al., in press).

Two other markers and types of specialized intervention are also used: (a) When a client describes not knowing what to talk about or having an unclear sense of something bothering him or her, the therapist uses Gendlin's (1978) Experiential focusing technique (the client is asked to focus inwardly to see what emerges and to try out different labels for the emerging experience). (b) When a client describes a puzzling personal reaction to something, Rice's (Rice & Sapiera, 1984) Evocative unfolding technique is used (the client is asked to describe the situation in which the reaction occurred in detail, step-by-step, leading up to the puzzling reaction, then to explore the issues raised by the reaction).

Data collection methods

OUTCOME MEASURES

We used a battery of measures to assess change in various areas of the client's life, specific depressive symptoms, general clinical status, social adjustment, individualized therapy goals, and experiential functioning. Nine measures of the client's clinical status were administered at five times: Immediately before treatment began, halfway through therapy (after session 8), at the end of treatment, and at 6- and 18-month follow-ups (the last are not yet complete). The measures included the following:

1. Hamilton Depression Scale (Hamilton, 1960), the most commonly-used interview measure of depression (assessed by an independent clinical observer).

2. Symptom Checklist-90 (SCL-90) (Derogatis, 1977), a standard self-report measure of psychiatric symptoms.

3. Beck Depression Inventory (BDI) (Beck et al, 1988), the most widely used self-report measure of depression.

4. Social Adjustment Scale (Weissman & Bothwell, 1976), a standard self-report measure of work and interpersonal functioning (SAS-SR).

5. Rosenberg Self-Esteem Scale-Revised (O'Malley & Bachman, 1979), a simple 10-item self-report measure.

6. Health-Sickness Rating Scale (HSRS) (Luborsky, 1962), a single

rating of client functioning by therapist and researcher (averaged together).

7. Millon Clinical Multiaxial Inventory (MCMI), a standard clinical personality and diagnostic inventory (Millon, 1983).

8. Walker-Rablen-Rogers (WWR) Process Scale (1960), a 7-item measure of client openness and self-awareness (rated by therapist).

9. Simplified Personal Questionnaire (PQ) (Phillips, 1986; Elliott, Shapiro & Barkham, 1985), a 10-item individualized change measure.

POSTTREATMENT CHANGE INTERVIEW

In addition to the outcome measures, we also interviewed clients at the end of therapy, asking them to describe in their own words the specific changes produced by therapy (Elliott & Mack, 1986).

SESSION MEASURES

Beyond measuring the effects of the treatment as a whole, there were a variety of weekly measures of the impact of particular sessions; we will focus here on two measures:1. Session Impacts Questionnaire (Wexler & Elliott, 1988), a 5-point scale measure of the specific immediate impacts of the session, completed by the client.2. Helpful Aspects of Therapy (H.A.T.) Questionnaire (Llewelyn, Elliott, Shapiro, Firth, & Hardy, 1988), a form which asked clients to describe in their own words the most helpful and hindering events in the session.

BRIEF STRUCTURED RECALL OF SIGNIFICANT EVENTS

Tape-assisted recall sessions with clients were conducted by trained interviewers after sessions 3, 6, 10 and 14, using the Brief Structured Recall procedure (Elliott, 1986; Elliott & Shapiro, 1988). Within two days after the designated session (usually immediately following it), client recall took place. During the recall process, the client was asked to locate the event he or she described on the above mentioned Helpful Aspects of Therapy Questionnaire (Llewelyn, et al., 1988) as the most helpful in the session. The interviewer (not the therapist) began by forwarding the videotape until the event was located. The client then established the precise beginning and end points of the event (events typically varied between 5 and 10 min. in length). Next, the interviewer conducted a structured interview focusing on the event using the Client Event Recall Form (Elliott, 1986). The therapist then completed the Therapist Event Recall Form, which provides information complementary to the client form. Of the complex data obtained from these two recall forms, we will report here only on client and therapist ratings on the two parallel Immediate Therapeutic Impact Scales (Elliott & Shapiro, 1988), which are a part of them; each consisting of 16 items (e.g. awareness, relief) rated on the same 5-point scales as the above mentioned Session Impacts Questionnaire.

RESULTS

Outcome of experiential therapy of depression

Table 2 summarizes the outcome data for study completers. We will describe the outcome of the Therapy using a variety of criteria, including clinical cut-off values (where available; including number of clients on the nondistressed side of the threshold); and pre- to post-change effect size, expressed in standard deviation units (using pretreatment assessment standard deviations) (cf. Jacobson, Follette, & Revenstorff, 1984).

BDI. Mean Beck Depression Inventory scores were about 22 before treatment, and dropped to 15 halfway through, 9 at termination, and 8 at 6-month follow-up. These results compare quite favorably with the average effects Nietzel, Russell, Hemmings , and Gretter (1987) found for 31 studies of psychotherapy of depression (80% involving cognitive or behavioral treatments; pre- to posttreatment BDI: 25 to 11). Using pretreatment mean and s.d. as a baseline, the change effect size was 1.55 s.d. for posttreatment and 1.72 for 6-month follow-up data.

The clinical cut-off we used for the BDI was 11 or greater; the average client passed this threshold between mid- and posttreatment assessments. Seven out of ten clients fell below the threshold at termination, while six of the nine clients for whom we have 6-month follow-up data remained below the clinical cut-off score.

Table 2
Change measure data for first ten cases

Measure	Clinical cut-off score	Initial Screening	Pre-treatment	Mid-treatment	Post-treatment	6-month Follow-up
BDI Mean:	11	22.4	21.6	15.0	8.7	7.3
(SD):		(6.1)	(8.3)	(9.0)	(9.6)	(6.8)
change:		-	0.00	.80	1.55	1.72
n:		0/10	0/10	2/10	7/10	6/9
Hamilton	14	19.4	-	13.9	7.7	6.6
		(4.9)		(3.6)	(4.3)	(5.7)
		0.00	-	1.12	2.39	2.61
		0/6		4/6	6/6	7/8
MCMI D	75	111.9	103.7	89.8	74.6	69.3
		(15.2)	(17.2)	(14.8)	(15.8)	(7.4)
		-	0.00	.81	1.69	2.00
		0/10	0/10	2/10	5/10	3/4
SCL-90 GSI	1.0	1.47	1.19	.90	.68	.42
		(.39)	(.31)	(.52)	(.61)	(.51)
		-	0.00	.24	1.65	2.48
		2/10	3/10	5/9	7/9	7/8
PQ		-	5.20	3.64	3.19	2.86
			(.69)	(1.19)	(1.44)	(1.06)
			0.00	2.26	2.91	3.39
			./10	./10	./10	./7
HSRS*	76	-	60.4	66.8	71.0	81.3
			(6.0)	(7.9)	(13.0)	(4.3)
			0.00	1.07	1.77	3.48
			0/6	1/8	3/10	6/7
Rosenberg*		-	3.57	4.25	4.95	5.40
			(1.46)	(1.45)	(1.70)	(1.42)
			0.00	.47	.95	1.25
			./10	./10	./10	./8
WRR*		-	2.83	3.40	3.90	-
			(1.02)	(1.07)	(1.07)	
			0.00	.56	1.05	
			./7	./6	./10	
SAS-SR		-	2.24	1.98	1.96	1.70
			(.19)	(.42)	(.40)	(.21)
			0.00	1.37	1.47	2.84
			./10	./10	./10	./8

Note:
BDI = Beck Depression Inventory. Hamilton = Hamilton Depression Scale.
MCMI D = Millon Clinical Multiaxial Inventory, Dysthymia Scale (BR score).
SCL-90 GSI = Symptom Checklist-90 Global Symptom Index. PQ = Personal
Questionnaire (mean). HSRS = Health Sickness Rating Scale. Rosenberg =
Rosenberg Self-Esteem Scale (mean). WRR = Walker-Rablen-Rogers Process
Scale (mean). SAS SR = Social Adjustment Scale - Self Report (mean).

For each outcome measure is given: The clinical cut-off score (if any) and at
various measurement times: Mean, standard deviation, pre- to post-change
effect size in pretreatment standard deviation units, and number of clients on
the nondistressed side of the threshold together with the number of clients for
whom data were available.

* For these scales higher scores indicate better health, self-esteem or openness
respectively. For the other scales higher scores indicate greater distress or
difficulty.

Hamilton. Mean Hamilton scores dropped from 19 at screening to 14
(the clinical cut-off score) at midtreatment, to 8 immediately after
treatment and 7 at 6-month follow-up. Change effect size values were
2.39 s.d. at termination and 2.61 at 6-month follow-up. Four of the six
clients for whom we have posttreatment Hamilton data were below the
clinical threshold at midtreatment, while all six were at posttreatment;
seven out of eight remained below threshold at follow-up.

MCMI D Scale. The MCMI Dysthymia scale complements the Beck
and Hamilton scales as a more conservative, inventory-based measure
which incorporates corrections for exaggeration and minimization of
symptoms. Millon (1983) defines a BR score of 75 or higher as a
clinical cutoff. As Table 2 shows, the average client scored at this
threshold at posttreatment and below it at 6-month follow-up. Five out
of ten clients scored below threshold at posttreatment assessment.
Change effect size values were 1.69 and 2.00 s.d. for posttreatment and
follow-up respectively.

SCL-90 GSI. The Global Symptom Index of the SCL-90 was used as
a measure of general clinical distress. 1.0 can be used as a cut-off on the
SCL-90; clients typically passed below this level between pre- and
midtreatment assessments. At the end of treatment, seven out of nine
clients were below threshold, while at 6-month follow-up seven out of
eight were below threshold. Change effect sizes were 1.65 and 2.48 s.d.
for posttreatment and follow-up respectively.

Personal Questionnaire. The Personal Questionnaire (PQ)
complements the SCL-90 and the other standard measures, by
providing an individual change measure of ten personal problems. At

the beginning of therapy, clients rated their problems as: Bothering them "considerably" (5 on a 7-point scale). This dropped substantially by midtreatment (2.26 s.d.), went on to drop to around "little" (scale point 3) at posttreatment and follow-up (2.91 and 3.39 s.d. respectively).

HSRS. The Health-Sickness Rating Scale provided a clinician- and therapist-based measure of global client functioning. The scale itself defines 76 or higher as indicating "everyday adjustment," with mild problems beginning at 75 and lower. Client change beyond this threshold was slow for the HSRS, with the average and majority of clients only passing the cut-off at 6-month follow-up (6 out of 7 clients). Change effect sizes were 1.77 and 3.48 s.d. for mid- and posttreatment.

Rosenberg. The Rosenberg Self-Esteem Scale was one of the two change measures selected for their particular relevance to experiential therapy. Surprisingly, self-esteem scores showed smaller standardized change than any other measure (change effect sizes of only .95 and 1.25 s.d. for posttreatment and follow-up).

WRR. The second theory-relevant change measure we used was the Process Scale developed by Walker, Rablen, & Rogers (1960). Change was also small on this scale, with clients moving approximately one point (to around scale point 4, corresponding to moderately good level of openness to experiencing; change-effect size: 1.05 s.d.).

SAS-SR. Finally, the Social Adjustment Scale-Self Report was used to pick up change relevant to Interpersonal Therapy, a contrasting therapy of depression, as well as to assess possible effects of the treatment on interpersonal and work functioning. Change effect sizes were 1.46 s.d. at termination and 2.48 at follow-up.

Summary of Outcome Data. Averaging change-effect sizes across measures provides one way to summarize treatment effects. At midtreatment, clients had changed an average of 1.04 s.d.; at posttreatment, this value reached 1.71 s.d.; and at 6-month follow-up it improved still further to 2.47 s.d.

Another kind of summary can be given in terms of the number of clients passing the five clinical threshold values (BDI: 11+; Hamilton: 14+; MCMI D BR: 75+; SCL-90: 1.0+; HSRS: 75 or lower). At the end of therapy, all ten clients bettered the threshold value on at least one of these five change measures; 6 out of 10 clients passed the cut offs on a majority of available measures; and 3 clients passed on all available measures. At follow-up, 8 out of 9 clients scored below clinical levels on a majority of the available measures; but only one passed on all available measures.

Comparison with First Sheffield psychotherapy project. The data also allow comparison to the First Sheffield psychotherapy project (Shapiro & Firth, 1987), which our study was designed to parallel. (Both studies used BDI, SCL-90, SAS-SR, and Rosenberg Self-Esteem Scale; clients were seen for 16 sessions in each study; in addition, most of the clients in the Sheffield-study were suffering from depression.) For these ten clients, our outcome results for mid- and post-treatment assessments on the four shared measures were virtually identical to those reported from the Sheffield study (Shapiro & Firth, 1987) for clients treated with cognitive-behavioral and interpersonal-dynamic therapies. In the Sheffield study, the mean effect sizes for the four shared change measures were as follows: Midtreatment: .93; posttreatment: 1.46; follow-up: 1.59. For our first ten clients the comparable values were: Midtreatment: .90; posttreatment: 1.41; follow-up: 2.07. The major difference between studies is in the follow-up data, which is higher for our study. This unexpected finding might be due to our use of a longer follow-up period (6 months vs. 3 months), or it may indicate a greater degree of "delayed impact" from experiential therapy.

Changes described by clients at the end of therapy

Describing the impact of experiential therapy using standard quantitative change measures satisfies many of the canons of psychotherapy outcome research. However, it neglects our clients' specific experiences of what changed in this therapy. During posttreatment interviews, the ten clients identified 48 changes as occurring since the beginning of therapy (mean: 4.8 changes; range 2-9). Four judges (the first author and three B.A.-level assistants) carried out a grounded theory analysis (Glaser & Strauss, 1967; Rennie, Phillips, & Quartaro, 1988) of these described changes (Grounded theory is a method of systematic qualitative analysis in which researchers attempt to discover naturally occurring categories in a set of accounts of some phenomenon, while setting aside preconceptions and previous theory). Judges independently developed categories for change descriptions, then met to agree upon the categories and the descriptions which fit into them.

We identified three major domains of change, divided into 7 categories and 11 subcategories. These are given in Table 3, along with frequencies of categories and examples. The three major domains of change were Improvements within the Self, Improvements in Dealing with Others, and Improvements in Life Situation.

Table 3
Changes described by clients at the end of therapy:
Grounded categories

I. *Improvements Within the Self:* (41 changes; 10 clients)
   A. *Positive Feelings:* (20 changes; 9 clients)
      1. *Improved General Mood, Optimism about Life* (decreased distress, depression) (12 changes; 6 clients)
      "I have a more cheerful outlook." (31-1 [see note])
      "I have not been thinking about death. I used to feel like it took too much energy to live, but now I have lots of energy." (64-3)
      2. *Improved Self-Esteem* (increased positive feelings, decreased negative feelings toward self) (8 changes; 6 clients)
      "I don't beat myself over the head over mistakes. I see myself as more human." (9-4)
      "I don't feel as strange as I used to. I had doubts about my normality. Now, those doubts are less." (70-3)
   B. *Action-Related Changes:* (11 changes; 6 clients)
      1. *Improved Ability to Cope with Life Situations* (7 changes; 4 clients)
      "I am able to approach other people differently now; (the way I deal with 'bossy' people [category IIA1])." (9-1)
      "I can deal with feelings in relationships." (31-4)
      2. *Preparing to Take Effective Action to Deal with Problems* (decisions, planning) (4 changes; 2 clients)
      "I was back and forth about getting an apartment at first, but not now." (1-1)
      "(I realize that) I need to do other things about my future rather than waiting for men to rescue me." (64-1)
   C. *Closer Contact with Self* (feelings, attitudes): (10 changes; 6 clients)
      1. *Realizations about Self* (5 changes; 3 clients)
      "I have a new understanding of my own sexuality." (67-3)
      "I realized my opinions and feelings matter." (59-1)
      2. *General Openness to Own Feelings* (3 changes; 3 clients)
      "I listen more to my emotions." (18-3)
      "I can deal with (my) feelings in relationships." (31-4)
      3. *Specific Wishes or Attitudes Strengthened* (2 changes; 2 clients)
      "I've made up my mind that my attitude towards the other woman will never change." (1-5)

"Deepening and clarifying the realization that I want to give something back to the world." (67-4)

II. *Improvements in Dealing with Others:* (24 changes; 8 clients)
    A. *Improvements in Interpersonal Style:* (17 changes; 6 clients)
        1. *Increased Independence/Assertion* (decreased dependence, inappropriate involvement with others) (9 changes; 5 clients)
        "(I am able to approach other people differently now [category IB1]); the way I deal with 'bossy' people. (9-1)
        "I don't take everything from everyone like I used to." (59-2)
        2. *Increased Positive Openness. Intimacy* (self-disclosure, expression; closeness, contact, incl. sexual) (8 changes; 5 clients)
        "I'm more able to talk to others about my problems." (1-8)
        "I've joined some groups and made some new friends." (64-2)
    B. *Changes in Interpersonal Perceptions* (7 changes; 6 clients)
        1. *Changes in C's Views and Attitudes towards Others* (new views; greater patience, tolerance, realism) (4 changes; 3 clients)
        "I am more tolerant of others." (57-2)
        "I have new ideas about my father." (67-2)
        2. *Reported Changes in Others' Views of Self* (3 changes; 3 clients)
        "My co-workers have noticed a change." (1-7)
        "(I don't take everything from everyone like I used to ... [category IIA1])
        My husband says he's glad, but I don't think he's used to it." (59-2)

III. *Improvements in Life Situation* (7 changes; 3 clients)
    A. *Improved Relationship Aspects* (4 changes; 3 clients)
        "It's gotten me closer to my husband." (1-3)
        "I've joined some groups and made new friends." (64-2)
    B. *Improved Non-relationship Aspects* (3 changes; 2 clients)
        "My husband has started on the house now." (1-6)
        "I am financially better." (9-8)

Note. $n = 48$ changes described by 10 clients. Grounded theory uses "open categories" (i.e. nonmutually exclusive); therefore, frequencies exceed 48. Examples are identified by: Client and number of change listed by client (e.g. 9-1 refers to the first change described by the client with the identification number of "9").

Consistent with the intrapersonal nature of experiential therapy, all clients described changes which are falling into the first and largest of these domains: *Improvements Within the Self.* Clients described three types of improvements in themselves: Positive Feelings, Action-Related Changes, and Closer Contact with Self. Not surprisingly, these depressed clients frequently reported changes in the form of enhanced Positive Feelings, including two subcategories, Improved General

Mood/Optimism and Improved Self-Esteem. The mood subcategory incorporated decreased depression as well as increased optimism about the world and the future. The self-esteem subcategory contained both decreased self-criticism and increased positive self-regard.

Action-Related changes made up about a quarter of the descriptions concerning Improvements Within the Self, and came from a majority of the clients. The two associated subcategories were Improved Ability to Cope with Life Situations, and Preparing to Take Effective Action. In the first of these, clients described specific abilities they had developed for resolving problems, or they stated that they had become more effective in general. In the second subcategory, clients described steps leading up to action, such as deciding, resolving or planning what to do.

Although a relatively small category, the third type of within-self change has particular relevance to the experiential model of therapy, because it involves clients achieving some form of Closer Contact with Self. This division consisted of three fairly small subcategories: (a) Realizations about Self involved insight or new awareness of specific ideas about oneself; (b) General Openness to Own Feelings referred to a general "in-touchness" with one's inner feelings; and (c) Specific Wishes or Attitudes Strengthened contained descriptions of the client feeling confirmed in particular important beliefs or desires.

About one-third of the changes described involved *Improvements in dealing with others,* which was divided into two separate categories. The larger of these, Improvements in Interpersonal Style, had two subcategories corresponding to Benjamin's (1974) two interpersonal dimensions of affiliation and independence, each described by half the ten clients: Increased Positive Openness, Intimacy contained descriptions of increased self-disclosure to significant others, and closer, warmer contact with others. Increased Independence/Assertion involved decreased dependence and decreased inappropriate involvement with others, including better limit-setting.

The third type of interpersonal change was Changes in Interpersonal Perceptions, which was further divided into two small subcategories: Changes in Client's Views and Attitudes Towards Others involved greater patience, tolerance and realism in one's attitudes towards others, while Reported Changes in Other's Views of Self consisted of descriptions of coworkers or spouse having observed or commented on changes in the client.

The final domain of changes described by clients was a small one of *Improvements in Client's Environment,* in which three clients located changes outside the self, in another's behavior or financial or job changes.

Rated impacts of experiential therapy sessions and significant events

The next set of results bear not on the broad effects of entire treatments, but on the more local impacts of particular sessions and events within experiential therapy. To assess session impact, we used a weekly measure of the immediate therapeutic impacts of sessions (Wexler & Elliott, 1988). The Brief Structured Recall method (Elliott & Shapiro, 1988) was used to allow clients to identify and rate on the same 5-point scales the most helpful events in 40 sampled sessions.

Table 4 summarizes averaged client ratings of sessions and client and therapist ratings of the sampled events. Client ratings of sessions and events were quite similar, with the highest ratings going to: Understood, Supported, Closer to the therapist, More involved, and Awareness. Therapists' ratings of the impacts they believed their clients experienced in significant events were highest for: Understood, Awareness, and Supported. Among helpful impacts, the least prevalent impacts included Insight into other people, Progress in solving problems, and Relief from painful feelings. These data are all consistent with the experiential model in placing the locus of the change process firmly in the therapeutic relationship and the process of enhanced self-awareness.

Hindering or negative impacts were endorsed by clients and therapists at much lower levels, but included being more bothered by unwanted thoughts and occasionally feeling confused and distracted from their problems.

Tabel 4
Therapeutic impacts of sessions and selected significant events:
Mean ratings

Impact	SESSIONS		EVENTS			
	Client		Client		Therapist	
	Mean	S.D.	Mean	S.D.	Mean	S.D.
Helpful Impacts:						
Insight-Self	3.1	1.4	3.0	1.5	3.0	1.4
Insight-Others	2.3	1.5	2.0	1.5	1.5	1.0
Awareness	3.4	1.3	3.6	1.2	3.7	1.2
Definition of Problems	3.0	1.4	2.6	1.5	2.5	1.3
Progress on Problems	2.4	1.4	2.3	1.5	1.8	1.2
Understood	4.0	1.0	4.1	.9	3.8	1.1
Supported	3.8	1.2	3.2	1.4	3.3	1.0
Relief	3.0	1.4	2.6	1.4	2.3	1.2
More Involved	3.4	1.3	3.3	1.3	2.7	1.0
Closer to Therapist	3.6	1.2	3.4	1.4	2.3	1.0
Hindering Impacts:						
Unwanted Thoughts	1.5	.8	1.4	.7	2.1	1.0
Unwanted Responsibility	1.2	.7	1.1	.6	1.3	.6
Misunderstood	1.1	.3	1.1	.5	1.2	.4
Attacked-Rejected	1.0	.3	1.1	.5	1.2	.3
Confused-Distracted	1.4	.9	1.1	.4	1.3	.7
Impatient-Doubting	1.2	.5	1.2	.5	1.0	.2

Note. Variables rated on 5-point scales (0 = not at all, to 5 = extremely). $N = 157$ for session ratings; 40 for ratings of significant events.

Content analysis of clients' descriptions of significant events

As reported above, ratings on predetermined scales are useful; however, they may not actually reflect the important features that significant events may have for clients. In order to explore clients' phenomenology of important events in experiential therapy, we carried out a content analysis of their descriptions of the most helpful or hindering events within each session (obtained using Llewelyn et al., [1988] H.A.T. Questionnaire). Three of the authors (RE, VK, & CC) used these descriptions in a partially-grounded research approach. That is, we started with the content analysis system developed by Elliott and colleagues (1985) and, using data from the first five clients to complete treatment in the present study, freely adapted the original system to more closely reflect the contents of the description given by our clients (Clark, Kemeny, & Elliott, 1987).

The resulting revised content analysis reflects the impacts (and several other domains not described here) most relevant to experiential therapy. We found that six of the impacts in the revised system involved some form of schema change: Insight into Self and Insight into Other involved the client seeing new *connections* (in self or other respectively); in Awareness of Self and Awareness of Other, some aspect of self or other (respectively) became more salient or available to the client; and in Positive Self and Positive Other, the client came to see self or other in a more positive light.

We also retained the Problem Clarification and Problem Solution categories from the previous version of the content analysis system (Elliott et al., 1985) to refer respectively to definition of goals or tasks for therapy and progress towards knowing what to do about problems. A Relief category was added, and four of the previous categories (Understanding, Reassuring, Personal contact and Involvement) were combined into one, Alliance Strengthening, because of their relatively low frequency in the data.

Descriptions of hindering events were relatively rare but consisted of four types: (a) the Unwanted Thoughts category was retained from the previous list of hindering impacts, and involved clients feeling that they had been made to experience unhelpful painful feelings, images, or thoughts. (b) A "Therapist Omissions" category was set up when clients complained of times in which the therapist refrained from some helpful intervention (e.g. did not give advice). (c) A third type of hindering event was Digressions, in which clients complained of having been thrown off or allowed to wander off track (cf. "Misdirection" in the old system). (d) Finally, clients several times described therapist interventions which simply did not fit the client's experience or for which the client felt unprepared; these we called Poor Fit.

Table 5

*Therapeutic impacts of most helpful and most hindering events
within sessions: Content analyses*

	Mean	S.D.	Mean inter-rater r	Alpha
Schema change impacts:				
Self-Insight	.17	.27	.58	.84
Other-Insight	.03	.12	.56	.83
Self-Awareness	.38	.32	.47	.78
Other-Awareness	.08	.20	.41	.69
Positive Self	.10	.20	.52	.81
Positive Other	.01	.07	.57	.83
Other impacts:				
Problem Clarification	.16	.23	.44	.75
Problem Solution	.11	.23	.63	.87
Alliance Strengthening	.11	.25	.69	.89
Relief	.08	.17	.38	.73
Hindering Impacts:				
Unwanted Thoughts	.02	.10	.40	.73
Therapist Omissions	.01	.09	.84	.96
Digressions	.01	.06	.44	.82
Poor Fit	.004	.04	.33	.61

Note. All ratings on a 0-1 confidence rating scale, averaged across 4 raters. Alpha gives reliability of averaged ratings.

After training to satisfactory levels of interrater reliability, four undergraduate judges rated descriptions of 192 significant events drawn from roughly 160 sessions with the first ten clients. The raters used a 0-1 confidence rating scale (to improve reliability), and ratings were averaged across all four raters. Interjudge reliabilities were good to excellent for all major categories (see Table 5).

Consistent with the treatment model, Awareness of self was by far the most common impact, occurring at a rate of almost 40% in the events described (see Table 5). Most of the other relatively frequent impacts were also in keeping with the treatment model, including Insight into self and problem clarification (occurring in about 15% of events), and Positive self and Relief (about 10%). Two other impacts which were less central to the model also occurred at a rate of about 10%: Awareness of others and Problem solution. Unwanted thoughts was the most frequent hindering impact, but occurred only 2% of the time.

DISCUSSION

The central question of this paper is, "What is the impact of experiential therapy on depression?" This question has been answered in a variety of ways, using different-sized pieces of the therapy process and standardized vs. open-ended methods of data collection and analysis.

The impact of the treatment as a whole: Outcome and perceived changes

Our first way of answering the question of impact was to look at outcome on a variety of measures of client change. In reviewing our results, it is important to keep in mind that, to date, we have only data on the first 10 clients. However, based on these cases, and subject to confirmation with the second wave of clients we are treating now, we tentatively conclude the following:

1. Most depressed clients change across a short-term experiential therapy.

2. By comparing our findings on the Beck, a key measure of depression, to the no-treatment control group data meta-analyzed by Nietzel and colleagues (1987), it is reasonable to infer that clients treated with our version of Experiential therapy changed more than if they had gone untreated. In other words, it appears likely that the treatment was responsible for the degree of client change observed.

3. The amount of change obtained was comparable to other treatments of depression which have been studied, primarily cognitive and behavioral treatments (cf. Nietzel et al., 1987).

4. Clients changed somewhat more during the first eight sessions of therapy (an average of 1 s.d., when effects are averaged across the measures used), but continued, substantial improvement also occurred during the second eight sessions (a further .67 s.d.). This result is comparable to the findings of Howard, Kopta, Krause and Orlinsky (1986) and Shapiro and Firth (1987).

5. After therapy, client change was maintained and substantially enhanced, on an order equivalent to the amount of change during the second half of therapy (. 76 s.d.). This result is at variance with Nicholson and Berman's (1983) meta-analysis of psychotherapy follow-up research, which found that levels of client improvement were stable for many months after treatment (and then gradually eroded). If this finding holds up, it may reflect the greater degree of autonomy which is given to clients in experiential therapy, autonomy which we believe leads clients to attribute change to themselves rather than to the therapist.

6. From our client's point of view, the most common changes were improved mood and self-esteem, on the one hand, and improved interpersonal behavior (in the form of both affiliation and independence), on the other. The improved mood was reflected on our standardized change measures, particularly the Hamilton Depression Scale, and to a lesser extent on the BDI and MCMI D scale. However, the Rosenberg Self-Esteem Scale showed the smallest amount of change among the measures used. The qualitative data, coupled with the fact that our results on the Rosenberg are very similar to those obtained by Shapiro and Firth (1987), lead us to the conclusion that this measure is insufficiently sensitive to the kinds of self-esteem change experienced by clients in our study. Finally, clients' changes in interpersonal behavior are probably reflected only in part by the Social Adjustment Scale, which showed respectable (but not large) changes at the end of therapy.

7. Not all clients attained clinically significant change. At posttreatment, four clients still exceeded clinical cut-offs on a majority of the change measures having such thresholds. We judged that these clients required further therapy at that point. In one instance, the effects of therapy required more time to become apparent; for another client, a further 8 sessions of experiential therapy brought about the desired change. Two clients remained in need of additional therapy at follow-up. Further study of clients who respond well vs. poorly to this

therapy is needed in order to develop clinical guidelines.

We recommend that future studies of experiential therapy attempt more systematic measurement of the types of change identified in our qualitative analysis. Better measures of self-esteem and interpersonal style are needed and could be based in qualitative data like that produced in this study. While we have no objection to global measures of outcome such as the SCL-90 or Hamilton Depression Scale, we would like to recommend further use of the Personal Questionnaire, which derives from research on behavior therapy (Phillips, 1986). This measure seems well-suited to research on the outcome of experiential therapy, both conceptually and in terms of sensitivity to change.

The impact of sessions and significant events in experiential therapy of depression

We also took a closer look at the impact of experiential therapy of depression, by examining the immediate effects of sessions and important events within sessions. Our results, expressed either in terms of mean ratings on scales or in content analyses of clients' descriptions, are generally consistent with the underlying model for experiential therapy. Taking either rating or free description data, the central change process appears to be that of enhancing awareness. However, the two sets of analyses offer complementary pictures of the additional effects of experiential therapy sessions and events.

When they used predetermined rating scales, clients gave much greater salience to what we have elsewhere called "interpersonal" impacts (Understood, Supported, Involved, Closer to Therapist; cf. Elliott, 1985; Elliott et al, 1985). In contrast, these impacts were so uncommon in clients' descriptions of most helpful events, that they had to be combined into one category (Alliance Strengthening). These interpersonal impacts parallel Rogers' (1957) facilitative conditions of empathy, warmth, and genuineness. However, although they occurred at relatively high levels, they were not usually valued by clients as "most helpful." We believe that Rice's (1983) formulation of task-relevant relationship factors applies here. These interpersonal impacts play an important supporting role in helping clients carry out therapeutic tasks (which enhance awareness in various ways), but we also believe that they are not sufficient for change in themselves.

In contrast, clients' descriptions of most helpful events sometimes contained descriptions of clients planning behavior change (the Problem Solution category), in spite of the fact that this change process is not at all a focus of the treatment. It appears that our clients sometimes used experiential work to spontaneously generate strategies for changing their own behavior. Client posttherapy descriptions of action-related changes are also consistent with this. Judging from the low mean ratings for Progress on problems, this appears to be a relatively low-base rate occurrence, at least as an immediate impact of events and sessions. Nevertheless, our clients appear to have valued it highly when it occurred. Thus, for both theoretical and practical reasons, we think that the process by which clients transform awareness and insight into problem solution is an important one for further study.

Negative, or hindering, impacts provide another topic for further study. These effects were relatively rare, but they did show up in both rating and free description data, and may help to explain what happened in our unsuccessful cases. Unwanted Thoughts was the most common negative effect, revealing the thin line between helpful awareness and unhelpful overstimulation of clients. We have found Gendlin's notion of "working distance" to be a useful way of thinking about and dealing with clients to help them reduce awareness, at least temporarily! Information about hindering events and their impacts has provided us with useful feedback for improving our therapy, revealing instances in which therapists were not active enough (negative impact: Unwanted Responsibility or Therapist Omissions), or in which they led too much or did not follow the client's train of experience closely enough (impact: Digressions or Misdirection).

In this paper, we have described the impacts of an experiential therapy of depression at both "macro" (outcome) and "micro" (events and sessions) levels. The picture for each is a predominantly positive one. However, we understand little as yet of what brings about these impacts at either level. For this, much more fine-grained work linking together contexts, client and therapist in-session actions, and impacts is needed. Task analysis (Rice & Greenberg, 1984) and Comprehensive process analysis (Elliott, in press) are two such approaches.

574

NOTE

The authors are grateful for the assistance of the following persons in the preparation of this paper: Victoria Morehouse (data analysis and rating); Julie Knapp (qualitative analysis and editorial assistance); Elizabeth Kazsa and Mark Wolever (qualitative analysis); Cheryl Anderson (editorial assistance); and Albert SanGregory, Teresa Norgaard, Jill Van Tassel (rating) and Carol Mack (she died on April 18, 1988).

REFERENCES

Beck, A.T., Rush, A.J., Shaw, B.F., & Emery, G. (1979). *Cognitive therapy of depression.* New York: Guilford.

Beck, A.T., Steer, R.A., & Garbin, M.G. (1988). Psychometric properties of the Beck Depression Inventory: Twenty-five years of evaluation. *Clinical Psychology Review, 8,* 77-100.

Benjamin, L.S. (1974). Structural analysis of social behavior. *Psychological Review, 81,* 392-425.

Brehm, S.S., & Smith, T.W. (1986). Social psychological approaches to psychotherapy and behavior change. In S.L. Garfield & A.E. Bergin (Eds.), *Handbook of psychotherapy and behavior change* (3rd ed., pp. 69-115). New York: Wiley.

Clark, C., Kemeny, V., & Elliott, R. (1987, June). *Helpful aspects of experiential therapy of depression.* Paper presented at the meeting of the Society for Psychotherapy Research, Ulm, West Germany.

Derogatis, L.R. (1977). *SCL-90-R Manual.*

Elliott, R. (1984). A discovery-oriented approach to significant events in psychotherapy: Interpersonal process recall and comprehensive process analysis. In L. Rice & L. Greenberg (Eds.), *Patterns of change* (pp. 249-286). New York: Guilford.

Elliott, R. (1985). Helpful and nonhelpful events in brief counseling interviews: An empirical taxonomy. *Journal of Counseling Psychology, 32,* 307-322.

Elliott, R. (1986). *Procedure manual and event description forms for brief structured recall.* Unpublished manuscript, University of Toledo, Toledo, Ohio.

Elliott, R. (1989). Comprehensive process analysis: Understanding the change process in significant therapy events. In M. Packer & R.B. Addison (Eds.), *Entering the circle: Hermeneutic investigation in psychology* (pp. 165-184). Albany, NY: SUNY Press.

Elliott, R., Greenberg, L.S., Rice, L.N., & Clark, C. (1987). *Draft manual for experiential therapy of depression.* Unpublished manuscript, Department of Psychology, University of Toledo.

Elliott, R., James, E., Reimschuessel, C., Cislo, D., & Sack, N. (1985). Significant events and the analysis of immediate therapeutic impacts. *Psychotherapy, 22,* 620-630.

Elliott, R., & Mack, C. (1986). *End of phase interview schedule.* Unpublished research instrument, Department of Psychology, University of Toledo.

Elliott, R., & Shapiro, D.A. (1988). Brief Structured Recall: A more efficient method for identifying and describing significant therapy events. *British Journal of Medical Psychology, 61,* 141-153.

Elliott, R., Shapiro, D.A., & Barkham, M. (1985). *Simplified Personal Questionnaire.* Unpublished questionnaire, Social and Applied Psychology Unit, Sheffield, England.

Fuchs, C.Z., & Rehm, L.P. (1977). A self-control behavior therapy program for depression. *Journal of Consulting and Clinical Psychology, 45,* 206-215.

Gendlin, E.T. (1978). *Focusing.* New York: Everest House.

Gendlin, E.T. (1979). Experiential psychotherapy. In R.J. Corsini, et al. (Eds.), *Current psychotherapies* (2nd ed.). Itasca, IL: Peacock.

Glaser, B.G., & Strauss, A. (1967). *The discovery of grounded theory: Strategies for qualitative research.* Chicago: Aldine.

Goldenberg, H. (1983). *Contemporary clinical psychology.* Monterey, CA: Brooks/Cole.

Greenberg, L.S. (1984). A task analysis of intrapersonal conflict resolution. In L. Rice & L. Greenberg (Eds.), *Patterns of change.* New York: Guilford.

Greenberg, L.S., Elliott, R., & Foerster, F. (in press). Experiential processes in the psychotherapeutic treatment of depression. In N. Endler & D.C. McCann (Eds), *Contemporary perspectives on emotion.*

Greenberg, L.S., & Safran, J.D. (1987). *Emotion in psychotherapy.* New York: Guilford.

Greenberg, L.S., & Webster, M. (1982). Resolving decisional conflict by means of two-chair dialogue: Relating process to outcome. *Journal of Counseling Psychology, 29,* 468-477.

Hamilton, M. (1960). A rating scale for depression. *Journal of Neurology, Neurosurgery and Psychiatry, 12,* 56-62.

Howard, K.I., Kopta, M., Krause, M.S., & Orlinsky, D.E. (1986). The dose-effect relationship in psychotherapy. *American Psychologist, 41,* 159-164.

Jacobson, N.S., Follette, W.C., & Revenstorf, D. (1984). Psychotherapy outcome research: Methods for reporting variability and evaluating clinical significance. *Behavior therapy, 15,* 336-352.

Llewelyn, S.P., Elliott, R., Shapiro, D.A., Firth, J., & Hardy, G. (1988). Client perceptions of significant events in prescriptive and exploratory periods of individual therapy. *British Journal of Clinical Psychology, 27,* 105-114.

Luborsky, L. (1962). Clinicians' judgements of mental health. *Archives of General Psychiatry, 7,* 407-417.

Mahrer, A.R. (1983). *Experiential psychotherapy: Basic practices.* New York: Brunner/Mazel.

Millon, T. (1983). *Millon multiaxial clinical inventory manual.* Minneapolis, MN: National Computer Systems.

Nicholson, R.A., & Berman, J.S. (1983). Is follow-up necessary in evaluating psychotherapy? *Psychological Bulletin, 93,* 261-278.

Nietzel, M.T., Russell, R.L., Hemmings, K.A., & Gretter, M.L. (1987). Clinical significance of psychotherapy for unipolar depression: A meta-analytic approach to social comparison. *Journal of Consulting and Clinical psychology, 55,* 156-160.

O'Malley, P.M., & Bachman, J.G. (1979). Self-esteem and education: Sex and cohort comparisons among high school seniors. *Journal of Personality and Social Psychology, 37,* 1153-1159.

Perls, F.S. (1969). *Gestalt theory verbatim.* Moab, UT: Real People Press.

Perls, F.S., Hefferline, R.F., & Goodman, P. (1951). *Gestalt therapy.* New York: Julian Press.

Phillips, J.P.N. (1986). Shapiro personal questionnaire and generalized personal techniques: A repeated measures individualized outcome measurement. In L.S. Greenberg & W.M. Pinsof (Eds.), *The psychotherapeutic process: A research handbook* (pp. 557-590). New York: Guilford.

Rennie, D.L., Phillips, J.R., & Quartaro, G.K. (1988). Grounded theory: A promising approach to conceptualization in psychology. *Canadian Psychologist,* 139-150.

Rice, L.N. (1983). The relationship in client-centered therapy. In M.J. Lambert (Ed.), *Psychotherapy and patient relationships.* Homewood, IL: Dow-Jones Irwin.

Rice, L.N., & Greenberg, L.S. (Eds.). (1984). *Patterns of change.* New York: Guilford.

Rice, L.N., & Greenberg, L.S. (1990). *Fundamental dimensions in experiential therapy: New directions in research.* See this volume.

Rice, L.N., & Saperia, E.P. (1984). Task analysis and the resolution of problematic reactions. In L.N. Rice & L.S. Greenberg (Eds.), *Patterns of change.* New York: Guilford.

Robins, L.N., Helzer, J.E., Croughan, J., & Ratcliff, K.S. (1981). National Institute of Mental Health diagnostic interview schedule: Its history, characteristics, and validity. *Archives of General Psychiatry, 38,* 381-389.

Rogers, C.R. (1951). Client-centered therapy. Boston: Houghton Mifflin.

Rogers, C.R. (1957). The necessary and sufficient conditions of therapeutic personality change. *Journal of Consulting Psychology, 21,* 95-103.

Rogers, C.R. (1959). A theory of therapy, personality, and interpersonal relationships as developed in the client-centered framework. In S. Koch (Ed.), *Psychology: The study of a science* (Vol. 3). New York: McGraw Hill.

Rogers, C.R. (1961). *On becoming a person.* Boston: Houghton Mifflin.

Rogers, C.R. (1980). *A way of being.* Boston: Houghton Mifflin.

Rogers, C.R., & Dymond, R.F. (1954). *Psychotherapy and personality change.* Chicago: University of Chicago Press.

Shapiro, D.A., & Firth, J. (1987). Prescriptive vs. exploratory psychotherapy: Outcomes of the Sheffield psychotherapy project. *British Journal of Psychiatry, 151,* 790-799.

Shaw, B.F. (1977). Comparison of cognitive therapy and behavior therapy in the treatment of depression. *Journal of Consulting and Clinical Psychology, 45,* 543-551.

Shlien, J.M., Mosak, H.H., & Dreikurs, R. (1962). Effect of time limits: A comparison of two psychotherapies. *Journal of Counseling Psychology, 9,* 31-34.

Smith, M.L., Glass, G.V., & Miller, T.I. (1980). *The benefits of psychotherapy.* Baltimore: The John Hopkins University Press.

Walker, A.M., Rablen, R.A., & Rogers, C.R. (1960). Development of a scale to measure process changes in psychotherapy. *Journal of Clinical Psychology, 16,* 79-85.

Weissman, M.M., & Bothwell, S. (1976). The assessment of social adjustment by patient self-report. *Archives of General Psychiatry, 33,* 1111-1115.

Wexler, M.M., & Elliott, R. (1988, June). *Experiential therapy of depression: Initial psychometric analyses of session data.* Paper presented at meetings of the Society for Psychotherapy Research, Santa Fe, Mexico.

Wolfe, B., Waskow, I.E., Lowery, H.A., & Docherty, J.P. (1984). *New directions in NIMH psychotherapy research program.* Forum presented at the June meeting of the Society for Psychotherapy Research, Lake Louise, Alberta, Canada.

Zajonc, R.B. (1980). Feeling and thinking: Preferences need no inferences. *American Psychologist, 35,* 151-175.

CLIENT-CENTERED THERAPY AND PSYCHIATRIC CRISIS INTERVENTION FOLLOWING SUICIDE ATTEMPTS

Luc HAMELINCK

Universitair Psychiatrisch Centrum, Leuven, Belgium

PSYCHIATRIC CRISIS INTERVENTION IN A GENERAL HOSPITAL

For the past seven years, I have been working in an emergency psychiatric hospitalization unit of the University Psychiatric Center in Leuven as clinical psychologist, client-centered and marital therapist. At foundation, ten years ago, this unit was intended as a crisis-intervention unit for acute psychiatric emergencies.

After some time however, our activity changed under the pressure of the necessities of the general hospital and the gaps in the mental health network. Most of all, clients changed from mostly "real" crisis clients to clients with more complex and lasting problems. Two factors in this process are worth mentioning. In the first place, many clients and their families prefer admissions in the psychiatric unit of a general hospital to the more stigmatising and lengthy admissions in a psychiatric hospital. Secondly, the intensive care provided by the unit according to the "multiple-impact-treatment" model (Weisman, Feirstein & Thomas, 1969) is very tempting for psychiatrists and psychotherapists when their outpatients drift into a crisis or impasse that exceeds their capabilities.

The "multiple-impact-treatment" model is personified in a team of four consisting of a psychiatric nurse, an assistant psychiatrist, a psychologist or a social worker and a supervising psychiatrist.

It is this socalled "mini-team" that takes care of the client and the client system during his admission. Treatment consists of various combinations of daily individual psychotherapeutic contacts, medication, marital or family therapy sessions and social work. Hospitalization is kept as brief as possible, so that the patient is not cut off too much from his social and professional network.

The short-term admission of about two or three weeks is considered long enough to reach the following aims: Provide the immediate response to the emergency situation, establish a correct diagnosis of the problem situation and its context, set the client on the right track to resolve the problem situation as well and as completely as possible during further treatment following discharge.

The crisis intervention model that we use, varies between an *individual crisis intervention* model and a *system oriented crisis intervention* model (Umana, Gross & Turner, 1982). In the individual crisis intervention model the individual personality is the key variable to be examined, including such facets as adaptability, flexibility, personal competence and coping ability. As far as possible, regression is halted by providing support and encouragement while working through traumatic events and by keeping an eye on the time limit of admission.

The assumption behind this model is that a period of time in a "safe" and supportive environment will allow the client to regain equilibrium and to be able to meet the stress situation more effectively. The client is supposed to be only temporarily overwhelmed by the intensity of the crisis. Insight into the causes of the breakdown and emotional discharge are considered to be important.

Using various degrees and combinations of individual and system oriented crisis intervention models is the result of our clinical experience and of our belief that interpersonal relations are not only potentially helpful in the rebalancing process, but are also potential causes of development of a crisis. In this system oriented model, a crisis is not only the result of an interaction between the personality of the client and the crisis stimulus, but also of the interaction of those factors with the interpersonal context of the client. The interpersonal context can provide the client with support, disqualification, condemnation or belittlement.

The goal of treatment is not just to enhance the client's strength but especially to provide individuals within the system with a means of dealing more effectively with future crises, by developing new patterns of interaction that provide more mutual support and decrease the need for further external intervention (Umana et al., 1982). This model also teaches us to respect the occasionally strong homeostatic forces of the client's system.

Most of our clients continue ambulatory psychotherapeutic treatment after their discharge. Choice of treatment is determined by our experience with the client during hospitalization. General and specific therapeutic capabilities of the client emerge through the intensive therapeutic contacts with the team. The kind of intervention or combination of interventions that has proved to be most successful during the hospital stay is the choice treatment following discharge[1].

AN ECOLOGICAL MODEL OF THE PERSON

We are strongly convinced that both the paradigms of individual and system oriented psychotherapy are too onesided. Indeed, we are all unique, above all for ourselves, but at the same time "more than anything else human" (Sullivan, 1953). Sullivans' conviction that our "unique" personality is in the first place formed by our patterns of interactions with significant others seems to be a rather correct approximation of reality.

Human relations both restrict the development of personality and at the same time provide the framework in which personality development is made possible.

Human development depends on "relational space" granted by significant others and built up by ourselves (Willi, 1987). The individual owes his existence to the group and exists in spite of the group (see also Pfeiffer, 1986).

Rogers stresses restrictions on personality development made by significant others, whereas Willi does not hesitate to state that "I depend on my partners for self-realisation" (Willi, 1987, p. 435). "In interaction with others, we gain a deeper consciousness of self, we are shaped and modeled, our potential takes on form and becomes visible by our behavior and action" (Willi, 1987, p. 434). Here, I would like to remind you of the fine text that Gendlin wrote on this subject, entitled "Existentialism and experiential psychotherapy" (Gendlin, 1970).

On the other side, the mistake of many system-oriented therapists is, according to Willi, their underestimation of the (relative) autonomy of the individual to withdraw or to change his participation in a system. The existence of human systems always depends on the motivation of individuals who want to collaborate and live together. Also, participating in many different systems (family, friends, school, professional groups, unions, political society, etc...), allows for individuals to behave with some independence of a specific system they take part in.

This ecological model of the person that stresses the interaction between person and interpersonal environment is not revolutionary. Apart from the notorious psychiatrist H. S. Sullivan, the notorious psychologist J.R. Nuttin (1968) - in his relational theory of personality - places personality in the interaction between person and world.

Changing rigid structures in the direction of more fluid processes is seen by many psychotherapy schools as an evolution in the direction of mental health. For an ecological model, intrapsychic and interpersonal structures and processes are only different sides of the same coin.

Change on one side will carry itself through to the other side. Changing interpersonal relations will change experience and changing experience will change interpersonal relations.

This model is also important for the understanding and treatment of suicidal behavior. Often, suicidal behavior appears in a context of social isolation. Suicidal behavior of adolescents can frequently be understood as a desperate solution to save the individual self and identity from alienation by a family system that does not allow "relational space" for the way of being of that person. This desperate self-protective and destructive reaction also indicates that this person cannot exist outside this rigid system (Pfeffer, 1981; Hendin, 1976). Likewise the strong social disapproval of suicidal behavior on the one hand and the heated debates concerning the right of the individual to commit suicide on the other hand, clarify the relationship between these behaviors and the paradoxical interactions between an individual person and the group to which he belongs. It follows as a matter of course that a therapist needs an ecological model of the person to guide his thinking and action in these matters.

FEATURES OF CRISIS INTERVENTION

Crisis intervention has become a concept that covers many different meanings and approaches.

Different schools of therapy have developed their own approach. Crisis intervention can consist of brief ambulatory psychotherapy in an outpatient clinic, short admissions to a psychiatric unit of a general hospital, family therapy sessions at home, intensive social work, etc...

By far the most popular use of crisis intervention is a form of psychotherapy. Originated from the work of Lindemann and Caplan, crisis therapy also has relations with more traditional theoretical frameworks such as ego psychology (with its emphasis on individual coping mechanisms), humanistic and existential orientations (which view crisis as a state with potential for psychological growth), behavior therapy (which sees crisis as an automatic response to environmental stimuli), family therapy (with its emphasis on homeostasis) and psychoanalysis (with its links between present and past threats) (Ewing, 1978).

Nevertheless, some features are common to different crisis intervention approaches. Crisis intervention is readily available and brief. It focuses not only on one definition of what a crisis is supposed to be, but on a wide range of human problems. Crisis intervention places the focus on current problems and tries not only to solve the current problems but also to help the client to develop more adaptive mechanisms for coping with future problems and crises. Crisis intervention is reality-oriented and requires therapists to take non-traditional roles in dealing with their clients. Last but not least: Crisis intervention may serve to prepare and motivate clients for further treatment (Ewing, 1978; Butcher & Koss, 1978).

1. Time-limited intervention

Crisis intervention is always limited in time because a crisis itself is considered limited, and one assumption of crisis theory is that people are most responsive to external intervention during this time-limited period (Caplan, 1964). In the case of hospitalization, a short time-limit has the advantage of providing a safe and supportive environment, while reducing the risk of keeping the client too long in a more isolated patient position.

Does this way of providing intensive help during a short period indicate low trust in the self-actualizing power of the client? Certainly not if we are dealing with a crisis stimulus of such severity that the acute break-down of the self of the client is very understandable to most empathic observers. This is also true if a client is surrounded by significant others with a strong negative attitude towards his person, his particular way of being, his values, etc... It is only if the third of the so called "balance factors", namely "ego-strength", comes to the front that the answer to our question is not so simple.

Translated into Rogers' personality model (Rogers, 1959), this means that there is such a widespread denial and distortion of self-experiences that even a minor crisis stimulus creates a high crisis effect. Rogers uses the term "vulnerability" to describe this state of "self-experience incongruity" that causes the crisis in the first place. In this case, it is important to remember that crisis theory holds the opinion that the period of disruption is self-limited and will result in a new equilibrium which may be better or worse than that which preceded the crisis.

The risk that the new equilibrium will be worse than the previous ones increases with the level of "vulnerability" of the client. This assumption places the crisis therapist in a dilemma which he can only resolve with the help of the client. On the one side, the crisis therapist knows that the mere existence of the crisis means that much has to be done by the client in order to change important aspects of his way of being. On the other side, the client himself has to find the equilibrium he needs for his psychological survival. So the crisis therapist has to sail between the Charybdis of overburdening the client and the Scylla of giving up the chances for growth of the client. The crisis therapist is less optimistic than the client-centered therapist. Two points are, in my view, important here.

Firstly crisis theory assumes that homeostasis is an important aspect of the human functioning. Secondly, there is the assumption that every aspect of human functioning is relatively dependent upon the interpersonal network in which it happens. This limited - and in my opinion more realistic - optimism of the crisis therapist forces him to stay in empathic contact with his client in order to be able to distinguish what the client wants, what frightens him and what he can do himself. So the crisis therapist hopes the crisis will stimulate the client to overcome his fear of change and of consequences, to explore new ways of relating to himself and to others. However, despite empathy, unconditional positive regard and congruence, a crisis can be an insufficient condition for change and growth.

2. A focus on current problems

Crisis intervention places the focus upon current problems, those responsible for the crisis, the admission or the request for help. This does not mean that the past of the client is not important, but only that the past will be explored in reference to current problems precipitating the crisis. The past is not considered as determining the client's chances to solve the crisis, but rather as a means of understanding the personal significance of the crisis stimulus for the client. It does not mean either that the client is not allowed to speak about his personal history, but that history will not be the focus of the intensive treatment. For instance, in the case of an incest-victim, the focus of the intensive treatment during hospitalization will be the current relationship with the partner or children. Working through the original trauma will be done in longterm outpatient psychotherapy.

The primary purpose of the intensive intervention is to re-establish or preserve the relative autonomy of the client, enabling him to function within his family, in his work and with his friends. In this process, the client must find the right distance from his emotions and problems: Far enough so that he is not overwhelmed, and close enough so that he cannot ignore the issue anymore.

Limiting our intervention to current problems also directs the self-actualization focus of the client on to the current most important problems, the aim being to break through a threatening impasse that obstructs the adequate and autonomous functioning of the self. This breakthrough can create hope and bring back progress on the self-actualization frontline.

Some optimism underlies this restriction: The past does not determine everything and one does not have to be "fully functioning" nor anywhere near this state in order to solve a serious, acute crisis or problem. In this way, the crisis therapist communicates hope and optimism as to the client's ability to handle his problems, without giving the client false reassurance (Ewing, 1978).

3. Improving coping mechanisms

While learning and experiencing how he can solve current problems, the client can learn something more general about how he behaves in a crisis situation. What are more constructive mechanisms of coping, both with internal conflicts and external realities? The client can learn how to deal with bodily or affective distress. The coping mechanisms he learns to use include combinations of cognitive strategies (like planning and focusing), physical actions and verbal strategies (like assertiveness training, relaxation or negotiation procedures) in order to deal with emotional and interpersonal problems. In this way, crisis intervention focuses on the interaction between the individual and his surroundings, and tries to teach the client alternative ways of dealing with the problems that arise there. Crisis intervention concentrates on the direct reality in which the client lives.

In this way, as Gutberlet (1985) pointed out, crisis therapy deals with a gap in the client-centered therapy model. In our personality and therapy model, we do not take into account disturbing factors in the surroundings of the client. Those factors can have so much influence on the behavior and experience of the client that they can freeze the actualization process activated in the therapy hour. The crisis therapist tries, with the client, to develop other ways of coping with these counteracting forces. To achieve this, it can be helpful to integrate significant others by marital or family therapy. These sessions will also give the therapist a more realistic view of what is going on between his client and his significant others, instead of viewing the process through the clients colored glasses. We have just introduced the next point of our discussion: Crisis intervention does not work only with the client's frame of reference but tries to include other views of reality.

4. Crisis intervention is reality-oriented

An important feature of crisis intervention is its orientation towards reality. The therapist provides the client with a view of reality as clear and correct as possible, including the client's own part in creating and maintaining his situation. "While continually offering emotional support, the crisis therapist may find it helpful, if not essential, to confront his client with the unrealistic or maladaptive nature of his goals, lifestyle, or belief system and to point out the possible negative consequences of current behavior patterns" (Ewing, 1978, p. 26). This is not only a process of creating intellectual insight but also a process of bringing the client into contact with his inner emotional reality. Thus catharsis is certainly a valuable experience for some clients. "Crisis therapists, however, generally do much more than simply offer a safe situation for the release of often highly charged emotions: The client is also helped to keep his affects at a conscious level, where they can be clearly identified and managed through direct effort" (Ewing, 1978, p. 27). Crisis therapists also point out real and potential negative effects of the client's emotional reactions upon others; they give advice and suggestions to their clients about more adaptive ways of understanding and about coping with feelings which play an important part in their problems and problematic relations.

Understanding what is going on in a crisis and how one can solve the crisis situation is, of course very important for someone who is very distressed and confused.

Experiencing the crisis helps the person to regain a grasp on reality. In cases where the crisis is a part of longerlasting problems or prolonged maladaptive patterns of behavior, confrontation is important not only to develop cognitive and emotional insight, but also to scan the limits of the client's ability to acknowledge his part in the entanglement and to take on responsibility for change.

5. A wide range of human problems

Crisis intervention started as a structured approach as to prevent negative consequences in victims of catastrophic events; it has now evolved into a broadspectrum approach. I can illustrate this by the range of problems found in our unit and for which our crisis intervention approach is considered useful. There are clients with a suicide attempt, a first psychotic breakdown, a postpartum depression, a pathological grief reaction, victims of incest, marital or family conflicts in which the situation at home became intolerable, agitation and anxiety conditions, and so on. For all these different psychiatric conditions, our crisis intervention program offers, in the first place, an intensive care program, in which the contribution of the different elements of treatment varies according to the particular case. The empathic contact with the client always plays a very important role as diagnostic as well as therapeutic tool, with a strong tendency to search for the client's strengths and with realistic optimism that a crisis can be an opportunity for growth.

6. Crisis intervention as preparation for further therapy

Because many of our clients have complex and longlasting problems, most of them are referred for further treatment after discharge. During hospitalization, a more confronting, directive and active type of psychotherapy is initiated. Combination of these two features brings about a situation that has much in common both with brief therapy and with the process of psychotherapy indication. During hospitalization, our team looks for the optimal approach to the client. How can we

588

make contact with the client and help him to understand and cope with
the crisis he is in? During therapy sessions, we alternate two basic
psychotherapeutic attitudes: Joining and deranging. In the process of
indication, De Jong (1987) calls this the method of "deranging
approximation".

Joining the client is composed of:
1. acceptation of the client and interest in making contact,
2. empathy and
3. authenticity.

Deranging is made of:
1. clarification of the situation and the chances for change,
2. confrontation and
3. interpretation (making connections between different elements that
   emerge in the interviews).

In this method of "deranging approximation", we cover the two
opposing tendencies of a crisis: The opportunity for change by
higherlevel integration and the need for balance, or self-actualization
opposed to self-preservation (De Jong, 1987).

I also have the impression that during crisis intervention we have to
keep an eye on another important balance: That of activity and control
versus passivity.

The crisis therapist has to be active but runs the risk of becoming too
active and too controlling. Maybe Gustafson and his colleagues are
right when they think that both clients and therapists have some
problems in that area (Gustafson et al., 1983). We have to take our
responsibility towards the client but without taking over his
responsibility. If the therapist pulls the client along, then he will miss
the inner feelings and pain of his client. The self-actualization process
will not develop, because the therapist gives the client a healthy reason
to resist his overcontrolling attitude.

CLIENT-CENTERED THERAPY AND CRISIS INTERVENTION

1. Rogers' personality model

Gutberlet (1985) is right when he says he is convinced that client-
centered therapists do not need any other crisis intervention model
than the personality model Rogers presented in 1959.

Indeed, Rogers' personality model is an implicit crisis model. A stimulus which is threatening or disturbing to the selfconcept and which gives rise to anxiety can break up the selfconcept and destroy the person's normal adequate functioning. Rogers also asserts that without a certain amount of anxiety no real therapy can be done (Rogers, 1957). So a crisis of the psychological system is a necessary condition for change and growth. Furthermore the absence of client-centered psychopathology and genetic psychology underlines the similarity between crisis-theory, which also focuses on the present, and client-centered therapy.

2. Meaningfulness of crisis behavior

According to the same author, a client-centered therapist considers the crisis behavior from the perspective of meaningfulness (Gutberlet, 1985). Crisis behavior can always be understood as a meaningful, understandable reaction, as a way of coping with an unbearable situation, in an effort to protect identity, self-esteem and self-cohesion. A depressive reaction, an anxiety attack, self-destructive or aggressive behavior, hallucinations or delusions are never only the symptoms of a psychiatric disease or of a certain type of personality. This certainly is an essential element of a client-centered view of crisis behavior but it is not an exclusive mark of client-centered therapy. Other psychotherapeutic schools defend the same position as well. Kohut (1971) tries to explain "narcissistic rage", even on a nationwide level, as a reaction of defense in favor of one's self-cohesion and self-esteem. Family therapists try to understand the symptoms of the "identified client" as meaningful for the client himself and for the other members of the system. This way of looking at crisis behavior is rather in conflict with a medical-psychiatric perspective and consistent with a psychotherapeutic view.

3. The role of confrontation

As I already mentioned, crisis therapy deals with what can be considered as a gap in client-centered therapy, it deals with the influence of reality outside the therapyhour of the client. In many cases a crisis means that a person tries to escape an unescapable truth. This is also the case in Rogers' theoretical model: It is something terrifyingly real that starts the crisis, an experience that is in contradiction with, or does not fit in the schemes of the self.

In client-centered practice, the therapist works patiently with the frame of reference of the client and tries to enlarge it step by step. In crisis intervention, the therapist does not wait until the client is able to find himself the truth that is bothering him, but confronts the client more rapidly with other frames of reference, with the views of other people about his or her problems and with the kind of solutions they offer.

The client's state of disregulation serves as an alibi for the crisis therapist not to postpone this confrontation, because only a clear view of the internal emotional world and of the outside reality will enhance control over it. In a normal lasting therapy, the therapist will also create crisis moments by confronting his client when he thinks that for the self-actualization process it is necessary to reduce the ambiguity and incongruities in the client's experiencing and communication. Confrontation can address discrepancies within the client (ideal versus real self), between what the client says and does, and between illusion and reality (Carkhuff & Berenson, 1967). Confrontation after a life-event-precipitated crisis (like ending the relationship with a girlfriend) aims at giving a meaning-structure to what happened to the client and indicates the part the client has in it. Many times we have to point out to our clients that their reaction is meaningful and understandable and sometimes they do not like that at all. But the crisis therapist's directiveness in confronting his client is only relative and is guided by his empathy for the client and his estimate of the amount of disorganisation the client and the unit can handle.

In this way, crisis intervention has much in common with "trial therapy" as used in the process of psychotherapy indication (De Jong, 1987).

4. The non-traditional role of the crisis therapist

Ewing (1978) agrees with other authors that a crisis therapist has to play an active, direct, involved role. He must do more than merely reflecting what the client says or does; he must show his own feelings, reactions and involvement. He must also speculate about his client's motives, intentions, vulnerabilities, resources, needs and feelings. And - not unimportant for client-centered therapists! - the author adds the following suggestion: "... turning to him (the client) regulary for validation while encouraging him to disagree where appropriate" (Ewing, 1978, p. 27). This may remind the client-centered reader of Gendlin's article on therapeutic procedures in dealing with schizophrenics and unexpressive clients (Gendlin, 1967). In this article, Gendlin advocates a specific approach for this special group of clients. In my opinion, the same holds true for clients in a crisis, where the self of the client is threatened by disintegration. This more active and specific approach is also valuable with unexpressive depressive clients as a way of creating movement instead of stagnation. Swildens (1982) likewise pleads strongly in favor of handling depressive clients differently in client-centered therapy during the premotivation phase of the therapyprocess. He expects the therapist to be talkative, to empathically guess the client's basic feelings, to communicate his understanding of the client's symptoms, but also to avoid advice and consolation.

The work of our team during hospitalization consists mainly of working through the client's request for help until it becomes treatable through some kind of psychiatric or psychotherapeutic aid. In my opinion, this socalled non-traditional role of the crisis therapist does not contain great problems for a client-centered therapist enlisted for a differentiated therapeutic approach.

CRISIS INTERVENTION AND THE PARADOX OF TREATING SUICIDAL BEHAVIOR

The problem of attempted suicide has become one of the major challenges facing health care services.

According to Hawton and Catalan (1982), deliberate self-poisoning has become the most common reason for acute medical admission of women to a general hospital in the United Kingdom and second only to heart attacks as the most common medical reason for admission of men.

General hospitals can play an important role in treatment and prevention of attempted suicide, if they are prepared to invest in trained mental health professionals and in units for intensive psychiatric intervention.

Attempted suicides account for 25% of our client population. Adding clients expressing suicidal ideas, this accounts for 36% of our population. The features of crisis intervention and client-centered therapy we discussed above are significant for this group of clients as well.

1. Serious and meaningful

Every suicide attempt has to be considered as a serious and meaningful reaction, a desperate way of coping with a very problematic situation. Wanting to be dead or to end all the painful thoughts and feelings can be an extreme expression of the desire to rescue one's own identity, to affirm one's autonomy, to get rid of terrible people or of a dilemma, to liberate others from oneself, to induce feelings of guilt, to prove one's love to someone else, to take revenge, or to require something. There usually is a combination of these motives. It is also important to take into account the fact that a suicide attempt can have very different backgrounds; in other words the end of many different courses of life. Like fever, it can be the symptom of very different processes. So, it is impossible and nonsensical to speak and think about suicide and suicide attempts in an absolute way. Considering every suicidal act either as a sign of sickness or as an expression of the basic freedom of the individual is enormously simplistic. As Scobel (1981) pointed out, neither view gives much support for the client nor helps to understand the client.

2. An ecological model

We will use our ecological model of the person to understand what is going on. What is the interpersonal context of the suicidal act? But also, what are the personal feelings of the client about his suicidal behavior, even if they are very vague?

This model also implies that we have no a priori opinion about the most appropriate subsequent treatment for the client or the client-system.

Preference should be given to the treatment format that will give the most chances to the self-actualization process of the client.

Because in most cases suicidal behavior is part of complex psychological processes of which the client himself often does not have a very clear view, I think it is advisable that the client-centered therapist gathers more knowledge about suicidal processes from other orientations than the client-centered one. I very much agree with Gendlin who wrote: "The more of the range of human feelings we have experienced, heard about and read about, and the more unique variants of it we have encountered, the more quickly we can sense this next unique one now being shared with us" (Gendlin, 1974, p. 282). Rogers' model of personality and therapy gives us a very general conceptual model that allows space for more specific articulations fitting in with the living reality of a specific client.

Clinical theories about suicidal behavior can be helpful on the condition that they are applied in a non-dogmatic and non-rigid way (see also Scobel, 1987).

3. A short admission

Short admission to the unit is only necessary for clients either with serious psychiatric disorders - depression, psychosis, organic states - or with a great risk of suicide or who require a short period of removal from stress situations (Hawton & Catalan, 1982). While providing a relatively safe environment, we will try to reach empathic contact with the client and to help him gain access to the darker sides of his emotional life.

It is the relative safety of the unit that enables us to confront the client with his feelings, with the discrepancies in his personality, behavior and emotional processes and with his selfdestructive emotions and behavior. We try to openly discuss the suicidal feelings of the client while maintaining a trustful relationship with him. When this is possible, even to a minor degree, we shall not forbid him to leave the unit, though we will pay great attention to any sign from him that more control from us is needed. We also tell the client very clearly that we are not able to prevent a suicidal act if he really wants to act that way.

4. Coping with current problems

Most instances of self-poisoning or self-injury are preceeded by stressful events. Events involving a key person stand out from all others. These events consist of quarrels with a significant other, separation from or rejecting behavior of a partner or relative. There are more chronic problems such as marital problems (mainly) and child abuse, work problems and physical health problems (Hawton & Catalan, 1982, Matthijs, 1985). About a quarter of our clients are diagnosed as suffering from depression.

During hospitalization, we try to start a process of problem solving, helping the client to look constructively at ways of tackling his problems. As most suicide attempts have to do with interpersonal problems, coping with the relations between partners or family members is a substantial area of therapeutic interventions. Besides conjoint marital therapy sessions, individual sessions remain important. Indeed, it is of equal importance that the client learns to deal with strong emotions like feelings of aggression, loneliness, sadness, anxiety and - last but not least - with the limitations of reality. In this way, the crisis therapist starts cutting through what Hinchliff et al. (1978) have called the three myths of modern man.

Hinchliff and his colleagues saw a connection between the growing incidence of depression and attempted suicide in all the Western countries and the following myths:
1. That the emotional pain of stressful life events is unbearable and,
2. That medicine has the cure for such pain readily available in the freely prescribed psychothropic drugs...
3. That all human relationships must be fruitful and satisfying and certainly never boring and irritating (Hinchliff et al., 1978, p. 125).

5. Confrontation and paradox

Confrontation with the limitations of reality, and especially of relationships, with unrealistic ambitions, with irrational thoughts, with the meaning underlying emotional pain and with discrepancies between expressed attitudes and actual behavior, plays an important role in crisis intervention after a suicide attempt.

It is important in two ways. It helps the client to solve his problems and it enhances the chances that he will become motivated for further psychotherapy after discharge from the unit, because of increased awareness of his own contribution to a distressful history. Confrontation will certainly only be effective when it is borne by a warm and accepting relationship.

The strength of a client-centered therapist lies in his relational capacity to make empathic contact with an isolated, desperate person who feels ambivalent about the presented help. To move in this paradoxical situation of a client who "cries for help" and does not believe there is a chance he will get it, the only possibility for the therapist is to introduce another paradox. Firstly, the client-centered therapist has to accept that suicide can be a way of coping with an unbearable situation; he has to free himself of the dangerous idea that he must prevent all suicidal behavior. Secondly, the client-centered therapist will introduce his own paradox: He will try to understand why the client wants to commit suicide or a suicide attempt, because he believes this is the only way to help the client to break out of his isolation and to prevent suicide.

6. Indication procedure

In view of the lack of irrefutable evidence for the superiority of a particular therapy orientation for well-defined problem areas or client-groups, it is important to proceed to indication as much as possible in consultation with the client. The client will be more committed to a therapy or care system that he has contributed to choose and if he understands the relationship of this method with his complaints and with the objectives he states (Frank, 1973; Lazare & Eisenthal, 1979).

In the near future, we will start a research project to investigate more systematically the kind of requests for treatment of attempted suicide clients and what kind of strategy gives the best results, in the sense of the client being satisfied with his therapist and therapy.

We plan to use two conditions of strategy: One where indication is done by negotiation like that advocated by Lazare and Eisenthal (1979), and one where we check after discharge if the client has followed up our proposal of subsequent treatment together with the possibility of discussing it with us again.

EPILOGUE

I want to conclude with some insights of our German colleague Pfeiffer (1986, p. 374), which I personally find very valuable. Pfeiffer mentions four polarities which serve me as "Leitmotiv" in my psychiatric work as a client-centered psychotherapist. I will only mention two of them dealing with the therapeutic relationship and most relevant for our discussion.

In my work with attempted suicide clients, I always have to move between poles. The first aspect is that, on the one side, I am aware of the existential equivalence of client and therapist, but on the other side, I am ' also aware of the asymmetrical relation between client and therapist and of their different, complementary roles. The second aspect is that, on the one hand, I have an unconditional positive regard for my client, but on the other hand, I take into account the fact that he is not free, a state resulting from pathological processes and self-destructive potentials.

NOTE

1. For a comparison of different stationary crisis intervention units: See C. Alzheimer, 1987.

REFERENCES

Alzheimer, C. (1987). *Nichtambulante Krisenintervention und Notfallpsychiatrie. Versuch einer Bestandsaufname der Lage in Westeuropa.* Berlin: Springer-Verlag.

Butcher, J., & Koss, M. (1978). Research on brief and crisis-oriented therapies. In A. Garfield & S. Bergin (Eds.), *Handbook of psychotherapy and behavior change.* New York: John Wiley & Sons.

Caplan, G. (1964). *Principles of preventive psychiatry.* New York: Basic Books.

Carkhuff, R., & Berenson, B. (1967). *Beyond counseling and therapy.* New York: Holt, Rinehart & Winston.

De Jong, A. (1987). *Intake voor psychotherapie.* Meppel: Boom.

Ewing, C. (1978). *Crisis intervention as psychotherapy.* New York: Oxford University Press.

Frank, J. (1973). *Persuasion and Healing. A comparative study of psychotherapy.* Baltimore: John Hopkins University Press.

Gendlin, E.R. (1967). Therapeutic procedures in dealing with schizophrenics. In C.R. Rogers (Ed.), *The therapeutic relationship and its impact* (pp. 369-400). Madison: University of Wisconsin Press.

Gendlin, E.T. (1970). Existentialism and experiential psychotherapy. In J. Hart & T. Tomlinson (Eds.), *New directions in client-centered therapy* (pp. 70-94). Boston: Houghton Mifflin.

Gendlin, E.T. (1974). The role of knowledge in practice. In G.F. Farwell, N.R. Gamsky & F. Mathieu-Coughlan (Eds.), *The counselor's handbook.* New York: Intext.

Gustafson, J. et al. (1983). Winnicott and Sullivan in the brief psychotherapy clinic. Part 1, 2 and 3. *Contemporary Psychoanalysis, 19(4),* 624-672.

Gutberlet, M. (1985). Entwurf zu einem Krisenmodell in der Gesprächspsychotherapie/Klientenzentrierten Psychotherapie. *GwG-info, 61,* 51-62.

Hawton, K., & Catalan, J. (1982). Attempted suicide. *A practical guide to its nature and management.* New York: Oxford University Press.

Hendin, H. (1976). Growing up dead: Student suicide. In E. Shneidman (Ed.), *Suicidology: Contemporary developments.* New York: Grune & Stratton.

Hinchliff, M. et al. (1978). *The melancholy marriage.* Chichester: Wiley.

Kohut, H. (1971). Thoughts on narcissism and narcissistic rage. *The Psychoanalytic Study of the Child, 27,* 360-400.

Lazare, A., & Eisenthal, E. (1979). A negotiated approach to the clinical encounter. In A. Lazare (Ed.), *Outpatient psychiatry diagnosis and treatment* (pp. 141-171). Baltimore: Williams & Wilkins.

Matthijs, K. (1985). *Zelfdoding en zelfdodingspoging.* Leuven: Universitaire Pers.

Nuttin, J.R. (1968). *La structure de la personnalité.* Paris: Presses Universitaires de France.

Pfeffer, C. (1981). The family system of suicidal children. *American Journal of Psychotherapy, 35(3),* 330-341.

Pfeiffer, W. (1986). Ist das Rogers'sche Persönlichkeits- und Therapie Konzept im Hinblick auf psychiatrische Erkrankungen angemessen ? *Zeitschrift für Personenzentrierte Psychologie und Psychotherapie, 5,* 367-377.

Rogers, C.R. (1957). The necessary and sufficient conditions of therapeutic personality change. *Journal of Consulting Psychology, 21,* 97-103.

Rogers, C.R. (1959). A theory of therapy, personality and interpersonal relationships as developed in the client-centered framework. In S. Koch (Ed.), *Psychology: A study of a science* (Vol. 3, pp. 184-256). New York: Mc Graw Hill.

Scobel, W. (1981). Suizid - Freiheit oder Krankheit ? In H. Henseler, & C. Reimer (Eds.), *Selbstmordgefährdung. Zur Psychodynamik und Psychotherapie.* Stuttgart-Bad Cannstatt: Frommann-Holzboog.

Scobel, W. (1987). Suizidalität. Erklärungsmodelle und Anleitung zur psychotherapeutischen Hilfe. *GwG Zeitschrift, 18,* No. 66, 78-84.

Sullivan, H.S. (1953). *Conceptions of modern psychiatry.* New York: Norton.

Swildens, J. (1982). De hulpverwachting in de therapeutische relatie III. *Tijdschrift voor Psychotherapie, 8,* 18-27.

Umana, R.S., Gross, S., & Turner, M. (1982). *Crisis in the family.* New York: Gardner Press.

Weisman, G., Feirstein, A., & Thomas, C. (1969). Three-day hospitalization: A model for intensive intervention. *Archives of General Psychiatry, 21,* 620-629.

Willi, J. (1987). Some principles of an ecological model of the person as a consequence of the therapeutic experience with systems. *Family Process, 26(4),* 429-436.

A COGNITIVE CLIENT-CENTERED PERSPECTIVE ON BORDERLINE PERSONALITY DEVELOPMENT

Arthur C. Bohart
California State University
Dominguez Hills, U.S.A.

Sandi, age 21, came to see me about a year after her hospitalization for a brief psychotic episode. This had been precipitated by her grandmother breaking up an affair she was having with a 16 year old boy. After her hospitalization she had rushed into a marriage with another man, who had abused and mistreated her. She was now getting divorced from him. Sandi's social history consisted of periods of substance abuse and sexual promiscuity. While she had graduated from high school, she had held no stable job since. She had started college several times, but had always dropped out without ever finishing a class. At the time she came to see me she had started a small part time job.

Sandi had had several previous therapists. She had been told by them that her demands for support and attention were manipulative, and that she had deep seated personality problems. At one point with her last therapist she had gotten so angry at him she had stormed out of his office.

When I saw Sandi she was depressed and had great difficulty getting up to go to work every morning. She experienced life as empty, and felt a general sense of abandonment. She reported having felt suicidal. These symptoms, along with her sense of identity confusion and negative self-esteem, led to a diagnosis of "borderline personality disorder." One theoretical perspective, object relations theory (Masterson, 1981; St. Clair, 1986), would portray Sandi as suffering from a developmental arrest within the first two years of life. This perspective holds that in the first few months of life the infant lives in an hallucinatory, delusional fantasy world where it believes itself to be fused with the mother. This belief allows the infant to feel "oceanic bliss," and a sense of omnipotence. The major developmental task of infancy is to relinquish this fantasy in order to separate and individuate from the mother. Sandi had not successfully accomplished this and therefore had a seriously defective self and ego structure, and would need years of psychoanalysis to "fix."

However this was not the Sandi I experienced. I perceived her as a courageous young woman who was struggling against great negative odds to make her life work. Sandi had had a difficult childhood. However, most of her difficulties started after the age of five, when she was diagnosed as having a serious medical condition. It was then that her parents' inability to support and nurture her became manifest. She was frequently left alone when she had to spend time in the hospital. She was criticized for demanding time and attention, and was generally given negative regard rather than support and empathy. At the age of 13 her parents divorced, and she overheard them saying it was because of her problems. After the divorce her mother became more involved with her own social life and ignored Sandi. At this point Sandi began to seek support among her peers. Eventually a conflict with her mother at age 15 led to the mother's banishing her from the house, and Sandi had to live with her grandmother. Her grandmother, while materially supportive, was also not nurturing. She gave Sandi double messages. For instance, Sandi was continually told she should go to college. Yet when she started college her accomplishments were belittled ("oh that class is easy!").

Compounding her problems, Sandi had been overweight since childhood (because of her medical condition). This had occasioned a good deal of rejection and abuse from her peers, to the point where she would often go to junior high school early to avoid being teased. With this background in mind, I will discuss Sandi periodically throughout the remainder of the paper.

BORDERLINE PERSONALITY DIAGNOSIS

Briefly, the DSM-IIIR (American Psychiatric Association, 1987) criteria for borderline personality disorder (BPD) are as follows: impulsive behavior; unstable and intense interpersonal relationships, including the use of manipulation, idealization, and devaluation; intense anger or lack of anger control; identity disturbance; affective instability; efforts to avoid real or imagined abandonment; physically self-damaging acts, including suicidal gestures; and chronic feelings of emptiness and boredom. However, there is considerable controversy over the borderline concept and its name, the criteria used to define it, and its diagnostic reliability (Gunderson, 1984; Kroll, 1988; Millon, 1981).

In addition to the above symptoms, a commonly noted one is the presence of transitory psychotic experiences (Gunderson, 1984). Behavior noted in therapy includes excessive demands for attention and accomodation to the client's wishes, as well as a tendency to become easily disappointed and negative towards the therapist (Gunderson, 1984).

A CLIENT-CENTERED/EXPERIENTIAL VIEW OF PERSONALITY

In order to consider BPD I must first develop some ideas about personality in general. In addition to client-centered/experiential (CCE) theory I will incorporate ideas from social learning theory (Bandura, 1986; Mischel, 1984), social cognitive theory (Dweck & Leggett, 1988; Markus & Nurius, 1987), cognitive therapy (Beck et al., 1979; Padesky, 1986), and strategic, family systems approaches (De Shazer, 1985; O'Hanlon, 1987; Watzlawick, 1984, 1987).

Client-centered/experiential theory has been more a theory of therapy than it has of personality and psychopathology. The main reason is that CCE has focused on issues of change and growth. This "process" orientation seems incompatible with theories that focus on personality structure, such as psychoanalysis. How does one account for the apparent continuity and organization in personality from a CCE perspective? My initial goal is to address this.

A core metaphor

A core metaphor for CCE would be of a tree growing towards sunlight in a forest. In an overcrowded forest the tree might have to grow in contorted ways in order to reach the light. Out of context that tree may look dysfunctional compared to its more fortunate fellows. Yet its "behavior" arises out of a positive attempt to grow and survive. Further, regardless of its "history", at any moment if "light" is provided in a new, more positive direction, it can positively alter its path. The tree has grown in an apparently distorted manner, not because it is trying to avoid painful truths about itself, or because it is clinging to infantile fantasies, but because it is the only way it "sees" to grow towards light. As we shall see, Sandi had had to "grow crookedly" (i.e. behave in ways that looked dysfunctional from outside) in order to survive at all. Yet she wasn't "crooked."

I believe this metaphor captures the core of the client-centered approach. CCE has a fundamentally positive view of the human being and of the forces underlying dysfunctional behavior. CCE shares this with strategic approaches (De Shazer, 1985; O'Hanlon, 1987). In contrast, psychoanalysis and object relational views portray the human being in negative, unflattering terms (Brandchaft & Stolorow, 1984; Hamilton, 1985; Wile, 1981).

Process and interaction

The tree is a process that continues to change throughout its lifespan. Not only is it a process, but it exists in continual interaction with its surroundings. It responds to those surroundings, and alters its "behavior" in order to achieve a more integrated "fit." Elsewhere (Bohart, in press) I have argued that all living creatures are characterized by this "process" nature. Humans have the capacity not only to profit from feedback and modify their immediate responses, but to "stand back" and modify the "programs" themselves (Hofstader, 1979) and to find creative "second order change" solutions in life problems (Watzlawick, 1987).

This image of the human being as "built to learn" and profit from feedback suggests a future oriented organism. Learning is for the purpose of developing tools to cope with "what comes next." Therefore, it does not make sense that an organism built to learn, with a childhood that extends twelve years or more, would then develop fixed, engrained personality structures at an early age. In fact, the development of fixed personality structures would be contrary to the very idea of a forward-looking, learning oriented organism. Even when we do exhibit continuities in behavior, I suggest that is because we are *anticipating* that these continuities are profitable ways of dealing with future events.

For CCE, then, what is most fundamental to human beings is their capacity for growth and change. No matter how many negative experiences a person has had, that capacity for future growth is always there, waiting to be mobilized. Implied in this is the idea that the goal of therapy is to help the person move creatively towards the future, rather than to "repair" the crooked path followed from (and in) the past.

Personality structure and continuity

I have already pointed out that this process emphasis does not seem to be able to account for continuity in personality. If we are a flowing, changing organism then why do we both perceive ourselves and are perceived by others as being "the same" in many ways from time to time?

The answer to this dilemma is found in an article by Gendlin (1964). He argues that theories that talk about personality structure cannot explain personality *change*. Gendlin proposes that process is primary, and structure secondary. Structure is seen as arising out of process. This idea forms the basis of this paper.

I propose that we think of personality structures as things created by humans in order to help them interact and cope with the world. Metaphorically, personality structures can be thought of as *devices* or as *tools* ("schemas" in certain social psychological theories are similar - see Markus & Nurius, 1987). Included as "tools" are concepts, beliefs, and behavioral "know-how." Also included are the perceptual skills of quickly and accurately identifying and perceiving events in the environment. Thus the person *uses* personality structures rather than *is* personality structure. There is continuity in the sense that persons adopt certain enduring goals and strategies which they believe will best help them cope with the world. Therefore the person's organized set of goals, characteristic strategies, and procedures, *is* what we call "personality."

The person will *identify* with certain of these strategies or goals more than with others, and see them as reflecting "himself." He may say, "I am a sensitive person." However this means "I am a person who has adopted sensitivity as a value and as a way I want to relate. I also have developed a lot of know-how about acting sensitively."

This view assumes that structure is in the *organization* of know-how, goals and skills. In other words, "structure" *means* a pattern of organization. It is in the same sense that a filing system in a library can be said to have structure.

Other personality models, most notably psychoanalytic ones, utilize a "physical" metaphor of structure. Analysts talk about "accreting self structure" (Kahn, 1985), "building a strong ego," "laying down a foundation for personality in early childhood," and so on. These metaphors call to mind the construction of buildings. As one builds a building by laying down a foundation first, so one builds personality. On this latter view personality structure is something relatively stable and fixed that is built up *inside* the organism, and *constitutes* the person. The "building up" process is started by early childhood experiences, and the basic structures are "laid down" then. One imagines a kind of internal lattice work of traits and characteristics that "drives" external behavior. Different personality "types" have different "internal lattice works." Since behavior is "driven" by these structures, there should be a good deal of consistency in behavior across situations. If early childhood experiences lead to the build up of defective structures, then the person will not "work right," and will exhibit strange behavior. Therapy then becomes the remodeling of these engrained structures.

In contrast, for the "tool" metaphor the difference between "personality types" would be the difference between the organized sets of strategies and goals characteristically used by individuals. Moreover, while a person may use a particular strategy in certain situations in his life, there is no reason to believe that he would necessarily use them in *all* situations. Therefore one would not expect cross situational consistency in behavior (Mischel, 1984).

The process that is the person synthesizes rules, procedures, goals, and schemas, out of experience. This synthesized set is also systematized and organized ("I like sex, but only in a loving relationship"). Then these "knowledge structures" (Markus, 1977) lead to feedback which further shapes and structures the person's experience of the world. In other words, these structures become the "envelope" or "lense" through which people experience feedback from the world. The tools with which we relate to the world orient our attention to selected aspects of experience, provide the means whereby we shape (interpret) that experience, as well as providing the means whereby we take action.

Therefore we may go "locked into" vicious circle feedback loops, where we continue to perceive and behave in the same way over and over. Or we may act in ways which create the very situation we are anticipating, thereby confirming our perceptions and actions and keeping us locked in (Watzlawick, 1984; 1987). If, for example, I conclude that I am no good with romantic relationships, I may avoid them, or interpret any awkward moment as a reflection of my inadequacy. Or I may be so nervous around a potential partner that I act unattractively. It is partially because we often get involved in these "self fulfilling prophecies" that we appear from the outside to have engrained personality structures.

An analogy of an organization illustrates these ideas. The organization (such as a counseling center) sets goals and creates rules, procedures and structure in order to function. Those structures influence how the organization interfaces with the world, the kind of feedback it receives, and how it processes that feedback. Members of the organization may even come to identify it with those structures and procedures. Yet the organization is really using the structure as a tool, and can change it at any time.

The view that personality is a set of structures used by the living process that is the human is compatible with Gendlin's (1981) focusing technique. "Clearing a space" helps the client to see that he is not his problems (including ones that are part of his "personality").

Role of the future

The human needs to be thought of as a "flowing towards." Even goals are anticipations or expectations of what will be fulfilling, exciting, fun, or enriching. Coping strategies are what one believes *will* work to one's benefit in the future. Interpretations and perceptions of situations are characterizations of what is going on, to be used for *predictions* about the future. With this in mind it could be argued that this is the *future* that determines one's present behavior more than the past (Bandura, 1986; De Shazer, 1985; Markus & Nurius, 1987; O'Hanlon, 1987; Shlien, 1988; Watzlawick, 1987). Research (Markus & Nurius, 1987; Nuttin, 1984) has found that current behavior correlates more highly with images of one's possible "future" selves than with one's current self-concept.

From this perspective, the past does not influence the person by "building in" a personality structure which then "drives" behavior. Rather, it influences behavior because past experience is the *basis* on which the person "builds models" of what to expect in the future. The past is a "well of resources" (Livson & Peskin, 1980).

Included in our images of possible future selves (Markus & Nurius, 1987) are images of what we think our deficits are, as well as our skills and talents. As an example, consider Sandi. From the neglect and rejection she experienced as a child and teenager, she came to believe that she lacked the qualities and attractiveness necessary to form a stable romantic relationship. She therefore decided to engage in transitory relationships as a way of gaining some of the rewards of relationships. Having no faith that she had the necessary skills and talents to go to college and create a "place" for herself in the world, she created a place by associating with others like her who didn't "fit in," and took drugs. Therefore her behavior of pursuing transitory relationships and using drugs were active attempts to create some semblance of a liveable, rewarding future for her. They were *not* infantile attempts to recreate a delusional childhood of perfect fusion, arising out of an internally defective self and ego structure.

The self

According to Shlien (1970) the self-concept is like a map "...to which the person refers when he is about to make a move" (p. 119). Thus the self-concept is a "tool." However, the self-concept may be a particularly important "tool" or set of tools, in that it is a hierarchically organized set of percepts and values, designed to provide some coherence and continuity to behavior. If it is negative, rigid and inflexible, then it will dysfunctionally constrain one's interactions with the world.

For instance, Sandi had grown up being told that she was a "bad" person. Even therapists had told her that she was "manipulative." She had been rejected by peers because she was unattractive. Therefore, she had developed a negative self-concept. How can a negative self-concept be a "tool"? I suggest that individuals adopt negative self-concepts because they are legitimately trying to control their futures. If they have been told often enough that they are "bad," then it is only realistic to "face up to it," and do the best one can to meet one's needs anyway. If one believes oneself to be "bad," one will not expect successes in the future to be gained through the normal means available to "good" persons. One may see no option but to seek engagements and gratifications in "deviant" ways.

Because the self (not the self-concept) is a flowing changing process, and is not to be identified with any of its products or structures, it is important that the self-concept be held tentatively, and re-evaluated against experience (Rogers, 1961). In addition attributing fixed character traits to ourselves would be incongruent with our nature as changing process, and therefore would be dysfunctional. Research support for this comes from Dweck and Leggett (1988). These authors found that children who believe that character traits are fixed are primarily concerned with whether they succeed or fail in a situation. As a result they give up easily at the first sign of failure, and exhibit defensive and avoidance behavior. In contrast mastery oriented children (process orientation in our terms) view personality traits as malleable (compatible with the current perspective which sees them as coping devices). Their orientation to task situations is towards learning, and they are not discouraged by failure because they see it as simply information to learn from. They are more likely to persist, and they do not exhibit defensive and avoidance behavior.

Since the self is not to be identified with any of its products, what is the self? Gendlin (1964) defines the self *as* "self process." It *is* the process of inwardly referring to experiencing. It is this ability to refer inwardly, and to explicate the felt meanings implicit in the experiencing process, which is the core of creativity. Therefore when one is able to focus, one is in touch with oneself, creative and forward looking, and one will have a sense of identity.

This process of inwardly referring is the sense of active, living engagement with the world, as well as of active, creative coping. It is therefore related to Bandura's (1986) concept of self-efficacy. Self-efficacy is defined as the perception that one is able to enact certain behaviors. Put another way, it could be conceived of as a sense of ableness or agency, a sense that one *can* actively cope with and engage the world.

CCE places a great deal of emphasis on self-trust. I see this as a sense of one's "ableness" or "agency" - of self as an active process that can engage the world creatively, even when things go wrong. This does not mean that to trust oneself one is to believe that one's feelings are right, one's ideas are correct, or one's behaviors are the appropriate thing to do. Rather, a process conception of self-trust is to trust that one *can* profit from feedback, learn, and eventually master a situation in some way or the other.

Sandi, as part of her negative self-concept, had no sense of self-trust. She did not trust her feelings, nor did she have any faith in her ability to establish fruitful relationships or career engagements. In addition, her fixed negative self characterization interfered with the ability to focus. Therefore she was unable to *find* a clear sense of herself when she inwardly referred on felt meanings. As a result she suffered from "identity confusion."

Identity

If we do not equate the self with a fixed self-concept consisting of generalized stable personality traits, then on what basis does the sense of identity exist? I believe that the "I" is that sense of the self as the *originator* of one's experience. Since experiencing is interactive, this means to sense oneself *in connection* with the world.

Therefore identity is the felt sense of one's place in the world. It is thus the felt sense of the *intersection* of all the "vectors" in one's life. It is defined in terms of one's relations to parents, family, friends, peers, work, leisure activities, political beliefs and values, past experiences, moral values, esthetic values, and so on. Put still another way, identity is the sum total sense of one's "engagements" in the world.

However one's engagements shift and change without completely altering one's sense of identity. This is because identity is also that unique vantage *point of intersection* of all one's continuing and changing engagements in the world. The analogy is to Gibson's (1979) argument that we are aware of our *physical* self because visually we are that unique and stable point of intersection of all the angles of light from the environment, no matter how much we or the environment move or change.

If one's engagements in the world are continually fruitless, frustrating, or result in negative feedback, then one may have an important or negative sense of identity. If one withdraws from engagements, then one literally begins to feel identityless ("empty").

Sandi had never had any support for forming positive engagements in the world - such as through school success, development of a talent, or through stable romantic relationships. As I have mentioned, she had no sense that she had the skills or talents to create positive engagements. Therefore she felt empty and depressed. Her only sense of *stable* identity came from consistently having been neglected or criticized, a negative set of "engagements" in the world.

Experiencing

In order to quickly and creatively interact with the world, we must be able to operate on a more rapid basis than we can by thinking, which is relatively slow (Langer, 1978; Zajonc, 1980). Therefore most of our behavior is of the perceptual-motor variety. It consists of "know-how." Such know how also involves the quick, rapid perceptual identification of a situation. This is learned through direct experiential interaction with the world. For instance, we may learn a great deal about "how to" interact with others through the visual and auditory observation of our parents, as well as through our fledgling efforts to interact with them. Much of this learning may never have included the verbal encoding of the implicit rules or concepts acquired. These rules are therefore "tacit" and "automatic."

For instance, in a family which revolves around an alcoholic we may learn rules that say (in effect) "one must accomodate to alcoholism." Then it may "feel right" to get in a relation with, and to enable, an alcoholic. The paradox is that our way of perceiving/behaving may "feel right," even though cognitively we "know" that it is self-destructive. Such perceptual-motor knowing is not unconscious in the strict Freudian sense, so much as it is simply unattended to (Shlien, 1970; Wexler, 1974) and unarticulated. That is why, when in therapy, we finally do articulate it, we often feel somehow as if we "knew it all along." I believe it is because many of our characteristic coping devices or tools are learned at the perceptual-motor level, and then enacted automatically and nonconsciously, that we *believe* them to be engrained personality characteristics.

From a client-centered perspective, what I have called perceptual-motor knowing is equivalent to *experiential* knowing. Gendlin (1984) says that at the experiential level we know far more than we can ever put into words. This knowledge can be utilized for change if we learn to tune into it properly, and articulate it (Gendlin, 1964, 1984).

The ability to creatively alter our "tools" for coping lies in the ability to focus our attention inwardly into the felt sense of our interactions, and then through a dialogic process, form new understandings. Such a process creates engagements in the world, and can be used to create a sense of inner richness. If, however, one's schemas for self-monitoring are rigid, judgmental, and undifferentiated (Beck et al., 1979: Padesky, 1986), then when an individual refers inwardly, the focusing/

experiencing process will not occur. The more crude, pervasive, and undifferentiated the person's schemas are for self-monitoring, the more crude and undifferentiated will be experiencing.

I have previously noted how Sandi's way of referring inwardly primarily involved making negative self judgements. The result was that she was unable to articulate her felt meanings in *her* words and thereby gain a sense of self. This was one of the areas of focus in therapy. Sandi had a potentially rich inner life and as she learned to trust her feelings and articulate her perceptions, a creative intelligent person began to appear.

Psychopathology

The basic hypothesis of this paper is that ways of perceiving and doing that we label "pathological" are actually attempts to cope. One can only talk of dysfunctional perception or coping in relation to specific situations. Therefore psychopathology is interactional (Gendlin, 1968).

The view that psychopathology is interactional is congruent with social learning theory (Bandura, 1986; Mischel, 1984). Mischel has found that aggressive and withdrawn children exhibit their "pathological" behavior precisely when they run into situations where their skills and talents do not match the demands of the situation. Pathological behavior is therefore situation-contingent. This is also congruent with the views of such family systems strategic therapists as Watzlawick (1987) and De Shazer (1985). They hold that psychopathology is actually behavior that was once functional (was once a "solution" to a problem), but which now is no longer functional in the current situation (and is therefore in some sense being inappropriately applied).

Psychopathological behavior therefore arises when a person attempts to use ways of perceiving and doing that originally developed in situations where they "made sense." Many pathological behaviors originally were the best the person could do at the time in coping with her environment. They make sense if one understands the context of their development, and they make sense (though they may not be effective) if one understands what the person is attempting to achieve in the current situation.

In this regard, pathological behaviors therefore contain implications as to what people are trying to accomplish - their images of the future.

Borderlines may have no stable image of the future. We have already seen that this characterized Sandi, who had no coherent sense of possibility (in contrast to depressives, whose sense of the future is that of "impossibility"). Furthermore she felt stuck, and did not know how to move towards the future (i.e. by focusing).

Psychopathology is also the inability of the person to profit from feedback (Bohart, in press). Why might the tree "persist" in growing in its old manner even when new feedback indicates that a change is in order? For client-centered therapy, the ability to note when one's schemas are not working with respect to the present situation, and then to work to creatively alter them, is based on the ability to utilize one's experiencing process and focus (Gendlin, 1964, 1969). If one is able to attend inwardly one can get a felt sense of the stuckness, and move towards creative reorganizations of experience (what Watzlawick, from another perspective, has called a "second order change"). Therefore when stuckness exists it can be assumed that at least in that problem area, the experiencing/focusing process is not happening.

BORDERLINE PERSONALITY DISORDER

Interactional nature of borderline behavior

Borderline symptomatology does not reflect an underlying disorder in the person: While the person may act in "borderline" ways, the person is not borderline. Furthermore, because borderline behavior is not a manifestation of an underlying engrained personality structure I would not expect "borderline" individuals to behave borderline all the time. This is congruent with observations of "borderlines" by many clinicians, who have noted that many behave quite effectively in some areas of their lives, and only act "borderline" under certain conditions. It is also congruent with Kroll's (1988) observations that borderline symptoms wax and wane, and that there are periods where borderlines do not act "borderline." In addition, other research (cited by Kroll, 1988, pp. 79-86) finds that many borderlines do not receive the same diagnosis if studied several years later, and that borderline symptomatology appears to subside starting around age 30.

I suggest that there are certain *kinds* of situations where individuals utilize "borderline" coping mechanisms. I am not prepared to present a full taxonomy, but from my observations they include ambiguous but yet stressful situations, situations of loss and deprivation, and situations of frustration and/or danger. Even here it is not clear that "borderline" individuals act borderline in all ambiguous situations, or in all frustrating situations.

As an example of the above, a "borderline" may act manipulatively in situations where she does not *know how* to cope in more direct self-affirming ways. Her behavior, however, does not reflect a "defective ego structure." While Sandi may have acted manipulatively with previous critical and confronting therapists, or with her nonsupportive parents, she never acted manipulatively with me. This is probably because I never presented her with criticism in a manner she could not cope with.

Development of borderline behavior

There may be many possible antecedents to borderline behavior, including biological, familial, and cultural/environmental ones, and they all could interact. To try to trace a "tight" causal pathway from one possible set of antecedents to adult behavior is therefore likely doomed to failure. Below I will sketch ideas about some possible antecedents, without assuming that they are the sole cause of borderline behavior.

It has been shown that many borderlines have grown up in "dangerous environments" in which they have either been abused (Briere, 1989), or subjected to conflict, criticism, and alcoholism (Loranger & Tulis, 1985; Soloff & Millward, 1983). However, Gunderson (1984) notes that the development of borderline symptomatology is not associated with a specific early-childhood developmental period. Rather, it is dependent on a dysfunctional family background that spans all of childhood.

At the same time, there are cases of some "borderlines" who do not appear to have grown up in dangerous environments (Masterson, 1981). I will first look at how a dangerous environment could predispose to borderline behavior, and then consider a possible nondangerous developmental path.

Growing up in a dangerous environment may create a "danger oriented" way of dealing with the world. This includes a sense of distrust, a focus on threatening aspects of the environment, and a readiness to act defensively and self-protectively. In other words, the "tools" one develops to cope with the world largely reflect attempts to identify danger, avoid it, or try to get what one wants despite its presence.

If, for instance, one grew up in a world where virtually all animals were dangerous predators, one would continually be wary. If an animal acted friendly, one might approach the animal cautiously but, at the first sign of danger, run. One would be unlikely to trust others, and one might take what one could get in the moment, rather than worry about the long term.

Thus, growing up in a danger-oriented environment might lead to the development of a "cognitive map" of the world that highlights all the potential dangers, rather than a map that highlights opportunities or possibilities. In such a world one might grab for whatever one could get in the moment ("impulsiveness") and one might "bond" excessively to figures perceived as safe and caring ("idealization") but then very quickly and easily experience rejection and get disappointed ("devaluation"). In such a dangerous and ungiving world one might be prone to rapid mood fluctuations and easily develop feelings of depression. Also one might experience feelings of abandonment when someone "safe" is away or leaves.

Identity in terms of stable long term values and commitments would be a luxury. Anger would be a fairly constant emotion, especially if the dangerous environment created the feeling that the world was unfair.

All of this would be true if the environment did not nurture the development of positive skills and commitments (engagements), as well as the ability to focus. Even in a dangerous environment, if there is someone to support (parent, teacher, minister) positive proactive ways of coping, the effects of the dangerous environment may be mitigated. Another possible mitigating factor would be if the person herself were lucky enough to chance on an activity that provided a positive source of engagement, commitment and esteem (perhaps discovering she is good at chess, or computers).

A dangerous environment will also focus one's attention *externally*. One will take one's cues for behavior from the immediate situation. Being able to quickly and flexibly change strategies, and grab for rewards when they are there, might be perceived as more adaptive than trying to plan and create stability for the future. When survival is all, focusing inwardly to create stable long term plans, commitments and goals might be a luxury. Therefore a person living in a dangerous environment may never develop the "tool" of a stable self-concept which includes images of long term goals, outcomes, and commitments. Furthermore, since she learns to take her cues from the environment, she will be at a loss when the environment fails to provide such cues. Finally, a dangerous environment might mitigate against the developing of the skill of focusing.

We have already seen that Sandi grew up in a dangerous environment. No significant other in her environment was ever able to respond to *her* as a person. Their pattern was either to neglect her, or tell her what to do. Until she came to therapy her uniform experience of people was of others who told her how she should be, instead of showing the slightest interest or support of how she was coping, or where *she* wanted to go. This continued into her adulthood. It is not surprising that Sandi therefore did not have a good sense of her own identity, nor that she felt "emmeshed with" or undifferentiated from others. She had had no experience of being responded to as a separate trustworthy person *for her whole life,* not just during the first two years of it.

It is not clear that all "borderlines" come from dangerous environments. Chaotic and nonlimit-setting environments may also predispose. Jennifer grew up in a family which was generally loving and stable. Yet she has had a history of manipulative behavior, feelings of emptiness, joining of cults, and so on. In Jennifer's environment, particularly when she was a teenager, what may have contributed to her "borderline" behavior was the fact that her parents never set any limits for her. They tolerated her wildest excesses. As an adult, Jennifer acts as if she has a sense of entitlement. There is no sense of a stable commitment to others, or to life tasks. She jumps from one cult movement to another, and acts manipulatively towards her family (but not, apparently, with her close friends). We can imagine that without limits, Jennifer never learned the necessity of developing assertive ways of dealing with her family, and so relies on manipulative ways. She also never learned how to make things happen in a stable, predictable way for herself. Therefore she seeks a model of stable coherence for her life in cults.

Aspects of borderline functioning

There are two things that appear to be characteristic of the symptoms of BPD as described in DSM IIIR. First, they all represent instability in behavior. Secondly, they could all be interpreted as to suggest that the "borderline" takes her cues for her behavior from the situation.

Psychoanalysis attributes this instability and external focus to a "weak ego" and "self structure." From the present perspective I suggest that the difficulty is that in *certain situations* the individual is unable to create a coherent meaning making context. This however represents the lack of the development of certain *skills* rather than a "weak ego." It manifests itself in two ways. First, the person is unable to assimilate the current situation into a broader framework that permits a sense of coherence and continuity over time. For instance, if there is a temporary problem in a romantic relationship, the "borderline" is unable to say to herself: "This is a temporary disturbance, which often happens in the context of long term involvements and engagements." She has no "map" of how long term commitments and engagements work to compare the present situation to. She therefore immediately concludes that the disruption means the worst possible thing: The other person is not right for her (devaluation) and the relationship is doomed. This may lead to anger, depression, and feelings of abandonment.

This suggests that the "borderline" has not developed good differentiated and/or coherent "maps" for functioning in certain important areas. This makes sense if the "borderline" has grown up in dangerous, chaotic, or nonlimit-setting environments.

Secondly, the person does not have the sense that she is *able* to create contexts of long term engagements and meaning in certain areas (low self-efficacy feelings). One needs practice in "staying with" difficult situations in order to learn to make sense out of them, to learn from them, and to master them.

A "difficult" situation is (by definition) one for which no good "maps" have been developed. A key to being a "mastery oriented" person (Dweck & Leggett, 1988) is to be able to *develop* workable maps or definitions for such situations. Gendlin (1984) has pointed out that we experience difficulties with a situation precisely when our maps or strategies are not sufficiently differentiated to handle the complexity involved. It is at these times that the individual must be able to struggle to articulate new and more differentiated "maps" or definitions of the situation. In order to do this the person must be able to focus. Further, focusing will lead to a sense of an unfolding, more differentiated continuous development of meaning in these areas.

The ability to focus is involved in the ability to learn from feedback. In areas where the person is acting "borderline," she is not learning from feedback, and remains stuck in a dysfunctional feedback loop. I suggest that one becomes aware when one's constructs and maps are not working at a "feeling" or experiential level. Discrepancies between maps and situations lead to an immediate sensing that there is "something wrong." That may manifest itself in dysphoric feelings (anger, depression, or anxiety). I assume that borderlines have the "sense" of things not fitting, but they do not respond to it in a productive way. When they do have this sense instead of focusing they either attempt to ignore it, or immediately implement "solutions" consisting of rigid, preset cognitive strategies (Padesky, 1986). For instance, a person may immediately conclude "I am being abandoned," rather than listen to his felt meanings, in order to develop a more functional "engagement" with the situation.

Therefore the borderline is unable to deal with ambiguous situations where he has to create meaning (such as on the Rorschach, see Singer & Larson, 1981). This is why he seeks for external guidance and structure, and fears being alone without such external structure. This also accounts for the extreme fluctuations in behavior that psychoanalysts attribute to "splitting."

By definition, the self-concept in borderlines is not a highly workable one. I have already discussed the consequences of a negative ·self-concept. If the self-concept is a "map," then negative areas can be thought of as directions in which the person cannot "go." If one has a *global* negative self-concept, then one may believe that all "normal" positive directions are banned. One may either give up and feel helpless (depression), or conclude that the only directions left are twisted and convoluted ones (drugs, promiscuity, etc.). In addition, a negative self-concept will most likely interfere with creative focusing, and therefore with feelings of self-efficacy.

A dysfunctional *positive* self-concept (as with Jennifer) could develop in a nonlimit-setting environment. If no limits are set for a person, she develops an unrealistically positive self-concept - "I'm good, justified, or entitled, no matter what I do." However such a self-concept will also foreclose the focusing process. In addition, such a self-concept includes no "map" of having struggled to *create* meaning and continuity. Nor does it include any map of coherent directions to go in.

Chaotic environments will lead to such an external, immediate "here and now" focus that a person growing up in one may never develop a "working map" of his own long term goals, values, commitments, or beliefs at all. He may therefore have a chaotic self-concept.

For all three of these ineffective "maps" the person will be left with an unclear "sense of self" (especially since he is unable to focus). This will feed into the tendency to seek definition externally. Further it will lead to a potential for "confusion" between self and other. For instance, if a significant other criticizes a person with either a negative or chaotic self-concept, the person does not have his own map to compare the criticism to. Having no well worked out self definition, he will be vulnerable to adopting the definitions of others, especially significant or admired others. It is for this reason that borderlines sometimes "copy" their therapists in mannerisms, beliefs, and dress, not because they are still unconsciously fused with their mothers.

A NOTE ON PERSONALITY DEVELOPMENT

I will only briefly note that from a CCE perspective, humans are active, curious creatures, who want to learn about the world. They do not "hide out" in a delusional fantasy of fusion with the mother. Nor do infants live in an hallucinatory world of "oceanic bliss" or omnipotence. Instead they are basically oriented towards wanting to see reality accurately and viably and towards wanting to learn how reality works. In contrast to the object relational view they have a sense of self at birth (see Stern, 1985 also). This view is more compatible with what is now known about the active, curious creatures infants are.

Because we are information hungry we soak up information from those who we see as the "experts" on reality. In this culture that is initially our parents. If they provide highly dysfunctional models of how to deal with the world we may learn distorted ways of dealing with reality. At the same time the whole context of childhood needs to be taken into account. Psychoanalytic theory focuses on simple linear causal relationships between early parent-child interactions and all significant adult interactions. Yet if we are active, future oriented organisms interested in learning we will want to "decode" our "place" in the set of relationships with all of our experienced world. That will include relationships with siblings, peers, and teachers, as well as with school activities, sports, and so on. It will also include sociocultural influences. These various relationships form a matrix or net of interactions, and feed into one another. One simply cannot "rip" the relationship with parents out of the matrix. That relationship will influence adult behavior to a greater or a lesser extent, in many different possible ways, depending on how it was and is embedded in the person's whole network of relationships.

Development will be continuous over the life span. Early childhood is not more important than other developmental periods (Chess & Thomas, 1984). Cairns (1979, p. 139) has concluded that "early social interchanges are tentative rather than rigid or 'foundational'." Further, we are called on to deal with complex social and physical environments. For those of us in modern industrialized society, social reality is especially complex and ambiguous, with changing mores and values. Any models of reality (values, goals, ideals) we develop to help us cope will need to be continually revised against experience. Thus the "tools" we develop to cope with life will never be "finished." Ideally experience will lead to further refinement and differentiation of our "tools," as well as "creative leaps" (Guidano, 1987; Watzlawick, 1987) and the development of new more complex understandings.

Because the world is complex and ambiguous, from time to time we all will find our tools inadequate, and feel anxiety, depression, loss, or confusion. This is not because each of us has some "pathology" built into us from childhood, but because life is complex. This further implies that even with good childhoods we may run into situations that overwhelm our abilities to cope, and become temporarily dysfunctional.

SANDI: A FINAL NOTE

I saw Sandi once a week for two years, and then off and on for another two years. My main emphasis was to facilitate her trusting and listening to her felt meanings. She got over her depression, learned to live by herself comfortably, and did not return to her "impulsive" ways of behaving. Even after she had to abandon the career she had just achieved as a preschool teacher because her chronic physical condition worsened, she did not let that set her back. She now works and is the president of a national organization for victims of her disease. Not only would she no longer merit the borderline diagnosis, but I do not believe she merits any psychiatric diagnosis. And we barely talked about her early relationship with her mother at all!

REFERENCES

American Psychiatric Association. (1987). *Diagnostic and statistical manual of mental disorders (DSM-IIIR)* (3rd ed., revised). Washington, DC: American Psychiatric Association.

Bandura, A. (1986). *Social foundations of thought and action: A social-cognitive analysis.* Englewood Cliffs, NJ: Prentice-Hall.

Beck, A.T., Rush, A.J., Shaw, B.F., & Emery, G. (1979). *Cognitive therapy of depression.* New York: Guilford.

Bohart, A. (1990). *Psychotherapy integration from a client-centered perspective.* See this volume.

Brandchaft, B., & Stolorow, R.D. (1984). A current perspective on difficult patients. In P.E. Stepansky & A. Goldberg (Eds.), *Kohut's legacy: Contributions to self psychology.* Hillsdale, NJ: Analytic Press.

Briere, J. (1989). *Therapy for adults molested as children: Beyond survival.* New York: Springer.

Cairns, R.B. (1979). *Social development: The origin and plasticity of interchanges.* San Francisco, CA: Freeman.

Chess, S., & Thomas, A. (1984). *Origins and evolution of behavior disorders.* New York: Brunner/Mazel.

De Shazer, S. (1985). *Keys to solution in brief therapy.* New York: Norton.

Dweck, C.S., & Leggett, E.L. (1988). A social-cognitive approach to motivation and personality. *Psychological Review, 95,* 256-273.

Gendlin, E.T. (1964). A theory of personality change. In P. Worchel & D. Byrne (Eds.), *Personality change.* New York: Wiley.

Gendlin, E.T. (1968). The experiential response. In E. Hammer (Ed.), *Use of interpretation in treatment.* New York: Grune & Stratton.

Gendlin, E.T. (1981). *Focusing.* New York: Bantam.

Gendlin, E.T. (1984). The client's client: The edge of awareness. In R.F. Levant & J.M. Shlien (Eds.), *Client-centered therapy and the person-centered approach: New directions in theory, research, and practice.* New York: Praeger.

Gibson, J.J. (1979). *The ecological approach to visual perception.* Boston: Houghton Mifflin.

Guidano, V.F. (1987). *Complexity of the self.* New York: Guilford.

Gunderson, J.G. (1984). *Borderline personality disorder.* Washington, DC: American Psychiatric Press.

Hamilton, V. (1985). John Bowlby: An ethological basis for psychoanalysis. In J.

620

Reppen (Ed.), *Beyond Freud: A study of modern psychoanalytic theorists.* Hillsdale, NJ: Analytic Press.

Hofstader, D. (1979). *Godel, Escher, Bach: An eternal golden braid.* New York: Random House.

Kahn, E. (1985). Heinz Kohut and Carl Rogers: A timely comparison. *American Psychologist, 40,* 893-904.

Kroll, J. (1988). *The challenge of the borderline patient.* New York: Norton.

Langer, E.J. (1978). Rethinking the role of thought in social interaction. In J.H. Harvey, W.I. Ickes, & R.F. Kidd (Eds), *New directions in attribution research* (Vol. 2). Hillsdale, NJ: Erlbaum.

Livson, N., & Peskin, H. (1980). Perspectives on adolescence from longitudinal research. In J. Adelson (Ed.), *Handbook of adolescent psychology.* New York: Wiley.

Loranger, A.W., & Tulis E.H. (1985). Family history of alcoholism in borderline personality disorder. *Archives of General Psychiatry, 42,* 153-157.

Markus, H. (1977). Self-schemata and processing information about the self. *Journal of Personality and Social Psychology, 35,* 63-78.

Markus, H., & Nurius, P. (1987). Possible selves: The interface between motivation and the self-concept. In K. Yardley & T. Honess (Eds.), *Self & Identity: Psychosocial perspectives.* New York: Wiley.

Masterson, J.F. (1981). *The narcissistic and borderline disorders: An integrated developmental research.* New York: Brunner/Mazel.

Millon, T. (1981). *Disorders of personality.* New York: Wiley-Interscience.

Mischel, W. (1984). Convergences and challenges in the search for consistency. *American Psychologist, 39,* 351-364.

Mischel, W., & Peaken P.K. (1982). Beyond déjà vu in the search for cross-cultural consistency. *Psychological Review, 89,* 730-755.

Nuttin, J.R. (1984). *Motivation, planning, and action: A relational theory of behavior dynamics.* Hillsdale, NJ: Erlbaum.

O'Hanlon, W.H. (1987). *Taproots: Underlying principles of Milton Erickson's therapy and hypnosis.* New York: Norton.

Padesky, C.A. (1986). *Personality disorders: Cognitive therapy into the 90's.* Paper presented in Umea, Sweden at the 2nd International Conference on Cognitive Psychotherapy, September 18-20, 1986.

Shlien, J.M. (1970). Phenomenology and personality. In J.T. Hart & T.M. Tomlinson (Eds.), *New directions in client-centered therapy.* Boston: Houghton Mifflin.

Shlien, J.M. (1988). *The future is more important than the past in determining present behavior.* Paper presented at the International Conference on Client-centered and Experiential Psychotherapy, Leuven (Belgium), September 12-16, 1988.

Singer, M.T. & Larson, D.G. (1981). Borderline personality and the Rorschach test. *Archives of General Psychiatry, 38,* 693-698.

Soloff, P.H., & Millward, J.W. (1983). Developmental histories of borderline patients. *Comprehensive Psychiatry, 6,* 574-588.

St. Clair, M. (1986). *Object relations and self psychology.* Monterey CA: Brooks/Cole.

Stern, D.N. (1985). *The interpersonal world of the infant: A view from psychoanalysis and developmental psychology.* New York: Basic Books.

Watzlawick, P. (Ed.). (1984). *The invented reality: How do we know what we believe we know?* New York: Norton.

Watzlawick, P. (1985). *Brief therapeutic interventions.* Paper presented at the Evolution of Psychotherapy Conference, Phoenix, AZ, December 13, 1985.

Watzlawick, P. (1987). If you desire to see, learn now to act. In J. Zeig (Ed.), *The evolution of psychotherapy.* New York: Brunner/Mazel.

Wexler, D.A. (1974). A cognitive theory of experiencing, self-actualization, and therapeutic process. In D.A. Wexler & L.N. Rice (Eds.), *Innovations in client-centered therapy.* New York: Wiley.

Wile, D. (1981). *Couples therapy.* New York: Wiley.

Zajonc, R.B. (1980). Feeling and thinking: Preferences need no inferences. *American Psychologist, 35,* 151-175.

CLIENT-CENTERED PSYCHOTHERAPY
FOR PATIENTS WITH BORDERLINE SYMPTOMS

Hans SWILDENS
Bakkum, The Netherlands

INTRODUCTION

The "borderline" concept encompasses three distinct associations. In the first place, of course, it has to do with the area between psychosis and neurosis: paranoid reactions, anxiety attacks and angry outbursts and even delusions and hallucinations are frequently observed. But unlike in psychotic patients, in borderline patients perception of reality is usually easily restored. Neurotic symptoms are also frequently found, but their significance is not the same as in the context of neurosis. Finally, psychopathic symptoms of sexual or aggressive nature are also common.

In the second place, the "borderline" concept should be considered when defining the boundaries of psychotherapy with such patients: Does counseling and supportive contact fall into the area of psychotherapy or should it be given a different description which reflects both the involvement as well as the uncertainty as to the method? Is it not a form of social psychiatric interfering or intermittant crisis intervention?

In the third place, the relevance of the "borderline" concept can be seen in the use of the related word "borderland" used to refer to the borderline patient who is a frontier inhabitant living partly in a clinical setting and partly in society with out-patient treatment. The borderline client often commutes between these two settings. In this chapter, I will refer to borderline clients whom I have treated in both the clinical and non-clinical settings.

A SHORT HISTORICAL OUTLINE

Freud was probably the first to use the term "borderline." In the second half of the 1930's, there arose a number of different descriptions and attempts to explain and categorize the syndrome. The disorder was described as ambulatory schizophrenia, atypical schizophrenia and pseudoneurotic schizophrenia. Some investigators have emphasized the triad of pan-anxiety, pan-neurosis and pan-sexuality, while others have emphasized the psychotic aspects or the psychopathic symptoms. Later, other clinicians stressed the following symptoms as core-symptoms of the disorder: Anger, depression (without guilt feelings), identity and interpersonal problems. During the late 1950's and early 1960's, a wave of speculative explanations and attempts at treatment occurred. We are now in agreement that we are dealing with a closed nosological entity with core and peripheral symptoms.

I wish to conclude this historical outline with an epidemiological note. This disorder - which still receives very modest attention in the DSM III and only gets a brief mention as the borderline personality disorder - must have increased dramatically if we consider that in 1977 (Rohde-Dachser), 30 to 70% of all psychotherapy clients belonged to this group. Several questions arise: Were there no borderline clients before and, if so, what accounts for this development, or did these clients exist but were they simply labelled differently? I think the latter hypothesis is indeed the correct one. I believe that the categories of atypical schizophrenia and of atypical manic depressive psychosis as well as of paraphrenia, schizoid, schizothymic, schizo-affective, and sensitive delusions were previously used whereas we now often speak of "borderline" symptoms. In addition, some self-mutilizers, klepto-maniacs and perverts who were categorized as psychopaths would today fall into the borderline category. Another possible reason for the increase in borderline clients has been suggested by Greenberg and Mitchell (1983), who pointed out that more and more use is being made of this concept because it offers promise of help for serious psychopathological disorders.

Finally, the shift from the psychoanalytic label of oedipal problems to the diagnosis of the pathology of the self remains inexplicable if it is not placed in the context of other possible explanations. Chessick (1977) emphasized social factors in his explanation of the rapid spread of the syndrome in the western world. He mentions the demise of the traditional family structure together with the stability and values that were associated with it. He also refers to the prosperity which is available to today's children, who, as a result, fail to learn to deal with boundaries and limitations. Finally, he refers to the declining influence of religion, the fear of the future, the rapid changes which allow for greater mobility, the pedagogical uncertainty of parents, the effects of the mass-media, specifically television, and the unbridled consumptive attitudes of adults.

Much has been written about the mothers of borderline patients. The role of the mother in the aetiology of the syndrome appears to be a special one in all the theories. Mothers of borderline patients are now described as cold, demanding and only accepting their children if the latter meet their demands; or they are described as insecure and hiding their fears and emotional deficits behind an overprotective façade, or as mothers who do everything possible to be seen in a good light. It appears as though the unproductive conflict surrounding the schizophrenogenic mother is once again being repeated.

Whatever the case, the mother is the first available and most important significant other, because it is she who lays the foundations for the child's self-concept.

THE DIAGNOSIS

As mentioned before, DSM III does not describe the borderline syndrome as such, but lists it under the section "Personality Disorders" as the "borderline personality disorder." This disorder, according to DSM III, does not refer to limited periods or attacks of illness but to long-term functioning, involving impulsivity and unpredictability with regard to spending, sex, eating, gambling, etc. In addition, there is a tendency to form unstable and intense interpersonal relationships; mention is also made of inappropriately intense anger or lack of control of anger, and of identity disturbances, affective instability, intolerance of being alone, physically self-damaging acts and, finally, chronic feelings of emptiness or boredom. These symptoms or symptom clusters do not all need to be present for a legitimate diagnosis, but five of the eight must be present.

In the above description, I believe many of the characteristics which belong to the borderline syndrome are missing, such as the symptoms of anxiety in its free-floating or phobic forms. Other characteristics which are missing are conversion symptoms and disturbances of consciousness, hypochondria and compulsive symptoms. Also absent are the polymorphous perverse sexual tendencies and the strong inclinations to sexualize relationships or to sexualize the intentions of others. Finally, isolated paranoid delusions, pseudohallucinations, thought disorders, depersonalization and derealization phenomena are also missing. A feature of nearly all the aspects of the description of the borderline disorder is that they include aetiological notions derived from psychoanalytic views regarding psychopathology.

PHENOMENOLOGY

Rogers has not given any indications with regard to borderline functioning; however, I believe that it is possible to gain an understanding of the "borderline" concept using Rogers' concepts of the phenomenological field and of the self.

Neurotic people have a deficient self-concept: Significant others determine their conditions of worth which leads to a negative self-concept. It is negative in that new experiences can only be allowed to enter into consciousness with the aid of neurotic defense behaviors making them innocuous to the self-concept. A characteristic of the neurotic self-concept is its rigid structure and its well-delineated boundaries. A great deal is required before threatening and incompatible new experiences are allowed to break through the safety net of the self-concept and to cause a psychotic disintegration. We can assume that in the case of the borderline client, significant others also impose their conditions of worth, but that it does not result in a safety net for the self, nor does it result in a clear self-concept. The self-concept that results is extremely vulnerable, and self-hate exists simultaneously with megalomanic ideas. In other words, although the client is aware of the logical inconsistencies, he insists on maintaining his position at least temporarily; one hour later, the therapeutic conversation can take a turn and a different self-concept may emerge, sometimes with other polarities arising and sometimes with the splitting off of negative aspects. The self-concept appears to lack structure and boundaries.

Here the difference between a neurotic self-concept and a healthy self-concept becomes clear. The neurotic self-concept is rigid and strongly guarded and allows little room for new experiences. The healthy self-concept is, on the contrary, flexible and flows actively and freely as an integrated "whole" characterized by continuity. The borderline self-concept, in comparison, lacks cohesion, continuity and protection. It is therefore always vulnerable and new experiences cannot be effectively integrated into the self-concept because of the contradictions inherent to it. It is therefore not consistently defensible. One may say that this self is at war and the battle-front is not clearly demarcated, the enemy is everywhere. The many disturbing symptoms that arise can be explained as ad hoc defense manoeuvres against surprise attacks by the enemy. In such a situation of permanent instability, the emergency laws that exist in times of war apply. Splitting, idealization and distortion fit into this pattern as do externalization and projection. It is of absolute necessity for the person's survival to localize the enemy and to know who his allies are. People are thus classified as being either good or bad. The differentiation has, however, to be constantly reviewed and readjusted. The conditions of war demand that the good are tested for their trustworthiness and those not found to be absolutely good are reclassified as bad.

The therapeutic relationship is also declared a war front and under certain circumstances it is a very threatening area. The therapeutic contact involves the self and the other, the therapist, who comes very close and concerns himself with the most essential and most vulnerable aspect of the patient, namely the self. The experience of the closeness of the other and the instability of the self-concept makes the avoidance of conflicts difficult. In discussions with the psychotherapist, new interpersonal experiences confront the self in an extremely intrusive manner.

It will become clear that one can hardly speak of existing, there is no question of "bad faith." The borderline patient has great difficulty in surviving. He does not lack good intentions with regard to the future but he lacks the possibility of projecting himself into the future; therefore he does not live authentically. Time, in the sense of the past and of the future, becomes less important in the face of the growing threat of disintegration. During the early phase of therapy, as well as in its later phases, we hardly hear of the borderline client's personal myth, his fundamental project (Swildens, 1988). Also absent is something similar to a neurotic alibi: It is not necessary for the client to demonstrate that it is impossible to go on existing in instances where he has to square up to the enemy, which can be either people with whom the client has to deal: the external enemy, or the enemy within, the bad parts of the self. From within, negative views and judgements of the self-concept may arise which, in turn, threaten the self-concept. There remains no other possible defense for the self than to split off, to project or to externalize the threatening contents and, if everything else fails, the client may then deny.

The borderline patient is not alienated from intersubjective reality, as is evidenced by the fact that in some important areas he appears to function without great difficulty. The battle-scene described above is limited to intrapsychic and interpersonal situations where the self is threatened by new experiences. Conflicts do not arise, nor does the disorder manifest itself in situations which are familiar and non-conflicting, and when the client does not have any ambivalent feelings with regard to the people surrounding him.

It would be incorrect to think that the borderline patient is usually depressed, anxious, enraged, dissociative, suicidal or aggressive. During their periods of normal functioning, borderlines are normal people with some neurotic symptoms which have the function of shielding them from having to do too much during the truce. It would also be incorrect to try to fight those symptoms since that would break the truce and the war would flare up once again.

PROCESS-ORIENTED PSYCHOTHERAPY

The first phase of therapy: Averting the danger of escalation

The war metaphor is useful when considering therapy with borderline clients. A phenomenological approach would focus on the feelings of diffuse anxiety as the departure point of the therapy. The reaction of the client in this early phase of therapy takes the form of acting out and destructive behaviors. The psychotherapist has to take into account the anxiety and the manner in which the client tries to make the situation safe for himself. The therapist must present a non-threatening attitude and he must try to win the trust of the client. At the same time, he must also provide support which will dam the flow of anxiety and anger. In practice, this restricts us - in the first phase of therapy - to supportive interventions, calming comments, not too deeply penetrating expressions of empathy, limited and conditional acceptance, active protection against the anxiety (possibly with the use of medication) and active support of the client's cognitive functioning with regard to reality. Only when the client feels that his safety is guaranteed within the therapeutic relationship can this phase of the therapy be terminated.

The client's trust in the therapist is not gained as a result of impressive interventions. Rather, interventions demand a large degree of empathy but, at the same time, another form of expression of empathy than reflecting feelings. Empathic reflection is not indicated in this phase but rather a deep understanding of the fear of the client, without trying to explain or verbalize it. A deep understanding of his hostile and acting-out behavior is also necessary, without getting involved in a conflict. And it is important to ensure that the client does not harm himself nor others. Only when the client feels secure and accepted, a climate in which he will have the courage to start reflecting on himself can be created. Gradually, self-protection will become less essential and self-evaluation less threatening. Even self-esteem becomes a possibility. Self-esteem must be distinguished from pathological megalomanic fantasies or megalomanic delusions, both of which occur simultaneously with feelings of inferiority, characteristic of the borderline syndrome. Only after this first phase has been more or less completed, and prospects with regard to self-esteem have been offered, can the defensive behavior be reviewed as well as the image of the other, their fellow-human beings ("die Mitdaseienden"). The conclusion of the first phase will also involve other interventions. The therapist can say more and confront the client who at this stage has less reactive behavior.

By using confrontations, the therapist can verbalize more precisely what he would like to say. In the beginning, only non-compelling tentative confrontations with reality are possible with supportive, structuring interventions offered in preference to the more confronting interventions. These interventions can be best illustrated with an example: A young man who was admitted to a psychiatric clinic for treatment was distrustful of a fellow female patient. He suspected her of wanting to seduce him. The woman was, however, clearly lesbian. The therapist reacted to the suspicion by confronting the client with the reality of the situation: "Irene? But she has a girl-friend?" The client reacted with the remark that it did not mean much and that he was still scared that she would come and sit on his lap. Thereupon, the therapist reacted: "But so far, she has always sat in her own chair ... or hasn't she?" This tentatively formulated confrontation with reality was accepted.

The second phase of therapy: Disarming

The second phase of the therapy is concerned with changing the survival strategies of the client. This phase also must be supported by empathic understanding which reflects the unsafe situation in which the client finds himself. Here also the usual client-centered empathic reflections are not advisable, since they can reactivate the client's anxiety. Furthermore, they may lead to the client clinging to the therapist and in this way the client can avoid, by means of what can be called regressive behavior any unpleasant confrontations. Interventions in this phase should be confronting, along with empathic understanding for what the client fears, and the process should be one of building bridges between the client's contradictory tendencies and strivings (Rohde-Dachser, 1986). The client finds it necessary, because of his internal dissensions, to defend himself against nuances. The client prefers polarized black and white statements since nuances obscure the enemy, the opposition in all its negativity, and the loyal allies as well. It is in the therapist's interest to build bridges between the black-and-white polarized aspects of the self-concept and the client's view of the "Mitwelt," the Other. The therapist should respond to the client's black-and-white statements with interventions and confrontations which have an "as well as" character. A short example may clarify what I mean: A 40-year-old woman constantly saw one or the other of her friends in diabolical terms. In an therapeutic session, she once again reported how cunning and mean one of her friends had been and how hard and relentless she had felt in this situation. The therapist responded with "hard and relentless as well as vulnerable and sensitive ... like your friend who is not only sly and unreliable but who has also been affectionate and caring towards you." This "as well as" confrontation was accepted with tears in her eyes and resulted in the client correcting her judgment.

Another example will highlight a second aspect of this disarming phase which is the fragile and delicate therapeutic relationship. If the client is confronted often and the internal inconsistencies of the self-concept are not respected, there is a risk that the client will feel rejected. A young woman who was particularly self-destructive and acting out in the first phase of the therapy and who had reached the stage where she could appreciate the newly attained strengths achieved as a result of the therapeutic relationship, remained concerned about the therapist's responses: Would the newly acquired independence result in him thinking that she no longer needed him? (See also Mahler, 1975). It resulted in the following conversation:

C: I want to stop with the therapy.
T: Why so suddenly?
C: I can see no further progress here ... I mean ... we have come to the end.
T: Did you reach this conclusion in the last few days? Did anything happen which has resulted in you not wanting to continue and feeling that we have come to the end?
C: No, nothing has happened ... I believe that others need your help more now and I can express myself better to John, my nurse.
T: Oh, I understand: You have the impression, the feeling, that I have distanced myself from you since I am spending relatively more time with new clients ... and you have chosen another, more dependable counselor.
C: You can say that again ... more dependable!
T: You feel that my changed schedule is a rejection, a mark of bad faith and now you feel that you need help, more than ever, before.

In the above case, the therapist is experienced as rejecting this client because of his understandable concern for new clients, and is split off as a bad therapist. It is very important that the therapist responds correctly to the threatening crisis in the trust relationship without feeling offended or changing his schedule. It is important that he should respond with empathy for the feelings of disappointment and rejection that the client is experiencing. But it is equally important that he does not allow the client to split him off into being good or bad.

The third phase: The existential phase

The third and very important phase of treatment of borderlines is no longer concerned specifically with achieving a disarmament and a cease-fire. Of course, the civil war may flare up again and the therapist will then be forced to switch back to strategies and subgoals which belong to the second and first phases of therapy. The subgoal of the existential phase, however, is to reconcile the client with his vulnerable, unstable, oversensitive side. The client must learn to accept these aspects of himself as being uniquely his own.

At the same time, the client has the right to expect help from his therapist who must teach him to cope with these aspects in his daily life.

The task of the therapist in this phase is two-fold. In the first place, he must help the client to work through his feelings of weakness, vulnerability and his specific defenselessness. The defects should not be viewed as unchangeable, but should be seen as dynamic weaknesses with which the client must learn to live but against which he can, under certain circumstances, arm himself. The deficiencies are part of his fate and destiny which he cannot avoid. The issue is whether he accepts or rejects them. This existential problem demands that the therapist should take a more equal position in the relationship with his client. Some of the problems of the client in this phase are sometimes overlooked.

A short example may highlight the necessary therapeutic interventions.

> C: Life is too much for me ... I'd rather not continue living.
> T: It is so hard that you'd rather not continue ... and, yet, there are things at which you succeed very well.
> C: You fail completely to see just how hard it is for me; you only pay attention to my achievements.
> T: You feel that I allow myself to be influenced too much by your external achievements and that I fail to see your profound vulnerability.
> C: Not entirely ... but you cannot really feel how much effort it takes to associate with people.
> T: That is true - there you stand completely alone.

Secondly, and finally, it remains a very important task of the therapist to help the patient to cope with daily life, and in addition to concern himself with the client's future choices. This demands an active supportive attitude on the part of the therapist, not using traditional client-centered interventions but presenting alternatives, discussing dangerous options which might arise and giving advice.

Another example will follow to illustrate the above.

> C: It is hard to choose: Should I rent the small house in Alkmaar or should I rather wait until something bigger presents itself in the country?

T: Small in the city or something bigger in the country ... does the choice have any other consequences for you?

C: Yes, and I must give it some serious thinking: Anonymity and perhaps loneliness, or many people I can get to know ... both possibilities have their pros and cons.

I would like to conclude this chapter with a few words about group therapy and hospital treatment. In the course of a long-term therapy of borderline patients, hospitalization is not always avoidable. Such hospital admissions are not necessarily problematic or bad; often hospitalization can be a valuable break on the context of a difficult life. Group therapy is often useful especially for in-patients (see also Eckert & Biermannn-Ratjen, 1986). The hospital setting offers more than a mere period of rest, if the psychiatrist and his therapeutic co-workers are able to create a situation which will facilitate, in a more or less casual and playful manner, the patients development of new relationships with himself, his fellow-patients and the nursing staff and readjustment of the image he has of others and of himself (see also Van der Linden, 1988). The psychotherapist has the possibility of using individual sessions to work through the patient's experiences in the hospital group. I know of no treatment situations in which individual psychotherapy is superfluous. Success in treatment cannot be achieved in clinical institutions if regular individual therapy is not available for clients who need to work through the problems they experience on the ward and who need a secure environment in which to do so. Individual therapy sessions do not necessarily have to be very frequent.

CONCLUSIONS

I have discussed client-centered therapy for borderline clients. I have described four very varied psychotherapeutic strategies, which do not fall into the traditional client-centered approach, namely:
- Anxiety-reducing strategies
- Confronting and interpretative strategies which facilitate insight and stability
- An existential strategy
- An approach in which counseling, support and advice is given.

It becomes clear that the treatment of borderline clients is not restricted to a specific psychotherapeutic orientation if one compares the therapeutic guidelines drawn up by Rohde-Dachser (1979) from the psychoanalytic perspective with the methodical criteria formulated by De Haas (1981) and Swildens (1981, 1988), who were both working as client-centered therapists.

To conclude this chapter I will repeat some of the most important guidelines to be observed in treating borderline clients.1. A non-threatening therapeutic situation is preferred. It is important to note that forced eye-contact can be anxiety-provoking. It is desirable to look for the least fear-provoking setting in therapy.2. A positive relationship between the client and the therapist must have a high priority and should not be threatened by any unnecessary interventions on the part of the therapist. A positive relationship includes, among other things, an optimal balance between distance and closeness.3. Acceptance, empathy and congruence must be reflected in the different phases in the therapy. Especially in the first phase, but also in later phases, the therapeutic attitude as defined by Rogers should be adjusted to the aims of the phase of the treatment and the appropriate strategies.4. The relationship with reality should first of all be restored. Confrontations with regard to the client's distortions of his actual situation should be made early in the therapeutic process.5. Only in the second place should the client's defense strategies be tackled by means of clarifying interventions, so that the client is partly disarmed, resulting in healthy interpersonal relationships.7. During the existential phase - which may take a long time - the existential burden caused by the limitations associated with the borderline personality disorder should be worked through. At the same time, attention should be paid to the client's actual situation. Sometimes a structured approach aimed at the practical daily life of the patient should be given priority.

Are phases, strategies, subgoals and guidelines still consistent with a client-centered treatment? What about the therapist's authenticity when treating borderline clients in accordance with the above guidelines?

I believe I can answer this question in the affirmative in view of the following:

1. The psychotherapist proceeds on the basis of phenomenology: He allows himself to be guided by his client's experience in that he listens carefully to what the pathological experiences of this unique client reveal to him.

2. Furthermore, he is guided by his empathic understanding of his client's needs even if these needs do not demand a traditional client-centered answer.

3. His aim is not to reconstruct the client's personality but to assist the client in overcoming the problems and symptoms which oppress him in the here-and-now and in helping him to exist as a complete human being.

REFERENCES

Chessick, R. (1977). *Intensive therapy of the borderline patient.* New York: Jason Aronson.

de Haas, O.P. (1981). Gestructureerde gesprekstherapie bij borderline cliënten. *Tijdschrift voor Psychotherapie, 7(5),* 70-80.

Eckert, J., & Biermann-Ratjen, E.-M. (1986). Ueberlegungen und Erfahrungen bei der gesprächspsychotherapeutischen Behandlung in Gruppen von Patienten mit einer Borderline-Persönlichkeitsstörung. *Zeitschrift für Personenzentrierte Psychologie und Psychotherapie, 5(1),* 47-54.

Greenberg, J.R., & Mitchell, S.A. (1983). *Object relations in psychoanalytic theory.* Cambridge (MA): Harvard University Press.

Mahler, M.S. (1975). Bedeutung des Loslösungs- und Individuationsprozesses für die Beurteilung von Borderline-Phänomenen. *Psyche, 29,* 1078-1095.

Rohde-Dachser, C. (1979). *Das Borderline Syndrom.* Bern: Huber.

Rohde-Dachser, C. (1986). Borderline Störungen. In K.P. Kisker (Ed.), *Psychiatrie der Gegenwart, Band 1.* Berlin: Springer.

Swildens, J.C.A.G. (1981). De hulpverwachting in de therapeutische relatie. II. Verkenningen in grensland. *Tijdschrift voor Psychotherapie, 7,* 15-23.

Swildens, J.C.A.G. (1988). *Procesgerichte gesprekstherapie.* Amersfoort/Leuven: Acco.

Van der Linden, P. (1981). How does the large group change the individual? *International Journal of Therapeutic Communities, 9,* 31-39.

POSITIVE EFFECTS AND LIMITATIONS OF CLIENT-CENTERED THERAPY WITH SCHIZOPHRENIC PATIENTS

Ludwig TEUSCH
Psychiatrische Uniklinik Essen, F.R.Germany

A fundamental aspect of schizophrenic disorders is a deep disturbance in the relationship with other human beings. Schizophrenic patients withdraw in an autistic way to a poor or to a bizarre and strange inner world. In other cases or at other times, excitement or delusions prevent them from coming into contact.The client-centered therapist tries to see the world through client's eyes and to describe and understand his ideas, feelings and needs. In the therapeutic relationship, the patient may feel sure and come to integrate the split part of his thoughts and feelings into his self-concept.

The fundamental theory of the client-centered concept as well as of recent psychoanalytic views is: 1. Even strange schizophrenic symptomatology is a comprehensible coded message. The assumption is that the patient has a hidden interest in communicating with others. 2. It is not neutral analysis that is important but an emphatic internal participation with the patient, to help him reorganize his personality.

In an acute psychotic crisis, client-centered therapy (CCT) may help the therapist to forge links with the schizophrenic patient. In that period, the therapist must work flexibly and abstain from standard conditions of setting, e.g. regular one-hour therapy sessions. Some case-reports (Pagel & Teusch, 1986; Rogers, 1967a; Shlien, 1960; Teusch, Köhler, & Finke, 1987) show positive effects, but there is a lack of empirical studies in this important field. Up to now, systematic studies of client-centered therapy of schizophrenic patients have been performed after the decline of acute symptomatology. The following results refer to this area of research.

WHAT DO WE KNOW ABOUT THE POSITIVE OR NEGATIVE EFFECTS OF CLIENT-CENTERED THERAPY (CCT) WITH SCHIZOPHRENIC PATIENTS?

How do schizophrenic patients experience CCT? Which personality changes occur? What is the influence on the psychopathological state? Does CCT influence the social prognosis or the further course of the schizophrenic disorders? What are the limitations of CCT with schizophrenic patients?

Some years ago, a systematic investigation was carried out in the Essen psychiatric university hospital in order to find out, how schizophrenic patients experience the client-centered therapy sessions (Teusch et al., 1983). The patients took part in a multidimensional in-patient therapy program including client-centered individual and group therapy for about 3 months.

In this study, 60 schizophrenic patients rated every individual therapy sessions by means of the Client-Experiencing-Questionnaire (KEB) of Eckert, Schwartz, and Tausch (1977) - totalling 517 sessions. Factor analysis of the items shows three dimensions (Zielke, 1980) which have proved valid for schizophrenics (Teusch et al., 1983):
- Insecurity and verbal inhibition caused by interaction;
- Reassuring change optimism;
- Physical tension and emotional stress.

The major part of the data indicate that the patients experienced the individual therapy sessions as reassuring, and helpful. Insecurity and verbal inhibition as well as physical tension and emotional stress connected with the therapy sessions were low.

There was a significant difference between patients of different psychopathological states in view of the factor "Reassuring change optimism" in the beginning of therapy. The less disturbed the schizophrenic patients were, the more they experienced CCT as helpful, except for a small group of uncritical patients. This indicates that severly disturbed patients have a sceptical attitude towards therapy which may be partly due to their impaired cognitive functioning. Rogers described corresponding findings based on the results of the Wisconsin study: "Evidently the deeply disturbed psychotic is simply not able to perceive or report understanding, warmth and genuineness to the same degree as the less disturbed person, even when these qualities may be objectively present in the relationship. Over the period of therapy, however, the schizophrenic patient comes to distinguish more sharply among the different therapist attitudes and also is able to perceive a higher level of these therapist conditions" (Rogers, 1967b).

PERSONALITY CHANGES UNDER THERAPY

In both the Wisconsin study and the Essen study positive personality changes were found. In Rogers' study, TAT records indicated definitely greater constructive changes in the group undergoing therapy than in the control group. One of the sharpest changes of the group undergoing therapy was a significant pretest-posttest difference in the emotional distance from the experience they described in the TAT pictures. " Evidently these therapy patients reduced their need to deny or emotionally distance themselves from their experience." (Rogers, 1967b). At the end, they were "less vulnerable, psychologically, and more capable of facing themselves and their environment." In the Essen study, pre-post tests were made with the Freiburger Personality Inventory (FPI). The most impressive positive changes were found in the dimensions of physical complaints, depression and sociability. Physical complaints declined as well as depressive mood. Patients' self-assessment showed more self-confidence and sociability. Furthermore, patients felt less frustrated and less strained. Evidently, CCT leads to positive shifts in personality, even though absence of a control-group in the Essen study leads to some reservations (Teusch, 1986a).

THE INFLUENCE OF CCT
ON PSYCHOPATHOLOGICAL SYMPTOMS

In the study of Rogers (1967b), there was an overall reduction of psychopathology in both groups: The additional CCT group and the standard therapy control group. This finding may be discouraging for client-centered therapists. However, psychopathological measurements, especially those concerning negative symptoms were coarse thirty years ago. In the future, modern rating scales (e.g. Andreasen, 1982; Mundt et al., 1985) should be used to discriminate psychotherapy effects. In the Essen study, the majority of patients (75%), - apart from early failure within the first 30 days of treatment - showed a distinct reduction of psychopathology and a distinctly better social adjustment on a global clinical rating. 18% Showed slight improvement, 7% were unchanged or deteriorated. Absence of a control group limits the importance of the findings.

THE INFLUENCE ON SOCIAL PROGNOSIS AND THE FURTHER COURSE OF THE DISEASE

There are no follow-up studies up to now, concerning the influence of CCT on subsequent social adjustment, including living and working conditions.

Truax (1970) reported on the nine years pretherapy and nine years posttherapy hospitalization of the patients of the Wisconsin study. The results were remarkable: There was no significant difference between therapy and control groups but a significantly different trend between on the one hand the patients, who had received high therapeutic conditions and, on the other hand, the low-condition group and the control group. There was a trend for number of days out of hospital to be worse for the low-condition group. If the results were confirmed, the conclusion would be that CCT with schizophrenic patients has either effective or adverse effects, and, furthermore, that even experienced therapists may provide negative therapeutic effects, which is in agreement with the well-known findings of Whitehorn and Betz (1975).

WHAT DO WE KNOW ABOUT THE LIMITATIONS OR THE NEGATIVE EFFECTS OF CCT?

Since there is no empirical basis to advocate for psychotherapy, including CCT, as the treatment of choice with schizophrenic patients, the role of psychotherapy must be defined within a multidimensional treatment plan. As a consequence, client-centered therapists must accept diagnostic procedures in this area and give up the myth of universality of the method.

In our rehabilitation unit, an initial interview serves to reject patients with no motivation or with too acute symptomatology. In addition schizophrenic patients with dependencies or dissociation are refused.

In spite of this selection before entering the rehabilitation unit, about 10% of patients drop out or must be transferred to the psychiatric emergency ward in the first 30 days. In the developmental period of our rehabilitation program, failures occurred even more frequently, which suggests the necessity of analysing treatment errors (Teusch, 1986b).

Within the observation period of one year, failures were studied on the basis of clinical case reports. Out of 73 patients, 10 (13,7%) dropped out and 5 (6,9%) were transferred to the emergency ward. Of all sociodemographic variables, the sex distribution was remarkable. Male patients failed significantly more frequently. This may be due to "masculine inexpressiveness, the myth of masculine competence and the avoidance of intimacy with other men" (Lohstein, 1978). So it could be useful to take into account the "masculine handicaps" in the therapeutic procedure.

Another important factor is the *psychopathological state*. A global rating of psychopathological disturbance at admission compared with occurrence of failures shows the following regular pattern: The more disturbed the patients in the beginning of the therapy, the more likely they were to fail. Disorganized schizophrenic patients deteriorated into extensive hebephrenic behavior and finally had to be transferred.

Schizophrenic patients of the residual and paranoid types were more likely to drop out than those of the disorganized type. Case 1: A 17-year-old male, going to secondary school, had been on a psychiatric ward for 6 months because of an acute disorganized schizophrenic disorder. We had followed the orders on the psychiatric ward during the last weeks before he came to the rehabilitation unit, but he now deteriorated extensively. He enjoyed the "freedom" of our setting and went by taxi to dance in neighboring cities and did not take part in the therapy program.

Patients may be overpressured by the extent of the therapy program, particularly by the emotional stimulation of the psychotherapeutic procedures and the demands concerning autonomy on a rehabilitation unit. Case 2: A 23-year-old janitor's assistant had been transferred to us from the emergency ward at the end of her acute paranoid psychotic episode. She was admitted against the will of her mother who dominated the family. In the first days, the patient had reservations about therapy. Then she spoke about her difficult position in the family and was pushed by some group members to leave her family. This confrontation led her to leave the hospital.

In this last case, the balance in the family was disrupted by premature interventions of the group members. The patient could not endure the tension between her mother and the therapy group.

The handling of neuroleptic *drug therapy* is important. In the beginning of the rehabilitation program, continuity of the drug dosage is important. Several cases of failure may have been due to premature reduction of neuroleptic medication particularly when psychopathology was severe and partly compensated by the medication. Drug dosage should not be reduced too quickly in the beginning of intensive psychotherapy. On the other hand, neuroleptic drugs usually can be markedly reduced in the course of therapy (Teusch, 1986a). Incidentally, few patients were treated without drugs, or came to accept drugs in the course of treatment.

CONCLUSION

CCT can be regarded as helpful and effective in the treatment of schizophrenic patients. However, CCT as other psychotherapeutic approaches is not the method of choice; it is necessary to integrate it into a multidimensional therapy plan which mainly includes social intervention and neuroleptic drug therapy (Gaebel, 1986).

As a consequence, diagnostic procedures are necessary to develop a therapy plan and to decide whether the patient will be appropriately helped by a defined psychotherapeutic setting. Standard conditions with regular individual and/or group therapy sessions are only possible or useful if the psychopathological symptomatology is not acute nor severe, and if the patient is at least minimally motivated in psychotherapy. If these conditions are taken into account, nearly all patients benefit from treatment in a measurable way:

- Reduction of psychopathological symptoms and improvement of social adjustment.

- Important changes in self-assessment, especially a reduced need to deny or emotionally distance themselves from their experience, a reduction of depressive mood and physical complaints and more self-confidence and sociability.

REFERENCES

Andreasen, N. (1982). Negative symptoms in schizophrenia. Definition and reliability. *Archives of General Psychiatry, 39,* 784-788.

Eckert, J., Schwartz, H.J., & Tausch, R. (1977). Klienten-Erfahrungen und Zusammenhang mit psychischen Aenderungen in personenzentrierter Gesprächspsychotherapie. *Zeitschrift für Personenzentrierte Psychologie und Psychotherapie, 5,* 399-408.

Gaebel, W. (1986). Die Bedeutung von psychiatrischer Diagnose und Indikation in der Gesprächspsychotherapie. *Zeitschrift für Personenzentrierte Psychologie und Psychotherapie, 5,* 399-408.

Lohstein, L.M. (1978). The group psychotherapy dropout phenomenon revisited. *American Journal of Psychiatry, 135,* 1492-1495.

Mundt, C., Fiedler, P., Pracht, B., & Rettig, R. (1985). Intentionalitäts-Skala. *Nervenarzt, 56,* 146-149.

Pagel, J., & Teusch, L. (1986). Otto K. In Gesellschaft für wissenschaftliche Gesprächspsychotherapie (Ed.), *Orientierung an der Person* (Vol. 1, pp. 66-70). Köln: Gesellschaft für Wissenschaftliche Gesprächspsychotherapie.

Rogers, C.R. (1967a). A silent young man. In C.R. Rogers, E.T. Gendlin, D. Kiesler, & C.B. Truax (Eds.), *The therapeutic relationship and its impact: A study of psychotherapy with schizophrenics* (pp. 411-416). Madison: University of Wisconson Press.

Rogers, C.R. (1967b). The findings in brief. In C.R. Rogers, E.T. Gendlin, D. Kiesler, & C.B. Truax (Eds.), *The therapeutic relationship and its impact: A study of psychotherapy with schizophrenics* (pp. 73-93). Madison: University of Wisconsin Press.

Shlien, J.M. (1960). A client-centered approach to schizophrenics: First approximation. In A. Burton (Ed.), *Psychotherapy of the psychoses* (pp. 285-317). New York: Basic Books.

Teusch, L. (1986a). Gesprächspsychotherapie schizophrener Patienten. *Zeitschrift für Personenzentrierte Psychologie und Psychotherapie, 5,* 391-398.

Teusch, L. (1986b). Behandlungsabbrüche and Verlegungen schizophrener Patienten im Verlauf der stationären Behandlung mit psychotherapeutischem Schwerpunkt. Eine systematische Untersuchung. *Psychiatrische Praxis, 13,* 177-184.

Teusch, L., Beyerle, U., Lange, H.U., Schenk, G.K., & Stadtmüller, G. (1983). The client-centered approach to schizophrenic patients. First empirical results. In W.R. Minsel & W. Herff (Eds.), *Research in psychotherapeutic approaches* (pp. 140-148). Frankfurt a/M.: Peter Lang.

Teusch, L., Köhler, K.H., & Finke, J. (1987). Die Bearbeitung von Wahnphänomenen in der klientenzentrierten Gesprächspsychotherapie. In H. Olbrich (Ed.), *Halluzination und Wahn* (pp. 168-173). Berlin: Springer.

Truax, C.B. (1970). Effects of client-centered psychotherapy with schizophrenic patients: Nine years pre-therapy and nine years post-therapy hospitalization. *Journal of Consulting and Clinical Psychology, 3,* 417-422.

Whitehorn, J.C., & Betz, B.J. (1975). *Effective psychotherapy with the schizophrenic patient.* New York: Jason Aronson.

Zielke, M. (1980). Untersuchungen der Gütekriterien des Klienten-Erfahrungsbogens (KEB). *Diagnostica; 16,* 57-73.

PRE-THERAPY:
A THEORETICAL EVOLUTION IN THE PERSON-CENTERED/EXPERIENTIAL PSYCHOTHERAPY OF SCHIZOPHRENIA AND RETARDATION

Garry F. PROUTY
University of Illinois at Chicago, U.S.A.

INTRODUCTION: THE WISCONSIN STUDY

Empirical findings: Rogers (1957) specifies his relationship theory of psychotherapy as a set of therapist attitudes. Unconditional positive regard, empathy and congruence. Gendlin (1964) describes his experiential theory of psychotherapy in terms of organismic phenomenology. Experiencing is a concrete bodily felt process. The application of relationship and experiencing to the psychotherapy of schizophrenia is well documented by Rogers, Gendlin, et al., (1967) through the Wisconsin Project. Basically these authors found: 1. Regardless of the reality of therapist attitudes, patients tended to perceive low levels of these conditions. 2. There was no significant difference in experiential process movement over therapy in the schizophrenic group as a function of therapist attitudes. 3. There was no significant difference in experiential process movement between treatment group and control group.

On a more positive note, it was found that where experiential process movement did occur, it was a function of therapist attitudes. Also it was found that clients receiving highest levels of therapeutic relationship, experienced the greatest reduction in schizophrenic pathology. Treated clients evidenced slightly better rates of hospital discharge and presented improvement on Thematic Apperception Test protocols.

RELATIONSHIP

Tsakanika (1987), reviewing the Wisconsin Study, stated "the learning shared from this study made apparent that severely disturbed individuals have difficulty perceiving empathic understanding and unconditional positive regard intended from the therapist. Empathic contact is thus not established and the therapeutic process is hindered."

This observation is supported by Rogers (1972, p. 188) who reported: "Another simple observation. Our schizophrenics tend to be either massively silent or to engage in continuous (and not very revealing) conversation. It has been found that half of our schizophrenics, in their second interviews show either less than 1% silence or more than 40% silence... This sharply differed from clinic clients. Our schizophrenic individuals *tend to fend off relationships* either by an almost complete silence - often extending over many interviews - or by a flood of over-talk which is equally effective in preventing a real encounter." *Obviously relationship is problematic* in the psychotherapy of schizophrenics.

EXPERIENCING

The Wisconsin clinical research findings prompted Gendlin (1970, p. 288) to theoretically formulate schizophrenia as arrested experiencing: "My conception of the illness: It is not so much what is there, as what is not here. The interactive experiential process is lacking, stuck, deadened in old hurt stoppages, and in the disconnection from the world. The psychosis is the curtailment or cessation of the interaction process of feeling and events." Clearly, *experiencing is problematic.* It is impaired, curtailed or absent in the schizophrenic psychosis.

Perhaps we conclude our review of relationship and experiencing in the psychotherapy of schizophrenia by citing Rogers (1959, p. 251): "An increased amount of experience with individuals classed as psychotic (...) would round out and enrich our *systematic thinking,* in an area in which it is presently inadequate."

A SHIFT IN PERSPECTIVE: METHODOLOGICAL QUESTIONS

The problematic status of relationship and experiencing in the psychotherapy of schizophrenia places a boundary on the person-centered/experiential treatment of psychosis and raises new questions.

Assuming relationship/experiencing are valid dimensions of psychotherapeutic process, how can these impaired psychological functions develop or be accessed in the schizophrenic population? What kind of *method* can facilitate impaired relationship and experiential capacities in this group? From these questions the notion of relationship/experiencing as therapeutic *goals* becomes formulated, and the question of a *"pre" relationship or "pre" experiential* method comes into focus.

A SHIFT IN PERSPECTIVE: THEORETICAL QUESTIONS

Prouty (1976) describes three contact deficits in chronic schizophrenics and schizophrenic retardates. Due to institutionalization, over-sedation, psychological withdrawal and social isolation, these clients exhibited impaired reality, affective and communicative contact.

These psychological functions emerge as necessary conditions of therapy for these populations. Without reality contact these clients cannot share a mutual "here and now" with the therapist.

Without affective contact the clients cannot access feeling or emotions. Without communicative contact the clients cannot be verbally expressive. Clearly, reality, affective and communicative contact are "pre" conditions for therapy that must be rendered functional.

Although Rogers (1959) parallels this observation by describing "psychological contact" as the first condition of a therapeutic relationship, the theory assumes its presence between therapist and client. Second, the theory provides no definitions of "psychological contact." E.g. Watson (1984, p. 18-19) writes: "If conditions 2-6 are operationally defined and shown to be present - it follows then that condition 1 is present, then condition 1 does not require operational definition..." Third, the theory provides no process to restore or develop "psychological contact" when it is impaired or absent.

Thus a *theoretical problematic* emerges. Chronic schizophrenics and schizophrenic retardates evidence impaired or absent reality, affective and communicative contact - yet Rogerian theory assumes "psychological contact" as present and it provides no observable definitions about its nature or what techniques are needed to restore or develop it. What does Rogerian theory specify in the *absence or impairment of the first necessary condition - "psychological contact"*? "Pre-" therapy is an attempt to answer this question.

PRE-THERAPY: A THEORY OF PSYCHOLOGICAL CONTACT

Introduction: Pre-therapy centers on the concept of "psychological contact" (Peters, 1986) - developing psychological contact with WORLD, SELF, and OTHER (Merleau-Ponty, 1962, p. 260). Psychological contact is theoretically described on three levels. First, it is a set of therapist techniques; i.e. CONTACT REFLECTIONS by which the therapist facilitates contact with the client. Secondly, it is a set of psychological functions necessary for therapy to occur, i.e. reality, affective and communicative contacts, the CONTACT FUNCTIONS. Thirdly, it is a set of "outcome-behaviors" or CONTACT BEHA-VIORS, i.e. the emergent behavioral manifestation of psychological contact which results in operationalization for research.

Psychological contact is thus: 1. A set of therapeutic techniques. 2. A set of psychological functions necessary for therapy to occur. 3. A set of measurable outcome behaviors.

1. Contact reflections

Rank (Rychlack, 1971, p. 410) developed reflection as a linguistic technique to elaborate therapist cognitive understanding. Rogers (1966) further evolved reflecting to concretize non-directiveness, empathy and unconditional positive regard - all elements in his relationship theory of therapy. Gendlin (1968) alternately described reflection as an experiential technique directed at facilitating the concrete felt process in the client.

Pre-therapy (Leijssen & Roelens, 1988) conceptualizes reflective technique as the concretization of the therapist's psychological contact. Contact reflections are the method by which the therapist makes "contact" with the client, thereby, facilitating the contact functions and contact behaviors. Contact reflections develop or restore the necessary functions for therapy with non-contactful clients (chronic schizophrenics and schizophrenic retardates).

a. Techniques

Essentially, the pre-therapy or contact modality of reflecting consists of techniques' that form a common method, in so far as they center on pre-expressive, pre-verbal and primitive levels of client behavior.

Contact reflections form a common style because they are distinctly literal, duplicative and concrete.

There are five contact reflections (Karon & Vanderbos, 1981): 1. Situational-(SR), 2. Facial-(FR), 3. Word-for-Word-(WWR), 4. Body-(BR), and 5. Reiterative-(RR):

(SR) Their psychological function is the development or restoration of Reality Contact (WORLD). These reflections are focused toward the client's immediate environment, situation or milieu.

(FR) Their psychological function is the development or restoration of Affective Contact (SELF). With these reflections the therapist verbalizes the implicit affect in the clients face. This helps the client express pre-expressive affect.

(WWR) Their psychological function is the restoration or development of Communicative contact (OTHERS), where it is absent or impaired. These reflections develop or restore functional speech and assist the client to prototypically experience self as expressor and communicator.

(BR) These are literal or verbal reflections of the client's bizarre movements or body states. These reflections are directed toward "body-sense" and to assist the client in a generalized "here-now" reality contact.

(RR) This is essentially re-contact - utilizing previously successful reflections. They assist in the interactive effect of contact and experiencing.

b. Clinical example

Prouty (Prouty & Pietrzak, 1988) describes a therapeutic vignette which involves the application of Contact Reflections to a hallucinatory experience. This particular vignette is chosen because it illustrates *all techniques* of the pre-therapy method.

Client "Roger" in his early twenties and single, was a resident of a "halfway house" for psychiatric patients. He was consecutively diagnosed as a Schizo/Affective with drug-dependence, Catatonic/Schizophrenic with suicidal tendencies and finally, Borderline Schizophrenic with chronic depression. A car accident had caused his leg to shorten and a blood clot to form in his brain. The client was receiving 10 mg. of Haldol, four times a day, by psychiatric prescription for his psychotic condition. He had a normal childhood, but, his adolescence was marked by polydrug use and Heroin addiction.

The client had been a resident of a "halfway house" for six months when client-centered/experiential therapy began. He was semi-catatonic, suicidal, and often in a lethargic stupor. This particular hallucinatory vignette occurred after six months of therapy.

C:	"Careful. Pink elephant there."
T: (WW)	"Careful. Pink elephant there."
T: (FR)	"Your face looks scared."
T: (FR)	"Your eyes are big."
T: (BR)	"Hands on legs."
C:	"Look out - Hurt - gonna get."
T: (WW)	"Look out - Hurt - gonna get."
T: (BR)	"Your whole body is stiff."
C:	"It's over there - a lot of animals."
T: (SR)	"Over there."
T: (FR)	"Your eyes got bigger."
T: (RR)	"Over there."
C:	"All kinds hurt you - it will hurt you."
T: (BR)	"You point."
T: (SR)	"You point over there."
T: (BR)	"You point, I point."
T: (BR)	"We both point."
C:	"They are big and pink and ugly."
T: (WW)	"They are big and pink and ugly."
C:	"They laugh and yell and hurt you."
T: (WW)	"They laugh and yell and hurt you."
C:	"They hurt me."
T: (WW)	"They hurt you."
	(a few minutes of silence)
T: (RR)	"Before, you pointed over there."
T: (RR)	"Before, you pointed there and said, 'They are big and pink and ugly'."
T: (RR)	"You said they laugh and yell and hurt you."
C:	"They you, 'Hurt me'."

C:	"Hurt me."
T: (WW)	"Hurt me."
	(a few minutes of silence)
T: (SR)	"We have been quite a long time in this little room."
T: (FR)	"You looked up."
T: (RR)	"Before you said, 'They hurt me'."
C:	"It will hurt me."
T: (WW)	"It will hurt me."
C:	"Yeah, she'll hurt me."
T: (WW)	"Yeah, she'll hurt me."
T: (FR)	"Little smile on your face."
C:	"I hate her."
T: (WW)	"You hate her."
T: (FR)	"Your eyes are big."
T: (BR)	"You rub your legs."
T: (BR)	"You rub, I rub."
T: (BR)	"You hate her."
C:	"Yeah, she is ugly."
T: (WW)	"Yeah, she is ugly."
C:	"She is ugly like a big elephant."
T: (WW)	"She is ugly like a big elephant."
C:	"She tramples me like an elephant."
T: (WW)	"She tramples me like an elephant."
C:	"My mother is all over me."
T: (WW)	"My mother is all over me."
C:	"My mother smothers me emotionally."
T: (WW)	"My mother smothers me emotionally."
C:	"I am angry - my mother runs my life."
T: (WW)	"I am angry - my mother runs my life."
T: (BR)	"You're angry - your body looks twisted."
	(silence for a few minutes)
T: (RR)	"You said you were angry and that your mother runs your life."
C:	"Yeah, what am I gonna do? Sharon where do I start?"

2. Contact functions

Rogers defines psychological contact as the first necessary condition of a therapeutic relationship. Rooted in this context and broadly conceived, pre-therapy conceptualizes psychological contact as the functions necessary for therapy to occur (to schizophrenics and schizophrenic retardates). Psychological contact (CONTACT FUNCTIONS) are described on three levels of functional awareness: 1. Reality contact (WORLD), 2. Affective contact (SELF), and 3. Communicative contact (OTHER).

Reality contact (WORLD) is defined as the literal awareness of people, places, things and events. Affective contact (SELF) is described as awareness of mood, feelings and emotions. Communicative contact (OTHER) is conceptualized as the symbolization of reality and affective awareness to others. Reality, affective and communicative functions are necessary for psychotherapy to proceed. As these CONTACT FUNCTIONS are the most impaired in chronic schizophrenics and psychotic retardates, they become the clinical goals in a "pre-therapy."

Clinical example

Prouty (1985) describes a vignette in which reality, affective and communicative contact (CONTACT FUNCTIONS) are facilitated. The client is a long term hospitalized chronic schizophrenic.

"Dorothy is an old woman, who is one of the more regressed women on the X ward. She was mumbling something (as she usually does). This time I could hear certain words in her confusion. I repeated only the words I could clearly understand. After about ten minutes, I could hear a complete sentence."

C:		"Come with me."
T: (WW)		"Come with me."
T:		Patient led me to the corner of the dayroom. We stood there silently for what seemed to be a very long time. Since I couldn't seem to communicate verbally with her, I watched her body movements and closely imitated them.
C:		Patient put her hand on the wall and said, "cold."
T: (WW)		I put my hand on the wall and repeated "cold."
T:		She had been holding my hand all along, but when I reflected her, she would tighten her grip.
C:		Dorothy began to mumble word fragments. I was careful to reflect only the words that I could hear. What she was saying began to make sense: "I don't know what this is anymore." (touching the wall) REALITY CONTACT. "The walls and chairs don't mean anything to me any more."
T:(WW-BR)		Touching the wall: "You don't know what this is anymore." The chairs and walls don't mean anything to you anymore."
C:		Patient began to cry; AFFECTIVE CONTACTC: After a while she began to talk again. This time she spoke clearly. COMMUNICATIVE CONTACT. "I don't like it here." "I'm tired, so tired."
T: (WW)		I gently touched her arm, and this time it was me who

	tightened my grip on her hand. I said: "You are tired, so tired."
C:	The client smiled and told me to sit in a chair directly in front of her and began to braid my hair.

3. Contact behaviors

As a result of contact reflections and the facilitation of contact functions, a client is more expressive about WORLD (Reality contact), SELF (Affective contact) and OTHER (Communicative contact). As a consequence, the client is more accessible to psychotherapy or remedial programming (social, vocational, educational).

Contact behaviors are the emergent behavioral manifestations of reality, affective and communicative contact. Behaviorally, reality contact is the client's verbalization of people, places, things and events. Affective contact is the client's verbalization of emotions through feeling words, (e.g. sad) - or through bodily/facial expression of emotion. Communicative contact is the client's use of social language - words or sentences. These specific behavioral categories serve as the foundation for scale development and statistical evaluation.

Intensive case study: Contact behaviors

Client "N" was one of five retarded clients who exhibited schizophrenic like symptoms and was referred for pre-therapy by a State of Illinois residential facility. These clients constituted the basis of study for pilot research about the effects of pre-therapy (Prouty, 1985).

All residents were treated twice weekly for two years by para-professional therapists (AAS in Mental Health), who tape recorded each session. All tape recorded sessions were transcribed verbatim to a data sheet for scoring by therapists and independent raters. All therapists and raters were pre-trained to a competency of .6 correlation with master raters. Each therapist and rater scored and tabulated the frequencies of contact behaviors. Variable length of sessions were statistically compensated. The data presented represent simple average scores of client contacts per minute.

Client "N", female, IQ 17, mental age three years one month, was alternately diagnosed schizophrenic and/or autistic. At the age of six, she was in an auto accident which further added brain damage to a complicated diagnosis. She was referred to pre-therapy because of her aggressive behavior and general lack of appropriate communication. As a result of this maladaptive behavior, she was unsuitable for vocational rehabilitation in a community workshop.

As a result of treatment, client "N" communicated more realistically, evidenced more integrated emotion and reduced her aggressiveness. Subsequently, she was placed in a pre-vocational program. Presented are "pre" and "post" treatment descriptions by the therapist, a staff psychologist and quantitative data outlining significant gains in reality, affective and communicative functions.

a. Therapist pre-treatment description, 1982

Client "N" spoke in a quiet, harsh voice with poor articulation. She spoke mostly unidentifiable utterances combined with neologisms. At other times she evidenced inappropriate laughter mixed with baby talk. She also evidenced sudden explosive talking accompanied by ritualistic touching of arms and legs. This was also accompanied by ritualistic stomping and yelling. There was very little eye contact. Her frustration tolerance was very low and this led to self-abusive behavior and aggression toward others. The client was very resistant to physical contact and very resistive to entrance of her play space. She would play with the therapist's body as a puppet. This involved pulling, hitting, and molding as a thing.

b. Therapist post-treatment description, 1984

Client "N" is motivated to articulate. She speaks more clearly with fewer neologisms and communicates her needs more. She makes more attempts at conversation. She is more sociable and makes more eye contact.

There was considerably less autistic, ritualistic and aggressive behavior. Her frustration tolerance is better because she attempts to find solutions. She is much more contactful bodily and is much more aware of therapist as a person. She exhibits better grooming habits and esteem over her achievements (entrance to pre-vocational workshop). She displays more emotional awareness and appropriateness. She also spends significantly less time hallucinating.

c. Staff psychologist report, 1984

The client has started to acquire patience with minimal frustration which leads to a reduction in her maladaptive behaviors. She has decreased tremendously in destructive and aggressive behavior at home and at school. Self control mechanisms have become internalized, increasing her ability to verbally express her emotions instead of acting out behaviorally. She seems, overall, more stable emotionally and behaviorally. This affective stability was not realized a year ago. Her ability to adjust to change has improved. She is more sociable than in the past.

d. Quantitative data

		Reality contact per minute			
1982	(T)	1.05	(IR)	1.03	
1983	(T)	6.46	(IR)	8.20	

		Affective contact per minute			
1982	(T)	.22	(IR)	.23	
1983	(T)	1.13	(IR)	1.12	(IR) 1.00

		Communicative contact per minute			
1982	(T)	1.33	(IR)	1.70	
1983	(T)	3.52	(IR)	3.77	

SUMMARY

Pre-therapy is a theory and methodology designed to develop or restore the reality, affective and communicative functions necessary for therapeutics with the psychotic/retarded or chronic schizophrenic clients. It theoretically expands Rogers' contention that client and therapist need to be in "psychological contact" as the first necessary condition of a therapeutic relationship. However, in contrast to classical theory, pre-therapy does not assume its presence with chronic regressed populations; rather, it assumes the need for its restoration or development. Pre-therapy, in the absence of theoretical definition by Rogers, also provides conceptualization of "psychological contact." Specifically, pre-therapy defines contact reflections, contact functions and contact behaviors as an interdependent theoretical system.

1. Contact reflections

Contact reflections are the techniques whereby the pre-therapist facilitates the contact functions (reality, affect and communication). Situational reflections facilitate reality contact. Facial reflections facilitate affective contact. Word for word reflections develop communicative contact. Body reflections assist generalized "here-now" contact. Reiterative reflections assist re-contact.

2. Contact functions

Contact is conceptualized as awareness of WORLD, SELF and OTHER. Reality contact (WORLD), defined as awareness of people, places things, and events. Affective contact (SELF) is defined as awareness of feelings, moods and emotions.

Communicative contact (OTHER) is defined as the symbolization of reality and affective awareness to others. Reality, affective and communicative contact are the psychological functions necessary for treatment.

3. Contact behaviors

Resulting from contact reflections, the client should be evidencing more reality, affective and communicative contact, i.e. the client expresses more contact with WORLD, SELF, and OTHER; thereby, becoming more accessible for programming or psychotherapy. As emergent behavioral manifestation, reality contact is the verbalization of people, places, things and events. Affective contact is the expression of emotion through feeling words or bodily/facial concretizations. Communicative contact is the utilization of social language in words and sentences. Contact behaviors result in operationalization for research.

REFERENCES

Gendlin, E.T. (1964). A theory of personality change. In P. Worchel & D. Byrne (Eds.), *Personality change* (pp. 102-148). New York: Wiley.

Gendlin, E.T. (1968). The experiential response. In A. Hammer (Ed.), *Use of interpretation in treatment* (pp. 208-228). New York: Grune and Stratton.

Gendlin, E.T. (1970). Research in psychotherapy with schizophrenic patients and the nature of that illness. In J.T. Hart & T.M. Tomlinson (Eds.), *New directions in client-centered therapy* (pp. 280-291). Boston: Houghton Mifflin.

Karon, B., & Vandenbos, G. (1981). *Psychotherapy of schizophrenia.* New York: Aronson.

Leijssen, M., & Roelens, L. (1988). Herstel van contactfuncties bij zwaar gestoorde patiënten door middel van Prouty's pre-therapie. (The restauration of contact functions in Prouty's pre-therapy). *Tijdschrift Klinische Psychologie, 18,* 21-24.

Merleau-Ponty, M. (1962). *Phenomenology of perception.* New York: Routledge and Kegan Paul.

Peters, H. (1986). Prouty's pre-therapie methode en de behandeling van hallucinaties: een verslag. *Ruit,* 26-34.

Prouty, G. (1976). Pre-therapy, a method of treating pre-expressive psychotic and retarded patients. *Psychotherapy, Theory, Research and Practice, 13,* 290-294.

Prouty, G. (1985). *The development of reality, affect and communication in psychotic retardates.* Unpublished manuscript.

Prouty, G., & Kubiak, H. (1988). The development of communicative contact with a catatonic schizophrenic. *Journal of Communication Therapy, 4(1),* 13-20.

Prouty, G., & Pietrzak, S. (1988). Pre-therapy method applied to persons experiencing hallucinatory images. *Person-Centered Review, 3(4),* 426-441.

Rogers, C. (1957). The necessary and sufficient conditions of therapeutic personality change. *Journal of Consulting Psychology, 21,* 95-103.

Rogers, C. (1959). A theory of therapy, personality and interpersonal relationships as developed in the client-centered framework. In S. Koch (Ed.), *Psychology: A study of a science* (Vol. 3, pp. 185-256). New York: McGraw Hill.

Rogers, C.R. (1966). Client-centered therapy. In S. Arieti (Ed.), *American handbook of psychiatry* (Vol. 3, pp. 183-200). New York: Basic Books.

Rogers, C.R. (Ed.). (1967). *The therapeutic relationship and its impact: A study of psychotherapy with schizophrenics.* Madison: University of Wisconsin Press.

Rogers, C.R. (1972). Some learnings from a study of psychotherapy with schizophrenics. In C.R. Rogers & B. Stevens (Eds.), *Person to person: The problem of being human* (pp. 181-192) New York: Pocketbooks.

Rychlak, J. (1971). *Introduction to personality and psychotherapy.* Boston: Houghton Mifflin.

Tsakanika, M. (1987). *Evolution of client-centered therapy: Theoretical comparison between C. Rogers and G. Prouty.* Paper presented at Humanistic psychotherapy of the psychoses and borderline conditions. Conference convened by Chicago Counseling and Psychotherapy Center.

Watson, N. (1984). The empirical status of Rogers' hypothesis of the necessary and sufficient conditions of psychotherapy. In J. Shlien & R. Levant (Eds.), *Client-centered therapy and the person-centered approach. New directions in theory, research and practice* (pp. 17-40). New York: Praeger.

CLIENT-CENTERED THERAPY WITH MENTALLY RETARDED PERSONS: CATHERINE AND RUTH[1]

Marlis Pörtner
Zürich, Switzerland

When, some years ago, I was asked for the first time to do therapy with a mentally retarded young woman, I was very sceptical. At that time, I was just beginning to work as a client-centered therapist and I deeply doubted the possibility to work that way with mentally handicapped people. I am glad that finally I overcame all doubts and hesitations and tried. From the experience with mentally retarded clients, I learned essential things for my work as a client-centered therapist.

The following examples are just two individual cases but they show how client-centered therapy with mentally retarded persons is possible and can be helpful. I will give a short summary of the therapy with Catherine (which had to be dropped after one and a half year because of her moving to another place) and a more detailed description of the one with Ruth with whom I worked for three years. Both women lived and worked in the same institution for mentally retarded adults. In both cases, the therapy had been suggested by staff members.

CATHERINE

She was twenty years old and considered imbecile but capable of learning practical skills. Her first years she had lived with her parents, later in an institution for children until she came to the place where she lived now. She saw her family frequently, went home for weekends and holidays. At the time we started to work together, her parents had just divorced.

Before Catherine came to the institution for adults, she had had to undergo surgery for sterilization, apparently without anybody telling her what was going to happen to her. One of the expectations of the staff members was that, in therapy, Catherine should have an opportunity to deal with that traumatic experience. Catherine's sexuality troubled her. She fell in love with each new male staff member and wanted him all to herself. She was very possessive and persistent and made it difficult for the young men to refuse her demands without being rude or hurting her. Catherine was constantly torn between unrealistic hope and deep disappointment. She was little interested in relations with her handicapped mates, or when she was, they could not cope with her possessive demands. Catherine did not feel good about her body. She treated herself very roughly, sometimes hit and scratched herself. Another problem for the staff was her periodical stealing.

I soon realized that I had to be careful not to let myself be pushed by all the expectations from the staff, but to work with just what came from Catherine herself. I thought that it would not be possible for her just to talk, so for the first session I took a lot of material with me: Color pencils, paper, pictures to look at - but fortunately also my tape-recorder.

To my surprise we did not need any of the material - except for the tape-recorder. Catherine talked and talked for the whole hour. Jumping abruptly from one level to another, she recounted what had happened to her during the week, referred to something she actually perceived in the room or outside the window or fantasized. It was not easy to follow her abrupt changes of times and levels, but I tried to take everything she said as her subjective reality, exactly as I would have done with "normal" clients.

From the beginning, I had a good relationship with her. Catherine liked the therapy hours which always took place in a similar way. Once or twice she wanted to listen to the tape and once she brought her own tape-recorder and made a tape of our conversation. Sometimes she got very angry about something that had happened in the institution and, for a certain time, she was angry at her father whose leaving from home deeply bothered her.

I did not care if what she told me was real or fantasy or even a lie, and I felt that this helped her to trust me more and more. But I was not at all sure if I was on the right track. Was I not pushing her even more into her fantasies? And was there any change with her at all? I could not tell from the therapy hours.

An interview with the staff reassured me: They had noticed several changes in Catherine's behavior. She related more to reality and withdrew less into her fantasies. Additionally, she was not angry in an excessive way. Obviously she was capable of using the therapy hour as a space for fantasies and the expression of strong feelings; consequently, she did not need to live them out quite as frequently in the institution. For a certain time, she even stopped stealing, but this did not last. I was most impressed by what they told me about Catherine's altered attitude towards her body: She now enjoyed taking long baths and washing carefully and tenderly whereas before she used to do this in a quick, rough and careless way.

Catherine fantasized very frequently about accidents, the police, ambulance, and hospitals. She often said that she had to go and help the doctor hold a patient or that the nurse had called her to come and help. Sometimes she told me that she had been at the hospital the day before or that she had to go there in the afternoon to have something done to her. Slowly, I realized that beneath all this confusion of hospital fantasies was hidden the real memory of the traumatic experience of her sterilization. Piece by piece, fragments of the memory emerged: How the nurse had held her hand in the elevator, how she had been "put to sleep," how she woke up in a hospital room and a doctor had been at her bedside, and how they "took something out of me down there." What I am telling here in a few words took many therapy hours to emerge, element by element in tiny fragments.

And then, each time, Catherine quickly changed the subject. It was impossible to concentrate for a while on one of those details. Obviously this was the way and the rhythm in which she could bear to approach this painful memory.

I had the feeling that something very important had started for Catherine and was very sorry that she had to move soon to another institution where the therapy was not possible anymore. I had not seen Catherine for eighteen months when, one evening, I got a phone call: Catherine. She laughed and seemed utterly pleased to have got me on the phone. A staff member explained to me afterwards that for many days she had been insisting on calling the number which she had on a little card among her belongings. As they did not know what it was all about, nobody paid any attention to it, but Catherine persisted until they let her call.

I went to see her on the following weekend. She seemed to be happy and to like the new place. But obviously, Catherine wanted to take up the therapy sessions again: She picked up the conversation exactly where we had left it eighteen months ago. Again and again, she told the people around us: "This is Marlis, with whom I used to talk about what is the matter with me." Unfortunately there was no possibility to continue the therapy.

RUTH

Ruth was twenty-four, mongoloid, and had lived in institutions since her early childhood. She never had any contact with her family. Her mother refused to see her though she lived nearby.

Ruth was isolated among the other handicapped, who did not like her. She clung to the staff members and required a large amount of their time. This was a burden for the persons in charge and it increased Ruth's isolation from her mates.

Ruth's situation was more difficult as she had - unlike the other handicapped in her group - no relatives who cared about her. When everybody else went home for the weekend, she had no place to go. A few times a woman from the neighborhood invited her to her house, but it turned out that this was mainly to have her help with the housework. Sometimes Ruth spent a weekend or a few days at a children's home where she had lived as a child. There too she had to do housework. But somehow she considered this place as her home. For as long as the people who knew her could remember, Ruth was always doing the same drawing: A house with a tree on each side.

In the beginning, Ruth's therapy hours always had the same pattern: She gave me a detailed report of her day beginning with how she got up in the morning until she went to sleep at night. When she was through, she started again at the beginning and repeated this many times in a very compulsive way. When she had had enough, she said "all" and wanted to go. I asked her if she wanted to come again next week, and she always said "yes."

Ruth was rather handicapped in speaking and difficult to understand, so I used to repeat carefully what I had heard her say, to make sure I got her right. She enjoyed this "reflecting." Later, when I omitted it sometimes because I was now more familiar with her language, she repeated her sentence again and again until I in turn repeated it. Then she was satisfied and went on. Obviously this form of communication reassured her that she was making herself understood. Because of her speech impediment, this was not at all granted. Very frequently, people who did not know her or did not have the patience just said "yes, yes," without understanding what she wanted to say. This added to her isolation.

It was not always easy for me to listen patiently to her minute report. She enumerated endlessly fact after fact and it was hard to guess what all this meant to her. When once in a while I tried to verbalize a feeling, she did not pay any attention to me and just repeated the fact she had just told me.

She obviously liked me. She asked me about my family, begged to be taken to my home, offered to "help cooking." At that time, I was often not at all sure if a therapy was what Ruth really needed. Would it not be much better to take her home from time to time and to take care of her in another way? I considered it seriously.

The day came when I began to trust the therapy. I had been away for a week and Ruth had not had her therapy hour. When I came back she told me that she had been "homesick" and angry at me. She could express her anxiety that I would never come back anymore and also talk about how it had often happened that people she cared for disappeared for good. During this session, we also agreed on something like a contract concerning our relation. She told me again and again that she did not want me to go away anymore, that I had to take her with me for the summer holidays. And I explained her as many times that I would sometimes be away, that I could not take her with me, but that I would always come back again, always on a Thursday for one hour. After a long while, she all at once stretched out her hand and said: "O.K." Then she nestled against me and said: "You are so kind." Obviously she accepted the - limited - kind of relation I could offer her. From then on, it was no problem for her when an hour had to be dropped or when I was away for holidays.

This did not mean that from now on the sessions had ceased to follow the old pattern. For the first time another possibility to express herself had emerged in Ruth, but it soon disappeared again behind the usual patterns. But it was there, it reappeared and disappeared again many times, and each time it grew a little bit more. But for many many hours there was just the usual stereotyped reporting of facts. In the meantime, there had been major changes concerning the working conditions in the institution, changes which at first caused a lot of insecurity and trouble among the handicapped people. This also showed in Ruth's therapy sessions. She was aggressive and blamed the others violently, especially Catherine, whose hour at eight thirty she claimed for herself. She was obviously jealous. When Catherine had to move away, Ruth was very content.

Sometimes I had a hard time bearing Ruth's endless scolding and it was not always easy to be empathic. When from time to time I made a rather helpless attempt to reflect her anger, Ruth did not pay any attention to it and started anew to tell me what the persons who so much irritated her had done and what was wrong with them and how they should do better and that it was "their own fault." But once in a while, when I was able to understand how she was feeling at that moment and express this to her, her face would become all radiant and she would say: "Exactly." After that she was able to change the subject.

So it suddenly occurred to me that her scolding did not mean just anger but that she also deeply enjoyed it. Ruth considered herself more and more as a grown-up person, and being grown-up to her meant to be obeyed. That was how she had experienced adults when she was a child: She had to obey them. Now she wanted to be the one who set the rules for the group. She had very specific ideas of how everything should be done and got very angry when the others did not agree. Of course, this did not help her to become more popular among her mates.

During the therapy hour, Ruth sometimes asked for pencils and did one of her usual drawings of the house with the two trees. One day there was a surprise: After not having done so for quite a while, she asked for pencils and began to draw, not the well-known house, but a boat on a lake and a bus. (The group had been on a excursion on Sunday.) She was very excited and repeated again and again: "This is great, this is really great." She paid no attention to my remark that now for the first time she had drawn something different than a house and trees. But after that she sometimes told me what drawings she had done during the week. For a while it was elephants, later other animals.

When Ruth had difficulties with somebody she now sometimes suggested to have "a meeting" together with that person and me. She seemed to trust the kind of conversation we had together. Once we arranged such a meeting. In the meantime, a family in the neighborhood invited Ruth from time to time to their house. But soon things went wrong. Ruth, in her usual compulsive way, told the children what they had to do. Of course they did not like that and began to oppose to Ruth's visits. It was a stressful situation for Mrs. B. As Ruth had suggested, we invited her to talk it over with Ruth, two staff members and myself. I was deeply impressed to see how Ruth tried to convince Mrs. B. that she would not "shout at the children" anymore. This was an important step for Ruth: To recognize that *she* had been wrong and not just the others, and to do something to improve the situation. Unfortunately this did not have the success we wished for her so much. The B. family avoided further contact with Ruth. So this time she was not reinforced in what she had learned.

Ruth seemed to use the therapy sessions more and more as an outlet for her anger. After scolding for a while, she took a deep breath and relaxed. When I said: "Now you feel better after having said all this," she answered: "Yes." The staff reported that Ruth was fairly balanced at home as well as at work.

During that time, she sometimes fantasized about her brother or her mother having come to see her, and sometimes memories of her childhood emerged. At least - after my experience with Catherine - I supposed that these were memories and not fantasies.

The children's institution which Ruth somehow considered her home was to be closed down. Ruth was upset. She said she would "go to the bank and buy the house." She was deeply worried where to spend Christmas. During those weeks she started again to ask me if I would take her to my home, but she did not insist like she used to at the beginning.

Fortunately M., another woman in the neighborhood, now, took care of Ruth from time to time. Soon Ruth told me that she had been "home with M." over the weekend. And she accepted without difficulty when M. went away for some weeks and she could not see her. I suppose that her experience with the limited but steady therapeutic relation helped her not to panic about M. leaving her for good.

For a longer period of time, Ruth was concerned with issues like "I want my peace," "I want to be left alone," especially when she did not feel well physically. Then she was irritated with the people around her, although it seemed to me that she did not hold others responsible for how she was feeling quite so often.

Towards the end of the second year of therapy, Ruth said more and more frequently: "I am happy and content" and she appeared quite relaxed. Although she still got annoyed about things happening at work or at the home, it took her less time to overcome it. Sometimes she could even tell how she felt about it and not just blame the others. When shortly before Christmas one of the handicapped men broke the television set, Ruth first scolded in her usual way and then all at once said: "A was sad and B was sad and ..." she enumerated all the people living or working at the group one after the other. When I added: "Everybody was sad and you were sad too," she took a deep breath and said: "Exactly."

I slowly began to think about ending the therapy, although I could not yet figure out how Ruth would take it. The staff felt that Ruth had made considerable progress in these two years. She did not "stick" to them so much anymore but was able to do things by herself. It was amazing how subtly she could express how she was feeling. For instance, she said: "I am a little sad," or even (after somebody died whom she did not like too much): "I am half sad and half pleased," which I think is quite remarkable considering how difficult it is for many "normal" people to be aware of and to accept contradictory feelings, and how in the beginning Ruth could not tell how she was feeling at all. Ruth's position in the group remained difficult. She still considered herself as a staff member and continued to order the others around. There was no visible change in this.

We thought it important that Ruth should not again loose what she had learned, so we decided to continue with the therapy, but in a different setting. As I had to work once a week anyway at the institution, Ruth should have the opportunity to decide for herself every week if she wanted her hour or not. For another year she came every week. Sometimes she just told me briefly how she was. Sometimes, when something bothered her, she required the whole hour. Once in a while she had one of her familiar violent scolding attacks. But very often when there was trouble in the group, she said: "They should not shout so much" or "they have to talk decently like grown-ups." Sometimes she suggested that the others should have "a meeting" with me. She considered obviously this way of talking together as a possibility to deal with conflicts.

The time came when our sessions did not last longer than twenty minutes, and somehow our relation had changed. Ruth still liked me very much and was always pleased to see me, but I was more and more convinced that now she would be able to deal with the termination of our therapy sessions.

The staff had noticed some more changes during that year. Ruth appeared more adult, more serious. She could express herself much better. Even her relations within the group had improved. My opinion was that Ruth did not need therapy anymore, but that the further development of what she had learned should happen in her daily environment. We agreed to end the therapy, not abruptly but in several steps. Ruth was told that she could ask to have her therapy sessions again anytime she wanted to. But she did not. She accepted that the therapy was over.

SOME CONCLUSIONS

What I have described here where the "highlights" when changes became visible. But there were also the long monotonous hours when nothing seemed to move, when I was troubled by doubts and sometimes got bored and had enough. Looking back I am sure that for Ruth something went on at those times, something I did not then perceive. This does not happen only with mentally retarded persons, but from them I learned to take it more patiently when at times "nothing happens" in therapy. Very often it later turned out that I just could not see what was going on at the moment. It seems to me that for Ruth the therapy simultaneously changed many and few things. Of course she will always need help from others. There will be very few things in her life she can decide for herself. She will never lose her compulsive behavior and it will still get her into trouble with other people. But within her limitations, she succeeded in widening her margins, in discovering new possibilities of reacting and, through this in improving somewhat the quality of her everyday life. I think that this is crucial and was worth the long and hard effort.

To become more aware of their internal and external possibilities, to learn to use them better and - if possible - to enlarge them, is one of the main goals in working with mentally retarded individuals. Considering its theoretical background, the client-centered/person-centered approach appears very appropriate for this goal, not only in terms of psychotherapy but also in terms of training people who work with mentally retarded persons. As it is extremely difficult to enter the inner world of mentally retarded persons "as if I were the other" (Rogers), it is all the more meaningful. Mentally handicapped persons do not often experience that they are understood, and this makes them withdraw more and more into their inner world and increases their isolation. With Ruth, changes became possible at times when I succeeded in understanding her inner world and in expressing that to her. It then seemed as if the veil of the mental handicap would tear open for a short moment.

Perhaps it cannot really be called self-exploration. Nevertheless, the long patient effort of empathy and understanding as well for Catherine (with whom this process just started) as for Ruth, changed their self-perception. They could not verbalize these changes - or at best in some kind of code - but they became visible in their behavior. Therefore the bi-annual interviews with the staff members were helpful and indispensable. Only through what they observed and reported did I become aware of the progress of the therapy. This is different from therapies with "normal" clients.

I also gave supervision to the staff. Many times I was amazed how clearly the tensions and conflicts within the institution were reflected in Ruth's therapy hours - of course again in a coded manner. As sensitive as a seismograph, she registered what was "in the air." By the way, no client gave me such striking feedback as Ruth when I happened to be temporarily distracted during a therapy session.

We learned from each other. By working with Catherine and Ruth I got - like through a magnifying glass - essential insights for my work as a client-centered therapist.

IMPLICATIONS ON MY WORK AS A THERAPIST

Experiencing the effects of client-centered therapy with mentally handicapped individuals consolidated my confidence in this therapeutic approach and in my daily work with other clients. To rely on the resources of the clients, to accompany them patiently in their rhythm, to put aside one's own conceptions, to trust the process is fundamental for a client-centered therapist. But it is not always easy to do: Often there are doubts about the efficacy of these apparently simple conditions, there is lack of patience to follow the client in his seemingly endless detours. The mentally handicapped clients impressively demonstrated for me how important it is to stay with these basic conditions.

Furthermore this work brought me some other insights that were not really new; but what happened was that I experienced them deeply and that they became crucial for me:

- Big break-throughs are not essential, but the *small steps* which the client is capable of integrating.

- Only a few changes happen during therapy sessions. The client makes the most important strides *outside the therapy environment.*

- The *interaction* between what the client *learns in therapy* and what he *experiences in his life* is crucial. The most amazing changes during the therapy session are not of much use for the client if they do not help him to make new and better experiences in his everyday life.

- As a therapist *I cannot "do"* anything. I can just create a space and conditions which make it possible for the client to change.

And this I think is important not only for me. The "boom" with psychology is over. Exaggerated, nearly religious, salvation pretentions on the one hand, disappointment and withdrawal on the other, as well as a growing mistrust in psychotherapy - often based on negative experiences - require a return to more modesty, to a reconsideration of the limits and possibilities of psychotherapy. The client-centered approach is a very good foundation for this.

NOTE

1. The names are changed.

CLIENT-CENTERED PSYCHOTHERAPY WITH MENTALLY HANDICAPPED ADULTS

Isolde BADELT
Werkstätten für Behinderte, Heidelberg, F.R.Germany

INTRODUCTION

Interest for this topic came out of the experience of fourteen years of counseling and psychotherapeutic work with mentally handicapped adults in a sheltered workshop and hostel of the "Lebenshilfe". When I started working, I used the client-centered approach in counseling the mentally retarded workers, their parents and staff members. As a client-centered psychotherapist who used to work with clients in a general practice, I soon tried to transfer psychotherapy to the mentally handicapped, though at this time the public opinion (expressed by the literature and by colleagues) was that, in general, psychotherapy would be impossible for persons with mental handicaps and intellectual deficiencies. But in my work I considered it necessary and so, by trying over the years, I found a way and developed a special form of client-centered psychotherapy for mentally handicapped persons in my sheltered workshop.

SPECIAL IMPLICATIONS OF CLIENT-CENTERED PSYCHOTHERAPY WITH MENTALLY HANDICAPPED ADULTS

Characteristics of mentally retarded persons concerning self competence and communication

I first want to give a short description of the sheltered workshop where the mentally retarded persons spend their day-time. The "Lebenshilfe", which is in charge of the workshop, is a community founded thirty years ago by experts and by the parents and friends of mentally retarded persons. Soon the movement spread all over Germany. Today, the "Lebenshilfe" is in charge of nurseries, kindergartens, schools, sheltered workshops, hostels and sheltered houses and appartments for mentally retarded children and adults.

The sheltered workshop in Heidelberg has 320 mentally retarded workers between the age of 18 and 65. They are mainly mentally retarded, but often have additional handicaps such as behavior disorders, psychotic symptoms, physical and sensory handicaps, etc.

About 25% of the 320 persons live in a hostel or in sheltered houses or apartments; most of them live at home. Some of them are very severely handicapped; they need help in eating or going to the toilet or are not able to speak or sit in wheel-chairs and cannot move their arms and hands; others are only mildly handicapped with some learning disabilities.

Concerning communication, only one third of them can speak in a normal way. Many of them can express themselves in one- or two-word sentences, or in a rudimentary language. Some persons cannot speak at all, and express themselves with mimics or develop a sort of body language. Many of them use stereotypes and repeat a sentence or a story several times.

Concerning self-competence, I soon realized in my work that mentally handicapped persons often complain about not feeling very competent. They have not had enough opportunities to learn to express their feelings and wishes. Sometimes they express the meaning and thoughts of someone else, i.e. their parents and cannot find their own position, or cannot defend their own position if another person tries to convince them. They feel a lack of self-esteem and self-confidence. So they often react with behavior disturbances or psychosomatic symptoms to the unsatisfying situation in which they have to live.

The effect of the client-centered approach on the personality of the mentally handicapped

From the very beginning of my work in the sheltered workshop I tried to meet the handicapped in a client-centered way when they came to me to talk about their problems. I listened to them carefully, trying to see the world as they saw it, trying to understand the frame of their inner world and accepting and valuing them as whole persons. I also tried to be as congruent as possible and to give them room to develop their own thoughts and feelings and their own solution to their problems. Soon I realized that in such a positive climate the mentally handicapped could profit in an impressive way from the person-centered approach.

They slowly lost their fears and tried to speak about very deep and important feelings and life events. They developed confidence in their abilities and changed dramatically to having more self-competence and more self-esteem.

I was encouraged by this positive experience and so began regular therapy sessions with clients showing severe symptoms or having significant problems with their parents, colleagues or staff members. A precondition for these clients was their readiness to communicate with me. With growing experience, I managed to develop a special form of communication for every individual client; and so, being able to communicate in a real client-centered way, I found out during the therapy process that in some cases it was reasonable to continue the therapy with persons of the client's environment, i.e. parents, educators in the hostel, or group leaders in the workshop.

With the years, it appeared that person-centered therapy is a successful way to help clients develop more identity and more satisfaction in their lives and to solve their problems in a more self-competent way.

Discussion about the difference between counseling and psychotherapy and the indication of psychotherapy in this area

The clients in my workshop often come to me to discuss a certain problem, i.e. they want to change to another working group, or they have a conflict with their group leader, their parents, their colleagues, their friends or their partners. I first try to listen very carefully until I get a feel of the whole problem with all its details and have realized the significance for the client's frame of reference. I accept whatever the client says without criticizing him and try to understand his feelings and wishes. Then I ask him if he has an idea of how to solve his problem. I encourage him to develop his own way, and if he does not know enough problem-solving strategies for this special problem, I show several strategies for him to choose his individual solution. This counseling process is centered on problem-solving; and 80% of my work consists in counseling not only the mentally retarded workers but also parents and staff members.

When a client is willing and able to come regularly to therapy sessions over a longer period and is very unhappy with his whole life situation and perhaps shows this unhappiness with severe symptoms such as phobic behavior, depression, aggression, or autoaggression, then the therapy does not center only on problem-solving, but on developing more self-competence. In an accepting, positive, trustful atmosphere the client can learn new and better attitudes towards himself and towards his social environment. Because of my restricted time, this was and is only a small part of my work; but for some clients it was very important, as without this therapy they would not have been able to stay in the workshop. The only alternative way for these clients would have been the psychiatric ward in a sanatorium.

My work in the sheltered workshop leads me to become closely related to all my clients. Because of this and because of lack of time, I would prefer to send the clients to an exterior psychotherapist. However, there are no psychotherapists offering person-centered psychotherapy in Heidelberg, let alone other psychotherapies for mentally handicapped persons.

Special methods in person-centered psychotherapy with mentally handicapped persons

As I mentioned before, mentally handicapped persons often do not speak in the usual way. An example may illustrate this.

A young woman comes in my office, sits down and begins to cry.

> T: It seems to me that you are very unhappy today.
> C: (Nods with her head).
> T: You had difficulties at home?
> C: (Shakes her head).
> T: With your group leader?
> C: No.
> T: With someone in your group...
> C: Walter spoke to Maria always...
> T: Your friend Walter spoke the whole morning only to Maria and did not realize that you were there, too...
> C: Yes. (Cries louder) I'm so unhappy...
> T: It has hurt you very much, hasn't it? Walter did not seem to see you, though you like him very much...
> C: Yes, I like him...
> etc.

Compared with normal clients, it seems necessary to be more active and in some cases to translate very sensitively mimics and gestures and body language into perceived feelings and wishes. So the therapeutic access requires more verbal and non-verbal offers and more creativeness in understanding the inner process of the client.

Another special feature which has implications for the communication of mentally handicapped persons in therapy is that there are more repetitions and more stereotyped sentences and contents. So the therapist needs much more patience and sensitivity in accepting the client even if he tells the same content twenty times. But if the therapist has this patience, the client can benefit very clearly in the area of self-confidence and self-esteem.

During the therapeutic process, I often realized that my clients lacked daily problem-solving strategies. They usually did not know whom to go to for help, or how to react in a conflict. It seemed to me that in their education they had never been trained in making decisions nor in handling conflicts the way non-handicapped children are taught. Often their parents and their social environment overprotected them. Thus they learned to rely on others. In cases where it was necessary, I offered various conflict-solving methods for the particular client to choose whatever seemed most helpful to him, or we tried to find solutions through role playing.

Another aspect that has special implications in the psychotherapy with mentally handicapped persons is their restricted ability to influence their environment. When they change their behavior and become more self-confident and critical, their social environment reacts with resistance and lack of understanding, as they are no longer as easy to handle as before. So it seems to be even more important to speak with the significant persons with whom the client has a good relation. It is necessary that the mentally handicapped person is not left alone in his process, but is helped by an understanding environment.

The last special characteristic I want to emphasize is the lack of intellectual strategies in changing attitudes or in finding patterns of traits and mechanisms in their own life concept because of a deficit of intellectual abilities. Mentally handicapped persons are usually not able to abstract a pattern or a concept out from recurrent events or situations and this has implications for their ability to change "scripts", self-concepts and behavior.

In one of the case studies (Miss. C.S.), a young woman had developed an agoraphobic behavior. During the therapeutic process, I found out that since the sudden death of her father she felt very insecure and had lost trust in the world. Her inner insecurity was expressed by her symptoms: She was only able to walk if she could hold on to a wall: She could not climb stairs if there were other people around; and she could not cross an open place. If a client with normal intellectual abilities realized the connection between his symptoms and his insecurity, he would try to find a way to regain security. For my mentally handicapped client to come to this conclusion was impossible; thus *I* had to create a climate in the workshop for her to feel more secure and then be able to reduce her symptoms.

Besides all these special implications, the problems reported by the clients are the same as in a normal practice: Partner conflicts, conflicts with parents, friends and colleagues; problems with the work situation, with lack of money, sexual problems and critical life events.

It seems to me that mentally handicapped persons can benefit even more from the client-centered accepting and warm atmosphere because they very seldom feel that they are taken seriously in their needs and wishes; it is an overwhelming experience for them.

PRESENTATION OF CASE STUDIES

Case studies with single clients

A crisis intervention

Miss E., Down-syndrome, 38 years old, attempted to commit suicide by jumping from the third floor railing, but was prevented by her colleagues and brought to my office. She explained through sobbing tears that her boy-friend left her and she felt that she could not live any more.

I arranged to meet with her on a daily basis for therapeutic discussions, which she was thankful for and attended regularly. She spoke at length of her feelings of jealousy, worthlessness and confusion, and that there was nothing she enjoyed anymore. Through sympathetic understanding and acceptance of her feelings of misery in many repetitions, she was better able to accept herself. She began to see options again and shared with friends and was able to find enjoyment in living again. After four weeks of daily discussions, she was so stable that she only came once a week and after a 2-month period she no longer needed therapy.

Brigitte S. (B.S.), a young woman of 26 years, mildly mentally handicapped, accepted her life until recently, and got along well with her family and in her work place; then suddenly she began to react with severely disturbed behavior. She had aggressive rages where she threw things, would suddenly physically attack colleagues and have fits of whining for no apparent reason. Eventually, she refused to do any work and verbally abused everyone and everything around her. This became so extreme within a short period (a few weeks) that her colleagues in the work group were no longer able to cope with the situation, and it was seriously questioned whether keeping Brigitte S. was beneficial to the workshop.

Through daily therapeutic sessions it was possible to determine that Miss B.S., when experiencing the pregnancy of her sister, also developed the desire to have children. However, her parents had to inform her that she had been sterilized at the age of 16. In retrospect, she considered this to be a terrible infringement on her rights as a person, and was unable to accept it. She felt worthless and desperate. I arranged to meet with her twice weekly for therapeutic consultations and by expressing and leaving her feelings of anger, sorrow and desperation, she managed to handle her problems and found a new meaning to her life. During this time she looked for and found a partner and could reintegrate her group. During the first three months of her therapy, her symptoms disappeared completely. After nine months, she considered she was now able to manage on her own and terminated the therapy.

An example of individual therapy combined with systemic therapy

Miss C.S., a 35 year-old woman, developed agoraphobic behavior during a period of several weeks as I mentioned above. Occasionally when she was not conscious of what she was doing, she suddenly was able to walk freely; but as soon as she realized this, she tried to find the next wall and became very anxious. Even her physical state changed; she got pale, began to sweat and visibly got into panic.

After many therapy sessions, I found out that she felt very insecure and had lost trust in the whole world since her beloved father suddenly died. She felt lost and had the feeling she was not getting enough protection. It took me a long time to understand this clearly because she spoke only rarely; and when she spoke, she used two- or three-word sentences.

In the therapy sessions, I gave her room to express and live out her feelings of sadness and desperation and loneliness; in addition, I talked to her group leader. This lady believed that Miss S. could sometimes walk when she forgot about the situation. So she wanted her to control herself and gave her no help. By talking several times to the group leader about such symptoms in general and about the reasons for this phobic behavior, I managed to persuade her that she could help the client by accepting her and giving her more security. The group leader talked with the working group; and as a consequence, they all tried to help the client by giving her the feeling that she was accepted and not lost, and that she could develop a new trust in the world. Slowly, she could reduce her symptoms and felt much more satisfied with her life.

An example of family therapy

A severely handicapped young man with auto-aggressive behavior (sticking fingers in his eyes, scratching his face until it bled, bumping his head against the table) was easily integrated in the sheltered workshop and his symptoms nearly disappeared. He found a job that was interesting for him, and his autoaggressive behavior regressed continuously. However, after two years, he became more and more disturbed; his autoaggressive activities increased tremendously; he was hardly able to work and he seemed to be very nervous and deeply unhappy. Since even at home his behavioral disorders worsened dramatically, his parents came to me and asked for help.

In bimonthly therapy sessions with the whole family, during nearly one year, it appeared that the young man, when he came to the workshop first, experienced a certain success by accomplishing a good job, which improved his self-competence and independency. His parents, however, still treated him as a child and did not give him enough freedom to make his own decisions. It became more and more difficult for him to accept this discrepancy and, in his helplessness, he reacted with increasing autoaggressive behavior.

During the course of therapy, his parents learned more and more to accept their son's new independence. Finally, they even agreed to his request to move in a sheltered hostel which they eventually regarded as a relief. The symptoms slowly improved and nowadays, this young man only very rarely shows autoagressive behavior. In general, he manages his life very well.

Group Therapy

I first asked some of my clients who had problems if they wanted to meet regularly in a group. They all accepted; so group sessions with six members took place every week for one hour. At the beginning, I told them that they could say all they wanted, that all that was said should remain within the group; that all they wanted to say is important for the group.

First the group could not handle the situation; the group members looked at me and wanted me to tell them what to say; for weeks, nearly nothing was said; even if I repeated the above-cited introduction several times, only some words were spoken. So I thought that the group members could perhaps not benefit from this form of group. But when I once had to cancel a session, I found all group members standing before my door, very disappointed and urgently wanting the group session to take place; so I tried to have more patience.

Gradually, some weeks later, a surprising process began to develop; the group members began to speak about their experience of being handicapped; they talked about feelings of being worthless and not sufficient. During the next months a very powerful process led to unexpected consequences: The group members gained much more self-confidence; their global dissatisfaction changed into knowing exactly what was bad for them; so they became more critical and wanted to change the environmental conditions; i.e they wanted to have more freedom at home, to go out alone and to meet friends; in the workshop they wanted to make decisions about their work, etc. So a difficult situation arose, and I had to talk for hours and hours with parents, with angry group leaders, etc.

So I found that client-centered group therapy is a good opportunity for personality development of mentally retarded persons, but it is important that the environment tries to follow the therapeutic process; once again, it is necessary that the mentally retarded are not left alone, but helped in their therapeutic processes.

RESULTS

The client-centered psychotherapy seems to offer mentally handicapped persons a very good opportunity for personal growth and for finding new ways of dealing with problems. It has to be really "client-centered"; this means it has to be adapted individually, even more than usual, to the abilities of the mentally handicapped to communicate and to express their thoughts and feelings. General problem-solving strategies are less known than usual, because of the way mentally retarded children are educated; so it is sometimes necessary to offer more information about ways of resolving conflicts.

My experience as a therapist has also led me to realize that mentally retarded clients need more help from their environment in support of their emancipation process; first, because they are not capable of abstracting concepts from their behavior, and cannot easily draw conclusions because of their intellectual deficits; second, because they often do not have enough power to influence others. So the therapist has to talk to significant others in order to encourage them to accompany the therapeutic process.

CONCLUSIONS

It was surprising how mentally handicapped persons could benefit from the positive climate created by the person-centered approach; they changed dramatically in their self-concept, increased their self-esteem, their self-competence and were able to find their own way of living a more satisfactory life.

For the moment, it is not common to do psychotherapy with mentally handicapped persons. My experience of many years has shown that it is possible and helpful. I hope that, in the future, more psychotherapists (and especially client-centered oriented therapists) will offer their abilities and skills to this - at least to this day - neglected minority.

REFERENCES

Badelt, I. (1984). Selbsterfahrungsgruppen geistig behinderter Erwachsener. *Geistige Behinderung, 4* (Fachzeitschrift der Bundesvereinigung Lebenshilfe).

Badelt, I. (1986). Selbsterfahrungsgruppen geistig behinderter Erwachsene. In J. Walter (Ed.), *Sexualität und geistige Behinderung* (2nd ed.). Heidelberg: Edition Schindele.

Buber, M. (1983). *Ich und Du.* Heidelberg: Lambert Schneider.

Linster, H.W. (1980). *Veränderung und Entwicklung der Person.* Hamburg: Hoffmann und Campe.

Rogers, C. (1974). *Encounter Gruppen.* München: Kindler.

Rogers, C. (1977). *Therapeut und Klient.* München: Kindler.

Rogers, C. (1981). *Der neue Mensch.* Stuttgart: Klette Cotta.

REFLECTIONS ON A PERSON-CENTERED APPROACH TO MEDICINE

Wolfgang M. PFEIFFER   &   Thomas RIPKE
Universität Erlangen   Heidelberg
F.R.Germany   F.R.Germany

Among the various areas of application of the "person-centered approach," certainly medical practice is of special importance (Barnard, 1984). No doubt, it is a classical challenge of medical ethics to meet the patient on a personal level. But even in favorable cases, this attitude was of a paternalistic quality. A proof is the book of E. Liek "Der Arzt und seine Sendung" which in the days of our studies was considered particularly progressive, a book in which you will find sentences such as: "Each patient is in need of his special doctor ... to whom he submits without restraint ... Each patient even in a high position, wants to be guided" (1926, p. 39). Today, this attitude is still reflected in familiar expressions such as "patient guidance," "compliance," etc. With them the opinion is expressed that the doctor is in possession of the relevant knowledge and that he brings healing from the exterior to the patient who - as far as he understands - complies conscientiously. This is certainly an opinion in contradiction with the person-centered approach which has its foundation in the respect for the patient's autonomy and his responsibility for himself.

A profound change has been introduced by the scientific development of medicine. To be sure, we owe to this development that medicine has become an impressive structure of various sciences of universal validity and practicability (Schoene, 1980). Yet the scientific approach calls for looking at the patient objectively, taking him as an object (e.g. in diagnostics with the help of technical equipment or in surgery); consequently, it suggests a change of the personal relationship between patient and doctor into a factual one. Thus it is not difficult to imagine computers being able to determine diagnosis and therapy on the mere basis of questionnaires and laboratory results without any interpersonal contact. Accordingly, in science fiction the doctor is already replaced by the "Medimat" (Piercy, 1976) completely depriving medicine of its medical, we dare say, its human qualities.

It is precisely this onesided form of scientism which provoked discontentment in patients as well as in doctors. Above all those departments with an intensive scientific-technological orientation (such as cardiac surgery, anesthesiology, oncology) were the ones that opened up for a close cooperation with psychologists. Yet most medical practitioners feel that a division of labor leaving the physical care to the doctors and the mental care to the psychologists only can be, at best, a momentary solution. To be sure, the collaboration of psychologists in medicine is indispensable. But all the doctors' activities have to be imbued with a person-centered attitude, because we are dealing with the patient as a whole human being. Accordingly it is necessary that the doctor unites both kinds of approach (the scientific-objectifying and the person-centered approach) and that he applies both of them in his relationship with the patient. This means applying them in a wide range of situations, stretching from counseling for daily indispositions and from attending in chronic ailments to providing support in the extremities of threatened and expiring life. When we try to apply the person-centered approach in these circumstances, we will find quite a few conformities with the psychotherapeutic situation, but also marked differences.

MEDICINE AND PSYCHOTHERAPY

An important parallel to psychotherapy is our confidence in the actualizing tendency of the organism which, in the case of illness, is expressed above all in its self-healing power (Ripke, 1987). Similarly to psychotherapeutic self-exploration, it is necessary for the patient to become aware of the reactions and needs of his organism and to articulate them. Certainly, there can only be limited reliance on the organismic tendencies. Frequently, the potential for self-healing has to be activated, and the danger of self-destructive tendencies calls for corrective intervention. Think in medicine of malign tumors or auto-aggressive diseases, in psychotherapy of anorexia nervosa or addictions.

Of course, the main correspondence between client-centered therapy and person-centered medicine is to be found in the basic attitudes, the Rogerian triad. But in medicine we have to pay attention to several peculiarities:

The demand *to be real* means that the doctor must neither become a mere functionary of the institution nor a mere agent of the patient. In order to prove as a real partner in the dialogue with the patient, it is necessary that he responds to the whole situation both with his professional skills and with his individuality, that he is available to the patient as a person. Yet there are limitations: The individual characteristics, the private circumstances of the doctor remain in the background and his professional role retains its binding quality. For it is to this role (and not so much to the private person) that the patient's confidence and his request for help are directed. Certainly, this may be a reduction of *congruence;* and that is even more valid with regard to the *transparency* of the doctor. But as much as we strive for sincerity, for transparency of our considerations and actions, we cannot possibly burden the patient with all the considerations and apprehensions welling up during the examination.

It is the basic attitude of *caring* which demands that we must not anguish the patient more than necessary and that we must not deprive him of hope. It also asks that we accept the patient on *his* level and do not reproach him (e.g. with regard to his lifestyle) nor that we employ therapy as a kind of punishment (e.g. by means of diet prescriptions). But there are ethical limits to tolerance; they are reached when the patient's conduct becomes destructive for himself or his environment, or when it comes into conflict with other social or ethical obligations of the doctor. Especially, we have to recognize the discrepancy between the patient's inclination for denial (which we have basically to respect) and the doctor's obligation to inform the patient for the sake of further treatment. It are precisely such conflicts that lend dynamics to the dialogue.

The attitude of *empathy* means the attempt to see the ailment, the diagnostic and therapeutic activities through the eyes of the patient and to look for the personal meaning even in conceptions which may seem abstruse. Empathy assumes a very special quality when we strive to comprehend altered bodily sensations and motor processes by a kind of tentative identification with the patient. If the doctor has already had similar experiences with illness, it will be much easier for him to empathize. But we have to realize how limited the possibilities are for empathizing with pathologically altered experiences. It is again the attitude of caring, the willingness to give support - even when unable to understand - which here claims priority among the basic attitudes. (I here point to the very understanding remarks of John Wood in his discussion with Carl Rogers in: Rogers & Wood, 1974).

EXCHANGE OF INFORMATION

By using different examples from the medical practice, I am going to demonstrate how the interaction between patient and doctor presents itself as a dialogue when the Rogerian principles are applied. To begin with, we will pay attention to the exchange of information (Pfeiffer, 1983). Seen from a traditional viewpoint, the doctor appears to play the active and initiative-taking role both when taking down the case history and the complaints and when informing the patient of the diagnosis and of possible therapeutic measures. The patient, on the other hand, appears to be the one who is merely reacting and accepting. This is a distribution of activities which is unsuitable as the basis for a cooperative relationship. In our opinion, it is necessary that doctor and patient meet as equal partners of the interaction from the very beginning. Of course, they are in quite different positions, but due to the mutual expectations and to the requirements of the situation, they complement each other.

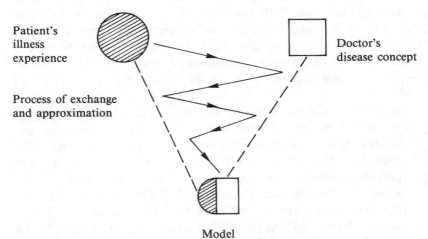

Patient's illness experience

Doctor's disease concept

Process of exchange and approximation

Model
Negotiation towards consensus on diagnosis
and therapy. (Adapted from Pfeiffer, 1983.)

At first the patient introduces the subjective experience of his suffering. It is characterized by his vital affliction and the emotional evaluation of the disturbance, by the biographical and the social context of the pathological process. This is indicated in the model by a hachured circle as going against the doctor's scientific disease-concept, represented here by a white square. The latter is detached from the individual case. It is factual and organ-centered, rather like the manner in which it is presented in scientific literature.

Initiated by the patient, a process of interchange and approximation begins which we term with Newcomb (1953, p. 393) "coorientation." In the course of this, the patient's experience of suffering turns into an objective matter of fact, he becomes more detached, which enables him to face and to contemplate his suffering and to form an intellectual concept of it. On the other hand, the scientific-abstract concept of the doctor is adapted to this particular patient: To the specific pecularities of his organism, to this concrete individual in his social entanglement. In this way, the doctor also becomes personally and emotionally involved.

In this part of the conversation, the main topic is the patient's altered state of bodily feelings. They are brought in correlation to the doctor's disease-concept by transformation into "symptoms".

By the very fact of diagnosing (labelling), the altered state of health is taken out of the muteness of private suffering and is transferred into the sphere of verbal communication and of the medical system. This takes away much of its threatening quality, corresponding to the "Rumpelstiltskin-principle" (Torrey, 1972, p. 15 ff), according to which the demon loses its power when called by its name. But there is more to it. When diagnostically classified, the pathological process becomes accessible for therapy in accordance with the rules of medical practice; moreover the requirements for social relief are fulfilled. Thus, medical diagnosis is an indispensable basis for joint therapeutic and social action ("cooperation"). But it can only have a solid foundation on today's circumstances if the diagnosis is not imposed on the patient from outside as something alien to him but if it has developed from the reciprocal activity of "coorientation," convincing and binding on both sides. In other words: It must represent a "consensus". By the term "consensus," we do not mean total conformity of opinion. Even if doctor and patient use the same term to name the illness, it represents qualitatively different things and has different connotations for both of them. This results from the different background of experiences and of personal affliction. It is neither possible nor desirable to remove these differences (their persistance is also indicated in the model); for it takes precisely this difference for the patient and the doctor to continue stimulating and complementing each other, in accordance with their complementary position in the therapeutic process. We will call this form of relationship "coexistence".

PHYSICAL EXAMINATION

Even the physical examination - in other words, the process in which the patient completely appears to be the object of medical action and observation - takes on the quality of a dialogue when the person-centered approach is applied (Ripke, 1987). Physical interaction begins during the first few moments of contact, it is already at this point that patient and doctor exchange important information, be it in an elementary, largely nonverbal way. The patient may indicate his apprehension and his demand for help by his movements, his bearing, and his facial expressions. In a similar way, the doctor indicates his readiness to have a personal relationship or his need for distance, e.g. by taking the patient into the consulting room himself or by flashing a number, by taking up physical contact or avoiding it. And each partner in the exchange responds by his conduct to the offer made by the other. Thus, these first moments of the interaction become the very foundations for the future relationship. In the consulting room the relationship of doctor and patient is entirely staged; the seating arrangement and the form of the conversation may stress the asymmetrical quality of the situation or mitigate it.

The actual examination of the body causes a vital closeness which is a characteristic of the medical occupations. It is precisely this characteristic which makes it necessary to analyze the situation in terms of the person-centered aspect. The patient must not become the mere object of a schematic course of examination; on the contrary it is necessary to give him enough freedom to be a comprehending and contributing partner also in the process of examination, which - in a way similar to what we have shown for the conversation - is determined as much by the needs and anticipations of the patient as by the factual interests of the doctor.

In contrast to a widespread opinion (so Morgan & Engel, 1977, p. 9), we feel that the role of the doctor does not include permission to implement the examination on his discretion only. The patient may request a mere verbal consultation or he may first want to prepare himself for the physical examination. Accordingly we consider it appropriate for the doctor to make sure of the patient's consent at each new stage in the examination and to choose the course according to the patient's needs. This may mean that the doctor begins with the aching parts or, on the contrary, that he begins with a neutral part and will only gradually approach the area protected by fear or shame. Such a procedure has to do with the growth of trust and the overcoming of timidity. This is apparent in the dialogue in which the patient's contribution is not so much verbal as manifested in facial expression, in muscular tension, or in the change of respiration. When informed about each step of the examination and its results, the patient becomes a contributing partner; he may even actively participate in the examination, e.g. feeling himself the defensive tension of the abdominal wall or a lump in the breast. This way, the patient turns from an object into a subject of examination, and this changes his relationship with his body. In a comparable manner to psychological selfexploration, he gains the freedom either to face the state of his body from the distant position of the observer or to live it out in a more or less conscious way (cf. Rogers, 1967, p. 188). Nonetheless, there certainly are limits to information we should give and thus to the discourse; we must always consider the adequacy of our communication. This does not only apply to the objective results but particularly to the feelings connected with the situation. The doctor may have different feelings of affinity, ranging from tender compassion to sexual attraction, or feelings of aversion, e.g. towards a highly neglected body or towards malodorous secretions. As in psychotherapy, the striving for congruence demands that one is aware of such impulses; yet after that, the doctor will put them aside, so that the patient does not perceive them. In order to feel free to undress, the patient must be able to trust that this will cause neither extremely positive nor extremely negative feelings in the doctor (Spital-Frenking, 1986, p. 110 ff); or that at least a demeanor of unemotional detachment is maintained. Correspondingly, the doctor must consider to what extent it is appropriate to voice his feelings of apprehension and helplessness in the given situation (Ripke, 1987, p. 191 ff).

On the other hand, the doctor should also be aware of the feelings evoked in the patient during physical contact, e.g. fear or shame. We have to respect them and to let them direct our actions. But again we are faced with the question of whether it is appropriate to mention them. In doing so, a sense of shame could turn into complete embarrassment and fear is often reinforced by verbalization. But if apprehensions are justified, it is often necessary to accept them and to work them through.

PLANNING OF THERAPY

The third topic we want to touch upon is the planning of therapy. Here again, the dynamics of the dialogue result from the tension between the positions of the patient and the doctor. It may be even more pronounced, because the doctor tends to associate a certain therapeutic procedure to a certain diagnosis, whereas the patient often has set ideas of what may be beneficial or damaging to him - opinions rooted in his biography (childhood, former diseases) and in his social environment (neighborhood, media).

Here again we have to take into consideration the asymmetrical quality of the positions: The doctor holds the position of the expert, which is officially recognized, supported and formulated by science and public health. The patient's position, however, is that of the layman, thus it lacks official recognition and his opinions are difficult to formulate. Therefore, in many cases the patient does not dare to express his view and in particular his objections to the doctor's prescriptions. A pseudo-consensus is the consequence and this leads to lack of cooperation and to "non-compliance". To avoid such misguided developments, it is necessary to encourage the patient to express his opinions. A mere facial signal (the frowning of an eyebrow) should be enough to frankly discuss the dissent and to give the patient support in formulating his view. Very often, it is only then that the patient's expectations and misgivings become evident to himself; then the way will be open for a frank exchange, for the "negotiation" of the therapeutic schedule.

If one has the basis of a stable consensus concerning diagnosis, it is usually not difficult either to reach consensus on the therapeutic procedure. But we have to be aware that here also such a consensus does not mean complete conformity: The positions and concepts of patient and doctor are genuinely distinct and so the consensus has to be reconsidered again and again.

Thus, in many cases we will recognize different opinions with regard to the right course of therapy. In this case, it is of special importance that the doctor takes the patient's opinions seriously and tries to explore the intrinsic meaning of the patient's concern. It may be that even behind seemingly eccentric intentions an elementary knowledge is to be found, e.g. of needs and reactions of the organism. Furthermore, the doctor has to reconsider his own conceptions: To what extent are his prescriptions based on real necessities or - as is often true - rather on speculations and habits. Through such differentiations, we can approximate a solution which will more or less do justice to both points of view. The solution may be simply tolerating the other's opinions with no mutual exclusion. But it may also result in the creative synthesis of a novel therapeutic approach.

We rarely meet real incompatibility. A specific case is that of the patient who insists on maintaining self-destructive behavior (e.g. drug abuse) or who rejects measures of vital importance. In this case, we have to examine how far the patient is able to assess the consequences of his behavior and to accept responsibility for it. If he is responsible, we certainly have to respect his decisions and, in many cases, we shall be able - in spite of our misgivings - to carry on with the medical care.

If the capability for responsible self-determination is not given, then it may be necessary to take steps in contradiction to the patient's will (e.g. hospitalization of a suicidal psychotic).

The problem presents itself differently when the patient makes demands that the doctor cannot answer, e.g. for continuous and progressive prescriptions of analgesic and sedative drugs, or for an excessively prolonged medical certificate. In this case also we should strive to maintain the dialogue. The earlier and the more clearly the doctor demonstrates the limits of his possibilities, the more the patient will understand the doctor's attitude and respect those limits (Ripke, in preparation).

SOME CONCLUSIONS AND PERSPECTIVES

In the present discussion, we were only able to characterize the interaction of patient and doctor in several areas and in a rather general way. In many areas, there still is a total shortage of relevant studies. The difficulty is still increased by the fact that most psychological methods (e.g. counting specified linguistic components or rating random sections) are not appropriate for the aim, because they look at the partners separately (which makes the interaction invisible) or they fragment the course of the dialogue. Therefore, we expect more from the methods of discourse-analysis which describe and analyze typical situations by means of recordings and transcriptions. But we consider it desirable to supplement the verbal exchange by taking into consideration the aspects of the situation and by adding interviews with the dialogue-partners, one possibility being the method of "process-recall" which involves reinspection of the recordings (Kagan, 1977). Several corresponding studies are already available, e.g. analyses of dental dialogues (Süssmann, 1986), of medical dialogues with labor migrants (Eser, 1985), of dialogues in general practice (Pfeiffer, 1983; Rellecke & Pfeiffer, 1985).

Yet, all these studies deal with discourses held in a traditional manner. Compared with this, current studies of Ripke (in preparation) are of special interest because they try to analyze discourses of a person-centered quality under a person-centered point of view. Of course, these efforts are but first steps into an area where a wide range of problems is awaiting research.

Another point to be taken into consideration is that viewing the doctor-patient relationship as isolated is an abstraction from reality. The activities of the doctor cover only a limited sector of the total of medical care. In hospitals as well as in long term home treatment, the more intimate and longlasting contacts lie in the relationship with nurses and other medical occupations, such as psychotherapists, social workers etc. The person-centered approach will only be translated into the reality of medical practice if it is supported by the members of all these occupations (Pfeiffer, 1986, p. 7). As a consequence, it is urgent that the Rogers-oriented associations pay attention to these occupational groups much more than they have done in the past, and it is imperative that doctors and all the other occupational groups who are active in medical care, strive for coordination of their efforts.

In a corresponding way, the patient is part of his social context: His family, his neighborhood, his business. Thus, the person seeking help does not come for consultation as a single individual. In an invisible way, all the members of his social context are also present in the apparently dyadic situation of the practice. Therefore, in many cases it is necessary to include in reality his relations and the members of his professional life. Consensus and cooperation which are restricted to doctor and patient may, ultimately, not be sufficient; the situation calls for consensus and cooperation of wider circles involved.

We hope that from all this it is evident that the person-centered approach can be crucial for the manner in which medical practice is conducted. As a conclusion, let us now switch perspectives and ask what medical practice can contribute to psychotherapy. Here we want to stress one point only. For us, there is an experience of great importance: That human freedom - the basis and target of client-centered therapy - is limited in several respects (see Wijngaarden, 1984). Man as a natural being is subject to the causality of biological processes; his organism in its fragility is prey to the laws of nature, but the freedom of man originates precisely from this bondage. There are still other restrictions: We are limited by society, without which we cannot exist. And there is also a level from which we are given to ourselves and taken away. We would call it - in Kant's and Jaspers' sense - "transcendence".

We realize these limitations of human freedom especially when confronted with chronic diseases such as a process of dementia, which destroys the mental faculties and with them the autonomy of the individual, or illnesses which cause physical destitution, as in the case of destructive somatic diseases. It would seem unwise and presumptuous if we tried to "heal" those cases with the help of psychotherapy. The task of medical or psychotherapeutic intervention is more modest, yet it is great precisely in this modesty: To help the patient live through his suffering and actualize his limited freedom, even to extend it.

But the above-mentioned cases (dementia, destructive processes) are extreme examples. In fact, in medical practice as well as in psychotherapy, we are permanently confronted with the finiteness and fragility of human existence and we ourselves - the therapists - are afflicted in a similar way as our patients and so are solidary fellows. This understanding addresses us in various ways. The knowledge of causal dependencies calls for the therapist as an expert. Hence it is our duty to do medical diagnostics, to give advice, to encourage, and to warn. But on the basis of our human solidarity, we are called upon - all the more as therapists - to stand by the suffering person also in a caring way:

- By offering support and encouragement against his resignation and despair;
- By giving structure if the patient is in confusion;
- By taking responsibility if the patient is not able to take responsibility for himself anymore.

Thus in medical practice as well as in psychotherapy, we attend to the patient as experts and at the same time as solidary fellow human beings. No doubt, in the first place we are the patient's personal proxies. But there are limits to our obligation to his intentions, because we are also indebted to society and to life in general. Here we bear in mind not only the physical functioning of the patient but also his human existence, which is put to the ultimate proof when it is threatened by serious illness or stands under the expectation of death.

In this context, we anticipate the objections of our psychologist colleagues, and this is also our own misgiving: Is it not precisely the doctor's claim to care for the patient, to take responsibility, to intercede for life, what restricts the patient's autonomy and incapacitates him? It is necessary that we recognize this danger and take it very seriously. In fact, we are subjected to tension arising from contradictory demands: Caring, intervening for the suffering person and respecting his autonomy. Yet this antagonism dissolves and becomes productive when turned into a dialogue, with patient and therapist face to face in different positions but as equal and communicating partners. In this way, content, form and aims of the interaction are not determined from one side, but therapy develops from the relationship of two real persons as something novel and unique. And this holds true for medical practice and for psychotherapy in similar ways.

REFERENCES

Barnard, D. (1984). The personal meaning of illness: Client-centered dimensions of medicine and health care. In R.F. Levant & J. Shlien (Eds.), *Client-centered therapy and the person-centered approach* (pp. 337-351). New York: Praeger.

Eser, U. (1985). *Symptompräsentation und Krankheitsverhalten bei türkischen und deutschen Patienten.* Unpublished Dissertation, Universität Münster.

Kagan, N. (1977). *Interpersonal process recall.* East Lansing, MI: Michigan State University, Department of Psychiatry.

Liek, E. (1926). *Der Arzt und seine Sendung.* München: Lehmann.

Morgan, L.W., & Engel, G.L. (1977). *Der klinische Zugang zum Patienten.* Bern: Huber.

Newcomb, T.M. (1953). An approach to the study of communicative acts. *Psychological Review, 60,* 306-322.

Pfeiffer, W.M. (1983). Konsens als Grundlage therapeutischen Handelns. *Zeitschrift für Personenzentrierte Psychologie und Psychotherapie, 2,* 306-322.

Pfeiffer, W.M. (1986a). Ist das Rogers'sche Persönlichkeits- und Therapiekonzept in Hinblick auf psychiatrische Erkrankungen angemessen? *Zeitschrift für Personenzentrierte Psychologie und Psychotherapie, 5,* 367-377.

Pfeiffer, W.M. (1986b). *Psychologie des kranken Menschen.* Stuttgart: Kohlhammer.

Piercy, M. (1976). *Women on the edge of time.* New York: Knopf.

Rellecke, E.-M., & Pfeiffer, W.M. (1985). Analyse und Interpretation eines Gesprächs aus der ärztlichen Allgemeinpraxis unter patientenorientierter Perspektive. *GwG-Info,* No 159, 151-167.

Ripke, Th. (1983). Erfahrungen mit der Gesprächspsychotherapie als Allgemeinarzt. *Zeitschrift für Personenzentrierte Psychologie und Psychotherapie, 2,* 367-376.

Ripke, Th. (1987). Patientenorientierte körperliche Untersuchung. *Zeitschrift für Personenzentrierte Psychologie und Psychotherapie, 6,* 185-192.

Ripke, Th. (in preparation). *Der therapeutische Bereich in der medizinischen Allgemeinpraxis.*

Rogers, C.R. (1961). *On becoming a person.* Boston: Houghton Mifflin.

Rogers, C.R., & Wood, J.K. (1974). The changing theory of client-centered therapy. In A. Burton (Ed.), *Operational theories of personality* (pp. 211-258). New York: Brunner-Mazel.

Schoene, W. (1980). Alternative Medizinen und die Medizin: Zum Kontrast ihrer sozialen Funktionsweisen. *Medizin, Mensch, Gesellschaft, 5,* 226-233.

Spital-Frenking, R. (1986). *Patientenerleben während der körperlichen Untersuchung.* Unpublished Dissertation, Universität Münster.

Süssmann, S. (1986). *Das Arzt-Patient-Gespräch. Analyse von zahnärztlichen Gesprächen während Extraktionsbehandlungen.* Unpublished Dissertation, Universität Münster.

696

Torrey, E.F. (1974). *The mindgame. Witch-doctors and psychiatrists.* New York: Emerson Hall Publications.

Wijngaarden, H. (1984). Client-centered therapy: een eigen identiteit? In G. Lietaer, Ph.H. van Praag, & J.C.A.G. Swildens (Eds.), *Client-centered psychotherapie in beweging* (pp. 41-53). Leuven-Amersfoort: Acco.

CLIENT-CENTERED PSYCHOTHERAPY WITH HEART-SURGERY PATIENTS

Heinz-Jörg MEFFERT
Chirurgische Universitätsklinik Hamburg, F.R. Germany

THE PSYCHOLOGICAL IMPACT OF HEART SURGERY

In the Federal Republic of Germany in 1988, about 30.000 people underwent open-heart-surgery. Before operation, more than half of the patients report changes in their emotions and behavior, exceeding the normal range. After the operation, about 50% of the patients show psychological and psychopathological reactions, ranging from emotional disturbances to delirium (Götze, 1981). During the first week after surgery, psychiatrists diagnose so-called post-operative psychoses in 10-20% of patients. Even years after the operation about 30% - including many patients who were free of psychopathology at the time of the operation - complain of personality changes, like lability of mood, sadness, irritability, hypochondrial anxiety, sexual and marital problems. This occurs mostly in combination with heart-related physical problems, which the patients (but not the physicians) judge as threatening diseases thus documenting a striking discrepancy between subjectively experienced and objectively diagnosed complaints.

The research efforts of the past years have clearly shown, that the peri-operative reactions to heart surgery cannot be understood as signs of morphological, metabolic or psychological complications but must be considered in the context of a complex psychosomatic crisis (Speidel & Rodewald, 1980; Becker et al., 1982). From research and experience, it also became obvious that the surgery itself does not evoke any new emotions and personality traits, as often reported by the patients, but strengthens and elucidates the patients' basic personal characteristics and psychological mechanisms (Meffert et al., 1983). Furthermore, the frequency and variety of psychological reactions to cardiac surgery exceed those of all other kinds of major surgery, again throwing light on the unique psychological impact of the heart as the center of physical and psychological life.

THE FANTASY OF DEATH AND REBIRTH

This section is inspired by the findings of the American psychoanalyst Blacher (1982), who, like the author works as a member of the staff in a cardiac surgery unit. These findings are:

1. At least in the western hemisphere and culture, the heart occupies a unique position in the psychological life of man: It is not only the central organ of the body but also, historically, the seat of emotions. In literature and in colloquial use, the word "heart" more often means "love" than the organ itself.

2. The heart is the only organ that can be felt and heard, and that works in an on-off mode. If it beats one lives; if it stops beating, one dies. When the heart stops beating, it has always meant and still means death, despite todays more scientific definition of death as a zero-line in the EEG for a definite time. The heart - not the brain - is seen as the indicator of life and death.

3. The on-off quality of the heart fits with the general opinion concerning the probability of danger, namely a 50-50 chance of survival; in this case, surviving a surgery during which the heart will be stopped. This subjective point of view contrasts with objective survival rates, reaching 99% in uncomplicated bypass procedures.

The cardiac surgery patient therefore has quite a different emotional task from any other surgical patient, namely coping with his death fantasies and later in his recovering from surgery - with his ideas of rebirth and resurrection. In contrast to the general surgery patient who fears that he will die because his heart may stop, the cardiac patient agrees that his heart will be stopped and that it will be restarted again at the end of the surgery. In other words, in his view, he must accept the fact that he will be dead and then brought back to life.

This is a difficult idea to deal with and most patients try not to think of it. Not all of them succeed.

Blacher's findings are one key to understanding the patients' irrational anxiety, his fantasies of death and rebirth, psychological disorders, catastrophic reactions and long-term psychological problems, despite successful operations.

HEART OPERATION AS A LIFE-CRISIS

The nature, the frequency and the drama of all short- and long-term psychological reactions around open heart surgery can be better understood if they are considered as reactions to a serious crisis in life, during which the patient's psychological balance becomes fragile.

Therefore, crisis nearly always follows the phases described by Kübler-Ross (1977), which originally concerned the course of grieving of terminally ill people facing impending death.

1. Shock, denial and isolation

In this first phase, the patient tries to protect himself against impending death by denying this threatening fact. He uses denial as a buffer, placing it between the shocking diagnosis and himself.

2. Anger, defiance and hostility

In the second phase the patient fights against fate. This phase is characterized by rigorous emotions, aggressive impulses, anger, rage and desperation, blaming others and oneself for this blow of fate.

3. Negotiations

In this phase, the patient tries to postpone or even avoid his death. By promising to lead a better (i.e. more healthy, religious) life, he hopes that fate will pass by.

4. Depression

This phase of grief is the reaction to pain, bodily weakness, loss of self-esteem and the near death.

5. Acceptance of the fate

The final phase is characterized by an indifferent, apathic silence; it is not a state of happiness, but it is mostly free of emotions.

Neither all terminally ill nor all heart surgery patients follow this pattern nor this course. The main difference between the two patient groups is that the terminally ill will die in true fact, whereas the heart patients die in their fantasy, but go on living in reality.

CRISIS AND CHANCE

In a crisis, something always comes to an end; something gets lost. Crises hurt because they bear the potential loss of man's inner and outer stability, i.e. thorough convictions, confirmed recognitions, family and intimate friends, familiar surroundings. But fundamentally, crises do not only bear pain, loss and fears, but also the chance of healing, developing and being safe in the future. In contrast to the terminally ill patient whose final and only chance is to come to an inner acceptance of the unavoidable death, the heart patient gets a second chance to live a more healthy and better life.

On his way through the course of the crisis another phase opens to him: That of a new start, new psychological identity, discovering new values in life. Rebirth (starting life anew like a newborn child) and resurrection (having another chance in the old surroundings) represent the patients concepts of this phase. The numerous short-term and long-term psychological problems following cardiac surgery, clearly show that the ideas of a new life does not guarantee the end of the crisis nor its successful current and future management.

Western culture has never established a positive, accepting attitude towards crises and therefore has never taught how to manage them successfully. Furthermore, there is in general only little sympathy with people who suffer from psychological problems, especially following successful medical treatment. Neither relatives and friends nor patients themselves understand and accept this mental crisis. The consequence is that the patients fight a lonely battle against their problems, their minds and their surroundings.

PERI-OPERATIVE PSYCHOTHERAPY:
BASIC ASSUMPTIONS AND CASE STUDIES

The description of the psychological impact of heart surgery, the frequency and nature of psychological reactions and fantasies, the course of the patients' crises and their often unsuccessful self-defence and self-help should have opened one's mind to psychotherapeutical considerations.

Client-centered psychotherapy, in the author's experience, offers ideal help to patients in this situation and is extremely satisfactory to the psychotherapist too. One reason for this is, that there is hardly any other situation in life, where patients' emotions are so obvious, where patients "open their hearts" to an understanding, empathic vis-à-vis, from person to person. Another reason is that, differently from psychotherapeutical work with terminally ill patients which many psychotherapists are afraid of, this work has an unlimited perspective. Many heart patients do not dare to think beyond the day of the operation, which in their fantasies often means death. The psychotherapist, on the other hand, can be very sure to resume work with the patient the day after the surgery. A third reason is that Blacher's findings about death and rebirth fantasies, together with Kübler-Ross' work about the phases of existential crises and the numerous research findings about the nature of peri-operative psychopathology compose a comprehensive mosaic of the patient's emotional course through surgery. It is like a guideline along a psychological development, like a key that also helps to understand psychotic events of which patients, families and hospital staff are afraid, and often also psychotherapists. This understanding uncovers the usual mystery of the patient's psychological reactions and psychotic episodes, and enables the psychotherapist to feel free and not scared, to follow and accompany the patient wherever his mind leads him.

The reasons for undergoing *pre-operative* psychological treatment are either a disabling ambivalence concerning a suggested operation, or extreme fears. The symptoms vary from lability of mood, restlessness, grief and anxiety to psychosomatic complaints like stomach ulcers or searching for reliable information about the operation and the chances of survival. In this emotional situation, the patient is grateful to find a person who provides him with emotional warmth, shows his unconditional positive regard and accompanies him with empathic understanding. Given these basic assumptions, the patient will open his heart to his vis-à-vis. As usual in client-centered psychotherapy, this work is based on the patient's current emotions, complaints or ideas. It is necessary to accompany the patient along the stages of his emotional crisis, from shock through denial, anger, bargaining, depression and apathy. Along this way, amongst discrepant emotions, he will talk about his fears; and once he has accepted to talk about his fears, he will be ready to talk about his fears and fantasies of death. Afterwards, he will feel relieved and often better prepared to accept the operation.

The typical case is that of a 56-year-old insurance agent, who, following a heart attack was suggested to undergo bypass surgery. During the fortnight between indication and date of operation his emotions and behavior changed daily, sometimes hourly, ranging from cool acceptance of the surgery to anxious refusal. The physicians and the ward staff found him very difficult to handle; whatever they said or did was not agreeable to him. In subsequent psychological sessions during the last week before surgery, it appeared that he was fighting against his fate, always aggressively blaming others for his illness but never himself. He tried to avoid the operation, suggesting alternative medical treatments and promising to live more healthily, to work less and keep strictly to medications and diet. During the last two days before surgery he became quieter, started talking about his life and his family in more detail, thought about his own faults in life, mentioned that he had written his will after he had been confronted with the diagnosis and the impending operation. He felt relieved after that and better prepared for the operation, which he finally accepted.

The pre-operative course of this patient is typical of someone whose main problem is the impending operation and his fears of death, but with no additional existential problems. This case study shows:

1. The course of the crisis, roughly following the Kübler-Ross phases, during a rather short period of time.

2. The opportunities and support of client-centered treatment during this crisis for the patient: The patient's emotions are obvious in all phases; although they are verbally denied in the beginning, they are accepted in the end. This course characterizes development in the client-centered psychotherapeutical process as documented by Rogers (1961). The patient experiences the psychotherapeutic process as moving from incongruence, unaccepted emotions and problems to congruence, self-empathy, acceptance of actual emotions and problems. Not all patients necessarily experience this process along the seven phases described by Rogers, all the way to the "fully functioning person," but they definitely have the opportunity to go some steps towards increased mental health.

Another typical example of effective pre-operative client-centered treatment can be demonstrated with the case of a 45-year-old patient, whose unresolved private problems were about to endanger the life-saving operation.

Following a heart-attack, this patient also was catheterized and urgently recommended a bypass operation. While in contact with surgeons, he was unable to make a decision, despite clear medical evidence. In the first psychotherapeutic contact, states of panic were followed by severe depressive moods and suicidal thoughts. His wife was an alcoholic and not only did the patient work as a plumber for his own and his family's living but he also took care of the children and did the housework. He devoted all his care to his wife, hoping that this would stop her from drinking. But the more he took care of her, the more she drank. He experienced his heart-attack as his own failure, as a sign of his own weakness and insufficiency. Concerning the operation, he felt a striking ambivalence: On the one hand, there was the expectation that this was a chance to recover and become strong enough to take care again of his "poor wife," which he was unable to do effectively since his heart attack, as he suffered from continuous anginous pain. On the other hand, he suffered from the fear that he might die during the operation and leave her alone, or that it could leave him as a disabled person, not being able any longer to give his wife the support which he felt was his obligation.

In a series of six psychotherapeutical contacts, the patient emotionally talked about his ideal of physical and mental strength and power - and he discovered his weakness and indulgence. At first tentatively and later very clearly and frankly, he experienced his disappointment with his wife and felt his anger and rage. He identified relations which he had never seen before, between his illness, his marital problems, his fears and depression. Thinking over a variety of new future perspectives, he delivered himself from his fears and depression and consequently decided to undergo the surgery.

At first glance, this case-description looks very similar to everyday client-centered psychotherapy with a psychoneurotic patient. The difference is that this happened on the background of the patient's impending death, either with or without operation. He was only able to accept the operation, whatever the outcome, after he had realized that there were several solutions to his current problems, even though he had not yet decided which one to try.

In this case-study again, the patient's course through the Kübler-Ross phases, as well as his stepwise movement along the Rogers process scale are evident. But in contrast to the previous case, this patient placed his actual life problem at the foreground, using it as a buffer between himself and the operation.

The stresses of an *early post-operative intensive care* treatment have often been described. Its psychological characteristics are, on the one hand, the patient's experience of being totally controlled and protected (by the medical and the ward staff) and, on the other hand, his absolute dependency on technical apparatus and ward staff.

The patient's emotions vary quickly in this situation. The euphoria of the first day after the surgery is often replaced in relation to the painful and exhausting post-operative illness, by fears of a surgical failure. With some patients, pain, weakness and fears lead the way to a breakdown of the physical and psychological defence mechanisms, very similar to a nervous breakdown; psychotic episodes, formed by the patient's basic personality characteristics may then show in the form of e.g. paranoid-hallucinatory fears, depressive silence or aggressive behavior.

In this phase again, the psychotherapist's task is to be with the patient; in addition to his empathic understanding of the overt emotions he needs to decode the emotional meanings of psychotic episodes and to use them for his work.

A typical, though dramatic, case study may illustrate the early postoperative situation and the psychotherapeutic implications: A 60-year-old patient underwent mitral valve replacement surgery. Before surgery, he had suffered in an intern ward from fear of death and depressive mood. When questioned, the consultant psychiatrist declared that psychotherapeutic support was ineffective in this situation and prescribed tranquillizers. In the intensive care unit after surgery, this patient became psychotic, with symptoms varying from paranoid hallucinations to delusions. Following extubation, the patient suffered from dispnea and experienced fear of death because of attacks of suffocation. Medical check up, including rethoracotomy, resulted in negative findings; the attacks of suffocation and hyperventilation continued resulting in the patient being reintubated and extubated several times during the first few post-operative days. Observing the patient from a psychological point of view, it became obvious that the hyperventilation and panic attacks were almost always connected with his wife's visits, or when she was mentioned to him. During a very careful client-centered approach, still in the intensive care unit, the patient initially described his partnership as very harmonious, but gradually criticized this during several short sessions which culminated dramatically to violent refusal of his wife's presence. He was full of rage and hate against her. He felt that she had pushed him into the operation against his own will; he felt fundamentally dependent on her, inferior, little, helpless, narrowed and suppressed; this culminated in a feeling of suffocation when she was around him. During his early post-operative delusions, he had killed her in fantasy. The more the patient encountered his true emotions and the more frankly he could express them, the more freely he was able to breathe. Still in hospital, the patient confronted his wife with his feelings and started arguing against her, which he had never dared to do before. (Later, they separated.)

This example clearly shows that psychological work in unusual situations, e.g. intensive care units, with intubated and/or psychotic patients needs thorough observation, psychological interpretation of behavior, facial expressions and gestures, and empathic understanding of psychotic episodes as signs of a serious crisis. In the early post-operative phase more than in any other situation, the psychotherapist has to be flexible and has to be present.

The main task for the patient in the postoperative course, is to cope with his new life or to consider this a new opportunity for a better life.

There is no single patient who does not know his date of operation by heart; many of them celebrate this date - openly or secretely - as another birthday. But being born again in the old familiar surroundings or starting life anew can be emotionally very confusing and may cause unexpected problems. In their deep desire to make the best out of their new life, which they take as a gift, patients want to make everything better, including work, family, leisure and health attitudes.

Psychotherapy must go on with patients who do not successfully manage their current and future life. Part of the patients fail because their ideas of a better life are neither accepted nor understood by their families, friends and work colleagues. Another part of the patients has never overcome the offence they experienced through their heart-diseases and operations, which left them as disabled people. Patients of both groups react with grief and resignation, sometimes suffering from suicidal ideas.

A final and short case study throws light on the difficulty of managing "new life."

A 60-year-old female patient postponed the indicated mitral valve replacement for several *years* because she suffered from fear of death. When she finally decided to undergo the surgery because her physical condition was very serious, the surgeon refused to operate on her because she was in sheer panic during their preparatory talks. Client-centered psychotherapy helped her to clear her emotions and she calmly underwent the surgery. She experienced her survival as a rebirth and began to rearrange her life-style. She withdrew from some of the family and old friends and very grateful for her new life, she turned towards ill elderly people and started to care for a number of them. Not long after, she experienced that she was no longer well-accepted by her family and friends. In addition, she increasingly experienced caring for others as a heavy burden. She came into moral conflicts, isolated and reacted with panic attacks, phobias, nightmares, depressive moods and even suicidal ideas like before the operation. It took about another sixty sessions of outpatient client-centered psychotherapy for her to feel fully stabilized emotionally.

IN-PATIENT AND OUT-PATIENT PSYCHOTHERAPY, CHANCES AND PROBLEMS

As carefully and mindfully as the surgeon is expected to handle the unique organ heart, so is the psychotherapist expected to handle the patient's soul, which is also unique; psychotherapy then is a success for the patient and also a satisfaction for the psychotherapist. This comparison between the surgical treatment of the heart and the psychological treatment of the heart-patient's soul underlines the common basis of both experts' work, in terms of responsibility and carefulness.

Successful psychotherapy is primarily based on a trustful, constant and reliable relationship with the patient.

Ideally, this relation is established before the operation, either in the hospital or on an outpatient basis, but it can also be established at any time during a psychological crisis. This can be in the intensive care unit, during the early postoperative period, on the open ward or even - on an outpatient basis - after the patient is discharged from hospital.

Consequently, whenever a psychotherapeutic relation with a patient is initiated, it must have perspective in the future. Limitation of this work to either preoperative work with the patient's fears or to supportive psychotherapy during the intensive care, or to psychological counseling from admittance until discharge may be helpful in certain cases but is not sufficient for patients struggling through an existential crisis.

In the author's experience, accompanying a heart surgery patient from the moment he is confronted with the diagnosis through the operation until he feels to have fully coped with his new life, is one of the most exciting experiences in psychotherapeutical work.

Only very few heart-surgery institutions provide their patients with inpatient and outpatient psychotherapy. The author therefore deeply appreciates the unambivalent agreement of the heads of the heart surgery department on his ideas of successful psychotherapeutic work, indicating the degree of these heart surgeons open-mindedness to the psychological importance of the heart and also their respect for psychological work.

Naturally, the everyday reality of all somatic institutions complicates psychotherapeutical work. In a setting other than a "normal" psychotherapy, the course, the frequency and the duration of contacts are determined by the patient's physical complaints and inpatient organizational problems. Patient-centered work in a cardiovascular surgery department, especially during intensive care, is limited by the patient's physical situation (e.g. artificial respiration or sedation), by the organizational inadequacy of the institution (e.g. in the presence of fellow patients) and by the daily hospital routine (e.g. practice of discharge), which hardly ever follows the individual emotional needs of patients but mostly habitual rules to which patients and staff have to submit.

Therefore the difficulties a psychotherapist encounters in this work and the possibilities he has, primarily depend on the situation and not on the patient's characteristics.

The description of the problems and limitations of inpatient psychological work was aimed at underlining once more the importance of normal-range client-centered psychotherapy, giving heart surgery patients a realistic chance to get the emotional warmth, empathy and positive regard which they urgently need to overcome an existential crisis in life.

708

REFERENCES

Becker, R., Katz, J., Polonius, M.-J., & Speidel, H. (Eds.). (1982). *Psychopathological and neurological dysfunctions following open-heart-surgery.* Berlin: Springer.

Blacher, R.S. (1983). Death, resurrection, and rebirth: Observations in cardiac surgery. *Psychoanalytic Quarterly, 52,* 56-72.

Götze, P. (1981). *Psychopathologie der Herzoperierten.* Stuttgart: Enke.

Kübler-Ross, E. (1977). *Interviews mit Sterbenden.* Berlin: Kreuz-Verlag.

Meffert, H.-J., Boll, A., Dahme, B., Götze, P., Huse-Kleinstoll, G., Polonius, M.-J., Prüssmann, Speidel, H., & Wessel, M. (1983). Der relative Anteil somatischer und psychischer Befunde an der Vorhersage psychopathologischer Auffälligkeiten nach Herzoperationen. In H.H. Studt (Ed.), *Psychosomatik in Forschung und Praxis.* München: Urban und Schwarzenberg.

Rodewald, G., & Speidel, H. (1980). *Psychic and neurological dysfunctions after open-heart-surgery. Intensivmedizin, Notfallmedizin, Anästhesiologie* (Vol. 19). Stuttgart: Thieme.

Rogers, C.R. (1961). *On becoming a person. A therapist's view of psychotherapy.* New York: Houghton Mifflin.

EXPERIENTIAL REMINISCENCE AND LIFE-REVIEW THERAPY WITH THE ELDERLY

Edmund SHERMAN
Ringel Institute of Gerontology,
State University of New York at Albany, U.S.A.

Reminiscence, oral histories, life narratives, and life reviews have all been growing areas of interest and study in the field of gerontology for various disciplines from the social and behavioral sciences to the humanities. The phenomenon of reminiscence has been studied in terms of its applied value as well as its possible theoretical value for the study of personality development in late adulthood. These applied and theoretical aspects of reminiscence have been the subject of ongoing research within the Ringel Institute of Gerontology since 1984, and in the course of this research some promising findings have emerged around experiential approaches to the subject.

Given these applied and theoretical concerns, the purpose of this paper is three-fold:

1. To report on an experimental study involving the application of experiential focusing to group reminiscence with the elderly.

2. To provide some preliminary findings and illustrations of the role of experiencing, as operationalized in the Experiencing Scale, within certain identified developmental patterns and processes in old age.

3. To present some implications of these findings for experiential therapy and research in the field of aging.

The primary objective of the initial experimental study in 1984-1985 was to determine whether reminiscence groups could be used to enhance the development of social and emotional supports, among community-dwelling elderly persons[1]. The social objectives had to do with enhancing socialization opportunities and the development of confidant relationships among elderly individuals, and the affective aspects of the study had to do with the enhancement of self-esteem and morale through the use of reminiscence as a coping mechanism and emotional resource.

The kinds and amount of data collected as well as many of the quantitative and qualitative findings from that study went well beyond the applied or demonstration purposes of the project (Sherman, 1987). Consequently, we carried out further analysis of the data after submission of the report on evaluation of effectiveness of the demonstration. This analysis revealed certain types of reminiscence at varying experiential levels that seemed to be related to life review processes, and to particular patterns of adaptation among the elderly subjects. In order to pursue some of the impressions and directions that were emerging from the analysis, selected follow-up interviews were carried out with individuals who appeared to represent certain patterns, processes and outcomes in the eight months of the demonstration phase of the project. Over 40 of these individuals have been seen at least once since then. Some have been seen as many as six times, and a few have been seen periodically right up to the present to gain some longitudinal impressions of processes that seem to have been set in motion during the demonstration phase.

Anecdotal reports of the socializing value of reminiscence among the elderly abound in the gerontological literature (Ingersoll & Goodman, 1983; Lesser, Lazarus, Frankel & Havasy, 1981; McMordie & Blom, 1979). Reminiscence appears to be ubiquitous among the elderly and it is a very natural interpersonal "ice breaker" to share common and unique personal past experiences with others. In addition to its potential for developing friendships and social supports, reminiscence has been found by a number of investigators to be associated with personal satisfaction, enhanced self-esteem, positive affect, and adaptive coping (Havighurst & Glasser, 1972: Lewis, 1971; McMahon & Rudick, 1964). Pinkus (1967) observed that reminiscence helped to deal with unresolved grief and to cope with stressful life experiences such as institutionalization.

It has also been proposed that remininiscence facilitates an introspective and integrative life review process in elderly individuals. Robert Butler (1963), a geropsychiatrist, proposed that reminiscence occurs within the life review, which he defines as "a naturally occurring, universal mental process characterized by the progressive return to consciousness of past experience and, particularly, the resurgence of unresolved conflicts." He felt that this introspective process is brought on by the realization of approaching death and that it can be beneficial when the result is the reintegration of past, present, and future, with ultimate acceptance of life experiences as they were actually lived. Thus, he described life review as reminiscence for the purpose of analysis and reintegration.

This integrative function is based upon Erik Erikson's (1963) theory, which posits the final developmental task of the human life cycle as one of achieving ego integrity over despair. Erikson's definition of integrity as "the acceptance of one's one and only life cycle as something that had to be and that of necessity permitted no substitution," would thus represent the positive outcome of a successful life review process. This review has to involve reminiscing about negative and unpleasant experiences as well as positive ones so that unresolved issues and conflicts can be brought into awareness, reworked, and reintegrated to achieve a more consistent and sustaining evaluation of the person's past life. Butler's psychiatric experience in facilitating such reminiscing was incorporated into an approach called life-review therapy (Lewis & Butler, 1973), which could be applied in groups as well as with individuals. This approach was the one we applied in the experimental groups of the demonstration study.

The experiential approach to group reminiscence in the study was based upon Gendlin's (1981) focusing method, which had been used for research purposes in a study of 639 elderly persons in Chicago who were undergoing the stresses of relocation from their own homes into nursing homes (Lieberman & Tobin, 1983). That study indicated that those individuals who coped best with the relocation actively used reminiscence in the process. In order to obtain more data on the nature of that reminiscence the investigators used Gendlin's (1981) six-step procedure for teaching a person how to focus on a bodily-felt inner referent or meaning of an experience. It was used procedurally to put the elderly respondents in a relaxed and introspective frame of mind so that they could recall, attend to, and relate their memories in a reminiscence process. Not only did the focusing evoke memories but the participants reported that they found it pleasant and helpful to do (Gorney, 1968; Gorney & Tobin, 1967). This finding led this author to speculate that focusing could be a valuable addition to group reminiscence practice, rather than just a facilitating device for research purposes. Therefore, focusing was incorporated into the experimental design so as to test its potential effectiveness in reminiscence group practice.

METHODS

Sample

A sample of 104 persons was randomly selected from pools of volunteers in three senior apartment dwellings in the City of Albany and in the Jewish Community Center of Albany. Individuals within each of these settings were randomly assigned to either a control group, a conventional reminiscence group or an experiential reminiscence group. There were thus 12 groups in the four settings. The 104 participants at the start of the study had a mean age of 73.8 with a range of 60 to 91. The 88 women accounted for 84.6% of the sample, and 61 of them were widowed (69.3%). For the whole sample, 58.7% were widowed and the next largest category was 28.8% who lived with their spouses. Since three of the four settings were sponsored by the Jewish Federation of Albany most participants (67.3%) were Jewish and all were white.

There was a pretest when the groups began and a post-test at the end of 10 group reminiscence sessions about three months later. A follow-up test was conducted three months after the post-test to determine whether any significant changes were maintained beyond the end of the reminiscence sessions.

The groups undergoing the experimental reminiscence conditions and those in the control conditions varied in size from six to ten members. The size of the groups in each setting was determined largely by the numbers in the sample pool of volunteers available. Attrition through the three testing periods was relatively low (17%), probably because of the $10 paid to participants at each testing. The number of participants at post-test was 86: 30 in control groups; 29 in conventional reminiscence groups; and 27 in experiential groups.

Testing procedures

Measures used in the three testing periods consisted of the Life Satisfaction Index-Form Z (Wood et al., 1969), the Monge (1975) Self-Concept measure, a scale of engagement in reminiscence, and the experiential level of reminiscence. The latter was measured by the Experiencing Scale (Klein, Mathieu, Gendlin, & Kiesler, 1970) based upon three to five minute audiotaped time samples of reminiscence of each participant for each testing period in all the groups, including controls. Judges were trained to determine Experiencing (EXP) Scale ratings based on the manifest content of these taped samples. After high levels of interjudge reliability were obtained in training, EXP ratings were assigned to each participant in each testing period.

The engagement in reminiscence measure consisted of a classification of the taped samples into a four-fold typology which reflected a continuum of inclusiveness of reminiscence going from: (1) non-engagement/avoidance, (2) selective avoidance, in which the participant explicitly avoids negative or unpleasant content, (3) selective engagement in which no negative content can be discerned but there is no explicit avoidance, to (4) full engagement/non-avoidance, in which negative as well as positive and neutral content are manifestly included. Other measures included self-reports of numbers of new friends made and maintained as well as frequency and degree of enjoyment of reminiscence.

It is important to note that participants in the control groups were tested in groups at three points in time in the same manner as experimental participants. Therefore, they engaged in audio-taped reminiscence in a group for the purposes of measuring type and experiential level of reminiscing. However, they did not meet at any other time as a group.

Group procedures

Group leadership was kept constant by having an MSW social worker conduct all eight reminiscence groups, i.e., two experimental types in each of four settings. She also conducted the three testing sessions with the help of a research assistant for all the groups including controls.

She conducted the conventional reminiscence groups using the life-review therapy format of Lewis & Butler (1974) in which group members share memories from earliest remembered childhood through young and middle adulthood up to the present. This was named "conventional" because it was not a newly developed approach to reminiscence. In it, members were encouraged to share their memories with the group, but they were reassured that this was entirely voluntary and that there was no expectation that they had to discuss subjects they were not comfortable with. The approach was open and conversational so as to encourage spontaneity in sharing and discussing memories.

They were also encouraged to bring in any photographs and other memorabilia they wished to share.

All groups had 10 sessions of 1 1/2 hours each. The planned format called for spending two sessions each on the following periods of life cycle: childhood, adolescence, adulthood, middle age, and senior adulthood.

Topics for each session were divised from a variety of sources and a set of flash cards with developmentally-related subjects and topics were used extensively to guide each session format (Fiedler, 1981; Quigley, 1981). The cards included such topics as childhood: (ages 1-11), recalling first memory, describing playmates, best friends, typical activities on weekdays and weekends, relationships with family members, describing favorite toys, pets, or other possessions; adolescence: (ages 12-19) describing the first date, first job, entering the service, and so forth; adulthood: (ages 20-40), describing courtship, engagement, marriage, occupations and the good and bad points of careers; middle age: (ages 40-60), naming one of the two things they were most proud of during this period, any mid-life problems, becoming a grandparent, sharing school or family reunions or anniversaries; senior adulthood: (ages 60-present), discussing pros and cons of being over 60, recalling if they ever had experienced prejudice because of their age and sharing these, relating how they were satisfied with the way their lives had turned out, as well as ways they would have preferred it to be different.

The experiential groups at each of the four settings were begun in the same way as the conventional reminiscence groups, following the format of developmental life-stage topics. Then, in the third session, members were told that their group would begin the remainder of sessions with a new and somewhat different way of focusing on personal experiences and memories. They would spend approximately one-third to one-half of each session doing this, and the rest of the session would continue with discussion of developmentally oriented topics. During that third sesssion the practitioner explained that this technique had been found relaxing and enjoyable in a research study in Chicago. Group members were told: "We will begin each meeting with a relaxing way of focusing on past life experiences. It is an individual and quiet process that I will guide you through and will take only a few minutes. After we finish, we will then discuss life experiences and memories."

At the beginning of the first focusing session, and all that followed, the practitioner first led the group members through guided relaxation. She instructed everyone to get in as comfortable and relaxed a position as possible and to breathe deeply, just focusing on the way their bodies felt. They were instructed to relax and breathe deeply and to allow their chairs to fully support their weight while they continued to be aware of how their bodies felt as they relaxed. After about 30 seconds of this relaxation, the practitioner guided them through the initial silent focusing process by asking them to think of something they feel or felt good about and liked a lot. It could be a favorite place, a possession, an event or anything else that would come to mind, except a person or pet. The exceptions were to avoid possible painful memories of recent loss. Participants were asked to focus on the bodily sensations experienced in thinking about the pleasant thing and to try to find "feeling words" to describe the sensations or bodily-felt sense of the pleasant thing. After about five minutes of silent focusing the practitioner opened discussion for sharing of individual experiences of guided focusing on memories.

In the second focusing session (fourth group meeting) the practitioner guided members through the pre-focusing relaxation, but this time the members were told that they could focus an a special person or pet if this involved pleasant memories.

Again, the practitioner opened up discussion for feedback regarding individual experience of the focusing. These first two focusing sessions were developed so that the groups' introduction to the process was positive. By having members focus on happy and positive experiences, it was presumed they would be more receptive to continuing with the problem-oriented focusing implemented during the remainder of the group meetings.

During the remaining meetings (fifth to tenth meetings of groups), the practitioner directed members through the full six-step focusing sequence (Gendlin, 1981), which included focusing on present and unresolved past problems and experiences, as well as positive ones.

RESULTS

Findings

The experiment demonstrated quite clearly that reminiscence groups could serve to enhance the development of social supports. The participants claimed to have made new friendships and to have maintained them into the follow-up period of testing. In fact, in three of the four study settings members of the experimental groups, and even a few controls, decided on their own to develop ongoing peer groups that continued well beyond the end of the project. This was an unanticipated outcome of some significance for gerontological practice.

The outcomes with respect to life satisfaction and self concept, however, were somewhat more equivocal and complex. The multiple analysis of variance showed that there was no significant difference in the amount of change from pretest to follow-up on those two outcome measures between the control and experimental groups. There was a clear positive increase, though not statistically significant, on both measures within the controls as well as the experimentals. There was, however, a statistically significant (p = .001) change in the type of reminiscence between the control and experimental groups. The control participants tended to remain more selective and avoidant in their reminiscence at follow-up, whereas the experimental group participants had become inclusive, less avoidant, and more fully engaged. Moreover, the experimental group showed significantly higher (p = .05) modal Experiencing (EXP) Scale scores than the control groups. Further, the experiential groups evidenced significantly higher (p = .05) EXP scores than the conventional reminiscence groups.

Interpretation

A number of questions arise about the statistical non-significance of change within the experimental groups as well as between the experimentals and controls. These questions become salient in the light of the clearly significant difference between experimentals and controls in the type of reminiscence and in the EXP levels.

The following interpretation of these findings is based on a subsequent and more detailed statistical analysis, the post-demonstration interviews with selected participants, and the correspondence of some of these findings with relevant findings of other investigators of reminiscence. The subsequent statistical analysis showed that there was a complex, non-linear relationship between type of reminiscence and the life satisfaction and self-concept measures.

There was considerable movement within the total sample from pretest to post-test of persons going from Type I (non-engagement/ avoidance) to Type II (engagement but explicit avoidance of negative content) or Type III (selective engagement on positive). This occurred even in the control group, probably because they actually did have to engage in audio-taped reminiscences in a group testing situation at both times. Further, there appeared to be a contagion effect in that reminiscence was "in the air" at the three senior apartment dwellings, and the controls admitted to being conscious of this. By the time of the third group testing at follow-up they were calling themselves "a group" and felt that they too had gotten something out of it. The fact that they, like the experimentals, were paid $10 for each testing might also be involved in their increases in reminiscence, life satisfaction, and self-concept measures.

These changes from Type I to Types II and III seemed to be associated with increases in life satisfaction and self-concept. This was true in the experiential as well as the control groups. On the other hand, the experimental groups showed significantly more participants who moved from Types I and II to Type IV (full engagement/non-avoidance). However, Type IV's showed a mixed relationship to life satisfaction and self-concept. Within Type IV were quite a few individuals who showed reduced life satisfaction and self-concept after moving from Types I, II, or II. The advent of negative and unpleasant content into their reminiscence serves to explain much of this. It appeared that the life review format had triggered off a life review process that led to some dissonant and unresolved issues. This is consistent with the findings of Romaniuk and Romaniuk (1981) who studied various triggers and uses of reminiscence and found that reminiscence associated with resolving such past issues and conflicts, fitted into a life review type of reminiscence they labelled "Existential/ Self Understanding." Their factor analysis also turned up a reminiscence dimension labelled "Self-Regard/Image Enhancement," and this was associated very highly with recall of *pleasant* events. It was also associated with entertaining and describing self to others as well as using recall to lift spirits. This is quite consistent with the Type II and

III reminiscence in this study, and would explain some of the enhanced satisfaction and self-concept measures.

Along with changes in type of reminiscence went a change in experiencing level based on EXP ratings. This was again a complex non-linear relationship but one that was very evident in cross tabulations. The few participants (11) who began in the pretest at a modal EXP level 1 moved up to level 2 as they moved from Reminiscence Type I to Type II at post-test or follow-up. EXP level 1 is characterized by either a refusal to participate or to present past experiences in terms of external events and in an impersonal and detached manner. Level 2 is characterized by some behavioral or intellectual self-description and even though the reminiscence content consists of external events, they are handled in interested and personal terms of self participation. Level 2 was the prevailing modal rating in all three periods of the study and in the experimental as well as the control group. However, the controls showed no appreciable change. They had a mean rating of 1.93 (SD = 0.38) at pretest and 2.11 (SD = 0.68) at post-test. The conventional reminiscence group participants had a change in means from 1.86 (SD = 0.35) to 2.11 (SD = 0.68) and the experiential participants a change from 1.85 (SD = 0.37) to 3.08 (SD = 0.80). The analysis of variance indicated a significant difference between experimental and control groups on the modal EXP measure (p = .05), with the experiential group participants also showing a significantly greater (p = .05) degree of change than conventional group participants.

The pattern of EXP change in relationship to life satisfaction and self-concept measures is probably of greater consequence than the significant change in EXP itself. Although there were some increases in EXP levels, there were 10 individuals in the experimental group and none in controls who showed a notable decrease in life satisfaction and self concept as their EXP levels went up from pretest to post-test. Some of these then showed an increase in life satisfaction and self-concept at follow-up while others went even lower on the two measures, although their EXP remained the same or went up.

The post-demonstration interviews with these individuals revealed that all of them were experiencing greater internal conflict and lowered morale while their EXP levels were going up. In fact, their higher EXP levels were much more evident in the individual interviews than in group testing situations. It appears that the interpersonal group context acts as a constraint on the manifest expression of painful memory affects which are apt to be at EXP levels 4 and 5 rather than the modal level 2 found in the group situations.

This is again consistent with findings of Romaniuk and Romaniuk (1981) who found differential uses of reminiscence in relationship to either the intrapersonal or interpersonal dimensions. The entertaining, teaching, and pleasure uses of reminiscence in their Self Regard/Image Enhancement category are obviously much more associated with the interpersonal dimension, which would be most likely found at an EXP level of 3. A shift to the more internalized, groping and tentative EXP level 5 would entail a certain linguistic dysfluency that would be dysfunctional for the above interpersonal functions. Yet, it would be much more appropriate for their Existential/Self-Understanding (life review) category or their Problem-Solving category, which includes coping with a loss, dealing with a current problem, or making future plans.

Three other investigators who examined reminiscence in relationship to Erikson's ego integrity-vs-despair dimension, found in their elderly sample a group very similar to the 10 individuals with decreasing morale in relationship to higher affective experiencing levels (Walaskay, Whitbourne, & Nehrke, 1983). They labeled this group "dissonant", which was made up of individuals who appeared to be unhappy and stressed. Yet, this was seen as a temporary state in comparison to the more chronically low sense of well-being in a group they called "despairing." It should be noted, parenthetically, that all four individuals who showed a decrease followed by an increase to a higher level of morale much like the dissonants were all members of experiential groups.

Lieberman and Tobin (1983) also found a group comprising about 15% of their sample who were like the dissonants. They appeared to be involved in a life review process, and they were labelled "conflicted." The same investigators also found a large group (51%) who were characterized as avoiding the past or reviewing their lives, and they were labelled "in flight." They had higher morale measures than the "conflicted," but they were more neutral or bland in affect. This is somewhat similar to a group in the Walaskay, Whitbourne, and Nehrke (1983) study who were labelled "foreclosed" and who would nor self-explore or self-disclose. Yet, they were relatively high on morale or well-being measures. Although we did not use the same morale or affect measures in our study it appeared that the largest single group in our sample was like the foreclosed.

Given these similarities, it would be helpful to recapitulate the four integrity statuses identified by Walaskay et al. (1983): Integrity achieving, dissonant (in crisis), forclosed (avoiding crisis), and despairing. A person in the integrity achieving status would have examined and accepted his or her unique life as it had been lived, in accordance with Erikson's formulation of ego integrity. The person in foreclosed status would defend against self-exploration and avoid the reflective processes of crisis and life review. They would sustain a relatively positive sense of well-being but at the expense of relative lack of integration of past, present, and future and of depth of insight and meaning.

The older person in dissonant status is one who is undergoing a shift from precrisis to crisis phase of integrity resolution and is in a state of dissonance and disequilibrium which impacts negatively on their sense of well-being and self. The despairing person is unhappy with his or her past and present life, is fearful of death, and sees life as too short to make up for past mistakes and regrets. This status is seen as a chronic one in that the integrity vs. despair crisis has been resolved in an unfavorable direction. There appeared to be about six individuals in our sample whom we could, with some degree of assurance, identify as despairing.

CASE ILLUSTRATIONS

One way of attempting to pull together some of the disparate points, patterns, and processes that have been touched on in the preceding interpretation of findings is to present some illustrative case material. Space does not permit a representative cross-section of cases, not even of the four integrity statuses. Therefore, two case vignettes will be presented which could serve to illustrate some of the more important points just covered.

When the experimental demonstration ended after approximately eight months we began our post-demonstration interviews with selected individuals. We had asked in the follow-up testing groups which participants would be willing to be interviewed individually to provide impressions, observations, and suggestions based on their experiences in the project. We also indicated that they might be able to help us interpret some possible quantitative or qualitative findings from our analysis based on their own first-hand experience in the project. The majority not only expressed willingness but also an interest in doing so. It has already been noted that in three of the four settings participants were planning for ongoing peer groups to be reconstituted from our project groups, so the positive interest did not surprise us.

We carried out interviews primarily with individuals who seemed to reflect some of the patterns that appeared to be emerging in the analysis and discussions of project staff. The interviews took place mostly in the participants' own appartments or homes, although a few from the Jewish Community Center preferred to be interviewed there. We made sure to interview those who appeared to be in the dissonant category, but we also included persons who seemed to fit in the achieving integrity, despairing, and forclosed statuses. However, a number of individuals asked to be seen because of personal issues that had been raised during the demonstration phase of the project. We had three project staff members with professional counseling experience, plus one other experienced Ringel Institute staff person, so we were prepared by design to meet these requests as well as the requests for a group facilitator to help get two of the peer groups started

The first case vignette concerns Mr. N., a widower who was 87 years old at pretest and 88 at the time of his four post-demonstration interviews. He was interviewed only because he appeared to be going through a life review and to be "dissonant", but also because of his age. It appeared very anomolous for him to be going through a life review at his advanced age (Butler, 1963). Lieberman and Tobin (1983) had found the majority octogenarians in their study to be somewhat resolved, contented, and mellow but infrequent reminiscencers.

Mr. N. was a very frequent reminiscer, both in terms of self-report and in his participation in his conventional reminiscence group in the Jewish Community Center. He had low life satisfaction and self concept scores at pretest, in the lowest quartile for the study. He had exactly the same low life satisfaction score for all three testing periods. However, his self-concept score fell another five points from post-test to follow-up, even though he was already 15 points below the norm for this sample. His pretest audiotape revealed that his reminiscences were already in the Type IV category in that there was a good deal of negative content. He began the pretest by saying that he didn't really have anything to say. His modal EXP level was 2 and the peak level 3. He related events in his life as external and largely with intellectual self-descriptions. He said, "I was an orphan when I was 10." "I went through the First World War and was a prisoner of war." "I came from a poor family in Lithuania, the youngest of eleven children, so I didn't have an education." These brief staccato, self-descriptions were characteristic of his early group verbalizations. Although he claimed to reminisce "all the time," he did not particularly enjoy it.

Mr. N. liked to discuss politics and current affairs in the group whenever there was a chance and he was one of the most verbally active members. However, as the group was nearing the end of its 10 sessions his reminiscence and his observation about current affairs began taking on an obsessive quality. He began expressing considerable personal distress about the current world and national situation in light of his own life. He had been a union organizer, leader, and social activist from the time he was a teenager in Europe. Two years after he came to the United States at age 21 he was jailed for his involvement in a long and bitter strike in an attempt to organize a cap and hat worker's union in Albany. After a life-time of social activism based on "a certain philosophy and ideals," he found himself not only dismayed but truly distressed over the current state of affairs under President Reagan. He exclaimed that the young people, instead of being idealistic as they should, were all for "consumer materialism, individualism, and self-interest."

This became something of a litany in his group participation. However, at the follow-up testing he appeared more demoralized and made more depressed statements, such as: "I didn't have a youth." They appeared to be more personal as compared to social or political regret and a concern that time was running out. His EXP levels were consistently at level 4 in the post-test: Immediate and expressive language, with much expression of affect and subjective association.

When this author contacted him about a month after the follow-up testing to see if he would be willing to be interviewed to get his observations about the reminiscence group experience he readily agreed. The first of four interviews with him began with his offering several suggestions. First, that more time should be spent in the groups on current affairs. Second, if "they want to reminisce, it should be about important social events out of the past ... about history." Then, without any change in direction on the interviewer's part, Mr. N. went back to the observation that he "didn't have a childhood" and proceeded to go back, recollect, and reflect on his family of origin and his wife and children for the first time.

The interviewer simply followed Mr. N.'s life review in a reflective manner, for it seemed to "take on a life of its own." The EXP levels were quite frequently in the 4 and 5 range in the first two interviews. At the start of the third interview Mr. N. asked that the session not be taped because he had "more personal things" he wanted to talk about. He then began talking about his wife and children and his concern that he had not been a good husband and father. He had spent "too much time away from them during all the union and social activities." If only things had changed in society because of his activities maybe he could justify his "neglect" of his family, but "things have turned out terrible" and he felt no justification for what he had done.

Although the last two interviews were not taped, and the EXP levels could not be evaluated by independent raters, it was this author's impression that Mr. N.'s self-questioning, tentative, and pained demeanor as well as his hesitating, dysfluent speech meant that he was working on his issues at level 5. He claimed to be unable to sleep or to eat adequately because of these concerns. He said they bothered him intensely, so much so that he said, "I can feel it all here," pointing to his stomach. He was asked if he could stay with that feeling in that place. He did that without hesitation and naturally. In fact, it appeared that he would have done just that without the interviewer's guiding question. His eyes were closed, and although the look on his face was pained he seemed to be focusing inwardly and following a process in which he needed no guidance.

He remained unselfconsciously focused inward and his body appeared to shift several times. His demeanor and facial expression seemed to become less pained. When he opened his eyes he took a few moments before saying that he had been struggling with feelings of failure and disillusionment in himself, that he felt like a "failure" because of the failure of social reform and progress in society in general. He said he had just realized that he identified himself with "the movement...with history." Then he went on to say ..."but that's not right." He then paused reflectively and said empathically, "I did what I had to do!" He hesitated and said again, more slowly, "I did what I had to do." At this, his body simply slumped and went loose. He sat in a slumped, relaxed posture for awhile, and then said that he had a lot "to think about...good things.." which he preferred to keep for the next scheduled interview the following week.

It can truly be said that this author was witness to a life review and its experiential process in Mr. N.'s case. Except for the mild intervention of asking if he could stay with "that feeling," Mr. N. did it all by himself. He had moved from level 5 to 6 as he was sensing that feeling, and he was at level 7 when he exclaimed, "I did what I had to do!" It was something that he now "knew" for himself.

In the fourth and last interview he was in an excited state. He claimed to have slept thoroughly for the first time in a long time. He was enthusiastic about what he had learned about himself and said, "I walked in the sun and it was worth it." He said he realized what he had done was right, but more important that it was right *for him*. It couldn't be any other way, regardless of what had happened with society in general. All of this was said with the declarative and fresh expressions characteristic of EXP level 6.

When asked somewhat later in the interview about what procedures worked best for him in the group, he said: "The sequencing ...starting with early childhood." He added, "It made me want to tell my story to someone ... and to myself ... straight through." This he had done, of course, with this author and without the interruptions and disjunctures of the group process.

The author had occasion to talk to Mr. N. again a year and half later at the Jewish Community Center. He was then 90 years old and he had just finished with his daily swim at the Center, something he had been doing since his participation in the reminiscence group. In fact, the peer group that was reconstituted from the reminiscence group at the Community Center had continued on as a combined reminiscence and current affairs, "Old times and New times," discussion group, which he continued to participate in enthusiastically.

The case of Mrs. A. is probably, not as dramatic as Mr. N.'s because she had not been involved in as many momentous historical events in her shorter life span of 78 years. She was a widow of two years and a practicing Roman Catholic who lived in a newly opened senior appartment dwelling under the auspices of the Greek Orthodox Church. However, the dwelling was non-denominational and there was a fairly even mix of Greek Catholics, Roman Catholics, Protestants and Jews.

This meeting presented some unique features as far as the purposes of the study were concerned. It had just been open for about two months, whereas all of the other study settings had been in existence for well over a decade. Consequently, there were not well-established friendships or informal social networks within the setting. This fitted well with the study's purposes, but there was some initial participant weariness which was an understandable result of not knowing one another. Added to this was the fact that most of the residents had experienced recent, frequently multiple, losses. Almost all had recently left their own homes of long standing, usually because of being widowed, alone, or physically unable to maintain the homes. We found that because of these losses and the associated painful memories, there was more defensiveness and less willingness to engage in memory-sharing about their personal pasts when the groups began.

Mrs. A. was randomly assigned to an experiential reminiscence group and like others in her group she had suffered a number of recent losses. Her husband had died almost two years earlier but only after prolonged illness and disability due to a series of strokes. Mrs. A. had to care for him at home for four years prior to his death. Shortly after his death she developed breast cancer and had to have a radical mastectomy. Although she was reassured that no signs of any cancer remained, she found it more and more difficult physically and emotionally to keep up the house she had lived in for over 30 years.

At the pretest she indicated that she sometimes thought about her parents and her siblings, but said, "there was a lot of sadness" and "I try not to think about it," for a Type II reminiscence. Her modal EXP score was 1 and the peak was 2. Her life satisfaction and self-concept scores were very close to the mean for the whole sample. However, at the time of the post-test her life satisfaction had dropped to the lowest quartile of the sample and was quite low relative to the norms of the test.

At the post-test she was very actively reminiscing and much of the content was negative, for a Type IV rating. She said that she thought often of her youth and that she would like to "skip over" her marriage and her children, but she was not able to. She said, "Since I've been ill, I think about death and I know it could happen - I'm in my seventies. I get a sad, sort of fatalistic feeling ... well, it's going to happen. It comes to everybody." Her modal EXP was 4 and the peak was 5 at that time.

In the follow-up testing, three months later, Mrs 's life satisfaction score had gone up into the second quartile. The self-concept score showed a similar pattern of down and then up within the three test periods but not quite as pronounced. She and seven other study participants in her setting indicated a strong interest in developing what they called a "coping group" to discuss and cope with different losses, illnesses, and other events that had befallen them in the recent past. They requested a professional group leader rather than attempt a peer-group approach at first.

The Ringel Institute was able to provide one. She was a mature psychiatric nursing instructor, with many years of geriatric experience, who was working on a Ph.D. through the Institute. She worked with the group for 15 sessions, a four-month period, in which the members (all women) were able to work through the losses and other issues that had brought them together. Interestingly, they continued on as a peer social action group to deal with issues concerning the quality of services in and maintenance of their apartment dwelling. They started and became the focal group in the residents' council for that new dwelling.

Mrs. A. was one of the key actors in both the coping and social action phases of the group. She was also very interested in being interviewed individually after the demonstration was over to share her thoughts about the reminiscence group experience. In that interview she admitted to being quite reluctant when the group started to share her memories "for fear of stirring them up." She also found the first focusing step of clearing a space to be problematic at first. She found that a lot of the same problems kept coming back, and she would have to put them "on the shelf" or at a distance for the time being. She did not seem to be able to work through any one of them in the remaining five steps of focusing. This served to prevent her from suppressing them as usual, but in the process this made her want to talk about them in the group. This urge to talk about them began in the seventh session, and it seemed to give her some relief. It also started some of the other women in her group to begin sharing some of their painful memories and thoughts

It was not until the end of the 10 sessions that she really learned to relax with the focusing and to do all six steps on her own. She found she could stay with her feelings and explore them by herself without having to share as much with the others, although that was still helpful, too. She reported that some of the feelings which came to her in the process were guilt over the anger she felt and was still feeling toward her husband for his prolonged illness and dependency. Deep frustration and resentment over her own illness after caring for him so long, and further guilt over not really mourning for him after he finally did die.

Then she began to find in the process of focusing that there was more to the feelings than the raw anger, hurt, sadness and so on. They were becoming "more complicated but not all bad anymore." They seemed to be changing and "falling more into place in a way that I could go on with my life." She was not through working on those feelings at the time of the post-project interview, so it could not be said that she had yet moved to the integrity achieving status at that time.

By the time the coping group had ended and it was moving into its social action phase, Mrs. A. did appear to have moved into the integrity-achieving status. The professional group leader reported that Mrs. A. had become a role-model for some of the other women in the group. She was seen as someone who had "put it all together" and had "come out on top." Although no testing or assessments were done in that later group, she appeared to have accomplished a great deal of reintegrative work.

DISCUSSION

These findings and illustrations suggest that reminiscence groups can provide a forum for initiating the life review process and that they can enhance the experiential level of memory processing and sharing among the elderly. It also appears that the experiential level can be enhanced even more through the addition of focusing. Whether this leads to more life review reminiscing of a reintegrative nature is still open to question, but it is a fruitful question to pursue in further research.

In drawing the implications of all this for an experiential approach to practice with the elderly, it is important to note that the foregoing dealt only with group reminiscence and the use of focusing within that modality. While groups can provide a forum for initiating a life review process, life review therapy conducted on an individual basis is not usually a strategy initiated by a therapist. Instead, "the therapist taps into an already on-going self-analysis and participates in it with the older person" (Lewis & Butler, 1974, p. 166). This suggests that it is a good strategy to have the option of individual life review therapy available when starting experiential reminiscence groups.

It is also important to note that individual therapy as described by Lewis and Butler (1974) has a much more open experiential flavor to it than the more structured group procedure described here. In individual work the practitioner takes a reflective and non-directive stance, provides supportive listening, and "taps into" an already on-going process. It is not difficult to see that experiential therapists should be particularly well suited to work with this type of process.

Several points need to be made about using a structured approach to reminiscence and life review therapy. An empirical study by Fry (1983) indicated that depressed older persons trained in structured reminiscence showed significantly greater improvement than those provided with unstructured reminiscence. The structure in that study consisted of a set of questions carefully designed to evoke problematic reminiscences. Haight (1988) used a structured set of questions to guide the home-bound older person through a life review reminiscence process, and she found that this approach led to significantly more improvement on measures of life satisfaction and psychological well being when compared to outcomes of an alternate treatment and a non-treatment condition. Her study also revealed that life review is most effective when carried out on a one-to-one basis with a therapeutic listener.

Question could be raised as to whether a structured approach is compatible with the essentially non-directive nature of experiential practice. It should be noted that in both the Fry and the Haight studies the therapists were instructed to use an empathetic listening and reflective style after each of the structured questions were asked. It should also be noted that the focusing training of the participants in our experiential reminiscence groups was basically a structured six-step procedure until the participants incorporated the steps more naturally into their own bodily felt sensing of problems and issues. Our experience suggests that there is no basic incompatibility here.

One of the unanticipated outcomes of this study was the extent to which our data and our clinical impressions correspond to the four integrity statuses found by Walaskay et al. (1983). Since we did not use their interview format or assessment instruments, we have no way of knowing how our sample would be statistically distributed in the four statuses, but it should be useful at this point to examine certain of our findings within each status in terms of their research and clinical implications.

It is clear that a number of individuals in the study entered or were in the dissonant status in the course of the experiment. The data show and the cases of Mr. N and Mrs. A. indicate that individuals entered this status in the course of either conventional or experiential group reminiscence. However, it was only in the experiential groups that we saw individuals, like Mrs. A., show evidence of reintegration and recovery of positive life satisfaction and self-concept levels following a period of dissonance and lowered scores. The numbers were too small to make a causal connection between focusing and reintegration, but the findings are suggestive.

It was noted that several persons appeared to be in the despairing status. This presumably chronic and negatively resolved status is frequently characterized by obsessive reminiscing about a particular situation that may not yield to life review therapy (Lo Gerfo, 1980-1981). It has been suggested that, instead of taking the broader view of the past ordinarily taken in life review therapy, "the goal should not be to cut off the obsessive reminiscence completely, but rather to focus it so that it can be used in the healing process until it is no longer needed" (Lo Gerfo, 1980-81, p. 44). Gendlin's (1981) focusing procedure is an excellent one for precisely this problem. This author found it to be notably effective in the case of a despairing and suicidal 71-year-old man (Sherman, 1984, pp. 102-116). This suggests that the despairing status does not have to be a chronic and unyielding one.

The foreclosed status prevents a different set of problems from an experiential perspective. Those who appeared to be foreclosed in our study did not seem to move beyond a modal EXP score of 2 or a peak of 3 in the manifest content of their shared memories and reminiscences. Since they do tend to be avoidant of unpleasant memories and associated negative affects, they are not apt to refer themselves for individual help. This certainly seemed to be the case in our study. However, "foreclosed" is not a process word and should not be taken as a "closed case." It is entirely possibly that sharp changes or crises in external life circumstances or interpersonal relationships could move forclosed persons into another integrity status. In fact, we do not really know whether a structured individual approach such as Haight's (1988) might not engage a forclosed person in a life review and experiential process that can result in a change in integrity status. This is another question we would like to address in our next phase of research.

Finally, the integrity-achieving status appears to show a particular pattern of reminiscing in relation to other data. These individuals show up statistically more positive on all measures, such as life satisfaction, self-concept, and psychological well-being, but they do not reminisce as frequently as the other three status groups (Walaskay et al., 1983). Lieberman and Tobin's (1985) study showed the same pattern, and they noted as we did that when the older person in this status reminisces negative as well as positive content emerges, but the positive outweighs the negative, which is put in an accepting life perspective. Further, they enjoy the reminiscing that they do engage in, but do not appear to show higher EXP levels in conjunction with their shared memories. However, we wonder whether this was a function of the group setting which tended to favor oral expression of personal anecdotes and stories. It is possible that the integrated older person may experience memories inwardly, with self as subject rather than object, and prefer to stay with that intrapersonal experiencing level without feeling the need to meet the social expectation of sharing each memory. This is another question we would like to explore in the next phase of research.

In summary, we can say that experiential reminiscence appears to be a natural inextricable aspect of the life-review process, as illustrated in the cases of Mr. N. and Mrs. A. Since this is based on our retrospective analysis and post-demonstration interviews it needs to be demonstrated with a newly designed study. This will be done in our next phase of research and in that study "experiential reminiscence" will probably have to be operationally defined as reminiscences experienced at an EXP level of at least 4, which is the beginning level commonly associated with significant personal change in experiential psychotherapy. In this regard it should also be noted that life review therapy and psychotherapy with elderly individuals in general could be greatly enhanced by the use of the Therapist Experiencing Scale and application of other new developments in psychotherapy process research (Mathieu-Coughlan & Klein, 1984). We need to look much more closely not only at change in our elderly clients but at the therapist behaviors that facilitate the change process, particularly in the life review and reintegrative processes of old age.

NOTE

1. This research was supported by a grant from the AARP Andrus Foundation.

REFERENCES

Erikson, E.H. (1963). *Childhood and society* (2nd ed.). New York: Norton.

Gorney, J. (1968). *Experiencing and age: Patterns of reminiscence among the elderly.* Unpublished doctoral dissertation. Committee on Human Development, University of Chicago.

Gorney, J., & Tobin, S.S. (1967). *Experiencing among the aged.* Paper presented at the 20th Annual Meeting of the American Gerontological Society, St. Petersburg, Florida.

Haight, B.K. (1988). The therapeutic role of a structured life review process in homebound elderly subjects. *Journal of Gerontology, 43(2),* 40-44.

Havighurst, R.J., & Glasser, R. (1972). An exploratory study of reminiscence. *Journal of Gerontology, 27,* 245-253.

Ingersoll, B., & Goodman, L. (1983). A reminiscence group for institutionalized elderly. In M. Rosenbaum (Ed.), *Handbook of short-term therapy groups* (Chap. 14). New York: McGraw-Hill.

Klein, M.H., Mathieu, P.L., Kiesler, D.P., & Gendlin, E.T. (1970). *The experiencing scale manual.* Madison: University of Wisconsin Press.

Lesser, J., Lazarus, L.W., Frankel, R., & Havasy, S. (1981). Reminiscence group therapy with psychotic geriatric inpatients. *The Gerontologist, 21,* 291-296.

Lewis, C.N. (1971). Reminiscing and the self-concept in old age. *Journal of Gerontology, 26,* 240-243.

Lewis, M.I., & Butler, R.N. (1974). Life-review therapy: Putting memories to work in individual and group psychotherapy. *Geriatrics, 29,* 165-173.

Lieberman, M.A., & Tobin, S.S. (1983). *The experience of old age.* New York: Basic Books.

LoGerfo, M. (1980-1981). Three ways of reminiscing in theory and practice. *International Journal of Aging and Human Development, 12,* 39-48.

Mathieu-Coughlan, P., & Klein, M.W. (1984). Experiential psychotherapy: Key events in client-therapist interaction. In L.N. Rice & L.S. Greenberg (Eds.), *Patterns of change: Intensive analysis of psychotherapy process* (pp. 213-248). New York: Guilford Press.

McMahon, A.W., & Rudick, P.J. (1964). Reminiscence: Adaptational significance in the aged. *Archives of General Psychiatry, 17,* 292-299.

McMordie, W.R., & Blom, S. (1979). Life review therapy: Psychotherapy for the elderly. *Perspectives in Psychiatric Care, 17,* 292-298.

Monge, R.H. (1975). Structure of the self-concept from adolescence through old age. *Experimental Aging Research, 1,* 281-291.

Pinkus, A. (1967). Toward a developmental view of aging for social work. *Social Work, 3,* 33-41.

732

Quigley, R. (1981). *Those were the days.* Buffalo: Potentials Development Inc.

Romaniuk, M., & Romaniuk, J.G. (1981). Looking back: An analysis of reminiscence functions and triggers. *Experimental Aging Research, 7(4),* 477-489.

Sherman, E. (1981). *Counseling the aging: An integrative approach.* New York: Free Press.

Sherman, E. (1984). *Working with older persons.* Boston: Kluwer-Nijhoff.

Sherman, E. (1987). Reminiscence groups for community elderly. *The Gerontologist, 27(5),* 569-572.

Walaskay, M., Whitbourne, S., & Nehrke, M.F. t1983). Construction and validation of an ego integrity status interview. *International Journal of Aging and Human Development, 18(1),* 61-72.

Wood, V., Wylie, M.L., & Shaefor, B. (1969). An analysis of a short self-report measure of life satisfaction: Correlation with rater judgements. *Journal of Gerontology, 24,* 465-469.

SOME ASPECTS OF COMBINING FOCUSING WITH PERSON-CENTERED THERAPY IN WORKING WITH PSYCHOSOMATIC CLIENTS

Eberhard Wolfgang FUHRMANN
Heidelberg, F.R.Germany

INTRODUCTION

Physicians and colleagues often refer psychosomatic clients to me with the following words: "Try it! But remember this (he/she) is a psychosomatic client!" To me that means: Perhaps it will be very difficult to help this person with my offer of psychotherapy. And depending on my own experience with psychosomatic clients that means I have to be extraordinarily alert when this client enters my practice.

I remember that several years ago, a 35-year-old civil engineer came to me with severe pain in his stomach. The physician had diagnosed "chronical gastritis" and advised him to start psychotherapy. All medical interventions had failed and so psychotherapy was his last opportunity of getting help. However, I did not succeed in getting in contact with his inner processes. There was a barrier. He said "I have no problems, but my stomach aches; apart from this, my life is okay!" (For me, his message seemed to be: There is this pain in my stomach. Please stop it at once, but do not touch me, stay away from my Self!) I failed with my offer of person-centered therapy and he did not even accept other interventions like role-playing according to Moreno. When we both decided to stop therapy and consider it ineffective, one part of him seemed to tell me: "I am the winner, I am not mentally ill, I don't need psychotherapy. You cannot help me either." But another part of him looked at me disappointedly. This part seemed to say: "Help me, but be careful not to hurt me!" It was hard for me to feel my own helplessness. I felt more at ease when I noticed through supervision that other colleagues had had similar experiences with psychosomatic clients.

SPECIFIC CHALLENGES

My experience has led me to suppose that persons suffering from severe symptoms classified as caused by psychological and somatic factors:

- Tend to have barriers against intensive warm contacts.
- Rarely directly refer to felt experience.
- Have a demanding attitude towards themselves and the therapist. This may put a strong pressure on the therapist to be quick and effective. There is great danger of becoming the "bad expert" who has good ideas about how to manage the client's problems.
- Attach extreme importance to the symptom as an isolated problem which seems unconnected to other topics of their life. There is like an implicite instruction to the therapist to eliminate the symptom, as if psychotherapy were surgery.
- Break off psychotherapy rather quickly, if they feel uncomfortable with the therapeutic situation. To me as a therapist, this means that I will have only a minimal chance to correct my mistakes.

Of course, this leads to the question of indication. Is it reasonable to start any kind of psychotherapy with persons who are initially motivated by the advice of physicians or of others? And the other question: Will this client be responsive to the specific offer of person-centered therapy and focusing? In most cases, I feel it is a challenge which I willingly accept. But I also see the danger of working under stress to prove something about myself. I agree with the position of Bierman-Ratjen, Eckert, & Schwartz (1979, p. 138-140) who summed up their considerations on indication as follows: "The 'responsiveness' of the client to the therapeutic process is the best guideline for indication and prognosis in client-centered psychotherapy." Thus the best criterion for deciding if person-centered therapy will be effective or not seems to be the responsiveness of the client in the first interviews. On the other hand, of course, the psychotherapist has the option and the responsibility to modify his psychotherapeutic procedure according to the client's specific abilities.

When I looked at other theoretical positions I found - in spite of significant differences - a surprising conformity among the psycho-analytical descriptions of psychosomatic patients. Freud (1892-1899, p. 255), as well as more recent authors (Marty et al., 1963; Mitscherlich, 1969, p. 198; Sifneos, 1973, p. 255-262; Uexküll, 1981, p. 217-218), characterized their psychosomatic patients as more or less unable to come in contact with their feelings. Furthermore, they agree that these patients cannot verbalize their feelings. Sifneos (1973) created the term "Alexithymia" which means the inability to "read" feelings and to express them by words (a = alpha privativum; lexis = word; thymos = feeling). Basing his research on a group of 20 persons in a Boston psychiatric hospital, he described 16 of them as handicapped in communication with the interviewer, as nearly unable to verbalize feelings, with a lack of fantasy and with a kind of automatical-mechanistic thinking (similar to the "pensée opératoire" of the Paris psychosomatic school). The discussion of these terms and its implications for therapeutic practice shows to me the differences and similarities between experiences: There is a well-known difficulty in working with psychosomatic clients, but on the other hand the problems of these patients are very different from those of psychosomatic clients I work with. This underlines the fact that very different disease processes are labeled under one term "psychosomatic" and it points out the great danger of classifying groups of clients, especially if it leads to a certain kind of negative countertransference.

Nevertheless, there is a need to organize one's own experience and to look for indicators, which will show where specific interventions are necessary and can be more effective. Pfeiffer (1987, p. 55-62) pointed out that specific types of resistance require specific procedures from the therapist. On the other hand, following Rogers, the therapist has to respect the defensiveness of the client as an important protection against disintegration of the self structure. However, another responsibility of the therapist is to encourage the clients readiness for introspection. Pfeiffer (1987, p. 58) showed, that empathy ("Verbalisierung emotionaler Erlebnisinhalte") and - among many other methods - focusing, can help the client to get more in touch with his own experiences, to react to them emotionally and to perceive a felt meaning. So the psychotherapist has the difficult task of finding the balance between a rather receptive and a more active attitude between respecting the defensiveness of the client and offering specific stimulation to ease the process of the client.

Another difficult task in the work with psychosomatic clients is to be sensitive to the right distance between client and therapist, since being too close may provoke termination of therapy.

INTRODUCING FOCUSING

When I started to use focusing in my psychotherapeutic work, I hesitated to teach focusing explicitly. It seemed to be easy only with persons who made good progress with "sheer" person-centered therapy. And then I noticed that I did not like to teach focusing. For me it seemed artificial, as an alien element in the process of psychotherapy. So I was lucky to experience focusing by Gendlin and his team in workshops in Chicago in 1986 and 1987 in a very integrated, flexible way.

In his paper "The use of focusing during psychotherapy" (1979, p. 7) Gendlin illustrated different modes of introducing focusing-instructions. "Instead of explicitly teaching the six focusing-movements ... the therapist who knows focusing will teach it to the client - perhaps not all at once as a ten minute set of instructions, but bit by bit, now and then, in the early hours. It is often quite enough just to slow the talking down now and then. The therapist can respond to a meaningful spot slowly, as it were savoring or slowly sensing the significance of what was said. During such a slower responding the client is quite likely to do the same thing, to sense inwardly how the words fit, or don't fit, and what more there is." Today it seems to me an appropriate way to teach focusing to psychosomatic clients with such small bit by bit invitations.

BRIEF ILLUSTRATION OF WORK WITH PSYCHOSOMATIC CLIENTS

I will now present some illustrations of therapies with psychosomatic clients:

Example A

Mrs. B. is a 24 year old medical student; who was sent by a physician after some years of medical treatment. She told me that she was suspicious of every kind of psychotherapy, but that she was willing to test this possibility. She suffered from severe heart neurosis with attacks of fear of death. And she was so terrified by the fantasy of further attacks, that she seemed to be totally captured by this fear. In the second session I carefully gave her some invitations to find a good place, a little bit separated from the overwhelming fear of these terrifying attacks. This enabled her to sense her fear as a whole, and suddenly there was a dramatic shift with a new meaning to this fear: It no longer was fear of death, but fear of life! It was like a sudden opening of a door to a room filled with a lot of specific fears, in the middle of this room was the fear of being insufficient and unattractive, unable to cope with life. This woman felt great relief at the end of this session. To my surprise she never since then (a year ago) had such heavy attacks again.

Nevertheless, she still had unpleasant bodily sensations around her heart and she suffered from feeling inferior. In the further course of therapy, she very often rejected my invitations to attend to the bodily felt sense of a problem. But sometimes, especially when we looked at the quality of what was going on between us right now, she was able to refer directly to her experience. So, from my point of view, the therapy process followed a zig-zag line between opening and closing, being close and far.

After 46 sessions, Mrs. B is at a point where she is able to enjoy herself by looking at her process with less criticism: She perceives her own strength, she can now be a little more empathic with herself and less dependent on her parents and her friend.

Example B

Mrs. K., a 29 year old social scientist initiated the first contact with some ironical comments on psychotherapy and psychotherapists in general. She had a diagnosis of chronical gastritis and she had extraordinarily severe pain during menstruation.

"Every well-educated person nowadays knows that chronical gastritis is a psychosomatic disease. So here I am."

She too was sent by a physician and she showed her distrust in an eloquent and elegant way. In the first three sessions she remained on the level of her theoretical concepts, ignoring my attempts to slow down her talking.

In the following session, she criticized the superficial character of the first three ones. There was no progress, only a standstill, she said.

I asked her to feel this "standstill." "Yes, I can feel it ... it is like swimming on the surface of the water, not being able to dive, there are to many swimming belts. I cannot reach depth ...(starts weeping)... there comes another picture, I am surrounded by fog, can see nothing, hear nothing, smell nothing. I have no sense of direction."

At the end of this session she felt her pain, her fear of being alone, her wish to have another person to be close.

She was deeply impressed by the depth she had reached now by herself! And she was frightened by the depth of her experience. In subsequent sessions, she developed a tremendous creativity with magnificent pictures of her inner processes. And she had a lot of dreams. She felt she was discovering unknown regions in herself.

The frequency of phases with a strong tendency to talk and to look only at her intellectual concepts diminished more and more.

Instead, she more often came spontaneously to the point of looking inside, being touched by her feelings and then developing these marvelous pictures. But in spite of this process of opening and obvious progress in her life "outside," she sometimes was doubtful of the value of therapy.

The frequency of her stomach-ache diminished significantly and she started to interpret the pain as a sign of "something is wrong now, clear it up!"

And there was another important step: "When I feel cramped and bodily tensed, I cannot feel any fear - but I know that if I relax the fear will come!" This was the beginning of searching for a way to produce deep release; finally, she was able to reduce her menstruation pain a little.

Looking back on the therapy at the end of it (47 sessions) she said: "I am so amazed that I could clear something by just following my own pictures and dreams without making it clear!" And: "Sorry, I told you so many dreams, knowing well that you aren't a psychoanalyst, but I thought, that's my session, and so you had to swallow it!"

SOME FINAL COMMENTS

For me, the most surprising therapeutic event is the sudden shift produced by focusing on the "leading psychosomatic symptom": At this point of the process, the bodily feeling of the symptom changes to the bodily felt meaning of the symptom. It seems as though the symptom becomes useless, sometimes even disappears!

For this dramatic process to occur it is most important to succeed in "making space," especially if fear is so overwhelming. Then it can be like opening a door to the inner rooms of the big palace of a person! And it is surprising too that this bit by bit teaching of focusing seems to many psychosomatic clients to be the correct middle way between a structured and an unstructured offer. The classical zig-zag line of focusing between the rather new, unknown, vague, implicit awareness and the well-known, safe, explicit awareness seems to reduce distrust and fear of going inside. Using pictures and dreams as a medium allows the client to look at it; there seems to be a third party between client and therapist to which both can refer without touching each other directly. This seems to provide a support for the safety of the client, which enables him/her to allow more intensity into the therapeutic relationship. So the combination of person-centered therapy and carefully introduced focusing seems to be an appropriate way of practising psychotherapy with so-called "psychosomatic clients."

REFERENCES

Biermann-Ratjen, E., Eckert, J., & Schwartz, H. (1979). *Gesprächspsychotherapie. Verändern durch Verstehen.* Stuttgart: Kohlhammer.

Freud, S. (1892-1899). *Gesammelte Werke* (Vol. I). Frankfurt a. Main: Fischer.

Gendlin, E.T. (1979). *The use of focusing during psychotherapy.* Unpublished manuscript. University of Chicago.

Marty, P. et al. (1963). *L'investigation psychosomatique.* Paris.

Mitscherlich, A. (1969). *Krankheit als Konflikt. Studien zur psychosomatischen Medizin.* Frankfurt a. Main: Suhrkamp.

Pfeiffer, W.M. (1987). Der Widerstand in der klientenzentrierten Psychotherapie. *GwG-Zeitschrift, 18(66),* 55-62.

Sifneos, (1973). The prevalence of "alexithymic" characteristics in psychosomatic patients. *Psychotherapie und Psychosomatik, 22,* 255-262.

Uexküll, T. von. (1981). *Lehrbuch der Psychosomatischen Medizin.* München: Urban & Schwarzenberg.

MEMBER AND THERAPIST PERCEPTIONS OF THERAPEUTIC FACTORS IN THERAPY AND GROWTH GROUPS: COMMENTS ON A CATEGORY SYSTEM[1]

Paul DIERICK & Germain LIETAER
Katholieke Universiteit Leuven, Belgium

INTRODUCTION

The systematic study of therapeutic factors in therapy and growth groups is generally considered to date from a review article by Corsini and Rosenberg (1955). Most publications since that time have used a common set of nine to twelve factors (Yalom, 1975, 1985; Bloch & Crouch, 1985). Many studies have used some variations of Yalom's (1975) therapeutic factor questionnaire. Bloch et al., (1979, 1980) solicited open statements from group members in the form of critical incidents, but the responses were analyzed according to an "a priori" set of ten therapeutic factor categories. Only three studies analyzed such critical incident statements without preset categories, allowing these to emerge from the answers themselves (Berzon et al., 1963; Dickoff & Lakin, 1963; Lieberman et al., 1973). Unfortunately in each of these studies the helpful factors are described only in a summary fashion with little concrete detail so that the wealth of information present in the answers of the group members is lost in the category descriptions.

In the present study, statements from group members and therapists were placed into clusters based on similar content themes. In this manner we hoped to address the question of whether or not the customary 9 to 12 therapeutic factors indeed constitute an exhaustive listing. In addition, we were interested in eliciting information regarding specific concrete experiences that members considered helpful. By utilizing a natural categorizing system rather than predetermined categories, we hoped to detect a broader range of categories than those traditionally used in the literature. In addition to these central questions, our study provides an opportunity to compare three perspectives: Events helpful for Self, events seen to be helpful for

742

Others in the group, and helpful events as reported by Therapists. Furthermore the reported incidence of helpful events are compared in group sessions rated by the members as useful or not useful. We are also able to look for differences in the nature of therapeutic events reported in sample subgroups concerning members' motivation, in groups run from different theoretical orientations, as well as viewing the results from the standpoint of group developmental stages.

METHOD

Sample and data collection

Fourteen small groups participated in the study, with a total membership of 115 members. These fourteen groups consisted of two outpatient psychotherapy groups, one intensive experiential learning group for trainees in client-centered therapy, and eleven growth groups for students in clinical psychology. All therapists were clinical psychologists with post-graduate therapy training and several years of experience. Five therapists were of a client-centered orientation, two of psychoanalytic and two of Gestalt orientation. Some therapists participated in two or three groups in the study. Group members completed a questionnaire (see below) during the initial phase of the group (i.e. after 4 to 15 hours) or during the middle phase of the group (i.e. after 17 to 60 hours). In total, responses were gathered from twenty five different sessions or series of sessions and consisted of 187 questionnaire forms completed by group members, and 27 forms completed by therapists or co-therapists.

The questionnaires and the three judgment viewpoints

The questionnaires for members and therapist consisted of the following parts:
1. A global evaluation of the session(s) on a seven point Likert scale ranging from "not good at all" to "very good."
2. An open-ended question regarding aspects of the group session(s) that were helpful for the individual personally. This viewpoint will be referred to as "Self."

"Did particular things happen in this (these) session(s) that you feel were particularly helpful *for you personally?* Can you say something about them?"

3. An open-ended question regarding helpful events for other group members or for the group as a whole. This viewpoint will be referred to as "Other."

"Did particular things happen in this (these) session(s) that you feel were particularly helpful *for other group members or for the group as a whole?"*

4. An open-ended question for the therapist regarding helpful events for group members or the group as a whole, similar in content to number 3 above. This viewpoint will be referred to as "Therapist."

5. A similar set of questions was posed regarding unhelpful or harmful experiences and events. In this paper only helpful events are considered.

Content Analysis

The responses to the open-ended questions concerning helpful events were broken down into meaningful segments, each containing a different element of the helpful aspect. Rating of these segments according to their correspondence or difference in meaning, permitted - in several stages on the basis of half the material - to establish mutually exclusive content categories, containing all segments (Holsti, 1968; Weber, 1985). Because of the close resemblance between the answers from the three viewpoints ("Self," "Other," and "Therapist"), a unitary category system could be devised for the analysis of all responses. Once the category system was formed, two independent raters evaluated one sixth of the questionnaire material with an 80% correspondence in decisions. The entire data base was then analyzed.

In order to reveal further structure of helpful events, we clustered the basic categories where possible, keeping to near-similarities in meaning. In this way we obtained a series of "main categories" which we consider the backbone of our findings.

RESULTS

The category system of helpful events

The *basic categories* are described below along with illustrative examples where useful, regarding "(S)elf," "(O)ther," or "(T)herapist" viewpoints. We indicate the percentage of all segments for S, O and T in brackets following each category name, so that the relative weight of each category in our material can be seen at a glance. Where further content clustering occurs basic categories are presented as subdivisions of a *main category*.

Considered generally, the helpful categories emerging from the responses, turn out to be classifiable in *three sections*. The answers which group members and therapists gave on the open-ended questions about helpful aspects, pertain to: Certain facets of the relational climate and structural aspects of the group (section A), specific interventions by therapist or other group members (section B), and certain aspects of the process which the member mainly goes through himself (section C).

Section A: Relational climate and structural aspects of the group

1. Structural aspects of the group
1a. Events related to the composition of the group. (S: 0.4%, O: 0.4%, T: 0.5%). The fact that all ages are represented; that there is someone in the group in whom I recognize aspects of my mother; that the group is composed of motivated members; that my sweetheart is not a member of the group...
1b. Structural aspects of the sessions. (S: 0.6%, O: 0.4%, T: 0%). The weekend structure; respecting time limits ...

2. Group cohesion
2a. Belonging and feeling at home. (S: 4.6%, O: 7.2%, T: 6.1%). The member feels accepted and "wanted" in the group; a feeling of belonging together; an atmosphere of confidence and safety...
2b. Dedication and involvement of others. (S: 3.3%, O: 7.9%, T: 3.7%). Motivation of other group members to work on their problems; attention, interest, empathy and warmth received from other members or therapist ... Ex. O: "The attentive discrete care of the therapist for the group members." T: "A decrease in resistance by an increase of

associations to which almost the whole group contributed; a better working alliance."

2c. Getting a reaction. (S: 1.1%, O: 1.3%, T: 0%). That one answers, takes up or returns to what a group member says or asks, that one does not ignore what he[2] says. The fact of getting a reaction from a particular person.

2d. Informal contact outside the sessions. (S: 0.4%, O: 0.9%, T: 0.5%). An opportunity to simply be together on a friendly basis, to try out new behavior: Experiences that one can eventually discuss later in the group. Ex. S: "The game of volleyball outside, and doing the dishes together, was more helpful; or was it soothing after the hurtful sessions?"

3. Space and freedom
(S: 3.7%, O: 4.3%, T: 0.9%). The group member experiences an atmosphere of openness, tolerance, acceptance; a non-judgmental, non evaluative atmosphere. There is room for all types of personal contributions and reactions, but also freedom and respect for one's own limits and intimacy.

4. Empathy and feeling understood
(S: 2.2%, O: 2.8%, T: 1.9%). One listens empathically. The group member feels understood on a deeper level in what he tries to contribute.

5. Confirmation, appreciation and support
(S: 4.6%, O: 3.2%, T: 4.7%)... for how the member is as a person; regard for certain interventions made in the group; encouraged and stimulated; when having a difficult time, feels supported and fortified by the group. Ex. S: "The therapist's remark that I am capable of actively listening and understanding was invigorating for me."

6. Authenticity and Self-revelation in others
(S: 3.1%, O: 4.3%, T: 1.9%). The group member feels that others in the group are more open and transparent than in everyday life, that they adopt a vulnerable attitude and bring personal matters to the group, that they speak directly from their personal experience... Ex. S: "The disappearance of "masks" in a group member, in the presence of others." S: " The therapist indicated that he felt impotent; this was

useful for me, because one feels it anyway when the therapist desperately tries by any means available, and ends up running into a blind wall."

Section B: Specific interventions by group members or therapist

7. Stimulating and structuring interventions
7a. Inviting and steering interventions. (S: 4.0%, O: 3.0%, T: 2.3%) ... to tell more about oneself, go deeper into a certain issue, describe something more concretely, remain with one's experience and feelings, or to direct attention to the here-and-now experience in the group... Ex. S: "The members ask questions, they wish clarification of your statement." O: "The therapist asked a member directly how he had experienced the behavior of another member."
7b. Offering of therapeutic techniques. (S: 0.9%, O: 0.6%, T: 1.4%) ... which lead the members to reach their own feelings. Ex. associate on words, write a fairy tale, use directed imagery, homework assignment.
7c. Interrupting a disturbing process. (S: 0.6%, O: 1.3%, T: 0.9%). Ex. T: "I have a feeling that I, as therapist, had to intervene to make sure that a couple of people would not suffer severe damage." O: "The fact that a member dared to do something (stand up and smoke), lightened the tense atmosphere."

8. Clarifying and interpretative interventions
8a. Clarifying and deepening empathic interventions. (S: 2.2%, O: 2.8%, T: 4.7%). The therapist or a member repeats what is heard and reformulates it in a clearer fashion, pointing slightly further than what the group member himself already sees; interventions in a clarifying and deepening way about communication between group members. Ex. S: "That the therapist guessed that more was happening in me than I expressed."
8b. Interpretative interventions. (S: 0.9%, O: 1.3%, T: 0.9%). The therapist or group member says something from a different frame of reference, by which he contributes verbal insight; making an interpretation; making connections; offering a broader perspective or an alternative viewpoint; making the group member see something which he did not see before. Ex. O: "What the therapist said about the group process, probably was clarifying for many of us."

9. Feedback and confrontation

(S: 6.1%, O: 7.5%, T: 16.4%). Group members or therapist give their own impression about a group member; point out certain things which they observe in him; or reveal thoughts or feelings which he evokes in them. A member is confronted with aspects of himself which he does not see, something which is difficult for him, but nevertheless helpful. Ex. O: "We have made it clear to him how he stops people in the group by always advancing and defending general statements."

Section C: Process aspects in the group member

10. Personal involvement, authenticity and self-revelation

10a. Personal effort and involvement. (S: 4.0%, O: 2.3%, T: 2.3%). The group member experiences his own active participation in the group as helpful for himself: His input in work on his own problems, and his involvement with another member or with what happens in the group. This may be reflected in a member "coming out of his shell," intervening more frequently, or empathizing with another member...

10b. Inner authenticity and openness. (S: 1.8%, O: 1.3%, T: 0.9%). The group member experiences that he is in touch with what happens deep down in himself, that he is open to his own feelings and to those of others. He experiences readiness to become known with both his positive and negative feelings, both his good qualities and shortcomings.

10c. Bringing something personal to the group. (S: 2.0%, O: 4.3%, T: 6.1%). To bring out personal problems and experiences; these often concern issues about which he does not talk elsewhere. The experience of "putting it into words" or "finally discussing this openly with a group of people" are often cited as helpful.

10d. Being able to, or daring to talk about. (S: 3.7%, O: 3.6%, T: 4.7%) ... about something which preoccupied the member intensely, about an intimate and difficult matter, about something which has been a long preoccupation. This basic category is emotionally more intense than the previous one; it contains a cathartic aspect. The group member surmounts here an inner resistance, either because of personal motivation or because he is invited to do so by others.

11. Self-Exploration

11a. Profound self-exploration. (S: 2.9%, O: 2.4%, T: 3.3%). The group member approaches a personal problem and explores it thoroughly, examines his own part in it. It concerns here an inner search. Ex. S: "I got in touch with things which were repressed in me. I was able to work through some of this, which continued even after therapy."

11b. Experiencing feelings thoroughly and expressing them. (S: 2.0%, O: 2.3%, T: 3.3%). The group member experiences feelings intensively, often physically; this may be accompanied by verbal discussion and eventually by the non-verbal showing of feelings and emotions; he can "blow off steam." Ex. O: "Being able to express his feelings of hate towards his father."

12. Interpersonal exploration

12a. Discussing mutual relations with other group members. (S: 1.6%, O: 6.0%, T: 2.3%). Based on things happening here and now in the group, mutual relations with other group members are thoroughly discussed and explored; conflicts and tensions are talked over, misunderstandings straightened out and prejudices dissipated.

12b. Expressing feelings towards other group members or therapist (S: 1.6%, O: 1.7%, T: 1.9%). The group member is able to directly express his positive and negative feelings towards others in the group and can give critical feedback. Ex. T: "For Carl it was important to be able to say to Bea how much he felt hurt, and not respected, because of what she told him in the last session."

12c. Getting a better understanding of other group members. (S: 2.2%, O: 3.2%, T: 0.5%). The group member gets a better understanding of the behavior of another member, and of his own reaction to it; he gets to know other members better, learns to see them from another viewpoint; this is often accompanied by an ability to accept the other more easily.

13. Becoming conscious of

13a. Starting to think about. (S: 4.6%, O: 1.9%, T: 4.7%). Something which is talked about or happens in the group evokes personal experiences or problems and leads to reflection; it leads the member to ask himself questions, to become conscious of something kept hidden, to put into perspective his own opinions. Ex. S: "The diversity of group members (cat. 1a) brought me back to various corners within myself."

13b. Discussing sensitive topics. (S: 2.1%, O: 1.9%, T: 2.3%). The fact that certain existential, sexual or other topics are discussed in the group. Ex.: that we talked about death; about the search for happiness; about dealing with limitations in life and more specifically in couple relations; about homosexual and heterosexual desires; about the approaching end of the group...

14. Insight in oneself

(S: 7.4%, O: 6.2%, T: 4.7%). The group member discovers new or half-conscious things about himself; he sees recurrent patterns in his dealings with others and with himself; he sees more clearly where his problem really lies; he begins to understand what he really wants; the connections between a present problem and experiences he has lived through in his youth become clearer... Ex. T: "Recognize and acknowledge an inner conflict: Wish and fear."

15. Spectator therapy

15a. Experiencing of communality. (S: 5.6%, O: 2.8%, T: 0.5%). The group member recognizes in himself things which others talk about, or after telling something personal himself, finds that others mention similar experiences; he notices that he is not alone with certain thoughts and questions, that others too have difficulties. Ex. S: "That everyone has some disturbances in ability to relate, and that I should therefore not take mine too tragically."

15b. Learning by observation. (S: 4.2%, O: 1.1%, T: 1.4%). The group member sees or hears how others, or the therapist tackle problems; they hence offer a model and he begins to see that a problem can be solved in other ways than he customarily uses. By hearing others interact, the member learns for example to react more empathically or may learn how to deal with confrontations. The discussion of a problem such as dependency by another group member, and the clarification which that member reaches, is also useful to him.

16. Experiences with new behavior

16a. Trying out new behavior. (S: 1.1%, O: 0.6%, T: 0%). The group member uses the group as a place to try out behaviors which he finds difficult; to experiment with new or rediscovered possibilities, to transform newly acquired insights into concrete behavior. In this way, he may learn to empathize with others, or to state his opinion in an open, direct way...

16b. Planning new behavior outside the group. (S: 1.1%, O: 0.2%, T: 0.9%). The group member makes concrete plans or resolutions to start behaving differently in certain everyday situations outside the group.

16c. Acquiring corrective experiences. (S: 3.1%, O: 0.9%, T: 3.3%) The group member experiences in the group that when he does something, the feared reaction fails to occur, or certain things that he did not think possible do occur. He experiences for example that he can ask a critical question without provoking aggressivity; that one can allow feelings of rage and revenge without necessarily acting them out; that conflicts and tensions in the group which seem dangerous can be resolved; that he can allow himself to be direct and yet secure; that he is not rejected when he expresses positive feelings towards another group member.

17. Experiencing hope and progress, the capacity to help others, and relief

17a. Experiencing one's own progress and hope. (S: 5.9%, O: 2.1%, T: 5.1%). The group member finds it helpful that he is more capable of doing certain things, or has less difficulty with certain things. For example, he finds comfort from the experience that he has already advanced quite a bit in establishing interpersonal contact; that he can be more receptive to others without having his own worries stand in the way; that he can even more easily express criticism; that he does not immediately become defensive when something is said to him; that he can accept himself better. He feels hopeful and looks at the future with (more) confidence because of these experiences.

17b. Being able to help others in the group. (S: 0.9%, O: 0.4%, T: 0.5%). Ex. S: "People have worked at understanding themselves and I have contributed to it. I feel confirmed in being capable of something."

17c. Experiencing a feeling of relief and relaxation. (S: 2.2%, O: 1.9%, T: 1.9%)... mostly after talking of something which is intensely personal; also sometimes after controlling one's respiration, after a "delivering" group laughter, or simply after the tension of a session. Ex. T: "Georges has become a totally different person, as if he was delivered of something which burdened him a lot. He became more sure, calmer, and eventually really helpful to others."

18. Experiencing the helpful potential of the group

18a. The group members are capable of helping each other (S: 0.4%, O:

2.3%, T: 1.4%). The helping potential of the group is confirmed by seeing members make progress and realizing that most interventions are made predominantly by the group members themselves; this leads to greater belief in the specific power of the group process.

18b. The group as enriching experience. (S: 0.9%, O: 1.5%, T: 0.5%). The group member indicates in general terms that he has had an enriching experience. Ex. S: "Certain experiences and events have touched me"; "Afterwards, I feel that I have emerged stronger and more mature from the group experience"; "I have received a piece of wisdom."

Rest categories

19. No helpful events reported (blank responses)

20. Unclassifiable answers.
20a. Unclear answers (n=9).
20b. Clear but unclassifiable answers (n=8). On closer inspection five of these answers appear to refer to receiving concrete advice and suggestions. Ex. T: "Ann found it was helpful when a group member suggested that she write a letter to her father, which she did not need to send, and in which she should write everything she needed to tell him."

QUANTITATIVE ANALYSIS

Table 1 describes the quantitative results of the content analysis applied to the total sample and to the High and Low satisfaction groups (see below). We have limited ourselves to the main categories, and a few additional groupings of basic categories. These groupings were devised to allow some general trends to emerge from our data, referring to therapeutic processes known from the literature (Ag1 to Ag4), or to an important difference between the judgment viewpoints (Ag5), to which we will return later. The quantitative data pertaining to the basic categories (see category system) will be discussed separately only inasmuch as they provide important additional information, above and beyond the findings in the main categories to which they belong.

To find out which categories are significantly more or less often

Table 1

Content analysis of helpful events: Main categories and additional groupings:
Frequencies and percentages of segments in the total Sample for the 3 Judgment viewpoints
(S = Self; O = Others; T = Therapist); Chi-square Test S-O; Frequencies of Segments in High- and Lowgroup;
Chi-square Test H-L (n.s. = not significant; ° = p < .10; * = p < .05; ** = p < .01; *** = p < .001; **** p < .0001).

SECTOR	Main Categories and Additional Groupings	Code	Frequency of segments S (N=187)	O (N=187)	T (N=27)	Percentages S %:544	O %:469	T %:214	Chi²-test S-O p-level	Freq. (Self) High (N=40)	Low (N=40)	Chi²-test H-L p-level
A: RELATIONAL CLIMATE AND STRUCTURAL ASPECTS OF THE GROUP	Structural aspects of the group (a, b)	1	5	4	1	0.9	0.9	0.5	n.s.	2		n.s.
	Group cohesion (a, b, c, d)	2	51	81	22	9.0	17.3	10.3	*	25	1	***
	Space and freedom	3	20	20	2	3.7	4.3	0.9	n.s.	12		**
	Empathy, feeling understood	4	12	13	4	2.2	2.8	1.9	n.s.	2		n.s.
	Confirmation, appreciation and support	5	25	15	10	4.6	3.2	4.7	n.s.	11	3	n.s.
	Authenticity and self-revelation in others	6	17	20	4	3.1	4.3	1.9	n.s.	9		**
	Total for A		130	153	43	23.9	32.6	20.1		61	4	
B: SPECIFIC INTERVENTIONS	Stimulating/structuring interventions (a, b, c)	7	30	23	10	5.6	4.9	4.7	n.s.	9	2	*
	Clarifying/interpretative interventions (a, b)	8	17	19	12	3.1	4.1	5.6	n.s.	5	1	n.s.
	Feedback and confrontation	9	33	35	35	6.1	7.5	16.4	n.s.	11	2	*
	Total for B		80	77	57	14.7	16.4	26.6		25	5	

C: PROCESS ASPECTS IN THE GROUP MEMBER

	No.							sig			sig
Personal involvement, authenticity and self-revelation (a, b, c, d)	10	63	54	30	11.6	11.5	14.0	n.s.	24	2	***
Self-exploration (a, b)	11	27	22	14	5.0	4.7	6.5	n.s.	7	3	n.s.
Interpersonal exploration (a, b, c)	12	30	51	10	5.5	10.9	4.7	*	9	4	n.s.
Becoming conscious of (a, b)	13	36	18	17	6.6	3.8	7.9	**	11	2	*
Insight in oneself	14	40	29	10	7.4	6.2	4.7	*	16	2	***
Spectator therapy (a, b)	15	53	18	4	9.7	3.8	1.9	****	11	8	n.s.
Experiences with new behavior (a, b, c)	16	29	8	9	5.3	1.7	4.2	****	12	2	**
Experiencing: hope and progress, the capacity to help others, and relief (a, b, c)	17	49	21	16	9.0	4.5	7.5	**	18	4	*
Experiencing the helpful potential of the group (a, b)	18	7	18	4	1.3	3.8	1.9	·	2	3	n.s.
Total for C		334	239	114	61.4	51.0	53.3		110	30	
Total Helpful Aspects A+B+C		544	469	214	100.0	100.0	100.0		196	39	

ADDITIONAL GROUPINGS

	No.							sig			sig
Group cohesion in the larger sense (2+3+4+5+6)	Ag1	125	149	42	23.0	31.8	19.6	n.s.	59	4	
Catharsis (10d+11b+12b+17c)	Ag2	52	45	25	9.6	9.6	11.7	n.s.	21	4	
Self-insight in larger sense (8+13+14)	Ag3	93	66	39	17.1	14.1	18.2	*	32	5	
Interpersonal learning in the here-and-now (9+12+15+16)	Ag4	145	112	58	26.7	23.9	27.1	**	43	16	
Internal experiencing (10a+10b+13a+14+17a)	Ag5	182	83	42	33.5	17.7	19.6	****	56	16	
Rest: No helpful aspects (blank responses)	19	41	44	1	21.9 (%:187)	23.9 (%:187)	3.7 (%:27)		24		****

mentioned in self-judgment as compared to judgment about other group members, statistical tests were carried out[3]. We mention the results when they reach or exceed a level of significance of p < .10.

First, we discuss the nature and frequency of those events which the group members experience as helpful for themselves. Within the Self viewpoint we examen additionally, by comparing the High and Low groups, which helpful events differenciate best between productive and rather unproductive sessions. Further we examen how helpful events are judged from a participating observer's viewpoint, i.e. by other group members and therapists.

1. Self-perception of helpful events

Nature and frequency

A general overview shows that more than 60% of the response-segments fall in with section C. What one sees as helpful pertains thus mainly to the process which the group member himself goes through during the grouptherapy.

Within section A, the *Structural aspects of the group* (i.e. the composition of the group and organization of the sessions) are seldom explicitly mentioned as helpful, although they form the framework in which the therapeutic process takes place. We should not be surprised that group members pay as little attention to these ever-present environmental factors as a fish to the water in which it swimms (Chuang Tsu, cited in Berk, 1986, p. 40). One points out what strikes what stands out, and seldom what exerts an influence along sub- or unconscious ways.

An important series of helpful events seems related to the *Relational climate in the group*. Group cohesion mainly comprising the basic categories Belonging and Feeling at home(2a), and Experiencing dedication and involvement on the part of others(2b), occurs in 9.4% of the segments. When we consider group cohesion in the larger sense of the word, by adding other group-relational climate categories (Ag1), the importance of this group of helpful aspects stands out even more. In 23% of the segments, at least one of these categories (2 to 6) is mentioned as helpful for oneself.

The second section of helpful events concerns *Specific interventions* by therapist and other group members. Remarkable here is that Feedback and confrontation (9) plays a major role. As to Stimulating and structuring interventions (7), it is worth mentioning that it consists mainly of Inviting and steering interventions (7a), while Offering of therapeutic techniques (7b) is reported only a few times. Of the three main intervention categories, the Clarifying and interpretative interventions (8) are the least frequent. But within these, the Clarifying and deepening empathic interventions (8a) occur twice as frequently as the Interpretative interventions (8b).

Section C, *Process aspects in the group member* contains the largest number of categories. We discuss them under five headings in order to allow the general trends to emerge.

1. Personal involvement, authenticity and self-revelation (10) is mentioned in 11.6% of the segments by group members as being helpful to them; this is the highest frequency in the main categories. That group members should be motivated to participate in the group process and "plunge themselves into it" appears to be a conditio sine qua non, to allow other helpful processes to occur, or to intensify them. However, this *active involvement* per se is already experienced as particularly helpful.

2. A second series of process aspects in the group member pertains to *self-exploration and cognitive reflection and assimilation.* Self-exploration (11) occurs in 5.0% of the segments. This process of intrapsychic exploration of one's own life situation and feelings seems to be about as frequent in our sample groups as Interpersonal exploration (12). In addition, our group members seem to put the emphasis on cognitive reflection and assimilation. This is evidenced by the relatively large percentage of segments belonging to the Insight in oneself category (14: 7.4%) and by the additional grouping "self-insight in the larger sense" (Ag3: 17.1%) which contains, besides Insight in oneself (14) also Becoming conscious (13) and Clarifying and interpretative interventions (8). It should be remembered here that our sample is composed of psychologically sophisticated group members, all with higher education: Over 80% were students at Master level in Clinical psychology or therapy trainees. Hence it is not surprising that cognitive reflection and assimilation is highly valued in this population, perhaps more so than in a psychologically less

sophisticated population or one with less formal education. The category Becoming conscious (13) reveals one of the typical forces in group therapy: A group process wakes up a lot of things; one is often "surprised" that one's own experiences emerge, elicited by particular happenings in the group.

3. As third point in section C, we discuss those helpful categories in which the typical *interpersonal learning* properties of the group situation are put to use. Interpersonal exploration (12) contains: Discussing of mutual relations, expressing of feelings towards others and getting better understanding of other group members. These aspects are mentioned in 5.5% of the segments in self-judgment.

Spectator therapy (15) contains two basic categories with, as common element, the gaining of a helpful experience from observation of what other group members say or do in the group, without being actively involved oneself: Experiencing of communality (15a) and Learning by observation (15b). In self-judgment, Spectator therapy (15) is mentioned in 9.7% of the segments. Group members thus seem to benefit a great deal from the group, even without participating actively.

Experiences with new behavior (16: 5.3%) is also a typical possibility of the group situation. It contains especially Acquiring corrective experiences (16c): Finding out, in the group, that the feared reaction does not occur when one does something, or that certain things which were not thought possible can happen anyway. Trying out new behavior in the group (16a) and Planning new behavior outside the group (16b) are however seldom mentioned. These two categories reflect perhaps a process more typical of behavior therapy, and were maybe not explicitly emphasized in these experience-oriented methods of guiding groups.

All these categories, together with Feedback and confrontation (9) reflect various aspects and forms of interpersonal learning in the here-and-now group situation. This additional grouping of data (Ag4) shows that it is a very frequently mentioned group of helpful aspects in the group members' self-judgment (26.7%). Testing reality in the microcosmos of the group appears thus to be central in these groups.

4. Experiencing hope and progress, the capacity to help others, and relief (17), is relatively often mentioned by the group in self-judgment (9.0%). It is Experiencing one's own progress and hope (17a) which predominates. *Getting results,* perhaps by means of other helpful group processes, is thus mentioned as a valuable support in itself.

5. Finally, in a number of previously discussed categories of the C section, we discover aspects of the emotional curative process which is called *"catharsis"* in the literature, i.e. Being able to, or daring to talk about (10d), Experiencing feelings thoroughly (11b), Expressing feelings towards other group members or therapist (12b), and Experiencing a feeling of relief or relaxation (17c). We have put these categories together in an additional grouping (Ag2) which shows that these emotional process aspects too, are an important part of the therapeutic process for group members (9.6%), even though they are not as often mentioned as the more cognitive process aspects.

From the grouping in our category system, on the other hand, we also notice the closeness in meaning of these emotional aspects to the more cognitive ones inside one same main category: See Self-revelation, Self-exploration, and Interpersonal exploration (10, 11, 13).

It is even possible that our category system separates too forcefully the cognitive and the emotional, which could be osmotic aspects of one and the same process. This was for example pointed out by Yalom (1975) and Lietaer and Neirinck (1986). The notion of "felt sense" in experiential therapy reflects very well the osmotic junction between cognition and emotion.

Comparison of High and Low satisfaction groups

In a further effort to differentiate the impact of helpful factors, the global 7-pointscale evaluation was used to create High and Low satisfaction subgroups. The helpful events contained in the forty top and forty bottom responses of the 187 member questionnaires were compared. In all main categories but one, helpful events were mentioned more frequently in the High satisfaction group than in the Low satisfaction group. On the other hand, No helpful events reported (19) occurred only in the Low satisfaction group. This clearly identifies the close connection between satisfaction and the reporting of helpful events. We also consider this as evidence for the validity of our selection criteria for the extreme groups.

This trend is particularly strong in section A where fifteen times more helpful segments are mentioned in the High group than in the Low group (61/4), whereas in sections B and C only 4 to 5 times more (25/5 and 110/30). The relational climate seems thus to be the best barometer for the quality of a session in the group members' experience. Within section C, we find the biggest difference between "productive sessions" and rather "unproductive sessions" in Personal involvement, authenticity and self-revelation (10). "Plunging into it" seems thus also to bear fruit. On the other hand, we see that Spectator therapy (15) does not differentiate at all between the two extreme groups (H: 11, L: 8), in spite of the fact that it is the second most frequent main category. Although Learning by observation (15b) still shows some difference (H: 5, L: 2), Experiencing of communality (15a) occurs as frequently in the Low group, as in the High group (H=6, L=6), and is, in the Low group, the most frequently mentioned category. Did this category obtain a certain prominence when no other helpful events had been experienced? Might we think of Experiencing of communality as a general facilitating therapeutic process, one which prepares for the real work, manifested in other helpful events which do indeed differentiate between productive and rather unproductive sessions? In any event, personal work and active involvement in the context of a cohesive group are seen clearly more productive than passive, receptive following.

2. Perception of helpful events from a participating observer's viewpoint

It has already been mentioned that the same content categories are found in material from each of the three viewpoints. Here, we look at the frequencies with which the categories are mentioned, on the one hand in self-perception, and on the other hand from the point of view of a participating observer: Other group members or therapist.

In this comparison, we started by assuming a fundamental difference in nature between self-perception and perception by outside observation. In the first case, the judge has direct access to the intra-subjective experience, since he observes himself, whereas in the second, the judge must rely on his perception and empathy with the other person. In order to verify, on the basis of this difference, whether those helpful events which happen mostly inside the private world of a group member and have thus fewer external correlates, whether they are mentioned more frequently in self-judgment than in both other judgments, we grouped together in an additional category the following basic categories, which seem to refer to a *more internally experienced content* (Ag5): Experiencing personal effort and involvement (10a),

Experiencing inner authenticity and openness (10b), Starting to think about (13a), Insight in oneself (14), Experiencing of communality (15a), Learning by observation (15b), and Experiencing one's own progress and hope (17a).

Other group members

In Table 1 we see that this additional grouping of basic categories (Ag5) indeed represents a very significantly greater part of segments in self-judgment than in judgment by other group members ($p < .0001$). The differences in these basic categories separately (see category system) form also the basis of the significant differences in the main categories to which they belong (13, 14, 15, 17). In other members, one has thus less of a view on those helpful aspects which operate mostly in the person's inner experience, and have fewer outside correlates.

On the other hand, group members as participating observers seem to pay significantly more attention to Group cohesion (2), Interpersonal exploration (12), and Experiencing the helpful potential of the group (18). This could be partly induced by the particular question asked. Indeed, these categories reflect events which are not only helpful to other group members, but also to the group as a whole, the participating observer included. Besides, these all focus on the overt process of the group interaction as benefiting members, which can be readily seen in others.

Remains the discussion of the main category Experiences with new behavior (16), in which we are surprised to see a significantly higher percentage in "Self" than in "Others." Indeed, Experiences with new behavior would seem to be clearly observable. This difference is, however, mainly determined by Acquiring corrective experiences (16c). And, in retrospect, the corrective nature of an experience may not be highly visible (cf. description of the category). One can clearly see what someone does, or what he participates in, but not "in which soil it falls"; what it exactly means to him.

Therapist's perception

In the additional grouping Internal experiencing (Ag5), we see that the therapist's judgment falls to the same level as the judgment by other group members, i.e. clearly lower than the self-judgment. This confirms that the therapist, as other group members, has a more limited view on the occurrence of a number of helpful factors in the group process, which happen mainly "inside" each group member. Remarkable is that Spectator therapy (15) went fairly unnoticed by therapists: Experiencing communality (15a) in fact only once. Compared with the individual therapist, the group therapist is thus less in touch with a number of process aspects. It seems important to us that group therapists be aware of this. They may for example regularly try to find out, by exploratory questions, what is happening within each of their group members.

On the other hand, we see that therapists mention specific therapeutic interventions roughly 10% more often (26.5%) than group members, and particularly more than twice as much Feedback and confrontation (16.4%). It seems reasonable that therapists, by virtue of theoretical training, may pay more attention to this typical process than do the members. Space and freedom (3) in turn was seldom mentioned by therapists, in contrast with group members. Perhaps for therapists, this is part and parcel of the therapeutic framework of a group (as water is for a fish) and does not strike particularly as a helpful aspect, although it does so occasionally for group members.

3. Group versus therapist source of help

For some of the basic categories (see Table 2) it was possible to compare response segments making explicit reference to help from the therapist (T) and those referring to help from other group members, the group as a whole, or giving no explicit reference to this point (G). It can be seen that in general the members reported a much higher number of helpful events in relation to group members or the group as a whole than in relation to the therapist. Explicit references to the therapist (in self-judgment) occur approximately in a proportion of one to six (50/278) in those categories suitable for such references, and in approximately one tenth of all response segments (50/544). This may be an underestimation of the frequency with which the therapist is experienced as contributing to helpful events because therapeutic activity may be implicitly included in the references to the group-as-a-whole (G). We can thus certainly not maintain that the therapist is seldom mentioned, but in general we see that experiencing of helpful

Table 2

Content analysis data for the subcategories "Therapist" (T) versus "Group" (G) Source of help:
Frequencies of segments for "Self", "Others" and "Therapist-judgment".

SECTOR	Basic categories with T-G subcategories	Code	SELF (N=187)		OTHERS (N=187)		THERAPIST (N=27)	
			frequency of segments	frequency of segments	frequency of segments	frequency of segments	frequency of segments	frequency of segments
A: SPECIFIC RELATIONAL CLIMATE	Belonging and feeling at home	2a	2	23	1	33	1	12
	Dedication and involvement of others	2b	3	15	3	34	0	8
	Getting a reaction	2c	1	5	0	6	0	0
	Informal contact outside the sessions	2d	0	2	1	3	1	0
	Space and freedom	3	4	16	5	15	1	1
	Empathy and feeling understood	4	2	10	1	12	0	4
	Confirmation, appreciation and support	5	6	19	1	14	0	10
	Authenticity and self-revelation in others	6	1	15	0	20	0	4
B: INTERVENTIONS	Inviting and steering interventions	7a	8	14	5	9	3	2
	Offering of therapeutic techniques	7b	5	-	3	-	3	-
	Interrupting a disturbing process	7c	0	3	1	5	1	1
	Clarifying and deepening empathic interventions	8a	8	4	5	8	5	5
	Interpretative interventions	8b	3	2	4	2	2	0
	Feedback and confrontation	9	3	30	2	33	6	29
C: PROCESS GROUP MEMBER	Expressing feelings towards others	12b	1	8	0	8	3	1
	Discussing sensitive topics	13b	1	10	0	9	0	7
	Experiencing of communality	15a	0	30	0	13	0	1
	Learning by observation	15b	1	22	0	5	0	3
	Total segments		50	228	32	229	24	88

events is not tied to the therapist. This is even clearer in the judgment about other group members than in self-judgment.

When the therapist is identified, it is primarily from Section B dealing with specific interventions. Clarifying and deepening empathic interventions (8a) represent here most typically the helpful power of the therapist, together with Interpretative interventions (8b). He also plays a large part in Inviting and steering interventions (7a). Therapeutic techniques are, of course, only offered by the therapist (7b), but this is, in the kind of groups under study here, seldom mentioned. Therapists themselves do not only attach more importance to specific interventions, as we already saw in Table 1; besides, they refer relatively more frequently to their own interventions as source of help than do members (a "narcissistic trait"?).

In contrast to this, Feedback and confrontation (9) seems to happen primarily between group members. The helpful events pertaining to the relational climate (section A), also refer more to other group members or to the group as a whole. This confirms that the relational climate in group therapy is mostly carried by group members. Finally, and in the same vein, we notice that the therapist is seldom or never mentioned as the one towards whom powerful feelings are expressed (12b), with whom one discusses particular topics (13b), with whom one experiences communality (15a) or from whom one learns by observation (15b). Thus, the therapist is not reported as playing an important role as a model or companion in fate. "Encounter" with a self-revealing therapist seems a rare occurrence in these groups.

These findings demonstrate that, in these experiential groups, the therapist was not seen to be the central figure, and that the group process played itself out primarily between group members. This does not mean that the therapist had an unimportant role, but rather that his role was more an indirect one: To ensure that the group functioned well. This is in keeping with Yalom's (1975) description of the three fundamental tasks of the group therapist: Composing and maintaining the group, developing a therapeutic culture, and initiating and clarifying the here-and-now in the group.

4. Helpful events in relation to: Member's motivation, therapeutic orientation, and phase in the group process

Without going into the concrete methodology, we discuss here the major findings. (For a more detailed discussion, see Dierick, in preparation).

From the comparison between the less motivated student groups and the strongly motivated groups of clients and therapist-trainees, the predominant role of *motivation* as a conditio sine qua non emerges clearly: Where motivation is weak, all helpful processes, especially the most productive ones where the group member has to be actively involved, occur less frequently, in spite of the appreciated interventions of the therapist.

Comparison between *therapeutic orientation* was possible for the client-centered and the Gestalt groups of our sample (114 vs 58 answer forms). Nearly all helpful categories were mentioned with approximately the same relative frequency in both orientations. The only exception appears in the Offering of therapeutic techniques (10a), which is not mentioned at all in the client-centered groups, as opposed to six times in the Gestalt groups ("Self" and "Others" added up). This difference was to be expected, but remarkable is that, even in Gestalt groups, this category is mentioned so rarely. There are however differences in theory and technique. In line with Perls, Gestalt groups would have more the character of individual therapy in a group, with the group member who works in the "hot chair", the therapist as central figure, and the group as chair. The differences in method between both types of groups seem however to have made little or no difference here in the type and frequency of the helpful events mentioned by the members. The similarity found in this is probably due to the fact that both orientations are experiential and maybe also to the fact that the group phenomenon brings about typical helpful events which remain constant in spite of differences in method.

About the *phase in the group process,* we investigated whether different helpful aspects came to the fore more in the initial phase of a group than in the middle phase, where the group is already more advanced. The initial phase was operationally defined as: The responses to the open questions after four to fifteen therapy hours (41 answer sheets). From 17 to 60 hours was considered the middle phase (146 answer sheets).

In the initial phase of the group, we notice a relative emphasis on the helpful events of the group relational climate. Especially the categories Experiencing space and freedom , and Group cohesion are mentioned very significantly more often in the initial phase than in the middle phase (together 21% vs. 10%). In the same vein, Stimulating and structuring interventions were mentioned more frequently in the initial phase than later in the group process (10% vs. 4%). In the other direction, there are no significant differences, although there is a trend for the section C process categories as a group to occur more frequently in the middle phase; a tendency which is also noticeable in the additional groupings Self-insight in the larger sense, and Interpersonal learning in the here-and-now.

These findings are in keeping with the phenomena observed by Butler and Fuhriman (1983), and are in keeping with Mackenzie's (1987) analysis of the stages of development in a group. These authors suggest that in the early sessions engagement, acceptance, and the development of a group identity, are central. Only later does one find increasing levels of polarization, exploration of differences between group members, and more intensive introspective and interpersonal work, contributing a.o. to an increased degree of self-insight.

CLOSING COMMENTS

In this study, we have chosen to investigate helpful processes in group therapy by asking the people involved to write down, in answer to open-ended questions, what they found helpful in a particular group session or series of sessions. In these closing comments, we first want to look at our experience-geared methodology. Next, we confront the helpful aspects which we discovered, with the therapeutic factors described in the literature. We close with a look at the typical therapeutic possibilities of group therapy as compared to individual client-centered therapy.

Subjective experience as angle of approach

Therapeutic processes that operate on an unconscious level or outside of full awareness will not be reached with this method. We can only trace what is represented in the conscious experience. While this is a limitation, we believe that material reported at a level of conscious experience is very important. We follow here MacKenzie's reasoning (1987, p. 26): "The basic idea of this approach lies in the concept that individuals interpret their interpersonal world and its experiences in an idiosyncratic fashion, and that subsequent behavior is highly influenced by this process of personalized meaning-attribution. Strategies to tap the patient's perception of therapeutic events may thus reveal mediating variables which are not accessible by more objective techniques of process measurement."

In this study, we complemented the subjective self-perception of the group members by also asking the group members and the therapist to report on what they saw as helpful for their fellow group members. It is remarkable that these participant observers fail to see a great deal of what happens in the experience of each group member. On the other hand, they appear to see particular other helpful events more often: Therapists seem to pay more attention to specific therapeutic interventions, and especially the process of feedback and confrontation, whereas fellow group members seem to notice more those events related to group cohesion. This study shows thus clearly the complementarity between the various judgment-viewpoints.

Helpful processes

Most of the "therapeutic factors" found in the group psychotherapy literature are quite recognizable in the helpful events we reported. Besides, generally speaking, we find the same processes appearing centrally, and the same ones to remain on the periphery. In this study we have in some instances found a more finely differenciated content.
- *Group cohesion* defined by Yalom (1975) in a general way as "the resultant of all the forces acting on all the members to remain in the group", has received a richer content and has been enlarged to include an array of Group relational climate dimensions. Within these, Rogers' basic relationship attitudes are easily recognizable.
- As far as *Self-revelation* is concerned, we find that here too the basic attitudes such as personal effort and involvement in the group process, personal authenticity, openness and readiness to let oneself be known, are important.
- *Self-insight* is broadened to include the whole process of cognitive

reflection and assimilation. Not only reaching the end result was reported as being helpful, but also the clarifying and interpretative interventions which lead to insight, as well as moments of budding consciousness, starting to think about something, asking oneself questions, spurred on by particular topics discussed, or events happening in the group. That reflection and working through does not only happen on a cognitive level but also on a feeling level, is especially highlighted by our category Self-exploration which contains a cathartic aspect. As mentioned earlier, our category system makes perhaps too sharp a separation between what may well be osmotic aspects of the same process.

- We distinguish several forms of *Interpersonal learning in the here-and-now:* Feedback and confrontation; Interpersonal exploration (which includes: Discussing of mutual relations, expressing feelings towards others, and acquiring insight into other group members); Experiences with new behavior (including trying out new behavior in the group and especially, having corrective experiences); and also "Spectator therapy", in which we recognize the therapeutic factors of *"universality"* and "vicarious learning" which were traditionally considered separately (a.o. Bloch & Crouch, 1985).

- Finally, we notice that certain aspects of *"catharsis"* are, in our category system, an essential part of Self-revelation, Self-exploration and Interpersonal exploration. This puts clearly in evidence that emotional working-through, means far more than pure "ventilation of feelings."

- Experiencing one's own progress and *hope,* Experiencing relief and relaxation, and Being able to help others in the group were taken together, all as expressions of the experience of positive results in the course of the therapeutic process. These experiences appear to constitute a marked encouragement for group members. Included in this category, we recognize the traditional therapeutic factor of *"altruism".* In line with findings from other studies done with out-patient therapy and growth groups of medium duration, the ability to help other group members - and thus temporally putting one's own problems in the background - is mentioned only very occasionally in our study. Perhaps this would be a more important factor for group members with more serious problems.

- *Receiving advice* is almost never mentioned as helpful. This is in line with most other studies of group therapeutic factors where experiential therapeutic approaches are investigated. Perhaps advice is given more often in such groups, but not seen in itself as helpful. The recipient could for example, especially sense the concern of others or the support reflected in the advice and mention this as helpful. It is also striking that the few instances of receiving advice, which were mentioned, seem to refer to suggestions which were closely in line with the experience of the receiver, and left him free to use it or not.

- Yalom's (1975) factor of *corrective re-experiencing one's family of origin* does not occur in our category system. Probably our groups did not have enough age differences to evoke parent-child relationships. In the outpatient group where younger as well as older people participated, we found a few segments indirectly referring to parent-child relationships: In the categories concerning the composition of the group, the discussion of sensitive topics and the expression of feelings towards others. There was however no reference to the re-experiencing of sibling-relationships, or parental relationships with the therapist - something which could theoretically occur in all groups. Indeed, Yalom himself and other researchers, have found similarly that this therapeutic factor is seldom mentioned as helpful by group members (cf. Yalom, Tinklenberg & Gilula, 1975, p. 97; Lieberman, Yalom & Miles, 1973, p. 374). Nevertheless this does not mean that reliving and correcting feelings and relationship patterns stemming from the family of origin, would not play an important part in the therapeutic process in the group. Quite the contrary, we think, even though it is not recognized as such by the parties involved. Indeed, as Yalom (1975, p. 97) mentions, it may involve a therapeutic factor
which operates at another level of consciousness.

Group versus individual therapy

We were able to compare the helpful events found in the present study, with those found in a methodologically similar study by Lietaer and Neirinck (1986) concerning individual client-centered psychotherapy. The content category systems in both studies were remarkably similar. In group therapy we find roughly, with a few minor exceptions, all the helpful aspects which were experienced in individual therapy, although sometimes in differently formulated categories. In this similarity, we find a confirmation of our opinion that group therapy is an equally valid form of therapy. That the group offers a number of additional possibilities is shown in the following helpful aspects which either do not occur at all, or occur in a more limited fashion, in individual psychotherapy.

- The events pertaining to the relational climate have perhaps a larger impact in group therapy, where they are experienced not only in relationship to the therapist, but also to other group members. A therapist's acceptance of a client can, for example still be perceived by the client as something belonging to his job, where this is less possible when the acceptance comes from other group members. The aspect "belonging and feeling at home in the group" appears to be very important.
- Being able to, or daring to talk about a difficult issue, whereby one has to transcend an inner barrier, as it were, was mentioned much more often as helpful by members of a group than by clients in individual client-centered therapy. This suggests that the therapeutic impact of self-revelation is greater in a group context.
- The field of interpersonal learning in the here-and-now is broader in a group. In such therapeutic processes as feedback and confrontation, interpersonal exploration, spectator therapy and experiences with new behavior, one is in an active and profound way confronted with the social reality which is the group, and especially with how one handles this reality oneself. Besides, we see that clients in group therapy experience their own effort and involvement with others as helpful for themselves, and similarly their "altruism": To be able to help others.
- Finally, because of particular events happening in a group, specific issues can be raised in a group member, which probably would otherwise not have come to the surface so soon.

On the other hand, our comparison reveals that intrapsychic exploration of personal problems and the resulting self-insight as helpful events were mentioned relatively twice as frequently in individual client-centered therapy than in our groups.

These differences between group and individual psychotherapy suggest that in problems which require mostly an intensive intrapsychic exploration, individual therapy would be more indicated. Group therapy, on the other hand, would be particularly useful - if not indispensable - to get movement in rigid dysfunctional relationship patterns.

NOTES

1. This exploratory study is part of the first author's doctoral dissertation (Dierick, in preparation), sponsored by the Belgian National Foundation for Scientific Research. We wish to thank Miss Martine Decroos for her contribution to this study by means of her master's thesis (Decroos, 1986), as well as Prof. L. Delbeke for his methodological advice. We thank Mr. R. Stroobants for his help with the computer treatment of the data, and our colleagues at the Counseling Centrum for their useful feedback about the first draft of this text. Finally, we are deeply endebted to Prof. K.R. MacKenzie for his critical review and linguistic improvement of the translation.
2. The group member as well as the therapist can always be "he" or "she." For the sake of simplification, we consequently use the masculine form throughout.
3. For more details concerning our statistical analyses, see Dierick (in preparation).

REFERENCES

Berk, T. (1984). *Groepstherapie: theorie en techniek.* Deventer: Van Loghum Slaterus.

Berzon, B.C., Pious, C., & Farson, R. (1963). The therapeutic event in group psychotherapy: A study of subjective reports by group members. Journal of *Individual Psychology, 19,* 204-212.

Bloch, S., & Crouch, E. (1985). *Therapeutic factors in group psychotherapy.* Oxford: Oxford University Press.

Bloch, S., & Reibstein, J. (1980). Perception by patients and therapists of therapeutic factors in group psychotherapy. *British Journal of Psychiatry, 137,* 274-278.

Bloch, S., Reibstein, J., Crouch, E., Holroyd, P., & Themen, J. (1979). A method for the study of therapeutic factors in group psychotherapy. *British Journal of Psychiatry, 134,* 257-263.

Butler, T., & Fuhriman, A. (1983). Level of functioning and length of time in treatment variables influencing patients' therapeutic experience in group psychotherapy. *International Journal of Group Psychotherapy, 33,* 489-505.

Corsini, R., & Rosenberg, B. (1955). Mechanisms of group psychotherapy: Processes and dynamics. *Journal of Abnormal and Social Psychology, 51,* 406-411.

770

Decroos, M. (1986). *Curatieve processen in groepspsychotherapie: onderzoek naar cliënt- en therapeutbelevingen via open vragen.* Niet-gepubliceerde licentiaatsverhandeling, Katholieke Universiteit Leuven.

Dickoff, H., & Lakin, M. (1963). Patients' views of group psychotherapy: Retrospections and interpretations. *International Journal of Group Psychotherapy, 13,* 61-73.

Dierick, P. (in preparation). *Therapeutische en nadelige processen in groepstherapie en groeigroepen: constructie van een vragenlijst en vergelijkend procesonderzoek.* Doctoral dissertation, Katholieke Universiteit Leuven.

Holsti, O.R. (1968). Content analysis. In G. Lindzey & F. Aronson (Eds.), *The handbook of social psychology. Vol. 2: Research methods* (pp. 596-692). Reading MA/London: Addison-Wesley.

Lieberman, M.A., Yalom, I.D., & Miles, M.B. (1973). *Encounter groups first facts.* New York: Basic Books.

Lietaer, G., & Neirinck, M. (1986). Client and therapist perceptions of helping processes in client-centered/experiential psychotherapy. *Person-centered Review, 1,* 436-455.

MacKenzie, K.R. (1987). Therapeutic factors in group psychotherapy: A contemporary view. *Group, 11,* 26-34.

Weber, R.P. (1985). *Basic content analysis.* (Quantitative applications in the social sciences, no. 49). Beverly Hills/London: Sage.

Yalom, I.D. (1975). *The theory and practice of group psychotherapy* (2nd ed.). New York: Basic Books.

Yalom, I.D., Tinklenberg, J., & Gilula, M. (1975). Curative factors in group therapy. Cited in: I.D. Yalom, *The theory and practice of group psychotherapy* (pp. 76-103). New York: Basic Books.

IMPROVING ROGERS' THEORY:
TOWARD A MORE COMPLETELY
CLIENT-CENTERED PSYCHOTHERAPY

Arnold MENTE
Bad Lippspringe, F.R.Germany

I AND THOU

Rogers frequently notes that in the development of his theory and practice of therapy and consultation, he was influenced by Martin Buber's concept of dialogue. And as far as the person of the therapist and his relationship to the client is concerned, Rogers has fully implemented the theory of the encounter between I and thou in the way Buber saw it. However, during the course of successful therapy, one often hears clients sharing experiences such as: "During the last few weeks, my husband and several friends told me that I have become much easier to talk with" or "I am now able to joke around at work, in the past never, and I know they like me there." We have every reason to assume that the influence of these others is also therapeutic. Influence doesn't belong to the therapist alone; in fact, clients have to exercise constructive behavior changes with people in their environment, much more than in the relationship with the therapist (for in the therapy these changes have perhaps an anticipatory quality).

The serene, trusting and trust-evoking way of being on the part of the therapist most certainly triggers and accompanies the therapeutic processes of the client. According to Rogers, therapeutic process is possible because the therapist's "existence" and specific ways of acting facilitate *self*-exploration in the client. This, then, changes the clients' self-concepts so that they become more congruent with their experiences. This again frees the client's own potential for self-actualization. Certainly, this view of the therapeutic process allows therapists to work successfully.

However, the account does fall short of Buber's approach; moreover, it does not fully explain the quality of the above-mentioned client experiences. With Buber (1947, p. 23) it is: "Alles wirkliche Leben ist

Begegnung" (All true life is meeting) and, more specifically: "Ich werde am Du" (I become through the Thou). It means "I can gain my real and more inhabitable I *with* and *through* the other." It follows from this that self-exploration - understood to be an increasingly deeper understanding and experiencing of only one's *own* person - is too narrow a track for gaining mental health. Rather, the human being must be understood as his own (inter)active *center*. Applied to group therapy, this means: *Clients can and must approach each other,* because the meaningfulness of their lives is contingent on connectedness with others.

In this context, Alain Finkielkraut's "nouvelle philosophie" (1987) becomes interesting. In its consideration of the phenomenon of human love, it puts extreme emphasis on the assertion that the basic experience of the lover is to bring out the otherness of the other.

CLIENT EMPATHIC UNDERSTANDING

Buber's and Guardini's (1955) concepts of dialogue and the significance of interpersonal reality have become increasingly meaningful to me since 1968, when I began to do client-centered group therapy. In the second group, I was concerned about the problem of the group's coherence. Careful analysis of tape recordings and observations about each individual's progress in therapy led to the conclusion: Clients who were able to take part in the feelings of others were not only most helpful to the group's interaction, and consequently to the group coherence; they were also personally more successful in their therapy.

Let me illustrate this with the following excerpt of a group session:

> *Cl 2:* "I only have to hear my boss' voice from way off, sometimes even if I just imagine it, and I get really anxious. In those situations I just want to smash something or yell at someone or at everybody. Sometimes the only way I can help the situation is to go outside and grumble there. - (Turning to *Cl 5*) You nod your head. I know you feel similar about your boss etc. I've been thinking about that; what I can't understand about you is that in the same situation, you just freeze, you totally withdraw, and you're so paralyzed with fear" (Mente & Spittler, 1980, Vol. 2, p. 20).

The second part of this quote illustrates the client's behavior discussed above. If one attempts to understand it from the viewpoint of traditional client-centered therapy, one would have to say: "What client 2 says here, contributes to the self-exploration of client 5." And also: "It will improve the group atmosphere." But is that enough? Is this second part merely patchwork? Are clients as "mere subjects" the center of action only in the sense that they utilize the other clients? That is, is the group atmosphere merely a means to make the individual's self-exploration possible? Or is a "good atmosphere" a state of positive tension, in which empathic understanding leads to significant events *between* one and the other?

Thus, client 2 attempts to connect with the other person. He follows the other, strives with involvement, amazement and curiosity, compassion and care, possibly even with sadness and doubt toward the other who experiences a similar situation very differently. Basically, he expects to find congruence with the other person, but must first establish his own boundaries. Also, he has to find out more from his fellow human being: Feelings which he knows from himself "as such" exist *differently* for this other person. It seems that he first has to grasp some of the personal meanings the other gives to these feelings. By participating empathically, he can relate these personal meanings to his own. This exchange creates conditions which enable him to sort things out as well as to "collect himself." With the other and through the other the client finds himself (Mente, 1986).

Undoubtedly, these are emotional as well as social learning processes. They include the whole interpersonal reality of the client which is frequently very complex and never limited to the relationship with the therapist. Since 1969 I have become increasingly convinced that here we are dealing with a *stable characteristic* in the client's behavior. The term Client Empathic Understanding (CEU) best expresses what is meant. In a nutshell, CEU is a group member's "experiencing of feelings and personal meanings of another person as they exist for and affect this other person" (Mente & Spittler, 1980, Vol. 1, p. 58).

Further experiences in client-centered outpatient group therapy with neurotic clients showed that the cohesion of such a group *depends* for the most part on the therapist's success in one of the most important tasks: to facilitate client behaviors to the curative factor CEU.

Throughout the course of therapy, one can observe how CEU-behaviors first guide clients to modify their perceptions. Via participation in other people's feelings and personal meanings, the client becomes familiar with various behavioral constructs of fellow human beings. These are often more realistic than his own. For example, a client is amazed that another realizes a specific behavior *without* being "punished" for doing so; in his own rigid attitudes, this same behavior had previously been completely "off limits." Such experiences present stimuli for emotional learning and can lead to positive changes in behavior. The other members also try to implement intended new behaviors of their own and bring fresh experiences into the group. This exchange of experiences creates an interaction in which clients positively challenge each other. The process of therapy is intensified in such a way that it "recharges" itself ("concrete dialectics").

Neurotic clients are often trapped in their preoccupation with thémselves. To become free, they need to gain new perspectives on certain aspects. If such clients implement CEU, they step out of the alienation of being locked into their own person only. Bandura frequently emphasizes that clients must make use of vicarious experiences. The social realm - like culture and technology - is much too complex for any one person to rely solely on their own individual experiences, collected tediously one by one. Only by integrating those aspects that are missing in one's own experience from *other* people's experiential and behavioral models, is it possible to gain the necessary "emotional width" (Bandura, 1961). Behaviors that may appear - in the short run - to be copying another person can be differentiated, internalized, and appropriately generalized through the process of therapeutic learning. Thus they become useful.

This view - that therapy succeeds if it enables the client to have specific socio-emotional experiences - corresponds to the assumption that the majority of emotional problems have developed because of inappropriate socio-emotional experiences (Hobbs, 1962). Many clients share this observation about themselves. They may talk about key experiences like this one: "Mother used to say: 'Why can't you be more like your sister; she is better in school (and looks better, too)'." Because the child was used to relying on the mother's observations, she would accept being disabled in this way; then she went on to make things worse through further inappropriate generalizations.

Since 1969, the author has structured group therapy (and later, individual therapy also) to include this factor of Client Empathic Understanding. In some way, this can be compared to Truax's and

Carkhuff's (1965) use of "pretraining" clients toward better self-exploration. Initially, I used explanations which clients often could not really relate to very well. Over a period of about ten years, the following exercise was developed, which, for the purposes of simplicity, will be referred to as "CEU-training" (Mente & Spittler, 1980, Vol. 2, p. 155):

> Get a small diary that you can lock up. Find a convenient time in your daily routine and very briefly enter the answers to the following questions:
> 1. Was it possible for me to share in another person's feelings, even if only for a short while? (Internally? Or even with words? This person does not have to be part of your family or occupational world, but might be a salesperson or bank teller).
> 2. Was it possible for me to gain some understanding of what this feeling meant to the other? For example, you know that one "angry" feeling can be very different from another.
> There may well be a day when you can't find anything to write.

CEU-training can be used in such a way that the phenomenal world of the client remains a priority. During the first few sessions, it is better if the therapist does not mention the CEU-training. However, almost every motivated client will ask at some point whether there is anything else that can be done for better success in therapy. This is a good opportunity to speak of the training. One merely offers it as a resource; whether and how clients implement it is up to them. Either way, after a while usually all clients stop following the exercise in its verbal sense and writing their experience down: The training then has turned into an emotional habit; i.e., CEU becomes an attitude. In any case, experiencing has to remain self-induced on the part of the client to be in accordance with a non-directive approach to therapy (Mente, 1986).

> The factor CEU was also addressed in the research which accompanied therapy. Between 1968 and 1980, Mente and Spittler (1980) observed 20 therapy groups. Each group met over a period of at least 13 months, with an average number of 47 sessions. For almost four years (1973-1977) tape recordings of sessions were rated.

> "To assess the different degrees of CEU, Mente and Spittler developed a nine-point unipolar CEU-scale. The lowest level is defined as follows: 'The client does not respond to other group members.' At level five, the client responds verbally to another client's external circumstances and communicates nonverbally that he participates in the other client's feelings and personal meanings. Level nine expresses the highest degree of CEU: 'The client is able to dwell on the feelings of another and expresses

his empathy verbally.' ... In summary, Mente and Spittler's study suggests that CEU is a crucial variable in group therapy. Self-exploration appears to be secondary as a predictor of therapy outcome. ... For a more detailed elaboration on what these findings mean for the practice of group therapy, see Mente and Spittler, 1980." (Giesekus & Mente, 1986).

CONCLUSION

1. In contrast to Buber's view of the human encounter, Rogers' approach to therapy does not apply the "person-centered" concept in a reciprocal way.

2. Therapeutic learning is facilitated to a large degree if client and therapist become familiar with the curative factor of Client Empathic Understanding. If clients get to empathize with the feelings of others (not so much with their problems; "problems" are often only a smokescreen), they can find a way out of the preoccupation with their own emotional sclerosis (a sort of desensitization takes place). Moreover, through CEU, one can get in touch with reality. Much of reality's wealth can be found in relational entities; specifically, if one is able to appreciate one's fellow human beings in the otherness which characterizes their existence. If clients experience encounter in this sense, they are presented with the specific stimuli which are needed for the desired changes in behavior.

3. Since this kind of therapy continuously challenges clients to take initiatives, the interaction often creates its own energy and thus recharges itself. There is very little room left for destructive behaviors: The group is maintained because of the quality of its interaction. There are very few drop-outs.

4. We have good reasons to believe that the resulting higher intensity of therapy leads to a decrease in the overall length of therapy. In current forms of "brief therapy" this problem is addressed by agreeing with clients on a maximal number of sessions from the very beginning (Budman et al., 1980). Spittler and I consider it beneficial for the therapy group to set a quantitative limit, and we do so in an unmechanical way (Mente & Spittler, 1980, Vol. 1, p. 84 and 133 ff). However, limiting therapy duration alone is no solution to the problem that neurotics "need" two to eight years of therapy. An effective remedy must be based on improving the quality of interaction.

5. The client who realizes CEU chooses the therapeutic "significant

other" himself, and from time to time this choice can change. As a result, the therapist (who, after all, does not have to find a way out of a neurosis) is not needed as the model for all possible situations (see Curtis, 1982). And by no means does the therapist have to assume the role of an orchestra conductor, directing who, when, where, and how to play. Analytically oriented psychotherapists often like the comparison with a conductor (e.g. Kanter, 1976). In the presently described form of therapy the client stands in the center as a person.

6. Client-centered therapy, as it is understood up to now, is certainly not intended to be therapist-centered; nevertheless, it is in effect. Correspondingly, a large amount of research is based on an (implicit) assumption: "If the therapist does (or does not or does in part) allow this or that behavior to occur, then, all in all, this or that specific behavior can be expected from the client." Should the client be limited to only *reacting?* This view ignores - or at least does not reflect on - the fact that the client in therapy is also his own *proactive center.*

7. By presenting a brief discussion of the curative factor of Client Empathic Understanding as Spittler and I discovered it during therapy, I have pointed out how client-centered therapy can become more efficient through inclusion of this factor. This is certainly a considerable extension of the concepts developed by Rogers. However, this extension can be closely tied to certain remaining aspects of Rogers' approach to therapy. In its effect, including Client Empathic Understanding into therapy corresponds more closely to human reality.

REFERENCES

Bandura, A. (1961). Psychotherapy as a learning process. *Psychological Bulletin, 58,* 143-154.

Buber, M. (1947). *Dialogisches Leben.* Zürich: Gregor Müller.

Budman, S.H., Bennett, M.J., & Wisneski, M.J. (1980). Short term group therapy: An adult developmental model. *International Journal of Group Psychotherapy, 30,* 63-76.

Curtis, J.M. (1982). The effect of therapist self-disclosure on patients' perceptions of empathy, competence and trust in an analogue psychotherapeutic interaction. *Psychotherapy: Theory, Research, and Practice, 19,* 54-61.

Finkielkraut, A. (1987). *Die Weisheit der Liebe.* München: Hanser.

Giesekus, U., & Mente, A. (1986). Client empathic understanding in client-centered therapy. *Person-centered Review, 1,* 163-171.

Guardini, R. (1955). Die Begegnung. Ein Beitrag zur Struktur des Daseins. *Hochland, 47(3).*

Hobbs, N. (1962). Sources of gain in psychotherapy. *American Psychologist, 17,* 741-747.

Kanter, S.S. (1976). The therapist's leadership in psychoanalytically oriented group psychotherapy. *International Journal of Group Psychotherapy, 26,* 139-147.

Mente, A. (1986). *Selbstentfaltung in der Gesprächspsychotherapie durch Einbeziehung der Klientenvariable "Mitfühlendes Verstehen".*

BEYOND GOOD AND EVIL:
FOCUSING WITH EARLY TRAUMATIZED CHILDREN
AND ADOLESCENTS

Bart SANTEN
Psychotherapeutisch Centrum De Mark,
Breda, The Netherlands

> Satan, being thus confined to a vagabond, wandering,
> unsettled condition, is without any certain abode; for though
> he has, in consequence of his angelic nature, a kind of
> empire in the liquid waste of air, yet this is certainly part of
> his punishment, that he is ... without any fixed place, or
> space, allowed him to rest the sole of his foot upon.
>
> Daniel Defoe (cited in Rushdie, 1988)

INTRODUCTION

Shortly before he died in 1924, Franz Kafka (1985b) wrote a note. It said: "Let the bad be bad, otherwise it will get worse." Kafka must have been painfully aware of what he was writing about. During his whole life, this man who was said to behave like a saint has been caught in struggling with his insistent inner demons and suicidal wishes. They had brought him to the brink of insanity. Somehow he had not been able to do what he intuitively sensed as a possibility to get out of this cage. "Is it possible," Kafka once wrote, "to think something inconsolable, without the trail of consolation? There might be a way out because of the fact, that acknowledgement as such is consolation. So you could think: You must dispose of yourself, and yet - without counterfeiting this statement - stand your ground, being aware of having acknowledged that. That would really mean having pulled yourself out of the moor by your own hair. That which is ridiculous in the physical world is possible in the mental world" (Kafka, cited in Santen-Post, 1986). It is this kind of acknowledgement that I want to explore here.

The children and adolescents described in these pages all mentioned feeling caged-in. Like Kafka, they were caught in the trap of encapsulating their feelings. However, these children turned out to be able to "pull themselves out of the moor" in the way Kafka described. In order to be able to do this, they needed the presence of someone who could just keep them company in an accepting way, refraining from interfering with their process. I will describe some of these processes, and the way I guided these children to facilitate their development.

Two of the three children presented here have been psychiatrically diagnosed as suffering from a borderline syndrome. Elsewhere I gave a description of this syndrome and presented in detail a focusing therapy with a borderline adolescent (Santen, 1988). I now want to go beyond that, and ask attention for an underlying mechanism operating in many severely disturbed children: The presence of an early trauma, which triggered unmanageable anger and fear. Consequently, these children vigorously repressed their feelings. They got caught in an inner conflict, causing them in a way to strike against life. I will illustrate part of this mechanism, and make some remarks on how to get out of it. I will try to show, that the framework of the focusing method can help these children to find a way of dealing with their trauma and the consequent intense feelings, so that they can give up inner repressing and become more acceptant of themselves.

THE FOCUSING METHOD

Gendlin learned from Rogers, that "if every bit of a client's self-expression is taken in by the therapist, checked, verified, and then left to stand as is, without editing, without adding, without 'correcting' and 'improving' and 'interpreting,' then this inner relief and space lets more and more come from inside until a self-propelled change process rises in the client" (Gendlin, 1986). In my work as a client-centered/ experiential therapist I found out, that this is not only true for solid grown ups, but also for the shaky children and adolescents I met, with whom almost anything was very touchy.

Gendlin dedicated his life to develop this insight further and to refine a method, by which we can help another person to go beyond rationalizing and inner attacking, to sense directly the vague complexity of what is going on inside, without us interfering with their process. Gendlin calls this way of inner attending focusing (Gendlin, 1981; Santen & Gendlin, 1985). Instead of giving a technical description of this focusing method, I shall try to clarify how this process can be furthered by presenting some therapy fragments. Before going into that, however, I shall point out the importance of making a space and finding a way to deal with the inner critic.

CLEARING A SPACE

Clearing a space is the first focusing step. When we guide someone in doing this, we ask him to silently direct his attention to the middle of his body and to see what comes up there if he asks himself if he can feel totally fine. If something comes up which is in the way of feeling fine, we ask the client not to work on it, but to make some space between himself and that. Then he is asked to find out what else is bothering him. This is done until each troublesome experience has got its place for that moment. This is done without denying the weight of what has emerged. It is just welcome to be there.

Over the years this first focusing step has turned out to be of major importance (Gendlin, 1982a; Grindler, 1982; McGuire, 1982; Coffeng, 1984); when clients have learned to develop this new stance towards their blockages, the rest of the focusing process unfolds relatively easily.

In our case-examples, we find confirmation of how essential this change in the way of self-relating is. Initially, these children seemed to be nothing but their overwhelming problems. Gendlin calls this way of experiencing structure-bound (Gendlin, 1964); certain cues tend to evoke, over and over, the same feelings and thoughts, which withdraw from the influence of the current situation. In our traumatized children, this structure-boundness was extreme. Their experiences not only repeated themselves, but they were also perceived as unowned. Experience just intruded upon them. They seemed to look at their own movies with empty hands, without a felt connectedness, without experiencing a sense of self. As we shall see, a distance that fits is needed as a first step to get out of this trap and get a felt process going.

Depestele (1983) has studied the underlying mechanisms involved in making space. As he says, in this way a "me" can become differentiated by a new relationship with several "its." Instead of just being all this, the client can sense the "its": An experiential difference gets installed. What the client just was and repeated incessantly, he now can sense as a distinct person. As a consequence, an active and observing ego can gradually develop. Also because of this act of separating out, ego-boundaries can be restored.

THE INNER CRITIC

We all have to deal with our inner critic. It tells us not to be so oversensitive, and calls us bad and silly if we feel or think something it dislikes or cannot stand. Especially the traumatized children we talk about; all have their painful history with this harshly attacking inner voice, which stands for the Good and fights the Evil. It prevents them from getting in touch with the multicoloredness, and especially the dark sides, of their inner world.

Gendlin (1982b, 1984), commenting on the influence of this belittling force, noticed that this voice, which originates from the criticizing attitudes of the parents, not only has become introjected, but has also become meaner and more demanding than the parents ever have been.

The children we talk about desperately tried to be perfect, but meanwhile bad behavior escaped from their hands; it was if the chased forces strangled the hunter (Kafka, 1985a). As a result, they felt worthless and helpless. They were observing an incessant inner fight between Good and Evil, incessant because their inner critic refused to acknowledge the right of existence of the opponent, which fought back in a destructive way. Because they did not allow themselves to want to steal, they found their hands stealing. Disgusted with their dirty body and their sexuality, they were obsessed with sexual themes.

The question is how to deal with these forces therapeutically.

In answering this, we must realize that in the original traumatic situation which triggered the described mechanism, this was a way to cope in order to make a frightening situation bearable. Extreme fear of retaliation and loss of love may have forced the child into a preventive operation. Better censor and repress part of your own feelings and needs yourself than to have to deal with the expected rejection of those you depend on.

Though a crippling solution, it was a solution anyway, and it is still experienced that way when the child enters therapy. The structure-bound child experiences the therapist as another person, ready to retaliate if he really knew how bad the child is somewhere inside. So not only is inner attacking going on, experienced as attacking "at me," but somehow also an attack from the therapist is feared. For this reason we should not implicitly take the side of the inner critic by allowing it to dominate the whole field and smother. We must implicitly detach a little from it, to allow the child "to experience the directly sensed difference between these super-ego attitudes and the client's own body-center coming from himself" (Gendlin, 1982b). However, we should not approach the inner critic in its own style either. We must acknowledge that it is there, and has good reasons to be there. We approach it as someone who is for some good reason constantly negative, and just ask it to step aside for a while to give the smothered inner voice a bit of air. If we succeed in respecting the inner critic, we may find out that behind its hard front there are underlying feelings of scare, anger or hurt which may open up. If all the forces are acknowledged by the child and by us, these fears may prove unnecessary, and an integrating feeling-process may occur.

TREATING THE EFFECTS OF EARLY TRAUMATIZATION THREE CASE-HISTORIES

At this point, I will present fragments of three therapies. Each one is meant to stress a somewhat different aspect. With the beginning of the therapy of Patsy I shall illustrate how a focusing process can be guided. The therapy of Hester illustrates the mechanism of inner censorship. Besides, it shows how the struggle between Good and Evil can be brought to awareness. Finally, the therapy of Ronald is presented to clarify that the development of space can be essential for a therapeutic process to occur.

Patsy

Patsy was born in Pakistan. Shortly after birth she was abandoned by her mother. After three years spent in an orphanage, she was adopted and flown to the Netherlands.

Just like her parents, Patsy did her very best. She tried to be remarkably good and grateful, in order not to get banned again. But Patsy stole money at home. Her envy made her spoil the atmosphere. When she tried to make steps forward, as a rule, almost as many steps backwards followed. Patsy had suicidal fantasies. Every now and then she ran away.

Patsy seemed to put lots of energy in encapsulating her hardly bearable feelings of hurt and anger at being deserted. It left her with an inner chaos, which made her contact transient. It was hard to make contact with her.

At age 14, Patsy came to our clinic. Her ego-boundaries seemed to be weak. She made overwhelming contact with some people she idealized, and rejected others; she considered people to be either Good or Bad.

Patsy seemed to show a relatively positive development. She became somewhat more self-accepting and gained some introspection instead of being mainly the product of her strong conflicting emotions. However, the people working with her were constantly puzzled at the extent of Patsy's authenticity. She was highly talented in showing off, as a strategy to keep control.

In our clinic, I was Patsy's third individual therapist. The first two therapies had to be broken off for different reasons.

When Patsy and I met for the first sessions (back then she was fifteen years old), she was quite willing to talk about personal matters, and showed some insight. However, this knowledge did not seem to help her. In some way it led off-track. For this reason, I suggested that I could teach her focusing when, during the fifth session, she mentioned that it bothered her that she never felt cheerful.

Patsy sat in a chair. She looked at the bench at the other side of the room, and imagined that the lacking cheerfulness was over there. I asked her to find out what interfered with cheerfulness, step by step. Two packages came up: *not-belonging anywhere/feeling alone and feeling inferior.* She wrote this down on two pieces of paper, and put them on the floor, somewhere where it felt right to put it for a while. Then she chose to focus on the first feeling mentioned.

To prevent Patsy from going back into her head again, I let her be in touch with her feeling by fingerpainting. As soon as she began to paint, the encapsulation of her feeling became visualized. A flat painted dark spot appeared with some sharply edged belts around it.

I asked Patsy to take a few steps back. She went back and forth: Alternatively, she looked at the painting and attended to the middle of her body. She awaited her bodily reactions to see if words would loom up referring to the felt quality of not belonging. Words pointing to feeling encaged came up:

"Terribly rotten ..., deserted ... it is sad in my stomach, like something big I can't ever get out of it ... a big cage."

Sadness was growing. We sat with it for a while. The next session, I asked Patsy to paint "the heart" of last week's painting. The dark pink turned into blue. When she focused on it, she felt the encagedness again. But while she referred to this "circle you never get out of," it already shifted a bit. Something moved, though she did not yet have words for it. "It does say something," she murmered, "I don't know why you do this, because it makes me feel sad... but it does help."

A week later the ice melted some more. The painting was brushed more vividly and aggressively. The edges of the belts were more fluid now. Patsy stepped back and focused on the vague complexity of all this. Again something moved inside. When she referred to feeling, it was done on a higher experiential level and less absolute than before.

"It is so unclear ... It looks like a crossword-puzzle ... It is sad in a way, it is difficult to make it out... Grrr ..., I hate this."

In the next painting, Patsy made a spot in the middle. This spot contained The Good, she explained. Several roads in different colours were leading up to it. But when she stepped back and focused, she felt it did not really fit. Her feeling shifted. Red hate was brushed in all over, and wiped out the words (The Good) she had written. Instead of that she wrote: "The H(ate) crosses the roads." When she looked at it from some distance and resonated, new aspects of meaning came up, connected to her ambivalence and fear. From the particular stance she had developed, Patsy had become able to contact very intense feelings in such a way that she could get in touch with them somehow without drowning into them. She concentrated quietly, and was rather peaceful while all this was going on. When she resonated, she commented:

"The road looks frightening... It is the hate that blocks everything ... Much pleasure in your hate, but it is also a nuisance ... It is a misty road."

The next session the hate streamed down like lava. Patsy experienced how rage was in the way of being good:

"The lava makes a sad sound... a kind of hate ... that sad sound makes it frightening, it blocks almost everything... it's like something that never leaves... It blocks the good. The sound of the lava is a part of my anger, a kind of rage, and the fuzzy good has trouble getting through the lava.. . It is a sad, softly crying sound."

While Patsy mentioned the never ending blockage, she noticed some change. By directly referring to it, it had already shifted:

"It stops the good... There is nothing to be seen... by the way it is coming: Behind it there is a piece of good that is growing." Patsy spontaneously began to whistle softly. She added some yellow paint behind the big red stream. I asked Patsy to sing her sad lava-sound in the tape-recorder. She kept it in her pocket during the week, just to be with it sometimes. The next week she painted her sound. She sang the nagging sound again. This time, she spontaneously added a tune. When she stepped back and turned inward, for the first time, she directly touched her pain, and hurt:

"Painful sadness... Madmaking pain all over the upper part of my body." A few seconds later the pain got located in her stomach and her head. I asked Patsy to silently go back and forth between both parts of her body. "It really hurts," she said, though in her head it was stronger than in her stomach. While a process of grief had begun, there was "more relief" all the same. Patsy yawned.

I just presented these focusing sessions to show how gradually different shades of strongly repressed feelings could become sensed. Touching the unbearable had become possible by providing Patsy the opportunity to take the right stance. Though involved in a deeply felt process of acknowledgement, she still could stand her ground.

Hester

Hester was an unplanned child. Her birth blocked her mother's plans to study architecture. Right from the beginning there seemed to be ambivalence between mother and daughter. Hester's mother was uncertain, overprotective and controlling.

From the time she was nine months old, Hester was dependent on insulin-injections because of diabetes. Her mother injected her. Hester resisted, but could not prevent the intrusions.

Later on, Hester's mother told her that she had wished a second child, but that she had given up that wish because of the trouble concerning Hester's diabetes. Hester felt guilty.

When Hester came to the clinic, she was described as troublesome and manipulative. She stole and endangered her health by sabotaging her diet; an auto-destructive medium, apparently directed towards her introjected mother.

Therapy started when Hester was fourteen years old. She had a somewhat theatrical appearance: a "cheerful" way of making easy-going contact, while in fact she was hiding a lot behind that facade. Initially Hester talked a lot about personal matters: The alienation and aggressive escalations between herself and her mother, her feelings of guilt, and her longing to improve that relationship.

After about ten sessions, Hester became more silent. Then she gave an indication of how she had frozen part of her feelings: She complained, that for a couple of days she had a "stone" in her head. I asked her to draw that stone. Hester described it as "dark territories" with some small roads, light spots, small eyes, an orange stoplight and a flashing light. She commented: "It looks like a kind of labyrinth... Paths should come into it, but I can't yet enter." As I described elsewhere (Santen, 1986b), I suggested her to focus on that stone by means of imagery.

Hester visualized the stone in front of her. She imagined herself putting it at a distance that somehow felt right. Then she attended inwardly, and asked herself if she could feel fine when she thought of everything that had to do with that stone in front of her. Some feelings came up. After resonating several times from the image to the feeling in her body, the image changed. Some liveliness evidenced the beginning of a feeling process. The stone became a bit lighter. Little flowers appeared around the edge. The image got a more affective undertone; it gradually developed into "an island, surrounded by boiling tar ... a whirling mass." We took some time to receive what had come up.

A few minutes later Hester imagined the stone in front of her again. She asked inside how it felt to see it. She said: "It's a bit like me... the warmth. But there is also a difference. It is also something which doesn't belong." When Hester had said this, she felt fear growing inside. She needed to put a wall around the imagined stone. She went back and forth: Looked at the wall, behind which the stone was hidden, and turned inside. Now she got in touch with her fear of intrusion: From the outside, as a residue of all those times when her mother disrespected her boundaries, but also from the inside, as fear of the breaking through of her own anger which she had frozen so fiercefully up to now. "He is angry," she said, "he wants to jump over the wall and penetrate into me to do evil there." Fighting at two fronts, she had needed to raise walls both against her own aggressive tendencies and against the aggressive outside world. The two "arch-enemies" were still fused into one.

Hester began to realize that she had been angry at this "arch-enemy", as she called it herself, for some time. She had "kicked him out," but it didn't really work. Sometimes, she said, he succeeded in penetrating, and that scared her.

Some awareness was dawning in Hester that she had trouble expressing her feelings, especially when the expression of anger was involved. She, who initially just felt a stone, now verbalized - on a higher experiential level - that in her "heart" sometimes "problems are clotting together," especially when she had had a quarrel and had not talked herself out.

During the next sessions it became clear that Hester had a fruitless struggle going on between her angel-like part that rigorously tried to deny and suppress everything she experienced as bad in herself, and her bad part which reacted destructively to being denied. She played this out on three chairs: In the first one she talked as Good Hester, in the second as Bad Hester, and in the third Observing Hester could follow the battle going on. Here I will just present one fragment, evidencing the harshness of the Good part, and the nagging of the Bad part, to which any acknowledgement was refused:

> BH: "I want to obstruct, to smuggle, steal, be a nuisance to everybody, quarrel and oppose to you ... You have no power over that..."
>
> GH: "Okay, you're in power, but I will use all my power to suppress you ... I want to go to the right side."
>
> BH: "You're not firm enough for that, because you are far too good for this world; you want to help everybody with everything, and that's no good. I won't give you a chance. I just like to embitter everybody's lives, and then it's okay for me if they are sad because of me. If anything sociable goes on, you intend to behave well, but not me: I just gobble up all the food, and if anybody asks how that is possible, I let you pay for that. Sickening is my hobby. I want to perform badly at school, smuggle and overdose on my insuline."
>
> GH: "I'm against that. I don't want to hurt my parents. I would like them to see the good inside of me. I am good. I do my best to be with them in a good way, and I don't want you to get in the way of that."

The fruitless struggle went on. Bad Hester said that she felt alone. She kept trying to connect with Good Hester, but in a destructive way. Good Hester, however, just wanted to split:

> GH: "Anyway, you can try to avoid me and I can try to avoid you. If I know where you are I can take care never to come there, and if you know where I am you must do the same. We must simply learn to split, because the way it is now doesn't work."

Bad Hester kept stressing that she would miss Good Hester, because she needed to nag someone. But Good Hester denied feeling attached. Finally she expelled Bad Hester into space. Once again, Satan was without any abode.

Hester sat in the Bad chair. She felt alone, inconsolable and deserted. She said she wanted to be consoled by her father. She would have liked him to touch her shoulders and be close to her. When she allowed me to take his place, she grew very sad.

During the following months Hester became more self-accepting. The maternal introjection seemed to fade away, enabling her to unify and repair her boundaries. She began to talk about the affective qualities she missed in her mother. She felt her mother constrained her, and took away her freedom. She told her parents that she doubted whether they really loved her. During the therapy sessions, Hester, who formerly had expelled parts of herself, fantasized about expelling her mother: She stressed that physically she did not look like her. If she had been able to choose between several mothers now, she said she would not choose her own. It took a long time before she could become more accepting of her mother again.

Generally speaking, Hester tuned in more with her own feelings and needs. Two years after the first session on the chairs, she looked back and commented: "It is strange, realizing that you really... you find it out afterwards; formerly you didn't notice it so much... That you really had two different opinions: One that was more the opinion of my parents, that yet I listened to and which in fact I wanted then, and myself. My parents had just crammed it in so much, that I didn't know of anything else anymore. But I didn't realize, back then, that it was my parents, more or less, who were speaking inside me. Then the good one was in fact the things my mother wanted, and the bad one - so "me" - who completely opposed to it... And now it is somewhere in between ... Then there was a clear line between those two things, and now those two in fact have melted into one. Sometimes the one predominates, and sometimes the other. It does differ sometimes, but yes, it can always happen with somebody that one has inner struggles in oneself, that one doesn't totally agree concerning oneself. But certainly it's much less than before."

As we see, inner conflict was still there, but basically there seemed to be one Hester now, who was able to sense her own needs and could relate better to the world from that perspective. A Hester who was more self-accepting, and could even accept her moments of inner conflict, without being tangled up in it.

Ronald

Ronald was described to me as solitary, and hardly able to bear proximity. As a small child his boundaries had been violated rudely. He had been battered. He had been forced to watch his mother's work as a prostitute. Also, he had been locked in regularly as a punishment.

Fear colored Ronald's life. Reality had become too frightening and unmanageable for him. Gradually he had withdrawn into bizarre behavior and a fairy-like world of fantasies. He preferred to relate to objects instead of people, as could be seen in his stereotyped activities and preoccupations. Sometimes he was said to be psychotic.

Ronald tried to behave well. He inhibited the expression of his strong aggressive feelings. He either directed aggression towards himself, or showed moments of sadistic behavior. Sometimes he charged into a temper tantrum. He was very fearful of punishment.

Verbalizing feeling was difficult for Ronald. He did not seem to grasp the emotional value of words. Things were just "nice" as opposed to "not nice."

Ronald was too obsessed to be flexible. He had no distance. His play was repetitive: When he built a tower, and something went wrong, he just tried the same way again.

In the clinic, it was hard to get close to Ronald. He never talked about his former experiences. He was obsessed with mischief and satisfying his feelings of lust; meanwhile he strongly opposed his persistent needs. Ronald was disgusted with himself. He punished himself to prevent the punishment of God.

Generally speaking, Ronald was too aroused and obsessed to reflect on his behavior and his underlying needs.

When Ronald and I met for the first time (he was then twelve years old) he had a permanently twisted smile. He was restless and agitated. He called me a "spy" and tried to humiliate me.

When I asked him something, he stressed that it was "private"; on the other hand he was evidently searching for contact. Again and again he hid himself and then wanted me to find him. When I found him he indicated his lack of boundaries. "Then I am lost," he said. "I allow you to do anything you like with me."

In his play, Ronald indicated that we might scan the darkness of his repressed past under my guidance. He crept into a wheeled box and blinded himself; then I had to drive him through the playroom. Each time we stopped, he searched with his hands to find out where we were.

During the fifth session, Ronald told me that thoughts flashed through his mind which immediately were chased away. He himself called the two involved instances "the devil" and "the angel."

Meanwhile, during his play it became evident that Ronald's suppressed need to behave badly beated all his efforts to behave well. Just when he declared that he always listened to the angel, his hands shot out to prove the opposite.

At that time, Ronald did not yet experience his behavior as originating from himself. His need was externalized, like a devilish overwhelming force, which makes one act defencelessly against one's own will.

At this point, I decided to teach Ronald a way of making space. I asked him to write a story called "the devil and the angel." At that moment and also later, I did not try to influence in any way what he wrote. I abstained from any comment.

Ronald wrote. As I had asked him, he recorded the text on the tape-recorder. We silently listened to his story. In this way, I tried to help him create an experiential difference between himself as a person and all he had symbolized in his writing about devils and angels.

After listening we had our play-therapy session. The story was preserved on tape.

During the following months we began each session in the same way. We listened to the tape together. Then Ronald was asked to make a new story. Except for the first time, I did not suggest any titles. Each story was put on tape after the former. Gradually, a series of thematically connected stories originated without any comment of mine concerning their contents. This turned out to be a vehicle which considerably facilitated Ronald's experiential process.

The first story was just a string of single sentences, written down excitedly and fearfully. Doing this was almost unbearable for Ronald. Distance was lacking. Repeatedly, Ronald had to interrupt his writing by releasing mischievous behavior. All the sentences went like this: "The devil wants to cheat me: 'You must be mischievous,' and the angel says: 'You must be sweet.' 'You must kick a child,' the devil says. 'Don't do it,' says the angel."

As we see, there is not yet any dialogue between these struggling forces from outside. Also there is no reference to Ronald's own needs. Besides, Ronald did not mention any feelings.

As the developing stories showed, this adapted focusing exercise enabled Ronald to experience new aspects of meaning. In his first few stories he took his first step: He sorted out the aggressive outer world from his own aggressive needs. Also he began to refer increasingly to his own reality.

The second story seemed to refer to Ronald's fear of me. In this story, called "the vicious man," an untrustworthy man seduced a boy. He imprisoned and kicked the child. Both victim and aggressor had facades in the story, hiding their true motivations and feelings. His structure-bound experiencing of me also coloured the next story, in which a policeman was hired by "a strange woman" to lock in the bad boy. I just silently let him have that feeling and kept him company. The theme of trustworthiness was also a central aspect in the play-therapy sessions of those weeks. In the stories, it faded away.

The series became longer. Each time, by listening to the former stories, Ronald let the sentences he had symbolized resonate from some distance with his current feeling, to see if it fitted. Consequently his feeling changed and got more differentiated.

In the next story, Ronald's distrust directed towards where it seemingly originated. The mother-figure became a cruel ugly witch, with a friendly seducing facade. But after he had been able to express this fantasied exaggeration of how frightening and cruel the mother-figure was, his next story became more realistic and showed growing insight in the multi-leveledness of relating:

> *The girl*
> Once there was a girl, who was mischievous. The mother was sad. The girl didn't give a damn about that. "What a queer child you are." "That is not true," says the girl, "because *I do regret what I have done.*" "Is that really true?", mama says. And she behaves well forever.

As we can see the child in the story did like to cause mother pain. The "bad" own needs were realized and fully accepted. Pretense was maintained only to the outside world; the child "behaves well forever," but her heart is not in it.

Ronald was changing. He became more relaxed when writing, began to type his stories on the typewriter, and from the distance he developed, he became interested in the esthetic aspects of the stories. During the play-sessions he began to set new limits. He asked me to stop the tape-recorder and explained why. He feared that if people heard the tape, they might think he was a fool or might punish him. He also played a dialogue between the devil and the angel. Both appeared to have feelings and expressed them towards each other.

Ronald openly began to disobey me; at the same time his need to be mischievous tended to cease. At the end of one of these sessions he said: "Do you know that joke of the devil? ... he was an angel!"

At this point a considerable change took place in the themes of Ronald's stories. He began to express feelings of trust: Trusting yourself to an expert, who really turns out to be able to help, with a healing effect. He wrote:

> *The wood*
> Once there was a boy who walked through the wood. He heard something moving..It was a deer. "Help," the boy screamed. But the deer was a bit ill and couldn't get up. "I guess the deer must be ill," the boy thought. He took him to the forest-keeper. "Within two days he will be cured." "Thank goodness," the boy said. The boy got a reward.

Increasingly tender feelings came in. The appearance of flowers and plants in Ronald's stories gave evidence to his fresh way of sensing new aspects of life. Ronald became increasingly cheerful and relaxed. Now that he became more open about his feelings, and trusted me more than before, he told me directly when his trust became shaky. He was learning to stand his ground. When I once raised my voice, he just let me know that he was not a dog.

At this point where his self-acceptance had grown, Ronald dared to open his cage in a new way. His repressed rage suddenly broke its way out. One day, shortly after a visit to his father, he wrote:

> *Storm*
> A boy walked outside. But how it began to blow. It looked like windforce twelve. The boy was startled by the wind. The boy went inside. Here I am safe.

Immediately afterwards he symbolized his dilemma. He told a frightening joke about a man who could choose between three hells: One with barbed wire and blood, a second with nails and glass, and a third in the shit. "OK," the man decided, "I'll take the third choice."

Ronald finally dared to face his frightening shit. He ran to the play-room and just let some of his frozen rage out. With tremendous power, he knocked over the big steel cabinet, and for several hours he tried to destroy whatever he would get his hands on. Though it was hard to guide this, and we even had to isolate him for a while together with someone else who kept him company, the feared retaliation did not take place. As usual, the next session we just listened to the tape. That same session again a newly sensed aspect came in. Ronald crept into the steel cabinet. I had to close its door. From the dark inside I heard him use the voice of a scary little child. When he asked me to let him out, he stepped out cheerfully. This had been evidently a corrective, emotional experience for him, to overcome the feelings that he formerly related to being locked in. Ronald's ability to enjoy was growing fastly now. He sought bodily contact. Sunny feelings and cosyness colored the new stories. Friends began to enter. His growing self-acceptance was symbolized by acceptance of "the way nature is."

The Flower
Once there was a boy who got a flower. He was very pleased with the flower. He walked with it the whole day. But the flower dried up. The boy felt it was a pity. But that's the way nature is.

A few weeks later the series dried up. All of his own, Ronald began to talk about his traumatic experiences as a young child, and the feelings they had evoked in him. He improved in daily life in the clinic, at home and in school.

One year after Ronald's first story, we listened to the tape again. I asked him to write once more, and gave him the same title he had started with. Ronald wrote:

The devil and the angel
I never feel a need for that anymore. That never keeps me busy anymore. Formerly that was important. I do know better. Ronald himself determines what happens in my life. Ronald simply does everything himself and does it well. Devil and angel are fairies and fables.

By just letting him have what came up, good and bad, in a caring way, a person in his own right had emerged.

FINAL REMARK

To end with, I want to stress one more point. For this, I invite you to go back to Franz Kafka. On one of his walks with Gustav Janouch, Kafka was told a Chinese story: "The heart is a house with two sleeping rooms. In one of the rooms lives sadness,in the other lives cheerfulness. You may never laugh too loudly, otherwise you'll wake up the sadness in the other room." But, discussing this, it was concluded that the cheerfulness is dull of hearing. It doesn't hear the sadness in the other room. "That's the reason why we often just pretend to be cheerful," Kafka said, " We plug our ears with the wax of cheerfulness (...). I pretend cheerfulness to hide behind it. My laughter is a wall of concrete (...) against myself." Janouch was amazed. In his opinion the wall they talked about was directed outside. But Kafka stressed: "The grip of the world is (...) always a grip inside (...) the inside and the outside belong together. If they are separated from each other, they are the two confusing aspects of one secret under which are all bowing down, but that we cannot solve" (Janouch, 1965).

As you may have noticed, during the therapy fragments presented here, I did not comment on these children's twisted cheerfulness. I refrained from talking about what happened in the relationship. We did not work directly on the walls these children needed to erect against me. I just took it as something they needed, and guided them to get in touch with their inner walls and work on that. When the inner walls melted down, their outer walls almost automatically melted too. Hester and Ronald began to talk spontaneously, in a more authentic way than before. At that point, it was early enough to start commenting on things happening in our relationship. I think we drive people back too often into their strategies by wanting to go too fast.

REFERENCES

Coffeng, T. (1986). Focusing en rouwtherapie. In R. Van Balen, M. Leijssen, & G. Lietaer (Eds.), *Droom en werkelijkheid in client-centered psychotherapie.* Leuven/Amersfoort: Acco.

Depestele, F. (1983). *Enkele notities bij de eerste beweging van focusseren.* Unpublished manuscript.

Gendlin, E.T. (1964). A theory of personality change. In P. Worchel & D. Byrne (Eds.), *Personality change.* New York: Wiley.

Gendlin, E.T. (1981). *Focusing.* New York: Bantam Books.

Gendlin, E.T. (1982a). An introduction to the new developments in focusing. *The Focusing Folio, 2(1),* 24-35.

Gendlin, E.T. (1982b). A process view on the superego. In E.T. Gendlin, *Experiential psychotherapy.* Unpublished manuscript.

Gendlin, E.T. (1984). The obedience pattern. *Studies in Formative Spirituality, 5(2),* 189-202.

Gendlin, E.T. (1986). Foreword. In L. Wright, F. Everett & L. Roisman,

796

Experiential psychotherapy with children. Baltimore: John Hopkins University Press.

Grindler, D. (1982). "Clearing a space" with a borderline client. *The Focusing Folio, 2(1),* 5-19.

Janouch, G. (1965). *Gesprekken met Kafka.* Amsterdam: Querido.

Kafka, F. (1985a). *Letters to Milena.* New York: Schocken.

Kafka, F. (1985b). *Letters 1910-1924.* New York: Schocken.

McGuire, M. (1982). "Clearing a space" with two suicidal clients. *The Focusing Folio, 2(1),* 1-4.

Rushdie, S. (1988). *The satanic verses.* London: Viking.

Santen, B. (1986a). Working with a "Frozen whole structure." *The Focusing Connection,* 3(5).

Santen, B. (1986b). Focusing en imaginatie. In R. Van Balen, M. Leijssen, & G. Lietaer (Eds.), *Droom en werkelijkheid in client-centered psychotherapie.* Leuven/Amersfoort: Acco.

Santen, B., & Gendlin, E.T. (1985). Focusing. *Psychologie,* jan.-feb., 29-35.

Santen-Post, A. (1986). *Het gebruik van symbolen in de kinderpsychotherapie.* Unpublished manuscript, Stichting post-doctorale opleiding Kinderpsychotherapie Breda.

CLIENT-CENTERED/EXPERIENTIAL PRACTICE
WITH PARENTS AND INFANTS

C.F. Zachariah BOUKYDIS

Brown University Medical School, Providence, R.I., U.S.A.

I have been working to develop a model for consultation on the parent-infant relationship which derives from client-centered/experiential theory and which integrates research on non-verbal communication between infants and their parents. This chapter will highlight some of the settings where this approach is relevant and discuss some of the principles of consultation.

THEORETICAL BACKGROUND

Research on non-verbal communication between parents and infants has done much to elucidate the subtle patterns or sequences of interaction which occur. Observers of parent-infant interaction have called this exchange "the behavioral dialogue" (Bakeman & Brown, 1978): Both participants go through cycles of attention and inattention and modify their behavior over time to promote optimal levels of attention (Tronick, Als, & Brazelton, 1980; Condon & Sander, 1974; Stern, 1971, 1985). High attentiveness promotes social learning, cognitive development and self awareness (Thoman, 1975). Infants seem to enjoy having their actions responded to contingently and this kind of exchange leads to an early awareness of the relationship between self and other; as well as promoting the feeling of efficacy (Goldberg, 1977) at being able to initiate and sustain interpersonal discourse.

From the perspective of non-verbal communication and sensory awareness, the relationship is not only experienced on visual and verbal modes, but with all senses including taste, smell and touch. Thus, the "knowing" which develops for both infants and parent must be based on information integrated from these sensory modalities as well. The parent-infant relationship, based on all senses, can lead parents back to a more basic experience of self and may call forth early memories either as an explicit knowing level or an implicit "felt in the body" level. What is felt, is felt in the body, at a level below ordinary awareness; before the distinction between body and mind. This kind of awareness can be disruptive. It is here that a perspective developed from client-centered/ experiential theory is important. We are interested in the relationship between the "observable" and the "felt" in the relationship.

The consultation context

Within the consultation context, we are asked to deal with a variety of parenting concerns where the difficulties arise from problems at management (feeding, sleeping, crying patterns), problems due to a mismatch of personalities between parent and infant, problems due to infant behavior or temperament, or problems due to parental perception of the infant and of their relationship. From the client-centered/experiential perspective, we would say that the relationship is structure bound: The natural self-correcting tendencies of parent and infant are not working and certain unproductive cycles of behavior are repeated.

The metaphorizing process

The core of consultation work leads from an understanding of the "metaphorizing process". In the metaphorizing process, words, images, or body sensations have a particular interactive relationship with the preverbal felt sense. In the context of consultation on the parent-infant relationship, we extend from words, images, sensations to the "behaving of the partner" as potentially metaphorizing one's preverbal felt experience. Therefore, the baby's behavior can be a metaphor for parental experience and vice versa.

As we shall see, consulting with the parent-infant relationship involves emphasis on situations where parents can attend to their preverbal felt experience "in" the relationship, can engage in the metaphorizing process, and can evolve steps which eventually amount to changes of perception of the relationship, feeling of self efficacy as a parent, and changes in structures or patterns of interaction with their baby.

OPPORTUNITIES FOR CONSULTATION

As a psychologist working often in interdisciplinary settings, I have the opportunity to integrate the principles of client-centered/experiential practice both into ongoing work with parents and infants, and in developing new services. The most typical contexts for integrating principles into an existing service are: 1. Structured assessments where parents are observing a neurobehavioral, communicative, or temperamental assessment of their infant; 2. Standardized assessments of parent-infant interaction where parent and infant are either interacting freely or are engaged in a structured task; 3. Interactional play therapy where the focus is on parental problems at management or dysfunctional patterns of interaction due to parental misperceptions, infant behavior, or both; 4. Training mental health clinicians on parent-infant consultations; 5. Consultations with self-help parenting groups; 6. Community workshops; 7. Media presentations.

PRINCIPLES OF CONSULTATION FROM A CLIENT-CENTERED/EXPERIENTIAL PERSPECTIVE

Respect for parent's experiencing

Any form of consultation begins with respect for parent's experiencing and their current articulation of their relationship with their infant. This means that consultation begins with what the parent defines as the problem, and that the ongoing task of consultation, if necessary, is to help a parent look at their behavior from a different "internally-evolved" perspective in order to expand their options for dealing with problems.

There are many instances in which we are trying to sort out where difficulties may arise from the infant, from the parent, or due to a mismatch in personalities. Rather than define where the "trouble is" from the outside of the relationship, consultation involves listening to the parent, helping them to touch their felt sense of the relationship, and devise new steps in relating to themselves and their infant out of this process.

In many Western countries, with greater separation of parents from extended family, many parents have less exposure to infants and infant care, are less sure of their capacity, and are more susceptible to influence - especially media (articles, magazines, parenting programs) on how to parent. Parents may have a high ratio of advice and a low ratio of opportunity to listen to themselves or find their own ground in relation to advice. Therefore, one major principle in consultation is to find ways to provide the opportunity for listening to parents and help them to hear themselves - strengthen their own voice distinct from the external voices on how to parent.

Enhancing parental self-reflection

From a client-centered/experiential perspective, one main principle is to find ways to enhance parental self reflection, to help parents listen to themselves to set up a productive dialogue with preconceptual being (Gendlin, 1962, 1964, 1969, 1981). The next section will describe a number of modes where this process may take place. It is common to encourage this kind of attentiveness during actual interaction with their baby, or while observing videotapes of interaction.

The basic overall process is to start with the felt experience of the interaction, feeling and clarifying feelings, focusing on the implicit felt experience, metaphorizing; and eventually to step out of the interaction, to conceptualize possible different strategies for relating.

Efforts to understand the infant's process

Behavior can be seen in the context of its communicative intent, in relation to internal self-regulatory processes, and as an indicator of maturing developmental processes. Take for instance, thumb sucking in a newborn. Viewed externally, the baby is eliciting the behavior of trying to get his or her thumb or fingers into the mouth. We might say that this behavior communicates a desire to suck, and take it at its face value. However, how does this behavior function for the baby? We can see thumb sucking as an attempt to self-soothe and from this effort, establish rhythmic sucking in order to gain homeostatic balance. Sucking is related to a better coordination of breathing, closer linking of breathing and heart rate patterns, more efficient metabolic use of oxygen, muscular relaxation and so on. The capacity to get thumb or fingers into the mouth and hold them there also reflect development changes in neural maturation and motor coordination.

Parents have an intuitive awareness of these different dimensions of behavior, but in the consultation process, the dimensions are articulated and made explicit in ongoing interaction. There are parallels which arise between the baby's efforts to self-regulate, and the parent's efforts to manage, to achieve an internal balance, and a homeostatic balance in the ongoing flow of the relationship. There even are instances where infant efforts to self regulate precede parental attempts to disconnect from a tense interaction and eventually lead to parental focusing or self reflection.

There are times when parents experience certain behavior, crying especially, as being "done to" them: "crying bothers me, he is bothering me, he is trying to bother me." These are examples of structure boundness in the interaction. By having the opportunity to "get outside" problematic interactions with their baby, yet still feel, parents are able to differentiate and recover the question of what can be learned from this disruptive feeling. As indicated, one dimension which evolves from this process is what their baby is doing "for" themselves, somewhat separate from where this "effects" the parents.

The analogy of focusing, or self-reflection is important. By referring to the felt sense of the relationship, or interactive event, parents use this preverbal, implicit knowing as a guide for how to make concrete steps of change in the relationship. The consultant provides an outside partner for those who may just "fall into" the feelings, and helps them to develop the capacity to just touch, and learn from the felt sense - with a friendly questioning part of themselves outside feelings, the relational feelings which arise in the "between" or "non-separateness", between parent and infant.

In viewing communicative, self regulatory and developmental aspects of behaving, we are led to consider how these aspects of behavior relate to the infant's developing sense of self. We can ask, given what we experience, what may he/she be feeling? - how does this behavior relate to self regulatory processes? - and how does this behavior confirm or violate expectations as to who this baby "should be"?

Another instance were focusing or self reflection is useful is where disruption in the relationship between parent and infant may be due to qualitative shifts in the development of the infant. These are periods such as the "biobehavioral shift" in 2-3 month old infants where there is a major reorganisation in physiological processes and where many infants who have been relatively predictable in daily patterns of waking, feeding, crying, etc. up until this point, become much less predictable and behaviorally labile. It is in periods of qualitative change, or rapid maturation of the infant where the relationship may be in disequilibrium. The experience of these periods may be disruptive to some parents, and they may take the changes personally as instances of their failure to parent adequately or where something personally disruptive is being done to them by their infant. In this context, focusing is internally self-righting for parents: They are able to change their "internal set" or fixed perceptions of the relationship and move to respond with a wider range of options or creative adaptations to the new behavior and capacities of their infant.

Behavioral reflection

As indicated, in understanding the metaphorizing process, both infant and parent "behavior" (gestures, sounds, facial expressions, body movements and posture) and "state" (deep sleep through active alert, to crying) can be a metaphor for ongoing experiencing. In the effort to understand the experience congruent with an infant's communicative acts and autonomic states, parents learn to listen to the explicit and the implicit signals. With a concerted effort in the consultation process to attend to, and actively reflect their infant's acts/states, parents also become aware of their own feelings, and the underlying questions of who initiated what; from whom feelings arose; how much comes from self, how much comes from the infant and how much arises synergistically in "the between." While in everyday interaction, parents may not be aware of the principle of behavioral reflection, there are instances such as violations of expectations where parents either notice a mismatch, or where their infant's behaving or autonomic state is a metaphor for the parent's own uncomfortable experience. For example, a parent in the "face-to-face paradigm" (Tronick, Als, & Brazelton, 1980) which is used for observing parent-infant face-to-face interaction, holds her face still and the infant shows wariness and an accelerated effort of gesturing, vocalizing and facial expressions. There has been a violation of expectations; the infant changes behavior, and the parent notices the change.

During consultation, attention to behavioral reflection occurs by observing interaction, and commenting on; or asking a parent how they feel during particular events, watching a videotape of interaction, or during exercises which highlight the question of what is reflection, and what is metaphorizing of parental experience.

Attending to non-separateness

So far I have said that there is a felt experience in interaction and behavior can relate to, or metaphorize felt experience. Parents sometimes attend to this felt experience with uncertainty as to - from whom feelings arose. At this time, attending inwardly, in one's body to the felt sense is akin to attending to non-separateness. The emphasis on autonomic metaphorizing, and the importance of both infant behavior and state as a metaphor for parental experiencing relates to a bodily felt energy which seems to have arisen synergistically and not from parent or infant alone. This experience can sometimes be disruptive or can lead as we have seen to attributions that the infant's behavior or state are causing parent's uneasiness, or guilt that parent's behavior or state are causing infant's upset. With principles derived from experiential focusing and sometimes, structured excercises, parents are asked to change their interaction, set aside their usual modes of conceptualizing, attend to the felt sense in the body, and notice metaphors arising. Parental feelings and metaphors are reflected or possibly further steps of focusing occur. The changes which occur feel better in the body, and give new energy to working out active solutions in the relationship, enable new perspective to arise on "who is doing what," change the structure boundness, and probably unfreeze the merging of personalities. For example, parental anger has the tendency to move outward and inward at the same time - "I am frustrated with my baby, I am frustrated with myself" - "He (my baby) is just like me, he's stuck just the way that I am." With the inward attention of focusing, and observing interaction, it eventually becomes clearer who is doing what in complex interactions, and parents can see their infant's personality and behavior in the context of the baby's own self regulating and self expressing tendencies.

Recognizing structure boundness

Relationships between parents and infants are compelling and a lot happens which can be felt but which is either below normal awareness or disorganizing to parent's usual conceptual modes. It is often difficult to step out of the relationship to notice certain patterns which cause disruption, increase tension, and block forward moving felt experience.

There are structure bound patterns which can be observed (for example, gaze aversion in the infant when too much is happening). And, there are other instances, not easily observable, where the recognition of structure boundness must happen through counseling attention to the felt experience of one of the participants in the interaction. A potential key to structure boundness happens when a parent feels "stuck" or says something particularly charged about their infant or about the interaction. This statement can begin a process where the parent is encouraged to attend to their felt sense and where the metaphorizing process is facilitated (Boukydis, 1985b).

Articulating implicit conflicts: Taking both sides

Babies are dependent beings. Many parents immerse themselves in caring for their babies and may lose touch with their own needs. They may have feelings which touch on their responsibility for their baby while also trying to care for themselves, but these feelings may be vague or threatening. In some situations, it may be helpful for the consultant to articulate a disparity or conflict in needs between parent and infant, as a beginning in metaphorizing the feelings implicit in the relationship. This process can lead to a connection between metaphor and that which was implicitly felt, and can release new energy toward resolution.

One strategy for articulating disparity or conflict is to ask a parent to alternately take their own voice, then the voice of their infant and undertake an exchange relating to the conflict. Then, the parent can be asked to step back and imagine being a mediator who has heard both sides, and is trying to develop a resolution which affirms and eventually answers both people's needs.

Parents as collaborators in the process

Rather than interview to gather information, and then exclude parents from the diagnostic phase, the consultation model enables practitioners to engage parents as collaborators in all phases. There are two areas of theory which are relevant to this perspective: Contextual assessment (Fischer, 1978) and enhancing self reflection (or focusing; Gendlin, 1969, 1981). Contextual assessment emphasizes ways to create typical interactive events between parent, infant and consultant so that the weighing of perceptions as to what occurred, and what caused particular behavior can become the focus of the collaborative process. Alternative explanations, and unforseen influences on behavior are weighed. Then, the contextual influence, the influence of the family system, and informal network on the parent-infant relationship are explored as possible influences on current patterns.

As indicated earlier, enhancing self reflection or focusing emphasizes how to help parents refer to feelings in interaction, and enables parents to articulate the implicit meaning in complex interactive events.

Integrating developmental and experiential input

The main emphasis from this perspective is to develop a receptive mode to hear parent's feelings and concerns about their child's development. In structured assessments there can be direct input about development, but the main emphasis is on how a child performs, imagining what he or she may be showing, or learning, and thinking about how this related to other areas of development. As in consultation on parent-infant interaction, there is a basic effort to hear what parents are feeling while they are watching their child, to compare how typical this behavior is - and to anticipate the next steps in development.

Emphasizing strengths/attitudes of will to improve or change

Another principle involves respecting and commenting on things that are going well in parents' relationship and in their ongoing interaction with their child. Parents are vulnerable to criticism and often find themselves in situations facing varied opinions about how they should relate to, or discipline their child. One of the important principles in client-centered/experiential practice is finding something to care about in each person as the basis for relating empathically to what they are feeling (Rogers, 1957, 1975). During consultation, one way that this respect can be engendered in the collaboration is by noticing and commenting upon what parents are doing well and respecting their efforts to grow and change. It is very moving when parent's of premature infants talk about the incredible will their baby had in order to survive the hardships of the early days. Parents of all babies are enraptured at times when they see their baby's efforts to accomplish a new skill. Attention to the felt sense of this will and this effort in their baby sometimes leads to an experience of will and effort experienced as non-separate - the "we-ness" has will and effort to explore, learn and grow. One parent said: "When I recover my sense of my baby's will, I am not only moved by his courage, but I recover this capacity of will, to go on with courage in myself." A return to memories of this will, this effort, are helpful when things are going badly in the relationship.

Using consultant's own feelings in interaction with the infant

There are times when parents find it helpful to watch someone else interacting with their baby. They can attend to how they feel about the interaction, possibly imagine more clearly what their baby is feeling and imagine how they would have responded. This kind of interaction draws on the authentic feelings of the consultant, for instance reporting on their efforts to soothe a fussy baby, and helps build trust toward a collaborative relationship.

STRATEGIES FOR PROCESS CONSULTATION: INTEGRATING CLIENT-CENTERED/EXPERIENTIAL PRINCIPLES WITH EXISTING PRACTICE

There are a number of strategies for consultation on the parent-infant relationship. Here is a list of strategies or modes of consultation from different areas of work on the parent-infant relationship.

focus while watching live interaction of self/others with own/other baby
    (parent attends to felt sense of interaction and gets listened to on how it feels)

running commentary on what parent is/baby may be - feeling; state alternate possibilities
    (parents go back and forth between what they are/were feeling and what their baby may be feeling, then state other possibilities for what

their baby may be feeling; then are listened to on this)

focus/listen while watching videotape segment of parental event
(parent watches videotape of parenting interaction and attends to felt sense; then is listened to on this)

focus/listen while listening to audiotape of baby crying
(parents listen to tape, attending to felt sense in their body, and are listened to on this) (Boukydis, 1985a, 1985b)

focus on baby personality - including of whom he/she reminds me
(parents explicate their sense of their baby's personality, and whom their baby reminds them of; how are they similar and different to those people?)

listen to parents while they observe structured assessment
(parents are listened to on their feelings about watching their child perform structured tasks in the assessment context)

behavioral/autonomic reflection
(from what they observe behaviorally and feel viscerally, parents try to imagine what their baby is feeling or communicating and return this or reflect this to their baby)

follow baby initiations, imitate or mirror; change give and take patterns
(parents spend a period of time returning or following their baby's initiations; they can imitate or mirror facial expressions, gestures; and can change give and take patterns so that the baby initiates and the baby responds) (Field, 1978)

give verbal reflections to baby's communicative acts
(parent responds to/reflects baby's sounds, gestures, facial expressions)

coach parent in interaction live or on tape then listen/focusing
(parents try changing patterns of responding, may watch this afterward on tape, then get listened to on how it felt)

take imagined voice of baby or parent/done by parent/consultant

(while either parent or consultant is interacting with the baby, the other takes the imagined voice of the baby)

accentuate body movement/posture/facial expressions

(parent tries mimicking or accentuating baby's body movement, posture, and facial expressions, and then gets listened to on what he/she thought was being communicated, and on how this felt)

slow down/accelerate initiations, speech; use one modality voice/touch/ facial

(parent is asked to change pace of interactions or use one modality, then is listened to on what happened, and how this felt)

carrying forward infant initiatives; structure environment to facilitate infant exploration

(without interfering, parent imagines what infant is doing in play, and when necessary helps infant to follow through with his initiatives without doing things for her/him) (Mahrer, 1978; Maher, Levinson & Fine, 1976; Stollak, 1978)

ask parent what are you feeling; how does it feel when he/she does such and such

parent coaches consultant in interaction

(parents using knowledge of their baby, and trying out new patterns make suggestions to consultant while consultant interacts with the baby)

watch someone else relating to baby/compare similarities and differences

(parent attends to feelings while watching someone else interact with baby, and then compares similarities and differences in how parent and other person interact and in how baby responds)

ask where in your body do you experience bodily energy while interacting with baby?

(parents attend to felt sense of interaction with baby and are asked how and where they feel during the interaction) *examine baby with hand; different energy patterns*

(parents are asked to explore their baby with their hands and notice differences in energy patterns that they feel) (Krieger, 1979)

how baby responds to different orientation in space; patterns of being held/soothed; response to different rhythms in play/caretaking; massage

(parent tries out these activities, attends to felt sense, notices how baby responds, and is listened to on how it felt)

listen to parent; feeling mainline; who is affecting who; influence of family climate, family patterns

(parent is listened to on these perspectives; what does the relationship with your baby feel like; who is affecting who; who is in charge of the interaction; how do other relationships or the family climate effect your relationship with your baby?)

negotiate with a preverbal being

(parents articulate their needs, their baby's needs, then are asked to take the outside stance of a mediator and make suggestions for how to solve differences so that both people's needs can be met)

CONCLUSION

Keeping in mind the principles outlined above, the main job of the consultant is to attend to parental feelings, return to the baseline of parental experiencing during and after structured exercises, and to empathise/imagine infant experience. Consulting on the parent-infant relationship has differences from verbal counseling or psychotherapy, but the parallels are also striking. As a counselor, one imagines the preverbal experience taking shape in their clients, focuses on their own ongoing experience, and attempts to hear and reflect both the explicit and implicit "edge" of feeling in the clients. A parent is often in a similar situation with his/her baby - without the benefit, or possible distraction, of the verbal mode. Empathy implies both an attention to preverbal experience (in the baby, in the between, in the parent), and an activity of exploration to elaborate or heighten an understanding of what the baby might be feeling. As indicated in this chapter, the use of principles derived from client-centered/experiential therapy are helpful in facilitating this process.

REFERENCES

Bakeman, J., & Brown, R. (1978). Relationships of human mothers with their infants during the first year of life: Effects of prematurity. In R.W. Bell & W.P. Smotherman (Eds.), *Maternal influences and early behavior.* New York: Spectrum.

Boukydis, C.F.Z. (1981). Adult perception of infant appearance: A review. *Child Psychiatry and Human Behavior, 11(4),* 241-254.

Boukydis, C.F.Z. (1982). Support groups for parents with premature infants in N.I.C.U.'s. In R. Marshall, C. Kasman, & L. Cape (Eds.), *Coping with care for sick newborns.* Philadelphia: Saunders.

Boukydis, C.F.Z. (1985a). Perception of crying as an interpersonal event. In B.M. Lester & C.F.Z. Boukydis (Eds.), *Infant crying: Theoretical and research perspectives.* New York: Plenum.

Boukydis, C.F.Z. (1985b). Empathic relations between parents and infants. *Focusing Folio, 4(1),* 3-28.

Boukydis, C.F.Z. (1986). *Support for parents and infants: A manual for parent organizations and professionals.* New York: Routledge & Kegan Paul.

Boukydis, C.F.Z. (Ed.) (1987). *Research on support for parents and infants in the postnatal period.* New York: Ablex.

Condon, W.S., & Sander, L. (1974). Synchrony demonstrated between movements of the neonate and adult speech. *Child Development, 45,* 456-462.

Field, T. (1978). The three R's of infant-adult interactions: Rhythms, repertoires, and responsivity. *Journal of Pediatric Psychology, 33,* 131-136.

Fischer, C., & Brodsky, S. (1978). *Client participation in human services: The Prometheus principle.* New Brunswick, NJ: Transaction Press.

Gendlin, E.T. (1962). *Experiencing and the creation of meaning.* Glencoe, IL: Free Press.

Gendlin, E.T. (1964). A theory of personality change. In P. Worchel & D. Byrne (Eds), *Personality change.* New York: Wiley.

Gendlin, E.T. (1969). *Focusing. Psychotherapy: Theory, Research and Practice, 6,* 4-15.

Gendlin, E.T. (1981). *Focusing.* New York: Bantam.

Goldberg, S. (1977). Social competence in infancy: A model of parent-infant interaction. *Merrill-Palmer Quarterly, 23(3),* 163-177.

Krieger, D. (1979). *Therapeutic touch.* New Jersey: Prentice-Hall.

Maher, B. (Ed.). (1969). *Clinical psychology and personality: The selected papers of George Kelly.* New York: Wiley.

Mahrer, A. (1978). *Experiencing: A humanistic theory of psychology and psychiatry.* New York: Bruner/Mazel.

Mahrer, A., Levinson, J., & Fine, S. (1957). Infant psychotherapy: Theory, research and practice. *Psychotherapy: Theory and Practice, 13,* 131-140.

McGuire, K.N. (1981). *Building supportive community: Mutual self-help through peer counseling.* 3440 Onyx St. Eugene, OR 97405.

Rogers, C.R. (1957). The necessary and sufficient conditions of therapeutic personality change. *Journal of Consulting Psychology, 21,* 95-103.

Rogers, C.R. (1975). Empathic: An unappreciated way of being. *The Counseling Psychologist, 5(2),* 2-10.

Stern, D.N. (1971). A micro-analysis of mother-infant interaction: Behavior regulating social contact between a mother and her 3 1/2 month-old twins. *Journal of the American Academy of Child Psychiatry, 10,* 50-517.

Stern, D.N. (1985). *The interpersonal world of the infant.* New York: Basic Books.

Stollak, G.E. (1978). *Until we are six.* Miami, Florida: Krieger.

Thoman, E. (1975). The role of the infant in the early transfer of information. *Biological Psychiatry, 10,* 161-169.

Tronick, E., Als, H., & Brazelton, T.B. (1980). Monadic phases: A structural descriptive analysis of infant-mother face-to-face interaction. *Merrill-Palmer Quarterly, 26,* 3-24.

Watson, J. (1967). Memory and "contingency analysis" in infant learning. *Merrill-Palmer Quarterly, 13,* 55-67.

FAMILY-CENTERED THERAPY

Ned L. GAYLIN
University of Maryland, U.S.A.

INTRODUCTION

In barely one generation, marriage and family therapy[1] has grown from an upstart - an idiosyncratic, subspecialty of counseling - to a major force in psychotherapy. Until relatively recently, marriage and family therapy was relegated to a corner of the counseling field, and had its primary roots in marital counseling. In the early 50's, Nathan Ackerman, a classical psychoanalytically trained child psychiatrist, moved beyond his traditional psychotherapeutic background and began working with parents and children together. Thus, from the diverse rootstocks of marital counseling and child psychiatry, the extant field of marriage and family therapy came into being. However, regardless of philosophic orientation, nearly all marriage and family therapists unite in viewing the client unit as two or more interconnected individuals. Although some marital and family practitioners (e.g. Thayer, 1982), additionally suggest parallels between the processes of group therapy and family therapy, most believe that the two differ significantly, in that the clients in family therapy are publicly committed to and intimately involved with each other.

As a longstanding student and advocate of the family, committed to the practice of family therapy and the application of the client-centered approach, I now find myself struggling with semantics. The recent transposing of the word "client" to the word "person" in Rogerian theory has made my stance as a client-centered family therapist an awkward one. Whereas the word "client" may lend itself to include two or more interconnected persons, the word "person" patently suggests a solitary individual. As a family therapist the ideation of a client-centered family therapy retains theoretical integrity: That is, it allows for both the person and the family to be seen as the client. However, the conceptualization of a person-centered family therapy is inherently contradictory.

It is axiomatic to virtually all family therapy systems models[2] that the family unit, rather than its individual members, is the client. Some family systems theorists go so far as to argue that working with an individual, even in the family context, is counterproductive to family systems work. My professional integrity and congruence as a client-centered family therapist arise from the premise that both the client-centered (i.e. individual) approach, and the family systems approach have common elements of therapeutic veracity, and that once those elements are identified, an intrinsically better model for understanding human interaction is possible. Therefore, for clarity, I have chosen the name *family-centered therapy* to describe the client-centered approach to psychotherapy with families.

THEORETICAL FOUNDATIONS: THE ACTUALIZING TENDENCY

Many of the early pioneers in marital and family therapy (e.g., Ackerman, 1958; Bowen, 1961; Minuchin, 1967), were child psychiatrists. Their orientation was in Freudian psychiatry which emphasized early psychosocial development and concommittant parent-child relationships. Contrarily, Rogers' work with individuals de-emphasized early childhood history and dealt with the pragmatics of the client's present. Ironically, Rogers also began his career focusing on children. His first written volume was on child psychotherapy, but actually, he (like Freud) dealt almost exclusively with adults.

Rogers' psychotherapeutic orientation was pragmatic and inductive: Theory followed research on practice (1951, 1959). Rogers was not committed to a unifying theory of personality, and only developed one after his methods of therapy became established. Rogers' special genius and contribution lay in his ability to cut through the tangle of accepted theory, and demonstrate empirically a more elegant and parsimonious set of principles to explain the process of psychotherapeutic change.

One of the basic elements, and for years, the only motive (or drive) postulated by the client-centered approach was that of the actualizing tendency. The actualizing tendency, assimilated from Kurt Goldstein's work with brain damaged patients (1939, 1940), was biologically based and empirically grounded. From Goldstein's organismic theory, Rogers (1951) borrowed the concept of the actualizing tendency to postulate the theoretical concept of self actualization. Too often, however, the two ideas - those of the actualizing tendency of the organism (common to all organisms), and self actualization (unique to the human organism) - are erroneously taken as synonymous.

The actualizing tendency is the propensity of any organism to "develop all of its capacities in ways which serve to maintain or enhance the organism" (Rogers, 1959, p. 196). The tendency towards self-actualization further requires the conceptualization of the self as distinct from others. Thus, the heart of Rogers' theory is the independent individual experience. For Rogers, as for the poet William Henley (1843-1903), we are each the master of our fate, the captain of our soul[3].

The evolution and subsequent preeminence of individual psychotherapy in the twentieth century have both paved the way and presented detours to the theoretical and practical development of family therapy. For example, family systems therapists are firm in the position that the family cannot be viewed simply as an aggregate of individuals living together, but rather as a holistic interactive ecosystem. I would suggest that the tension between individual and family therapy concepts is a specious one arising, in part, from a reaction by family therapists to the dominance of individual psychotherapy. Furthermore, I believe that a family-centered therapy represents a progressive integration of the two positions into a theoretically different framework - that of the person in intimate context. Finally, I contend that a client-centered approach to working with families is fully consonant with such interpolation and integration.

Just as individual client-centered theory rests upon the actualizing tendency of the organism, so does family-centered theory, for the basic family unit is a true biological extension of the human organism. Moreover, the assumption of such an organismic base to family-centered therapy easily allows for the incorporation of the "formative tendency," one of Rogers' (1980) last major theoretical propositions. The formative tendency is the second basic human motive - the anti-entropic, creativeness motive.

The formative tendency might well be applied metaphorically to the creative endeavors of humankind. However, it does not quite work biologically as a construct for individual growth and development, which follow more accurately the entropy principle - at least for the majority of our adult lives. That is, from biological maturity onward, the individual is basically in a state of organic decline. It is only through progenation that this decline is transcended. Thus, the formative tendency works with perfect validity when applied to the family, because the actualizing tendency of the family, by its very nature includes the formative tendency. The primary goal of the family is the creation and maintenance of the next generation and the species.

Despite the various forms it takes across cultures and through time, no other social institution is either so indigenous to us or so defining of us as a unique species, as the family. Although marriage is the precursor to family, the dyad is by nature an unstable unit which via the biological imperative leads to the triad and beyond. It is the birth of the first child and the taking on of the responsibility for the next generation that defines the mature organism of any species. Comprehension of propagation and the lifelong concern for the physical and psychological well-being of mate and offspring distinguish humankind from all other mammalian species, even its closest infrahuman cousins. This comprehension and concern require the development of a special kind of temporal consciousness: Awareness of past, present, and future. Such awareness does two things: It enables human love to transcend both sexuality and simple parental nurturance, and initiates the development of complex communication - nonverbal, spoken, and written. These are but some of the creative, anti-entropic or formative tendency elements which define the family and make it so basic to who we are and what we do (Gaylin, 1985).

Van der Veen (1959) demonstrated that like a concept of self, each of us has a personal concept of family[4]. To some degree each individual family member's perception of his or her family is a shared experience. However, each family member's perception is also colored by the unique experience of that individual, e.g., the extended family history (if a spouse), the difference created by order of birth for each of the children (Toman, 1969). These experiences are augmented by each individual's observation of other families both real (our extended families, friends, and neighbors), and unreal (those we read about in books and see in movies and on television).

Furthermore, I submit that the family concept, and the corresponding ideation of an ideal family concept, are not merely analogues to the self and ideal self concepts, but that family concepts are actually primary and subsume the self concepts. Genetic and biologic proclivities aside, this premise of a self rooted in family is a natural one. Virtually all of us formulate our ideas about ourselves and who we are while growing up in a family.

The child is introduced to society through the family. The shared meanings of the parents are conveyed to the child, and help shape the child's view of the universe - including the child's view of self. Thus, one might say that within the family there is an amalgam of subjectivities by which our views of ourselves and the world around us are shaped. One might conjecture that the chances of having an adaptable, relatively happy individual development are in some way contingent upon the roles played by the joint and individual congruences of the parents as they shape an intimate environment for their developing family. Assuming that neonates also come into the world with their basic perceptual predispositions relatively intact, their approaches to the world cannot help but be filtered at first through the individual and combined subjective perceptions of those interacting with them in their immediate interpersonal environment, i.e., parents, siblings, extended family, and friends.

To understand the unique interactive ecosystem of any family, one must gain entrée to the shared meanings and values of the individuals within that system. The family therapist must be attentive to both the intrapersonal and interpersonal elements which are presented during the family therapy hour. A more finely tuned sense of integration and well-being of the individual affects the well-being of the family system as a whole. More broadly developed, interpersonal well-being reflexively has positive impact on the individual. Thus, a therapy model of the individual in intimate context holds promise of being more efficacious than one minimizing or ignoring that context.

THE NECESSARY AND SUFFICIENT CONDITIONS FOR CHANGE[5]

Having sketched a basis for the application of the principles of client-centered theory to the practice of family therapy, the rest of this discussion attempts to demonstrate how the six basic conditions Rogers deemed "necessary and sufficient" for therapeutic change may be transposed accordingly. The intent of offering parallel structure is to show that the practice of family-centered therapy retains the philosophical character as well as integrity of client-centered thinking.

Thus, family-centered therapy defines no norm or ideal by which family behavior is measured, and maintains respect for the ethos of each family (see McGoldrick, Pearce, & Giordano, 1982). The family-centered practitioner also sees the curative power within the family unit, with the therapist acting as facilitator of a blocked process rather than as the manager of that unit and the purveyor of "truth."

Rogers' (1951) theory of therapy defines six conditions as necessary and sufficient for therapeutic change to take place. These are: 1. a relationship or psychological contact exists between client and therapist; 2. the client experiences incongruence; 3. the therapist is congruent; 4. the therapist experiences empathy for the client; 5. the therapist experiences unconditional positive regard for the client, and finally; 6. the client perceives the therapist's empathy and unconditional positive regard.

In individual therapy Rogers' first condition - that of psychological contact, or the therapeutic relationship - seems straightforward and obvious. In family therapy the establishment of a relationship between the therapist and client becomes complex because the family therapist relates to all family members, both individually and in concert. Thus, the family therapist becomes aware of and attentive to the subtle ecology of the family context through the complex interactions played out directly in the therapy hour.

The different perspectives of the family members afford the family therapist a rich multidimensional view of the individual members' relationship to their intimate environments, to one another and to the family as an interactive whole. Such a view is rarely if ever available to therapists who work solely with individuals. It is common for family therapists to report that once they have become immersed in family therapy process, the experience significantly alters the manner in which they think about and practice therapy with individuals as well.

Rogers' second condition, the state of client incongruence, perhaps more than any of the other five conditions, becomes more profound when one moves from the individual to the family context. Transposing the concept of incongruence - that is, the feelings of distress that occur when the experience and perception of self are not consistent - to the milieu of the family, greatly extends the richness of the concept. The incongruence of each family member, the incongruence within subsystems, as well as that of the system as a whole, all require attention.

Drawing on the previously mentioned analogue between self concept and family concept, one form of familial incongruence exists when there is a discrepancy between how individuals perceive and actually experience their family. Thus, a family may seek aid because of the distress (i.e. severe incongruence) of one or more of its individual members, an incongruence within one of the familial subsystems (i.e. spousal, parent-child, or sibling), and/or a generalized incongruence within the system as a whole.

Systemic incongruence may result from a temporary acute stress placed on an individual or on the system (e.g., severe illness, financial difficulty, pregnancy, unexpected death, substance abuse, etc.). Alternately, the incongruence may be chronic, having developed over a long period of time (e.g. a husband's and wife's disaffection, a child's failure to meet parental expectations, etc.). It is not unusual for an individual's incongruence to create a familial incongruence. When the family comes to a family therapist with the incongruence of an individual as the presenting problem, the dilemma is often whether or not the incongruence of that individual is primary or, rather, an expression of the incongruence of the family system.

This last situation is commonly observed in family therapy: An individual is presented as "the family's problem" when, in fact, the individual may actually be one of the more congruent family members who is being used by the family to deflect or express the incongruence of the system. Such might be the case of children who assume blame for their parents' marital problems and exhibit symptoms ranging from withdrawal to inappropriate outward displays of behavior. In this situation, the individual who impels the family to seek therapy is commonly referred to as a "lightning-rod," or "scapegoat."

Another example is that of the family with a handicapped member. In this complex situation, the issues may include: 1. the individual's incongruence associated with the handicap itself; 2. the corresponding incongruences of other members in their relationship to the handicapped individual; and 3. the incongruence of the family system. It is the unfolding of these complexities and their implications, facilitated by the therapist, that is integral to the family-centered therapy hour.

Regarding the emergence of client congruence with therapeutic progress, the difference between working with individuals and families is subtle but pivotal, and demonstrates how aptly suited client-centered theory is to therapy with families. In individual therapy, when the client begins to feel more congruent, the assuaging of psychological distress is experienced and the individual feels freer, more integrated, etc. This is often accomplished through a coming to terms (i.e. becoming more realistic) with expectations of oneself. In the family session, that kind of simple congruence seldom suffices. Rather, the family often seeks a kind of consensual congruence. Accomplished neither as simply nor as easily as the mitigation of incongruence in individual therapy, consensual congruence, when it occurs, affords the family as a whole and its individual members relief, as well as a sense of shared meaning, belonging, and unity.

Yet, during the course of family therapy, despite the manifestations of progress regarding the resolution of conflicts and/or the diminution or elimination of those presenting problems which brought the family to seek help, certain (and in some cases, all) family members ironically may experience greater discomfort and distress than they did at the outset of therapy. Much of this has to do with the state of the individual family members and their differing: 1. initial perceptions of the nature and scope of the family's problems; 2. thresholds of tolerance; 3. timing of achievable change; and 4. abilities to lower protective defenses. Indeed, apparent therapeutic "failure" or abortion of the course of therapy may actually be engineered (usually unconsciously) by one or more family member(s) for whom the process may be going too rapidly or taking a frightening direction; the resulting distress may be intolerable. Thus, in the case of the lightning-rod, once the dynamic becomes exposed, other difficulties - particularly those for which the lightning-rod had been created - may be more easily discerned. An example is the dread revealing of a shared but unmentionable family secret (Ackerman, 1966; Roman & Blackburn, 1979). This point in the therapeutic process is often a critical juncture, where the family must decide to tolerate the potential anxiety of the unknown and to create new and perhaps unfamiliar behavior patterns for dealing with each other and the world, or to return to former familiar (albeit dysfunctional) behavior patterns.

Rogers' third condition, that of therapist congruence, often poses more difficulty for those working with families than with individuals. Family therapists must simultaneously communicate openly with more than one individual. Ideally, the family therapist needs to feel and express a genuine prizing and empathy (see next two conditions) for each family member, even though these individuals may be in open conflict with one another. Family therapists must be able to draw upon many aspects of their own beings in order to be concurrently empathic with individuals of different genders and ages. Moreover, concurrent empathy with these individuals must be maintained despite the possible evocation of the therapist's unresolved feelings surrounding family issues from the therapist's own family history. Again, Rogers' conditions frame the dynamics faithfully, although the number of interpersonal facets and synchronicity of these events within the session distinguish individual from family psychotherapy.

Regarding the fourth condition, that of unconditional positive regard, the family-centered therapist must simultaneously maintain a prizing attitude toward more than one individual. This attitude must be sustained often in an atmosphere of acrimony by family members towards one another. Thus, there is a contrast presented to family members when the therapist expresses feelings of unconditional positive regard for the very same individuals who claim or display a loss of positive regard for each other, and where feelings of caring and prizing have been replaced by those of alienation and condemnation.

Frequently, particularly early in the course of therapy in such cases as marital discord or parent-child conflict, family members may attempt to place the family therapist in the role of arbiter. In these instances, given family members may be locked into a struggle in which validation of their position requires the invalidation of another's. It is not at all unusual for a family member to resist the nonjudgmental stance of the therapist towards an opposing family member as he or she strives to seek validation for his or her own position in a conflict. If the family therapist can maintain a nonjudgmental stance towards all parties, the family may be able to "reframe" (see Watzlawick, Weakland, & Fisch, 1974) the situation from a winner-take-all conquest to a new and, ideally, mutually acceptable view of the situation.

With regard to the fifth condition, empathy, the family-centered therapist must be able to shuttle back and forth between the internal frames of reference of each family member. If the therapist is able to convey empathy for each individual, family members may each become aware of their separate realities, and thus become more accepting of differing perceptions, even of their common experiences. If these separate realities can be accepted by the family, then rich complementarity can supplant clashing polarity, and shared meanings can be enhanced. Thus, a reconceptualization of the situation is made possible, one which may engender greater empathy among family members for one another. For example, when a family member concurs with the therapist's reflection of his or her internal frame of reference, it is not uncommon for another member, who is listening to the therapist, to exclaim in wonder, "I never realized you felt that way!" or, "I never understood what you meant when you said that before[6]!"

Furthermore, in the family therapy session, as a result of an authentic prizing and prehension of multiple frames of reference, the therapist may often have a sense of the various subsystems and the family system as a whole - an understanding often not easily accesssible to family members themselves. In such cases the therapist's reflection of a systemic vantage point may have the impact of holding up a mirror to the family, ideally enabling the family members to see their interactions in a new light.

Finally, in Rogers' sixth and last condition, that of the client(s)' perception of the therapist as empathic and prizing, the family therapist may have an easier time than the individual therapist. Since the condition suggests at least a minimal perception by the client(s), it may be sufficient if, at times, only certain family members perceive the therapist as caring and understanding. However, as noted throughout the preceding discussion, the more able the therapist is at communicating these attitudes to each family member, and thus to the system at large, the more available (and more accepted) the therapist will be as a facilitator of change. In the family therapy hour the therapist's active empathy and conveyed unconditional positive regard may serve, in part, as role model for disaffected family members, while figuratively reminding them of each member's positive attributes and worth.

Conversely, when some family members see the therapist as insensitive and/or condemning, a greater likelihood exists for abortion of the therapeutic process because of disengagement or even subversion by the alienated family member(s). However, even when parts of the system have been so negatively affected, change may be engendered from within even after therapy has ended. That is, once some of the barriers have been mitigated and the family members jointly experience the power of the family's actualizing potential, a process of growth has been set in motion that is likely to continue.

In sum, the family-centered therapist sees the family as an organismic ecological unit with an actualizing potential, and each individual member as a vital, integral part of that dynamic whole, who also strives to self actualize within the system. Thus, the therapist relates to each member empathically, in an effort to understand: 1. the internal frame of reference of each member; 2. the delicate interpersonal connections among members; and 3. the ecology of these connections and interactions.

SOME ADDITIONAL THOUGHTS ON FAMILY-CENTERED PRACTICE

In the foregoing discussion, the attempt has been to demonstrate that family-centered therapy follows the same philosophic underpinnings and basic principles as individual client-centered therapy. The following discussion attempts to demonstrate some pragmatic variations which occur in shifting from the individual to the family as client.

Very often the family-centered therapist starts out by responding in a manner not unlike the individual client-centered therapist. One listens empathically to a family member and reflects empathically that member's message. Often, particularly if there is a point of disagreement, other family members will counter with their perceptions of the given situation, and the therapist in like fashion will empathically respond to each family member in turn. Once this has been accomplished, the therapist may continue by sharing an amalgamated understanding of each person's internal frame of reference to reflect the shared or conflicted meaning of the family unit.

For example, it is common, particularly because family members may have had difficulty in hearing each other, for initial sessions to be laden with attributions. The following scenario represents such a situation.

Mary: *You have never understood how I felt about such and such.*

The family therapist can rechannel such attributions by reflecting them, and might say: *When you tell John about your feelings about such and such, it seems to you he never understands you.*

The returning salvo from John to Mary may often be something like: *I want to understand, but every time I try and talk to you about it, you*

824

walk away.

Then the therapist might respond to John: *When you try and understand what Mary is concerned about, you feel she does not listen to your questions.*

At a moment like this the therapist is in the position of reflecting what I refer to as the interspace between the two members, and might comment accordingly: *Whenever you two try to talk about such and such there seems to be some kind of barrier between you.*

In this manner both individuals have been heard and the problem couched in such a manner that neither person is blamed but, rather, the situation is put on the table.

Despite the apparent simplicity - the reduction of attribution and blame-laying and the heavy use of experiential description regarding family incidents that previously have been counterproductive - an atmosphere for greater understanding and creative problem solving on the part of family members is occasioned. Note that in family-centered therapy, as opposed to many other family therapy modalities, the therapist does not personally attempt to resolve the problem, but creates the facilitative and engendering atmosphere in which the family may reconceptualize their problems, concerns, and goals. In this manner, the family's actualizing tendency can be disencumbered and psychotherapeutic change can take place.

In working with families, particularly families in which there are young children, there are certain complications with which the client-centered therapist working exclusively with individuals is rarely, if ever, concerned. Many of these have to do with the normative development of children. A parent worried about a child's not walking or talking by the age of two may indeed have a child with a pragmatic developmental problem. This is not to deny the reality and necessity of dealing with the emotional anguish and concern that invariably accompany such developmental difficulties, but it would be both dangerous and professionally derelict to deal with the latter without dealing with the former. On the other hand, there are occasions when parental expectations of a child may be inappropriately high vis-à-vis the child's stage of development, thereby creating both intrapersonal and interpersonal incongruence.

Thus, it is highly desirable for therapists working with the families of young children to have a basic knowledge of child development. While I believe it is important for a family-centered therapist to be comfortable and able to work in a child guidance mode, it may be sufficient for some therapists to know when it is necessary to make an appropriate referral. Note that there is a distinction being made between family therapy and child guidance. Although I do both within the context of a family therapy hour, I consider it essential to recognize and separate the two processes, and know when I am doing which and why. Such recognition is crucial to my own congruence and integrity as a family-centered therapist.

Respect for the family as an organismic whole faces the family-centered therapist with the need for additional awareness. There is a natural hierarchy within all families: Parents are accorded respect by dint of their ages and their parental roles. Although American culture tends to de-emphasize this hierarchy, it is nonetheless a feature of all families in all cultures. In families with teenage children, the therapist's empathic stance towards a teenager attempting to come to grips with struggles of independence may too easily be misinterpreted by a parent as the therapist's approbation and support of the child's disrespectful position towards the parents.

Out of recognition and respect for the responsibility and authority of the parents, I invariably ask them to come alone for the first session in order to give them an opportunity to know me and establish a relationship; listen to their perceptions of the problem(s); and allow me to explain how, on occasion, my attention and empathy may appear more focused on their child. I have never had a parent misunderstand my position during the therapy hour when I have contracted in this manner. On the other hand, severe misunderstandings have been created on those exceptional occasions when I have not followed this procedure. Once the initial contracting stage has been accomplished, I am comfortable in being guided by the family's expressed needs regarding which family members should attend the therapy hour.

This introductory approach to the family is at odds with many family therapy modalities which advocate seeing the entire family from the outset. My approach is also counter to some other family-centered therapists (e.g., Levant, 1984; and Tayer, 1982) who see the family as the sole decider of who is to attend sessions and when. I consider these opening decisions on my part well within the client-centered framework, in the same way that an individual client-centered therapist sets the length of the hour, the time and spacing of the visits, etc. to meet the mutual needs of both client and therapist.

SUMMARY

The attempt of this discussion has been to demonstrate how the practice of family-centered therapy, despite morphological differences, retains the essential philosophy, character, and principles of individual client-centered therapy. As in individual client-centered therapy, the family-centered therapist sees the wellspring of change residing in the actualizing tendency of the client, and in no way attempts to direct the family. Moreover, for the family-centered therapist, there is no normal or ideal state of family health by which family behavior is measured. If the therapist is congruent (i.e. authentic), maintains a stance of empathy and unconditional positive regard in relation to the client both individually and in concert, and if the family, in whole or part, perceives the therapist's empathic understanding and prizing, the family's natural actualizing tendency will be facilitated and therapeutic change engendered.

NOTES

1. For simplicity's sake, the term "family therapy" as used throughout this paper should be understood to refer to psychotherapy with both couples and families.
2. There are many systems theories extant in the practice of family therapy. Because they have provided family therapists with an alternative to models of individual psychotherapy, these systems models have dominated theoretical thinking and practice for the past two decades. It is only recently, that some (e.g. Shields, 1966; Erickson, 1988) have begun questioning these models and their ability to account adequately for the complex behavior of individuals in a family context. In this paper the word systems is used generically, and does not refer to any particular school of thought.
3. The person's symbolization, and actualization of the self, as a separate and distinct individual is the core of Rogers' conceptual thinking. However, the self, like the concept of consciousness, is a relatively new social invention dating back, perhaps, only 400-500 years. There is considerable evidence (Aires, 1962; Jaynes, 1976; Stephenson, 1980) that the idea of an individual consciousness was preceded by a far longer period of group consciousness. In a current exploration related to these ideas, Sampson (1988) proposes, as more explanatory of the human condition, the idea of "ensembled" as opposed to "self-contained" individualism. He suggests that there is no simple way to bridge the two positions because of basic ideological differences.
4. More recently Reiss and Klein (1987) have discussed and elaborated upon a

similar concept which they term the "family paradigm."
5. The following section is a condensed and modified version of an earlier paper entitled *The necessary and sufficient conditions for change: Individual versus family therapy*, (Gaylin, 1989).
6. Recently Johnson and Greenberg (1988) have identified this "increased accessibility and responsiveness" in spousal interaction in marital therapy and labelled it "softening."

REFERENCES

Aires, P. (1962). *Centuries of childhood: A social history of family life.* New York: Knopf.

Ackerman, N. (1958). *The psychodynamics of family life.* New York: Basic Books.

Ackerman, N. (1966). *Treating the troubled family.* New York: Basic Books.

Bowen, M. (1961). Family psychotherapy. *American Journal of Orthopsychiatry, 30,* 40-60.

Erickson, G. (1988). Against the grain: Decentering family therapy. *Journal of Marital and Family Therapy, 14(3),* 225-236.

Gaylin, N. (1985). Marriage: The civilizing of sexuality. In M. Farber (Ed.), *Human sexuality: Psychosexual effects of disease.* New York: Macmillan.

Gaylin, N. (1989). The necessary and sufficient conditions for change: Individual versus family therapy. *The Person-centered Review, 4(3),* 263-279.

Goldstein, K. (1939). *The organism.* New York: American Book Co.

Goldstein, K. (1940). *Human nature in the light of psychopathology.* Cambridge: Harvard University Press.

Henley, W. (1970). Invictus. In O. Williams (Ed.), *Immortal poems of the English language: British and American poetry from Chaucer's time to the present.* New York: Washington Square Press.

Jaynes, J. (1976). *The origin of consciousness in the breakdown of the bicameral mind.* Boston: Houghton Mifflin.

Johnson, S., & Greenberg, L. (1988). Relating process to outcome in marital therapy. *Journal of Marital and Family Therapy, 14(2),* 175-183.

Levant, R. (1984). From person to system: Two perspectives. In R. Levant & J. Shlien (Eds.), *Client-centered therapy and the person-centered approach: New directions in theory, research and practice.* New York: Praeger.

McGoldrick M., Pearce, J., & Giordano, J. (Eds.). (1982). *Ethnicity and family therapy.* New York: Guilford.

Minuchin, S., Montalvo, B., Guerney, B.G., Rosman, B.L., & Schumer, F. (1967). *Families of the slums.* New York: Basic Books.

Reiss, D., & Klein, D. (1987). Paradigm and pathogenesis. In T. Jacob (Ed.), *Family interaction and psychopathology.* New York: Plenum.

Rogers, C.R. (1951). *Client-centered therapy: Its practice, implications, and theory.* Boston: Houghton Mifflin.

828

Rogers, C.R. (1959). A theory of therapy, personality and interpersonal relationships, as developed in the client-centered frame work. In S. Koch (Ed.), *Psychology: A study of a science. Vol. 3. Formulation of the person in the social context* (pp. 184-256). New York: McGraw-Hill.

Rogers, C.R. (1980). *A way of being.* Boston: Houghton Mifflin.

Roman, M., & Blackburn, S. (1979). *Family secrets.* New York: Times Books.

Sampson, E.E. (1988). The debate on individualism. *American Psychologist, 43,* 15-22.

Shields, C. (1986). Critiquing the new epistemologies: Toward minimum requirements for a scientific theory of family therapy. *Journal of Marital and Family Therapy, 12(4),* 359-372.

Stephenson, W. (1980). Newton's fifth rule and Q methodology. *American Psychologist, 35(10),* 882-889.

Thayer, L. (1983). A person-centered approach to family therapy. In A.M. Horne & M.M. Ohlsen (Eds.), *Family counseling & therapy.* Itasca, IL: Peacock.

Toman, W. (1969). *Family constellation: Its effects on personality and social behavior* (2nd ed.). New York: Springer.

Veen, F. van der, Novak, A.L. (1969). Perceived parental attitudes and family concepts of disturbed adolescents, normal siblings and normal controls. *Family Process, 8,* 327-341.

Watzlawick, P., Weakland, J., & Fisch, R. (1974). *Change: Principles of problem formation and problem resolution.* New York: W.W. Norton.

CLIENT-CENTERED PARTNERSHIP THERAPY AS RELATIONSHIP THERAPY

Ulrich ESSER & Ingrid SCHNEIDER
Erziehungsberatungsstelle, Köln, F.R.Germany

INTRODUCTION

As a real life couple and therapists in an educational counseling center, we have been working on relationships for many years, expecting implicitly that the children of the couples will do better when the relationship of their parents is clarified (Grawe, 1976). Our central orientation is client-centered, but with psychoanalytic and Adlerian traditions being integrated to a certain degree. We would like to describe our position within the context of two questions:

- Do the theoretical outlines presented by Rogers lead to the derivation of a therapy of both individuals (client-centered psychotherapy with couples), and/or to the derivation of a therapy of the relationship (client-centered partnership therapy)?

We use the expression "client-centered psychotherapy with couples" (as does Anna Auckenthaler) if therapeutic endeavors focus on the personal growth of both partners. If emphasis is put on changes of the relationship, we call it "client-centered partnership therapy." The differentiation of an individual-centered approach and a relationship-centered approach within the client-centered orientation was introduced by the authors and by Van Stein (1988).

- Is the classical setting of therapist/client sufficient for partnership therapy or psychotherapy with couples, or is co-therapy with one male and one female therapist more adequate?

THERAPY WITH COUPLES AND
THERAPY OF THE RELATIONSHIP

Description of the individual-centered approach and its effects (client-centered psychotherapy with couples)

It is the goal of client-centered psychotherapy with couples "to change the client's relationship with themselves towards more selfempathy, self-esteem, and congruence" (Auckenthaler 1980, p.176). In order to achieve this goal, the therapist will lead both partners to engage in a process of self-exploration by offering the typical relationship of client-centered therapy: Empathy, unconditional positive regard, congruence. According to Auckenthaler (1980, 1983), Henning (1984), and Plog (1975), it is therefore necessary to treat both partners with empathy and positive regard, and to react equally to their communications. In this way, the therapist initially stays in the center of the communication. According to Henning, however, he will gradually be able to withdraw more and more from this center.

Schall (1981) refers to the work of Plog, Rogers, and Pavel, and concludes that marital counseling is possible by means of the client-centered model. He is, however, also the first to point out that besides trying to help improve the individuals, the therapist should "conceptualize the two people plus their relationship as one organism." "Each of the partners do have their very own and individual background of experience, but the (marital) couple can also be viewed as an experiential world" (p.1-11). Schall does not elaborate further on these holistic thoughts. He introduces the idea, though, that partnership might be viewed as a kind of feedback system.Auckenthaler (1980, p. 179) suggests the following criteria of indication:
- Both partners suffer from an incongruence in their experience that shows in the form of discontent with their relationship.
- The clients are able to take up a relationship to themselves, to the partner, and to the therapist.
- Both clients are able to accept the relational offer of the therapist.
- Abolishing the incongruency is at least a first step in solving the clients' problems.

In a later work Auckenthaler (1983, p.97) extended these criteria with one item :
- Both partners are able not only to perceive their own incongruency

but also to have at least a vague idea of the partner's incongruency.

While Henning (1984) thinks that partner therapy is indicated when a couple wants it, Auckenthaler follows the principles of classic selective indication, and considers application of these criteria necessary.

Even though many client-centered psychotherapists say that they are working with couples, no research has been done on the outcome of this approach. Anna Auckenthaler (1983, p. 162) presents some examples of positive effects. Concerning one of these examples, she concludes: "Mr. and Mrs. A. have learned a certain style of communication with each other, and their sexual relationship has improved. These visible changes, however, simply are manifestations of changes in their relationship to themselves and to each other."

Description of the relationship-centered approach (client-centered partnership therapy) and its effects

According to Pavel (1978, p. 125) the primary task of a partner therapist is to initiate and facilitate a process of open and highly empathic communication between the partners. The (two) therapists have a catalytic function in helping to perceive in a more differentiated manner, in sending messages more exactly and more consciously, and in receiving verbal and nonverbal signals more accurately. It is the main task of the therapists to improve the partners' mutual understanding of feelings for and attitudes towards each other, to talk about success and failure openly, and to introduce and conduct experiential exercises, if indicated.

In addition, the therapists can be role models in the clients' process of growth by demonstrating how they deal with each other and with the partners, how they present their perception of the therapeutic situation, or how they present themselves as a person, as a relationship, as a partner, or as an expert.

Special attention should be given to the situation in which the couple therapists are also a real life couple. Inevitably, the therapist couple's style of dealing with their own relationship will show in therapy, on a personal as well as on a professional level. We never had any doubts that we should tell our client couples that we live together as a couple, not only work together. As a matter of fact, we have learned in many years of experience to consider it as a favorable opportunity. We both have been, separately and as partners in a relationship, personally as well as professionally, available to the other to turn to. There was uncertainty at times, however, as to when we should tell our clients. We did not want to do it right at the beginning, when it was not yet clear, whether both partners really were ready to engage in a therapy of their partnership. Why should we put something on someone that may not even be relevant to him or her in the end. In our work we found that if during the initial 3 to 5 focal interviews (Esser 1985, 1987) a contract for therapy of the relation develops and is accepted by both, it is time for us to not only present our conditions of work, but also to tell the clients about our personal situation. This has always been connected with a definite offer to ask questions like "do you know something like that ?," or "how is that in your relationship ?," or "how do you deal with certain things ?" Couples in therapy have reacted very differently to this situation. A few couples saw us as therapists, who, even though living together, are here primarily to work together. The majority, however, saw us as a couple that could also be addressed on a "private" personal level.

Pavel does not report any outcome studies, with one exception, a study of Grawe (1976). Grawe's work is based on the program of Berlin (1975); the study clearly shows positive effects of a partner therapy group on the educational style of parents of behaviorally disturbed children. The outcome of a case study reported by Pavel may be considered highly disputable (a homosexual man stays in a heterosexual relationship).

The goal of our approach to client-centered therapy of the relationship is to foster open communication between partners and to guarantee the transfer of this style of communication to real life. This work requires a certain degree of insight in both clients. If initial interviews (Esser 1985, 1987) give reason to assume that there are too many problems related to a client's self, we offer to do individual therapy before couple therapy or, individual therapy while already starting couple therapy. In partnership therapy we work on the congruence of both partners, particularly in regard to their mutual messages, and on their empathy for each other.

The first aspect should be quite clear: an honest interpersonal relationship is not possible without congruence. The other aspect may be astonishing at first sight as, therapeutically, it means improving processes of the perception of others. We believe however, that a constructive dialogue is not possible without empathy for the partner. There would only be power plays, fight rituals, symmetrical escalation, and more. Our emphasis concerning improvement of the perception of others differs considerably from Auckenthaler's (1980, 1983). While Auckenthaler also takes both aspects into consideration, she stresses self-perception to a much higher degree. By fostering the capability for congruence and empathy for the other person in therapy, we can find out with the clients if unconditional basic regard is even possible or if the partners have first to set up conditions to make mutual positive regard possible. Fear of losing the other person or of hurting him/her so much that the relationship will appear more disturbed than before often prevents couples from interacting openly (Leichter, 1980). Therapists should then, as they would in individual or group psychotherapy, create a climate or an atmosphere which allows the partners to learn to communicate directly and openly, and to understand and accept each other without having to fulfill all the partner's desires. Clarifying the relationship is essential in this process: "Do I really want to live with you? If I want to, what do we want from each other, for each other, and what does each of us want for himself of herself ?" Van Stein (1988) statistically analysed test materials and conducted personal interviews with some of the former clients after 3 to 5 years, and could show changes in the self-concept and in the concept of the partner as a result of client-centered group therapy with couples. However, changes showed predominantly in personal basic attitudes and feelings.

During the personal interviews, the clients hardly talked about the changes in the self-concept that were found by the analysis of the tests, while changes in the concept of the partner where referred to frequently. This fact may reflect the emphasis of the partner therapy they went through, focusing on the relationship of the partners, rather than on individual problems. Personality changes were found concerning "depression," "sociability," and "extraversion." The most striking result of the groups was the increase in openness in their relationship. Almost all our clients report more frequent and more intense talks. The interviewees also stated a considerable increase in sensitivity for partner problems resulting, in many cases, in a helping function for other couples. Partner therapy was experienced as positive, as well as negative. Participants' expectations were frustrated insofar as: a) client-centered therapy turned out to be not as "soft" as generally believed to be, b) the couples who were tested were rather limited in their involvement, and c) the model of therapy and human relations seemed rather technical. In one sentence, most of the interviewees had expected an easier way to improve their partnership (Van Stein, 1988, p. 18-21).

These results may not allow for generalization, due to the small number (N=30) of former clients of therapy of the partnership,. They provide first evidence, however, that clients experience strong changes in their relationship as a result of partnership work, while working on individual problems (self-concept) seems to lose importance.

Derivation of both forms of client-centered couple therapy from Rogers' theoretical positions through emphasizing of different aspects

According to Rogers (1975, 1979), summarized by Plog (1975), successful partnership requires four conditions:
1. Willingness to become an independant self
2. Willingness to communicate and empathize
3. Dealing with supposed or real expectations of the social environment (e.g. attitudes towards male/female)
4. Dealing with the question "What does this relationship mean to us, how do we want to see our ourselves ?"

In Rogers' words (1975, p. 172): "We each commit ourselves to working together on the changing process of our present relationship, because that relationship is currently enriching our love and our life and we wish it to grow." Auckenthaler and Henning emphasize condition 1. We agree with Auckenthaler, Henning, Schall, Plog, and Pavel in regard to the importance of conditions 2 and 3. We share with Pavel the emphasis on condition 4. We are endeavouring to better understand the individual, as well as a to better understand the quality of the relationship.

Rogers (1959) analyzed the characteristics of a disturbed relationship as follows: Two people want to get in contact and to communicate with each other. One person shows significant incongruency in regard to the following elements: (a) his experience of the content of the communication with others (which may be the communication itself or some other object); (b) the symbolization of this experience in his awareness and its relation to the self-concept; (c) his consciously communicated expression (verbal and/or non-verbal) of this experience.

Rogers explains this incongruence as follows: If there is an incongruence between the experience of an object on the one side, and its symbolization, including its consciously communicated expression, on the other side, this person is psychologically maladjusted and the immediate consequence of this condition is a personal one (meaning, we assume, personal problems). If incongruence exists between experience and symbolization on the one side, and the consciously communicated expression, on the other side, this state can be named deceit, and the immediate consequence is a social one (that is, somebody else is affected).

In 1979 (p. 331), Rogers says it even more clearly. "We should pay attention, then, to the fact that we talk about defense, or repression from awareness if there is an incongruence between experience and consciousness. If incongruence occurs between consciousness and communication, we generally call it falseness or deceit".

W. Pfeiffer (personal correspondence) suggested that incongruence between experience and consciousness might also be based on a lack of cognitive schemata that would allow for the adequate integration of certain impressions. We are trying to find out how far this additional thought may be relevant, beyond Rogers, to relationship therapy.

We now postulate that the individual-centered approach puts the emphasis on the incongruence between experience and symbolization, whereas the relationship-centered approach focuses on the incongruence between experience and symbolization on the one side, and conscious messages on the other. As relationship-centered therapists of partnership, we are dealing with topics that are consciously avoided, with taboos not talked about, with feelings that are consciously withheld in their intensity, and with conscious lies. Conscious avoidance occurs as a result of the inability to communicate adequately and effectively, and out of fear of losing the other person.

Therapeutic work must focus on the relationship in order to come to the question: "What do I really want from you ?, What do I not want from you ?, What do I want for both of us, together ?" Someone, unable (for neurotic reasons) to get there, may benefit from client-centered psychotherapy with couples or from client-centered individual psychotherapy.

Auckenthaler, referring to the same basic framework (e.g. Rogers,

1959), maintains that the discrepancy between self and message is the primary object of her work. As long as the discrepancy between experience and symbolization exceeds a certain point, willingness to communicate may not yet exist (1983, p. 97). Many couples are likely to agree with Auckenthaler's criterion number 2 on a verbal level (1983, p.97): "Both partners would like to communicate with each other. They are willing to better understand and accept the other person and to be better understood and accepted by him or her." However, when the process leads to topics of central importance to the relationship, the difference between defensiveness and deceit is quite remarkable. The following example from a partnership therapy may illustrate it.

> A woman complains about her husband's lack of sexual impulses. The husband, in therapy, tries to gain access to experiences fundamental to his present lack of sexual interest in his wife. His "defense" is being challenged, carefully, understandingly. What is the reason that he is no longer sexually desirous of his wife. Is it changes in her, arguments, lack of acceptance, organic reasons ...? Two years of partner therapy did not bring about any progress, because the husband never admitted he had a girl friend.

The difficulty of differentiating between defensiveness and avoidance by mere behavior observation can also be demonstrated by the following case example from a group therapy:

> A man states, loudly and with a red face, that he expects his wife to be in the house when he comes home. His anger is clearly felt by members of the partner group. They give feedback, but he says he did not feel angry. He only wanted to get his expectation straight. The way he said it, however, makes his wife understand: "My husband is mad at me !."

This example underlines the fact that a chain of interaction is made understandable by both forms of incongruence: If the husband really is not aware of his anger (unable to accept his experience due to his self-structure, devaluing his anger), this is a case of defense. If, however, he is aware of his anger, it is deceit.

This difference is of minor importance to Auckenthaler, who does not see a necessity to challenge avoidance behavior. She even says (1983, p. 93): "The differentiation regarding the effects of incongruence on the individual himself or others must not be interpreted as Rogers' intention of introducing different forms of incongruence. Incongruence between experience and symbolization versus conscious communication of the experience, as well as incongruence between experience versus symbolization of the experience and conscious communication are only different aspects of one form of incongruence: Concentrating on one or the other aspect is more a matter of emphasis than of exclusion of the aspect not emphasized." While stating at this point that a differentation should not be made, later she is more radical, psychologically combining both forms of incongruence in one melting pot (1983, p. 94): "A person withholding a certain message due to certain experiences with the partner or changing the message in relation to the content of the experience, may be based on the fact that he cannot stand the reactions he expects from his partner. It is important, in regard to indication of client-centered partner therapy" (please note here that Auckenthaler's terminology is different from our's), "that a partner's decision to deceive is not based totally on free volition because it is the result of an incongruence, an incongruence within himself or in his partner. What it comes down to is that the person who deceives would simply like to talk to the partner in a different way." Here, the liar is therapeutisized into a neurotic who, if only he could, would want to communicate differently with his partner!!

Summarizing, we come to the conclusion that both forms of client-centered couple work can be derived from Rogers' theoretical framework.

CO-THERAPY

The question whether co-therapy by a couple of therapists (one male and one female) is adequate and helpful has long been under discussion. Anna Auckenthaler (1983), by a thorough review of studies on the topic, is led to the conclusion that there is no sufficient evidence to support the preferability of co-therapy in partner therapy or psychotherapy with couples. In her concept of conditions for change (Auckenthaler, 1980) it is sufficient, like in individual therapy, that *one* relevant person offers the necessary and sufficient conditions to the client or, in our case, the couple, enabling them to deal with themselves. Striving to provide Rogers' three basic conditions is sufficient, thus making couple therapy no more difficult than individual therapy: Improving self-acceptance, empathy, and congruence should automatically result in a better relationship.

Favoring the four people setting means to Auckenthaler, leaving the Rogerian concept and adding different approaches. Modeling, to name one example, is considered not appropriate, because the clients are primarily supposed to learn to deal with themselves, striving for self-empathy, positive self-regard, and congruence.

In our approach, to the contrary, we do favor cotherapy, and especially therapist couples, i.e. one male and one female therapist. Our decision is not based on the question of what is more successful. It is rather based on considerations that are client-centered, as well as therapist-centered. The polarity of client-centered versus therapist-centered was first introduced in the field of initial interviews (Esser 1985, 1987). We believe that a three people setting is not appropriate for clients nor for therapists in client-centered therapy of the partnership as decribed above.

From the clients' perspective the four people setting has the following advantages:

- Take for instance, a mother's first interview in the counseling center. A partnership problem becomes evident. The husband can be offered one or more therapy sessions with a colleague who, later, might be one of the co-therapists in a couple therapy, if it is agreed upon. According to our experience it is easier for clients to accept therapy if they know there is somebody who does not know anything yet and so has no preconceived opinion. Would the husband end up with his wife's counselor, he might feel, like a client once said, in her own words: "I feel naked in front of you, as you know so much about me already." The therapist could also be seen as taking the wife's side, especially after having worked with her therapeutically for a while.

- If partner therapy takes place, there is the possibility of splitting up into parallel individual sessions. This might be indicated if one of the partners exhibits a great deal of self-related problems or, if a high level of fear of the partner occurs. In partner therapy or therapy of the relation, the partner is present, unavoidably, not allowing the other person - as in individual therapy - to blame her for all his problems. As Leichter (1980) reports about marital groups: The partner, while present, is being talked about, but not necessarily in a loving and kind way. He is more likely to be accused, blamed, attacked, and hurt. The presence of the partner may increase the fear of really talking honestly.

One has to expect the other person's reaction: "Will he be agressive, sad? Will he punish me, pay me back? Will he withdraw completely and not deal with it at all ?"

Fear of the partner sometimes is a kind of avoidance behavior. It helps to protect oneself against talking about things that are really important. The relationship itself, for instance, is not to be jeopardized, everything should stay the way it is. Splitting up the four people group during one or more individual sessions offers a possibility to express such fear, inducing topics to oneself and to a neutral therapist, prior to presenting them in the four people setting and in front of the partner.

- Changes of design are possible within partner therapy. There is a considerable range for variation from a group of four to one-to-one sessions. A single therapist, in contrast, will hardly be able to work with each of the partners individually, as knowledge of the position of one partner will supposedly restrict empathy for the inner framework of the other to a considerable degree.

- The presence of a male and a female therapist allows for a special understanding of and for adequate answers to gender-specific problems, professionally, as well as personally. Analysis of follow-up questionaires (Schneider) of members of partnership therapy groups shows that clients experience this constellation as comforting and helpful. Verbatim answers to part (b) of question (8) of the questionnaire:

> What did you think of being treated by a) a single person - male or female counselor, b) a counselor couple (male/female) ?", were:
> "The risk of gender-specific responses seemed reduced".
> "Very good, with men and women feeling differently, there was a broader basis of acceptance".
> "Very good, I had the impression there was a kind of a professional understanding, exchange and mutual control".
> "Conversations are less bound to go towards 'typical male / typical female'; balanced attitudes are more likely".
> "Partner therapy should be done by a couple of therapists".
> "No opinion".
> "Very adequate. Marital conflicts occur between husband and wife, too. In the case of a single therapist, the partner of the opposite sex might feel at a disadvantage".

- Crisis situations and dangerous developments (such as suicidal or homocidal thoughts, intentions, fantasies) require therapeutic interventions like high self-disclosure (e.g. limits of acceptance for homicidal tendencies), or safety procedures (e.g. initiate hospitalization). They are easier to realize if the other partner has therapeutic assistance himself.

The experienced reader in marital counseling and partner therapy will, at this point, be reminded of clients turning to a general counseling center for educational and family problems, rather than of couples, who are economically and professionally well-to-do, physically healthy, psychologically slightly neurotic, and in search of a co-evolution process such as the one offered, for instance, in Anna Auckenthaler's (1983) client-centered psychotherapy with couples.

- If relationship therapy results in separation, the clients benefit from having separate therapists they can turn to. Relational difficulties, such as jealousy, do not occur as might happen in the case of one therapist continuing to work with both clients on an individual basis.

From a therapist's perspective, the four people setting can offer the following advantages:

- The therapists are able to support each other in very difficult situations in relationship therapy.
- The intensity of experiencing is easier to bear, as the other person can take over.
- Empathic and confrontative functions do not have to stay within one person, but can go back and forth between the therapist couple.

This advantage applies to clients, as well as to therapists. The myth of the "typical male" or the "typical female" still exists, as we found out in our work with couples. A woman in one of our groups, for instance, wants her husband to be more agressive, to put his fist down now and then. Another participant describes her husband as very domineering, leaving her without a chance against him.

As a result of insecurity (female therapist) at the beginning, we as the 'expert couple' fitted this role stereotype quite well at times, with the male therapist dominating functions such as structuring, setting limits, confronting, and the female therapist being empathic and understanding. Dealing with this issue resulted in a dissolution of the male/female distribution of functions. A new attribution (e.g. dissolution of expected role behaviors) exerts some influence on client couples and can, by serving a model function, be classified as client-centered.

Some relationship problems are common to the four people and the three people setting. It is not any better in a four-people than in a three-people setting that one partner does not feel sufficiently understood by the therapist. It may even happen that two therapists have more understanding for one of the clients. A great deal of consideration should also be given to what we express non-verbally, by mere action, when conducting partnership therapy or relationship therapy (a) by one therapist, or (b) by a couple of therapists. Situation (a) might model to the client an individual existing for himself or herself, able to achieve a great deal. Situation b) might express, contrarily, something like "It can be nice to be together, to share ones work and achievements".

In client-centered therapy of the partnership, when we favor co-therapy of one male and one female therapist, we also expect special qualities in the therapist couple: They both are required to feel real empathy, acceptance, and congruence for each other. They have to know each other well, especially in regard to their personal partnership. There is a need for constant self-reflection dealing with the therapists' relationship with one another, their partner relationship, and their self. We try, in our team of relationship therapists, to achieve these goals by even engaging the real life partners of the therapists.

Teamwork and talking about our experience right after therapeutic sessions thus have become part of our personal hygiene. If sometimes we felt overwhelmed by the problems or by the way two people treated each other or, finally, by thinking that the couples, who turned to us for help really represent "normality," we never gave up. With help from the team, in mutual supervision, we regained the courage to proceed and get the couple closer to the basic question: "Do you want to continue living with me, and if "yes," under what conditions ?" Especially the supervisory talking after partner groups led to the question: "What about us? How do we as a couple handle problems like those presented in the group tonight ?" That makes the work 'heavy' (and most likely even more so, when you are a couple yourselves), but it is constructive, and provides us with a constant confrontation with the process of our very own personal relationship.

Two aspects should demonstrate that working and living together as a couple can contribute to certain problems as well: (a) If I know or feel that some central aspect in our relationship is troublesome, and we do not talk about it or deal with it otherwise, I or we should not get involved with a partner group; (b) If you live and work together, there is a constant risk that work time takes over (e.g. "let's talk something over"), leaving little or no space for private matters.

CONCLUSION: SOME IMPORTANT ADDITIONAL FACTORS

Rogers himself did little work on partner therapy or relationship therapy. In his book "Becoming partners" he describes different forms of partnership which he had learned to accept. In an interview with German TV (Westdeutscher Rundfunk, Channel III, series "Wege zum Menschen"), he referred in very personal statements to his private partnership. A colleague talked to Carl Rogers about the topic in Hungary. She said he was very humble about it, stating that he was not a great expert in the field of partner therapy or therapy of the relationship and that he would prefer somebody else working on it.

Rogers' (1959) theoretical framework, as presented in the Koch volume, allows for the derivation of work on a constructive relationship (e.g. Anna Auckenthaler, 1983). We think, however, that additional factors such as environmental factors (job, place of living, and so on), forms of partnership, and the developmental stage of a partnership (age, children) are important for the understanding of therapy with couples and relational therapy.

Clarifying environmental conditions

In client-centered partnership therapy, we consider a series of initial interviews (socalled "focal interviews," Esser, 1985, 1987) sufficient for the understanding of the clients' environmental conditions and his personal development. It is the goal of the focal interview, through a transparent and empathic process, to structure the client-therapist relationship in such a manner as to allow the client and the therapist to come to an agreement concerning the factors to which the development and maintenance of the problems of the client or the client family can be attributed.

Only after the assessment of concrete environmental circumstances will true empathic understanding of the clients be possible. Even in the case of clients asking for couple therapy or relationship therapy when they first come, therapists should devote thorough consideration to clarify if couple therapy or a therapy of the relationship are really indicated or if instead personal problems of the individuals, although exerting negative influence on the relationship, rather indicate individual therapy or both forms of therapy simultaneously. It may also show that the reasons for marital problems are simply of an economical nature. Whatever the case, it is most important for all people involved (clients as well as therapists) that the goals and conditions for working together are agreed upon in a process of open and transparent interaction. This applies to the attributions of the clients, as well as to the expectations and the conditions for working of the therapists.

Forms of partnership from a social-psychological perspective

Typologies as developed by Eva Jaeggi (1985) are helpful in understanding the special holistic character of partnership, beyond the individual people it is made of. In becoming a couple, two people create a new cosmos, trying to develop a mutual understanding of the world. Acquaintances, friends, family, work, and many other constituents of one's environment are given a new meaning, are put in a new order of importance, the order most likely differing from the one in the own family. This process makes the partner an important factor in creating a new and/or own identity. Partners develop a kind of a "marital identity," and it provides stability. According to Eva Jaeggi there are five types which can be differentiated along the dimensions: Open versus closed systems; dominance versus mutual agreement.

Specific forms of partnership result in specific forms of separation. The new meaning, the new quality created in becoming a couple, generally is well beyond the individual partner's understanding of it. Clarification of this rather abstract theoretical statement requires an example:

> A married couple owning a business frequently work together in the business as well as at home. It is the goal of their cosmos to "decently raise the kids" and "to create something, like buying a home." There are power problems and as a result of that the husband no longer wants his wife's help in the business. He invests in technical equipment and in this way finally does not even need her anymore. She withdraws to the household sector and to raising the children, extending her position there and preventing him from playing a major part. When the home is built and the kids are grown up, there is little they share. They have different interests (laying on the beach, for instance, versus sightseeing). The common cosmos is falling apart, and the partners feel that their mutual attraction and positive regard are not strong enough anymore to keep them together

as a couple. They may even realize that they never would have been a couple without their common cosmos.

Forms of partnership from a developmental perspective

Cöllen (1984) has introduced ideas that we consider relevant to our approach to client-centered partnership therapy. In his opinion three factors are important in creating relationship conflicts: "Social-normative deformation," "sequential dynamics, specific to couples," and "personal difficulties." Developmental aspects of partnership problems can be derived from the couple-specific sequential dynamics. Cöllen thinks that "choosing a partner is based, centrally, on a desire for common self-realization and mutual support, thus normally presenting a very healthy striving for personal growth, depending strongly on one's own state of maturation (p.85). Everyone will be faced with typical phases in his or her relationship with a partner and will be forced to deal with the possible crises they bring about (e.g. the empty nest syndrome). Nothing is neurotic in these phases and crises, but the way people deal with them, may be troublesome.

Taking another look at our abovementioned example will aid to demonstrate the fact that the developmental perspective can help a couple to better understand their relationship. The couple presented there has apparently reached the phase of "mid life." Both are troubled by the question if what they have achieved so far is really all they can do. Discontentment and feeling of hurt take over. There are complaints about the loss of tenderness and sexuality. In client-centered relationship therapy, they painfully realize that they never fully achieved a phase of unconditional attention and "dedication." It does not seem likely, at this point, that they will be able to achieve a satisfying relationship. They will have to ask themselves: "Should we continue living next to each other, depressed and frustrated about our relationship, and look for something else separately," or "Should we get separated, and try a new start with new partners ?"

Sequential phenomena deserve serious attention in client-centered relationship therapy. It is important to realize that different phases of a partnership are characterized by specific central issues, and that different periods require different and specific solutions (in regard to togetherness versus individual action for example). For a more expanded elaboration of these ideas: see Esser & Schneider (1989).

In summary, we have come to the conclusion that the analysis of environmental conditions, as well as social psychological contributions and the phase (or sequential) model of partnership are extremely helpful in perceiving and describing partnership processes, and basically, are essential to the empathic understanding of our clients. In addition, we have started to study psychoanalytical models of understanding - such as the Adlerian "Priorities approach" (Pew & Pew, 1971; Ruthe, 1981), and the approach of "Changing relationship fantasies" (Kast, 1987) - in regard to their compatibility with and their helpfulness to the client-centered approach.

REFERENCES

Auckenthaler, A. (1980). Klientenzentrierte Partnertherapie: Überlegungen zur Gültigkeit des klientenzentrierten Konzeptes für die Psychotherapie mit Paaren. In M. Hautzinger, & W. Schulz (Eds.), *Klinische Psychologie und Psychotherapie. Band 4.* Tübingen, Köln: Steinbauer und Rau.

Auckenthaler, A. (1983). *Klientenzentrierte Psychotherapie mit Paaren,* Stuttgart: Kohlhammer.

Auckenthaler, A. (1983). Gemeinsam sind wir stark? Cotherapie als Antwort auf die Bedrohlichkeit der partnertherapeutischen Situation. *Zeitschrift für Personenzentrierte Psychologie und Psychotherapie, 2(4),* 449-458.

Berlin, J. (1975). *Das offene Gespräch,* München: Pfeiffer.

Biermann-Ratjen, E. M., Eckert, J., & Schwartz, H.J. (1979). *Gesprächs-psychotherapie. Verändern durch Verstehen.* Stuttgart: Kohlhammer.

Binder, U., & Binder, H.J. (1979). *Klientenzentrierte Psychotherapie bei schweren psychischen Störungen.* Frankfurt: Fachbuchhandlung für Psychologie.

Cöllen, M. (1984). *Lass uns für die Liebe kämpfen.* München: Kösel.

Dreikurs, R. (1976). *Die Ehe eine Herausforderung.* Stuttgart: Klett.

Eckert, J., & Biermann-Ratjen, E. M. (1985). *Stationäre Gruppenpsychotherapie.* Berlin: Springer.

Esser, U. (1985). Das Erstinterview in der Erziehungsberatung. *Zeitschrift für Personenzentrierte Psychologie und Psychotherapie. 4(1),* 73-89.

Esser, U. (1987). Das Erstinterview in der Erziehungsberatung (Part 2). Ein Beitrag zur Entwicklung des Fokalinterviews. *Zeitschrift für Personenzentrierte Psychologie und Psychotherapie. 6(1),* 101-114.

Esser, U., & Schneider, I. (1989). Klientenzentrierte Partnerschafttherapie als Beziehungstherapie. Eine Positionsbestimmung. In M. Behr et al. (Eds.), *Jahrbuch für Personenzentrierte Psychologie und Psychotherapie.* (Vol. 1, pp. 206-228). Salzburg: Müller.

Grawe, S. (1976). Ehepaartherapie in Gruppen mit Eltern von verhaltensgestörten Kindern. In P. Jankowsky, D. Tscheulin, H. J. Fietkau,

846

& F. Mann (Eds.). *Klientenzentrierte Psychotherapie Heute.* Göttingen: Hogrefe.

Gesellschaft für wissenschaftliche Gesprächspsychotherapie. (1985). *Sondern-Info* (no.59) zur Geschichte, Durchführungsform und den Ergebnissen des 6. Symposions der Gesellschaft für wissenschaftliche Gesprächspsychotherapie in Köln.

Henning, H. (1984). Klientenzentrierte Partnertherapie. *GwG-info, No 43,* 49-52.

Jaeggi, E. (1985). Trennung und die Destruktion des Sinnes. *Zeitschrift für Personenzentrierte Psychologie und Psychotherapie, 4(2),* 115-134.

Kast, V. (1987). *Partnerschaft zwischen Anspruch und Verzicht.* Paper presented at: Westdeutschen Psychotherapieseminar in Aachen, 10. Januar 1987.

Leichter, E. (1980). Behandlung von Ehepaar-Gruppen. *Zeitschrift Gruppenpsychotherapie und Gruppendynamik, 16,* 107-128.

Pavel, F.G. (1978). *Klientenzentrierte Psychotherapie.* München: Pfeiffer.

Pew, W.L., & Pew, M.L. (1971). Marital therapy. In A.G. Nikelly. *Techniques for behavior change (pp.125-133).* Springfield: Charles C. Thomas.

Pfeiffer, W.M. (1987). Der Widerstand in der Sicht der Klientenzentrierten Psychotherapie. *GwG Zeitschrift, 18, No. 66,* 55-62.

Plog, U. (1975). Partnertherapie. In Gesellschaft für wissenschaftliche Gesprächspsychotherapie, *Die Klientenzentrierte Gesprächspsychotherapie.* München: Kindler.

Rogers, C.R. (1959). A theory of therapy, personality, and interpersonal relationships, as developed in the client-centered framework. In S. Koch (Ed.), *Psychology: A study of a science. (Vol. 3). Formulations of the person and the social context* (pp.184-256). New York: McGraw Hill.

Rogers, C.R. (1975) *Partnerschule.* München: Kindler.

Rogers, R. (1979). *Die Entwicklung der Persönlichkeit.* Stuttgart: Klett Verlag.

Ruthe, R. (1981). Die Priorität Nummer Eins in der Paar-Therapie. *Zeitschrift für Individualpsychologie. 6,* 159-168.

Schall, T.U. (1981). Ehe- und Partnerberatung in der Klientenzentrierten Gesprächspsychotherapie. *GwG-Info,* No. 42.

Schneider, I. (1988). *Nachbefragungsbogen: Klientenzentrierte Partnertherapie.* Unpublished manuscript (Erziehungsberatungsstelle der Stadt Köln, Buchheimer Str. 64 - 66, 5 Köln 80).

Tausch, C., Langer, I., & Bergeest, H. (1984). Personenzentrierte Gruppengespräche bei Paaren mit Partnerschwierigkeiten. *Zeitschrift für Personenzentrierte Psychologie und Psychotherapie, 3(4),* 489-497.

Van Stein, E., (1988). *Auswirkungen Klientenzentrierter Partnertherapie auf Selbst- und Partnerbild sowie auf die Partnerschaft.* Unpublished Master's thesis, Universität Köln, Psychologisches Institut.

Willi, J. (1978). *Therapie der Zweierbeziehung.* Reinbek bei Hamburg: Rowohlt.

CONJOINT COUPLE THERAPY IN
CLIENT-CENTERED PRACTICE

Jan ROMBAUTS   &   Monica DEVRIENDT
Katholieke Universiteit Leuven   Linden
Belgium   Belgium

In the field of couple therapy, there are very few client-centered publications. Well known surveys like Gurman & Rice (1975) and Paolino & McCrady (1978) give a detailed summary of the psychoanalytic, behavioral, systems, and communication theory approaches. The client-centered approach is mentioned briefly, and only in connection with educational programs like that of Guerney (1977).

Rogers wrote the noted book on partner relationships (1972). In *On personal power* (1976) he also dealt with family and partner relationships over three chapters. But to our knowledge he has not written about conjoint couple therapy.

An elaborated client-centered viewpoint on family therapy (including conjoint couple therapy) has been described by Raskin & Van der Veen (1970) and by Levant (1978a, b, c ; 1984). These authors stress the fact that both the psychodynamic approach and the family therapy approach drawing on the systems theory are to a large extent "therapist-centered." In both approaches the family is viewed as dependent on external help from an expert in order to be able to change. In the client-centered perspective, however, the family is considered to be "a selfdirected unit" (Levant, 1978a, p.37). Just as individual therapy, family and couple therapy must have a strong emphasis on the potentialities of the clients, and on their own search for growth. This also goes for other aspects of the basic therapeutic attitude: Non-possessive caring, empathic understanding and genuineness. Levant (1978a, p.41; 1978c, p.6-7; 1984, p.256-259) mentions only a few typical aspects of therapeutic interaction in couple therapy. And he does not describe the therapeutic process in couple therapy in such a way that it could be connected with the theory that Gendlin (1968, 1970, 1974, 1979) has elaborated for individual therapy.

Auckenthaler (1983) also leaves aside Gendlin's work and prefers Rogers' original contributions (1957, 1959) as a starting point for elaborating her view on couple therapy. She sees couple therapy as a simultaneous (individual) therapy for the two partners. The therapist tries to promote the personal growth of each partner individually, and thus only enhances the relationship indirectly. For Auckenthaler many interventions which originate from more system-oriented approaches are incompatible with the basic client-centered principles. In this she differs greatly from Vansteenwegen (1984) and Pavel (1985) who are in favor of an integration of these techniques in couple therapy.

A QUESTIONNAIRE FOR THERAPISTS

In order to have a more concrete and experiential picture of client-centered couple therapy, we have tried to put together a questionnaire whose questions stem from the literature and from our own practice. They relate more particularly to aspects and problems which are proper to working with the partners together. Besides we asked two questions which deal with the therapeutic process. We also asked with which relational conflicts the therapists are most frequently confronted, and to what extent the opinions of the therapists about an ideal relationship (and their experiences in their own partner relationship) play a part in their work with partners. This is also the reason for including questions about communication and separateness. At the beginning and at the end of the questionnaire we have put an open question in order to enable the therapists to elaborate upon other aspects when they considered it to be useful.

The complete questionnaire follows:

1. In your opinion, what are the specific stresses which a client-centered background brings into conjoint couple therapy?
2. Is your attention as a therapist mainly (or even exclusively) directed at what goes on between the partners, or do you also concern yourself (and to what extent) with the individual problems of both partners?
3. Do you experience that there is still enough time and space to listen to the message of both partners on a deep empathic level during fierce interactions between them? (see 5.).
4. When you are listening to and accepting the experience of one partner, does the other partner sometimes feel rejected by you? In what way can this difficulty be overcome? (see 6.).

5. According to Gendlin, empathic listening to the client still leaves sufficient space for the therapist to assess his own subjective reactions. Do you feel that this is also true during fierce interactions between partners? (see 3.).

6. Is it true that your own subjective reactions often link up better with the experience of one of the partners than with the other? Could communicating your own reactions not be felt as a rejection by the latter? (see 4.).

7. According to Gendlin the therapeutic process consists of making the "felt sense" more and more explicit so that it can be carried further. The presence of another person can further this process on condition that the latter is present during this process with a great deal of goodwill and respect. In your opinion, what is the effect of a partner who behaves as an adversary in the relationship?

8. According to experiential therapists like Gendlin and Whitaker it is important that the therapy itself becomes a new experience, a "living further" for the client. To make this possible it is necessary that the therapist is present in the therapy in such a way that one can "live" with him. Levant also speaks about the client-centered family therapist as a "co-participant." How can this be realized in couple therapy? (see 5. and 6.).

9. Rogers puts great importance on the open communication within a partner relationship. Farson believes that humanistic psychologists exaggerate open communication. O'Neill says that too much openness can be detrimental to a partner relationship. Do you feel that it is possible to define an optimal degree of openness? Or are there certain instances where openness is indeed desirable and others where this is not the case?

10. Is the tension between the role patterns of men and women a topic which occurs frequently in your couple therapies? What are other important points of conflict?

11. Rogers stresses the importance of the independence of both partners for an optimal relationship. This also implies that there should be space for relationships with others. He is, however, hesitant about intimate extramarital relationships. Also, as to the jealousy regarding these relationships, he does not give a clear opinion (whether it is essential - even biological - or whether it is a learned and cultural phenomenon). Do you believe that intimate extramarital relationships are possible without damaging the partner relationship? Can jealousy be avoided, mitigated or done away with?

12. To what extent and in what way do your personal opinions concerning an optimal partner relationship play a role in the way you practice partner therapy? And your personal experiences in your own partner relationship? To what extent do you feel able to support a gradual change in the partners which leads to a way of living together that differs from your own ideal?

13. Do you believe that there are still other topics or points which ought

to be mentioned in connection with a client-centered approach to conjoint couple therapy?

We have sent this questionnaire to thirty therapists with client-centered training or background. We also knew or suspected that they had experience with conjoint couple therapy. This proved to be the case with half of them. In a conversation with these therapists, we took a closer look at the different questions, and recorded this on tape. In doing so, it seems that we have gathered important information on the client-centered practice of conjoint couple therapy. We will try to explain the important aspects in a systematic way.

COUPLES IN CONFLICT

Although the relational problems the clients present tend to be rather different, it appears that certain topics keep coming back. The questioned therapists named the battle for power as one of the most frequently recurring and most fundamental conflicts. The issue at stake is often, in a more or less explicit way, the preservation or the rejection of the traditional male or female role patterns. But the conflict can be situated in a broader context: The partners have a different hierarchy of values and try to impose it in their concrete style of living and in the education of their children, e.g. regarding discipline versus freedom, material property versus spiritual and moral values. Another topic that often comes to the fore is that of being disappointed in the expectations about the relationship with the partner. These expectations easily run high, are not realistic, and tend to come from a lack of healthy independence. It also happens that the personal change which one partner goes through clashes with the rigidity and lack of change in the relationship or in the other partner. Other topics which are mentioned: Lack of contact or communication, unsatisfactory sexual contact, the existence of an extramarital relationship, clinging too strongly to the parents and the own family. In some cases the conflict concerns the continuance of the relationship itself: One partner wants to keep it up and continue to invest in it, whereas the other wants to end it.

It is not the diversity of problems which renders the therapeutic practice difficult. The real difficulties are sometimes the limited motivation and the onesided expectations which the client has about the therapy. Many of the therapists indicate that some of their clients are not highly motivated to do something about their relationship with their partner. This is more often true at the beginning of therapy, but it is also true, to a lesser extent, throughout the therapeutic relationship. This results from both the setting and the type of client with which these therapists work. Some clients are so entangled in their own personal problems that they have little or even no attention at all for the relationship. In other instances, it occurs that one partner views the other as the patient who has to change, without him or her being aware of the interplay between the personal problems and the relationship. In still other cases, there is a deep and persistent hostility and little willingness to listen to the other. In all these instances the therapist has to ask himself what is feasible. Mostly concrete solutions and arrangements are looked for. Sometimes it is only possible to try to make the situation a bit more liveable. It is also common for the therapist to recommend individual therapy for one or both partners.

It is obvious that this differs greatly from what one could call "the ideal application." This implies that both partners are motivated to do something about their relationship, that they are aware of the fact that both have a part in the difficulties, and that they are ready to explore it further and correct it if possible. They are also ready to make a more serious attempt to listen to the other. There is still significant goodwill towards the other, and therefore also a feeling of safety which enables the person to explore his own experience and to communicate about it more adequately. It almost appears that these people do not need therapy! But it is precisely the task of the therapist - and here his work is a lot easier than in the instances mentioned above - to support and stimulate what is already basically present.

We can simply state that the therapists questioned are not "therapist-centered" but truly work in a "partner-centered" way. They stress the fact that couples who come for therapy should find their own way. It is the task of the therapist to help them with this, and not to orientate or influence them to choose a way that the therapist approves of.

This can be seen from the therapists' opinions on the importance of open communication in a partner relationship. Of course a minimal openness is necessary before we can speak of a personal relationship. The extent of real openness, however, largely depends on the persons living in this relationship. There can be great differences. It would be wrong to fix a standard here, and certainly wrong to define an ideal for maximal openness. Freedom in this respect, however, seems to be very important: Both the feeling of being able to talk about something when one feels the need to, and the feeling one does not have to talk, if one does not want to. As a conclusion, one can say that optimal openness may be different for each couple. The same also goes for the independence of both partners. For the therapists this independence is of great value. Time and again it has been suggested, that during the therapy, we should be concerned with letting the weaker partner become stronger and more independent. But here also each couple has to find the best equilibrium between the personal development of each partner, and a satisfactory relationship. For example the existence of a intimate extra-marital relationship is not excluded by the therapists in principle. Yet for the couples coming for therapy, it continuously gave rise to great problems. Most of the time the personal maturity needed for maintaining (and accepting) a limited satellite relationship was lacking. And also the primary relationship of these clients was too unsafe and too unsatisfactory.

So the therapists try to keep their own opinions about a good relationship in the background as much as possible. They are, however, aware that they do not always succeed in this: Sometimes they listen selectively and also are influencing somewhat because of these opinions. Furthermore they find that they understand some experiences of certain clients better from a background of related experiences in their own partner relationship. Yet they want to remain very conscious of this. And when they notice that one or another of their interventions is too subjectively colored they sometimes point it out explicitly to the clients and thus try to weaken a possible influence.

So it seems that most of the time, the therapists do succeed in accompanying and supporting their clients in a change towards different ways of living in a relationship, even if this differs from what the therapists would wish for themselves. But sometimes there are difficulties arising in this respect. This is particularly true when the clients seem to change in a direction which is completely contrary to the fundamental values of the therapist. For instance, when the relationship is evolving with a strong desequilibrium between the two partners and especially when one of the partners is oppressing the other. At this point personal development is in great danger. Letting someone be a person in his own right, with space for personal development and growth, is a basic value for a client-centered therapist. It is understandable then, that it is hard for him to let such an unbalanced relationship evolve. Such a reaction can also arise when the children threaten to become the victims of the situation or when they suffer significantly, or are substantially hindered in their personal development. A similar difficulty arises - although it is less frequently mentioned - when the clients are unsuccessful in building up their relationship in accordance with their own experience, or even do not wish to do so. In this instance, the therapist may believe that adopting values from the outside, without due consideration, will be a shaky basis for living in a relationship. That is why it is hard for him to consider the end of a therapy to be a success when both partners have not progressed any further than a superficial way of life which is not their own. But as stated above, this is usually linked to the deficient motivations and limited potentialities of some clients. In this context, the therapist will concentrate mainly on what is feasible.

That the clients have to find their own way does not mean that the therapist remains passive. On the contrary, it appears that he is more active in conjoint therapy than in individual therapy. For instance, although he may be aware that being angry, quarrelling, and calling each other names, can be a phase of the therapeutic process, he will intervene when he feels that the partners get stuck in this phase, and do not succeed in communicating with one another. He sometimes gives instructions, such as: "Let the other finish," "paraphrase before you react" and so on. Or else the therapist asks them to quiet down a bit because he cannot follow them. He also tries to hear the message which is expressed by this fierceness, and to verbalize it. In doing so he alternately addresses himself to each partner in order to avoid allowing one of them to dominate the conversation. Also, the therapist will intervene actively when the form of therapy is being decided. The therapist may take the initiative when clients are switched from conjoint therapy to individual therapy. While one cannot speak about a strategy of treatment, the working method of the therapist obviously changes as the therapy proceeds.

THE CENTRAL PLACE OF EMPATHY

All therapists stress the central place of empathy both in individual and in couple therapy. But this has a proper shape in couple therapy. There is not only the individual experience of the two persons, but there is also their interaction, their relation on which the empathic attention of the therapist is mainly focused. Moreover the individual and relational problems are interwoven with one another. The personal reality of each partner also encompasses the relationship, and this relationship is a relationship between two concrete individuals with their own specific problems and personality. The relational problems influence the personal problems and vice versa. When an improvement occurs this interplay can also work in a positive sense. Therefore both relational and personal topics are dealt with in the conversations. Usually the emphasis is on the relational aspects, although this can vary. Thus, in the beginning stage of the couple therapy for instance, the focus will not be on the more individual problems of both partners: The main attention of the therapist will be devoted to the interactional behavior. This is certainly the case when these interactions are vehement. The therapist tries to get in touch with what actually happens between the people, at the deepest level of the conflict. When the storm has spent itself somewhat, he can try to make this meaning explicit for the partners, along with the experiential message of each of the partners. While doing so, it is important that he has an eye for the possible positive meaning of a negative behavior. For instance he may point out that jealous reactions indicate how important the partner and the relationship are, or that disappointment points to expectations or appreciation of the partner. This positive translating of negative or hostile behavior can contribute to defusing the aggressive atmosphere and can bring the still existing positive aspects of the relationship to the foreground.

A difficulty which tends to occur in couple therapy is that listening empathically to one of the partners, sometimes provokes a feeling of rejection or counter-reaction from the other. Even at the beginning of the therapy, when one only reflects briefly on individual experience, this reaction can occur. It seems that clients have not formed sufficient trust in their therapist at the early stages of therapy. Or else some clients expect the therapist to take sides. When one partner looks upon the other as the patient or the guilty one, then he sometimes cannot understand why importance is attached to the message and the experience of the other. In any case, when this happens, it is completely opposed to his expectations. He is convinced that he is right and that the other person should change. The attitude of the therapist who tries to give both partners the opportunity to express their opinions appears to the client as a rejection of his own "justified" indignation. Also in less extreme instances, when this atmosphere of being in the right or being put in the right prevails, the therapist has to be aware of this risk and must take this into consideration. This is one of the reasons why they do not, at the start of a therapy, linger too long on one of the partners but, very consciously, alternate their attention to both of them. Thus they try to avoid the impression of partiality. At the same time they remain especially alert to every trace of partiality they would recognize in themselves. They also occasionally explicitly emphasize that they are trying to listen to the subjective input of each person and that this listening implies neither a judgement nor approval. Working with a co-therapist can sometimes be an aid in getting around this rock of suspected partiality. In some cases individual therapy can be the solution to let the confidence between the therapist and the clients grow. In spite of all these precautions, it can still happen that a feeling of rejection arises which often will not be verbalized explicitly, but will be expressed nonverbally. Then the therapist tries to remedy this disturbance by discussing this feeling of rejection. But this direct approach is not always accepted by the client concerned. So it is sometimes better to go about it in an indirect way by giving extra attention, in the next conversations, to the person who feels rejected in the hope that he will gradually feel accepted again. In extreme and exceptional cases the rupture of confidence will persist. As a consequence, the client sometimes will withdraw from therapy.

Is it possible in a later stage of the therapy, after the confidence in the therapist has been established with both partners and after there is more serenity in the conversations, that more space can be given to the individual experience and problems ? This seems to vary according to the type of clients. The therapists had different opinions about it. A few believed that the therapist can engage in the deeper personal problems of one of the partners during one or even more sessions, on condition that the other is open to it, and agrees to it. The person must be certain that what he says will not be used by the partner against him or her later on. These therapists observe, that the topics which are discussed, do not constitute a conflict. Therefore the partners can communicate better with, and listen better to, one another. This contributes to making the atmosphere of the therapy warmer, and is a good preliminary for a better communication on points which are more conflictual. On this issue most therapists take a more reserved approach though. When the individual problems are big or remain prominent, then they prefer to discuss this in individual sessions. There are different ways to go about that: Regular individual sessions varied with regular conjoint sessions, occasional individual sessions combined with a continued conjoint therapy, or vice versa. These therapists want to bring in individual sessions because they believe that there is too little space in conjoint therapy to go into the personal problems thoroughly. The client often feels too unsafe in the presence of the other partner and does not want to show too many weaknesses to the other. Also there is fear that the latter will use it against him later on as well as the danger that in conjoint sessions the therapist might influence them to reveal deeper issues to their partner, issues they are not ready to reveal.

TRANSPARENCY OF THE THERAPIST

All therapists stress the fact that they try to be present in the therapy as a real person, not by telling a lot about themselves, but by their real involvement, their acceptance and their true attempt to facilitate the process between the partners in an empathic way. When the therapist feels relaxed and receptive himself, he is able to create a positive atmosphere. In a verbal or nonverbal way (sometimes with a tinge of humor) he can contribute to building up a relationship of confidence and letting a good working atmosphere arise. That is when he will be experienced by the clients as a real presence. Consequently a feeling of solidarity is created: "The three of us are working on this relationship together."

There is agreement among the therapists about communicating subjective reactions to their clients. It should rarely take place and certainly, less frequently than in individual or group therapy. The main reason for this is that it requires a great amount of energy and attention to keep in touch with both partners, and with what is going on between them. Therefore the therapist can hardly afford to focus on the subjective and complex reactions arising in him. Of course, he has to go further into these reactions after the sessions because they give an indication of his attitude during therapy, of what is a hinderance and what can be set right.

A positive feeling towards what is happening between the partners may be expressed once in a while, but negative reactions are kept in the background. In fact, negative reactions are only communicated when they are so strong that they render it impossible to listen further in an empathic and accepting way. Such reactions frequently occur when there is vehement and persistent quarrelling between the partners - a situation we have already described above. The feelings which flood the therapist at that time can be very complex: Feeling of powerlessness, resentment, irritation and anger. When this makes him feel like slipping away from what is happening as well as from his clients, he may indeed verbalize this in an attempt to break this sterile climate. Such interventions usually turn out to have a positive effect. First of all, for the therapist himself, who feels relieved afterwards and is better able to listen empathically, but also for the partners. At first the partners may be surprised by the unusual reaction of their therapist, but at the same time their attention is drawn to the inadequate manner in which they have behaved towards one another. Moreover, such reactions strengthen their feeling that the therapist is really committed, whereas always and continuously calmly listening (or the appearance of it) may give the impression of indifference.

In the above we have dealt with the subjective reactions of the therapist towards what is happening between the partners. But what about such reactions - be they negative or positive - that the therapist has towards one of both ? In this instance the therapists are still more prudent. They indeed observe that their feelings towards the individual partners are often different. Sometimes this is only an impression during the first sessions, which disappears for the most part later on, and consequently rarely entails any problems. In many cases, however, a difference remains. This usually does not involve the sex of the client, but rather the personality characteristics of the client (and of the therapist). He feels more attracted to one partner than to the other (sometimes because of experiences in his own partner relationship). Spontaneously he has better contact with one of the partners. In this case the therapist tries - very consciously and deliberately - not to express these feelings. There is one case though - which we have discussed before - where such an impartial attitude is very difficult. Almost all therapists underline this, namely when they are confronted with one partner who is not respected by the other and is dominated and oppressed time and time again. Here it may happen - "by accident" the therapists say - that their annoyance shows itself. Then of course, the client who is the target of the annoyance feels strongly put down and rejected. Actually, the therapist may not reject the person, but may be upset by the client's behavior which he cannot accept. After such an incident, however, it often requires great efforts to make this clear to the person involved. As we have written above in connection with empathy, the therapist tries to handle this feeling of rejection in different ways. But this is sometimes very hard to do and the risk of breaking off the therapy remains imminent.

For the sake of completeness, we have to add here that certain therapists sometimes voice their subjective reactions more freely in the last stage of a well-evolved couple therapy. At this point, there is a completely different climate. Here safety, warmth, confidence and familiarity have grown in abundance. These conversations consist of glancing back at what they have been through together. Memories are exchanged in a relaxed atmosphere. Among other things, the participants also discuss how they have experienced one another at various times. This is no longer difficult therapeutic work, but rather a chat together after many hours of struggle. It is part of the agreeable end of a successful couple therapy. It might also be a way of postponing the final termination.

THE THERAPEUTIC PROCESS

According to the current client-centered conceptions, the therapeutic process is substantially seen as an experiential process. As the client focuses on his experiencing and, with the support of the therapist, continues to explore this experiencing further, a felt sense forms and the felt experiencing changes. But according to most therapists whom we questioned, the description of the therapeutic process such as Gendlin (1970) elaborated it, is more evident in individual therapy than in couple therapy. In fact there are many gradations. Sometimes one has to content oneself with a very limited result (concrete solutions for problems and agreements, a somewhat more liveable situation) and sometimes one succeeds in substantially improving the communication between the two partners. At best there is still space for a deeper selfexploration, analogous to what happens in individual therapy: There is a similar, but less clear process, that develops.

It seems that practically in each couple therapy the improvement of the communication between the two partners gets paramount attention and that it is the condition for a more deep-going therapeutic process. Indeed, a thorough selfexploration is not possible unless there is a good interactional climate. Good communication implies, among other things, that one speaks less about facts and behavior and more about feelings and experiences. This is less accusatory and more acceptable for the partner. The therapist plays an important part in this. By continuously focusing on experiences, he draws the attention of the clients to the experiential reality underlying the words and the behaviors. And also thanks to the relationship of confidence which is growing between the clients and the therapist, they will readily take him as a model. This is also true for the ability to listen. By intensely listening to the message of both partners, the therapist also influences them to listen better. In order to arrive at good communication - and with certain clients not much headway is made in this respect - many hindrances have to be swept away. The lack of respect, the unwillingness, and the hostility between the partners can be so strong at the beginning of the therapy, that it will be a long time before the inhibitions to communicate get unblocked. As mentioned before, these early inhibitions can be addressed by discussing what is individual and less conflicting. Even here, a lack of security can cause defensiveness. But when the therapy evolves well, the climate gradually becomes better. There is a greater desire and ability to listen to one another. The partners will also discover that it is possible to have contradictory experiences and opinions without it necessarily leading to a serious conflict, and that there can be a respect for each other's opinion. Moreover they begin to see that, besides the topics on which they have different opinions, there are also areas where they feel close, and where a strong solidarity remains.

As to the depth of the self-exploration and of the therapeutic process, there are great differences between the several therapies - as we have mentioned before. In some couple therapies there is never sufficient security present for a real self-exploration or the persons themselves seem incapable of it. In other instances the change is clearly seen. Also here there is too little safety and too much emotionality at the beginning. But gradually the climate becomes more quiet and then there is the possibility for a process that is similar to what occurs in an individual therapy. In this context there is an interplay as well: When one of both partners (or both) succeeds to explore his experience in a serene way, then this definitely has a favorable effect on the relationship and on the interactional climate. A greater warmth, willingness to listen and involvement with one another is the result. From this, the possibility for still more self-exploration and continuation of the individual experiencing process gradually grows. Thus the partners will be able to experience themselves, as well as their relationship and their partner, in another way. In this sense it can be said that both the individual experiencing is carried forward and the stopped relationship is lived onward. Consequently, the interwovenness of the personal and the relational problems is revealed in this favorable interplay. This is definitely a specific aspect of the process in marital therapy.

Finally we still want to stress that the favorable change, as it has been described above, occurs only infrequently or to a limited extent. Practically all therapists questioned believe that the clients in a couple therapy rarely succeed in exploring themselves and rarely go through a experiential process that is as deep and intense as in the usual individual therapy. That is why many of them prefer individual sessions for the personal exploration and the experiential process.

CONCLUSIONS

In retrospect on this exploration of couple therapy, we want to highlight some points and make some personal reflections about them.

To us the flexibility of the therapists is striking. They accomodate themselves easily to what is possible, according to the motivation and the possibilities of the clients. Their flexibility also appears in their facility to change from conjoint sessions to individual ones, and often combine both. Therefore most client-centered therapists are not always willing to define themselves as "couple therapists," even though they practice conjoint therapy. They are rather therapists who, according to the situation, accept the clients in individual or in conjoint sessions.

They often take the initiative in introducing the form of the therapy, but the ultimate decision is left to the clients. During the conjoint sessions the therapists are also very active when it comes to stimulating the appropriate course of interaction. One could even say that they are "directive" when they inform the clients explicitly of the rules of a good communication. But this directivity is "formal." It is aimed at the method of communication and not at the content. This "formal direction" is also found in individual therapy. There the therapist tries to make the client turn towards his experience, explore it, and communicate from it. However, only the client can give content to the communication. Couple therapy is first of all directed at the relationship between the partners. Certainly on this point, the therapist does not want to give any directives: He does not try to present an ideal for the partner relationship. The partners themselves search for their own direction. At most, if it is necessary, the therapist will point out that what matters is a relationship between two persons with each having their own value so that one can hardly speak of a relationship when one of both is oppressed.

Also in couple therapy we see that empathy in client-centered therapy takes a central place. Listening to the interaction and to the message of the two persons in an empathic way, requires practically all the attention and engagement of the therapist. Even more than in individual therapy, the therapist's presence as a real person in the relationship coincides with the empathic involvement. Anyhow there is very little space for the therapist to explore his own subjective reactions in the conjoint sessions. So the therapist only communicates his reactions to keep his relationship with the couple intact. Since the therapist mainly wants to focus on the interaction and the relationship between the partners, his subjective reactions towards one of both partners are experienced by him as a disruption, and so he avoids them when possible. Finally, there is the fear of partial interventions because these could damage or break the clients' confidence in the therapist and possibly prevent further therapy.

The therapeutic process in couple therapy is essentially viewed in function of the relationship. That is the reason why so much importance is attached to creating a better interaction. This implies both that one listens better to the message of the partner, and that the communication starts more from one's own experience. To this end it is necessary to explore this experience and make it explicit. Although there may be little space in a conjoint therapy for a protracted selfexploration, still a personal experiential process in the partners will take place, as a side effect, as the interaction improves. Just as the personal and relational problems are tightly interlinked with one another, there is a parallel and an interplay between the constructive change in the relationship, and the personal growth of the partners.

With this we want to conclude our outline of the client-centered approach of conjoint couple therapy. In our opinion it appears that client-centered therapists have developed their own approach when they practice this form of therapy. Their presence as a real person in the therapeutic relationship, their deep empathic involvement and their respect for the the couples' own direction, creates a climate that may be defined as "person-centered."

REFERENCES

Auckentaler, A. (1983). *Klientenzentrierte Psychotherapie mit Paaren.* Stuttgart: Kohlhammer.

De Chenne, T.K. (1973). Experiential facilitation in conjoint marriage counseling. *Psychotherapy: Theory, Research and Practice, 10,* 212-214.

Gendlin, E.T. (1968). The experiential response. In E.F. Hammer (Ed.), *Use of interpretation in treatment (pp.208-227).* New York: Grune and Stratton.

Gendlin, E.T. (1970). A theory of personality change. In J.T. Hart & T.M. Tomlinson (Eds.), *New directions in client-centered therapy* (pp.129-173). Boston: Houghton Mifflin.

Gendlin, E.T. (1974). Client-centered and experiential psychotherapy. In D.A. Wexler & L.N. Rice (Eds.), *Innovations in client-centered therapy* (pp.211-246). New York: Wiley.

Gendlin, E.T. (1979). Experiential psychotherapy. In R.J. Corsini (Ed.), *Current psychotherapies* (2nd ed., pp. 340-373). Itasca, IL.: Peacock.

Guerney, B.G., Jr. (1977). *Relationship enhancement.* San Francisco: Jossey-Bass.

Gurman, A.S., & Rice, D.G. (Eds.). (1975). *Couples in conflict: New directions in marital therapy.* New York: Aronson.

Kempler, W. (1981). *Experiential psychotherapy within families.* New York: Brunner-Mazel.

Levant, R.F. (1978a). Client-centered approaches to working with the family: An overview of new developments in therapeutic, educational and preventive methods. *International Journal of Family Counseling, 6,* 31-44.

Levant, R.F. (1978b). Family therapy: A client-centered perspective. *Journal of Marriage and Family Counseling, 4,* 35-42.

Levant, R.F. (1978c). Client-centered family therapy: Discussion for research and clinical exchange. *American Journal of Family Therapy, 10,* 72-75.

Levant, R.F. (1984). From person to system: Two perspectives. In R.F. Levant & J.M. Shlien (Eds.), *Client-centered therapy and the person-centered approach: New directions in theory, research and practice* (pp.242-260). New York: Praeger.

Paolino, Th.J., & McCrady, B.S. (Eds.), (1978). *Marriage and marital therapy:*

Psychoanalytic, behavioral and systems theory perspectives. New York: Brunner-Mazel.

Pavel, F.G. (1985). Klientenzentrierte Therapie von Systemen. *GwG-info, No. 59,* 35-54.

Raskin, N.J., & van der Veen, F. (1970). Client-centered family therapy: Some clinical and research perspectives. In J.T. Hart & T.M. Tomlinson (Eds.), *New directions in client-centered Therapy* (pp.387-406). Boston: Houghton Mifflin.

Rogers, C.R. (1957). The necessary and sufficient conditions of therapeutic personality change. *Journal of Consulting Psychology, 21,* 95-103.

Rogers, C.R. (1959). A theory of therapy, personality and interpersonal relationships. In S. Koch (Ed.), *Psychology: A study of science* (Vol. 3, pp.185-256). New York: McGraw Hill.

Rogers, C.R. (1970). *What it means to be married. Mental Health,* (Cassette Recording No.7). Chicago: I.D.I.

Rogers, C.R. (1972). *On becoming partners: Marriage and its alternatives.* New York: Delacorte Press.

Rogers, C.R. (1975). Empathic: An unappreciated way of being. *The Counseling Psychologist, 5,* 2-10.

Rogers, C.R. (1976). *On personal power: Inner strength and its revolutionary impact.* New York: Delacorte Press.

Vansteenwegen, A. (1984). Client-centered partnerrelatietherapie: Mogelijkheden en grenzen. In G. Lietaer, Ph.H. van Praag, & J.C.A.G. Swildens (Eds.), *Client-centered psychotherapie in beweging. Naar een procesgerichte benadering* (pp.503-520). Leuven-Amersfoort: Acco.

Whitaker, C., Greenberg, A., & Greenberg, M.L. (1981). Experiential marital therapy: A synthesis. A subsystem of existential family therapy. In G. Pirooz Sholevar (Ed.), *The handbook of marriage and marital therapy* (pp.181-217). New York: SP Medical and Scientific Books.

Drukkerij-Binderij Scheerders van Kerchove N.V. - 2700 Sint-Niklaas